Twenty Years of Inflation Targeting

There is now a strong but not universal consensus among academics and professional economists that central banks should adopt explicit inflation targets and that all key monetary policy decisions, especially those concerning interest rates, should be made with a view to ensuring that these targets are achieved. This book provides a comprehensive review of the experience of inflation targeting since its introduction in New Zealand in 1989 and looks in detail at what we can learn from the past twenty years and what challenges we may face in the future. Written by a distinguished team of academics and professional economists from universities and central banks around the world, the book covers a wide range of issues, including many that have arisen as a result of the recent financial crisis. It should be read by anyone concerned with better understanding inflation targeting and its past, present and future roles within monetary policy.

DAVID COBHAM is Professor of Economics at Heriot-Watt University, Edinburgh.

ØYVIND EITRHEIM is a director at Norges Bank Monetary Policy.

STEFAN GERLACH is Professor of Monetary Economics at the Institute for Monetary and Financial Stability, University of Frankfurt.

JAN F. QVIGSTAD is Deputy Governor of Norges Bank.

Twenty Years of Inflation Targeting

Lessons Learned and Future Prospects

Edited by

David Cobham

Øyvind Eitrheim

Stefan Gerlach

Jan F. Qvigstad

%NB% NORGES BANK

CAMBRIDGE
UNIVERSITY PRESS

The Edinburgh Building, Cambridge CB2 8RU, UK

Published in the United States of America by Cambridge University Press, New York

Cambridge University Press is part of the University of Cambridge.

It furthers the University's mission by disseminating knowledge in the pursuit of education, learning and research at the highest international levels of excellence.

www.cambridge.org
Information on this title: www.cambridge.org/9781107696891

© Cambridge University Press 2010

First published 2010
First paperback edition 2013

A catalogue record for this publication is available from the British Library

ISBN 978-0-521-76818-4 Hardback
ISBN 978-1-107-69689-1 Paperback

Contents

Figures

Tables

Contributors

CHRISTOPHER ALLSOPP University of Oxford

MAGNUS ANDERSSON European Central Bank

IDA WOLDEN BACHE Norges Bank

STEPHEN G. CECCHETTI Bank for International Settlements

DAVID COBHAM Heriot-Watt University

CHRISTOPHER CROWE International Monetary Fund

SPENCER DALE Bank of England

ØYVIND EITRHEIM Norges Bank

GEORGE W. EVANS University of Oregon and University of St Andrews

ANDREW FILARDO Bank for International Settlements, Representative Office for Asia and the Pacific

HANS GENBERG Bank for International Settlements, Representative Office for Asia and the Pacific

STEFAN GERLACH Institute for Monetary and Financial Stability, University of Frankfurt

CHARLES GOODHART London School of Economics

CRAIG S. HAKKIO Federal Reserve Bank of Kansas City

LARS HEIKENSTEN European Court of Auditors

BORIS HOFMANN European Central Bank

SEPPO HONKAPOHJA Bank of Finland

JAMES MITCHELL National Institute of Economic and Social Research

ATHANASIOS ORPHANIDES Central Bank of Cyprus

CAROLINA OSORIO University of Oxford

THÓRARINN G. PÉTURSSON Central Bank of Iceland and Reykjavík University

JAN F. QVIGSTAD Norges Bank

FRANCESCO RAVAZZOLO Norges Bank

SCOTT ROGER International Monetary Fund

KLAUS SCHMIDT-HEBBEL Catholic University of Chile

DANIEL L. THORNTON Federal Reserve Bank of St. Louis

DIMITRIOS TSOMOCOS University of Oxford

SHAUN P. VAHEY University of Melbourne

SUSHIL B. WADHWANI Wadhwani Asset Management

ANKE WEBER International Monetary Fund

1   Introduction

David Cobham, Øyvind Eitrheim, Stefan Gerlach
and Jan F. Qvigstad

The first country to adopt inflation targeting (IT) in its formal definition
was New Zealand, which first announced a consumer price index (CPI)
inflation target in 1989 as part of its economic reform and restructuring
effort. IT was therefore twenty years old by the time of the conference in
Oslo at Norges Bank, Norway's central bank, in June 2009 at which the
contributions in this volume were originally presented – a conference
sponsored jointly by Norges Bank and the Institute for Monetary and
Financial Stability (IMFS) of the Goethe University in Frankfurt. The
anniversary seemed a good time for some deeper and longer reflection.
In organising the conference and putting together this book, we therefore
sought answers to a wide range of questions, from the nature and causes of
the spread of IT through the degree of its success as a monetary policy strategy to the ways in which it is developing and may develop in the future.

Formal inflation targeting can be considered as involving (i) the prior
announcement of a quantitative target for a specific measure of inflation;
(ii) an emphasis by the central bank as policymaker on communicating
both the reasons for the decisions it has taken and the type of decisions
it is likely to take in the future, including in particular the publication
of its inflation forecasts; and (iii) a high level of accountability for the
central bank via the publication of information on its decisions and regular appearances before relevant public bodies. While many researchers
in this area, and most of the contributors to this volume, regard the
announcement of a target as a *sine qua non* for inflation targeting, some
focus more on the operation of policy by central banks, and consider the
Federal Reserve Board in the United States and the European Central
Bank (ECB) of the European Union (EU), for example, as (informal
or implicit) inflation targeters (ITers). However, these two banks have
shown no inclination so far to announce the targets that would qualify them as formal or explicit inflation targeters under the conventional
definition.

The opening remarks by Jan F. Qvigstad, deputy governor of Norges
Bank, provide a brief Norwegian perspective on IT, with an illustration

of the application of Norges Bank's five criteria for a good interest rate path. Athanasios Orphanides, governor of the Central Bank of Cyprus and member of the Governing Council of the ECB (and before that an economist at the Federal Reserve Board for nearly twenty years), offers some perceptive reflections on IT from an agnostic point of view.

Scott Roger's overview, which updates his earlier work with Mark Stone (2005), covers the introduction and spread of IT, the key features of its operation in different countries, its contribution to macroeconomic and inflation stability, and the challenges it faces in the future. He finds, for example, that IT countries have typically had larger improvements in macro-performance than non-IT countries, but have not ended up with better performance than non-ITers. On the other hand, ITers seem to be doing better than non-ITers in the financial crisis period (so far). Klaus Schmidt-Hebbel brings together a large amount of very recent work in this area, looking more closely at the reasons countries have adopted IT and at the effect on inflation of adopting IT. In terms of the latter, a range of different results have been found, depending on what countries ITers are compared with. However, there is evidence that industrial ITers have lower long-run inflation than industrial non-ITers. He also finds that ITers have improved the efficiency of their monetary policy, but remain less efficient than a control group of high-performing non-IT industrial countries.

Daniel L. Thornton takes a rather different tack in his examination of how monetary policymaking arrived at IT, with particular reference to the United States (which he considers an implicit ITer). He argues that the old (1950s to 1960s) proposition that monetary policy is ineffective, because the transmission mechanism is weak and obscure and the velocity of money is endogenous, has not in fact been refuted. As the result of various experiences, central bankers and others have become convinced that monetary policy matters, and now formulate policy on that basis, but the intellectual underpinnings remain weak. In addition, he warns against multiple objectives or dual mandates for central banks, and supports more openness by central banks about what they can and cannot achieve.

The chapter by Thórarinn G. Pétursson returns to the issue of the effect of IT adoption on macroperformance, but examines it from a different perspective. He focuses on the volatility rather than the level of inflation and sets out to identify the factors responsible for countries' different rates of success in reducing inflation volatility in a sample of forty-two developed and emerging market countries. His initial cross-section work highlights the roles of the volatility of the exchange rate risk premium, the exchange rate pass-through to inflation, and monetary policy predictability. He then introduces a dummy variable for the effect of

adopting IT on inflation volatility, and it turns out to be significantly negative in a panel regression in which the three factors already mentioned
remain significant.

Andrew Filardo and Hans Genberg investigate a very different sample:
twelve Asia-Pacific countries, including both industrial and developing,
large and small, from Australia via China and Hong Kong to Indonesia,
of which six are formal ITers and the other six take inflation very seriously.
They find that the macroeconomic performance of the two groups has
been broadly similar, particularly in terms of inflation control and private
sector inflation expectations. This leads them to suggest that, in their
sample at least, there is no clear advantage for formal over informal IT:
'[T]argeting inflation is important but there are many ways to skin that
cat.' They also speculate briefly about the possibility of a central bank
having multiple objectives with state-dependent priorities.

While the macroeconomic impact of IT is fundamental, a second
major issue is that of the correct response of monetary policy to asset
prices (which is also touched upon by Roger, Schmidt-Hebbel and others). Christopher Allsopp re-examines, and broadly reasserts, the conventional majority view that policy should not respond except after a
bubble has burst. He argues that an important part of the contribution
of IT is that it simplifies the assignment problem: the control of inflation
is assigned to central banks as the single objective to be pursued with a
single appropriate instrument – the policy interest rate. Ideas of responding pre-emptively to rises in asset prices, or 'leaning against the wind',
risk diluting that clarity and losing the benefits it confers. At the same
time, he calls for more emphasis on improved financial regulation and on
understanding and dealing with the global imbalances that underlie the
'savings glut' of recent years.

Charles Goodhart, Carolina Osorio and Dimitrios Tsomocos present
an emphatically non-DSGE (dynamic stochastic general equilibrium)
model, with heterogeneous households and banks, securitisation,
endogenous default, an essential role for money, and incomplete financial markets. This allows them to analyse the impact of different policy
responses in the context of a financial crisis. The key finding is that the
policy interest rate is a superior instrument to changes in money supply. They also emphasise the need for better financial regulation, and
for house prices to be included in the price index that the central bank
targets.

George Evans and Seppo Honkapohja also deal with the issue of the
appropriate policy instrument in a crisis or liquidity trap situation, but
they model the private sector's ability to learn to make accurate expectations. They analyse an infinite-horizon learning – as opposed to an

Euler equation learning – economy in which agents need to forecast variables such as output, inflation, interest rates and taxes. In their model, a large pessimistic shock to expectations can drive the economy into a highly undesirable deflation trap. Aggressive monetary easing on its own is not sufficient to rescue the economy if the expectations shock is large. However, aggressive monetary easing coupled with expansionary fiscal policy when required eliminates the possibility of a deflationary spiral and ensures global stability.

Anke Weber also uses learning models, but with a different focus, to address empirically the development of expectations in a group of EU countries. She finds that expectations can be reasonably modelled as reflecting adaptive learning behaviour, and identifies some interesting but plausible contrasts between the learning behaviour of households and expert forecasters (the former learn more slowly) and between high- and low-inflation countries (households in high-inflation countries update their information sets more frequently than those in low-inflation countries). She also finds that the inflation expectations of professional forecasters broadly converge on the ECB's definition of price stability (under but close to 2 per cent), but that this is not true of households: German households underestimate the ECB's target while Spanish households overestimate it.

The next two chapters examine professional forecasters' expectations of inflation in IT as opposed to non-IT regimes. Morris and Shin (2002) raised the possibility that increased transparency could be destabilising if forecasters put too much weight on information published by the central bank (as opposed to their private sources of information), because this makes the economy too sensitive to common forecast errors. Stephen Cecchetti and Craig Hakkio study the impact of inflation targeting on the dispersion of inflation forecasts (as collected by Consensus Economics). Broadly, they find no clear evidence that (greater transparency of policy under) IT reduces that dispersion, which means that the Morris and Shin concern is not of practical importance. Christopher Crowe focuses on individual forecasters (using the same data source). He finds that IT improves individual forecasters' forecasts, and does so by more for those with initially poorer forecasts but with no loss for those with already good forecasts. However, he also finds that forecasters' rationality may be adversely affected by IT, as they tend to overweight the central bank's published information, and this enables him to reconcile his findings with those of Cecchetti and Hakkio.

Magnus Andersson and Boris Hofmann investigate one of the most recent (and contested) innovations in IT: the publication by IT central banks of their own forecasts of the policy interest rate. It has been argued that such publication could improve central banks' ability to manage expectations and so facilitate the transmission of monetary policy. Andersson and Hofmann test this by comparing ITers that do and do not publish own interest rate paths, across countries and across time. Their findings suggest that the publication of an interest rate path may not significantly improve the short-term predictability of future monetary policy or the anchoring of long-term inflation expectations, but that it may enhance central banks' leverage on the medium-term structure of interest rates.

Ida Wolden Bache, James Mitchell, Francesco Ravazzolo and Shaun P. Vahey discuss, and recommend, a new technique for central bank forecasting under IT. They propose that forecasters should take a leaf out of the book of meteorologists by using 'ensemble modelling', in which uncertainties about model specifications (e.g. initial conditions, parameters and boundary conditions) are explicitly accounted for by constructing ensemble predictive densities from a large number of component models. This allows the modeller to explore a range of uncertainties, and the resulting ensemble 'integrates out' these uncertainties using time-varying weights on the components. The authors illustrate this technique using Norwegian data, first for alternative measures of inflation and then for DSGE models forecasting inflation.

We also publish here five shorter pieces that are revised versions of oral presentations at the conference. Charles Goodhart spoke at the conference dinner about the effects of the crisis and of quantitative easing on the autonomy of central banks. He argues that the experiences of the last two years have reopened the previously closed issue of central bank independence, with unpredictable consequences.

The conference also included a panel discussion on the future of inflation targeting, in which the panel speakers were asked to focus on two questions. First, did inflation targets play any role in setting the stage for the current crisis? Second, does inflation targeting need to be modified as a consequence of the crisis (and, if so, how)? Their contributions, revised in the light of the discussion, are included here. Spencer Dale broadly adheres to the conventional view that monetary policy should not respond to asset prices, but argues for additional financial regulatory instruments in order to minimise bubbles. Hans Genberg argues that the correct response to the crisis is to improve the monetary framework, and, in particular, that there is scope within inflation targeting for the central bank to be more 'sensitive' to concerns other than inflation, and to operate a policy of 'leaning against the wind' (LATW) of asset price movements. Lars Heikensten suggests that some element of LATW would have moderated, but not prevented, the crisis; and that in the future central banks should, cautiously and judiciously, include some element of LATW within their inflation-targeting procedures. Finally, Sushil Wadhwani criticises the prevailing consensus against LATW, which, he argues, would have mitigated the crisis; he also suggests that observers are now exaggerating the crisis-precluding capacity of the new financial regulatory measures (time-varying capital requirements) that are being discussed, in which case, he argues, LATW will remain a necessary policy for ITers.

REFERENCES

Morris, S., and H. Shin (2002). 'Social value of public inflation', *American Economic Review*, 92(5): 1521–34.

Roger, S., and M. Stone (2005). 'On target? The international experience with achieving inflation targets'. Working Paper no. 05/163. Washington, DC: International Monetary Fund [IMF].

2 Welcome remarks: a Norwegian perspective

Jan F. Qvigstad

Dear conference participants, it is a great pleasure for me to welcome all of you to the Sixth Norges Bank Monetary Policy Conference. Norges Bank and the Institute for Monetary and Financial Stability are privileged to host this conference, which has attracted the interest of such a distinguished group of international experts.

Given that we are going to talk about inflation targeting, I will take this opportunity to set the stage by summarising the Norwegian experience. Since the beginning of the 1980s there has been a broad international consensus that monetary policy must be geared towards price stability. This paradigm shift also reached Norway, but not until the end of that decade.

The starting point for us in Norway was a high and variable inflation rate of around 8 to 9 per cent combined with frequent devaluations. In the period from 1976 to 1986 the government carried out no fewer than ten de facto devaluations of the krone. The devaluation in 1986 would become the last in the series, however. The government recognised that the repeated devaluations were ineffective; confidence had been lost, and inflation had soared without a fall in unemployment. There was a broad political agreement that Norway should follow the rest of the world.

In the first phase of the new era (see Figure 2.1) Norway pursued a fixed exchange rate against European currencies with no devaluations. In practice, we tried to borrow credibility and anchor expectations via linkage to low-inflation countries. The crisis in the European Monetary System (EMS) in autumn 1992 changed the situation, as we had to let the krone float.

In the second phase we no longer operated a formal fixed exchange rate system, but in the following years monetary policy was still oriented towards maintaining a stable exchange rate at all times. We also used this phase to learn and prepare for inflation targeting, and received valuable assistance from international academics and other central banks. In 1998,

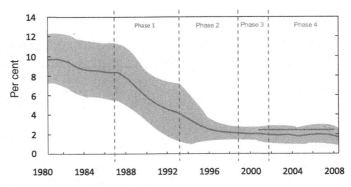

Figure 2.1 Inflation in Norway

Notes: Moving ten-year average and variation in CPI.
Sources: Statistics Norway and Norges Bank.

however, we faced the dilemma that the interest rate that was needed to stabilise the exchange rate was different from the interest rate needed to stabilise the economy. In August Norges Bank shifted its policy to one of setting the interest rate with a view to keeping inflation low and stable over time.

In the following period – the third phase – Norges Bank gave greater weight to influencing inflation developments as a prerequisite for a more stable krone exchange rate over time. These developments led to the formalisation of the inflation target in March 2001, a good eleven years after New Zealand began implementing its inflation-targeting policy, ten years after Canada, nine years after the United Kingdom and eight years after Sweden.

The fourth phase indicates that the paradigm shift has been successful. We have managed to move from high and variable to low and stable inflation.

The question that arises, though, is this: how should we then set the interest rate under inflation targeting? Norges Bank has developed the following set of criteria for a good interest rate path (see Qvigstad 2006 and Holmsen *et al.* 2008 for more detailed descriptions of the criteria and how they are used).

(1) Inflation close to the target in the medium term.
(2) A reasonable balance between the path for inflation and the path for capacity utilisation.
(3) Robustness.
(4) Gradualism and consistency.
(5) Cross-checks: simple policy rules.

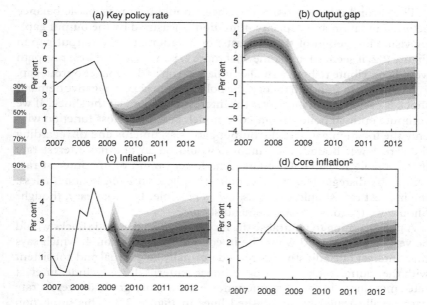

Figure 2.2 Baseline scenario in *Monetary Policy Report 1/09*

Notes:
[1] CPI.
[2] CPI adjusted for tax changes and excluding temporary changes in energy prices.
Sources: Statistics Norway and Norges Bank.

It was Lars Svensson, currently the deputy governor of the Sveriges Riksbank, the central bank of Sweden, who inspired us to develop these criteria. He said that we needed to find an interest path that 'looks good'. The criteria serve the purpose both of communicating the reasoning behind the interest rate path to the public and of providing an agenda for the board's discussion. The criteria are not equal, however. The first one has priority.

Let me give a simple analytical illustration of how these criteria may be used, by using the forecasts from Norges Bank's *Monetary Policy Report 1/09 (MPR 1/09)* as an example (see Figure 2.2). With this interest rate path, we expected inflation to reach the inflation target of 2.5 per cent in what we considered to be the 'medium term'. Thus, the first criterion was satisfied. However, there are many possible interest rate paths that may cause inflation to reach the target in the medium term. Which path should we take? Is there a trade-off between flexibility and credibility? How long can the horizon for achieving the target be without jeopardising credibility?

The second criterion states that there should be a reasonable balance between inflation and capacity utilisation (measured by the output gap). By visual inspection of the forecasts for inflation and the output gap in Figure 2.2, it seems that a somewhat more expansionary interest rate path would contribute to both a smaller inflation gap and a smaller output gap.

According to standard theory, the policy response to a negative demand shock is easy: you should lower the interest rate to offset the shock. If we compute optimal policy in our core model, based on a loss function with only the inflation gap and the output gap as arguments and disregarding the zero lower bound, the outcome would be an optimal interest rate that is highly negative. Of course, the lower bound on the interest rate cannot be disregarded, but the policy implication is clear nonetheless: the interest rate should be set as low as possible. Is it that easy, though? Should we try to neutralise demand shocks?

A policy aiming to neutralise the recent negative demand shocks would be very aggressive and would be in conflict with criterion 4, which says that 'interest rate adjustments should normally be gradual and consistent with the central bank's previous response pattern'. If we include 'interest rate smoothing' in the loss function, we get a more gradual interest rate path, as illustrated by the dashed lines in Figure 2.3. This projection implies that the interest rate should reach a lower level of about 0.5 per cent, which is perhaps close to the lower bound in practice. All the same, criteria 1, 2 and 4 imply a somewhat lower interest rate path than what we ended up with in the last report. Then again, though, is gradualism a good thing? What is the case for 'interest rate smoothing'?

The way we assess economic developments and the economic mechanisms may be wrong. Criterion 3 says that the interest rate path should also result in acceptable developments in inflation and output under alternative, but not unrealistic, assumptions about the economy. I will not go deeply into the issue of robustness, but let me briefly mention two aspects. First, from a robust control perspective, one could imagine a worst-case scenario involving a severe international economic meltdown. The policy implication of such a worst case is to react with more aggressive interest rate cuts. On the other hand, uncertainty about the effects of an expansionary monetary policy points towards a more cautious policy – that is, higher interest rates. There are therefore arguments for both higher interest rates and lower interest rates. What is a robust strategy in the current situation? We welcome advice from academia on how to organise the arguments in a systematic way.

A more practical approach to model uncertainty is to cross-check the path with simple policy rules, such as the Taylor rule. In addition to the standard Taylor rule, we usually consider a version with an additional

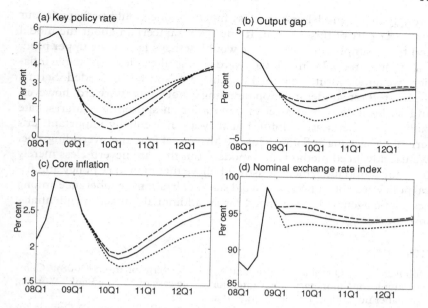

Figure 2.3 Baseline scenario in *MPR 1/09*, optimal policy with interest rate smoothing, and Taylor rule

Notes: Baseline scenario = solid lines; optimal policy = dashed lines; Taylor rule = dotted lines.
Source: Norges Bank.

term on the foreign interest rate, and a version in which the output gap is replaced by gross domestic product (GDP) *growth*.

If we had decided to follow the Taylor rule mechanically, the forecasts would have looked something like the dotted lines in Figure 2.3. The Taylor rule is usually considered to be relatively robust to model uncertainty, but it does not, among other things, distinguish between supply and demand shocks. The higher interest rate path implied by the Taylor rule would lead to more negative output and inflation gaps. Inflation would not reach the target for about ten years. John Taylor and others have advocated that central banks should not follow simple rules mechanically, however, but use them as rough guides for policy. In other words, central banks should place some weight on such rules, but depart from them when they have good reasons to do so.

Based on the criteria, we get an interval for the interest rate, in which the lower limit can be represented by optimal policy (with interest rate smoothing) and the upper limit by the Taylor rule. If one believes very strongly in the model and the loss function, one would perhaps favour the lower part of this interval. If one is very uncertain about the model and trusts simple rules more, one would perhaps favour the upper part.

Let me sum up. From 1986 onwards our goal was low and stable inflation: we aimed for it, we hoped to achieve it, and we succeeded. Setting the interest rate under inflation targeting is not straightforward, however, and we have developed a set of criteria for an appropriate interest rate path. The criteria are helpful, but they are not equally important: criterion 1 – getting inflation close to the target – is the overriding one. We use advanced methods and models, but they are nevertheless merely tools for sound judgement. Lastly, I believe that monetary policy and fiscal policy are not sufficient to avoid states of irrational exuberance among economic agents. There is need for an additional – macro-prudential – instrument.

REFERENCES

Holmsen, A., J. Qvigstad, Ø. Røisland and K. Solberg-Johansen (2008). 'Communicating monetary policy intentions: The case of Norges Bank'. Working Paper no. 2008/20. Oslo: Norges Bank.

Qvigstad, J. (2006). 'When does an interest rate path 'look good'? Criteria for an appropriate future interest rate path'. Working Paper no. 2006/5. Oslo: Norges Bank.

3   Reflections on inflation targeting

Athanasios Orphanides

Starting with the Reserve Bank of New Zealand (RBNZ), over the past twenty years a large number of central banks have adopted inflation targeting as their framework for monetary policy. As the second decade of inflation targeting comes to a close, a retrospective assessing how well it has worked, what lessons have been learned and what challenges may lie ahead is most appropriate. During much of the past twenty years I have observed the introduction and practice of inflation targeting at various central banks around the world with great interest. Throughout this period, though, I have been affiliated with central banks that did not espouse the inflation-targeting approach, and have thus observed its practice as an outsider. I would like to thank Norges Bank for giving me the opportunity to be part of this event, and I am especially thankful to its deputy governor, Jan Qvigstad, for the invitation to offer my personal reflections on inflation targeting. Before I proceed, I should note that the views I express are my own and do not necessarily reflect those of the Governing Council of the European Central Bank.

What is inflation targeting? There are several and sometimes competing or conflicting definitions, reflecting the numerous variations encountered in policy practice and the evolution of the framework itself. In a thorough study of the first experiences with inflation targeting, Bernanke *et al.* (1999: 4) have suggested the following description:

Inflation targeting is a framework for monetary policy characterised by the public announcement of official quantitative targets (or target ranges) for the inflation rate over one or more time horizons, and by explicit acknowledgement that low, stable inflation is monetary policy's primary long-run goal. Among other important features of inflation targeting are vigorous efforts to communicate with the public about the plans and objectives of the monetary authorities, and, in many cases, mechanisms that strengthen the central bank's accountability for attaining those objectives.

In my view, inflation targeting, as originally developed and practised, is a robust way of achieving and maintaining price stability. It is certainly

13

not the only way of achieving this goal, however. That said, inflation targeting can be more effective than other alternatives in achieving price stability under some circumstances. If so, it would be useful to identify what these circumstances may be. At the same time, judging from the experience of the past two decades, one can conclude that several central banks around the world, including banks that characterise themselves as inflation targeters and others that do not, have had similarly good macroeconomic performances overall, and similar success in achieving and maintaining price stability. A pertinent question, then, is to identify what the commonalities are among alternative strategies that make the best contributions to good policy practice.

A distinguishing characteristic of inflation targeting is that it is a monetary policy framework that focuses maximum attention on the ultimate objective of price stability, and, indeed, demands close monitoring of current and prospective developments in aggregate prices as a means both to guiding current policy and to evaluating past policy actions. By encouraging an ongoing open dialogue between the central bank and the government, the public and financial market participants, the inflation-targeting approach leaves little room for neglecting price stability, which further reinforces its unique focus. For these reasons, inflation targeting may be particularly effective as a monetary policy framework for central banks that are institutionally challenged in some way, for instance because they lack a history of political independence or because they have an impaired credibility in pursuing monetary-stability-oriented policies. The intrusion of politics into monetary policy decisions and the pursuit of multiple and possibly conflicting objectives are potential sources of such impaired credibility with regard to a central bank's commitment to achieving and maintaining price stability. Inflation targeting helps guard against these forces.

Ensuring the stability of a currency's value has long been recognised as a prerequisite for the efficient working of a capitalist economy. As early as the end of the nineteenth century, Knut Wicksell (1898 [1936]) proposed that monetary policy should aim at maintaining a stable price level. However, achieving and maintaining price stability has been elusive over the short history of monetary policy practice with a fiat currency, with deflation and inflation frequently undermining price stability over time. Highlighting the common understanding of the destructive potential of an unstable currency among both supporters and opponents of our economic system, John Maynard Keynes attributed to Vladimir Ilyich Lenin the remark that 'the best way to destroy the Capitalist System was to debauch the currency'. Keynes continued: 'Lenin was certainly right. There is no subtler, no surer means of overturning the existing basis of society than to debauch the currency. The process engages all the hidden forces of economic law on the side of destruction, and does it in a manner which not one man in a million is able to diagnose' (Keynes 1919 [1971]: 148–9).

In a similar vein, Irving Fisher argued that it was imperative to find a way to maintain monetary stability, concluding: 'It is not too much to say that the evils of a variable monetary standard are among the most serious economic evils with which civilization has to deal' (Fisher 1922: ix). As Meltzer (2003) documents in his history of the Federal Reserve, for much of the 1920s price stability as a goal of monetary policy became a recurrent issue for discussion in the United States. However, the central bank opposed focusing on price stability as a policy guide, and the approach was never adopted. During the 1930s Sweden offered a unique example of a monetary regime targeting a price level, but that experience lasted for only a few years (Berg and Jonung 1999).

Although price stability was considered a worthwhile objective for macroeconomic policy to varying degrees throughout the course of the twentieth century, this would have been rather hard to infer from observing price developments. Price instability instead of stability seems to have been the norm throughout much of the last century.

A useful starting point for understanding the origins of inflation targeting is to comprehend the sources and magnitude of the failure in some of the countries that adopted it. The case of New Zealand, the pioneer of inflation targeting, is instructive. As Don Brash, the governor who first implemented the new approach, explained in a retrospective on inflation targeting, prior to the mid-1980s New Zealand had one of the worst inflation rates among the Organisation for Economic Co-operation and Development (OECD) countries, exceeding 10 per cent per year for virtually a whole decade. Why was that? Wasn't low inflation one of the aims of the RBNZ? Apparently, one problem was exactly that. Price stability was merely *one* of multiple goals. Brash explains the multiple-goal-oriented approach pursued by the RBNZ before the adoption of inflation targeting as follows: 'The legislation under which we operated required us, in formulating our advice, to have regard for the inflation rate, employment, growth, motherhood, and a range of other good things' (Brash 1999: 36). Another problem was that the central bank's role was to provide advice to the minister of finance on monetary policy decisions, instead of having the power to implement the decisions itself. This lack of operational independence allowed the possibility of short-term political considerations to creep into the implementation of policy.

The Reserve Bank of New Zealand Act of 1989 corrected both these shortcomings. First, in place of the multiple goal orientation, section 8 of the act clarified the primacy of price stability as the RBNZ's objective: 'The primary function of the Bank is to formulate and implement monetary policy directed to the economic objective of achieving and maintaining stability in the general level of prices.' Second, section 9 of the act stipulated that the minister of finance and the governor were to enter into a 'Policy Target Agreement' that defined the numerical objective to be pursued during the governor's term, while section 10 provided the governor with complete operational independence to pursue the agreed policy targets.

The Reserve Bank of New Zealand Act of 1989 therefore described two defining characteristics of the canonical inflation-targeting approach it originated: first, defining a hierarchical mandate for the central bank with price stability as the primary objective; and, second, providing the central bank with the operational independence to pursue this objective. The approach quickly succeeded in bringing inflation down in New Zealand, and thus captured the attention of other central banks.

Not all inflation-targeting central banks have an explicit mandate defining price stability as the primary objective. Nonetheless, the primacy of price stability may be implicitly recognised in practice. One example is the Reserve Bank of Australia (RBA), for which the adoption of inflation targeting was an evolutionary process influenced by the New Zealand experience. The RBA's legislated mandate, dating back to 1959, is multiple-goal-oriented and directs it to set monetary policy so as to 'best contribute to: (a) the stability of the currency of Australia; (b) the maintenance of full employment in Australia; and (c) the economic prosperity and welfare of the people of Australia' (Reserve Bank Act: 6–7). However, following the adoption of inflation targeting in 2003, the RBA and the government signed a letter of agreement recognising that price stability is the main contribution that monetary policy can make to sustained growth in output and employment. This helps mitigate the possible tension between the multiple goals in the Reserve Bank of Australia Act and the practice of inflation targeting (Debelle 2009). In principle, an independent central bank with a legislative mandate that mentions multiple goals but is not clear on the primacy of price stability could choose to interpret its mandate in a hierarchical manner if it espouses the inflation-targeting policy framework. A legislated hierarchical mandate would be superior, however, as without it there is always the risk of backsliding away from the primacy of price stability towards the pre-inflation-targeting multiple goal orientation.

Conversely, not all central banks with a mandate specifying price stability as the primary objective and having operational independence to pursue this objective are inflation-targeting central banks. An example in this category is the European Central Bank (ECB), part of the European System of Central Banks (ESCB). The ECB's monetary policy framework identifies price stability as its primary focus. Indeed, both the independence of the ECB as well as its price stability mandate are enshrined in the treaty establishing the European Community. According to the treaty: 'The primary objective of the ESCB shall be to maintain price stability' (European Union 2006: 87). However, the ECB is also instructed to do whatever else it can to enhance the welfare of European citizens. This is why the treaty continues: 'Without prejudice to the objective of price stability the ESCB shall support the general economic policies in the Community' (87). The mandate is explicitly hierarchical, though, with emphasis on the primary nature of price stability as the ECB's objective.

Against this background, it may be of interest to understand key elements that are not unique to inflation targeting but may be seen as contributing to good policy practice. I would like to focus on three such elements.

The first, and arguably the most fundamental, element of inflation targeting is the announcement of an explicit quantitative definition of price stability and the acknowledgement that the achievement of this target over time is the primary objective and responsibility of the central bank. Typically, the quantitative definition of price stability is specified as a low inflation rate or a narrow range. There is considerable variation in the exact specification but annual inflation rates of around 2 per cent are compatible with most definitions. Some central banks focus on an exact point target (e.g. 2 per cent) while others focus on a zone target (e.g. 1 to 3 per cent), with or without special emphasis on the midpoint. There is also variation regarding the specificity of the time horizon. Early implementations specified a rather rigid horizon for achieving the objective – e.g. two years – but other implementations are more flexible – e.g. specifying the objective as 2 to 3 per cent inflation over the business cycle (what is sometimes referred to as a 'thick' target in the case of the Reserve Bank of Australia).

Recognising price stability as the overriding objective of monetary policy does not imply that the central bank is blind to other policy goals. Nor does it replace the policymaker with an automaton, in the manner that adoption of a rigid policy rule would. Inflation-targeting central banks retain considerable discretion in policy implementation and remain sensitive to other objectives that are important for economic welfare, including the stability of real economic activity and employment as well as financial stability. As suggested by Bernanke *et al.* (1999), inflation targeting is not a policy *rule* but, rather, a *framework* that allows policy to operate in an environment of 'constrained discretion'. In practice, the flexibility aspect of inflation targeting is exercised by deciding how to deal with shocks to the economy and how quickly to plan to bring inflation back to its target rate in response to destabilising shocks. This flexibility has tended to increase somewhat over time, as inflation-targeting central banks accumulated credibility that their focus on price stability was meaningful. With increased confidence that policymakers would not backslide to the days of a multiple-goal-oriented approach, expectations are more likely to stay well anchored in the face of shocks, thereby enabling greater flexibility in policy. In practice, inflation targeting can be more or less flexible, depending on the circumstances and the success of the central bank in establishing and maintaining a high degree of credibility.

A commitment to price stability as the key operational objective of a central bank is by no means unique to inflation targeting. Rather, it is a characteristic common to all monetary policy frameworks that may possibly be identified as broadly consistent with good policy practice. Avoiding both prolonged inflation and deflation, and safeguarding price stability, is now widely understood as contributing to high levels of economic activity and employment.

Price stability facilitates better planning by businesses and households, preventing an arbitrary redistribution of wealth and income as a result of unexpected inflation or deflation. It also improves the transparency of the price mechanism, raising efficiency.

As already mentioned, the monetary policy framework of the ECB also identifies price stability as the primary focus of the institution. In implementing this mandate, the ECB uses an explicit quantitative definition of price stability that, since 2003, has been stated as corresponding to a rate of increase in consumer prices of below but close to 2 per cent over the medium term.

Among non-inflation-targeting central banks, it is of interest to mention that the US Federal Reserve is also, as would be expected, committed to price stability in a manner not dissimilar to that of an inflation-targeting central bank. Indeed, the case of the Federal Reserve is quite close to that of the RBA mentioned earlier. The Federal Reserve Act (as amended in 1977) directs the Federal Reserve to pursue policies that promote 'maximum employment, stable prices, and moderate long-term interest rates'. One of the most significant changes in Federal Reserve policy following the reform introduced in 1979 by its then chairman, Paul Volcker, can be identified with the reaffirmation of price stability as the most important operational objective for monetary policy, and as a means of achieving the Federal Reserve's other objectives (Lindsey, Orphanides and Rasche 2005). Although the Federal Reserve does not have an explicit numerical objective for inflation, in January 2009 the

Federal Open Market Committee provided some pertinent guidance. In particular, the Committee decided to disclose its members' assessments of the appropriate long-run inflation rate. A large majority of the Committee indicated that their assessment was close to or equal to 2 per cent. Interestingly, according to the minutes of the 27–8 January meeting, the Committee considered adopting a numerical target, but ultimately made no decision on the matter. Some members noted that providing information on the appropriate long-run inflation rate would probably yield the benefits of a more formal declaration. In light of these developments, the Federal Reserve policy framework is now quite close to inflation targeting with respect to providing explicit numerical guidance on its price stability objective.

Why is an explicit numerical objective helpful, beyond a general commitment to price stability? Specification of an explicit quantitative definition of price stability – in the form of a numerical inflation target – can be particularly helpful in facilitating long-term planning. Critically, it facilitates the public's formation of more accurate expectations and helps anchor longer-term inflation expectations with well-known benefits to the overall effectiveness of monetary policy and success in promoting greater stability in general (Orphanides and Williams 2005).

The second key element of the inflation-targeting framework is a forward-looking policy orientation and the associated monitoring of inflation forecasts and inflation expectations. As long and variable lags are an inherent feature of monetary policy, the latter should exhibit a forward-looking approach. Central banks pursuing inflation targeting regularly publish extensive reports on economic conditions and the outlook for inflation, including their projections for these variables. Similarly, since the public's inflation expectations can provide valuable information about the outlook for inflation, the evolution of these expectations receives special emphasis in any forward-looking policy approach. Monitoring short-term inflation expectations is valuable because they are important determinants of actual price- and wage-setting behaviour, and thus actual inflation, over time. Expectations over longer horizons are particularly useful for gauging any possible reversal in the central bank's credibility regarding its commitment to price stability. They are also embedded in asset prices and long-term interest rates, and therefore, importantly, influence economic decisions with long-term outcomes, such as investment in capital, housing and durable goods.

Monitoring the stability of inflation expectations is also important for gauging the extent to which a central bank can accommodate real economic disturbances without compromising its price stability mandate. When private inflation expectations become unmoored from the central bank's objectives, macroeconomic stabilisation can be considerably harder to achieve. Well-anchored inflation expectations facilitate the monetary policy response to adverse supply shocks, thereby enabling central banks to stabilise economic fluctuations more effectively. For these reasons, inflation-targeting central banks place particular emphasis on inflation forecasts and inflation expectations. However, the same applies to *any* policy framework focused on achieving price stability, and indeed the forward-looking policy orientation and close monitoring of inflation forecasts and inflation expectations are also common to other policy frameworks, including those of the ECB and the Federal Reserve.

The third element of inflation targeting is a transparent communication strategy that aims to explain to the markets and the public at large the mandate of the central bank and its actions towards achieving this mandate over the medium term. The opacity that accompanied monetary policy in the past has been replaced by transparency. The merits of this transparency have been understood and incorporated into other strategies as well. Increased transparency in monetary policy has been espoused by both inflation- and non-inflation-targeting central banks during this period. I believe that, although an increase in transparency may not have been an integral part of the framework followed by non-inflation-targeting central banks, its value was recognised, in part, because of the early success of inflation targeting. As a result, today the public is in a better position to comprehend the rationale for policy decisions. A better-educated public regarding the systematic component of monetary policy implies a smaller element of surprise and increased effectiveness in terms of monetary policy actions.

All in all, when considering crucial aspects of policy strategy, such as recognition of the primacy of price stability, the forward-looking policy orientation, the emphasis on maintaining well-anchored inflation expectations and transparency in communications, there are many similarities between the frameworks of the ECB, the Federal Reserve and inflation-targeting central banks. Differences in the practices of these central banks should not be exaggerated.

Although it is straightforward to identify some key elements of inflation targeting, modelling this policy approach has not been as straightforward. One strand of the academic literature identifies inflation targeting with the solution to a central bank optimisation problem in a linear rational expectations model of the economy. To capture the flexibility aspect of inflation targeting, a quadratic loss function with multiple objectives is imposed on a linear model of the economy, and sufficient assumptions are made for the solution to fit within the confines of the familiar linear-quadratic optimisation framework. Typical assumptions include perfect knowledge of the underlying structure of the economy and complete transparency and credibility with regard to the multiple objectives of the central bank. In that context, inflation targeting is seen as the policy that implements the linear first-order conditions obtained from the related optimisation problem (see, for example, Svensson 2002, Svensson and Woodford 2005 and Giannoni and Woodford 2005).

Such models can certainly be useful for advancing macroeconomic theory, but I question their practical usefulness for formulating policy under inflation targeting. By rendering inflation targeting observationally equivalent to the earlier approach of optimal control monetary policy, this modelling approach fails to appreciate and does not adequately reflect some of the special features of inflation targeting (Faust and Henderson 2004). Indeed, the optimal control approach misses the central focus that inflation targeting places on price stability, as well as the rationale for this focus.

An optimisation problem based on a quadratic loss function with multiple goals hardly reflects the hierarchical nature of the objectives of an inflation-targeting central bank. When this difference is acknowledged, the term 'flexible' inflation targeting is often used to distinguish this modelling approach from inflation targeting. In my view, this is an unfortunate and confusing use of terminology. A more accurate term would be 'multiple goal targeting', to distinguish the parallel emphasis on multiple goals as opposed to the unique focus that inflation targeting places on price stability. Recalling Brash's description of the multiple goal orientation of the Reserve Bank of New Zealand before the adoption of inflation targeting also suggests that the multiple-goal-targeting modelling approach is more suitable for modelling monetary policy prior to the adoption of inflation targeting than monetary policy under inflation targeting.

A danger in using such models for policy analysis is that they may suggest the feasibility of misleadingly ambitious outcomes. Under the imposed assumption of rational expectations with perfect knowledge, inflation expectations are always well anchored and central bank communication loses any meaningful independent role. Economic shocks have more benign consequences, and the fine tuning of policy appears able to deal with them more easily than is feasible in practice.

To appreciate the effectiveness of the inflation-targeting approach better, Orphanides and Williams (2007) argue that it is essential to acknowledge economic agents' imperfect understanding of the macroeconomic environment within which the public forms expectations and policymakers formulate and implement monetary policy. This requires relaxing the assumption of perfect knowledge in our models and accommodating learning dynamics in order to achieve a better approximation of how economic agents update their beliefs and form expectations on the basis of incoming information.

In models that introduce such additional layers of complexity to approximate reality better, implementation of the inflation-targeting policy can be approximated with simple policy rules that specify how the central bank adjusts its interest rate policy instrument in response to deviations of inflation projections from the inflation target. Certainly, no simple rule can accurately capture the constrained discretion of inflation targeting. Nevertheless, macroeconometric policy evaluations of simple rules in various models can usefully help identify those factors that are most important for guiding policymakers in achieving the robust stability results that inflation-targeting central banks seek (see, for example, Batini and Haldane 1999, Levin, Wieland and Williams 2003 and Orphanides and Williams 2007).

Another reason for utilising simple policy rules as descriptive devices for implementing inflation targeting is their value in communicating the simplicity of the framework. An outline of the implementation of monetary policy under inflation targeting could be simply stated in terms of the deviation of inflation projections from a central bank's target over time. A rule of thumb could be: if it appears that inflation will be notably higher than the target for a considerable period, the policy rate should be raised; if it appears that inflation will be notably lower than the target for a considerable period, the policy rate should be eased. I find it remarkable how similar this rule of thumb for inflation targeting appears to be to Wicksell's (1898 [1936]: 189) suggested rule for achieving and maintaining a stable price level:

If prices rise, the rate of interest is to be raised; and if prices fall, the rate of interest is to be lowered; and the rate of interest is henceforth to be maintained at its new level until a further movement in prices calls for a further change in one direction or the other.

In closing, I would like to highlight the methodological challenge I see in modelling inflation targeting. I am not convinced that we have reached a good equilibrium in the allocation of modelling resources to capture the essence of the approach. I am concerned about the appeal of relying on optimal control techniques to construct multiple-goal-targeting models that are then used for policy analysis regarding inflation targeting. As has been the case in the past, I see a risk of over-promising on what monetary policy can do and losing our focus on inflation. The search for ever-increasing flexibility in implementing inflation targeting should not tempt policymakers towards the tendency to overreach much beyond what inflation targeting can deliver.

To conclude, the key elements of inflation targeting – namely the public announcement of a numerical inflation target along with the recognition of the primacy of price stability, the forward-looking policy orientation with an emphasis on maintaining well-anchored inflation expectations and transparency in communications – lie at the centre of what constitutes good monetary policy practice more generally. As originally formulated and practised, inflation targeting appropriately respects the limits of our knowledge and should help avoid major monetary policy mistakes. Inflation targeting has contributed to improved policy practice over the past twenty years. Importantly, I believe that it has had a positive influence on policy even among central banks that have chosen not to adopt it. The increased transparency in monetary policy that has been espoused by inflation- and non-inflation-targeting central banks alike is confirmation of this. With the success of inflation targeting and other frameworks in maintaining price stability, however, new challenges have appeared. At present, we are dealing with an extreme episode of financial instability and a truly globalised economic downturn. I hope that over the next two decades we are as successful in dealing with these new challenges as we have been in dealing with the problem of price instability over the past twenty years.

REFERENCES

Batini, N., and A. Haldane (1999). 'Forward-looking rules for monetary policy', in J. Taylor (ed.). *Monetary Policy Rules*: 157–202. Chicago: University of Chicago Press.

Berg, C., and L. Jonung (1999). 'Pioneering price level targeting: the Swedish experience 1931–1937', *Journal of Monetary Economics*, 43(3): 525–51.

Bernanke, B., T. Laubach, F. Mishkin and A. Posen (1999). *Inflation Targeting: Lessons from the International Experience*. Princeton, NJ: Princeton University Press.

Brash, D. (1999). 'Inflation targeting: an alternative way of achieving price stability'. Address on the occasion of the fiftieth anniversary of central banking in the Philippines, Manila, 5 January.

Debelle, G. (2009). 'The Australian experience with inflation targeting'. Remarks at the Banco Central do Brasil, Brasília, 15 May.

European Union (2006). Monetary Policy, Article 105; consolidated version of the treaty establishing the European Community *OFFICIAL JOURNAL OF THE EUROPEAN UNION*.

Faust, J., and D. Henderson (2004). 'Is inflation targeting best-practice monetary policy?', *Federal Reserve Bank of St. Louis Review*, 86(4): 117–43.

Fisher, I. (1922) *The Purchasing Power of Money: Its Determination and Relation to Credit, Interest, and Crises* New York: Macmillan.

Giannoni, M., and M. Woodford (2005). 'Optimal inflation-targeting rules', in B. Bernanke and M. Woodford (eds.). *The Inflation-Targeting Debate*: 93–162. Chicago: University of Chicago Press.

Keynes, J. (1919 [1971]). *The Economic Consequences of the Peace*, repr. *The Collected Writings of John Maynard Keynes*, vol. II. London: Macmillan, for the Royal Economic Society.

Levin, A., V. Wieland and J. Williams (2003). 'The performance of forecast-based monetary policy rules under model uncertainty', *American Economic Review*, 93(3): 622–45.

Lindsey, D., A. Orphanides and R. Rasche (2005). 'The reform of October 1979: how it happened and why', *Federal Reserve Bank of St. Louis Review*, 87(2, part 2): 187–236.

Meltzer, A. (2003). *A History of the Federal Reserve*, vol. I, *1913–1951*. Chicago: University of Chicago Press.

Orphanides, A., and J. Williams (2005). 'Imperfect knowledge, inflation expectations, and monetary policy', in B. Bernanke and M. Woodford (eds.). *The Inflation-Targeting Debate*: 201–34. Chicago: University of Chicago Press.

    (2007). 'Inflation targeting under imperfect knowledge', in F. Mishkin and K. Schmidt-Hebbel (eds.). *Monetary Policy under Inflation Targeting*: 77–123. Santiago: Banco Central de Chile.

Reserve Bank of Australia (1959). Reserve Bank Act. Available at www.complaw.gov.av/comlaw/Legislation/Act/Compilation   1.nsf/0/5F58E3B25BE82A57CA256F71004DA83C/$file/RBA59.pdf.

Reserve Bank of New Zealand (1989). Reserve Bank of New Zealand Act. Available at www.legislation.govt.nz/act/public/1989/0157/latest/viewpdf.aspx?search=ts_act_Reserve+Bank+New+Zealand_resel&p=1.

Svensson, L. (2002). 'Inflation targeting: should it be modeled as an instrument rule or a targeting rule?', *European Economic Review*, 46(4–5): 771–80.

Svensson, L., and M. Woodford (2005). 'Implementing optimal policy through inflation-forecast targeting', in B. Bernanke and M. Woodford (eds.). *The Inflation-Targeting Debate*: 19–83. Chicago: University of Chicago Press.

Wicksell, K. (1898 [1936]). *Interest and Prices*. (trans. R. Kahn). London: Macmillan, for the Royal Economic Society.

4   Inflation targeting at twenty: achievements and challenges

Scott Roger[1]

4.1   Introduction

Inflation targeting was first adopted in the early 1990s by industrial countries, but now it is being adopted by a growing number of emerging market and developing countries. As of mid-2009 twenty-six countries are classified as inflation targeters, including eleven high-income countries and fifteen lower-income emerging market and developing countries. This chapter provides a review of the experience with inflation targeting, together with an overview of some issues and challenges facing the future of inflation targeting.

Section 4.2 briefly documents the spread of inflation targeting and, in particular, the increasing dominance of emerging market and developing country inflation targeters – a trend that is expected to continue.

Section 4.3 begins with an overview of the major elements of inflation-targeting frameworks, including (i) the specification of the inflation target and the handling of policy trade-offs; (ii) governance and decision-making frameworks; and (iii) communications and accountability arrangements. Broadly speaking, the analysis finds that a fairly standard model of inflation targeting has emerged. Inflation target specifications are generally quite similar – perhaps too much so – and a broad consensus has developed in favour of 'flexible' inflation targeting, which takes not only inflation but also output considerations into account in policy formulation. Policy accountability and communications arrangements also appear to be converging on an increasingly transparent model.

Section 4.4 reviews macroeconomic performance under inflation targeting, focusing on three main issues: (i) how well countries have done in meeting their inflation targets; (ii) whether inflation targeting has tended to deliver better macroeconomic performance than alternative policy frameworks; and (iii) whether inflation targeting has delivered better macroeconomic results than alternative frameworks in response to the global commodity price and financial shocks. The results indicate that inflation target ranges are missed frequently in most countries, but

25

Table 4.1 *Adoption of inflation targeting*

Country	Effective IT adoption date	CPI inflation rate at start of disinflation	Disinflation period	CPI inflation rate at start of stable targeting	Stable inflation-targeting period
New Zealand[1]	1990Q1	3.3	1990Q1–1992Q4	1.8	1993Q1–present
Canada[1]	1991M2	6.9	1991M2–1994M12	0.2	1995M1–present
United Kingdom[1]	1992M10			4.0	1992M10–present
Sweden[1]	1993M1			1.8	1993M1–present
Finland[1]	1993M2			2.6	1993M2–1998M12
Australia[1]	1993M4			2.0	1993Q2–present
Spain[1]	1995M1	4.2	1995M1–1997M12		1998M1–1998M12
Israel[1]	1997M6	8.1	1997M6–2002M12	6.5	2003M1–present
Czech Republic[1]	1997M12	6.8	1997M12–2001M12	4.1	2002M1–present
Poland[2]	1998M10	10.6	1998M10–2003M12	1.7	2004M1–present
Brazil[2]	1999M6	3.3	1999M6–2005M12	5.7	2006M1–present
Chile[2]	1999M9	3.2	1999M9–2000M12	4.5	2001M1–present
Colombia[2]	1999M9	9.3	1999M9–present		
South Africa[2]	2000M2			2.6	2000M2–present
Thailand[2]	2000M5			0.8	2000M5–present
Mexico[2]	2001M1	9.0	2001M1–2002M12	5.7	2003M1–present
South Korea[1]	2001M1			2.8	2001M1–present
Iceland[1]	2001M3	4.1	2001M3–2003M12	2.7	2004M1–present
Norway[1]	2001M3			3.6	2001M3–present

Hungary[1]	2001M6	2001M6–2006M12	10.8	6.5	2007M1–present
Peru[2]	2002M1	2002M1–present		−0.1	2002M1–present
Philippines[2]	2002M1	2002M1–present	4.5	1.8	
Guatemala[2]	2005M1	2005M1–present	9.2	0.2	
Slovakia[1]	2005M1	2005M1–2008M12	5.8		IT concluded 2008M12
Indonesia[2]	2005M7	2005M7–present	7.4		
Romania[2]	2005M8	2005M8–present	9.3		
Turkey[2]	2006M1	2006M1–present	7.7		
Serbia[2]	2006M9	2006M9–present	10.8		
Ghana[2]	2007M5	2007M5–present	10.5		
All countries			5.7	3.1	
14 high-income[1]			4.8	3.2	
15 low-income[2]			6.5	3.0	

Notes: Q = quarter, M = month.

[1] High-income countries, based on the World Bank's *World Development Indicators* classification.

[2] Low-income countries, based on the same classification.

especially in countries that are in the process of disinflation. Tentative evidence also indicates that inflation targeters have coped better with the commodity price and financial shocks in 2007–9 than non-inflation targeters.

Section 4.5 concludes with a discussion of issues and challenges in inflation targeting. These include challenges in adapting inflation targeting to emerging market and developing countries, and incorporating financial stability issues more effectively into inflation-targeting frameworks.

4.2   The shift towards inflation targeting

Since New Zealand first adopted inflation targeting in 1989, twenty-nine countries have introduced inflation-targeting frameworks (see Table 4.1).[2] In addition, several other central banks, including the European Central Bank, the Swiss National Bank and the Federal Reserve in the United States, have moved towards regimes that have many of the attributes of inflation targeting. Through the 1990s inflation targeting was almost entirely confined to advanced 'industrial' countries. Since the late 1990s, however, an increasing number of developing and emerging market economies (EMEs) have adopted the framework, and such countries are now the substantial majority of inflation targeters.

The spread of inflation targeting has often been prompted by exchange rate crises. As shown in Figure 4.1, exchange rate pegs of various kinds accounted for two-thirds of monetary policy regimes in industrial countries in 1989.[3] The ERM crisis in 1992 served as a spur to the adoption of inflation targeting in Europe. Among EMEs, the shift towards inflation targeting has been a more gradual process. In Latin America the movement towards inflation targeting began in the early 1990s, but full-fledged inflation targeting was adopted only in the late 1990s and early 2000s, following the 1998 financial crisis. In Europe the transition economies of central and eastern Europe began introducing inflation targeting in the late 1990s as part of their comprehensive economic reforms, while in east Asia inflation targeting began to be adopted in the early 2000s, as countries emerged from monetary targeting under IMF-supported programmes following the 1997 Asian financial crisis. At least until the global financial crisis erupted, inflation targeting was expected to continue to spread among emerging markets and developing economies.[4] The outlook for the spread of inflation targeting now seems likely to depend very much on how well the framework is perceived to

(a) Industrial countries

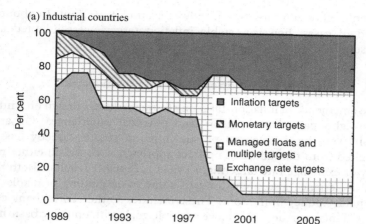

(b) Non-industrial countries

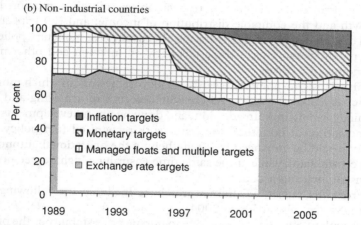

Figure 4.1 Evolution of monetary policy regimes, 1989–2006
Source: IMF.

have coped with the oil price shock and the subsequent global financial shock.

In most countries adopting inflation targeting, there has been an initial phase of disinflation. This phase has typically involved setting year-by-year targets for reducing inflation. Disinflation has typically begun from a level of about 4.8 per cent among high-income countries, and from 6.5 per cent in low-income countries. Once inflation has been brought down, the regime shifts to targeting stable, multi-period or indefinite horizon targets, typically of around 3 per cent. In about one-third of cases, however, stable inflation targets were adopted at the outset.

4.3   Elements of inflation-targeting frameworks[5]

The emergence of inflation-targeting frameworks has drawn on a number of insights gained from theory and practical experience.[6] On a practical level, the decision to pursue inflation targets directly has often resulted from the failure of indirect approaches, based on either monetary or exchange rate targeting, to yield acceptable results.[7] Both theory and experience also point towards some basic guiding principles for a monetary policy framework. These include: (i) the central bank cannot consistently pursue and achieve multiple goals with only one basic instrument – the policy interest rate; (ii) over the long term, monetary policy can control nominal but not real variables; (iii) high inflation harms growth and the equitable distribution of income; and (iv) expectations and credibility matter greatly for the effectiveness of monetary policy and the potential short-term trade-offs between inflation and other macroeconomic objectives.

These insights pointed towards a policy framework in which monetary policy is assigned a clear and credible objective of achieving and maintaining low inflation. In addition, and drawing upon developments in the principal–agent literature, the framework recognised that policy credibility would be enhanced by strengthening the operational autonomy of the central bank while at the same time ensuring a high degree of policy transparency and accountability.

From the outset, IT frameworks have included the following basic elements (see also Mishkin 2004):
- an explicit central bank mandate to pursue price stability as the primary objective of monetary policy, together with accountability with regard to performance in achieving the objective;
- a high degree of transparency in terms of monetary policy strategy and implementation;
- explicit quantitative targets for inflation; and
- policy actions based on a forward-looking assessment of inflation pressures, taking into account a wide array of information.

Central bank mandates

The objective of price stability is frequently embedded in central bank legislation and the target specification. However, legislated goals often do not clearly define price stability as the primary objective of monetary policy (see Table 4.2). Consequently, the specification of the inflation target plays a particularly important role in defining the IT mandate. In most countries, target specifications are established jointly between the central bank and the government, but, even in countries in which one or the other has sole authority to specify the target, close consultation is the norm.

IT central banks typically have a high degree of instrumental or operational autonomy. In several emerging market economies, revisions to central bank acts have explicitly ruled out the provision of credit to the government, eliminated government vetoes over policy decisions and strengthened measures to insulate central bank policy decision-makers from potential pressures from the government.

Even when there are limits on instrument autonomy, these do not appear to be binding in practice. As indicated in Table 4.2, in many countries in which inflation targeting has been implemented successfully, instrument autonomy is, in principle, constrained by the potential for central bank financing of government, government powers to override the central bank's instrument-setting decisions, or direct participation by government officials in monetary policy decision-making. This underlines the fact that de jure autonomy matters less than de facto autonomy. In this regard, a strong government commitment to the inflation-targeting framework is crucial.

Policy accountability and transparency

Central bank accountability for performance in relation to the inflation target is a natural corollary of autonomy in policy implementation, and helps to reinforce such autonomy. Having to account for inflation performance provides strong incentives for the central bank to focus on meeting its targets and to communicate its decisions and actions transparently. The need to explain policy decisions to the public also serves as a powerful internal discipline on the central bank's approach to policy analysis and decision-making. Moreover, public accountability provides an incentive for the central bank to resist external pressures to let factors outside its remit unduly influence policy. From this perspective, high standards of policy accountability help the central bank to maximise its autonomy to pursue its mandate, while minimising its incentives to be distracted by other considerations.

Mechanisms for providing central bank policy accountability vary between countries, with some having quite formal arrangements and others less formal (Table 4.3; see also Roger and Stone 2005, Tuladhar 2005

Table 4.2 *Central bank autonomy*

Country	Goal autonomy (legislated goal)	Target autonomy — Target specification	Instrument autonomy — Government override	Instrument autonomy — Credit to government	Instrument autonomy — Government participation in policymaking
Australia	Multiple goals	G+CB	Yes	Yes	Voting member
Brazil	Inflation target	G	No	No	No
Canada	Multiple goals	G+CB	Yes	Yes, limited	Non-voting
Chile	Price + financial stability	CB	Yes	No	Non-voting[1]
Colombia	Price stability	CB	Yes	No	Voting member
Czech Republic	Price stability	G+CB	No	No	Non-voting
Ghana	Price stability	G+CB	No	Yes, limited	Voting member
Guatemala	Price stability	CB	No	No	Voting member
Hungary	Price stability	G+CB	No	No	Non-voting
Iceland	Price stability	G+CB	No	No	No
Indonesia	Currency stability	G+CB	No	No	No
Israel	Price stability	G	No	No	No
Mexico	Price stability	CB	No	Yes	Non-voting
New Zealand	Price stability	G+CB	Yes	Yes	No
Norway	Low, stable inflation	G	Yes	No	No
Peru	Monetary stability	CB	No	No	Voting member
Philippines	Price stability	G+CB	No	Yes, limited	Voting member

Poland	Price stability	CB	No	No	Non-voting
Romania	Price stability	G+CB	No	No	No
Serbia	Low, stable inflation	G+CB	No	Yes, limited	Non-voting
Slovakia	Price stability	CB	No	No	No
South Africa	Currency stability	G+CB	Yes	Yes	No
South Korea	Price stability	G+CB	No	Yes	Non-voting
Sweden	Price stability	CB	No	No	Non-voting
Thailand	Monetary stability	CB	No	Yes	Non-voting
Turkey	Price stability	G+CB	No	No	Non-voting
United Kingdom	Price stability	G	Yes	No	Non-voting

Notes: G = government, CB = central bank.

[1] Finance minister may delay implementation of decisions for two weeks.

Sources: Government override – Roger and Stone (2005: tab. 3); credit to government – Tuladhar (2005: tab. 6); government participation in policymaking – Tuladhar (2005: tab. 3).

Table 4.3 *Central bank accountability and policy transparency*

Country	Publication of policy minutes	Testimony/ reporting to parliament	Monetary policy report	Specific reporting on large target misses	Use of escape clauses
Australia	No	Yes	Quarterly	No	No
Brazil	Yes, 8-day lag	Yes	Quarterly	Yes	No
Canada	No	Yes	Semi-annual + update	Yes	No
Chile	Yes, 90-day lag	Yes	3 per year	No	No
Colombia	No	Yes	Quarterly	No	No
Czech Republic	Yes	Yes	Quarterly	No	Explicit description
Ghana	No	No	4–6 per year	No	No
Guatemala	No	Yes	Semi-annual	No	No
Hungary	Yes	Yes	Semi-annual + update	No	No
Iceland	No	No	Quarterly	Yes	No
Indonesia	No	Yes	Quarterly	Yes	No
Israel	Yes	Yes	Semi-annual	Yes	No
Mexico	No	Yes	Quarterly	No	No
New Zealand	No	Yes	Quarterly	Yes	Explicit description
Norway	No	Yes	3 per year	No	No
Peru	No	No	3 per year	No	No
Philippines	Yes	Yes	Quarterly	Yes	Explicit description
Poland	No	Yes	Quarterly	No	Explicit description
Romania	No	No	Quarterly	No	Explicit description
Serbia	No	Yes	Quarterly	Yes	No
Slovakia	No	No	Quarterly	No	Explicit description
South Africa	No	No	Semi-annual	No	Explicit description
South Korea	No	Yes	Semi-annual	No	No
Sweden	Yes	Yes	3 per year	Yes	Explicit description
Thailand	No	No	Quarterly	Yes	No
Turkey	Yes	No	Quarterly	Yes	No
United Kingdom	Yes	Yes	Quarterly	Yes	No

Sources: Specific reporting on misses – Roger and Stone (2005: tab. 3); use of escape clauses – Tuladhar (2005: tab. 2).

and Lybek and Morris 2004). The main mechanisms used to hold the central bank accountable for its policy performance and actions include:

- the publication of regular inflation or monetary policy reports;
- the publication of special reports or open letters in the event of significant misses of the target;
- the use of 'escape' clauses to limit central bank accountability in particular circumstances, as well as to indicate, in advance, how policy will react to certain kinds of shocks;
- parliamentary testimony by the central bank governor;
- the publication of minutes of policy meetings within a reasonable time frame; and
- press conferences and analyst briefings following the release of policy decisions and monetary policy reports.

Over time, policy accountability has tended to become more forward-looking. In the early years of inflation targeting, accountability arrangements tended to stress fairly formal accountability procedures in the event of target misses, such as the use of 'escape clauses' to limit central bank accountability in certain circumstances, as well as special reporting requirements in the event of target misses. In more recent years the trend appears to be to put more emphasis on explaining policy decisions to the public in a timely manner and de-emphasising the importance of target misses. To some extent this may reflect the fact that keeping inflation within a fairly narrow range has proved to be harder, or perhaps less sensible, than was believed in the early days. More fundamentally, it may also reflect the view that, with a forward-looking policy framework, the focus of accountability should be primarily on forward-looking decision-making, and less on outcomes that are affected by factors outside the close control of the central bank.

Effective, forward-looking accountability depends heavily on policy transparency. This includes, in particular, providing a clearly explained picture of the policy transmission mechanism, the macroeconomic outlook and the risks and uncertainties that need to be taken into account in setting policy. It also requires a better understanding of monetary policy by key audiences. As a consequence, IT central banks have moved to increase the transparency of policymaking, including through means such as the publication of inflation projections, the publication of minutes of policy meetings, the increased provision of information on websites, and so on. Practices vary widely, and many central banks are well short of best practice, but the direction of movement is clearly towards greater emphasis on good communications and transparency.

Inflation targets

Specifications of inflation targets have become fairly standardised. In the early years of inflation targeting there were considerable debates over the appropriate rate and measure of inflation to target, whether to use point or range targets, the appropriate length of target horizons, and so on. Over time, however, target specifications appear to have converged on a fairly standardised – perhaps too standardised – set-up.

- In almost all inflation-targeting countries, the target is specified in terms of the twelve-month change in the headline CPI. This reflects the familiarity of the public with the headline CPI, the importance of the CPI in the formation of inflation expectations and wage determination and the fact that it is calculated by the statistics agency, and is usually the best quality of the price measures available.[8]
- Central banks also monitor and report on a range of measures of core inflation. Typically, these include exclusion-based measures (most commonly excluding exceptionally volatile prices, such as those for fresh fruit and vegetables and fuels, and non-market-determined or administered prices) and limited-influence measures, such as trimmed means or the weighted median.
- Inflation target midpoints and ranges are similar for most countries (see Figure 4.2). For countries that have adopted stable inflation targets, the midpoints of targets almost all lie between 2 and 3 per cent. The target is usually specified as a point, with bands of plus or minus one percentage point. In a few countries, however, targets are defined as ranges, without specifying a centre, while in others a point or 'thick' point is specified without a range.
- Target horizons are also fairly standardised. During disinflation, targets are typically set for the end-of-year inflation rate, and set at least a year ahead. It is less common for the central bank to set out a full target path for disinflation, but several central banks indicate what the medium-term inflation objective is. Once disinflation has been accomplished, it is standard for countries to announce a shift from end-of-year inflation targets to continuous or indefinite-horizon targets.

Policy formulation and implementation

Details of policy formulation and implementation differ substantially between inflation targeters, but some basic features are generally similar. ITers all pursue 'flexible' inflation targeting; the pursuit of inflation targets is tempered by a desire to minimise output volatility. This is reflected partly in the attention paid to output developments and prospects in

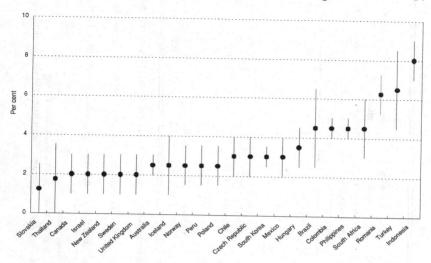

Figure 4.2 Inflation target rates and bands, 2008
Source: Central bank websites.

inflation reports, the use of core inflation measures in policy analysis and formulation, and the typical emphasis on developing forecasting models that pay as much attention to forecasting growth as inflation. ITers also generally seek to take a forward-looking approach to policy formulation, and to that end have worked to strengthen their forecasting and modelling capabilities. Clearly, however, there are marked differences in capacity, typically accentuated by very large differences in the availability of the timely, good-quality data needed for forecasting purposes.

There are some important differences between inflation targeters, however. One is with respect to the role of the exchange rate in the policy framework (see Stone, Roger, Shimizu *et al.* 2009). In several emerging market and developing country inflation-targeting countries the exchange rate has a much more prominent place in the policy framework than in most advanced economies, but even in some of the latter there is some evidence that exchange rate movements tend to elicit systematic policy reactions (see, for example, Wei 2008). There are also significant differences between inflation targeters in terms of financial sector development and in the ability of the central bank to implement policy using indirect, market-based instruments. Although the primary policy instrument is almost always the central bank interest rate, a number of countries also

Table 4.4 *Inflation outcomes relative to targets, 1990–2008*

	Inflation rate at IT start (%)	Target range width (+/−) (%)	Mean deviation from range centre (percentage points)	Standard deviation around mean (outcome percentage points)	Frequency of target range misses: total/below/above (percentage of outcomes)	Average absolute magnitude of misses (percentage points)	Persistence of deviations from range centre (months)
All countries	5.7	1.1	1.0	1.9	54.5/18.3/36.3	1.5	8.5
High-income[1]	4.8	1.0	0.1	1.3	49.1/23.9/25.3	1.2	7.3
Low-income[2]	6.5	1.2	1.8	2.4	59.6/13.0/46.6	2.3	10.3
Disinflation phase							
All countries	7.2	1.2	1.4	2.1	64.0/17.0/47.0	1.8	10.2
High-income[3]	6.3	1.0	0.1	1.7	59.6/29.4/30.2	1.2	8.3
Low-income[4]	7.9	1.3	2.3	2.4	66.9/8.8/58.1	2.4	12.8
Stable inflation target phase							
All countries	3.1	1.1	0.4	1.4	42.7/17.9/24.8	1.0	6.9
High-income[5]	3.2	1.0	0.4	1.3	46.6/21.4/25.2	0.9	7.1
Low-income[6]	3.0	1.3	0.5	1.6	35.5/11.3/24.2	1.2	6.9

Notes: Data calculated as equally weighted averages of corresponding statistics for individual countries in relevant groups. Individual country figures are based on monthly data (quarterly for Australia and New Zealand).

[1] 14 countries: Australia, Canada, Czech Republic, Finland, Hungary, Iceland, Israel, New Zealand, Norway, Slovakia, South Korea, Spain, Sweden, United Kingdom.

[2] 15 countries: Brazil, Chile, Colombia, Ghana, Guatemala, Indonesia, Mexico, Peru, Philippines, Poland, Romania, Serbia, South Africa, Thailand, Turkey.

[3] 8 countries: Canada, Czech Republic, Hungary, Iceland, Israel, New Zealand, Slovakia, Spain.

[4] 12 countries: Brazil, Chile, Colombia, Ghana, Guatemala, Indonesia, Mexico, Philippines, Poland, Romania, Serbia, Turkey.

[5] 13 countries: Australia, Canada, Czech Republic, Finland, Hungary, Iceland, Israel, New Zealand, Norway, South Korea, Spain, Sweden, United Kingdom.

[6] 7 countries: Brazil, Chile, Mexico, Peru, Poland, South Africa, Thailand.

use reserve requirements or foreign exchange market intervention as supplementary instruments.

4.4   Performance under inflation targeting

This section reviews evidence on three aspects of the performance of inflation-targeting countries. The first is how well inflation-targeting central banks have succeeded in meeting their stated inflation objectives. Second is a broader assessment of macroeconomic performance under inflation targeting compared with alternative policy frameworks. The third is how well inflation-targeting countries have been coping with the most recent oil price and global financial shocks compared with other countries.

Performance in achieving inflation targets[9]

ITers miss their target ranges frequently, especially during the process of disinflation. Table 4.4 and Figure 4.3 present data on the inflation performance of twenty-nine inflation-targeting countries in relation to their targets. The analysis distinguishes between high- and low-income countries and between performance during disinflation and in the context of stable inflation targets. The main results to highlight include the following.

- High-income countries have typically started disinflating from around a 6 per cent inflation rate, while emerging markets have usually started at a higher rate of around 8 per cent. For both groups, however, stable inflation targeting has begun at around 3 per cent.
- During disinflation, the performances of high- and low-income countries have been significantly different from each other. Although both groups of countries have missed their targets around 60 per cent of the time, the misses by low-income countries have been biased upward, while those of high-income countries have been almost balanced.[10]
- The performance of both high- and low-income countries is generally better under stable inflation targeting. Inflation volatility is much less than during disinflation, which results in substantially fewer misses of inflation target ranges; in the case of high-income countries, the frequency of misses falls to under a half, while for low-income countries the frequency of misses falls to just one-third.[11]
- Both the dispersion of inflation outcomes and the bias with respect to the centres of target ranges are distinctly less with core inflation measures than with headline measures of inflation. Moreover, with core inflation measures the inflation performances of high- and low-income

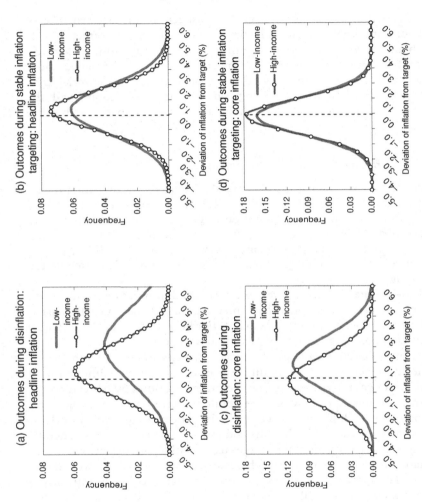

Figure 4.3 Distribution of inflation outcomes relative to targets

Source: Author's calculations.

countries are very similar, indicating that much of the difference seen in terms of headline inflation outcomes is attributable to the existence of larger and more frequent supply shocks in low-income countries.

Econometric analyses of deviations of inflation from targets help to account for these results. In particular, Albagli and Schmidt-Hebbel (2004), Lostumbo (2007) and Gosselin (2007) all find that policy credibility has an important effect on the volatility of inflation around the target. The higher frequency, magnitude and persistence of target misses during disinflation are likely in part to reflect relatively weak policy credibility during the early stages of inflation targeting. Céspedes and Soto (2005) also note that with weak credibility the output–inflation trade-off is worse. In such circumstances, monetary policy responses to supply shocks will tend to be more muted than otherwise, which results in larger and more persistent deviations of inflation from target. The analyses also find that relative price shocks, including significant movements in exchange rates and energy prices, are important factors for explaining deviations of inflation from targets.

Macroeconomic performance under alternative monetary policy regimes

Comparing macroeconomic performances under alternative monetary policies is a challenging task. A critical issue in making comparisons is the selection of relevant comparators. As discussed by Vega and Winkelried (2005), the ideal analysis would compare performance in countries that had adopted IT with how they would have performed had they not adopted IT. Since this is not possible, the challenge is to find another group of countries that can be used as relevant comparators.

There is likely to be some self-selection among countries adopting IT – that is, countries with conditions more suited to IT may be more likely to adopt it – making comparisons with non-targeters more difficult. Mishkin and Schmidt-Hebbel (2007) emphasise that the selection of comparators should take into account the endogeneity of the decision to adopt IT. This aspect may be overemphasised, however, insofar as many adopters of IT did so in crisis circumstances, as noted earlier, rather than deliberately. Moreover, as Batini and Laxton (2007) document, countries adopting IT often did not have in place many of the conditions regarded as important requirements for successful IT.

The main differences in the results in the various papers making such comparisons largely reflect differences in the selection of comparator countries.

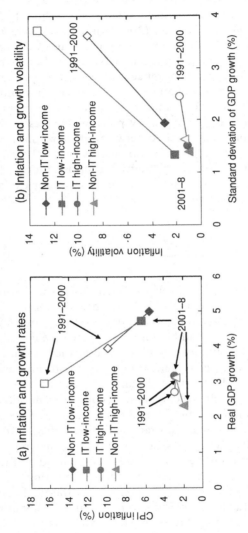

Figure 4.4 Inflation and growth performance, 2001–8 versus 1991–2000

Notes: Panel (a) figures are based on median country values of median annual values for inflation, and averages of median values for growth.

Panel (b) figures are based on median country values of the standard deviation of annual percentage changes.

Source: Author's calculations.

- The IMF (2005) analysis is based on a comparison of performance in the then thirteen emerging market inflation targeters with twenty-nine non-inflation-targeting emerging market countries.[12]
- Mishkin and Schmidt-Hebbel (2007) compare performance in the same group of emerging market economies with a number of alternative control groups. One control group includes thirteen non-IT industrial countries, deliberately established to provide a best (non-IT) benchmark.[13] A second control group adds the pre-IT experience of subsequent IT countries to make the comparison more realistic. The authors also seek to adjust for the endogeneity of the adoption of IT by using a parsimonious instrumental variable technique.
- Vega and Winkelried (2005) compare the performance of all inflation targeters, including industrial and non-industrial countries, with a group of eighty-six non-IT countries. To match IT country performances to relevant comparators, the authors use a 'propensity score matching' approach that seeks to identify relevant comparators for each IT country by comparing their pre-IT performance on a range of macroeconomic criteria with the corresponding performance of countries that did not adopt IT.

A second important issue is how to control for external factors. In this regard, the analyses are fairly consistent in approach: (i) using similar starting dates for the adoption of IT by the various IT countries; and (ii) using the average date of IT adoption by the relevant group as a break point for comparing the performances of non-IT countries.[14] This helps to minimise the influence of developments in the global economic environment on the relative performance of the different policy frameworks.

In this chapter, updated comparisons are based on essentially the same country groups as in the IMF (2005) analysis.[15] A comparison of macroeconomic performances suggests that low-income economies that have adopted inflation targeting have outperformed low-income economies with other policy regimes. Figure 4.4 compares the inflation and growth performances of high- and low-income IT and non-IT countries, in the 1990s and 2000s. In the case of the low-income IT countries, the macroeconomic performance indicators for the earlier period correspond to their pre-IT regimes, while the figures for the later period cover their experience under IT.[16] Panel (a) shows changes in performance in terms of inflation and growth rates, while panel (b) shows performance in terms of inflation and output volatility.

The figures indicate the following.

- Both IT and non-IT low-income countries saw major reductions in inflation rates, together with improvements in growth rates, but the countries adopting IT saw larger improvements in both dimensions.

The typical reduction in inflation in the low-income IT countries was 5.8 percentage points (p.p.) relative to the reduction in non-IT countries, while the relative improvement in growth was 0.7 p.p. Among the high-income countries, both IT and non-IT countries maintained low inflation rates, but the IT countries experienced a modest increase in growth, while non-IT countries typically experienced a decline in growth.

• Both low-income groups also experienced large reductions in the volatility of inflation and output, with the countries adopting IT again registering the biggest reductions in both kinds of volatility. Typically, the low-income IT countries experienced a 4.9 p.p. decline in the standard deviation of inflation relative to non-IT low-income countries, and a 0.7 p.p. reduction in relative growth volatility. Among the high-income countries, the performance of IT countries converged on the good performance of the non-IT countries.

More formal statistical analyses of the benefits of adopting inflation targeting are also based on a 'difference in differences' approach, comparing how performance for key macroeconomic variables has changed in countries adopting inflation targeting with performance in other countries under alternative monetary regimes over the same period. Ball and Sheridan (2003) applied this approach to industrial countries, and find no significant benefit from the adoption of inflation targeting. Using similar methodology, however, Mishkin and Schmidt-Hebbel (2007), the IMF (2005) and Vega and Winkelried (2005) find clearer evidence that inflation targeting in EMEs has been associated with better macroeconomic performance than alternative policy regimes.

The results of these analyses suggest that, when otherwise similar countries are compared over the same time periods, countries adopting IT have tended to outperform non-IT countries. The results from the IMF (2005) analysis are indicative. Over the period and countries examined, inflation targeting has been associated with a 4.8 p.p. reduction in average inflation relative to other monetary policy regimes. Interestingly, this is very close to the figures obtained by Mishkin and Schmidt-Hebbel (2007) and by Vega and Winkelried (2005).[17] Inflation targeting was also associated with a reduction in the variability of inflation (as measured by the standard deviation of inflation) by 3.6 p.p. relative to other strategies.

The resilience of inflation targeting

An issue of particular relevance in the wake of the global commodity price and financial shocks of the past two years is whether inflation targeting is more robust to shocks than other policy frameworks. Through most

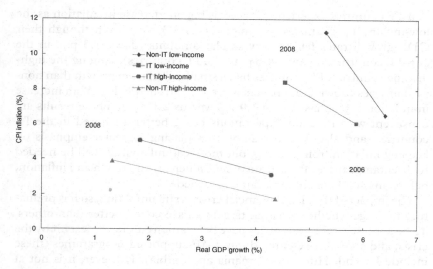

Figure 4.5 Inflation and growth rates, 2006–8
Note: Figures are averages of annual percentage changes.
Source: Author's calculations.

of the period since the widespread adoption of inflation targeting global macroeconomic conditions have been relatively benign compared with earlier periods. As a result, there is only limited evidence on the robustness of inflation targeting regimes to major shocks. The main examples prior to 2007 include the impact of the Argentina crisis on Brazil and other Latin American inflation targeters, Brazil's political crisis in 2002, South Africa's experience with a loss of investor confidence and sharp currency depreciation in 2001/2 and Hungary's massive fiscal shock in 2002.[18] Shocks of similar magnitude have destabilised these countries in the past, suggesting at least that the framework has contributed to the economies' resilience to shocks.

How well have inflation targeting frameworks performed in handling the 2007–9 global commodity price and financial shocks? It goes beyond the scope of this study to address this issue in depth. Moreover, in the case of the global financial shock, the full effects on macroeconomies are far from over. Consequently, this chapter offers only a very preliminary and limited perspective.

Inflation-targeting countries appear to have done better than others in minimising the inflationary impact of the surge in commodity prices in 2007.[19] As shown in Figure 4.5, all country groups saw significant increases in inflation and declines in growth. However, the low-income non-IT countries experienced twice as big an increase in inflation as the low-income IT countries (4.7 p.p. versus 2.3 p.p.), even though their GDP growth rates fell by very similar amounts (down 1.3 p.p. in the non-IT countries versus 1.6 p.p. in the IT countries). Among the high-income countries, IT countries had a smaller decline in growth than non-IT countries (down 2.5 p.p. versus 3 p.p.) and slightly less of an increase in inflation (up an average of 1.9 p.p. versus 2.1 p.p.). These results are consistent with inflation expectations being better anchored in the IT countries, and also with the authorities placing a greater emphasis on keeping inflation from surging, but more careful analysis will be needed to disentangle these effects from other influences on growth and inflation, before any solid conclusions can be reached.

The impact of the global financial crisis is still unfolding, so it is premature to judge whether inflation targeters have coped better than others. To be sure, several IT countries have been amongst the hardest hit by the crisis, and several have entered into IMF-supported programmes (these include Iceland, Hungary, Romania and Serbia). However, it is not at all clear that inflation targeting made these countries more susceptible to crises, or that their macroeconomic downturns are more severe than in comparable countries with other policy regimes. Indeed, there is some evidence to suggest that the IT countries are expected by market participants and private sector forecasters to weather the crisis somewhat better than non-IT countries.

Credit default swap (CDS) spreads suggest that IT countries are expected to be less vulnerable to full-blown financial or exchange rate crises. Figure 4.6 shows the evolution of CDS spreads in low-income non-IT countries as well as in low- and high-income IT countries. In 2007H2 spreads for low-income countries were very similar, at 50 to 60 basis points (b.p.). Spreads increased gradually through 2008, but remained similar until the eruption of the full-blown crisis in October 2008. Although spreads for both groups, as well as high-income countries, rose sharply, spreads for low-income non-IT countries rose to around 100 basis points over those of low-income IT countries. This suggests that market participants viewed, and continue to view, non-IT countries as riskier than IT countries. Of course, several other factors may play an important role in explaining the evolution of CDS differentials, but they may also reflect a difference in the perceived resilience of inflation-targeting policy frameworks.

Macroeconomic forecasts also suggest that IT economies are expected to be less adversely affected by the effects of the financial crisis. June 2009 Consensus Economics forecasts indicate that average growth for all groups of countries in 2009/10 is expected to fall well below the

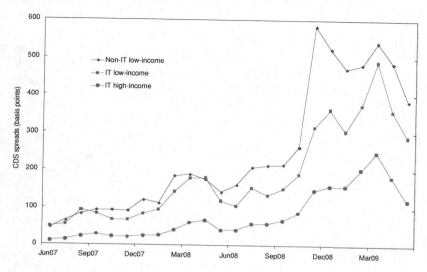

Figure 4.6 CDS spreads, 2007–9

Note: Figures are median country values.
Source: Datastream.

typical growth rates experienced in the 2001–8 period (see Figure 4.7).
Together with declines in commodity prices, this is expected to lead to
below-average inflation. Median inflation is projected to fall by close to
2 p.p. in low-income countries and by close to 0.9 p.p. in high-income
countries. Forecast differences between IT and non-IT countries are
negligible. Non-IT countries are forecast to experience larger declines in
growth, however. Among low-income countries, median growth in non-
IT countries is forecast to fall by 5 p.p. versus 3.8 p.p. in IT countries.
Among high-income countries, growth is forecast to fall by 4.3 p.p. in
non-IT versus 3.1 p.p. in IT countries.

4.5   Issues and challenges for inflation targeting[20]

Although the evidence to date suggests that inflation targeting can perform well in many quite different kinds of economies, a number of issues
and challenges arise for the future. Given the growing number of emerging market and developing economies adopting IT, a key challenge is to
adapt the framework to their circumstances. The second crucial challenge, relevant for all countries, is how to take better account of financial
structures and vulnerabilities in the IT framework.

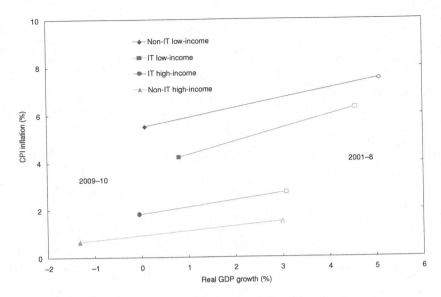

Figure 4.7 Growth and inflation: 2009–10 forecasts versus 2001–8 performance

Note: Figures are median country values.
Source: Author's calculations, with forecasts based on June 2009 Consensus Economics figures.

Adapting inflation targeting to emerging market and developing economies

Emerging market and developing countries adopting inflation targeting face a number of challenges that differ in character or in degree from those faced in more advanced industrial economies. Calvo and Mishkin (2003) highlight five particularly important challenges for non-industrial countries. These are: (i) weak public sector financial management; (ii) weak financial sector institutions and markets; (iii) low monetary policy credibility; (iv) the extensive dollarisation of financial liabilities; and (v) vulnerability to sharp changes in capital flows and international investor sentiment (see also Fraga, Goldfajn and Minella 2003). In addition, many of these countries face considerably greater uncertainty about the structure of their economies, the monetary policy transmission mechanism and the cyclical position of the economy than is typical of industrial country inflation targeters. These challenges are discussed in turn below.

The credibility of any systematic monetary policy framework requires the bringing of public sector finances under control. Fiscal dominance, or the threat of it, may completely undermine the credibility of inflation targeting. Indeed, fiscal policy that is fundamentally inconsistent with the inflation target can trigger an exchange rate crisis just as it may lead to the collapse of an exchange rate peg. It is also possible that the adoption of inflation targeting may serve as a catalyst for public sector financial reform, however, precisely by highlighting the inconsistency of fiscal indiscipline with the goal of stable, low inflation.

The adoption of inflation targeting as part of a more comprehensive package of economic reforms complicates the conduct of monetary policy. Such reforms often involve structural changes affecting long-run equilibrium values and the dynamics of key macroeconomic variables, making it extremely difficult to forecast or react with any degree of policy precision to economic developments. These challenges are often compounded by a lack of good-quality, timely macroeconomic data. Such complications do not necessarily preclude inflation targeting (see Batini and Laxton 2007), but they do imply that achieving targets is likely to be particularly challenging, as appears to be borne out by the earlier evidence on the high frequency of target misses during disinflation. In such circumstances, countries might opt for relatively wide target ranges until the structure of the economy has settled down and policy transmission is better understood. In addition, a high premium needs to be placed on policy transparency and accountability in order to ensure that target misses are not misinterpreted as reflecting lack of policy commitment.

Weak financial sector institutions and markets need to be taken into account in the formulation and implementation of inflation targeting. As discussed by Laurens, Arnone, Carare *et al.* (2005), such weaknesses alter the relative efficiency and speed of monetary policy transmission through different channels, and these need to be taken into consideration in policy formulation, on a country-by-country basis. Weak or incomplete financial markets may also limit the scope for reliance on the use of market-based instruments for implementing policy, but this is not essential. What *is* essential is for the central bank to be able to move the interest rates faced by households and businesses, and to do so in a manner that is clearly linked to the inflation objective. Weaknesses in the financial system itself may complicate the conduct of inflation targeting, as with any other monetary policy. In such circumstances, development of the inflation-targeting framework should also entail prudential measures and other reforms to strengthen the financial system.

The role of the exchange rate in an inflation-targeting framework is a particularly important issue for emerging markets and developing economies.[21] The conventional wisdom has long been that an inflation-targeting central bank should not react directly to exchange rate movements, but only insofar as they affect the outlook for inflation and output.[22] Such a benign approach to the exchange rate may not be appropriate, however, in economies in which there is a high degree of liability dollarisation, or in which access to international financial markets is limited. The global financial crisis has highlighted the importance of financial vulnerability and high dollarisation for emerging market inflation targeters. As noted by Mishkin (2003), extensive dollarisation of the economy can substantially alter the transmission of monetary policy. In particular, high dollarisation of the financial system will tend to amplify the importance of exchange rate changes relative to domestic interest rate movements in policy transmission, and may generate aggregate demand effects opposite to those in industrial countries. A number of highly euro-ised economies in central and eastern Europe appear to be encountering precisely this type of problem. In such circumstances, leaning against exchange rate movements may improve macroeconomic performance under inflation targeting, as long as the degree of exchange rate dampening is low (see Céspedes, Chang and Velasco 2004, Morón and Winkelried 2005 and Roger, Restrepo and Garcia 2009).

Inflation targeting and financial stability

The global financial crisis is forcing central banks to reassess the relationship between monetary and financial stability policies. To some extent, the assessment of what should be done depends on a diagnosis of the underlying causes of the crisis. One line of argument is, basically, that monetary policy in the United States and the euro area was too loose for too long, and this fuelled housing price bubbles in both regions (Taylor 2009). An alternative argument is that the crisis is a consequence of monetary policy in the major economies having been too narrowly focused on medium-term inflation, paying insufficient attention to financial developments and their implications for longer-term inflation risks (see, for example, Borio and Lowe 2002). A third line of argument is that financial sector deregulation and regulatory arbitrage led to a loosening of monetary conditions in the United States and elsewhere that was not adequately taken into account in setting monetary policy.

The issue of whether or how monetary policy should respond to financial stability developments is analogous to the issue of responding to exchange rate developments. From this perspective, it could be argued that there is unlikely to be much benefit from responding directly to financial sector developments, such as asset price changes, but that there could be some benefit from an indirect response, to the extent that financial sector developments affect the outlook for excess demand and inflation (Bernanke and Gertler 2001 and Bean 2004). This line of argument is reasonable to the extent that financial sector developments are, in fact, captured in the macroeconomic analysis and forecasts of central banks. The plain fact, however, is that most inflation-targeting central banks' analytical frameworks are seriously deficient with regard to macro-financial interactions.

At a minimum, the crisis highlights the need for inflation-targeting countries to pay greater attention to macro-financial interactions. In virtually all inflation-targeting economies, the workhorse macroeconomic models used in monetary policy analysis and forecasting lack any substantial representation of the financial sector, any determination of key asset prices such as equity and property prices, and any interaction between the financial sector and household and corporate sector behaviour. Nor is there any representation of interaction within the financial sector. Remedying such weaknesses will not be easy, but it is important to do so if financial developments are to be better integrated into policy analysis and forecasting.

A possible alternative is for central banks to react directly to financial stability indicators (see, for example, Borio and Lowe 2002 and Cecchetti et al. 2000). In other words, some indicators of financial stability would enter the central bank's reaction function directly. If the financial sector is already adequately represented in the central bank's policy model, then reacting directly to financial indicators might worsen macroeconomic performance, at least for some types of shocks. If the financial sector is not properly captured in the model, then reacting directly to financial indicators might improve performance. Walsh (2009) argues that reacting to financial indicators can be welfare-improving if financial frictions give rise to economic distortions, analogous to the rationale for including output in the policy reaction function. Research is needed in this area, including determining the appropriate financial indicators to take into account.

Another possibility is to extend the inflation-targeting horizon so as to be able to take into account the longer-term inflation risks associated with asset price cycles (see, for example, Borio and Lowe 2002). An advantage of this approach is that it would be less mechanical than responding directly to asset prices (or some other financial stability indicator). Nonetheless, a number of practical challenges would need to be addressed. In particular, a lengthening of the forecast horizon would also require an improvement in central banks' medium- to long-term forecasting capabilities. In addition, even with the extra room for manoeuvre afforded by a longer policy horizon, there would be difficult issues to sort out in terms of the appropriate timing of actions to counter the development of asset price bubbles (see, for example, Bean 2004 and Gruen, Plumb and Stone 2003). Policy communications would also need to be strengthened to ensure that the broadening of the central bank's effective mandate did not have an adverse impact on the credibility of its long-term commitment to low and stable inflation.

A potential alternative, or complement, to extending the policy horizon would be to introduce an element of price path targeting (see, for example, Svensson 1999 and Ambler 2007). Price path targeting would, in effect, extend the monetary policy horizon in a way that might facilitate taking into account financial stability considerations, but in a manner that might more credibly ensure a long-term commitment to price stability. In addition, as noted by Walsh (2009), price path targeting would have important benefits in influencing the formation of expectations, which should help minimise the potentially adverse effects of the zero lower bound on nominal interest rates.

NOTES

1. The author is grateful to participants at the Sixth Norges Bank Monetary Policy Conference, as well as to IMF colleagues, for useful comments and suggestions, which have enabled the author to update this contribution from the version presented at the conference. Any remaining errors and omissions are the author's own. The views expressed in this study are the author's own, and do not necessarily represent those of the IMF. The author would also like to thank Claudia Jadrijevic Zenteno for excellent research assistance.
2. New Zealand passed the legislation for inflation targeting in late 1989, with implementation from the beginning of 1990. Finland and Spain ceased inflation targeting when they entered the euro area in January 1999, and Slovakia ceased inflation targeting in January 2009 with its entry into the European Union's second Exchange Rate Mechanism (ERM II).
3. To facilitate comparisons over time, panels (a) and (b) of the figure include separately the various republics of the former Soviet Union and Yugoslavia, which became independent during the 1990s. In the pre-independence period each of the constituent republics is treated as having the same monetary policy as the federation. This avoids having the break-up of the federations affecting the relative proportions of different policy regimes. The establishment of the Eurozone is shown as a shift by ERM countries from exchange rate targeting to a multiple targets framework.
4. IMF discussions with member states in 2006 suggested that the number of inflation targeters in developing and emerging market economies was likely to increase fourfold over the next decade, consistent with the estimate by Husain, Mody and Rogoff (2005) that the number of countries with exchange rate pegs may almost halve in the next ten to fifteen years.

5. This section draws on Heenan, Peter and Roger (2006).

6. A revealing review of the development of the original IT framework in New Zealand is provided by Reddell (1999).

7. In the case of monetary targets, instability in money demand relationships – commonly associated with financial system reforms and the opening of capital markets – undermined the usefulness of monetary aggregates as policy guides. In the case of exchange rate pegs, real exchange rate targets provided no nominal anchor, while nominal exchange rate pegs left both prices and activity vulnerable to shocks affecting equilibrium real exchange rates.

8. In the Czech Republic and South Korea, targets were initially defined in terms of core or underlying inflation measures, but both have subsequently switched to headline inflation. Thailand is currently the only country setting its target in terms of core inflation.

9. This subsection updates the analysis in Roger and Stone (2005), which was based on data for twenty-two countries through to mid-2004. The analysis here covers twenty-nine countries to the end of 2008.

10. Moreover, given the high variance of inflation outcomes relative to target, if the average target range in low-income countries had been of the same width as it was in high-income countries, and on the assumption of an approximately normal distribution of outcomes, misses of target ranges would have been much higher: close to 80 per cent.

11. If the low-income countries had target ranges, on average, of about the same width of those in high-income countries, misses of target ranges would have been closer to 55 per cent, all other things being equal.

12. These consisted of twenty-two non-IT countries in the JP Morgan Emerging Market Bond Index (Algeria, Argentina, China, Côte d'Ivoire, Croatia, Dominican Republic, Ecuador, Egypt, El Salvador, Indonesia, Lebanon, Malaysia, Morocco, Nigeria, Pakistan, Russia, Serbia, Tunisia, Turkey, Ukraine, Uruguay and Venezuela) plus seven similarly classified countries (Botswana, Costa Rica, Ghana, Guatemala, India, Jordan and Tanzania).

13. These are described as a 'selective set of countries that are at the international frontier of macroeconomic management and performance: Austria, Belgium, Denmark, France, Germany, Greece, Ireland, Italy, Japan, Luxembourg, Netherlands, Portugal, and United States'.

14. The end-1999 break point used in the analyses reflected the fact that the average and median number of quarters of experience with inflation targeting among emerging markets at the time corresponded to the beginning of 2000.

15. The differences between the groups used in this analysis and the IMF 2005 analysis (described in endnote 12) are as follows: (i) the group of non-IT economies excludes Guatemala, Ghana, Indonesia, Serbia and Turkey, which have subsequently adopted IT; and (ii) Bulgaria has also been added to the group of relevant non-IT comparators. For high-income IT economies, the group of comparator non-IT economies includes Cyprus, Denmark, the euro area, Hong Kong SAR (Special Administrative Region), Japan, Singapore, Slovenia, Switzerland, Taiwan and the United States. Additionally, the data sample is extended to the end of 2008, and the break point between the earlier and later periods is shifted by one year (to the end of 2000) to reflect the change in the median date for the adoption of IT.

16. For IT countries the sample periods are split before and after the adoption of IT, while for non-IT countries the split is set at the end of 2000, corresponding to the median adoption date for the countries adopting IT.
17. The most comparable result in the Mishkin and Schmidt-Hebbel analysis is from the use of instrumental variables with their Control 1 group of countries, to maximise allowance for the fact that the emerging market countries adopting IT have generally been far from the frontier of macroeconomic management. In this case, the authors obtain the same estimated reduction in inflation due to the adoption of IT: 4.8 per cent. In the Vega and Winkelried analysis, the relevant comparisons are for developing countries adopting full-fledged IT. Their estimates of the benefit of the adoption of IT in terms of inflation reduction fall in the range of 3.3 to 5.4 percentage points.
18. See Bevilaqua and Loyo (2004) for a discussion of how Brazil's fledgling inflation targeting regime was stress-tested in the first few years following its introduction.
19. Habermeier, Ötker-Robe, Jácome et al. (2009) provide a comprehensive discussion of the inflation surge and monetary policy responses in emerging market and developing economies.
20. See also Batini et al. (2006).
21. See Stone, Roger, Shimizu et al. (2009) for an extensive overview of the role of the exchange rate in emerging market economies.
22. See Taylor (2001) for a succinct summary of the literature on this issue up to that point.

REFERENCES

Albagli, E., and K. Schmidt-Hebbel (2004). 'By how much and why do inflation targeters miss their targets?'. Mimeo. Santiago: Banco Central de Chile.
Ambler, S. (2007). 'Price-level targeting and stabilisation policy: a review'. Discussion Paper no. 2007–11. Ottawa: Bank of Canada.
Ball, L., and N. Sheridan (2003). 'Does inflation targeting matter?' Working Paper no. 9577. Cambridge, MA: National Bureau of Economic Research [NBER].
Batini, N., P. Breuer, K. Kochhar and S. Roger (2006). 'Inflation targeting and the IMF'. Board Paper no. SM/06/33. Washington, DC: IMF.
Batini, N., and D. Laxton (2007). 'Under what conditions can inflation targeting be adopted? The experience of emerging markets', in F. Mishkin and K. Schmidt-Hebbel (eds.). Monetary Policy under Inflation Targeting: 1–22. Santiago: Banco Central de Chile.
Bean, C. (2004). 'Asset prices, financial instability, and monetary policy,' American Economic Review, 94(2): 14–18.
Bernanke, B., and M. Gertler (2001). 'Should central banks respond to movements in asset prices?', American Economic Review, 91(2): 253–7.
Bevilaqua, A., and E. Loyo (2004). 'Brazil's stress test of inflation targeting'. Working Paper no. 23. Basel: Bank for International Settlements [BIS].
Borio, C., and P. Lowe (2002). 'Asset prices, financial and monetary stability: exploring the nexus'. Working Paper no. 114. Basel: BIS.

Calvo, G., and F. Mishkin (2003). 'The mirage of exchange rate regimes for emerging market countries'. Working Paper no. 9808. Cambridge, MA: NBER

Cecchetti, S., H. Genberg, J. Lipsky and S. Wadhwani (2000). *Asset Prices and Central Bank Policy*. Geneva: Centre International d'Etudes Monétaires et Baneaires [CIMB].

Céspedes, L., R. Chang and A. Velasco (2004). 'Balance sheets and exchange rate policy', *American Economic Review*, 94(4): 1183–93.

Céspedes, L., and C. Soto (2005). 'Credibility and inflation targeting in an emerging market: lessons from the Chilean experience', *International Finance*, 8(3): 545–75.

Fraga, A., I. Goldfajn and A. Minella (2003). 'Inflation targeting in emerging market economies'. Working Paper no. 10019. Cambridge, MA: NBER.

Gosselin, M.-A. (2007). 'Central bank performance under inflation targeting'. Working Paper no. 2007–18. Ottawa: Bank of Canada.

Gruen, D., M. Plumb and A. Stone (2003). 'How should monetary policy respond to asset-price bubbles?', in A. Richards and T. Robinson (eds.). *Asset Prices and Monetary Policy*: 260–80. Sydney: RBA.

Habermeier, K., I. Ötker-Robe, L. Jácome, A. Giustiniani, K. Ishi, D. Vávra, T. Kisinbay and F. Vázquez (2009). 'Inflation pressures and monetary policy options in emerging and developing countries: a cross-regional perspective'. Working Paper no. 09/1. Washington, DC: IMF.

Heenan, G., M. Peter and S. Roger (2006). 'Implementing inflation targeting: institutional arrangements, target design, and communications'. Working Paper no. 06/278. Washington, DC: IMF.

Husain, A., A. Mody and K. Rogoff (2005). 'Exchange rate durability and performance in developing versus advanced economies', *Journal of Monetary Economics*, 52(1): 35–64.

IMF (2005). *World Economic Outlook: September 2005*. Washington DC: IMF.

Laurens, B., M. Arnone, A. Carare, G. Iden, K. Iwatsubo, R. Maino, O. Nyawata, A. Schaechter and S. Swaray (2005). *Monetary Policy Implementation at Different Stages of Market Development*. Occasional Paper no. 244. Washington, DC: IMF.

Lostumbo, N. (2007). 'Success in hitting the inflation target: good luck or good policy?'. Mimeo. Chestnut Hill, MA: Boston College.

Lybek, T., and J. Morris (2004). 'Central bank governance: a survey of boards and management'. Working Paper no. 04/226. Washington, DC: IMF.

Mishkin, F. (2003). 'Comments on Fraga, Goldfajn, and Minella, "Inflation targeting in emerging market economies"', in NBER. *NBER Macroeconomics Annual 2003*: 403–11. Cambridge, MA: NBER.

(2004). 'Can inflation targeting work in emerging market countries?'. Working Paper no. 10646. Cambridge, MA: NBER.

Mishkin, F., and K. Schmidt-Hebbel (2007). 'Does inflation targeting make a difference?', in F. Mishkin and K. Schmidt-Hebbel (eds.). *Monetary Policy under Inflation Targeting*: 291–372. Santiago: Banco Central de Chile.

Morón, E., and D. Winkelried (2005). 'Monetary policy rules for financially vulnerable economies', *Journal of Development Economics*, 76(1): 25–51.

Reddell, M. (1999). 'Origins and early development of the inflation target', *Reserve Bank of New Zealand Bulletin*, 62(3): 63–71.

Roger, S., J. Restrepo and C. Garcia (2009). 'Hybrid inflation targeting regimes'. Working Paper no. 09/234. Washington, DC: IMF.

Roger, S., and M. Stone (2005). 'On target? The international experience with achieving inflation targets'. Working Paper no. 05/163. Washington DC: IMF.

Stone, M., S. Roger, S. Shimizu, A. Nordstrom, T. Kisinbay and J. Restrepo (2009). 'The role of the exchange rate in inflation-targeting emerging economies'. Occasional Paper no. 267. Washington, DC: IMF.

Svensson, L. (1999). 'Price-level targeting versus inflation targeting: a free lunch?', *Journal of Money, Credit and Banking*, 31(3): 277–95.

Taylor, J. (2001). 'The role of the exchange rate in monetary policy rules,' *American Economic Review*, 91(2): 263–7.

   (2009). 'The financial crisis and the policy response: an empirical analysis of what went wrong'. Working Paper no. 14631. Cambridge, MA: NBER.

Tuladhar, A. (2005). 'Governance structures and decision-making roles in inflation targeting central banks'. Working Paper no. 05/183. Washington, DC: IMF.

Vega, M., and D. Winkelried (2005). 'Inflation targeting and inflation behavior: a successful story?', *International Journal of Central Banking*, 1(3): 153–75.

Walsh, C. (2009). 'Using monetary policy to stabilize economic activity'. Paper presented at the 2009 Federal Reserve Bank of Kansas City symposium on financial stability and macroeconomic policy. Jackson Hole, WY, 20 August. Available at www.kc.frb.org/publicat/sympos/2009/papers/Walsh.09.11.09pdf.

Wei, D. (2008). 'Do central banks respond to exchange rate movements? Some new evidence from structural estimation'. Working Paper no. 2008–24. Ottawa: Bank of Canada.

5 Inflation targeting twenty years on: where, when, why, with what effects and what lies ahead?

Klaus Schmidt-Hebbel[1]

> The ability to deal with demand shocks and financial crises can be enhanced by a commitment to an explicit [inflation] target.
>
> Carl Walsh (2009a: 1)

> Today, inflation targeting is being put to the test – and it will almost certainly fail.
>
> Joseph Stiglitz (2008: 1)

5.1 Introduction

Two decades have passed since the Reserve Bank of New Zealand pioneered modern monetary policy practice by adopting inflation targeting. Since then, IT has gained followers and reputation, becoming the monetary regime of choice among many central bankers and academics. This preference has been revealed by the fact that no central bank endowed with monetary sovereignty that has adopted IT since 1989 has abandoned it – until now, at least.[2] Although at the time of this writing, in the midst of the worst financial crisis and global recession in a lifetime, it seems a bit adventurous to provide a firm forecast on IT's future prospects, my bet is that Walsh will be proved right in his quote and Stiglitz wrong.

The widespread adoption of IT as the frontier monetary regime around the world poses some questions about the economic and institutional factors that lead countries to adopt and sustain IT, and about the potential policy and performance benefits of IT. On what drives countries to implement IT, earlier studies point towards the role of initial institutional and economic conditions satisfied when adopting and maintaining IT adoption (see, for example, Mishkin and Schmidt-Hebbel 2007a). In contrast, Batini and Laxton (2007) show that the initial conditions do not matter for adopting IT: most countries, after starting IT, gradually build up better macroeconomic conditions and the institutional features of full-fledged IT.

The literature on the benefits of IT is older and deeper, spanning a decade of empirical research on its potential effects on inflation rates,

58   *Schmidt-Hebbel*

output and inflation stability, inflation expectations, exchange rate to inflation pass-through, monetary policy efficiency and the anchoring of inflation expectations, among other policy performance indicators. Such research includes, *inter alia*, country and cross-country empirical work reported by Corbo, Landerretche and Schmidt-Hebbel (2001, 2002); Mishkin and Savastano (2000); Schmidt-Hebbel and Werner (2002); Carare and Stone (2003); Vega and Winkelried (2005); Mishkin and Schmidt-Hebbel (2007a, 2007c); Gürkaynak *et al.* (2007); and other contributions published in the volumes published by Bernanke *et al.* (1999), Bernanke and Woodford (2005), Mishkin and Schmidt-Hebbel (2007b) and Schmidt-Hebbel and Walsh (2009). An outlier is the finding by Ball and Sheridan (2005) that IT does not improve macroeconomic performance in industrial countries, compared to other industrial countries that do not target inflation, at least explicitly.

IT also enhances the transparency of monetary policy, largely because it relies heavily on inflation forecasts (hence Svensson's (1997) labelling of IT as 'inflation-forecast targeting') and private sector inflation expectations. This feature enhances the efforts of IT central banks in strengthening their forms of communication with the markets and the general public, upgrading and reinforcing their transparency and governance (see Eijffinger and Geraats 2006 and Geraats 2009).

Against IT's generally remarkable record, however, the world economy's 2002–2010 boom-bust cycle, triggered and deepened by a massive financial crisis in industrial economies, has put into question the analytical foundation, forecasting and policymaking of modern monetary policy – with or without explicit IT. For example, Buiter's (2009) scathing indictment of modern macroeconomics, finance and monetary policy started a timely debate on the limitations and failures of the analytical foundations and policy practice in the latter fields, which found in Lucas (2009) a strong defender of the 'dismal science'. This debate and its implications for theory and policy are just starting, and will also certainly affect our future understanding of best monetary policy practice in general and under IT in particular.

This chapter is structured as follows. I start in section 5.2 by describing the where and when of IT adoption, focusing on the world sample of (currently) twenty-eight countries that have IT in place. Next I focus on the why of IT adoption, by assessing empirically the main determinants that lead central banks to choose this monetary regime. In section 5.4 I review the cross-country performance of IT central banks in attaining their targets, assessing empirically the role of institutional factors that drive those results. Then I present and survey evidence on the role of IT in three areas of monetary policy performance: inflation rates, policy

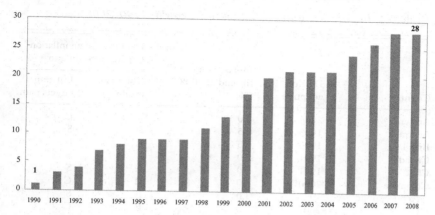

Figure 5.1 Number of inflation-targeting countries, 1990–2008
Sources: Mishkin and Schmidt-Hebbel (2007c) and Leyva (2008).

efficiency and policy transparency. In section 5.6 I discuss some questions posed for the conduct of monetary policy at large – and under IT in particular – by the still ongoing boom-bust cycle/financial crisis. Brief conclusions close the chapter.

5.2 Where and when? The spreading of IT

The number of IT countries has increased from one in 1989/90 (New Zealand, the 'mother of all inflation targeters') to twenty-eight in late 2008 (see Figure 5.1).[3] Among industrial countries, IT is not particularly popular; only eight of them have joined the IT club to date, the last two in 1999. One reason for this is the continuous erosion of monetary sovereignty in Europe as a result of the gradual growth of the euro area. The second is that the big three – the Fed, the ECB and the Bank of Japan – have not adopted IT, at least not of the explicit sort favoured by the twenty-eight countries included in this study.[4]

Among developing and emerging market economies, IT spread early and quickly, starting with Chile in 1991 and extending to twenty countries spread over four continents by late 2008. Many EMEs initially adopted partial IT, and shifted only later, and often quite gradually, to full-fledged IT, with all the bells and whistles of frontier-practice IT, including a floating exchange rate regime and high levels of policy transparency. Moreover, many EME inflation targeters used IT initially as a price stabilisation device, adopting the new regime at initially moderate and even high rates of inflation and pre-announcing a sequence of annually declining inflation targets – what is termed 'converging-target

Table 5.1 *Inflation-targeting countries in the world, 1990–2008*

Country	Date of adoption	Inflation target at the end of 2008 (%)	Definition of an inflation targeter according to	
			Country group	Inflation targets path
Armenia	2006	4.0	E	C
Australia	1993	2.5	I	S
Brazil	1999	4.5	E	C
Canada	1991	2.0	I	S
Chile	1991	3.0	E	S
Colombia	2000	4.0	E	C
Czech Republic	1998	3.0	E	S
Ghana	2007	5.0	E	C
Guatemala	2005	5.0	E	C
Hungary	2001	3.0	E	C
Iceland	2001	2.5	I	S
Indonesia	2005	5.0	E	C
Israel	1992	2.0	E	S
Mexico	1995	3.0	E	S
New Zealand	1990	2.0	I	S
Norway	2001	2.5	I	S
Peru	1994	2.0	E	S
Philippines	2002	4.0	E	S
Poland	1999	2.5	E	S
Romania	2005	3.8	E	C
Serbia	2007	4.5	E	C
South Africa	2000	4.5	E	S
South Korea	1998	3.0	E	S
Sweden	1993	2.0	I	S
Switzerland	2000	1.0	I	S
Thailand	2000	1.75	E	S
Turkey	2006	4.0	E	C
United Kingdom	1993	2.0	I	S

Notes: Adoption dates are taken from Leyva (2008) and Mishkin and Schmidt-Hebbel (2007c). The midpoint of the target is reported when the inflation target is defined as a range. If the IT adoption date is July or later in any year t, the annual date reported is for year $t + 1$. IT country groups are defined as E = emerging and I = industrial, and inflation targets paths as S = stationary and C = converging.
Sources: Based on Mishkin and Schmidt-Hebbel (2007b) and Leyva (2008).

IT'. As of late 2008 there were ten EME ITers that had graduated from target convergence by attaining low-inflation stationary inflation targets, while ten other EMEs were still converging towards stationary targets (Table 5.1).

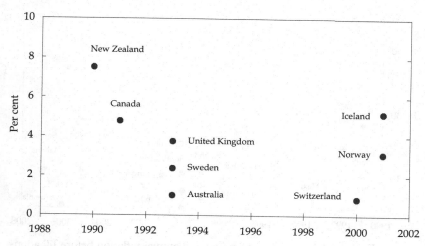

Figure 5.2 Dates of IT adoption and annual inflation before IT adoption, industrial economies, 1990–2001

Note: Depicted points reflect annual inflation rates during the twelve months that precede the month of IT adoption.

Source: Author's calculations based on IMF data.

Adoption dates and inflation rates during the twelve months before adoption show the contrasting experience of industrial economy (IE) ITers (with low initial inflation rates: see Figure 5.2) and many EME ITers (with moderate to high initial inflation rates: see Figure 5.3).

5.3   Why? The determinants of adopting IT and holding on to it

Central banks devote time to evaluating if their country's macroeconomic conditions and their own institutional set-up and policy framework are ripe for IT adoption – i.e. if they meet the so-called preconditions for successful IT adoption and operation. The standard initial conditions identified by the earlier literature include central bank operational independence, an absence of fiscal and financial dominance, and moderately low inflation (see, for example, Mishkin and Savastano 2000 and Mishkin and Schmidt-Hebbel 2007b). In contrast, Batini and Laxton (2007) show that the absence of some of the latter prerequisites at the time of adoption does not inhibit the start of IT.

Next I report selective results from work by Calderón and Schmidt-Hebbel (2008a) on the empirical determinants of the likelihood of

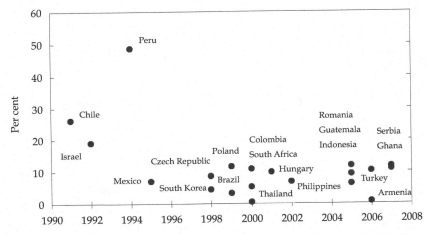

Figure 5.3 Dates of IT adoption and annual inflation before IT adoption, emerging market economies, 1991–2007

Note: Depicted points reflect annual inflation rates during the twelve months that precede the month of IT adoption.

Source: Author's calculations based on IMF data.

choosing and having in place IT rather than alternative monetary regimes. The panel data specification is the following:

$$y_{i,t} = 1(x_{i,t}'\beta + u_i + e_{i,t} \geq 0) \tag{5.1}$$

where y is a discrete-choice variable that is set equal to one if the argument (the IT choice) is positive and zero otherwise. The set of possible determinants is grouped in matrix x. The country-specific effect is u, e is a zero-mean disturbance term, and i and t are country and time subscripts, respectively.

Equation (5.1) is estimated by using discrete-choice panel estimation techniques applied to annual data covering 1975 to 2005 for ninety-eight IT and non-IT countries.[5] Selective results are reported in Table 5.2. Inflation affects negatively the likelihood of adopting IT. The fiscal position (measured by the ratio of the government balance to GDP) and the level of domestic financial development (proxied by the ratio of private credit to GDP) raise the probability of having IT in place. The two latter variables suggest that a country is more likely to adopt IT in the absence of fiscal and financial dominance, which conforms to the earlier literature on IT preconditions. Also in line with previous policy views, I report results that IT is more likely in countries with a floating exchange rate regime in place.[6] GDP per capita – a proxy of overall institutional development, including, for example, central bank independence – is also a significant determinant. Trade openness, which stands as a proxy for the influence of best monetary policy practice abroad, also contributes to having IT in place. Most of the latter variables, as reflected in alternative specifications, are significant and robust determinants of the choice of IT.

Unfortunately, this estimation approach drops the country-specific effects and therefore precludes proper computation of the marginal effects of individual determinants on the likelihood of having IT in place. Leyva (2008) overcomes this limitation by estimating jointly the individual (country-specific) effects and the slope parameters, at the cost of restricting the country sample to twenty-five ITers, spanning the years 1989 to 2005 – i.e. including at least one year before IT adoption for each country included.[7] His estimation results, based on a similar specification, are similar to those reported in Table 5.2. The estimated marginal effects for the main IT choice determinants are reproduced in Table 5.3. The largest marginal effects stem from changes in overall development: a rise in income levels from, say, Indonesia's level to Poland's raises the likelihood of having IT in place by a massive 66 per cent. Significant improvements in the three other determinants – lower inflation, higher financial development, larger trade openness – have smaller effects on the choice of IT.

5.4   Deviations of inflation from target

Monetary policy success hinges on consistent central bank behaviour and strong credibility on the part of the central bank with the private sector. ITers have been aiming at the latter by committing to explicit inflation targets. Have they succeeded in meeting their targets? What explains their success? I answer these questions in two steps. First, I measure inflation deviations from targets using three alternative measures and I estimate the half-lives of inflation shocks, for each and every IT country experience and several country groups. Second, I report empirical estimations of the role played by institutional and macroeconomic performance measures in explaining the panel data variation in inflation deviations from targets, based on the findings of Albagli and Schmidt-Hebbel (2004).

For measuring inflation deviations from targets I use (at most) 1990–2008 quarterly data for year-on-year consumer inflation in the world population comprised by the twenty-eight IT countries and official data on the corresponding inflation targets announced since the dates when the countries started inflation targeting.[8]

Table 5.2 Determinants of the likelihood of having an IT regime in place

	Fixed effects					Random effects		
	(1)	(2)	(3)	(4)	(5)	(6)	(7)	(8)
Inflation	−130.026***	−117.311***	−35.392***	−36.295***	−43.349***	−36.421***	−39.508***	−33.487***
	(2.95)	(3.18)	(5.10)	(5.46)	(6.13)	(5.88)	(6.63)	(6.46)
Government budget balance	−25.066	—	19.307**	20.685**	15.040**	17.909**	—	—
	(1.45)		(2.07)	(2.31)	(1.98)	(2.53)		
Financial development	19.872***	16.881***	0.775	—	3.299***	3.186***	2.633***	2.677***
	(3.07)	(3.39)	(0.55)		(3.19)	(3.40)	(2.99)	(3.22)
Exchange rate regime	−20.320***	−17.824***	−4.958***	−5.068***	−4.978***	−4.464***	−3.990***	−3.655***
	(3.03)	(3.22)	(5.27)	(5.54)	(7.04)	(7.20)	(7.74)	(7.49)
GDP per capita	104.027***	90.130***	5.042***	5.249***	4.605***	3.478***	4.822***	3.829***
	(3.19)	(3.56)	(4.78)	(5.29)	(5.08)	(3.49)	(5.90)	(4.19)
Trade openness	46.763***	42.343***	1.156	—	2.289**	0.837	3.185***	2.134**
	(2.83)	(3.03)	(0.82)		(2.06)	(0.68)	(4.01)	(2.53)
Money growth volatility	—	—	−0.142	−0.126	—	—	—	—
			(0.44)	(0.39)				
Terms of trade volatility	—	—	1.760	0.959	—	—	—	—
			(0.28)	(0.15)				
Dummy	—	—	6.986***	6.741***	7.789***	—	7.433***	—
			(3.84)	(4.11)	(4.63)		(4.85)	

Constant	—	—	−45.403***	−45.517***	−43.798***	−30.343***	−47.961***	−36.263***
			(5.01)	(5.27)	(5.68)	(3.44)	(7.01)	(4.57)
Observations	491	554	1,143	1,163	1,854	1,854	2,305	2,305
Number of countries	19	24	71	71	76	76	98	98
Countries with an IT regime	19	24	19	19	19	19	24	24
Countries without an IT regime (control group)	0	0	52	52	57	57	74	74
Likelihood ratio (LR) statistic	450.19	499.19	76.03	75.10	126.91	126.90	177.77	161.95
p-value	0.00	0.00	0.00	0.00	0.00	0.00	0.00	0.00

Notes: Absolute value of z statistics in parentheses. * = significant at 10 per cent; ** = significant at 5 per cent; *** = significant at 1 per cent.
Source: Calderón and Schmidt-Hebbel (2008a).

Table 5.3 *Marginal contribution of key determinants to IT regime likelihood*

Variable	Marginal contribution (per cent)	Measure	Impact of ...
CPI inflation	13.19	rate	a reduction of π^n by 10 p.p., which amounts roughly to a reduction of π from 17% to 5%
Financial development	6.79	ratio	an increase of the indicator by 10 p.p.
GDP per capita	65.64	logs	an increase of the log of GDP per capita by 1.2, which accounts for passing from 2 (8.1 Indonesia) to 3 (9.3 Poland) in income category
Trade openness	8.82	ratio	an increase of the indicator by 10 p.p.

Note: The figures for Indonesia and Poland correspond to the log of the 2001–5 average per capita GDP.
Source: Leyva (2008).

Three alternative inflation deviation measures are reported for each country since its corresponding IT starting date in Table 5.4: the mean absolute error (MAE), the mean squared error (MSE) and the root mean squared error (RMSE). Countries are ordered from smallest (Switzerland) to largest (Ghana) MSE or RMSE. The country ranking by MAE is slightly different from the rankings based on any of the two alternative measures, but the value or rank correlation between MAE and any of the two alternatives is very high. Interestingly, the persistence of inflation shocks – as measured by the half-life of monthly inflation deviations from targets[9] – is largely orthogonal to the size of inflation deviations across countries, as shown by the second column of Table 5.4. Half-lives of inflation deviations range from lows of six to eight months (Armenia, Mexico, Turkey and Norway – although some of these include very few observations) to highs of twenty-seven to twenty-nine months (the United Kingdom and the Philippines).

Figures 5.4 to 5.7 depict quarterly inflation deviations measured as the MAE for each country over time, reported separately by regional country groups. Figures 5.8 and 5.9 report the RMSE for each country by four main country groups. The average RMSE for EMEs is equal to 3 p.p., more than twice the IE average RMSE of 1.4 p.p. (Figure 5.8). The average RMSE of stationary ITers is 2 p.p., close to a half of the converging ITers' RMSE of 3.8 p.p.

Table 5.4 *Measures of inflation deviations from targets and inflation deviation in IT countries, IT starting quarter to 2008Q4*

Country	Number of observations	Half-life (months)	MAE	MSE	RMSE
Switzerland	36	11.6	0.4	0.3	0.5
United Kingdom	69	27.1	0.9	1.1	1.1
Canada	72	14.2	0.9	1.3	1.1
Sweden	56	25.3	1.1	1.6	1.3
Norway	32	8.0	1.1	2.0	1.4
New Zealand	76	20.1	1.1	2.0	1.4
Australia	64	20.0	1.1	2.1	1.4
Colombia	37	15.7	1.2	2.8	1.7
Romania	14	–	1.3	2.9	1.7
South Korea	44	18.9	1.1	3.1	1.8
Thailand	36	23.2	1.2	3.1	1.8
Chile	72	14.7	1.1	3.1	1.8
Philippines	28	29.3	2.1	5.1	2.3
Czech Republic	44	14.4	1.7	5.8	2.4
Poland	42	24.4	2.0	6.1	2.5
Israel	68	14.6	2.1	7.0	2.6
Guatemala	16	14.5	2.2	7.1	2.7
Iceland	32	16.6	2.2	8.1	2.8
Armenia	12	6.8	2.5	8.2	2.9
Peru	60	9.1	1.7	8.5	2.9
Hungary	32	18.4	2.3	9.2	3.0
South Africa	36	24.7	2.4	9.5	3.1
Serbia	10	24.9	3.6	19.4	4.4
Brazil	40	22.6	2.9	19.4	4.4
Mexico	56	7.6	2.8	24.6	5.0
Turkey	12	7.1	4.9	25.3	5.0
Indonesia	16	10.3	3.9	30.4	5.5
Ghana	8	–	6.2	40.1	6.3

Notes: Country samples comprise inflation targets and inflation rates from the start of IT in each country until the fourth quarter of 2008. The half-life of an inflation deviation is defined as the number of months that an inflation deviation from target is reduced to one-half its initial value. Half-lives are computed from an AR(1) process for inflation deviations for each country.
Source: Author's calculation based on central bank and IMF data.

In order to describe how inflation deviations have changed over time, I compute rolling estimations of RMSEs, using a window size of eight quarters (Figure 5.10). Before 2007 both industrial and emerging economies exhibited downward RMSE trends, during the period that has been labelled as the 'Great Moderation' (see, for example, Calderón and Schmidt-Hebbel 2008b). This came to an abrupt end during the

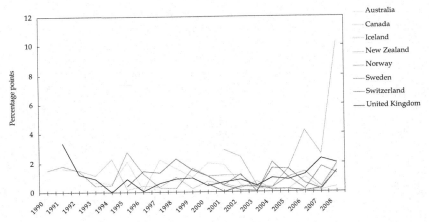

Figure 5.4 Annual absolute inflation deviations from targets in industrial economies, 1990–2008

Sources: Author's calculations based on central bank and IMF data.

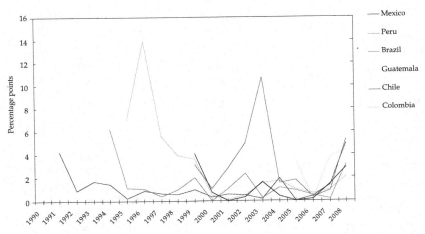

Figure 5.5 Annual absolute inflation deviations from targets in Latin American economies, 1991–2008

Sources: Author's calculations based on central bank and IMF data.

late phase of the boom, as unprecedented commodity price inflation was passed through to consumer prices all over the world – especially in EMEs, and even more so in converging-target EMEs. For the full 1992–2008 period, however, Figure 5.10 confirms that RMSEs were

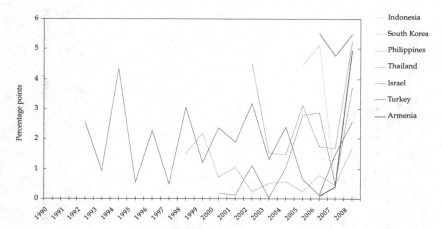

Figure 5.6 Annual absolute inflation deviations from targets in Asian economies, 1992–2008

Sources: Author's calculations based on central bank and IMF data.

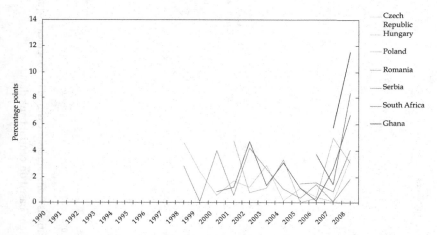

Figure 5.7 Annual absolute inflation deviations from targets in central/eastern European and African economies, 1998–2008

Sources: Author's calculations based on central bank and IMF data.

consistently larger in EMEs than in IEs, as they were in converging as compared to stationary ITers.

Next I focus on potential determinants of inflation target deviations. I follow Albagli and Schmidt-Hebbel (2004) in specifying the deviation of

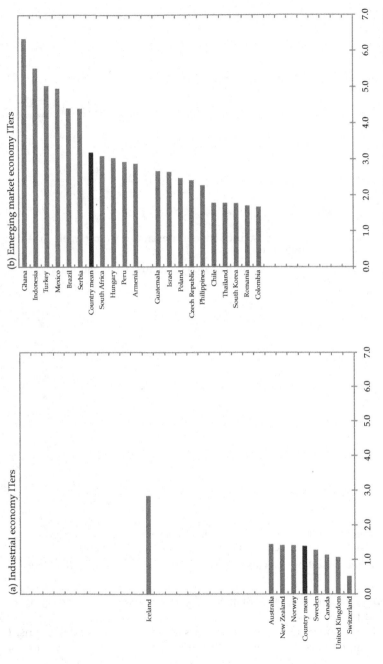

Figure 5.8 Inflation deviations from targets measured by root mean squared errors in IE and EME inflation targeters, 1990–2008

Source: Author's calculations based on central bank data.

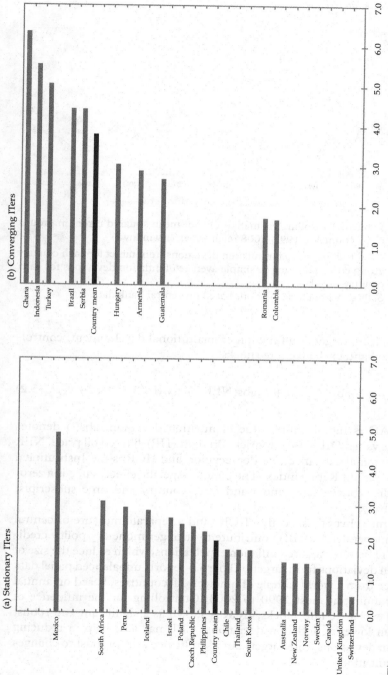

Figure 5.9 Inflation deviations from targets measured by root mean squared errors in stationary and converging inflation targeters, 1990–2008

Source: Author's calculations based on central bank data.

72   *Schmidt-Hebbel*

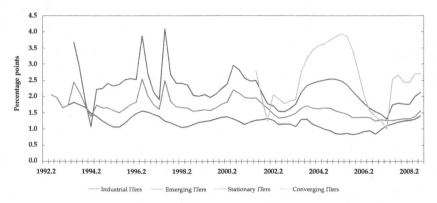

Figure 5.10 Rolling estimation of root mean squared errors in groups of IT countries, 1992–2008 (eight-quarter windows)

Note: Rolling series for inflation deviations from target for each country group correspond to the simple average of inflation deviations for each country member.

Source: Author's calculations based on central bank data.

inflation from target as a function of institutional development, controlling for oil and exchange rate shocks:

$$AD_{i,t} = \beta_1 abs(OIL_{i,t}) + \beta_2 abs(NER_{i,t}) + \beta_3 IICR_{i,t} + u_i + e_{i,t} \quad (5.2)$$

where AD is the absolute value of inflation deviation, abs(·) denotes absolute value, OIL is the Hodrick–Prescott (HP)-filtered oil price, NER is the nominal exchange rate depreciation and IICR is the Institutional Investor Credit Rating index. The country-specific effect is u, e is a zero-mean disturbance term and i and t are country and time subscripts, respectively.

The main hypothesis is that IICR (and a separate measure of central bank independence, CBI) contribute to stronger monetary policy credibility and better-anchored inflation expectations, which reduce the size of inflation deviations from targets. Table 5.5 reports unbalanced panel data evidence from a world sample of nineteen IT countries, based on annual data spanning at most 1990 to 2003. Controlling for the influence of oil and exchange rate shocks, IICR is shown as a significant and robust factor in lowering inflation deviations. CBI may also help in reducing inflation deviations from targets but its influence is less robust to changes in specification.

5.5   What other effects?

In this section I report other effects of IT, also drawing from cross-country and panel data evidence. I focus on three performance measures: long-term inflation rates, monetary policy efficiency and central bank transparency.

Mishkin and Schmidt-Hebbel (2007c) assess empirically the effects of IT on long-term inflation, taking as starting point previous cross-section studies on differences in long-term inflation between ITers and non-ITers. Table 5.6 summarises the results of previous studies, together with new estimates by these authors, which show that long-term inflation rates are higher in IT countries than in a stringent control group of high-performing non-IT industrial countries. The diversity of the cross-section results reported in the table, all based on similar specifications, illustrates the fact that empirical results are highly sensitive to the choice of treatment and control groups. In addition, the latter results are based on weak estimation techniques (inflation is not instrumentalised) and lack a time-series dimension. Mishkin and Schmidt-Hebbel (2007c) therefore specify a dynamic equation for the difference in long-term inflation rates in IT and non-IT countries and estimate it using an instrumental variable panel data model for a large panel sample. Table 5.7 summarises a wide range of long-term inflation differences between alternative treatment and control groups. The reported differences in results confirm that the choice of treatment and control groups is key for the corresponding results. It is interesting to note, however, that long-term inflation is 1.1 p.p. lower in the subset of IE ITers than in the control group of IE non-ITers, in contrast to the cross-country result of Ball and Sheridan (2005), who report no differences between IE ITers and non-ITers.

Calderón and Schmidt-Hebbel (2008a) find that adopting IT and having it in place lowers inflation rates. They assess the role of non-monetary factors in determining inflation in a world panel based on the following specification:

$$\pi_{i,t} = \beta_0 + \beta_1 \mathrm{INFR} + \beta_2 \mathrm{MERR} + \beta_3 \mathrm{OPN} + \beta_4 \mathrm{STIN} + \beta_5 \mathrm{CYC} + u_i + e_{i,t} \tag{5.3}$$

where π is the normalised inflation rate,[10] INFR stands for inflation-related variables (high inflation and hyperinflation dummy variables; lagged inflation), MERR is a set of dummy variables for monetary and exchange rate regimes, OPN comprises openness variables (measures of trade and financial openness; external inflation), STIN is a set of structural and institutional variables (democratic accountability, per capita GDP and the ratios of the fiscal surplus to GDP and private credit to

Table 5.5 *Determinants of inflation deviations from targets, panel of nineteen IT countries, 1990–2003*

	(1) AD1	(2) AD2	(3) AD3	(4) AD1	(5) AD2	(6) AD3	(7) AD1	(8) AD2	(9) AD3
c	1.444 (0.000)	0.860 (0.000)	1.147 (0.000)	1.914 (0.000)	1.294 (0.001)	1.880 (0.001)	1.962 (0.001)	1.277 (0.002)	1.925 (0.001)
abs(AD1(−1))	0.800 (0.000)	0.876 (0.000)	0.871 (0.000)	0.725 (0.000)	0.844 (0.000)	0.824 (0.000)	0.724 (0.000)	0.822 (0.000)	0.824 (0.000)
abs(AD1(−2))	−0.191 (0.000)	−0.246 (0.000)	−0.195 (0.000)	−0.190 (0.000)	−0.261 (0.000)	−0.186 (0.000)	−0.190 (0.000)	−0.225 (0.000)	−0.185 (0.000)
abs(AD1(−3))	−0.055 (0.104)		−0.076 (0.037)	−0.087 (0.016)		−0.104 (0.004)	−0.088 (0.016)	−0.059 (0.098)	−0.104 (0.004)
abs(NER)	(0.022)	0.009 (0.031)	0.009						
abs(NER(−1))	0.015 (0.000)			0.012 (0.007)	0.009 (0.039)	0.010 (0.019)	0.012 (0.007)	0.009 (0.043)	0.011 (0.018)
abs(OILG)	0.007 (0.020)	0.007 (0.013)	0.006 (0.035)	0.007 (0.018)	0.007 (0.013)	0.006 (0.025)	0.007 (0.018)	0.007 (0.009)	0.006 (0.025)
abs(OILG(−1))	−0.010 (0.006)	−0.010 (0.002)	−0.006 (0.065)	−0.010 (0.005)	−0.010 (0.001)	−0.006 (0.049)	−0.010 (0.005)	−0.010 (0.002)	−0.006 (0.049)
abs(OILG(−2))	0.009 (0.002)	0.006 (0.016)	0.006 (0.049)	0.008 (0.004)	0.006 (0.021)	0.005 (0.063)	0.008 (0.003)	0.005 (0.044)	0.005 (0.062)

abs(GAP(−3))	−0.040 (0.005)		−0.033 (0.024)			−0.025 (0.108)			−0.025 (0.104)
CBI	−0.161 (0.010)	−0.149 (0.007)	−0.144 (0.015)						
IICR	−0.011 (0.000)	−0.007 (0.000)	−0.010 (0.000)	−0.020 (0.002)	−0.012 (0.034)	−0.020 (0.001)	−0.021 (0.002)	−0.011 (0.063)	−0.021 (0.001)
R^2	0.51	0.58	0.59	0.53	0.61	0.62	0.53	0.58	0.62
Adj. R^2	0.50	0.57	0.58	0.50	0.59	0.60	0.50	0.55	0.60
U-root test	−22.02	−21.56	−21.84	−22.26	−21.58	−21.46	−21.46	−22.09	−18.10
N	517	536	517	517	536	517	517	517	517
Intercept	C	C	C	F-effects	F-effects	F-effects	F-effects	F-effects	F-effects
Method	OLS	OLS	OLS	OLS	OLS	OLS	TSLS	TSLS	TSLS

Source: Albagli and Schmidt-Hebbel (2004).

76   *Schmidt-Hebbel*

Table 5.6 *Estimates of differences in long-term inflation rates between IT and non-IT countries in four cross-section studies*

Authors	Sample	Method	Long-term inflation rate differences (percentage points)
Ball and Sheridan (2005)	IE: 7 IT, 13 non-IT	Cross-section OLS	zero[a]
Vega and Winkelried (2005)	World: 23 IT, 86 non-IT	Propensity score	$(-2.6, -4.8)$[b]
IMF (2005)	EMEs: 13 IT, 22 non-IT	Cross-section OLS	−4.8
Mishkin and Schmidt-Hebbel (2007a)	World's 21 IT, 13 IE non-IT	Cross-section OLS	1.2

Notes: OLS = ordinary least squares.
[a] Zero = statistically not significantly different from zero.
[b] Range of estimates reported by the authors.

Table 5.7 *Estimates of differences in long-term inflation rates between different groups of IT and non-IT countries, panel data results*

Treatment group/ control group	Method	Long-term inflation rate differences (percentage points)		
		Non-Iters and pre-ITers	Non-ITers	Pre-ITers
All ITers	OLS	−1.9	zero	−5.0
All ITers	IV	−4.8	zero	−5.0
Industrial ITers	IV	zero	−1.1	zero
Emerging ITers	IV	−7.5	zero	−6.4
Stationary ITers	IV	−2.1	zero	zero
Converging ITers	IV	−8.0	zero	−8.2

Notes: Zero = statistically not significantly different from zero. IV = instrumental variables.
Source: Mishkin and Schmidt-Hebbel (2007c).

GDP) and CYC denotes cyclical variables (the domestic and foreign output gaps; the cyclical component of international oil prices).

The panel data estimation results for equation (5.3), reported in Table 5.8, are based on a world sample of annual data covering the period 1975 to 2005 and comprising sixty-five countries, including both ITers and non-ITers. The main result for this chapter is that having an IT regime in place lowers annual inflation by roughly 5 p.p. Note that here the control group is comprised of all the non-IT countries in the world included in this study, among them many non-IT EMEs with at least moderate inflation rates.

This result is robust to using different samples, estimating techniques and specifications that control for a sizable number of statistically significant inflation determinants, as reported by Calderón and Schmidt-Hebbel (2008a). Other than the IT regime, significant and robust variables that reduce inflation in the world are financial openness, the fiscal balance, income per capita, the output gap and a fixed exchange rate regime.

Next I turn to the issue of monetary policy efficiency. Focusing only on inflation volatility – or inflation deviations from targets, as in section 5.4 – is a partial and hence potentially biased way to assess the efficiency of monetary policy. The usual, more comprehensive approach involves measures of both inflation and output variability. Mishkin and Schmidt-Hebbel (2007c), following Cecchetti, Flores-Lagunes and Krause (2006), solve for the minimisation problem of a central bank loss function based on inflation and output volatility, subject to a highly stylised structure of an economy reflected by aggregate demand and supply equations. Extending the previous empirical work by Cecchetti, Flores-Lagunes and Krause on individual countries, Mishkin and Schmidt-Hebbel estimate the system of equations on panel data for different treatment (IT) country groups and different control (non-IT) country groups, based on quarterly data for 1989 to 2004. Using the parameter estimates and the model solution, they construct inflation–output variability frontiers that represent measures of economic performance and monetary policy efficiency. Supply shock variability is interpreted as a change in the position of the efficiency frontier, while the efficiency of monetary policy is measured by the distance from the economy's observed volatility performance to the policy efficiency frontier.

Figure 5.11 depicts two efficiency frontiers and two observed points of output and inflation variability: one for inflation targeters before they adopted IT and one for stationary ITers after they converged to stationary targets. The more outward efficiency frontier and observed volatility performance represents a control group of subsequent IT countries from 1986 up to the quarter before they adopted IT. The more inward efficiency frontier and observed volatility performance represents a treatment group of stationary-target ITers that extends from the first quarter

Table 5.8 *Determinants of inflation in the world, panel data results*

| | Fixed effects (FE) and random effects (RE) instrumental variables estimates | | | | |
	(1) FE IV	RE IV	(2) FE IV	(3) FE IV	(4) FE IV
Inflation-related variables					
Lagged inflation					
Normalised and instrumented value	0.160***	−0.033	0.196*	0.141	0.139
	(1.97)	(0.22)	(1.87)	(1.42)	(1.39)
Hyperinflation	0.348***	0.488***	0.357***	0.363***	0.364***
	(9.29)	(6.54)	(8.24)	(8.83)	(8.82)
High inflation	0.232***	0.308***	0.226***	0.230***	0.232***
	(14.02)	(8.29)	(11.14)	(11.85)	(11.72)
Monetary and exchange rate regime					
Inflation targeting					
Lagged	−0.051***	−0.045***	−0.051 †***	−0.054 †***	−0.055 †***
	(5.41)	(4.25)	(3.80)	(4.16)	(4.27)
Exchange rate regime					
Lagged	−0.029***	−0.037***	−0.031***	−0.033***	−0.033***
	(7.70)	(5.97)	(6.77)	(7.70)	(7.82)
Openness					
Trade openness					
Lagged	−0.009	−0.012**	−0.019	−0.010	
	(0.81)	(2.15)	(1.43)	(0.73)	
Capital openness					
Lagged	−0.013***	−0.011***	−0.013***	−0.013***	−0.013***
	(5.94)	(4.90)	(4.79)	(5.09)	(5.06)
Relevant external inflation					
Normalised	0.210***	0.412***	0.169**	0.080	0.127
	(3.11)	(4.77)	(2.10)	(0.96)	(1.57)
Structural/institutional variables					
Fiscal surplus					
Lagged	−0.204***	−0.179***	−0.251 †***	−0.459 †***	−0.427 †***
	(5.30)	(4.46)	(5.17)	(5.15)	(5.00)

	(1)	(2)	(3)	(4)	(5)
Income per capita					
Lagged	−0.040***	0.012***	−0.045***	−0.051†***	−0.047†***
	(3.67)	(3.09)	(3.46)	(4.06)	(4.20)
Domestic private credit					
Lagged	0.018*	−0.059***	0.028**	0.025**	0.024**
	(1.87)	(4.65)	(2.37)	(2.26)	(2.29)
Democratic accountability	−0.002	−0.003*	−0.002	−0.002	
	(1.22)	(1.65)	(1.05)	(0.74)	
Cyclical domestic and foreign variables					
Cyclical component of oil prices	0.019**	0.017	0.013	0.026**	0.021**
	(2.01)	(1.48)	(1.14)	(2.34)	(2.05)
National output gap					
Lagged	0.238***	0.057	1.182†***	0.724†**	0.709†**
	(3.60)	(0.55)	(3.06)	(2.07)	(2.02)
Foreign output gap (weighted by GDP)	−0.204	−0.406	−0.565**	−0.366	
	(0.93)	(1.40)	(2.11)	(1.45)	
Constant	0.467***	0.086***	0.504***	0.557**	0.512***
	(4.80)	(3.68)	(4.47)	(5.09)	(5.22)
Hausman test (RE vs FE) p-value	0.00	0.00	0.00	0.00	0.00
Observations	1,574	1,574	1,574	1,570	1,619
Country number	65	65	65	65	65
R^2 overall	0.75	0.79	0.71	0.68	0.69

Notes: The dependent variable is normalised inflation. Estimation is fixed effects with instrumented variables. Absolute values of t-statistics in parentheses. * = significant at 10%; ** = significant at 5%; *** = significant at 1%. † = not lagged but instrumented. The Hausman test favors FE regressions in all cases; thus RE, being inconsistent, is not reported from equation (5.2).

Source: Calderón and Schmidt-Hebbel (2008b).

Output variability

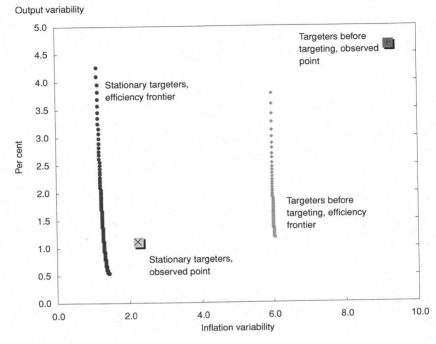

Figure 5.11 Efficiency frontiers and observed inflation and output volatility in IT countries before IT adoption and in stationary-target IT countries

Source: Mishkin and Schmidt-Hebbel (2007c).

of stationary targets through to the last quarter of 2004. Figure 5.12 plots efficiency frontiers and observed volatility points for the treatment group of stationary ITers (again) and for the control group of non-IT economies. The main findings represented in these two figures are that IT has helped to improve massively the efficiency of monetary policy of ITers but that monetary policy efficiency still falls short of the efficiency levels observed in the stringent control group of high-performing non-IT industrial countries.

Finally, I refer briefly to the contribution of IT in attaining higher levels of central bank transparency, based on simple unconditional analysis derived from the data collected by other researchers. Policy transparency is a key issue for IT central banks as they aim at policy credibility in general and anchoring inflation expectations in particular. Eijffinger and Geraats (2006) have developed an aggregate central bank transparency

Output variability

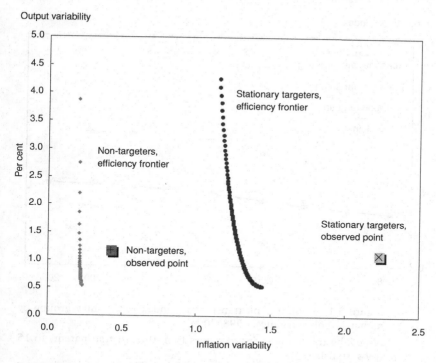

Figure 5.12 Efficiency frontiers and observed inflation and output volatility in non-IT countries and in stationary-target IT countries
Source: Mishkin and Schmidt-Hebbel (2007c).

index based on performance indicators grouped into five measures: political transparency (related to policy objectives), economic transparency (related to information disclosure on data, models and forecasts), procedural transparency (which refers to the release of minutes and votes), policy transparency (related to the announcement and explanation of policy decisions) and operational transparency (regarding the implementation of policy decisions). They apply these transparency measures to several industrial countries. Dincer and Eichengreen (2007) extend this database by including more countries and differentiating between IEs and EMEs.

Figure 5.13, borrowed from Geraats (2009), plots average transparency indexes for different country groups classified by four alternative monetary policy regimes over the period 1998 to 2006. ITers achieve by far the highest levels of aggregate central bank transparency among all

Transparency index

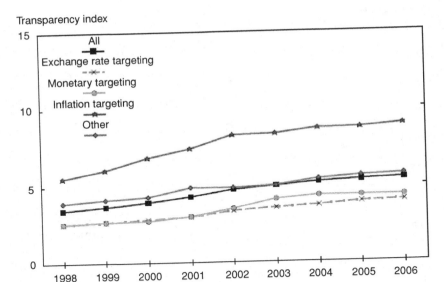

Figure 5.13 Central bank transparency index for country groups by monetary policy regimes, 1998–2006

Note: The transparency index ranges from 0 (least transparent) to 15 (most transparent).

Sources: Geraats (2009), based on data by Dincer and Eichengreen (2007).

countries pursuing different monetary regimes. Moreover, ITers have been able to increase over time the distance in transparency from countries under other regimes. Figure 5.14 shows the transparency attained by IE and EME ITers from 1998 to 2005. While transparency in IE ITers is much larger than in EME ITers, the gap is narrowing over time.

5.6   What lies ahead for IT regimes?

I now refer to two sets of challenges that lie ahead for IT central banks. The first relates to demands for the enhancement of monetary policy transparency. The second set is comprised of systemic challenges to the conduct of policy and the design of IT derived from questions posed by the monetary policy experience of the 2002–9 boom-bust cycle (for more detailed discussions, see Walsh 2009a, 2009b, and Hammond 2009).

The evidence discussed in this chapter and other research quoted above on the comparative achievements of monetary policy under IT suggests

Transparency index

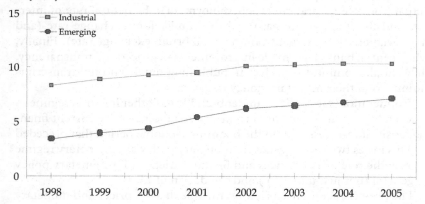

Figure 5.14 Central bank transparency index for IE and EME IT country groups, 1998–2005

Note: The transparency index ranges from 0 (least transparent) to 15 (most transparent).
Sources: Geraats (2009), based on data by Dincer and Eichengreen (2007).

that explicit IT dominates other successful monetary regimes (including implicit IT and other monetary regimes different from explicit IT, such as those pursued by the US Federal Reserve, the European Central Bank and the Bank of Japan) in several dimensions. First, IT enhances transparency and accountability more effectively than other regimes, as shown in the evidence reported by Dincer and Eichengreen (2007) and Geraats (2009). IT also provides more predictability, because there is less discretion in monetary policy decisions (Walsh 2009a, 2009b). Third, IT guarantees better anchoring of inflation expectations (see, for example, Gürkaynak *et al.* 2007). Finally, IT does not imply higher output volatility than other monetary regimes, as shown by Mishkin and Schmidt-Hebbel (2007c) among others (see also Walsh 2009a).

Many inflation-targeting central banks still face important transparency and communication challenges, however. First, following the advice of academics and the encouragement of several IT central banks to date, all ITers should aim at publishing their interest rate forecasts and fan charts, complementing the publication of inflation and output growth forecasts and fan charts. Second, to make a clearer, more transparent connection between the monetary policy decisions and published projections of central banks, they should include their backcasts and forecasts of key unobservable variables, including potential or efficient-level output (and the output gap), the natural unemployment rate (and the deviation of the actual from the natural rate of unemployment), the neutral rate of interest (and the interest rate gap) and the equilibrium exchange rate (and the deviation of the actual from the equilibrium exchange rate). Finally, while central banks have made improvements in procedural transparency, they should commit themselves to publishing timely and full transcripts (minutes) of their monetary policy meetings.

Frontier monetary policy – under both IT and other inflation regimes – is severely challenged by our current understanding of the current financial crisis-cum-recession and the boom-and-bubble period that preceded it. This raises two sets of issues for monetary policy and monetary regime choice: the role of asset prices and financial frictions for monetary policy in general (not just under IT) and the design of IT.

The pre-crisis consensus view on the role of asset prices and monetary policy was that the latter should react to asset price shocks only to the extent that they affect inflation forecasts or if the real interest rate were affected by financial shocks (Bernanke and Gertler 2001). Financial frictions (like real frictions) affect monetary policy transmission and interact with nominal rigidities, however, which calls for monetary policy to mitigate the effects of that interaction.[11] The crisis has highlighted the latter role for monetary policy (as shown in recent theoretical work by Cúrdia and Woodford 2009, De Fiore and Tristani 2009 and Demirel 2009), although, as pointed out by Walsh (2009b), the appropriate monetary policy response will depend on the type of financial friction and shock.

A separate, much longer discussion has been about whether central banks should lean against the wind of asset price bubbles. Cecchetti *et al.* (2000), Cecchetti, Genberg and Wadhwani (2002) and Borio and White (2003) have argued that monetary policy should attempt to mitigate the development of bubbles. Against the latter, the widely shared consensus view was that monetary policy was too ineffective to deal with bubbles, that bubbles were difficult to identify *ex ante* and that the more effective alternative would be to address the effects of a bursting bubble by easing policy after the event (Bernanke and Gertler 2001, Bernanke 2002 and Gertler 2003). The latter consensus view has been seriously shattered by the massive real costs and deflationary consequences of the housing and equity price bursts observed in many industrial economies, with worldwide consequences. While this bubble-and-bust experience certainly has other causes as well, in the many market and regulatory imperfections that require separate regulatory reform, it is likely to lead to changes in the conduct of monetary policy – both with and without IT – with the aim of deflating incipient asset price bubbles.

Another issue brought to the forefront by monetary policy actions during the current crisis is the need to come to a better theoretical and practical understanding of how conventional monetary policy – whether under IT or other monetary regimes – is complemented by unconventional monetary (and credit) policy, as reflected by the massive deployment of quantitative (and credit) easing to provide liquidity to illiquid financial markets and firms.

Finally, the crisis has brought into the open the problems faced by monetary policy under conditions of severe deflationary demand shocks that lead to policy rate cuts to near zero – i.e. when the zero lower bound (ZLB) is binding. Three design corrections to the actual implementation of IT in most countries could reduce the likelihood of attaining the ZLB: first, raising the numerical inflation target (at the cost of having higher average inflation); second, adopting a target for core inflation, which exhibits less volatility around the central target value than headline inflation (at the cost of reducing the usefulness and credibility of a headline inflation target); and, third, an extension of standard policy horizons under IT (typically between two and three years) to five years or more, as suggested recently by Mishkin (2008). These three alternatives have been widely discussed in the literature on the initial conditions and optimal design of IT and at central bank conferences. Until recently they were largely dismissed, but the recent experience of binding ZLB and the 2008/9 recession make their discussion relevant again.

The most radical challenge to IT comes from the proposal to adopt price level targeting (PLT). Long before the current crisis, Svensson (1999) and Vestin (2006) were among the first to evaluate seriously the relative merits and possible adoption of price level targeting. PLT's main theoretical advantage over IT is that the expectation that prices will return to their target level influences current inflation when price setting is forward-looking. This benefit is particularly strong when the ZLB holds and the economy is in a deflationary liquidity trap. Deflation bygones under IT are not bygones under PLT; they require future inflation that is on average higher than the inflation target level (or the price level target growth). As this is anticipated by forward-looking agents, the likelihood of getting into a deflationary situation is lower under PLT, and, when it materialises, the likelihood of getting out more quickly is greater under PLT.[12] PLT is therefore likely to emerge as a viable and possibly superior alternative to – or improvement of – IT in the future.

5.7   Concluding remarks

IT has come a long way since its birth two decades ago. The evidence shows that IT is not observationally equivalent to other monetary regimes used by frontier central banks (such as implicit IT) or to best-practice monetary policy – neither in design nor in performance. Moreover, IT dominates alternative monetary regimes (including implicit IT and non-explicit regimes) in several dimensions. Nevertheless, the current crisis and the preceding boom-and-bubble period pose serious challenges to IT as we know it – and to the frontier conduct of monetary policy generally, under IT or other monetary regimes.

Many more emerging economies are likely to adopt a variant of IT in the future. It is also possible that some current ITers in Europe will drop out of the club as they join the euro area. The specific form that frontier best-practice IT in a broad sense – including price level targeting – will take in the next (third) decade of its existence is far from clear now, however, just as the current frontier IT regime was not anticipated at the birth of IT two decades ago.

NOTES

1. A preliminary version of this study was delivered as the luncheon address at the eleventh annual inflation targeting conference of the Banco Central de Brasil (Rio de Janeiro, 14–15 May 2009). The author thanks Stefan Gerlach and other participants at the Sixth Norges Bank Monetary Policy Conference for valuable comments on a previous draft. The author also thanks Gustavo Leyva for outstanding research assistance.
2. Three European countries (Finland, Spain and Slovakia) that had adopted IT in the past have relinquished monetary sovereignty subsequently by adopting the euro and hence abandoning IT. They will be followed by more currently IT and non-IT European countries in the future.
3. Hammond (2009) presents a detailed overview of the key features of IT in twenty-six IT central banks and a discussion of the main issues faced by IT today.
4. It is debatable as to whether Switzerland should be counted as an IT country. The Swiss National Bank does not define its monetary policy framework as that of an explicit inflation targeter. I have decided to include Switzerland in my world count of ITers, nonetheless, on account of the close similarity of its monetary policy regime to those of other ITers.
5. Fixed-effects and random-effects models are both estimated. The fixed-effects approach drops the country-specific effects in order to ensure consistency in the estimation of slope parameters (in contrast to the individual effects). The random-effects model typically assumes a joint normal distribution between individual effects and the rest of the inflation determinants. The drawback of the former approach is that the estimator is restricted to those individuals whose regime choice changes over time (the so-called 'movers'), while the second is not. This explains the difference in sample size between fixed-effects and random-effects results reported in Table 5.2.
6. The exchange rate regime is measured by a dummy variable that takes a value of one for fixed and intermediate exchange rate regimes.
7. Although the number of countries is severely restricted, he shows that the bias in the estimation of the slope parameters is reasonably small.

8. Quarterly inflation rates are taken from the IMF's International Financial Statistics (IFS) database. I use annual inflation targets publicly reported on central bank web pages. For converging ITers that announce annual calendar-year inflation targets, I calculate quarterly targets by linear interpolation, assuming that the fourth-quarter inflation target is the annual target announced for the corresponding year.

9. Half-lives are computed from a simple first-order autoregressive (AR(1)) process for each country's monthly inflation deviation from target, by calculating the impulse response for a unitary (1 p.p.) shock.

10. INF is defined as (annual inflation)/(1 + annual inflation).

11. Walsh (2009a) makes the important point that this monetary policy acts as a second-best policy. If an effective time-varying fiscal policy instrument (based on taxes and subsidies) were available to counteract the effects of mark-up (real) shocks, monetary policy would not be necessary to mitigate the inflation and output effects of interactions between real frictions and nominal rigidities. In the same vein, if an effective time-varying financial regulation (for example, counter-cyclical capital and liquidity requirements) were available to counteract financial shocks such as changes in credit spreads, monetary policy would not be necessary to mitigate the consequences of interactions between financial frictions and nominal rigidities.

12. Walsh (2009b) reports counterfactual simulation results for the stabilising effects that PLT would have had on inflation expectations if the United States had had PLT in place at the start of the crisis instead of its actual monetary regime.

REFERENCES

Albagli, E., and K. Schmidt-Hebbel (2004). 'By how much and why do inflation targeters miss their targets?'. Mimeo. Santiago: Banco Central de Chile.

Ball, L., and N. Sheridan (2005). 'Does inflation targeting matter?', in B. Bernanke and M. Woodford (eds.). *The Inflation-Targeting Debate*: 249–82. Chicago: University of Chicago Press.

Batini, N., and D. Laxton (2007). 'Under what conditions can inflation targeting be adopted? The experience of emerging markets', in F. Mishkin and K. Schmidt-Hebbel (eds.). *Monetary Policy under Inflation Targeting*: 1–22. Santiago: Banco Central de Chile.

Bernanke, B. (2002). 'Asset price "bubbles" and monetary policy'. Remarks before the New York Chapter of the National Association for Business Economists. New York, 15 October.

Bernanke, B., and M. Gertler (2001). 'Should central banks respond to movements in asset prices?', *American Economic Review*, 91(2): 253–7.

Bernanke, B., T. Laubach, F. Mishkin and A. Posen (1999). *Inflation Targeting: Lessons from the International Experience*. Princeton, NJ: Princeton University Press.

Bernanke, B., and M. Woodford (eds.) (2005). *The Inflation-Targeting Debate*. Chicago: University of Chicago Press.

Borio, C., and W. White (2003). 'Whither monetary and financial stability? The implications of evolving policy regimes', in Federal Reserve Bank of Kansas City. *Monetary Policy and Uncertainty: Adapting to a Changing Economy*: 131–211. Kansas City: Federal Reserve Bank of Kansas City.

Buiter, W. (2009). 'The unfortunate uselessness of most "state of the art" academic monetary economics', *Financial Times*, 3 March. Available at http://blogs.ft.com/maverecon/2009/03/the-unfortunate-uselessness-of-most-state-of-the-art-academic-monetary-economics.

Calderón, C., and K. Schmidt-Hebbel (2008a). 'What drives the choice of inflation targets in the world?'. Mimeo. Santiago: Banco Central de Chile.

(2008b). 'What drives inflation in the world?'. Working Paper no. 491. Santiago: Banco Central de Chile.

Carare, A., and M. Stone (2003). 'Inflation targeting regimes'. Working Paper no. 03/9. Washington, DC: IMF.

Cecchetti, S., A. Flores-Lagunes and S. Krause (2006). 'Has monetary policy become more efficient? A cross-country analysis', *Economic Journal*, 116: 408–33.

Cecchetti, S., H. Genberg, J. Lipsky and S. Wadhwani (2000). *Asset Prices and Central Bank Policy*. Geneva: CIMB.

Cecchetti, S., H. Genberg and S. Wadhwani (2002). 'Asset prices in a flexible inflation targeting framework'. Working Paper no. 8970. Cambridge, MA: NBER.

Corbo, V., O. Landerretche and K. Schmidt-Hebbel (2001). 'Assessing inflation targeting after a decade of world experience', *International Journal of Economics and Finance*, 6(4): 343–68.

(2002). 'Does inflation targeting make a difference?', in N. Loayza and R. Soto (eds.). *Inflation Targeting: Design, Performance, Challenges*: 221–69. Santiago: Banco Central de Chile.

Cúrdia, V., and M. Woodford (2009). 'Credit Frictions and Optimal Monetary Policy'. Working Paper no. 278. Basel: BIS.

De Fiore, F., and O. Tristani (2009). 'Optimal monetary policy in a model of the credit channel'. Working Paper no. 1043. Frankfurt: ECB.

Demirel, U. (2009). 'Optimal monetary policy in a financially fragile economy', *B. E. Journal of Macroeconomics*, 9: article 15. Available at www.bepress.com/bejm/vol9/iss1/art15.

Dincer, N., and B. Eichengreen (2007). 'Central bank transparency: where, why, and with what effects?'. Working Paper no. 13003. Cambridge, MA: NBER.

Eijffinger, S., and P. Geraats (2006). 'How transparent are central banks?', *European Journal of Political Economy*, 22(1): 1–21.

Geraats, P. (2009). 'Trends in monetary policy transparency'. Working Paper no. 2584. Munich: CESifo.

Gertler, M. (2003). 'Commentary: "Whither monetary and financial stability? The implications of evolving policy regimes"', in Federal Reserve Bank of Kansas City. *Monetary Policy and Uncertainty: Adapting to a Changing Economy*: 213–23. Kansas City: Federal Reserve Bank of Kansas City.

Gürkaynak, R., A. Levin, A. Marder and E. Swanson (2007). 'Inflation targeting and the anchoring of inflation expectations in the Western Hemisphere', in

F. Mishkin and K. Schmidt-Hebbel (eds.). *Monetary Policy under Inflation Targeting*: 415–65. Santiago: Banco Central de Chile.

Hammond, G. (2009). *State of the Art of Inflation Targeting*. Handbook no. 29. London: Centre for Central Banking Studies, Bank of England.

IMF (2005). *World Economic Outlook, September 2005: Building Institutions*. Washington, DC: IMF.

Leyva, G. (2008). 'The choice of inflation targeting'. Working Paper no. 475. Santiago: Banco Central de Chile.

Lucas, R. (2009). 'In defence of the dismal science', *The Economist*, 6 August. Available at www.economist.com/businessfinance/displaystory.cfm?story_id=14165405.

Mishkin, F. (2008). 'Whither Federal Reserve communication?' Presentation delivered at the Bank of Canada conference 'International experience with the conduct of monetary policy under inflation targeting', Quebec, 22 July.

Mishkin, F., and M. Savastano (2000). 'Monetary policy strategies for Latin America'. Working Paper no. 7617. Cambridge, MA: NBER.

Mishkin, F., and K. Schmidt-Hebbel (2007a). 'One decade of inflation targeting in the world: what do we know and what do we need to know?', in F. Mishkin (ed.). *Monetary Policy Strategy*: 405–64. Cambridge, MA: MIT Press.

(eds.) (2007b). *Monetary Policy under Inflation Targeting*. Santiago: Banco Central de Chile.

(2007c). 'Does inflation targeting make a difference?', in F. Mishkin and K. Schmidt-Hebbel (eds.). *Monetary Policy under Inflation Targeting*: 291–372. Santiago: Banco Central de Chile.

Schmidt-Hebbel, K., and C. Walsh (eds.) (2009). *Monetary Policy under Uncertainty and Learning*. Santiago: Banco Central de Chile.

Schmidt-Hebbel, K., and A. Werner (2002). 'Inflation targeting in Brazil, Chile, and Mexico: performance, credibility, and the exchange rate', *Economia*, 2(2): 30–89.

Stiglitz, J. (2008). 'The failure of inflation targeting', Project Syndicate. Available at www.project-syndicate.org/commentary/Stiglitz99/English.

Svensson, L. (1997) 'Inflation forecast targeting: implementing and monitoring inflation targets', *European Economic Review*, 41(6): 1111–46.

(1999). 'Price-level targeting versus inflation targeting: a free lunch?', *Journal of Money, Credit and Banking*, 31(3): 277–95.

Vega, M., and D. Winkelried (2005). 'Inflation targeting and inflation behavior: a successful story?', *International Journal of Central Banking*, 1(3): 153–75.

Vestin, D. (2006). 'Price-level targeting versus inflation targeting', *Journal of Monetary Economics*, 53(7): 1361–76.

Walsh, C. (2009a). 'Inflation targeting: what have we learned?' Mimeo. Santa Cruz: University of California.

(2009b). 'Using monetary policy to stabilize economic activity'. Paper presented at the 2009 Federal Reserve Bank of Kansas City symposium on financial stability and macroeconomic policy. Jackson Hole, WY, 20 August. Available at www.kc.frb.org/publicat/sympos/2009/papers/walsh.09.11.09.pdf.

6   How did we get to inflation targeting and where do we need to go to now? A perspective from the US experience

Daniel L. Thornton

6.1   Introduction

This chapter provides a perspective on the evolution to inflation targeting based on economic theory and the US experience. The Federal Reserve is not formally inflation targeting. Nevertheless, it is commonly believed to be an implicit inflation targeter. While the analysis presented here is based largely on the US experience, I believe that it applies broadly to all central banks.

The economics profession has made considerable progress towards understanding the role of central banks in controlling inflation in the forty-five years since I took my first economics course. Until at least the early 1970s the majority of the economics profession believed that central banks could do little to control inflation. Conventional wisdom had it that monetary policy was relatively ineffective for controlling inflation or for economic stabilisation. Fiscal policy, not monetary policy, was the principal way that governments could stabilise the economy and keep inflation low, by filling the gap between private demand and potential output. I review the evolution of economic thought from 'there is little central banks can do to control inflation' to 'inflation targeting'.

My thesis is that policymakers' belief in the efficacy of monetary policy for inflation control changed dramatically in spite of the fact that there was no fundamental refutation of what I call the monetary policy ineffectiveness proposition (MPIP). The evolution to inflation targeting occurred because central banks, most importantly the Federal Reserve, demonstrated that monetary policy could control inflation. It was not a consequence of fundamental advancements in the profession's understanding of how monetary policy affects the economy. Consequently, the profession and policymakers returned, perhaps reluctantly, to the Phillips curve framework for conducting monetary policy. I argue that this framework endangers the continued effectiveness, and perhaps even the viability, of inflation targeting. I then recommend three steps that inflation-targeting central banks should take to preserve and strengthen inflation targeting.

6.2 The monetary policy ineffectiveness proposition

It is difficult to envisage a central banker who would have recommended inflation targeting in the 1950s and 1960s. As Cagan (1978: 85) points out, 'The quantity of money was not considered important, indeed was hardly worth mentioning, for questions of aggregate demand, unemployment, and even inflation.' This view of monetary policy's effectiveness extended well into the early 1970s. Just as today, the conventional view of inflation was that it was caused by an excess of aggregate demand at or near the 'full employment' level of output. The MPIP was the belief that monetary policy had relatively little effect on aggregate demand; unable to affect aggregate demand, there was little that monetary policy could do to control inflation.

The MPIP has several components.[1] Important among these is the belief that monetary-policy-induced changes in the money supply have little or no *direct* effect on aggregate demand. The theoretical basis for the direct link between the supply of money and prices is the quantity theory of money, or, more simply, the equation of exchange. As today, the quantity theory was widely viewed as a tautology, rather than an economic theory.[2] It was agreed that, if the central bank simply handed everyone money, prices would increase; this was not how central banks increased the money supply, however. Policy-induced changes in the money supply were a consequence of open market operations, discount window lending and changes in reserve requirements. These actions would have an immediate effect on bank reserves and, hence, short-term interest rates. Critics argued that a policy-induced increase in the supply of money would cause interest rates to fall, which would in turn increase the quantity of money demanded. The effect of an increase in the money supply would be largely offset by an endogenous decline in money's velocity. Consequently, there would be little or no effect on aggregate demand and, hence, on prices or output.[3]

The effectiveness of monetary policy is determined by the extent to which monetary policy actions affect interest rates – not the supply of money. The so-called interest rate channel of monetary policy was also thought to be relatively weak. Evidence suggested that consumption and investment spending were relatively interest-inelastic. Consequently, the monetary authority would have to produce a relatively large change in interest rates to have a significant impact on aggregate demand. Investment decisions were determined more by expectations of future earnings than by interest rates. Changes in the interest rate not accompanied by changes in expectations about the economy would be of little consequence for aggregate demand. Some thought that the efficacy of monetary policy might be asymmetric: reducing interest rates during a period of economic slack would be less effective than raising interest rates during a period of economic expansion.[4] Monetary policy, it was said, cannot *push on a string.*

This tenet of the MPIP was reinforced by the fact that monetary policy actions only directly affect very short-term rates. Spending decisions were thought to be determined by the behaviour of long-term rates, however; but central banks' ability to affect long-term rates was problematic.

The last fifty years have done little to change economists' and central bankers' views about the basic tenets of the MPIP. As of 2009 the supply of money is thought to be inconsequential, consumption and investment spending are thought to be interest-inelastic, short-term rates are thought to be relatively unimportant for spending and the monetary authority's ability to influence long-term rates remains questionable.

Acknowledging that there is little agreement 'on exactly how monetary policy exerts its influence' on the real economy, Bernanke and Gertler (1995: 27) note that the conventional model, whereby 'monetary policymakers use their leverage over short-term interest rates to influence the cost of capital and, consequently, spending on durable goods, such as fixed investment, housing, inventories and consumer durables', is incomplete in several important ways. Important among these is the fact that 'empirical studies of supposedly "interest-sensitive" components of aggregate spending have in fact had great difficulty in identifying a quantitatively important effect of the neoclassical cost-of-capital variable'. This evidence motivated Bernanke and Gertler (and others) 'to explore whether imperfect information and other "frictions" in credit markets might help explain the *potency of monetary policy*' (Bernanke and Gertler 1995: 28; emphasis added).[5] One such attempt is called the credit channel of monetary policy, which has two separate channels: the 'balance sheet' channel and the 'bank lending' channel.[6] The balance sheet channel suggests that restrictive monetary policy increases the wedge between the cost of internal finance and that of external finance. Specifically, monetary-policy-engineered increases in short-term interest rates adversely affect the value of potential borrowers' assets, their cash flow and, consequently, their creditworthiness. This increases the external finance premium. For small borrowers, the external finance premium increases by more than the rise in short-term rates. While heterogeneity is important for the effect of changes in interest rates on firms and individuals, the empirical importance of the balance sheet channel for the macroeconomy is unclear (see, for example, Hubbard 1995).[7]

The bank credit channel (see, for example, Bernanke and Blinder 1988, Bernanke 1993 and Gertler and Gilchrist 1993), which asserts that restrictive monetary policy actions have a direct effect on bank lending, is generally recognised (see, for example, Thornton 1994 and Bernanke 2007) to be 'quantitatively important', because banks have access to external funds that are not constrained by the availability of reserves.[8]

Economists continue to believe that long-term rates, not short-term rates, matter for spending decisions (see, for example, Blinder *et al.* 2001, Woodford 2001, Broaddus 2002, Freedman 2002 and Eggerts-son and Woodford 2003). Many economists and policymakers believe that central bank actions have a limited effect on long-term rates, however. For example, in his 20 July 1993 congressional testimony, Chairman Greenspan noted: 'Currently, short-term rates, most directly affected by the Federal Reserve, are not far from zero; longer-term rates, *set primarily by the market*, are appreciably higher' (Greenspan 1993; emphasis added).

Conventional wisdom sees central banks influencing longer-term rates in accordance with the expectations hypothesis (EH) of the term structure of interest rates. The EH asserts that the long-term rate is determined by the market's expectation for the short-term rate over the maturity of the long-term asset plus a constant risk premium. The risk premium compensates investors for the higher degree of market risk associated with holding longer-term assets. The empirical evidence against the EH is overwhelming (see, for example, Campbell and Shiller 1991, Sarno, Thornton and Valente 2007 and Della Corte, Sarno and Thornton 2008, and the references cited therein).[9] Nevertheless, because the ability of central banks to affect long-term rates in accordance with the EH depends on the predictability of the short-term rate and the duration for which the market believes the rate will stay at that level, a number of central banks have attempted to provide 'forward guidance' about their policy rate.

As was the case with inflation targeting, the Reserve Bank of New Zealand took the lead. It began announcing a path for its policy rate in 1997. Norway followed in 2005, Sweden in 2007. It is thought that announcing the path for its policy rate permits the central bank to 'steer' expectations. Irma Rosenberg, the first deputy governor of the Riksbank, Sweden's central bank, suggested in 2007 that, 'by affecting expectations of short-term interest rates, we as the central bank can also indirectly affect interest rates with a slightly longer duration, which in turn increases the effect of monetary policy' (Rosenberg 2007; see also Gjedrem 2006).

Rudebusch (2007), Goodhart and Lim (2008) and Andersson and Hofmann (Chapter 15 of this volume), however, show that forward guidance has not increased the predictability of the path of the policy rate beyond a few months.

The Federal Reserve was a latecomer here. In response to a presentation by Rudebusch on monetary policy inertia (see, for example, Woodford 1999) at the January 2003 Federal Open Market Committee (FOMC) meeting, the then governor of the Federal Reserve System, Ben Bernanke, asked Rudebusch 'if there had been evidence on whether or not the responsiveness of long-term interest rates to movements in the fed funds rate was consistent with the predictability of the type' proposed by Woodford (FOMC transcript, 28–9 January 2003: 31). Rudebusch responded that he did not 'think we have the empirical evidence of monetary policy inertia' (for a description of his argument and evidence, see Rudebusch 2007). Bernanke suggested that this meant only that it had not been tried: 'There should be more [inertia in the policy rule] in order to get more effect on long-term rates. I think that's an open question' (FOMC transcript, 28–9 January 2003: 32).

The Fed's first attempt at providing forward guidance came in August 2003. At the June 2003 FOMC meeting, Bernanke responded to several committee members who voiced reservations about the Fed's ability to influence longer-term interest rates by saying (FOMC transcript, 24–5 June 2003: 45–6):

If the policy is one in which we essentially try to lower the whole path of long-term interest rates and we enforce that with a package of complementary actions that includes trying to manage expectations along the term structure and taking a series of other actions such as purchasing long-term bonds and other kinds of instruments, I think that's one of the first things we ought to be doing. I believe that would actually work and would in fact be a good approach.

Consistent with Bernanke's suggestion, the August 2003 FOMC policy statement included the sentence 'In these circumstances, the Committee believes that policy accommodation can be maintained for a considerable period'.[10] At the September meeting, Alan Greenspan said he thought it a 'mistake' to include the sentence (FOMC transcript, 16 September 2003: 80).

Despite the concern among some members about the usefulness of forward guidance language, the FOMC's May 2004 statement read 'The Committee believes that policy accommodation can be removed at a pace that is likely to be measured', suggesting the FOMC might start increasing its target for the federal funds rate at the next meeting (Board of Governors' press release, 6 May 2004).[11] The FOMC began increasing

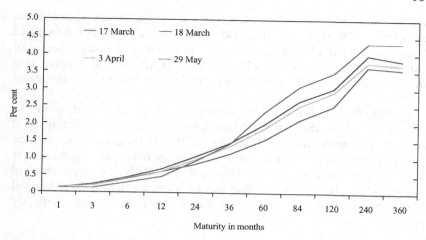

Figure 6.1 The yield curve announcement effect, 2009.

the funds rate from the then historically low level of 1.0 per cent at its June 2004 meeting and by 25 basis points at each of its next sixteen meetings. Forward guidance was dropped at the December 2005 meeting.

Forward guidance had relatively little effect on long-term rates. Not only did yields on longer-term securities generally increase from August 2003 to June 2004, but the yields across the term structure increased despite the historically low and unchanged target for the funds rate, and the FOMC's commitment to keep the funds rate low. Moreover, longer-term rates declined during the first few months following the initial target increases in 2004. Indeed, Greenspan (2005) termed the fact that longer-term rates edged lower despite the 150 b.p. increase in the funds rate target a 'conundrum'.[12]

The Fed's next attempt with forward guidance occurred at the 17–18 March 2009 meeting, when it implemented the Eggertsson and Woodford (2003) strategy, which Bernanke had outlined at the June 2003 FOMC meeting.[13] Specifically, the FOMC announced that 'economic conditions are likely to warrant exceptionally low levels of the federal funds rate for an extended period' and that the Fed would purchase 'up to $300 billion of Treasury securities over the next six months' (Board of Governors' press release, 18 March 2009).

This attempt was also unsuccessful. While there was an immediate 'announcement effect' as yields on ten-year Treasuries and most other long-term securities declined by about 50 b.p. on 18 March, the marked flattening of the yield curve, shown in Figure 6.1, was short-lived.

Figure 6.1 shows that the announcement effect had essentially vanished by 6 April 2009. By 27 July the yield was considerably steeper than it had been on 17 March. This experience is consistent with a high degree of substitutability across assets with differing maturities, and suggests that the Fed's ability to influence the behaviour of long-term rates is limited at best.

Finally, there is little to indicate that the economics profession has changed its view about the effectiveness of changes in monetary and reserve aggregates. Indeed, Svensson (2007: 4) suggests that, over the past fifty years, economists have learned that 'monetary aggregates matter little, or even not at all, for monetary policy'. The lack of importance of money is reflected in the fact that money is not explicit in the canonical New Keynesian model, which is commonly used to evaluate monetary policy.[14]

6.3   The evolution to inflation targeting

Scepticism about the ability of central banks to control inflation vanished despite essentially unchanged views about how monetary policy affects the economy. Consequently, it is natural to ask 'What then caused the dramatic shift towards inflation targeting?'. It is seldom, if ever, true that such an event is attributable to a single factor. Indeed, I believe a number of factors, in some way or another, contributed to the shift. Nevertheless, three factors or events were critical. The first, and most important, was the demonstration that central banks can control inflation. The cornerstone event was Paul Volcker's decision to reduce inflation by focusing on monetary aggregates. Inflation was in double digits when Volcker became chairman of the Federal Reserve in 1979 and about 4 per cent when he departed in 1987. This remarkable experience demonstrated beyond reasonable doubt that central banks could control inflation.[15]

The West Germans and Swiss also affected perceptions of inflation control. Both central banks were committed to keeping inflation low (Rich and Béguelin 1985; Kohli and Rich 1986; von Hagen 1999), and both emphasised monetary aggregates in the conduct of monetary policy. Moreover, both countries fared much better than most of their European counterparts. This is illustrated in Figure 6.2, which compares the year-on-year CPI inflation rates for West Germany and Switzerland to the envelope (the shaded area) of the lowest and highest monthly inflation rates of twelve European countries in the period 1970 to 1985.[16] West German inflation was low relative to the other countries over the entire period. Swiss inflation was in the middle of the range until the mid-1970s,

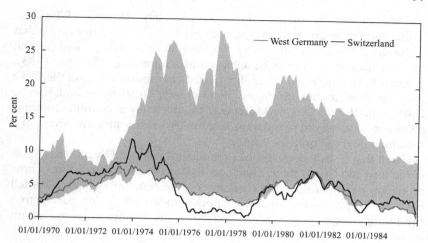

Figure 6.2 European inflation rates, 1970–85

but at or well below the envelope from the mid-1970s onwards. Had the United States continued on its high-inflation path, it is possible that these experiences would have led to inflation targeting. At a bare minimum, the US experience accelerated the evolution to inflation targeting.

My second event is likely to be controversial. Nevertheless, I believe it to be extremely important, at least in the United States. Beginning around 1970 the United States went from having cyclically balanced budgets, except during wars, to having what wars, by the standards of the time, large and persistent deficits. The practice of running large, persistent deficits played an important role in the shift to inflation targeting, because it took counter-cyclical fiscal policy out of the policy mix. With fiscal policy sidelined, the reduction in inflation and, perhaps more importantly, the subsequent Great Moderation could be attributed only to monetary policy. Had the government continued to conduct activist counter-cyclical fiscal policy, the relative importance of monetary and fiscal policy for inflation control and economic stabilisation would have been less clear. Even those who continued to embrace the tenets of the MPIP conceded that monetary policy was effective, even if they were not exactly sure how it worked (such as Bernanke and Gertler, 1995: 28, talking about the desire to 'explain the potency of monetary policy').[17]

A third factor that deserves credit for the shift to inflation targeting is the insightful 'impossibility theorem' known as the Lucas critique. Lucas's (1976) work was motivated by the 'mysterious transformation' of an 'obvious fallacy [a permanent Phillips curve trade-off] to the cornerstone of the theory of economic policy' (Lucas, 1976: 19). Economists were quick to understand that Lucas's insight meant (i) that any effort to reduce inflation permanently had to be credible and (ii) that credible disinflation might be achieved at a lower cost (Sargent 1983). There is little doubt that credibility played an important role in the Fed's decision to announce its intentions (Lindsey, Orphanides and Rasche 2005; Goodfriend 2007). Moreover, the need for a credible commitment is a cornerstone of inflation targeting – i.e. the announcement of a specific numerical inflation target.

Given that (i) inflation has been significantly reduced by monetary policy actions and (ii) no change had occurred in their understanding of how monetary policy worked, the economics profession and policymakers fell back on the pre-monetary-policy-appears-to-work inflation paradigm – the Phillips curve. The modern version of the Phillips curve paradigm takes the general form

$$\pi_{t+1} = E_t \pi_{t+1} - \beta y_t \qquad (6.1)$$

where $E_t \pi_{t+1}$ denotes the expected rate of inflation, y_t denotes some measure of economic slack (e.g. the gap between potential and actual output, or the gap between the actual unemployment rate and the non-accelerating inflation rate of unemployment (NAIRU) and the coefficient β is strictly positive (note that equation (6.1) implies that the long-run Phillips curve is vertical). Inflation-targeting central banks anchor inflation by announcing a numerical inflation target to establish $E_t \pi_{t+1}$. Of course, the inflation target must be credible. This requires the central bank to take actions to keep inflation close enough to the target. Because the only thing that determines inflation, given inflation expectations, is the degree of slack in the economy, policymakers have to adjust their policy instrument to changes in the measure of slack even if they have no specific objective for stabilising the real economy – even if they are what the then deputy governor of the Bank of England, Mervyn King (1997), referred to as 'inflation nutters'.

The profession and policymakers have adopted this framework despite still believing that changes in short-term rates should have a relatively small impact on aggregate demand. Moreover, they adhere to the Phillips curve framework despite the facts that (i) the Phillips curve framework provides relatively poor forecasts of future inflation and (ii) the marginal contribution of the slack measures to in-sample or out-of-sample inflation forecasts is small (see, for example, Atkeson and Ohanian 2001, the FOMC transcript for 25–6 June 2002, Fisher, Liu and Zhou 2002 and Stock and Watson 2008).

6.4   Implications for inflation targeting

I believe that the return to the Phillips curve framework may be a problem for the continued success, and even the viability, of inflation targeting.[18] There are three main threats. The first is the increasing belief in the need for central banks to have a 'dual mandate'. Meyer (2004) makes a distinction between a dual mandate – in which 'monetary policy is directed at promoting both full employment and price stability, *with no priority expressed*' – and a hierarchical mandate – in which 'price stability is identified as the principal objective, and central banks are restricted in pursuing other objectives unless price stability has been achieved' (Meyer 2004: 151; emphasis added). It is important to note that (i) monetary policy affects only aggregate demand and (ii) the appropriate monetary policy response to aggregate demand shocks is invariant to inflation or output stabilisation; when there are shocks to aggregate demand, inflation stabilisation and output stabilisation are complements, not substitutes (Svensson 2007: 3). For example, Bernanke (2004) notes that 'the ultimate source of this long-run trade-off [between the variance of prices and the variance of output] is the existence of shocks to aggregate supply'. As a result, having a dual mandate means that policymakers should *promote both full employment and price stability* when confronted with shocks to aggregate supply. Is this possible? Bernanke (2004) describes the problem:

According to conventional analysis, an increase in the price of oil raises the overall price level (a temporary burst in inflation) while depressing output and employment. Monetary policymakers are therefore faced with a difficult choice. If they choose to tighten policy (raise the short-term interest rate) in order to offset the effects of the oil price shock on the general price level, they may well succeed – but only at the cost of making the decline in output more severe. Likewise, if monetary policymakers choose to ease in order to mitigate the effects of the oil price shock on output, their action will exacerbate the inflationary impact. Hence, in the standard framework, the periodic occurrence of shocks to aggregate supply (such as oil price shocks) forces policymakers to choose between stabilising output and stabilising inflation.

Bernanke appears to suggest that the answer is 'No'. What should policymakers do? If the shock is temporary (a temporary oil price shock), it might be best to do nothing. If the shock is permanent, nothing might still be the best option, since there is no way for monetary policy to affect aggregate supply, and the effect on inflation will be temporary, as the price level adjusts to a permanent new higher or lower level. This policy choice is reinforced by monetary policy neutrality. In any event, just how and under what circumstances policymakers should respond to aggregate supply shocks is unclear.

Moreover, in a thoughtful analysis of the causes of the Great Moderation, Bernanke (2004) describes four ways that improved price stability has reduced the volatility of output (see also Taylor 2008). If long-run price stability generates greater economic stability for the reasons Bernanke suggests, and perhaps others, it is difficult to understand why policymakers would sacrifice price stability in order to offset temporarily the effect of a permanent adverse supply shock on output and employment.[19]

While most inflation-targeting central banks do not appear to give equal weight to economic stability and price stability, many (perhaps all) follow a hierarchical mandate – the second threat to inflation targeting. Meyer (2004: 151) indicates that 'inflation-targeting countries today have moved away from the initially austere implementation, more in line with the spirit of a hierarchical mandate, and have become flexible inflation targeters, close cousins of dual mandate central banks'. Consistent with Meyer's statement, the former deputy governor of the Reserve Bank of New Zealand, Murray Sherwin, has noted that the RBNZ has moved along the 'spectrum between what Svensson refers to as "strict" and "flexible" inflation targeting' (Sherwin 1999). The danger of a hierarchical mandate for inflation targeting comes from three sources. First, while both economic theory and experience suggest that central banks can achieve price stability, there are important reasons to be sceptical of central bankers' ability to stabilise output around potential. This scepticism is embedded in the MPIP and supported by empirical evidence. For example, Rasche and Williams' (2007) review of the empirical literature of the effectiveness of monetary stabilisation policy 'failed to determine a major role for monetary policy in short-run stabilisation' (2007: 469, 474).

Indeed, much of the evidence that monetary policy actions affect the real economy comes from a handful of episodes in which an economic recession appears to be 'caused' by a monetary contraction (see Rasche and Williams 2007 for a discussion of these 'case studies'). Such episodes provide no basis for believing that monetary policy can successfully stabilise the economy. Moreover, because they are one-sided, these episodes are not a basis for concluding that expansionary monetary policy can significantly increase output.

Successful economic stabilisation policy requires a good, or at least reliable, measure of potential output. It is widely accepted, however, that potential output is difficult if not impossible to measure (see Orphanides 2003, and the references cited therein, and the July/August 2009 issue of the *Federal Reserve Bank of St. Louis Review* (volume 91, issue 4), entitled 'Projecting potential growth: issues and measurements'). A failure to have good and reliable measures of the output gap or NAIRU can result in destabilising policy errors. Indeed, Orphanides (2004) argues that overemphasis on the output gap and its mismeasurement contributed significantly to the Great Inflation.

At a more fundamental level, economic theory suggests that the conventional 'steady-state' definition of potential output, which is commonly used by policymakers to construct the output gap and the NAIRU, is ill-suited for economic stabilisation policy. The policy-relevant definition is 'the rate of output the economy would have if there were no nominal rigidities, but all other (real) frictions and shocks were unchanged' (Basu and Fernald 2009: 3).[20] This policy-relevant definition accounts for the effect of supply shocks on potential output.[21] Consequently, even if the conventional definition of the output gap could be measured precisely, monetary policy actions based on it run a significant risk of being destabilising.

Successful stabilisation policy also depends on the ability of policymakers to forecast what would happen if they did nothing. Economic forecasting has always been difficult, and forecasting economic turning points, which is critical to successful economic stabilisation policy, is particularly difficult. This is evidenced by the significant lag in dating both the beginning and end of recessions.[22] There is considerable evidence that both survey and econometric forecasts have considerable difficulty improving upon naïve forecasts. This has been particularly true since the mid-1980s (Atkeson and Ohanian 2001; Tulip 2005; d'Agostino, Giannone and Surico 2006; Campbell 2007; Stock and Watson 2007, 2008; d'Agostino and Whelan 2008).[23]

The inability to make accurate forecasts beyond very short horizons means that it will be very difficult, if not impossible, for policymakers to anticipate the longer-run consequences of their actions. For example, the FOMC reduced its funds rate target to the then historically low level of 1.0 per cent at the June 2003 meeting and kept the target at 1.0 per cent until the June 2004 meeting. The staff had revised up its forecast for the output gap for 2003 and 2004 at the previous meeting, noting that '[a]ny serious delay in the recovery . . . would imply a larger output gap . . . and by our analysis would result in an even lower inflation rate; (FOMC transcript, 6 May 2003: 13). The presumption was that the FOMC would reduce the funds rate target at the June meeting unless there was new evidence. Governor Ferguson summarised the evidence, noting that 'the output gap still closes relatively slowly, . . . the unemployment rate hangs up above the NAIRU through next year [and] . . . core PCE [personal consumption expenditure] even before the adjustment stays at what I would consider to be the very low end of an acceptable range' (FOMC transcript, 24–5 June 2003: 130). The funds rate target was reduced to the then historically low level of 1.0 per cent, while several members had a desire or a willingness to accept a larger cut. Only President Moskow voiced concern about the action, saying: 'Of course the data we talk about are always looking backward, and the key is the forecast going forward. As we've often said in these meetings, sometimes the last cut or the last increase in the funds rate target is the one that's not needed because we didn't have perfect information at the time we made that cut or increase' (FOMC transcript, 24–5 June 2003: 153).

By the December 2003 meeting the data suggested that the economy had grown by 3.3 per cent in the second quarter and at an extremely rapid rate of 8.2 per cent in the third quarter. Greenspan summarised the situation (FOMC transcript, 9 December 2003: 88–9) by noting that

it has almost invariably been the case that the Federal Reserve would tighten under such conditions. Indeed, preemption is something that has filtered its way into the monetary policy lexicon. The issue of preemption implies, of course, that we will adjust our policy ahead of anything that we can readily foresee. In current circumstances, therefore, there is and there will continue to be a lot of pressure on us to move rates higher. We have resisted because of a quite considerable and significant difference in the present economy from what we have observed in the past. In recent decades, the turning point toward accelerating economic activity usually occurred when the inflation rate was 3 percent or 4 percent, sometimes even higher, and the necessity for preemption was critically obvious. The problem with preemption, though it is something that is very interesting to observe in retrospect, is that it doesn't necessarily follow that we are preempting future developments that will actually occur the way we expect. So, we have to be careful not to try to preempt something that is not fairly likely to happen. There is a risk and indeed a cost to being wrong.

No one expressed concern about the longer-run consequences of what was recognised as an excessively easy policy.[24] Even though inflation had increased substantially and by December the FOMC had acknowledged that 'the probability of an unwelcome fall in inflation has diminished in recent months and now appears almost equal to that of a rise in inflation' (Board of Governors' press release 9 December 2003), the FOMC did not increase the target until June 2004.

The FOMC was effectively pursuing a hierarchical mandate. With inflation in check, presumably because of well-anchored inflation expectations, the FOMC was free to pursue its objective of 'maximum sustainable economic growth'. Taylor and others have suggested that 'this extra-easy policy was responsible for accelerating the housing boom and thereby ultimately leading to the housing bust' (Taylor 2009b: 343–4).

While there will undoubtedly be much analysis and debate over the
Fed's role, the decline in housing prices and the resulting financial market
turmoil generated an unprecedented monetary policy response. Initially,
the Fed attempted to ease credit conditions by simply reallocating credit
(see, for example, Thornton 2009).[25] When the Fed was no longer able
to sterilise the effects of its credit allocation programme on the monetary
base, the base increased rapidly to an unprecedented level. The massive
quantitative easing has generated concerns of future inflation (see, for
example, Taylor 2009a). As Al Broaddus noted at the June 2003 FOMC
meeting, 'Common sense tells us . . . that a determined expansion of the
monetary base has to be effective against deflation at the zero bound. If
that were not the case, we could eliminate all taxes, and the government
could permanently finance its operations with money creation alone'
(FOMC transcript, 24–5 June 2003: 35).[26] What the ultimate verdict will
be is uncertain. That the Fed's behaviour was motivated by a hierarchical
mandate is not.[27]

Policymakers appear to have replaced their belief in a permanent
Phillips curve trade-off with the belief that 'a little inflation is good for
economic growth' – which is the third threat to inflation targeting. Most
policymakers believe that the long-run Phillips curve is vertical, which
implies that the same long-run real outcome can be achieved with zero
inflation as it can with 2 or 3 per cent inflation. Nonetheless, most policymakers also profess that the 'optimal', 'appropriately measured', inflation
rate is positive. The theoretical justification for the various hypotheses
that motivate the belief that a little inflation is good for economic growth
are highly questionable or simply unsound (Marty and Thornton 1995).
Nevertheless, many policymakers believe that 'inflation can be too low
as well as too high' (Meyer 2004: 160).[28]

The belief that positive inflation is somehow optimal is reflected in the
fact that all inflation-targeting central banks have a non-zero inflation
target. It is also consistent with the fact that nearly all inflation-targeting
central banks have a recent inflation performance that is in the upper end
of their target ranges. It could be that central bankers might simply believe
that the inflation measures they target overestimate the true unobservable
inflation rate. It seems unlikely, however, that the bias is large enough to
explain the observed behaviour.

6.6   Implications for inflation-targeting central banks

The analyses in the previous sections have implications for the evolution
of inflation targeting. First and foremost, inflation-targeting central banks
should be dissuaded from having a dual mandate. If they decide to have

a dual mandate, they should inform the public of this policy and the rationale for adopting it.

Second, inflation-targeting central banks should carefully and honestly evaluate the extent to which they can effectively stabilise the real economy around potential output. This analysis should provide a realistic assessment of their ability to measure potential output, the extent to which they believe inflation is related to the output gap, and the other impediments to successful economic stabilisation discussed above, as well as some others not discussed here (such as lags in the effect of policy actions on the economy). The end product of this analysis should be a statement indicating the extent to which the inflation-targeting central bank believes that it can pursue a hierarchical mandate.

Third, inflation-targeting central banks should engage in a serious dialogue with their constituents about the optimal rate of inflation. In particular, if they believe that the appropriately measured, long-run inflation rate is positive, they should state the reasons for this belief.

NOTES

1. There was also a belief that inflation was caused by 'cost-push' factors, not amenable to monetary policy actions (see, for example, Nelson 2005). For example, Arthur Burns attributed inflation to a variety of 'special factors'. As these special factors dissipated, but inflation did not, Burns blamed inflation on government deficits (Hetzel 1998). Hence, cost-push inflation was not an essential element of the MPIP.
2. Cagan (1978: 86) notes that 'textbooks in basic economics and even in money and banking mentioned the quantity theory of money, if at all, only to hold it up to ridicule'.
3. Monetarists made two attempts at incorporating money into the canonical model. One was to suggest that money affects aggregate demand through a 'wealth effect'. The other was the buffer stock model of money demand. The profession was not impressed.
4. Another reason is that, if the central bank reduces the money supply, individuals are forced to alter their behaviour. On the other hand, if the central bank increases the supply of money, individuals can simply hold the money in idle balances.
5. In essence, Bernanke and Gertler are saying that we know monetary policy is efficacious, we just don't know why. The credit channel of monetary policy, as it is called, is an attempt to provide a theoretical basis for the belief in the efficacy of monetary policy. See also Bernanke (2007).
6. Scepticism over the interest rate channel also arose out of the Great Inflation and Sargent and Wallace's (1975) demonstration that interest rate targeting can lead to price level indeterminacy. McCallum (1981) changed that by demonstrating that indeterminacy can be eliminated if policymakers have a 'nominal anchor' – i.e. if policymakers care about inflation.

7. The lack of empirical support for the interest rate channel of money policy led some analysts (such as Mishkin 1995, Meltzer 1995 and Taylor 1995) to broaden the financial asset price channel of monetary policy to include exchange rates, equity prices and even land prices. There has been relatively little interest in or empirical support for these alternative asset price channels of monetary policy, however.

8. Bernanke (2007) also suggests that restrictive monetary policy may affect banks by increasing the external finance premium paid by banks in much the same way that the balance sheet channel is thought to affect individuals and firms. He does not say why restrictive monetary policy will increase banks' external finance premium, however. The spread between the equivalent-term London Interbank Offered Rate (LIBOR) (the rate at which banks lend to each other) and the certificate of deposit (CD) rate (the rate at which banks borrow externally) has been small historically.

9. One reason for the empirical failure of the expectations hypothesis is that conventional tests of the EH are based on the assumption that the expected future short-term rate deviates from the actual future short-term interest rate by a white noise error. Interest rates are notoriously difficult to predict, however. The empirical failure of the EH is probably a consequence of the incompatibility of the assumption upon which tests of the EH are based and the unpredictability of interest rates (see, for example, Guidolin and Thornton 2008).

10. This sentence was not voted on by the committee. Rather, at the conclusion of a lengthy discussion of the sentence, Greenspan took a vote of all FOMC participants. The vote was eleven to seven in favour of the sentence. Greenspan concluded, 'On the basis of that vote it's right on the margin. But I would say that we have to put in the truncated version of the final sentence' (FOMC transcript, 12 August 2003: 95).

11. The committee considered several courses of action, including dropping the sentence. However, the sentence appeared unchanged in both the September and October FOMC statements. On a suggestion from Greenspan, the sentence was modified at the December 2003 meeting. Most thought that Greenspan's rewording made the statement more 'conditional'. Four participants expressed a preference for removing the statement, however.

12. Elsewhere (Thornton 2007), I show that there was a marked break in the relationship between the overnight funds rate and the ten-year Treasury yield that pre-dates the conundrum period. Moreover, it coincides with the FOMC switch from using the funds rate as an operational target to using it as a policy target. I hypothesise that the change in behaviour reflects the fact that the FOMC, and not the market, began determining the path for the funds rate in the late 1980s. I also present evidence to support this hypothesis.

13. Eggertsson and Woodford (2003: 200) note that the 'effect [on long-term yields] follows not from the purchases themselves, but from how they are interpreted', but that purchases may help overcome 'private sector skepticism about whether the history-dependent interest rate policy will actually be followed'.

14. McCallum (2001: 146) argues that money is implicit because 'the central bank's control over the one-period nominal interest rate ultimately stems from its ability to control the quantity of base money in existence'. He suggests, however, that the 'error thereby introduced [by omitting money] is extremely small' (2001: 150). This conclusion is not surprising, because money has no effect on economic activity, except through its effect on the interest rate. Hence, there is little difference in money being implicit or explicit in such models (see, for example, Leahy 2001).

15. Others share my view, such as Goodfriend (2007: 8).

16. The countries are Austria, Belgium, Denmark, Finland, France, Italy, Luxembourg, the Netherlands, Norway, Spain, Sweden and the United Kingdom.

17. A contributing factor was the experience of the Great Depression, which made economists and policymakers sceptical of the self-equilibrating nature of market economies. With fiscal policy sidelined and little or no faith in the self-correcting nature of market economies, the experience of the Great Moderation led many economists to conclude that monetary policy was much more effective than previously thought. The monetary and fiscal response to the most recent financial market turmoil suggests that policymakers remain sceptical of the self-equilibrating nature of market economies and the ability of existing institutions to deal with the current 'crisis' (see, for example, Miron 2009).

18. For evidence on the success of inflation targeting, see Rasche and Williams (2007) and Chapters 4 and 5 of this volume.

19. This point is directly related to the theoretically correct measure of the output gap, which is discussed later.

20. For estimates of the theoretically correct output gap, see Nelson and Neiss (2005).

21. The idea that aggregate supply shocks reduce potential output relative to its steady-state level is not new. For example, see Rasche and Tatom (1977) and the references therein.

22. For example, the NBER dating committee announced on 2 December 2008 that the recession began in December 2007.

23. Reifschneider and Tulip (2007) analyse the forecasting accuracy of the FOMC, the Greenbook (produced before each meeting of the FOMC), the Congressional Budget Office, the administration, the Blue Chip consensus forecast and the Survey of Professional Forecasters' short-run forecasts of GDP growth, the unemployment rate and CPI inflation over the period 1986 to 2006. Their estimates suggest that, with the exception of the unemployment rate, the forecasts provide little information beyond that contained in the historical average.

24. Greenspan noted that 'the current federal funds rate is well below any estimate of the equilibrium rate. That is, when we start to raise the rate, we may have the problem of having to return to the equilibrium rate relatively quickly' (FOMC transcript, 9 December 2003: 91).

25. Taylor (2009a) calls this 'industrial policy'.

26. Arthur Burns, Fed chairman from 1970 to 1978, had a similar belief. At the 18–19 March 1974 FOMC meeting, Burns noted that, while he was 'not a monetarist, he found a basic and inescapable truth in the monetarist position that inflation could not have persisted over a long period of time without a highly accommodative monetary policy' (FOMC memorandum of discussion, 18–19 March 1974: 110–12).

27. This danger associated with a hierarchical mandate is exacerbated by political pressures. In his Per Jacobsson Lecture, which was delivered just six days prior to Volcker's dramatic change in the FOMC's monetary policy, Burns (1979: 15) noted prophetically that 'the Federal Reserve System had the power to abort the inflation at its incipient stage fifteen years ago or at any later point, and it has the power to end it today. At any time within that period, it could have restricted the money supply and created sufficient strains in the financial and industrial markets to terminate inflation with little delay' but political pressures limited the 'practical scope for restrictive actions'.

28. In addition, at the June 2003 FOMC meeting Governor Bernanke, as he was then, stated: 'I think the May 6 statement left the mistaken impression with some that the Fed was concerned about the threat of imminent deflation as opposed to what really concerned us – namely, the possibility of a decline in inflation to a level that, *while below the desirable range*, would still be greater than zero' (FOMC transcript, 24–5 June 2003: 131; emphasis added).

REFERENCES

Atkeson, A., and L. Ohanian (2001). 'Are Phillips curves useful for forecasting inflation?', *Federal Reserve Bank of Minneapolis Quarterly Review*, 25(1): 2–11.

Basu, S., and J. Fernald. (2009). 'What do we know (and not know) about potential output?', *Federal Reserve Bank of St. Louis Review*, 91(4): 187–214.

Bernanke, B. (1993). 'Credit in the macroeconomy', *Federal Reserve Bank of New York Quarterly Review*, 18(1): 50–70.

(2004). 'The Great Moderation'. Speech at the meeting of the Eastern Economic Association. Washington, DC, 20 February.

(2007). 'The financial accelerator and the credit channel'. Speech at the conference 'Credit channel of monetary policy in the twenty-first century', Atlanta, 15 June.

Bernanke, B., and A. Blinder (1988). 'Credit, money, and aggregate demand', *American Economic Review*, 78(2): 435–9.

Bernanke, B., and M. Gertler (1995). 'Inside the Black Box: the credit channel of monetary policy transmission', *Journal of Economic Perspectives*, 9(4): 27–48.

Blinder, A., C. Goodhart, P. Hildebrand, D. Lipton and C. Wyplosz (2001). *How Do Central Banks Talk?* Geneva: CIMB.

Broaddus, J. (2002). 'Transparency in the practice of monetary policy', *Federal Reserve Bank of St. Louis Review*, 84(4): 161–6.

Burns, A. (1979). 'The anguish of central banking'. Per Jacobsson Lecture. Belgrade, 30 September.

Cagan, P. (1978). 'Monetarism in historical perspective', in T. Mayer (ed.). *The Structure of Monetarism*: 85–93. New York: W. W. Norton.

Campbell, J., and R. Shiller (1991). 'Yield spreads and interest rate movements; a bird's eye view', *Review of Economic Studies*, 58(3): 495–514.

Campbell, S. (2007). 'Macroeconomic volatility, predictability, and uncertainty in the Great Moderation: evidence from the Survey of Professional Forecasters', *Journal of Business and Economic Statistics*, 25(2): 191–200.

D'Agostino, A., D. Giannone and P. Surico (2006). '(Un)Predictability and macroeconomic stability'. Working Paper no. 605. Frankfurt: ECB.

D'Agostino, A., and K. Whelan (2008). 'Federal Reserve information during the Great Moderation', *Journal of the European Economic Association*, 6(2–3): 609–20.

Della Corte, P., L. Sarno and D. Thornton (2008). 'The expectation hypothesis of the term structure of very short-term rates: statistical tests and economic value', *Journal of Financial Economics*, 89(1): 158–74.

Eggertsson, G., and M. Woodford (2003). 'The zero bound on interest rates and optimal monetary policy', *Brookings Papers on Economic Activity*, 1: 139–211.

Fisher, J., C. Liu and R. Zhou (2002). 'When can we forecast inflation?', *Federal Reserve Bank of Chicago Economic Perspectives*, Q1: 32–44.

Freedman, C. (2002). 'The value of transparency in conducting monetary policy', *Federal Reserve Bank of St. Louis Review*, 84(4): 155–60.

Gertler, M., and S. Gilchrist (1993). 'The role of credit market imperfections in the monetary transmission mechanism: arguments and evidence', *Scandinavian Journal of Economics*, 95(1): 43–64.

Gjedrem, S. (2006). 'Monetary policy in Norway'. Speech given at Norges Bank's conference 'Evaluating monetary policy'. Oslo, 30 March.

Goodfriend, M. (2007). 'How the world achieved consensus on monetary policy'. Working Paper no. 13580. Cambridge, MA: NBER.

Goodhart, C., and W. Lim (2008). 'Interest rate forecasts: a pathology' Discussion Paper no. 612. London: Financial Markets Group, London School of Economics [LSE].

Greenspan, A. (1993). 'Testimony of Alan Greenspan, chairman, Federal Reserve Board', in Federal Reserve. *Monetary Policy Objectives: Midyear Review of the Federal Reserve Board*: 3–13. Washington, DC: Federal Reserve.

(2005). 'Testimony of Chairman Alan Greenspan before the Committee on Banking, Housing, and Urban Affairs, US Senate'. Washington, DC, 16 February.

Guidolin, M., and D. Thornton (2008). 'Predictions of short-term rates and the expectations hypothesis of the term structure of interest rates'. Working Paper no. 977. Frankfurt: ECB.

Hetzel, R. (1998). 'Arthur Burns and inflation', *Federal Reserve Bank of Richmond Economic Quarterly*, 84(1): 21–44.

Hubbard, R. (1995). 'Is there a "credit channel" for monetary policy?', *Federal Reserve Bank of St. Louis Review*, 77(3): 63–77.

King, M. (1997). 'Changes in UK monetary policy: rules and discretion in practice', *Journal of Monetary Economics*, 39(1): 81–97.

Kohli, U., and G. Rich (1986). 'Monetary control: the Swiss experience', *Cato Journal*, 5(3): 911–26.

Leahy, J. (2001). 'Commentary', *Federal Reserve Bank of St. Louis Review*, 83(4): 161–3.

Lindsey, D., A. Orphanides and R. Rasche (2005).'The reform of October 1979: how it happened and why', *Federal Reserve Bank of St. Louis Review*, 87(2): 187–236.

Lucas, R. (1976). 'Econometric policy evaluation: a critique', *Carnegie-Rochester Conference Series on Public Policy*, 1(1): 19–46.

Marty, A., and D. Thornton (1995). 'Is there a case for "moderate" inflation?', *Federal Reserve Bank of St. Louis Review*, 76(1): 31–49.

McCallum, B. (1981). 'Price level determinacy with an interest rate policy rule and rational expectations', *Journal of Monetary Economics*, 8(3): 319–29.

 (2001). 'Monetary policy analysis in models without money', *Federal Reserve Bank of St. Louis Review*, 83(4): 145–60.

Meltzer, A. (1995). 'Monetary, credit and (other) transmission processes: a monetarist perspective', *Journal of Economic Perspectives*, 9(4): 49–72.

Meyer, L. (2004). 'Practical problems and obstacles to inflation targeting', *Federal Reserve Bank of St. Louis Review*, 86(4): 151–60.

Miron, J. (2009). 'In defense of doing nothing'. *Cato's Letter*, spring 2009. Washington, DC: Cato Institute.

Mishkin, F. (1995). 'Symposium on the monetary transmission mechanism', *Journal of Economic Perspectives*, 9(4): 3–10.

Nelson, E. (2005). 'The Great Inflation of the seventies: what really happened?', *Advances in Macroeconomics*, 5(2): 1–48.

Nelson, E., and K. Neiss (2005). 'Inflation dynamics, marginal cost, and the output gap: evidence from three countries', *Journal of Money, Credit and Banking*, 37(6): 1019–45.

Orphanides, A. (2003). 'The quest for prosperity without inflation', *Journal of Monetary Economics*, 50(3): 633–63.

 (2004). 'Monetary policy rules, macroeconomic stability and inflation: a view from the trenches', *Journal of Money, Credit and Banking*, 36(2): 151–75.

Rasche, R., and J. Tatom (1977). 'The effects of the new energy regime on economic capacity, production, and prices', *Federal Reserve Bank of St. Louis Review*, 59(5): 2–12.

Rasche, R., and M. Williams (2007). 'The effectiveness of monetary policy', *Federal Reserve Bank of St. Louis Review*, 89(5): 447–89.

Reifschneider, D., and P. Tulip (2007). 'Gauging the uncertainty of the economic outlook from historical forecasting errors'. Finance and Economics Discussion Paper no. 2007-60. Washington, DC: Federal Reserve.

Rich, G., and J.-P. Béguelin (1985). 'Swiss monetary policy in the 1970s and 1980s: an experiment in pragmatic monetarism', in K. Brunner (ed.). *Monetary Policy and Monetary Regimes*: 76–111. Rochester, NY: Center for Research in Government Policy and Business, University of Rochester.

Rosenberg, I. (2007). 'Monetary policy and the Riksbank's communication'. Speech Stockholm, 10 August.

Rudebusch, G. (2007). 'Monetary policy inertia and recent Fed actions'. *Federal Reserve Bank of San Francisco Economic Letter*, 2007–03. San Francisco: Federal Reserve Bank of San Francisco.

Sargent, T. (1983). 'The ends of four big inflations', in R. Hall (ed.). *Inflation: Causes and Effects*: 41–97. Chicago: University of Chicago Press.

Sargent, T., and N. Wallace (1975). 'Rational expectations, the optimal monetary instrument, and the optimal money supply rule', *Journal of Political Economy*, 83(2): 241–54.

Sarno, L., D. Thornton and G. Valente (2007). 'The empirical failure of the expectations hypothesis of the term structure of bond yields', *Journal of Financial and Quantitative Analysis*, 42(1): 81–100.

Sherwin, M. (1999). 'Inflation targeting: 10 years on'. Speech given to a conference of the New Zealand Association of Economists. Rotorua, 1 July.

Stock, J., and M. Watson (2007). 'Why has US inflation become harder to forecast?', *Journal of Money, Credit and Banking*, 39(1): 3–33.

  (2008). 'Phillips curve inflation forecasts'. Working Paper no. 14322. Cambridge, MA: NBER.

Svensson, L. (2007). 'What have economists learned about monetary policy over the past 50 years?' Paper presented at the conference 'Monetary policy over fifty years'. Frankfurt, 21 September.

Taylor, J. (1995). 'The monetary transmission mechanism: an empirical framework', *Journal of Economic Perspectives*, 9(4): 11–26.

  (2008). 'Better living through monetary economics'. Unpublished manuscript. Palo Alto, CA: Stanford University.

  (2009a). 'The need to return to a monetary framework'. Unpublished manuscript. Palo Alto, CA: Stanford University.

  (2009b). 'Economic policy and the financial crisis: an empirical analysis of what went wrong', *Critical Review*, 21(2–3): 341–64.

Thornton, D. (1994). 'Financial innovation and deregulation and the "Credit View" of monetary policy', *Federal Reserve Bank of St. Louis Review*, 76(1): 31–49.

  (2007). 'The unusual behavior of the Federal Funds and 10-year Treasury rates: a conundrum or Goodhart's law?'. Working Paper no. 2007–39. St Louis, MO: Federal Reserve Bank of St Louis.

  (2009). 'The Fed, liquidity, and credit allocation', *Federal Reserve Bank of St. Louis Review*, 91(1): 13–21.

Tulip, P. (2005). 'Has output become more predictable? Changes in Greenbook forecast accuracy'. Finance and Economics Discussion Paper no. 2005–31. Washington, DC: Federal Reserve.

Von Hagen, J. (1999). 'Money growth targeting by the Bundesbank', *Journal of Monetary Economics*, 43(3): 681–701.

Woodford, M. (1999). 'Optimal monetary policy inertia', *Manchester School*, 67(supp. 1): 1–35.

  (2001). 'Monetary policy in the information economy'. Working Paper no. 8674. Cambridge, MA: NBER.

7 Inflation control around the world: why are some countries more successful than others?

Thórarinn G. Pétursson[1]

7.1 Introduction

During the last two decades the rate and variability of inflation has fallen across the world, including in many former high-inflation countries in Latin America and eastern Europe. This development has coincided with a general decline in overall economic variability and an increased emphasis on price stability in the conduct of monetary policy, in many cases formalised with changes in the monetary policy framework towards an explicit inflation target.

This general trend towards increased price stability and monetary policy reform notwithstanding, it remains the case that some countries have been more successful in controlling inflation than others, and the fact is that these countries are more or less the same countries that have been more successful over longer periods. Thus, relative inflation performance has remained stable over time, with the worst performers usually to be found among emerging market economies and very small, open economies (VSOEs).

This chapter focuses on these two issues. First, it tries to find out which factors explain this difference in inflation volatility between countries. Second, it seeks to establish what it is that explains the decline in inflation volatility over time. To tackle these issues, a country sample of forty-two of the most developed countries in the world is used, with countries chosen on the criteria that their per capita income is at least as high as that of the poorest OECD member and that their GDP level is at least as high as that of the smallest OECD member.

To try to explain relative inflation performance, a large menu of potential explanatory variables is used. These variables are related to economic structure, trade intensity and patterns, output volatility and exposure to external shocks, exchange rate behaviour and monetary policy performance. By sequentially eliminating non-significant variables, I am left with three statistically significant explanatory variables accounting for the cross-country variation in inflation volatility: the volatility of the exchange rate risk premium; the exchange rate pass-through to inflation; and monetary policy predictability. Further analysis suggests that these results are robust to a number of alterations of the empirical set-up.

I then move on to the second question of the chapter, namely what can explain the general improvement in inflation performance over time observed in the data. Using a panel set-up, I start by replicating the common finding documented in many other studies: that the adoption of inflation targeting plays a significant role in reducing the rate and volatility of inflation and that this effect remains significant even after taking account of the overall improvement among the non-targeting countries in the sample.

The next step is to add the three significant explanatory variables from the cross-country analysis to the panel, using an instrumental variable approach to allow for the possible endogeneity of the explanatory variables and the decision to adopt inflation targeting. The results show that all four variables are statistically significant with the expected sign: the contribution of inflation targeting to reducing inflation volatility remains significant and the three variables found important in explaining the cross-country variation in inflation volatility are also found important in explaining inflation volatility over time. Inflation targeting is therefore found to be statistically significant in a country sample that includes many countries that have not been used in similar analyses previously, and after allowing for additional controls that are found to be important in explaining the cross-country variation in inflation volatility.

The remainder of the chapter is organised as follows. Section 7.2 discusses the country group and the sample period used, with section 7.3 comparing inflation performance between country groups. Section 7.4 focuses on explaining the cross-country variation of inflation volatility from a large menu of possible structural variables and policy variables. Section 7.5 moves on to explain the declining inflation volatility observed in the country sample in a panel set-up, while section 7.6 concludes. Appendices explain the derivation of key explanatory variables, document the robustness of the cross-country results and detail the data sources and description.

7.2   The data

The country sample

This section describes the country sample analysed in this chapter. The focus is on reasonably developed, market-based economies, the aim being to include countries of similar income levels and size to OECD member countries. Hence, countries with a 2006 per capita GDP adjusted for purchasing power parity (PPP) that is lower than the poorest OECD member country (Turkey: $8,900) and a PPP-adjusted 2006 GDP lower than the smallest OECD member country (Iceland: $11.4 billion) are excluded.[2] This gives a sample of sixty-five countries in total from the 226 countries recorded in the *CIA World Factbook*.

It turns out that quarterly data for a sufficient time span are not available for some key variables in some of these sixty-five countries. Furthermore, a number of these countries cannot reasonably be described as decentralised, market-based economies, while others have experienced serious military conflicts within the sample period analysed here. As a result, twenty-three additional countries are excluded from the sample. This gives a sample of forty-two countries – i.e. all the current thirty OECD member countries, plus Chile, Cyprus, Estonia, Hong Kong, Israel, Latvia, Lithuania, Malta, Slovenia, South Africa, Taiwan and Thailand.

The sample period

The sample period in general runs from 1985 to 2005, but there are a few exceptions, as in some cases quarterly data for the entire period are not available or are not used. In most cases this involves the former communist countries in eastern Europe, for which any meaningful economic analysis would usually use data starting in the early 1990s. There are also three former hyperinflation countries, for which the analysis starts only after inflation has reached lower double-digit rates: Israel (analysis from 1986), Mexico (from 1989) and Poland (from 1992).

Different country groups

There are several interesting subgroups in the country sample (see Table 7.1). The first is a group of seven very small, open economies with population levels below 2.5 million. A second group comprises the emerging and developing countries in the sample. These are defined as the total country sample excluding both countries that have been OECD members since 1961 and Hong Kong, Israel, South Korea and Taiwan, which are more naturally thought of as developed countries. Turkey is treated as an EME country, however, as it most closely resembles an emerging market economy despite being an original OECD member. This gives a sample of fifteen countries. Compared to groups

Table 7.1 *Different country groups in the sample*

Emerging market economies	Very small, open economies	Euro12 members	Inflation-targeting countries (adoption dates)		Remaining countries
Chile	Cyprus	Austria	Australia	1993Q2	Denmark
Cyprus	Estonia	Belgium	Canada	1991Q1	Hong Kong
Czech Republic	Iceland	Finland	Chile	1990Q3	Japan
Estonia	Latvia	France	Czech Republic	1998Q1	Taiwan
Hungary	Luxembourg	Germany	Hungary	2001Q2	United States
Latvia	Malta	Greece	Iceland	2001Q1	
Lithuania	Slovenia	Ireland	Israel	1992Q1	
Malta		Italy	Mexico	1999Q1	
Mexico		Luxembourg	New Zealand	1990Q1	
Poland		Netherlands	Norway	2001Q1	
Slovakia		Portugal	Poland	1998Q4	
Slovenia		Spain	South Africa	2000Q1	
South Africa			South Korea	1998Q2	
Thailand			Sweden	1993Q1	
Turkey			Switzerland	2000Q1	
			Thailand	2000Q2	
			United Kingdom	1992Q4	

of large and more developed countries, such as the Group of six (G6) countries or the original twelve euro countries (Euro12), these two country groups have experienced much more volatile inflation rates (see below).

The final group consists of the seventeen inflation-targeting countries in the country sample. Of the countries that followed IT at the end of the sample period, this leaves out four countries: Brazil, Colombia, Peru and the Philippines, which are all excluded as they fall below the per capita income criterion described above. Furthermore, Finland and Spain, which temporarily adopted IT in the mid-1990s before entering the European Union's Economic and Monetary Union (EMU) in 1999, are treated as non-targeting countries in the analysis.

For the timing of IT adoption, this chapter uses the dates given by Pétursson (2005), which mainly follow the timing convention used by Fracasso, Genberg and Wyplosz (2003). The exceptions are Australia, for which the adoption date is as given by Schaechter, Stone and Zelner (2000); Chile, for which the adoption date is as given by Truman (2003); and New Zealand for which the adoption date is as given by Mishkin and Schmidt-Hebbel (2002) (see Pétursson 2005 for a further discussion of the targeting dates and the targeting group).

Table 7.2 *Inflation performance and predictability*

	Inflation	Inflation volatility	Inflation forecast errors
All countries	6.17	4.76	3.38
EMEs	11.62	8.08	5.52
VSOEs	6.01	5.81	3.14
G6	2.50	1.64	1.29
Euro12	3.44	2.23	1.59
ITers	6.78	5.66	3.59

Notes: The table reports average values for different country groups. Inflation is defined as annualised quarterly changes in seasonally adjusted headline consumer prices and inflation volatility as the standard deviation of inflation (both in percentages). Inflation forecast errors are standard deviations of one-quarter-ahead forecast errors (in percentages) from a rolling-window vector autoregressive (VAR) model.

7.3   Inflation performance

I start by looking at average inflation and inflation variability in the forty-two countries for the period 1985 to 2005, or the available sample period. Table 7.2 reports average values for different country groups.

Average inflation is 6.2 per cent for the whole-country sample but is found to be significantly higher in the VSOEs and the EMEs than in the larger and more developed countries. The same applies to inflation volatility, which is roughly 2 per cent in the large, developed countries but roughly three times as high in the VSOEs and about four times as high in the EMEs.

As previously discussed, inflation has fallen and become more stable worldwide during the last two decades (Cecchetti *et al.* 2007), coinciding with a general decline in overall macroeconomic volatility (McConnell and Perez-Quiros 2000). This decline in the rate and volatility of inflation is also apparent in the country sample used here: average inflation is 4.4 per cent during the period 1995 to 2005, compared to 6.2 per cent for the whole sample period, while the standard deviation of inflation falls from 4.8 per cent on average to 3.4 per cent in the 1995–2005 period. Section 7.5 analyses this improvement in inflation performance with respect to the adoption of IT in many countries included in the sample.

An alternative measure of inflation volatility comes from estimating out-of-sample, one-quarter-ahead inflation forecast errors from a fourth-order VAR model. The VAR(4) model includes domestic and import price inflation, the output gap (measured as the deviation of output from its Hodrick–Prescott trend) and the short-term interest rate, and is re-estimated over a rolling forty-quarter window to capture the learning behaviour of private agents.[3] The resulting standard deviations of the forecast errors are reported in the third column of Table 7.2. The pattern is very similar to the one using unconditional standard deviations (rank correlation equal to 0.74): conditional inflation volatility is higher in the VSOEs and the EMEs, although the difference is smaller than when using the unconditional standard deviations.

The observation that very small, open economies and emerging and developing countries tend to experience more volatile and less predictable inflation rates than the large, developed countries therefore seems to be robust. The focus of the next section is to try to understand what factors explain this difference.

7.4   Cross-country analysis of inflation performance

Variables used

This subsection describes the variables used to explain the cross-country variation in inflation volatility and the motivation for including them in the analysis. Where necessary, Appendix 7A explains the technical issues involved in measuring the variables.

Economic structure   There are several channels through which the level of economic development can affect economic volatility in general and inflation volatility in particular. For example, Acemoglu and Zilibotti (1997) present a model in which higher-income countries are more able to undertake investment in indivisible forms of capital and therefore obtain a more balanced sectoral distribution of output than lower-income countries. The overall level of economic development is also likely to coincide with financial market development which tends to smooth economic volatility by facilitating the intertemporal smoothing of households and firms and adding liquidity to financial markets. Seigniorage financing of government expenditure is also likely to be more important in low-income countries, for example because there may be a fixed cost to building an effective tax collection system, leading to higher and more volatile inflation (Végh 1988). Finally, per capita income can be thought of as a proxy for other economic and institutional developments that serve to reduce the time inconsistency problem.

The relationship between economic size and inflation volatility is less clear, perhaps. It can be argued, however, that larger countries should experience lower inflation variability, other things being equal. Larger markets make financial risk diversification easier and help economies to absorb shocks. The economy will also be less dependent on a relatively small number of industries, which can have disproportionately large effects on overall economic performance. This effect may be further enhanced if there is a fixed cost to building institutions that are more effective in containing inflationary pressures, for example if there is a limited pool of skilled people to draw from.

To analyse the relationship between economic structure and inflation volatility, this chapter includes economic size (SIZE), measured as PPP-adjusted GDP, and the level of economic development (INC), measured as PPP-adjusted GDP per capita, as potential explanatory variables.

Trade openness Romer (1993) argues that economies that are more active in international trade should, on average, have less inflation; this was extended to inflation volatility by Bowdler and Malik (2005). The reason is that an unanticipated monetary expansion will lead to a real exchange rate depreciation that directly raises import price inflation and the amount of domestic inflation for a given expansion of domestic output, for example if wages are partially indexed to inflation or if imported goods are used as intermediate inputs in domestic production. As both these effects are likely to be more pronounced in more open economies, the incentive to inflate should be smaller compared to less open economies. This suggests that countries more open to international trade should have lower and more stable inflation rates, with openness measured here as the sum of imports and exports of goods and services over GDP (constant prices, average for the period 2000 to 2005) (OPEN).

Trade patterns Different trade patterns can affect inflation performance to the extent that they reflect a different degree of exposure to external shocks. For example, a country that exports a narrow range of goods is bound to lose some diversification benefits and may experience more difficulties in stabilising the domestic economy and inflation than a country with a broad export product range. The same should apply to countries for which primary commodities constitute a large share of the export product base. Many resource-based goods tend to experience large relative price swings in response to changes in international economic conditions, which can lead to large changes in domestic conditions in economies in which these goods are relatively important.

Two measures of trade patterns are used here. First, to measure the extent of trade diversification, an index constructed by the United

Nations Conference on Trade and Development (UNCTAD) is used
(DIVER). This index ranges from zero to one and measures the extent
to which a country's export structure differs from that of the average
country. A country exporting only a few goods will have a value closer
to unity.[4] The second measure used is the share of commodities, defined
as all food items, agricultural raw materials, fuels and ores and metals
(including non-ferrous metals) in merchandise exports (COMM).

Output volatility and exposure to external shocks One would
expect countries with more volatile real economies to face an inferior
trade-off between inflation volatility and output volatility, so that greater
output gap variability would be reflected in greater inflation variability.
The standard deviation of the output gap is used to measure the variability of real output (REAL).

One would also expect a country's exposure to external shocks to have
a significant effect on the performance of the domestic economy and
its ability to control inflation. One indicator of this exposure is the co-
movement of the domestic economy with the rest of the world, which is
here proxied by the contemporaneous correlation between domestic and
world output gaps (INTER).[5] The idea is that countries with little co-
movement with the rest of the world face greater challenges in controlling
inflation than countries that are more closely tied to the world economy.
Frequent and large idiosyncratic shocks, often associated with large terms
of trade fluctuations, are likely to make domestic monetary policy more
challenging, especially in the modern world of freely flowing capital,
where asymmetric business cycles can generate huge capital flows in and
out of countries. These procyclical capital flows could easily amplify
economic volatility, making inflation control more difficult (see Aghion,
Bacchetta and Banerjee 2004 and Kaminsky, Reinhart and Végh 2004).

Another indicator of a country's exposure to external shocks is the
contemporaneous correlation between the cyclical part of private consumption and the effective exchange rate (CONS), which, according
to Lucas (1982), is the key determinant of the exchange rate risk premium. In his model, holding a particular currency is risky if it moves
in the same direction as the consumption cycle – i.e. if the currency is
weak in the low consumption state and strong in the high consumption
state. In the standard sticky price model, a monetary policy tightening
would generally lead to an exchange rate appreciation and a contraction
in consumption, generating counter-cyclical exchange rate movements.
However, procyclical exchange rate movements could reflect the importance of balance sheet effects, for example in small countries in which
foreign-currency-denominated borrowing is widespread, which can

counteract the usual contractionary effects of monetary policy tightening on consumption. Procyclical exchange rate movements could also reflect the importance of terms of trade shocks for exchange rate developments. In both cases this would imply a relatively large exchange rate premium according to Lucas's (1982) model, which might contribute to increased inflation variability if the risk premium was volatile (see the discussion below).

Exchange rate developments   This chapter uses two measures of the importance of exchange rate fluctuations for inflation volatility. The first is the volatility of the risk premium in multilateral exchange rates (EXRISK).[6] To measure this, I use the standard monetary model of exchange rate determination, but allow for a time-varying exchange rate risk premium (represented as the rational expectations deviation from the simple interest rate parity condition). A signal extraction approach suggested by Durlauf and Hall (1988, 1989), described in Appendix 7A.1, gives an estimate of the lower bound of the variance of the expected present value of the exchange rate risk premium. The argument is therefore that the more volatile the exchange rate risk premium is (or the more noisy the exchange rate is), the more unpredictable the exchange rate will be and, in turn, the more difficult inflation control becomes.

The second exchange rate indicator is the degree of exchange rate pass-through to consumer price inflation (PASS). It seems reasonable to expect countries with a high degree of pass-through to experience more difficulties in controlling inflation than countries with a low degree of pass-through, as exchange rates tend to be volatile and hard to predict. Furthermore, as shown by Betts and Devereux (2001), a high degree of pass-through should coincide with a negative co-movement of domestic and world output in the face of monetary policy shocks, thus creating an additional complication in conducting independent monetary policy as discussed above. To identify exchange rate shocks and estimate the degree of exchange rate pass-through, I use a VAR model that includes domestic and foreign inflation, exchange rate changes, the short-term interest rate and the output gap. Further details on the estimation approach are given in Appendix 7A.2.

Monetary policy   The final two variables measure the effects of monetary policy performance on inflation variability. The first measures monetary policy shocks or, alternatively, the predictability of monetary policy (POLICY). There is a large literature showing how a credible and transparent monetary policy can determine the level and variability of inflation directly through anchoring inflation expectations or indirectly

Table 7.3 *Descriptive statistics for the whole sample period*

	All countries	EMEs	VSOEs	G6	Euro12	ITers	RANK
SIZE	901	290	25	4,214	768	552	−0.35**
INC	27.3	16.1	29.6	33.1	33.4	24.8	−0.67***
OPEN	1.05	1.25	1.54	0.47	1.06	0.86	0.13
DIVER	0.46	0.50	0.57	0.30	0.41	0.50	0.39***
COMM	0.26	0.27	0.30	0.13	0.19	0.35	0.22*
REAL	1.68	2.06	1.76	1.03	1.35	1.86	0.60***
INTER	0.36	0.21	0.27	0.47	0.54	0.35	−0.47***
CONS	−0.11	−0.15	−0.11	0.00	−0.02	−0.22	−0.24*
EXRISK	13.69	20.86	17.74	10.53	8.04	14.96	0.68***
PASS	0.23	0.31	0.39	0.11	0.21	0.25	0.43***
POLICY	1.24	2.50	0.84	0.35	0.38	0.94	0.63***
INDEP	0.84	0.86	0.81	0.89	0.85	0.81	−0.10

Notes: The table reports average values for different country groups. RANK denotes the rank correlation of the given variable with inflation volatility. * = significant at 10%; ** = significant at 5%; *** = significant at 1%.

through its effects on other determinants of the inflation process (see, for example, Taylor 2000, and for empirical evidence see, for example, Kuttner and Posen 1999, Corbo, Landerretche and Schmidt-Hebbel 2001 and Roberts 2006, among others). To measure monetary policy shocks, a forward-looking Taylor rule similar to that used by Clarida, Gali and Gertler (2000) is estimated.[7] Further details on the estimation approach are given in Appendix 7A.3.

The second monetary policy indicator is a measure of central bank independence (INDEP), often found to be an important explanatory variable for inflation performance (see, for example, Alesina and Summers 1993). The basic idea is that central bank independence helps insulate monetary policy from political pressures and therefore reduces the time inconsistency problem. This chapter uses the independence index constructed by Fry *et al.* (2000), which covers all the countries in the sample except Luxembourg, which is given the same ranking as Belgium, as these two countries were in a monetary union up to the adoption of the euro in 1999. The variable ranges between one and zero, with a higher value indicating a more independent central bank.

Descriptive statistics for the cross-country analysis

This subsection reports some descriptive statistics for the explanatory variables used in the cross-country analysis below. Table 7.3 shows average values of each variable for the whole-country sample and the five different country groups discussed above.[8] The table also reports rank correlations between each variable and inflation volatility (INFVOL).

When comparing the outcomes for the EMEs and VSOEs with the larger and more developed countries, a number of features should be noted. First, as previously discussed, there is a strong negative correlation between SIZE and INC, on the one hand, and INFVOL, on the other – again suggesting that the larger and more developed countries have had greater success in controlling inflation than the smaller and less developed ones.

Second, the VSOEs and EMEs tend to be much more open to trade than the larger and more developed countries, but, in contrast to the results of Romer (1993) and Bowdler and Malik (2005), openness is not found to be significantly correlated with inflation performance. However, the results in both these studies suggest that the negative relation is mainly confined to the poorer and less developed countries in their large country samples, most of which are not included in the country sample used here. Terra's (1998) results also suggest that the negative relationship is mainly due to the performance of highly indebted countries during the debt crisis in the 1980s – of which only one country is included in the sample in this chapter (Mexico). It is therefore perhaps not surprising that no significant link between openness and inflation performance can be found in the country sample used here.

Third, the two indicators of trade patterns suggest that the EMEs and, especially, the VSOEs seem to have less diversified export product ranges and to be more resource-based than the larger countries. The rank correlation coefficients further imply that a narrower and more commodity-dominated export base significantly coincides with higher inflation volatility.

Fourth, output in both the VSOEs and EMEs is much more volatile than in the larger and more developed economies, and this greater output volatility is strongly positively correlated with inflation volatility.

Fifth, the correlation between the domestic and world business cycles is found to be lower for the VSOEs and EMEs than for the larger and more developed countries, even though the former are much more open to international trade. The rank correlation suggests that countries with more stable inflation rates seem to have stronger links to the world economy, even though they are somewhat less open to international trade, as discussed above.

Sixth, the correlation between consumption and exchange rate appreciation tends to be small and slightly negative in the case of the VSOEs and EMEs but more or less zero in the larger and more developed countries. Interestingly, the correlation is found to be much more negative in the IT countries. The sign of the rank correlation coefficient is consistent with the discussion above: a more procyclical exchange rate tends to coincide with higher inflation volatility.

Seventh, both exchange rate indicators suggest less favourable conditions for inflation control in the VSOEs and EMEs: both country groups have a more volatile exchange rate risk premium and a higher degree of exchange rate pass-through, and both indicators are found to be significantly positively correlated with inflation volatility.

Eighth, monetary policy shocks are found to be slightly greater in the VSOEs than in the larger and more developed countries, but the difference between the EMEs and other country groups is much larger, suggesting that monetary policy is much less predictable in the EMEs than in the other country groups. This could imply that monetary policy is less systematic in the EMEs or that the inflation goal of the monetary authorities is more likely to be changed in the face of adverse inflationary developments. The reasons for this could include political distortions, weak monetary policy institutions or capital market imperfections. However, the finding could also reflect the simple fact that measuring the output gap is probably more difficult in the EMEs than in other countries; national accounts may be less reliable and timely, and the estimation of potential output may be more difficult due to frequent structural changes. In addition, these structural changes may lead to changes in the equilibrium real interest rate, which could also show up as large 'monetary policy shocks'. As expected, the size of these monetary policy shocks is found to be strongly positively correlated with inflation volatility.

Finally, the central banks of the VSOEs and EMEs are found to be slightly less independent than those in their larger and more developed counterparts. The correlation with inflation volatility is negative, suggesting that greater central bank independence tends to coincide with less inflation volatility, but the correlation is not significant.

Basic cross-country results

This subsection attempts to explain the cross-country variation in INFVOL using the variables described above. In the empirical analysis below, SIZE and INC enter in logarithms, while other variables are measured in decimals (i.e. INFVOL of 1 per cent enters as 0.01).[9]

The results are reported in Table 7.4. I start with all the potential explanatory variables, sequentially deleting the least significant one until all the remaining variables are significant at the 5 per cent critical level.

As with the simple bilateral rank correlations in the previous subsection, no significant effects can be found for OPEN and INDEP. Furthermore, the results indicate that the cross-country variation in inflation volatility is not significantly explained by variations in SIZE, CONS, INTER, REAL and DIVER. The final two variables to be excluded, COMM and INC, are in fact not far from being significant from zero at the 10 per cent critical level, and both are correctly signed.

Eliminating all the insignificant variables leaves three significant variables, all with t-values above four: the volatility of the exchange rate risk premium and of monetary policy shocks, and the extent of exchange rate pass-through to consumer price inflation. Thus, the more volatile the exchange rate risk premium, the greater the pass-through of exchange rate shocks; or, the less predictable monetary policy is, the more volatile inflation tends to be. These three variables turn out to account for a large and significant fraction of the cross-country variation in inflation volatility, with R^2 equal to 0.75.

The impact of these three variables on inflation volatility is also quantitatively large. The point estimates in column (10) in Table 7.4 suggest, for example, that a 1 standard deviation decline in EXRISK from its sample mean decreases INFVOL by 0.3 standard deviations from its mean, or by 1.4 percentage points (from 4.8 per cent in Table 7.2 to 3.4 per cent). A 1 standard deviation decline in POLICY decreases INFVOL by 0.5 standard deviations, or by 2.3 p.p., while a 1 standard deviation decrease in PASS decreases INFVOL by 0.4 standard deviations, or by 1.8 p.p. These three explanatory variables are therefore not only statistically significant but also economically important.

Finally, as reported in Appendix 7B, these results are found to be robust to various alterations in model specification and estimation methods, such as adding country-group dummy variables or changing the country sample, possible effects of large outliers using robust estimators or possible endogeneity of the explanatory variables using instrumental variables estimation.

7.5   Inflation control and inflation targeting

This section focuses on explaining the decline in inflation volatility over the sample period and the potential role of the three factors found to be important in explaining the cross-country variation in inflation volatility in accounting for this development. Furthermore, a large and growing literature suggests that the adoption of inflation targeting has played a critical role in this improvement by reducing inflation rates, volatility and persistence, and that it has, by providing a better anchor for long-term

Table 7.4 Cross-country results for INFVOL

	(1)	(2)	(3)	(4)	(5)	(6)	(7)	(8)	(9)	(10)
log(SIZE)	0.000 (0.99)									
CONS	0.001 (0.91)	0.001 (0.91)								
OPEN	0.002 (0.81)	0.002 (0.77)	0.003 (0.73)							
INTER	0.009 (0.64)	0.009 (0.63)	0.009 (0.63)	0.007 (0.69)						
INDEP	0.000 (0.57)	0.000 (0.56)	0.000 (0.55)	0.000 (0.52)	0.000 (0.50)					
REAL	0.640 (0.48)	0.636 (0.45)	0.594 (0.41)	0.666 (0.33)	0.583 (0.37)	0.492 (0.43)				
DIVER	-0.032 (0.49)	-0.032 (0.40)	-0.032 (0.39)	-0.030 (0.41)	-0.029 (0.41)	-0.032 (0.36)	-0.021 (0.51)			
COMM	0.046 (0.07)	0.046 (0.07)	0.046 (0.06)	0.043 (0.06)	0.041 (0.06)	0.038 (0.08)	0.032 (0.10)	0.024 (0.11)		
log(INC)	-0.012 (0.33)	-0.012 (0.33)	-0.012 (0.32)	-0.011 (0.34)	-0.011 (0.34)	-0.012 (0.26)	-0.014 (0.18)	-0.016 (0.11)	-0.016 (0.12)	
EXRISK	0.113 (0.12)	0.113 (0.09)	0.114 (0.08)	0.114 (0.07)	0.107 (0.07)	0.115 (0.05)	0.121 (0.04)	0.111 (0.04)	0.125 (0.02)	0.174 (0.00)
POLICY	0.725 (0.00)	0.725 (0.00)	0.725 (0.00)	0.719 (0.00)	0.719 (0.00)	0.696 (0.00)	0.728 (0.00)	0.709 (0.00)	0.701 (0.00)	0.774 (0.00)
PASS	0.089 (0.00)	0.088 (0.00)	0.088 (0.00)	0.088 (0.00)	0.090 (0.00)	0.088 (0.00)	0.090 (0.00)	0.086 (0.00)	0.082 (0.00)	0.087 (0.00)
Constant	0.007 (0.92)	0.008 (0.91)	0.008 (0.91)	0.005 (0.94)	0.009 (0.88)	0.039 (0.34)	0.048 (0.22)	0.050 (0.20)	0.054 (0.17)	-0.006 (0.41)
R^2 (adj.)	0.728	0.737	0.746	0.753	0.760	0.764	0.766	0.770	0.760	0.750
SE	0.022	0.021	0.021	0.021	0.020	0.020	0.020	0.020	0.020	0.021
Excl. test	–	0.990	0.994	0.988	0.991*	0.980	0.969	0.972	0.855	0.849

Notes: The exclusion test is an F-test that tests for the exclusion of all the variables eliminated up to the given stage. The numbers in parentheses and values reported for the exclusion test are p-values. SE = standard error.

inflation expectations, made inflation more predictable. Many of these studies have also found that these effects are especially important for IT emerging market economies.[10] The possible role of IT in the decline of inflation volatility is therefore also analysed.

Descriptive statistics for the pre- and post-targeting periods

Table 7.5 reports descriptive statistics for the pre- and post-targeting periods for inflation volatility and the three potential explanatory variables. As is standard in this literature (see Mishkin and Schmidt-Hebbel 2007), I use the average IT adoption date as the break date for the non-targeting countries. In this sample, this date is 1996Q4: the pre-targeting period for the non-targeters is therefore 1985 to 1996, while the post-targeting period is 1997 to 2005.

To capture the time variation in the volatility of inflation, the exchange rate risk premium and monetary policy shocks, I use rolling two-year standard deviations.[11] To obtain some time variation in the degree of exchange rate pass-through, I follow Edwards (2006) in using a simple regression approach to obtain estimates of the pass-through coefficient before and after IT (or before and after 1997 for the non-targeting countries); Appendix 7A.2 gives a more detailed description of the approach.

Inflation volatility is found to decline in all country groups, with average volatility declining from 4.5 per cent to 2.7 per cent for the whole-country sample. The biggest reductions are found in the VSOEs, the EMEs and the IT countries. This improvement in inflation performance has occurred despite the fact that the volatility of the exchange rate risk premium seems to have increased. That increase seems to be restricted to the VSOEs and EMEs, however, and declining volatility of the exchange rate risk premium is observed in other country groups.[12] In contrast, the predictability of monetary policy seems to have improved in all country groups, even though monetary policy shocks continue to be much larger in the EMEs than in the other country groups. Finally, the table shows that the rate of exchange rate pass-through has declined in all country groups, with the largest decline observed in the VSOEs and EMEs, although pass-through continues to be higher than in the larger and more developed countries.

The declining volatility of inflation reported in Table 7.5, and the role of the three other variables from the table in this improvement, are studied more systematically in the next subsection, which includes the potential impact of IT adoption in the analysis.

Table 7.5 *Descriptive statistics, pre- and post-targeting*

	Pre-targeting	Post-targeting
INFVOL		
All countries	4.47	2.65
EMEs	7.59	4.47
VSOEs	5.86	2.72
G6	1.56	0.94
Euro12	2.11	1.19
ITers	5.46	2.39
Non-ITers	3.80	2.83
EXRISK		
All countries	9.44	11.00
EMEs	10.39	15.60
VSOEs	6.54	15.19
G6	11.02	10.04
Euro12	8.61	7.27
ITers	11.58	11.13
Non-ITers	7.98	10.91
POLICY		
All countries	2.28	1.29
EMEs	3.84	2.62
VSOEs	1.06	0.85
G6	0.67	0.32
Euro12	0.91	0.40
ITers	1.84	0.99
Non-ITers	2.40	1.49
PASS		
All countries	0.36	0.11
EMEs	0.72	0.20
VSOEs	0.74	0.23
G6	0.09	0.03
Euro12	0.13	0.07
ITers	0.36	0.15
Non-ITers	0.36	0.08

Notes: The table reports average values for different country groups before and after inflation targeting or before and after 1997 for the non-targeting countries. INFVOL, EXRISK and POLICY are reported in percentages.

Panel analysis of inflation performance

To estimate the role of IT and the three explanatory variables from the cross-country analysis above in the declining volatility of inflation, I use a panel approach that incorporates both the country and the time dimensions of the data. The panel approach also allows me to analyse the importance of the composition of the treatment (the IT countries) and the control (the non-targeting countries) groups, which Mishkin and Schmidt-Hebbel (2007) show plays a key role in the final analysis of the importance of IT for comparative inflation performance.

The treatment group in this chapter includes the seventeen IT countries, while the control group consists of the remaining twenty-five countries of the forty-two-country sample. The control group therefore includes countries ranging from very small emerging market countries, such as Cyprus and Malta, to very large developed countries, such as Japan and the United States, in addition to the twelve highly developed EMU countries. This should give a control group that is sufficiently heterogeneous to offer an interesting comparison to the treatment group, which also contains a similarly heterogeneous group of countries ranging from small to large, and from emerging to highly developed. The control group also offers a country set with a wide array of monetary policy frameworks, ranging from exchange rate pegs, currency boards and monetary unions to floating exchange rates with monetary targets or other hybrid frameworks.[13] Results for a narrower control group of the seventeen non-targeting industrial countries are also reported as a robustness check (the Euro12 countries plus the five remaining countries from Table 7.1).

The panel model estimated is specified as

$$INFVOL_{i,t} = \mu + \gamma_1 INFVOL_{i,t-1} + \gamma_2 INFVOL_{i,t-2} + \beta D_{i,t}$$
$$+ \varphi' \mathbf{Z}_{i,t-1} + \alpha_i + \delta_t + \varepsilon_{i,t} \qquad (7.1)$$

where μ is the overall constant in the model, α_i denotes the country-specific fixed effects, δ_t the time-specific fixed effects and $\varepsilon_{i,t}$ is the error term. $INFVOL_{i,t}$ is the volatility of inflation in country i at time t and $D_{i,t}$ is the IT dummy variable that equals unity from the first quarter after IT adoption if country i is a targeter but zero throughout for non-targeters. Two lags of $INFVOL_{i,t}$ are found to be sufficient to capture the persistence in inflation volatility (which can either be intrinsic or reflect other omitted determinants of volatility). Finally, $\mathbf{Z}_{i,t}$ is a set of the three additional control variables: $EXRISK_{i,t}$, $POLICY_{i,t}$ and $PASS_{i,t}$. These three control variables are included lagged by one quarter to reduce any potential bias that may stem from including them contemporaneously.[14]

As discussed by Mishkin and Schmidt-Hebbel (2007), the adoption of IT may be an endogenous decision that is based, *inter alia*, on past inflation performance. Thus, estimating equation (7.1) can give biased results if this potential endogeneity is not accounted for. As shown by Mishkin and Schmidt-Hebbel (2002), initial inflation plays an

Table 7.6 *Panel results for INFVOL*

	Country group 1				Country group 2			
	Fixed cross-section effects		Fixed cross-section and time effects		Fixed cross-section effects		Fixed cross-section and time effects	
Constant	0.0034 (0.000)	0.0025 (0.000)	0.0033 (0.000)	0.0025 (0.000)	0.0026 (0.000)	0.0018 (0.000)	0.0025 (0.000)	0.0018 (0.002)
$INFVOL_{i,t-1}$	0.9729 (0.000)	0.9390 (0.000)	0.9722 (0.000)	0.9407 (0.000)	1.0779 (0.000)	1.0618 (0.000)	1.0780 (0.000)	1.0665 (0.000)
$INFVOL_{i,t-2}$	−0.1069 (0.040)	−0.1581 (0.008)	−0.1085 (0.040)	−0.1595 (0.008)	−0.1969 (0.001)	−0.2298 (0.000)	−0.1972 (0.001)	−0.2343 (0.000)
IT dummy	−0.0021 (0.003)	−0.0013 (0.015)	−0.0013 (0.094)	−0.0012 (0.026)	−0.0019 (0.004)	−0.0011 (0.018)	−0.0013 (0.061)	−0.0011 (0.033)
$EXRISK_{i,t-1}$		0.0207 (0.005)		0.0212 (0.007)		0.0148 (0.012)		0.0152 (0.014)
$POLICY_{i,t-1}$		0.0628 (0.017)		0.0621 (0.020)		0.0586 (0.000)		0.0610 (0.000)
$PASS_{i,t-1}$		0.0018 (0.097)		0.0020 (0.090)		0.0004 (0.677)		0.0004 (0.709)
R^2	0.90	0.91	0.90	0.91	0.90	0.89	0.90	0.90
SE	0.0093	0.0072	0.0092	0.0072	0.0068	0.0054	0.0068	0.0053
Countries	42	42	42	42	34	34	34	34
Observations	2,941	2,680	2,941	2,680	2,507	2,374	2,507	2,374

Notes: Country group 1 includes all forty-two countries. Country group 2 includes the seventeen IT countries and the seventeen non-targeting industrial countries in the sample. The panels are estimated with the instrumental variables method, using average pre-targeting (or pre-1997 for the non-targeting countries) inflation, two lags of INFVOL and one-quarter lags of the inflation-targeting dummy, and the three additional explanatory variables (where applicable) as instruments. The numbers in parentheses are *p*-values using robust cross-section panel-corrected standard errors.

important role in the decision to adopt IT. Countries with high inflation in the past therefore seem more likely to adopt inflation targeting than countries with better inflation records. I therefore follow Mishkin and Schmidt-Hebbel (2007) in estimating the panel model applying IV panel estimation techniques, using pre-targeting average inflation (or pre-1997 average inflation for the non-targeting countries) in addition to the lagged IT dummy and lags of $INFVOL_{i,t}$ and $Z_{i,t}$ as instruments.

The estimation period uses all the available data, which cover 1987Q2 to 2005Q4, generating a large panel with the number of observations ranging from 2,374 to 2,941. Table 7.6 reports the results, allowing for country-specific fixed effects or country- and time-specific fixed effects. The table reports the results with and without the three additional controls in $Z_{i,t}$ for the two control groups.

As the table shows, the IT effect is found to be statistically significant at the 5 per cent critical level, except when the model is estimated without the three controls in $Z_{i,t}$ and using the fixed cross-country effects, in which case the IT dummy is found to be statistically significant at the 10 per cent critical level. The impact effect of the dummy variable ranges from −0.11 per cent to −0.21 per cent. Taking account of the lagged dynamics of $INFVOL_{i,t}$, this implies that IT adoption reduces inflation volatility by 0.6 to 1.6 p.p. in the long run, depending on control group and model specification.[15]

Including the three additional controls in $Z_{i,t}$ tends to reduce the size of the IT effect, but it remains statistically significant, and, in fact, is found to be more significant when allowing for $Z_{i,t}$ in some specifications. Moreover, all the additional controls are found to be statistically significant when using the whole-country sample (country group 1): $EXRISK_{i,t}$ and $POLICY_{i,t}$ at the 5 per cent critical level or lower and $PASS_{i,t}$ at the 10 per cent critical level. Taking account of the lagged dynamics of $INFVOL_{i,t}$ gives a long-run coefficient on $EXRISK_{i,t}$ of just below 0.1, while the coefficients on $POLICY_{i,t}$ and $PASS_{i,t}$ are close to 0.3 and 0.2, respectively. A 1 standard deviation decline in $EXRISK_{i,t}$ will therefore reduce $INFVOL_{i,t}$ by the same amount as in the cross-country analysis, while the effects of $POLICY_{i,t}$ and $PASS_{i,t}$ are somewhat smaller.

Comparing the results for the two control groups shows that, while the effects of $EXRISK_{i,t}$ and $POLICY_{i,t}$ remain statistically significant and similar in size when using the second, narrower, control group (country group 2), the effects of $PASS_{i,t}$ are now found to be insignificant from zero. This is not surprising, perhaps, given the nature of the countries left out of this control group. Of the eight EME countries excluded, three belong only to the EME group (Lithuania, Slovakia and Turkey), while the other five also belong to the VSOE group (Cyprus, Estonia, Latvia,

Malta and Slovenia), with the consequence that only two VSOE countries remain in the analysis: Iceland in the treatment group and Luxembourg in the control group. Most of the eight countries excluded are therefore either very small or rather small open economies and somewhat less developed countries, which the previous analysis has shown to have the highest degree of exchange rate pass-through overall (see Table 7.3) but to have experienced the biggest reduction in pass-through (see Table 7.5). It is interesting to note that the cross-country results from the previous subsection are robust to excluding these eight countries from the sample. This highlights how the cross-country and the panel analyses capture different aspects of the data. The cross-country analysis shows that a higher degree of pass-through tends to coincide with higher inflation volatility, while the panel analysis shows how the declining degree of pass-through has contributed to declining inflation volatility. The panel results suggest, however, that the small and less developed countries are needed in the control group to capture this latter feature of the data.

Comparison of the cross-sectional and panel estimation results also suggests that part of the estimated effects of $\mathbf{Z}_{i,t}$ on INFVOL$_{i,t}$ found in the cross-country analysis is now captured by the IT dummy variable. This is also seen when the IT dummy variable is excluded from the panel analysis, so that the same three explanatory variables are used as in the cross-section analysis. In this case, the p-values on the PASS$_{i,t}$ coefficient are well below 5 per cent in the first control group and, although still insignificant, decline substantially in the second group. Hence, it seems that the IT dummy captures some of the improvement observed in inflation performance that previous studies, such as that by Gagnon and Ihrig (2004), have attributed to declining pass-through. For the other two variables, however, the parameter estimates and p-values remain unchanged.

7.6   Conclusions

The focus of this chapter has been twofold. First, to try to identify what factors explain why some countries have had more success in stabilising inflation than others and, in particular, why inflation seems more volatile in very small, open economies and in emerging and developing countries than in the large and more developed ones. Second, to try to discover the explanation for the general decline in inflation volatility observed over the last two decades. To do this, I have used a country sample of forty-two of the most developed countries in the world. The results imply that three factors can explain most of the cross-country variation in inflation volatility: the volatility of currency risk premiums, the degree of exchange rate pass-through to inflation and the predictability of monetary policy. Other variables, related to economic development and size, international trade, output volatility, exposure to external shocks, and central bank independence, were not found to be significant. The three significant variables, in addition to the adoption of inflation targeting, are also found to play a critical role in explaining the developments in inflation volatility over the last two decades.

The results therefore confirm the general findings from the empirical inflation targeting literature, that the adoption of inflation targeting has played a key role in the observed improvement in inflation performance over the last two decades. The chapter also shows that the effect of inflation targeting continues to be significant even after adding the three variables found important for explaining the cross-country variation in inflation volatility to the analysis. Furthermore, the importance of inflation targeting is found to be robust to using a heterogeneous country group that includes many small, open economies that have not been included in previous studies. Finally, the results are found to be robust to variations in the country sample and to allowing for the possible endogeneity of the adoption of inflation targeting.

There are several policy implications that can be drawn from this analysis. For example, the results suggest that very small, open economies and emerging market economies may have to live with more volatile inflation rates than the larger and more developed countries, as greater exposure to idiosyncratic supply shocks and their small and relatively inefficient foreign exchange markets are likely to continue to contribute to larger and more volatile exchange rate risk premiums. Small and less efficiently traded currencies therefore seem to come at a cost of more volatile inflation rates. This excessive exchange rate volatility and the relatively high degree of pass-through of exchange rate shocks to domestic inflation seem to make inflation control particularly difficult in these countries. Notwithstanding this drawback of being small and less developed, however, the results suggest that a more predictable monetary policy backed by a formal adoption of inflation targeting can contribute significantly to stabilising inflation.

Appendix 7A   Derivation of explanatory variables

7A.1   *Measuring the exchange rate risk premium*

Durlauf and Hall (1988, 1989) suggest a general signal extraction approach for rational expectations present-value models to obtain a lower bound for the variance of the unobserved model noise component. This approach is adopted here, using the standard monetary model of exchange rate determination, which can be represented by a money market relation, a purchasing power parity condition and an interest rate parity condition:

$$m_t - p_t = \varphi y_t - \lambda i_t \tag{7A.1}$$

$$p_t = s_t + p_t^* \tag{7A.2}$$

$$i_t = i_t^* + \mathrm{E}(s_{t+1} | \Theta_t) - s_t + \xi_t \tag{7A.3}$$

where m_t is domestic money, p_t and p_t^* are the domestic and foreign price levels, respectively, y_t is real domestic output, i_t and i_t^* are the short-term domestic and foreign nominal interest rates, respectively, s_t is the multilateral spot exchange rate (the domestic currency price of one unit of a basket of foreign currencies) and $\mathrm{E}(s_{t+1} | \Theta_t)$ denotes rational expectations of the one-quarter-ahead spot rate, conditional on the public information set Θ_t available at time t.

The variable ξ_t denotes deviations from the rational expectations interest rate parity condition, and can be interpreted as a time-varying exchange rate risk premium that investors require to compensate for investing in domestic assets or, alternatively, as capturing deviations from the standard monetary model – i.e. the non-fundamental part of exchange rate behaviour, or exchange rate noise.

From (7A.1) to (7A.3), using the law of iterative expectations and imposing a no-bubble condition, the spot exchange rate can be written as

$$s_t = \sum_{j=0}^{\infty} \left(\frac{\lambda}{1+\lambda} \right)^j \mathrm{E}(f_{t+j} | \Theta_t) + \kappa_t \tag{7A.4}$$

where f_t denotes the economic fundamentals:

$$f_t = \left(\frac{1}{1+\lambda} \right) (m_t - \varphi y_t - p_t^* + \lambda i_t^*) \tag{7A.5}$$

and κ_t is the expected present value of the risk premium ξ_t:

$$\kappa_t = \sum_{j=0}^{\infty} \left(\frac{\lambda}{1+\lambda} \right)^{j+1} \mathrm{E}(\xi_{t+j} | \Theta_t) \tag{7A.6}$$

By defining

$$s_t^* = \sum_{j=0}^{\infty} \left(\frac{\lambda}{1+\lambda} \right)^j f_{t+j} \qquad (7A.7)$$

as the perfect foresight (risk-neutral) exchange rate, the following relation between the actual spot rate and s_t^* is obtained:

$$s_t = E(s_t^* | \Theta_t) + \kappa_t \qquad (7A.8)$$

The assumption of rational expectations implies that

$$E(s_t^* | \Theta_t) = s_t^* - v_t \qquad (7A.9)$$

where v_t is the rational expectations forecast error, which satisfies $E(v_t | \Theta_t) = 0$. Inserting this into (7A.8) gives

$$s_t - s_t^* = \kappa_t - v_t \qquad (7A.10)$$

Hence, a linear projection of $(s_t - s_t^*)$ on the econometrician's information set $\Psi_t \subseteq \Theta_t$ gives

$$\text{proj}(s_t - s_t^* | \Psi_t) = \text{proj}(\kappa_t | \Psi_t) = \hat{\kappa}_t \qquad (7A.11)$$

where $\text{proj}(x_t | \Psi_t)$ denotes an operator that linearly projects x_t onto the information set Ψ_t. A linear projection of $(s_t - s_t^*)$ on Ψ_t is therefore the same as a linear projection of κ_t on Ψ_t. Finally, by defining

$$\zeta_t = \text{proj}(\kappa_t | \Theta_t) - \text{proj}(\kappa_t | \Psi_t) = \kappa_t - \hat{\kappa}_t \qquad (7A.12)$$

the following is obtained:

$$\kappa_t = \hat{\kappa}_t + \zeta_t \qquad (7A.13)$$

The variance of κ_t can therefore be decomposed into two orthogonal components:

$$\sigma_\kappa^2 = \sigma_{\hat{\kappa}}^2 + \sigma_\zeta^2 \qquad (7A.14)$$

Thus, following Durlauf and Hall (1988, 1989), a lower bound on the variance of κ_t is obtained as

$$\sigma_{\hat{\kappa}}^2 \leq \sigma_\kappa^2 \qquad (7A.15)$$

Durlauf and Hall (1989) show that, if the information set Ψ_t includes current values of s_t and f_t, this signal extraction approach corresponds to an optimal Kalman filter smoothing estimate of κ_t (or model noise more generally).

The first step to obtaining this lower bound is to estimate the money market equation (7A.1) for the sample period available to get values of φ and λ, using the dynamic OLS (DOLS) approach of Stock and Watson (1993) with one lead and lag of the data. For those countries for which $\varphi > 1$, a unit income elasticity is imposed. Once estimates of φ and λ have been obtained, data for the fundamentals from equation (7A.5) can be generated using the endpoint approximation suggested by Shiller (1981):[16]

$$s_t^* = \sum_{j=0}^{T-t} \left(\frac{\lambda}{1+\lambda} \right)^j f_{t+j} + \left(\frac{\lambda}{1+\lambda} \right)^{T-t} s_T \qquad (7A.16)$$

The final step is to generate κ_t. This is done by projecting $(s_t - s_t^*)$ on the information set Ψ_t, which is assumed to include a constant and current and four lags of s_t and f_t, using a Newey–West adjusted covariance matrix. This gives the lower bound estimate of σ_κ.

7A.2   *Measuring exchange rate pass-through*

To obtain values for the degree of exchange rate pass-through, a VAR model that includes domestic and foreign inflation, exchange rate changes (annualised quarterly changes), the short-term interest rate and the output gap is estimated for each country for the sample period available, with the lag order chosen using the Akaike information criterion.[17]

To identify the exchange rate shocks, the generalised impulse response approach suggested by Pesaran and Shin (1998) is used. This identification approach is based on the historical covariance structure of idiosyncratic shocks and is not sensitive to the exact ordering of the variables in the VAR as when using a Cholesky ordering (although the results turned out to be very similar). The degree of exchange rate pass-through is measured as the accumulated impulse responses of inflation after two years to a 1 per cent shock to the exchange rate.[18] The reason for using the accumulated shock after two years is that the impulse responses typically peak at around that time and are less sensitive to the exact identification of the contemporaneous shocks than impulse responses at shorter lags.

This VAR approach is not suitable for obtaining the degree of exchange rate pass-through before and after IT used in the panel analysis, however, since the sample period in either sub-sample turns out to be too short for many countries. Instead, I follow Edwards (2006) in using a simple regression approach to obtain estimates of the pass-through coefficient before and after IT. Accordingly, the following equation is estimated (the regressions also include the tax dummies from the VAR analysis):

$$\pi_t = \alpha + [\gamma(L) + \eta D_t]\pi_{t-1} + [\beta(L) + \delta D_t]\Delta s_t$$
$$+ \varphi(L)\pi_t^* + \theta x_{t-1} + u_t \tag{7A.17}$$

where π_t is domestic inflation, π_t^* is foreign inflation, Δs_t denotes nominal exchange rate changes (all three measured as annualised quarterly changes), x_t is the output gap and u_t an error term. D_t is a dummy variable, equal to unity from the first quarter after IT adoption for the IT countries and from 1997Q1 for the non-targeting countries. Finally, $\gamma(L)$, $\beta(L)$ and $\phi(L)$ are lag polynomials to be determined by the data for each individual country. Thus the pass-through coefficient changes from $\beta(1)/(1 - \gamma(1))$ to $(\beta(1) + \delta)/(1 - \gamma(1) - \eta)$ after IT adoption (or from 1997Q1 for the non-targeting countries).

Overall, the resulting pass-through estimates are quite similar to the ones obtained using the VAR approach from above. Estimating (7A.17) for the whole sample without the regime dummy variable gives an average pass-through coefficient of 0.20, compared to 0.23 from the VAR approach. Furthermore, the results from the cross-country analysis are found to be robust to using this estimate of the pass-through coefficient in the cross-country analysis instead of the VAR estimate: all three explanatory variables, including the pass-through coefficient, continue to be highly significant.

7A.3 Measuring monetary policy shocks

To obtain a measure of monetary policy predictability, the following monetary policy rule is estimated for each country:

$$i_t = \gamma i_{t-1} + (1 - \gamma)[(r + \pi^T) + \beta(\mathrm{E}(\pi_{t+1}|\Omega_t) - \pi^T) + \eta x_t] + \varepsilon_t \tag{7A.18}$$

where i_t is the short-term nominal interest rate, r is the equilibrium real interest rate, π_t is the inflation rate, π^T is the targeted inflation rate, x_t is the output gap, $\Omega_t \subseteq \Theta_t$ denotes the monetary policymaker's information set, and ε_t is a random shock to the interest rate – i.e. the monetary policy shock. Many studies, such as that by Clarida, Gali and Gertler (2000), have found that the above rule characterises actual monetary policy in a number of countries quite well.

The policy rule is estimated by IV for the sample period available, assuming that the information set, Ω_t, includes four lags of i_t, π_t and x_t, using a Newey–West adjusted covariance matrix (the results are more or less the same if current values of π_t and x_t are also included in the information set).

An alternative measure of monetary policy predictability tried is obtained using a rolling-window VAR model that includes domestic and import price inflation, the output gap and the short-term interest rate. This gives conditional out-of-sample one-quarter-ahead forecast errors for the short-term interest rate. The empirical results using this measure of monetary policy predictability are practically identical to the ones reported in the chapter.

Appendix 7B   Robustness of cross-country results

Various alterations in model specification or estimation methods were made to check the robustness of the cross-country results. First, I checked whether the results were sensitive to the country sample or possible outliers. To do this I tried adding dummy variables for a number of different country groups to the final model specification in column (10) in Table 7.4. I also re-estimated the final specification excluding every country in the sample, one at a time. I then checked whether the inference was sensitive to possible heteroscedasticity problems, using White's heteroscedastic-consistent standard errors. Finally, I re-estimated the model using two robust estimators (the least absolute deviations and least trimmed squares estimators). The results were not found to be sensitive to any of these alterations.

Second, I tested for a possible endogeneity problem, using instrumental variables. Simple regression results suggested that OPEN, INTER, CONS, SIZE, DIVER, plus a country-group dummy variable for the EMEs and the three countries that have followed a hard currency peg throughout the sample period (Estonia, Hong Kong and Luxembourg), respectively, could serve as instruments. Shea's (1997) test for instrument relevance suggested that the instruments were relevant and the Sargan and J statistics suggested that the instrument set was valid. Finally, the Durbin–Wu–Hausman test failed to reject the null hypothesis that the IV and OLS estimates were equal, suggesting that there were no potential endogeneity problems affecting the consistency of the OLS estimates. Further detail on the robustness analysis can be found in the working paper version of this chapter (www.sedlabanki.is/?PageID=238).

Appendix 7C   Data sources and description

Structural data

PPP-adjusted GDP and PPP-adjusted GDP per capita: 2006 country data from *The World Factbook*: www.cia.gov/cia/publications/factbook.

Trade diversification: A modified Finger–Kreinin index of trade similarities that ranges from zero to one, measuring the extent to which a country's exports structure differs from that of the average country, with higher values indicating a bigger difference from the world average (2005 data from the UNCTAD *Handbook of Statistics*: www.unctad.org/Handbook).

Commodity share of exports: Share of primary commodities, including all food items, agricultural raw materials, fuels and ores and metals (including non-ferrous metals) in total merchandise exports (SITC (Standard International Trade Classification) codes 0, 1, 2, 3, 4 and 68) (2005 data from the UNCTAD *Handbook of Statistics* again).

Individual country data

Individual country data are obtained from different sources, ranging from Reuters/EcoWin, Eurostat and the IFS to national monetary authorities and statistical offices. The sample period is 1985 to 2005, or the period available. All the data (except exchange rates and interest rates) are seasonally adjusted from source or by the author using X–12.

Consumer prices: Headline consumer price index or implicit private consumption deflator, depending on availability.

Import prices: Implicit price deflator of imports of goods and services.

Effective exchange rate index: The value of the domestic currency per one unit of foreign currencies.

Short-term interest rate: The interest rate is a short-term money market rate, commercial bank deposit rate, Treasury bill rate, policy rate, repo rate or swap rate.

Broad money: M2 or M3, depending on availability.

National account data: Private consumption, exports of goods and services, imports of goods and services and GDP at constant prices.

International data

Consumer prices: OECD countries excluding high-inflation countries (Hungary, Mexico, Poland and Turkey) from Reuters/EcoWin.

GDP: Original twenty-five OECD countries for the period 1985 to 2005 from Reuters/EcoWin.

Interest rate: Weighted average of OECD countries (from the OECD's *Main Economic Indicators*), excluding high-inflation countries (Hungary, Mexico, Poland and Turkey), using truncated current OECD country weights.

Prices and GDP are seasonally adjusted from source or by the author using X–12.

Further detail on the data and sources can be found in the working paper version of this chapter (www.sedlabanki.is/?PageID=238).

NOTES

1. The author would like to thank the participants at the Sixth Norges Bank Monetary Policy Conference, and especially the discussant, Benoit Mojon, for helpful comments and suggestions. Thanks must also go to Andreas Mueller, Ásgeir Daníelsson, René Kallestrup, Már Gudmundsson, Tjörvi Ólafsson, Jón Steinsson, Mark A. Wynne and participants at conferences held by the Central Bank of Iceland/IMF, Reykjavík University/Ministry of Commerce, and the Reinventing Bretton Woods Committee for comments on an earlier version of the study. The author is also grateful to Gudjón Emilsson, Helga Gudmundsdottir, Anella Munro, Mary Ryan, Ricardo Vicuna and Sandra Zerafa for assistance with the data. All the remaining errors or omissions are the author's own. The views expressed do not necessarily reflect those of the Central Bank of Iceland.
2. There is one exception, however: Malta is included even though its GDP is only $8.1 billion, in order to add one observation of a very small, open economy.
3. There are a few countries for which shorter sample periods were all that was available, and a second-order VAR with a twenty-quarter horizon is used to preserve degrees of freedom.
4. UNCTAD also publishes an alternative index on trade concentration that is highly correlated with the one used here. The results, therefore, are not sensitive to which index is used. Gerlach (1999) finds a strong correlation between these two measures of trade concentration and the volatility of the terms of trade.
5. Note that the simple correlation may overstate the co-movement for the large economies, as they represent a significant part of the world output measure used here. To adjust for this, an alternative measure of world output excluding the largest economies individually was constructed (using constant US dollar price data obtained from Eurostat). Hence, to calculate the US

correlation, US output was compared to world output excluding the United States. A similar adjustment was made for the other five large economies (France, Germany, Italy, Japan and the United Kingdom). This led to a significant reduction in the correlation for Japan, the United Kingdom and the United States, but had no effect on the measured correlation for the other three countries.

6. This variable can equivalently be interpreted as the variability of exchange rate noise – i.e. the non-fundamental part of exchange rate movements.

7. A potentially important targeting variable for many emerging market and small, open economies could be the exchange rate. As a test for the robustness of the chosen measure of monetary policy shocks to omitted variables, the real exchange rate was therefore added to the policy rule and information set. The resulting variability of policy shocks was practically identical to the one used.

8. Individual country estimates for each variable are available from the author; Pétursson (2008) provides most of them as well.

9. A common practice in the literature is to use logarithm transformations of the dependent variable (whether inflation or inflation volatility) to reduce the effects of large outliers on the regression results, although a drawback is that very low observations would receive undue weights. The rate is used in this study, as there are no extremely large observations in this sample, but using logarithm transformations gives very similar results, both in the cross-country analysis described here and in the panel analysis discussed in the next section.

10. See Bernanke *et al.* (1999), Corbo, Landerretche and Schmidt-Hebbel (2001), Truman (2003), Vega and Winkelried (2005), Pétursson (2005), Batini and Laxton (2007) and Mishkin and Schmidt-Hebbel (2007), to name just a few studies that provide empirical support for the important role of IT in these developments, while Ball and Sheridan (2005) provide a more sceptical view. Many studies have also analysed the effects of inflation targeting on other key macroeconomic variables. See, for example, Mishkin and Schmidt-Hebbel (2007) for a recent overview of the main results.

11. Changes in indirect taxes create jumps in the measured volatility of headline inflation that can lead to a bias in the analysis. To avoid this, I have removed the effects of known indirect tax changes in the rolling-window standard deviations. These tax changes are for Australia (2000Q3), Canada (1991Q1 and 1994Q1/Q2), Japan (1997Q2), Norway (2003Q1 and 2003Q2) and the United Kingdom (1990Q2).

12. Pétursson (2009) finds that the adoption of IT has not led to increased volatility in the exchange rate risk premium, whereas membership of EMU has contributed significantly to declining volatility in the exchange rate risk premium.

13. It should be kept in mind that some of these countries do not pursue a truly independent monetary policy for some part of the sample period (e.g. the EMU countries), or pursue a monetary policy that is similar to that of the IT countries (e.g. the European countries, Japan and the United States). This may reduce the number of truly independent observations in

the control group and make the identification of the treatment effect more difficult. Including the emerging market countries is therefore important to help reduce this potential identification problem.

14. Allowing for interactive terms between $D_{i,t}$ and $Z_{i,t-1}$ does not give any additional significant non-linear effects.

15. Estimating the panel model for the inflation rate, for comparison with previous studies (without the additional controls), gives a highly significant IT effect (p-values of 1 per cent or lower). The long-run effect equals 3.3 p.p. for the first control group and 4.3 p.p. for the second control group. This can be compared to the result of roughly 5 p.p. found by Mishkin and Schmidt-Hebbel (2007) for a similar treatment group. Pétursson (2005), also using a panel set-up but with a relatively narrow set of industrial countries as a control group, finds a smaller effect of 1 to 2 p.p. long-run reduction in inflation.

16. In some cases the terminal value of (7A.16) tends to jump for the last few observations. To avoid this problem, data for 2006 and observations for what is available for 2007, plus artificial data, are used to generate three further years of data. The artificial data are constructed by assuming a 2 per cent annual steady-state rate of inflation, a 3 per cent steady-state rate of growth, a 5 per cent (the sum of inflation and output growth) steady-state growth rate of money and unchanged interest and exchange rates from the last observations. The results are not sensitive to these assumptions.

17. The VAR includes the special dummy variables for changes in indirect taxes discussed in note 11. The dummy variables are unity in the given quarter and zero elsewhere, except for the Canadian 1994Q1 and 1994Q2 dummies (0.75 in 1994Q1 and 0.25 in 1994Q2). In addition, there are dummy variables to account for large outliers in the case of Chile (1991Q1 and 1991Q2), Malta (2001Q3), New Zealand (1998Q4), South Korea (1997Q4 and 1998Q1) and Thailand (1997Q3 and 1998Q2).

18. The results for Slovenia are missing, as it turns out that a stable VAR model over the short sample period available is not obtainable (interest rate data are available only since 1998) and the estimated impulse responses are implausibly high and very sensitive to slight changes in model specification and the sample period used.

REFERENCES

Acemoglu, D., and F. Zilibotti (1997). 'Was Prometheus unbound by chance? Risk, diversification and growth', *Journal of Political Economy*, 105(4): 709–51.

Aghion, P., P. Bacchetta and A. Banerjee (2004). 'Financial development and the instability of open economies', *Journal of Monetary Economics*, 51(6): 1077–106.

Alesina, A., and L. Summers (1993). 'Central bank independence and macroeconomic performance: some comparative evidence', *Journal of Money, Credit and Banking*, 25(2): 151–62.

Ball, L., and N. Sheridan (2005). 'Does inflation targeting matter?', in B. Bernanke and M. Woodford (eds.). *The Inflation-Targeting Debate*: 249–82, Chicago: University of Chicago Press.

Batini, N., and D. Laxton (2007). 'Under what conditions can inflation targeting be adopted? The experience of emerging markets', in F. Mishkin and K. Schmidt-Hebbel (eds.). *Monetary Policy under Inflation Targeting*: 1–22. Santiago: Banco Central de Chile.

Bernanke, B., T. Laubach, F. Mishkin and A. Posen (1999). *Inflation Targeting: Lessons from the International Experience*. Princeton, NJ: Princeton University Press.

Betts, C., and M. Devereux (2001). 'The international effects of monetary and fiscal policy in a two-country model', in G. Calvo, R. Dornbusch and M. Obstfeld (eds.). *Essays in Honor of Robert A. Mundell*: 9–52. Cambridge, MA: MIT Press.

Bowdler, C., and A. Malik (2005). 'Openness and inflation volatility: cross-country evidence'. Economics Working Paper no. 2005–W14. Oxford: Nuffield College, Oxford University.

Cecchetti, S., P. Hooper, B. Kasman, K. Schoenholtz and M. Watson (2007). 'Understanding the evolving inflation process'. Chicago: Graduate School of Business, University of Chicago.

Clarida, R., J. Gali and M. Gertler (2000). 'Monetary policy rules and macroeconomic stability: evidence and some theory', *Quarterly Journal of Economics*, 115(1): 147–80.

Corbo, V., O. Landerretche and K. Schmidt-Hebbel (2001). 'Assessing inflation targeting after a decade of world experience', *International Journal of Finance and Economics*, 6(4): 343–68.

Durlauf, S., and R. Hall (1988). 'Bounds on the variances of specification errors in models with expectations'. Unpublished manuscript. Palo Alto, CA: Stanford University.

    (1989). 'Measuring noise in stock prices'. Unpublished manuscript. Palo Alto, CA: Stanford University.

Edwards, S. (2006). 'The relationship between exchange rates and inflation targeting revisited'. Working Paper no. 12163. Cambridge, MA: NBER.

Fracasso, A., H. Genberg, and C. Wyplosz (2003). *How Do Central Banks Write? An Evaluation of Inflation Reports by Inflation Targeting Central Banks*. Geneva: CIMB.

Fry, M., D. Julius, L. Mahadeva, S. Roger and G. Sterne (2000). 'Key issues in the choice of monetary policy frameworks', in L. Mahadeva and G. Sterne (eds.). *Monetary Policy Frameworks in a Global Context*: 1–216. London: Routledge.

Gagnon, J., and J. Ihrig (2004). 'Monetary policy and exchange rate pass-through', *International Journal of Finance and Economics*, 9(4): 315–38.

Gerlach, S. (1999). 'Who targets inflation explicitly?', *European Economic Review*, 43(7): 1257–77.

Kaminsky, G., C. Reinhart and C. Végh (2004). 'When it rains, it pours: procyclical capital flows and macroeconomic policies'. Working Paper no. 10780. Cambridge, MA: NBER.

Kuttner, K., and A. Posen (1999). 'Does talk matter after all? Inflation targeting and central bank behavior'. Staff Report no. 88. New York: Federal Reserve Bank of New York.

Lucas, R. (1982). 'Interest rates and currency prices in a two-country world', *Journal of Monetary Economics*, 10(3): 335–59.

McConnell, M., and G. Perez-Quiros (2000). 'Output fluctuations in the United States: what has changed since the early 1980s?', *American Economic Review*, 90(5): 1464–76.

Mishkin, F., and K. Schmidt-Hebbel (2002). 'One decade of inflation targeting in the world: what do we know and what do we need to know?', in N. Loayza and R. Soto (eds.). *Inflation Targeting: Design, Performance, Challenges*: 117–219. Santiago: Banco Central de Chile.

(2007). 'Does inflation targeting make a difference?', in F. Mishkin and K. Schmidt-Hebbel (eds.). *Monetary Policy under Inflation Targeting*: 291–372. Santiago: Banco Central de Chile.

Pesaran, M., and Y. Shin (1998). 'Generalized impulse response analysis in linear multivariate models', *Economics Letters*, 58(1): 17–29.

Pétursson, T. (2005). 'Inflation targeting and its effects on macroeconomic performance'. Study no. 2005/5. Vienna: Société Universitaire Européenne de Recherches Financières.

(2008). 'How hard can it be? Inflation control around the world'. Working Paper no. 40. Reykjavík: Central Bank of Iceland.

(2009). 'Does inflation targeting lead to excessive exchange rate volatility?'. Reykjavík: Working Paper no. L3. Central Bank of Iceland.

Roberts, J. (2006). 'Monetary policy and inflation dynamics', *International Journal of Central Banking*, 2(3): 193–230.

Romer, D. (1993). 'Openness and inflation: theory and evidence', *Quarterly Journal of Economics*, 108(4): 869–903.

Schaechter, A., M. Stone and M. Zelner (2000). 'Adopting inflation targeting: practical issues for emerging countries'. Occasional Paper no. 202. Washington, DC: IMF.

Shea, J. (1997). 'Instrument relevance in multivariate linear models: a simple measure', *Review of Economics and Statistics*, 79(2): 348–52.

Shiller, R. (1981). 'Do stock prices move too much to be justified by subsequent changes in dividends?', *American Economic Review*, 71(3): 421–36.

Stock, J., and M. Watson (1993). 'A simple estimator of cointegrating vectors in higher order integrated systems', *Econometrica*, 61(4): 783–820.

Taylor, J. (2000). 'Low inflation, pass-through and pricing power of firms', *European Economic Review*, 44(7): 1389–408.

Terra, C. (1998). 'Openness and inflation: a new assessment', *Quarterly Journal of Economics*, 113(2): 641–8.

Truman, E. (2003). *Inflation Targeting in the World Economy*. Washington, DC: Institute for International Economics [IIE].

Vega, M., and D. Winkelried (2005). 'Inflation targeting and inflation behavior: a successful story?', *International Journal of Central Banking*, 1(3): 153–75.

Végh, C. (1988). 'Government spending and inflationary finance: a public finance approach'. Working Paper no. 88/98. Washington, DC: IMF.

8   Targeting inflation in Asia and the Pacific: lessons from the recent past

Andrew Filardo and Hans Genberg[1]

8.1   Introduction

Central banks in Asia and the Pacific have overwhelmingly chosen inflation as the principal objective of monetary policy. Some central banks have declared themselves to be inflation targeters, while others pursue their objective without referring to this particular label. Moreover, whether or not they refer to their strategy as inflation targeting, central banks in the region have chosen diverse approaches to achieving their inflation targets, for example with respect to how explicit the target is, the choice of inflation indicator and the choice of instrument. All this suggests that the region constitutes a good sample with which to examine the lessons from the experiences of central banks that have adopted formal inflation targeting and those with more eclectic approaches to targeting inflation.

To this end, we examine monetary policy institutional changes in Asia and the Pacific to assess whether these can be traced to subsequent inflation performance. Section 8.2 highlights trends in twelve regional economies towards greater central bank focus on inflation control, institutional independence and transparency over the past two decades. Contrasting the experiences of the six formal inflation-targeting economies with those of the six others, section 8.3 explores the impact of these trends on inflation dynamics and on private sector inflation expectation formation. Section 8.4 then addresses some policy implications associated with the evolving views of targeting inflation in the region, and concludes that our results add to the growing body of evidence that formal inflation targeting is not the only monetary policy framework capable of delivering price stability; in other words, targeting inflation is important, but there are many ways to skin that cat.

144

8.2   Monetary policy objectives and institutional arrangements in Asia-Pacific

Objectives and strategies

As shown in Table 8.1, all but one of the twelve central banks in the region have price stability as a target for monetary policy. While for a majority of them the target appears unambiguously to refer to domestic price stability, in the case of three central banks – the People's Bank of China, Bank Indonesia and Bank Negara Malaysia – the goal is stated as maintaining the stability of the value of the currency, which could mean either the internal value in terms of goods and services (the price level) or the external value (the exchange rate). Bank Indonesia makes it explicit that the term refers to both aspects. Two central banks – the Reserve Bank of India and Bank Negara Malaysia – state that an adequate supply of credit to the economy is also an explicit goal of the central bank. Finally, the Hong Kong Monetary Authority (HKMA) puts exclusive emphasis on exchange rate stability (vis-à-vis the US dollar) and pursues this goal by means of a currency board arrangement.

The strategies that have been adopted to achieve the objectives differ. Six central banks are self-proclaimed inflation targeters – the Reserve Bank of Australia, Bank Indonesia, the Bank of Korea, the Reserve Bank of New Zealand, Bangko Sentral ng Pilipinas and the Bank of Thailand. While the Reserve Banks of Australia and New Zealand are 'old hands' at inflation targeting, having started in 1993 and 1990 respectively, the other four central banks are relative newcomers, with South Korea starting in 1999, Indonesia and Thailand in 2000 and the Philippines in 2002. All inflation-targeting central banks use an interest rate as the operating target for monetary policy.

The Monetary Authority of Singapore has been described by outside observers as an inflation targeter, albeit one that follows an unorthodox strategy in pursuing price stability by announcing the level as well as the rate of change of the target band for the nominal effective exchange rate of the Singapore dollar.

The People's Bank of China (PBC) uses growth rates of monetary aggregates as intermediate targets and typically employs several instruments in the implementation of its monetary policy: the exchange rate, the required reserve ratio, interest rates and open market operations. While it is undoubtedly the case that these instruments are not completely independent of each other, controls on the domestic financial system and on international capital flows arguably give the PBC additional degrees of freedom in implementing its monetary policy.

Table 8.1 *Central bank policy objectives*

Central bank	Policy objective	Objective as stated on the central bank's official website	IT?
Reserve Bank of Australia	Price stability	To focus on price (currency) stability while taking account of the implications of monetary policy for activity and, therefore, employment in the short term.	Yes, 1993
People's Bank of China	Value of the currency	To maintain the stability of the value of the currency and thereby promote economic growth.	No
Hong Kong Monetary Authority	Exchange rate stability	The primary monetary policy objective . . . is to maintain exchange rate stability.	No
Reserve Bank of India	Price stability and adequate credit supply	Maintaining price stability and ensuring an adequate flow of credit to productive sectors.	No
Bank Indonesia	Price stability and exchange rate stability	One single objective of achieving and maintaining stability of the Rupiah value, [which] comprises two aspects [: . . .] stability of Rupiah value against goods and services and . . . stability of the exchange rate of the Rupiah against other currencies.	Yes, 2000
Bank of Japan	Price stability	The Bank of Japan Law states that . . . monetary policy should be 'aimed at, through the pursuit of price stability, contributing to the sound development of the national economy'.	No
Bank of Korea	Price stability	The Bank of Korea takes price stability as the most important objective of its monetary policy. The Bank of Korea Act stipulates price stability as the purpose of the Bank of Korea.	Yes, 1999
Bank Negara Malaysia	Price stability and exchange rate stability	To issue currency and keep reserves safeguarding the value of the currency; to promote monetary stability and a sound financial structure; to influence the credit situation to the advantage of the country.	No
Reserve Bank of New Zealand	Price stability	The Reserve Bank of New Zealand Act 1989 specifies that the primary function of the Reserve Bank shall be to deliver 'stability in the general level of prices'.	Yes, 1990
Bangko Sentral ng Pilipinas	Price stability	The primary objective of BSP's monetary policy is to promote a low and stable inflation conducive to a balanced and sustainable economic growth.	Yes, 2002
Monetary Authority of Singapore	Price stability	The primary objective of monetary policy in Singapore is to promote price stability as a sound basis for sustainable economic growth.	No
Bank of Thailand	Price stability	Setting the monetary policy direction which is consistent with the nation's economic conditions, with the ultimate objective of maintaining price stability and sustainable economic growth.	Yes, 2000

Source: Adapted from Genberg and He (2009).

Central bank governance and independence

The ability of a central bank to achieve its objective depends in part on the institutional environment in which it operates. A large literature has investigated the link between measures of economic performance – usually inflation – and various indicators of central bank governance and independence (CBGI). The general conclusion is that central bank independence tends to be associated with better inflation performance, although there is some evidence that this result applies to developed economies only (Cukierman, Webb and Neyaptı: 1992).

A recent paper in this genre focuses on Asia and the Pacific (Fry 1996 is a forerunner in this respect). Ahsan, Skully and Wickramanayake (2008: hereafter ASW) study thirty-six countries in the region, including eleven of the countries in our sample.[2] The authors construct indexes of CBGI using twenty-seven different variables in order to capture different aspects of governance and independence. Apart from an overall index they tabulate indicators of (i) legal independence ('Legal' in the figures that follow), (ii) political independence ('Political'), (iii) independence to pursue price stability as the main and sole objective ('Price stability'), (iv) independence to pursue exchange rate policy ('Forex policy'), (v) independence in the control of monetary policy instruments and non-obligation to finance government deficits ('Deficit finance') and (vi) accountability and transparency ('Account. and transp.'). Using these indicators in regression analysis, the authors find that each of them is negatively associated with the inflation rate of the corresponding economy.

Rather than pursuing the link between CBGI and macroeconomic performance in the region, we examine the evolution of the ASW indexes with a view to detecting any trend over time and to seeing whether there is any appreciable difference between the inflation-targeting central banks and the others. We also look at whether the crisis in the region in 1997/8 acted as a wake-up call for the authorities in the most affected countries, in the sense that they altered the governance structure of their respective central banks after the crisis.

Figure 8.1 shows the overall value of the CBGI index for two years, 1996 and 2005; the overall value is the simple average of the six sub-indexes. The first date is chosen to represent the situation before the Asian financial crisis and the second is the latest available value in the ASW data set. With the exception of India and New Zealand, for which there is no change, all countries show some improvement over time. This is consistent with the notion that policymakers have, at least in part, accepted the view that greater central bank independence is desirable. The sets of bars on the right-hand side of the figure show

148   *Filardo and Genberg*

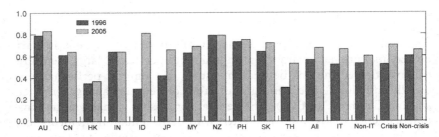

Figure 8.1 Index of central bank independence and governance

Notes: AU = Australia; CN = China; HK = Hong Kong; IN = India;
ID = Indonesia; JP = Japan; MY = Malaysia; NZ = New Zealand; PH
= the Philippines; SK = South Korea; TH = Thailand; All = average
for all countries; IT = average for inflation-targeting countries; Non-
IT = average for non-inflation-targeting countries; Crisis = average
for Indonesia, Malaysia, Philippines, South Korea and Thailand; Non-
crisis = average for Australia, China, Hong Kong, India, Japan and New
Zealand. There were no data available for Singapore.
Source: Ashan, Skully and Wickramanayake (2008).

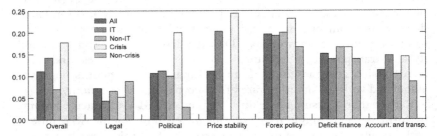

Figure 8.2 Differences in the overall index between 1996 and 2005
Source: Ashan, Skully and Wickramanayake (2008).

averages of five groups of jurisdictions: all jurisdictions in the sample,
the inflation-targeting countries, central banks that are not inflation
targeters, the countries most affected by the Asian financial crises
(Indonesia, Malaysia, the Philippines, South Korea and Thailand) and
the 'non-crisis' countries. These bars reveal that both inflation-targeting
and crisis countries have experienced larger changes in the overall index
than their respective counterparts. Figure 8.2 explores these differences
at a more disaggregated level.

The bars in Figure 8.2 represent the change in the values of the indexes
from 1996 to 2005 for all countries, inflation-targeting and non-inflation-
targeting countries, and crisis and non-crisis countries. The figure shows

that there are improvements in all aspects of CBGI in all groups, with the exception of the ability to pursue price stability in the non-inflation-targeting central banks. Particularly large increases are seen in (i) political independence in the crisis countries, (ii) the ability to pursue price stability in inflation-targeting and crisis countries (note that there is a large overlap in these groups, as the inflation targeting classification is based on the situation in 2005) and (iii) the ability to determine exchange rate policy independently.

The differences between country groupings, not surprisingly, are also illuminating. Compared to their non-inflation-targeting counterparts, central banks that are inflation targeters have been given more independence to pursue price stability as the sole objective of monetary policy. In general, inflation-targeting central banks have become more accountable and transparent relative to their non-inflation-targeting colleagues. This latter finding is consistent with the notion that, while greater accountability and transparency are desirable for all central banks (see Figure 8.2), they have been given particular emphasis in the context of inflation-targeting monetary policy strategies. With respect to legal independence and the ability to set monetary policy independently from fiscal policy (the 'Deficit finance' bars), the greatest changes have actually occurred for non-inflation-targeting central banks, somewhat contrary to the idea that a lack of fiscal dominance is particularly important for inflation-targeting strategies.[3]

The differences in the CBGI indexes as between the 'old' inflation-targeting countries in the region (Australia and New Zealand) and the newcomers were very large before the crises and have fallen substantially thereafter, the only exception being the legal independence sub-index. This confirms that the introduction of inflation targeting coincided with a more general overhaul of the central banks' governance structures.

Comparing the crisis with the non-crisis countries confirms that the Asian financial crisis did seem to lead to particularly significant reforms in the areas of political independence and the ability to set price stability objectives, the latter probably due to the overlap between crisis countries and new inflation-targeting countries.

Transparency Dincer and Eichengreen (2007) focus on the determinants and effects of central bank transparency in a large (100) sample of central banks from developed and developing economies, including those in our sample. Their empirical analysis implies that greater transparency reduces inflation volatility and persistence. Focusing exclusively on central banks in the Asia-Pacific region, Filardo and Guinigundo (2008) offer a more recent assessment of the transparency and communication strategies on the basis of a survey of the central banks themselves. The responses to the survey give a snapshot of current practices in the region and indicate that central banks use 'a fairly sophisticated set of communication strategies . . . [reflecting] . . . the greater conscious effort within the policy making circle to clearly communicate policy-relevant information to financial markets, the media and the public at large' (Filardo and Guinigundo 2008: 33). Although it does not contain an explicit comparison with past communication practices, the message of the Filardo–Guinigundo study is consistent with the statistics reported above, which show a general increase over time in the transparency and accountability of central banks in Asia and the Pacific.

Finally, it is of interest to note the study by Garcia-Herrero and Remolona (2008), which argues that central banks in Asia and the Pacific have learned to conduct policy so as to take advantage of the expectations channel of monetary policy – i.e. to become more transparent as to their future policy intentions. Their conclusion is based partly on examining the content of central banks' policy statements and partly on evidence showing that yield curves reflect expectations of future policy interest rates. They also note, however, that 'policy statements still appear to contain a larger element of surprise than do macroeconomic news, suggesting that there is still scope for central banks in the region to communicate more effectively the way they interpret economic data and the strategies that guide their decisions' (Garcia-Herrero and Remolona 2008: 13).

Summary   Inflation control is the main objective of all but one of the central banks in the region but the strategies for achieving this objective vary. Half the twelve central banks characterise their policy as one of inflation targeting, and use a short-term interest rate as the policy instrument. Other central banks, with the exception of the HKMA, target inflation and use a more eclectic set of policy instruments.

Whether they are inflation targeters or 'merely' target inflation, most central banks in the region have gained legal and/or political independence during the past decade. They have also seen improvements in other aspects of governance usually associated with an enhanced ability to achieve inflation control.

Although there are differences in the evolution of central bank independence and governance between the inflation-targeting central banks and the other central banks in our sample, it is an open question whether these differences have resulted in differences in macroeconomic performance, in particular inflation performance, between the corresponding economies. In the next section we present evidence bearing on this question as well as on the more specific issue of whether the adoption of inflation targeting as such confers some additional benefits.

8.3   Assessing the comparative performance of Asia-Pacific inflation targeters

There is no doubt that inflation performance in inflation-targeting countries in the region has been remarkable when compared to the pre-inflation-targeting days. In this section, we examine various statistical measures of inflation stability to explore whether the adoption of explicit inflation targeting was particularly effective in achieving the goal of inflation control in Asia and the Pacific. In addition to examining performances before and after the adoption of inflation targeting, we contrast the experiences in controlling inflation between inflation-targeting and non-inflation-targeting central banks in the region.

Inflation performance among Asia-Pacific inflation-targeting economies was strong

For the inflation-targeting central banks, two performance criteria are central: the achievement of their inflation targets and reducing inflation volatility (i.e. fostering inflation stability). Despite the challenging policy environment of the last several years, inflation-targeting central banks have been able to avoid some of the inflation control problems they used to experience in the past.

Hitting inflation targets

Inflation performance can be assessed in a variety of ways. The most stringent is whether the numerical target was hit. Figure 8.3 illustrates the fact that, by this metric, Asia-Pacific ITers have been far from perfect. Nearly all the inflation-targeting central banks breached the announced inflation targeting bands, with some of the deviations being quite large and persistent.

Such deviations from target may be too strict a criterion for assessing performance, however. Indeed, inflation-targeting central banks in the region have not generally defined success as always being at the target or even inside the target bands. Rather, the more conventional approach is to announce a target range over a medium-term horizon. For example, Australia's target range is 2 to 3 per cent for headline CPI inflation 'over the medium term', and South Korea's is 2.5 to 3.5 per cent in terms of a

152   *Filardo and Genberg*

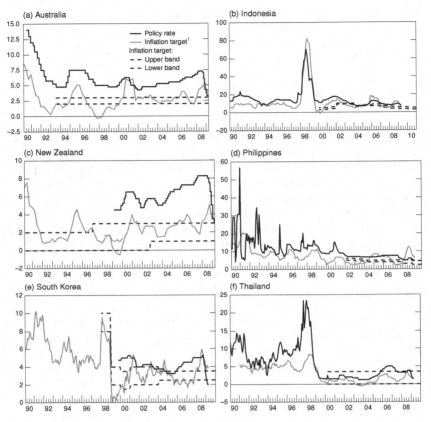

Figure 8.3 Inflation, inflation targets and policy rates

Notes: Inflation is defined as the twelve-month percentage change in the CPI index. Policy rates are given in per cent per annum. Between 1998 and 1999 New Zealand was monitoring the CPI the excluding credit services.

[1] In terms of the headline CPI, except in the case of Thailand, where it refers to core inflation.

Sources: CEIC and national data.

three-year average annual inflation for headline inflation. Operationally, central banks choose a path for policy rates that puts inflation on a general trajectory towards the middle of the inflation target range.

Using this looser criterion, one could reasonably argue that central banks in the region have achieved their respective goals. Figure 8.3 shows that inflation rates in the region have consistently gravitated to the centre of the target ranges whenever deviations arose. The success stands in stark contrast to the more volatile inflation behaviour evident prior to the adoption of inflation targeting.

Notwithstanding this success, it is noteworthy that the deviations from the inflation targets have hardly been symmetric. While there have been breaches both on the upside and the downside, most have been on the upside. Moreover, the biggest deviations from target have generally been on the upside.

There may be several explanations for this asymmetry. One view is that the period of inflation targeting has been so short that a full range of symmetric shocks, especially large and persistent ones, has yet to be experienced. This view would argue that more symmetry would be observed over time. Another view would suggest that, despite the constraining features of explicit inflation-targeting frameworks, central banks are still somewhat more concerned about sub-par GDP growth and deflation than periodic but modest breaches of the upper end of the inflation target ranges. This would suggest that, on average, inflation would exceed the middle of the inflation target range.

Achieving lower inflation volatility

Another performance criterion is inflation volatility. Here the record is far clearer. Inflation volatility has generally declined across the region. Indeed, the GDP-weighted average of inflation volatility from 1986 to 1990 is 64 per cent higher than that in 2008.

The decline in inflation volatility was hardly monotonic across the region during the period, however. For example, the Philippines and New Zealand certainly achieved much better inflation performance with respect to this measure of volatility, but Indonesia exhibited higher volatility after the adoption of inflation targeting than in the early 1990s, although part of the earlier stability may have been somewhat illusory because of the extensive use of administered prices for important staples.

Comparative performance with non-ITers

The experience of the non-inflation targeters over the same period is equally noteworthy. Inflation volatility for the non-inflation-targeting central banks was either low or falling across the region. While this behaviour underlines the favourable inflation environment in the region as a whole, it does raise questions about the marginal contribution of explicit inflation-targeting regimes in achieving this outcome. In other words, it is not clear that the adoption of inflation targeting per se has yielded qualitatively different inflation performance – at least with respect to the inflation volatility criterion – from that in the non-inflation-targeting countries.

In terms of rates of inflation, non-inflation-targeting central banks have shown roughly the same success as inflation-targeting central banks in achieving low inflation (see Figure 8.4). For the non-ITers, inflation rates have generally been lower in the past ten years than they were in the previous decade. Two notable exceptions to this trend towards greater success at controlling inflation are evident for inflation-targeting and non-inflation-targeting central banks alike: the Asian financial crisis in the late 1990s led to a spike in inflation, especially in Indonesia, Thailand and South Korea; and, more recently, the boom-bust in commodity prices led to a transitory rise in inflation.

Another similarity between the inflation-targeting and non-inflation-targeting central banks is that short-term policy interest rates have become lower and smoother for those central banks using this rate as their primary policy tool. In the 2000s most policy interest rate cycles exhibited lower frequency swings than in the 1980s and early 1990s. This central bank behaviour was seen outside the region as well, and was consistent with the greater central bank transparency documented in the previous section. The greater clarity about the goals and policy frameworks of central banks has been seen as elevating the role of private sector expectations in influencing economic decisions (Woodford 2003). The similarity in behaviour between inflation-targeting and non-inflation-targeting central banks is consistent with the findings of Eijffinger and Geraats (2006), that remarkable enhancements of public communication during the period from 1998 to 2002 in central banks from advanced industrial economies were achieved without significant changes in formal disclosure policies in central bank legislation.

Delving deeper into the inflation record   Given the close comparative performance of the inflation targeters and the other central banks, we now delve more deeply into the characteristics of each country's inflation process to see if more subtle differences between ITers and non-ITers emerge. We look first at various measures of inflation persistence and examine how inflation persistence has evolved over time, focusing on the permanent and transitory components of the inflation process. Then we explore the implications of the choice of inflation targeting on private sector expectations, using panel regression methods. Theory would suggest that a significant change in monetary policy regimes, such as the adoption of explicit inflation targeting, should influence the time series behaviour of inflation and the expectations of the private sector.

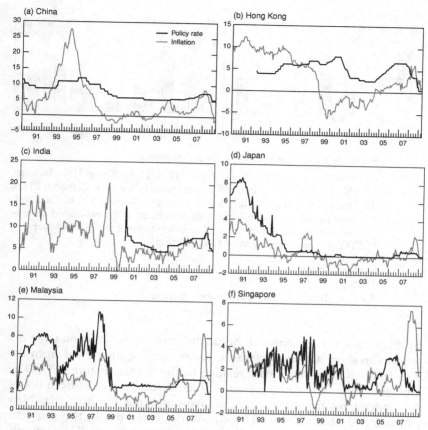

Figure 8.4 Inflation and benchmark rates

Notes: Inflation is defined as the twelve-month percentage change in the CPI index. Benchmark rates are given in per cent per annum. China: one-year working capital; Hong Kong: discount window base rate; Japan: uncollateralised overnight rate; India: repo rate; Malaysia: overnight interbank rate; Singapore: overnight rate.

Sources: Datastream and national data.

AR(1) persistence measures

One conventional measure of persistence is the AR(1) parameter of an autoregressive representation of the inflation process:

$$\pi_t = C + \beta \pi_{t-1} + \zeta_t$$

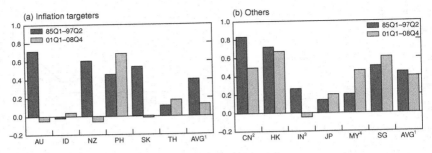

Figure 8.5 Changing AR(1) inflation persistence

Notes: AU = Australia; CN = China; HK = Hong Kong; ID = Indonesia; IN = India; JP = Japan; MY = Malaysia; NZ = New Zealand; PH = the Philippines; SG = Singapore; SK = South Korea; TH = Thailand. Inflation persistence on this measure is defined as the estimated autoregressive coefficient for annualised quarter-on-quarter CPI inflation.
[1] AVG = cross-country average coefficient.
[2] 93Q2–97Q2.
[3] 89Q2–97Q2.
[4] 85Q2–97Q2.
Sources: BIS calculations and national data.

By this measure, persistence of the inflation process for inflation targeting appears to show a more systematic decline during the period from the mid-1980s to the mid-1990s relative to the 2000s (Figure 8.5). The average decline across the region for the inflation targeters from 0.4 to 0.1 understates the much more dramatic declines for Australia, New Zealand and South Korea. These countries stand out in two respects. First, they are well developed, economically and financially, especially when compared to the rest of Asia and the Pacific. Second, they have adopted strong inflation-targeting regimes. The Philippines, by way of contrast, is a small, open economy that has experienced much greater inflation variability. In panel (b) of Figure 8.5, the non-inflation-targeting central banks have experienced very little change in the estimated AR(1) persistence across the two sub-periods.

One interpretation of this result is that inflation expectations were more firmly anchored in some inflation-targeting central banks. The firmer the anchor, the smaller the low-frequency drift in inflation expectations. Some conventional theories suggest that inflation represents a mixture of three stochastic processes:

$$\pi_t = E(\pi_{t+1}) + \gamma y_t + \varepsilon_t \tag{8.1}$$

For credible inflation targeters, expected inflation might be considered nearly a constant and y, the output gap, would be trendless (i.e. an I(0) variable); the error term would be transitory white noise. In this case, actual inflation persistence would largely reflect the inherent persistence of the output gap. If central banks were not so credible, however, then inflation expectations might move gradually up and down with the rate of inflation. In this situation, the AR persistence would be higher than that implied by the output gap alone. From this vantage point, the decline in the AR persistence of the inflation-targeting central banks could be seen as a sign of relative success in achieving inflation-fighting credibility. However, this cannot be the whole story, because some economies characterised by a low AR persistence estimate, such as Indonesia and India, have relatively chequered histories of inflation control.

IMA(1,1) persistence measures

To investigate the role of the persistent component in inflation expectations (i.e. the permanent stochastic component) and a transitory component (i.e. I(0) variables), we turn to an alternative measure of persistence along the lines developed by Stock and Watson (2007). Although the full implementation of Stock and Watson's trend-cycle model proved to be unstable for many of the Asia-Pacific economies, a simplified integrated moving average, or IMA(1,1), representation fared much better.

In this implied IMA(1,1) representation, changes in inflation from period to period are decomposed into two statistical components: one that arises from a shift in the permanent stochastic trend component of inflation and another one that arises from purely serially uncorrelated transitory fluctuations:

$$\Delta \pi_t = a_t + \theta a_{t-1} = \Delta \tau_t + \Delta \eta_t \tag{8.2}$$

Underlying this representation is a model of the rate of inflation, $\pi_t = \tau_t + \eta_t$. The permanent component, τ_t, is envisaged to evolve as a random walk, $\tau_t = \tau_{t-1} + \varepsilon_t$, with ε_t and η_t being serially uncorrelated error terms. Under these assumptions, the statistical model of interest can be estimated as an IMA(1,1).

Some inferences about the relative role of the permanent and transitory components can be inferred from the moving average (MA) estimate of θ. If θ is close to zero, the permanent component plays a relatively large role in driving the inflation variance. The greater $|\theta|$, the greater the proportion of the inflation variance accounted for by the transitory component; intuitively, this would correspond to inflation fluctuating around its mean.

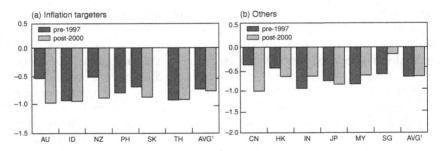

Figure 8.6 Changing IMA(1) inflation persistence

Notes: AU = Australia; CN = China; HK = Hong Kong; ID = Indonesia; IN = India; JP = Japan; MY = Malaysia; NZ = New Zealand; PH = the Philippines; SG = Singapore; SK = South Korea; TH = Thailand. Inflation persistence on this measure is defined as the estimated IMA(1,1) coefficient through unobserved component decomposition on the basis of a ten-year sample subject to data availability.

[1] AVG = cross-country parameter mean.

Sources: BIS calculations and national data.

Figure 8.6 plots the MA parameter estimates for the inflation-targeting and non-inflation-targeting economies. Various noteworthy features of the two panels stand out. First, the MA estimates are fairly large and the averages are between −0.5 and −1.0 for inflation-targeting and non-inflation-targeting central banks alike. This suggests that the role of permanent and transitory shocks is not exactly unique to whether a central bank chooses to adopt inflation targeting explicitly or not.

Second, for Australia, New Zealand and South Korea the absolute value of the MA estimate increases, as might be expected with a successful inflation-targeting regime. A time-varying measure of the MA parameter (not shown) confirms a nearly monotone change for each country since the end of the 1990s.

Third, a notable exception to the pattern observed for the inflation-targeting economies is the Philippines. This appears to reflect the more challenging inflation conditions for this small, open economy. During the past decade inflation rate swings have been pronounced and persistent, more often undershooting or overshooting the inflation target bands than being inside them. Moreover, the inflation target bands have moved down during the decade, which could induce a bias towards a more prominent permanent component.

Fourth, for Indonesia and Thailand the estimate of θ is nearly −1 and reflects the fairly favourable inflation behaviour before and after the tumultuous period of the Asian financial crisis in the late 1990s (note that the regression samples exclude this period). Somewhat surprisingly, the MA estimate for Indonesia does not appear to have fallen even though inflation target bands have been both increased and then decreased over the past decade. These findings indicate that transitory shocks, often related to large relative price adjustments, have been a very important part of these countries' inflation records.

Finally, Hong Kong and Singapore also stand out as having relatively low estimates of θ. This might not be so surprising given their exchange rate regimes. Hong Kong has adopted a currency board, which has kept the bilateral exchange rate with the US dollar within a narrow corridor. Singapore, in contrast, controls its exchange rate against a trade-weighted basket of currencies of major trading partners; the Monetary Authority of Singapore uses this exchange rate as its policy tool to promote price stability and sustainable economic growth.

The technical nature of the discussion in this section should not obscure the basic point. The time series econometric findings indicate that inflation performance has improved in Asia and the Pacific, and that improvements in regional price stability do not appear to correspond closely to the decision of some central banks to adopt formal inflation targeting.

Exploring the cross-sectional dimension of inflation expectations

While instructive, the time series measures of inflation performance above are *ex post* realisations that may obscure some of the *ex ante* benefits of explicit inflation targeting. Indeed, one of the putative advantages of transparency associated with inflation-targeting regimes is the self-reinforcing impact on private sector inflation expectations. Theory suggests that greater clarity about the intentions of a central bank should lead to reduced dispersion of private sector expectations, which in turn should promote the firmer anchoring of inflation expectations and, hence, greater inflation control. We explore this role of explicit inflation targeting in the Asia-Pacific region by comparing the impact of inflation targeting on the cross-sectional inflation expectations of the private sector using survey data from Consensus Economics.

Does inflation targeting account for the narrowing of the forecast distributions?

One natural question is whether shifts in the cross-sectional distribution of inflation forecasts are correlated in some way with the adoption of formal inflation targeting in the region. Figure 8.7 illustrates the shifts

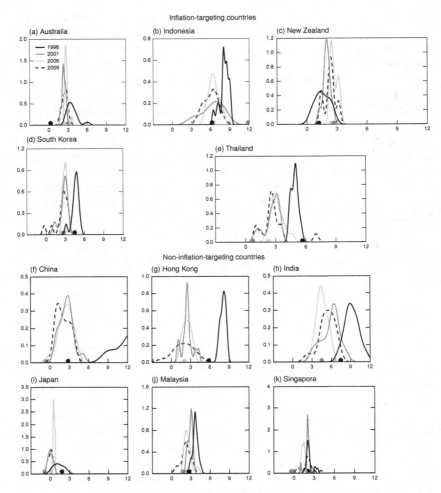

Figure 8.7 Cross-sectional distribution of next year's inflation expectations

Notes: Estimated distribution of individual forecasts from Consensus Economics for January. The dots represent the actual inflation corresponding to the forecast.
Sources: Consensus Economics, BIS calculations and national data.

in the location as well as the shapes of the distributions.[4] The estimated distributions represent the range of views that private sector forecasters had for inflation for the years 1996, 2001, 2006 and 2008 (the forecasters were surveyed in the January of each preceding year).

All else the same, the adoption of inflation targeting should lead to a shift to the left, indicating a move to lower inflation, and a sharpening of the distribution, indicating less dispersion among the private sector forecasters. Indeed, this general tendency can be seen in the behaviour of the estimated cross-sectional distributions for the region. A few caveats are important to note, however.

First, we have data only from mid-1990 onwards, owing to the data limitations of the Consensus Economics surveys. At the date that our data begin, both New Zealand and Australia had adopted explicit inflation targeting several years previously. For New Zealand, which adopted inflation targeting early on, the cross-sectional distribution shifts a little to the right from 1996, reflecting the raising of the upper inflation range bound from 2 per cent to 3 per cent in the mid-1990s and the raising of the lower bound in the early 2000s from 0 per cent to 1 per cent. Notwithstanding the shift in the modes of the estimated distributions, the dispersion of inflation expectations noticeably sharpened over time. For Australia, even though the inflation target bands did not change, the cross-sectional dispersion of inflation expectations sharpened too.

For Indonesia, South Korea and Thailand, which adopted inflation targeting in the 2000s, the shift in the mode of the cross-sectional distributions is much more dramatic. In addition, there is less evidence of a monotonic sharpening of the distributions.

Turning to the non-inflation-targeting countries, the shifts and shape changes are much more diverse. For low-inflation economies such as Japan, Malaysia and Singapore, the cross-sectional evidence does not appear to be out of line with the experiences of the inflation-targeting countries. In general, there were fairly sharp distributions of inflation expectations with some shifting of their modes. For China, Hong Kong and India, there was a pronounced shift to the left after the mid-1990s. The dispersion for China and India remained fairly wide in the 2000s while Hong Kong has experienced periods of sharpness and periods of diffuse expectations. These results are also consistent with the findings of Mishkin and Schmidt-Hebbel (2007), that inflation-targeting economies do not necessarily attain better monetary policy performance relative to highly successful non-inflation targeters.

Overall, the evolution of the private sector forecast distributions is consistent with the view that there has been a greater focus on inflation control in the region. To delve further into the links between these shapes of the forecast distributions and the monetary policy regime, it is important to distinguish the role of the regime from the size of the nominal shocks hitting the economy in each year. To achieve this, we now turn to panel regression methods.

Econometric exploration of the dispersion of beliefs of private forecasters of inflation

An immediate difficulty in assessing the statistical significance of the changing inflation forecast distributions is converting the graphical shapes into a useful statistical metric. We use the Kullback–Liebler (KL) divergence metric.[5] A higher KL statistic indicates a reduction in the dispersion of private sector views about the likely inflation outcomes – i.e. a sharper shape of the forecast distribution.

Armed with these KL divergence statistics, we use panel regression analysis to examine the relationship between information in the KL divergence and the timing of the adoption of explicit inflation-targeting regimes in the region. The estimated equation is

$$KLn_t^i = C^i + \beta_j KLc_t^i + \gamma_{IT} I_t^i + \gamma_{AIT} \sum_{n=1}^{11} I_t^n + e_t^i \qquad (8.3)$$

where KLn_t^i is the KL divergence statistic that applies to the subsequent year's inflation forecast distribution for each country i, KLc_t^i is a similar statistic for the current year's inflation forecast distribution, I_t^i is a dummy variable that indicates whether a country i had adopted a formal inflation-targeting regime at time t and $\sum_{n=1}^{11} I_t^n$ is an aggregator of the inflation targeting dummy variables. In the reported results, we also allow for interactions between these dummy variables and the constant (C) and slope parameters (β_j). We use panel regressions with fixed effects and report the coefficient estimates along with t-statistics calculated with robust standard errors.

In Table 8.2, the results for the January Consensus Economics surveys are consistent with the view that the adoption of explicit inflation targeting was correlated with less dispersion of private sector forecasts of inflation. The coefficient estimates for KL levels have the intuitively plausible signs, and standard statistical diagnostics indicate a good fit.

The positive and statistically significant sign on KLc (β) reflects the fact that uncertainty about the inflation environment is seen to be fairly persistent from year to year. The estimate is robust to the alternative specifications in columns (2) to (5) in Table 8.2.

The inflation targeting dummy coefficient (γ_I) is statistically significant. The positive sign of the parameter in column (2) indicates that, if a country is an inflation targeter, one-year-ahead inflation expectations

Table 8.2 *The impact of the adoption of inflation targeting on the cross-sectional distribution of inflation forecasts in Asia-Pacific*

$$KLn_t^i = C^i + \beta KLc_t^i + \gamma_{IT} I_t^i + \gamma_{AIT} \sum_{n=1}^{11} I_t^n + \beta_{IT} \left(I_t^i \times KLc_t^i \right) + \beta_{AIT} \left(\sum_{n=1}^{11} I_t^n \times KLc_t^i \right) + e_t^i$$

			Using January sample				
	(1)	(2)	(3)	(4)	(5)	(6)	(7)
			KL in levels			ΔKL	
β	0.62 (6.8)	0.61 (6.8)	0.57 (6.1)	0.57 (6.1)	0.58 (4.7)	0.87 (4.6)	0.86 (4.6)
γ_{IT}		0.21 (4.2)		0.06 (0.9)	0.01 (0.6)		0.17 (2.2)
γ_{AIT}			0.05 (2.8)	0.05 (2.1)	0.05 (2.1)		-0.0 (-0.5)
β_{IT}					-0.04 (-0.3)	-0.13 (-0.8)	-0.13 (-0.8)
β_{AIT}						-0.08 (-1.9)	-0.08 (-1.9)
Obs.	163	163	163	163	163	149	149
R^2	0.66	0.66	0.66	0.67	0.67	0.34	0.34

Notes: t-statistics in parentheses based on robust standard errors.

are, on average, distributed with less dispersion, owing to the higher predicted KLn (of 0.21).

Including the inflation targeting aggregator dummy yields intriguing results. The aggregator dummy variable is a common regional dummy for all countries in the panel regression, which contrasts with the country-specific inflation targeting dummy I_t^i. The coefficient on the common aggregator dummy (γ_{AIT}) in specifications (3) to (5) in Table 8.2 is positive and statistically significant. The sign is intuitively plausible. As an indicator of the region's focus on inflation control, there was a general sharpening of private sector inflation forecast distributions. The coefficient may look rather small compared to the coefficient on the inflation targeting dummy variable, but in the 2000s the value of the aggregator dummy is 5 (it is not 6 owing to the paucity of data for the Philippines); to get a sense of the quantitative importance in the 2000s, multiplying γ_{AIT} by five is a useful benchmark.

In addition, the inclusion of the aggregator dummy variable in the panel regression leads to a reduction in the size and statistical significance of γ_I. The smaller size and lower statistical significance in specifications (4) to (5) of γ_I indicate that the aggregator dummy variable dominates the country-specific inflation targeting dummies.

These findings support the view that a common regional trend toward greater inflation control, as might be reflected in the aggregator dummy, could account for many of the similarities in inflation performance across the region. (This conclusion using the aggregator dummy was confirmed in results (not shown) using an analogously constructed regional price stability variable as defined in section 8.2).[6] Such a view would downplay the importance of adopting explicit inflation-targeting regimes as a necessary condition for improved inflation outcomes. This can be seen as being consistent with the basic conclusions of Ball and Sheridan (2005). They find evidence in OECD countries in favour of the hypothesis that greater emphasis on price stability, but not the adoption of inflation targeting per se, is important.

Specifications (6) to (7) include interactions between the country-specific and regional inflation targeting dummies with the slope estimates on ΔKLc_t^i (namely β_{IT} and β_{AIT}):

$$\Delta KLn_t^i = C^i + \beta \Delta KLc_t^i + \gamma_{IT} I_t^i + \gamma_{AIT} \sum_{n=1}^{11} I_t^n + \beta_{IT} \left(I_t^i \times \Delta KLc_t^i \right)$$

$$+ \beta_{AIT} \left(\sum_{n=1}^{11} I_t^n \times \Delta KLc_t^i \right) + e_t^i \qquad (8.4)$$

This first-difference specification is useful for examining the robustness of our conclusions from the panel regressions in levels. Intuitively, if central banks can anchor inflation expectations more firmly, inflation expectations at longer horizons should be less sensitive to transitory inflation shocks. In other words, the dispersion of inflation expectations for future years should be less variable to short-term inflation variability. In terms of the KL metric, this translates into a prediction that changes in KLn should become less sensitive to variations in KLc as central banks become more transparent and more interested in inflation stability. This prediction is borne out in Table 8.2, with β_{AIT} being negative and statistically significant. This indicates that the slope of the relationship between ΔKLn_t^i and ΔKLc_t^i became flatter $(\beta + \beta_{AIT})$ as the region as a whole became more focused on inflation control.

Taken as a whole, the panel results appear sufficiently strong to underline the basic point that central banks in the region have been effective in getting out their message about price stability, and, in the process, have had an important impact on private sector expectations. In turn, private sector expectations arguably have been supportive of the central bank price stability goals.[7] Further research is needed to establish more subtle and possibly intricate interlinkages among changing central bank practices and communication strategies, private sector expectations and macroeconomic stability.

Overall, the results confirm that greater emphasis on targeting inflation – though not explicit inflation targeting – has been important in Asia and the Pacific. Central bank inflation-fighting credibility appears to have risen generally, reflecting the intellectual, social and economic consensus that central banks control the inflation destiny of a country and that low, stable inflation promotes sustainable growth. The initial motivation for this study remains an open empirical question, though: what is the marginal contribution of explicit versus implicit inflation targeting? The panel evidence in this section suggests that the contributions are not so obvious, even though we cannot rule out the possibility that further research might find that subtle differences could be linked back to the particular features of explicit inflation-targeting regimes.

Conclusions from the empirical evidence

The empirical evidence confirms that inflation performance in Asia and the Pacific has been admirable. The greater focus on inflation control has translated into a lower and more stable inflation environment.

However, it is difficult to document big differences in inflation performance over the past decade between explicit ITers and non-ITers. This is not to say there were no differences, but that the differences appear to be rather subtle.

Additional research and experience with inflation targeting will help to clarify the reasons for these performance patterns. In the interim, two competing, though not mutually exclusive, views are supportable. One is that inflation dynamics in the region have been dominated by common nominal shocks. The swings in import prices during the mid-2000s and then the boom-bust cycle in global commodity prices towards the end of the 2000s surely left their imprint on the inflation record.

Another view emphasises the role of central bank mindsets. Over the past decades central banks in the region and elsewhere saw a broad intellectual, social and economic consensus emerge about the importance of inflation control. Not only was low, stable inflation seen as a key policy goal, but it was also felt that central banks had the means to achieve the goal.

In addition, supportive changes in central bank governance (as documented in section 8.2) and in the general policy environment have taken place. Of particular importance in the past decade, Asia-Pacific policymakers have strengthened medium-term policy frameworks, not least those associated with fiscal probity and financial stability. With respect to the fiscal side, the region has adopted sound fiscal practices that have strengthened sustainability and lowered debt levels. With respect to financial stability, soundness in terms of the region's banking system has been achieved, through prudent capital provisioning and a reduction in non-performing loans. All these developments have not only strengthened the ability of central banks to achieve their primary goal of inflation control but also helped to boost the public's confidence in the underlying competence of the region's policymakers.

Hence, the Asia-Pacific evidence indicates that there are many different ways to ensure price stability. In other words, there is more than one way to skin a cat.

8.4   Policy implications and conclusions

Although the past decade has witnessed greater interest and determination in controlling inflation, central banks' thinking about their responsibilities continues to evolve. Exchange rate misalignments associated with periods of sustained capital inflows have long been of concern because of their impact on inflation and economic growth, and because of fears that the inflows may suddenly stop or reverse, leading to stress in local banking systems (see Committee on the Global Financial System (CGFS) 2009). The international financial crisis has naturally led to an even greater focus on the nexus between monetary stability and financial stability, not least owing to some views that the crisis could be attributed in part to lax monetary policy conditions during periods when inflation appeared to be consistent with medium-term trends. This section considers some challenges facing Asia-Pacific central banks as they seek to maintain a primary focus on inflation in a context in which concerns about financial system stability, the potential volatility of international capital flows and the variability of economic growth are taking on greater importance in pursuit of central bank policy objectives.

Some would argue that pursuing multiple independent goals with monetary policy – i.e. with one policy interest rate – is futile, or at least inadvisable. The classic assignment problem in macroeconomics emphasises the need for one independent policy tool for each independent policy goal. Moreover, others might argue that such competing goals would naturally lead central banks to lose sight of their primary goal of price stability.

There are two basic counter-arguments to this view. First, even though the logic of the assignment problem is impeccable, the theoretical assumptions are rather stark when compared to the practical trade-offs facing central banks. Goals related to financial, foreign exchange and capital flow volatility are not truly independent of the goal of price stability. Achieving price stability is a much more difficult task if stresses associated with these other factors are present in the economy. For example, if a strict focus on inflation control over a certain time horizon is associated with a build-up of imbalances in the economy that leads to inflation (or deflation) pressures further out in the future, then it may be argued that monetary policy faces a trade-off between near-term and longer-term inflation stability. Second, some central banks in the Asia-Pacific region have been able to achieve strong inflation performance while at the same time placing an emphasis on exchange rate volatility, capital flows and financial stability concerns (e.g. India, Indonesia and China). This success should not be ignored. Indeed, with respect to exchange rate stability and inflation control, Singapore and, of course, Hong Kong stand out.

This is not to say that central banks have an absolute or, in most cases, a comparative advantage in taking on these particular goals. Nonetheless, the experience in the region demonstrates that one need not abandon inflation control when taking some actions to address these alternative, albeit subordinate, goals.

A key question for the future is how best to incorporate these experiences from the region, and elsewhere, into our evolving understanding of the conduct of monetary policy. Is it necessary to construct monetary policy frameworks that focus exclusively on inflation control (as in strict inflation-targeting regimes) or is it possible to construct monetary policy frameworks that reflect the wide range of trade-offs that central banks face? If so, what would these frameworks look like?

The answer to the questions depends on how central banks perceive their responsibilities other than strict inflation control. A few stylised approaches help to illuminate the key issues. At one extreme is a view that central banks need to compartmentalise their policy priorities. A lexicographical approach provides a succinct way to summarise this perspective (Fischer 2008). Under this view, central banks would target inflation, and only when inflation was under control would they take counter-cyclical actions intended to smooth output. Likewise, only when inflation and output stability had been achieved would central banks entertain issues associated with exchange rates, capital flows and financial stability. While such priorities may have a theoretical appeal in certain stylised models of the economy, it is less clear that they could be implemented in a context in which the evolution of inflation, output and measures of financial stability depend on each other in a complex fashion. Moreover, such a set of priorities appears to be at odds with the actions taken by central banks during the international financial crisis.

An alternative approach is to trade off output and inflation stabilisation smoothly, while emphasising the key risks associated with auxiliary goals for a range of relevant policy horizons. As noted above, exchange rates, capital flows and financial stability issues have implications for inflation and output at some horizon. The policy conundrum is how best to weigh medium- to long-term concerns against those, say, at the one- to two-year horizon. One could interpret the fact that most central banks in the Asia-Pacific region have adopted price stability targets over the *medium term* as being consistent with the view that strict inflation control at all horizons is not paramount but, rather, that there are a range of concerns that need to be addressed. Finally, from a technical point of view, such preferences may be best thought of as being state-dependent (Svensson 2003; Disyatat 2005).

We would argue that the monetary policy responses in the region and elsewhere to the international financial crisis have been consistent with state-dependent preferences, but from a somewhat different motivation. Consider central banks that may find themselves in somewhat awkward positions at times when government authorities may not have adequately addressed regulatory or external issues, which then result in a crisis environment (Filardo 2009). At that point, central banks may have a comparative advantage (in the short run) in addressing such concerns with monetary policy tools. Of course, central banks would not like to be in such a situation, and moral hazard issues certainly arise. As the international financial crisis has shown, however, sometimes a central bank is called on to address such extreme situations.[8]

Practically, what might these state-dependent priorities mean for central banks, especially those that have adopted strict inflation targeting in the past? One implication is that inflation-targeting regimes need to be flexible. Overly strict, non-state-dependent criteria are not realistic.

Another implication is that conventional inflation-targeting regimes and state-dependent priorities may be odd bedfellows. While it is possible to argue that flexible inflation-targeting regimes can take into account economic and financial undershooting and overshooting, it is not so clear that stretching the reach of such policy regimes contributes in the best way to transparent and hence credible policymaking. Rather, monetary frameworks that explicitly reflect a full range of relevant policy risks would seem appropriate, especially given the different horizons that apply to short-term inflation and output fluctuations, on the one hand, and the longer-term boom-bust dynamics, on the other. Frameworks such as those adopted by the Bank of Japan (a two-perspective approach) and the European Central Bank (a two-pillar approach) would appear more consistent with these types of concerns. In these regimes, there is a clear distinction between the inflation and output dynamics that economists have a reasonable handle on, and those phenomena that defy easy characterisation with conventional forecasting tools. In the case of the latter, the nature of the low-probability/high-impact risks are qualitatively different from standard macro-risks on short-term inflation and output.

However, the suggestion that multi-pillar or multi-perspective monetary policy frameworks should arguably dominate strict inflation-targeting frameworks does not imply that one size fits all. Quite the contrary; a broader implication from the wide range of policy experiences in Asia-Pacific is that monetary policy strategies may have to be tailored to each central bank depending on the nature of the economic environment. For example, instrument rules would naturally look different in economies depending on a diverse set of factors, not the least being: whether the country is a commodity producer or not; the degree of exposure to food price shocks; the exposure to volatile international capital flows, which in turn depends on the sophistication of the domestic financial system in dealing with such shocks; and openness and the role of the exchange rate in the inflation and growth process. These factors are, furthermore, likely to change over time, which means that monetary policy strategies cannot be static, even if the main objective of policy remains price stability.

NOTES

1. The views expressed in this chapter are those of the authors and do not necessarily represent the views of the Bank for International Settlements. The authors thank Már Gudmundsson, James Yetman, Anella Munro and participants of the Sixth Norges Bank Conference on Monetary Policy for helpful comments. The authors also thank Marek Raczko for superb research assistance.
2. Singapore is not included. Ahsan, Skully and Wickramanayake (2008) also include an exhaustive survey of the literature relating to CBGI and economic performance.
3. This result is not the consequence of non-inflation-targeting central banks catching up. On the contrary, they have a higher index in both 1996 and 2005.
4. The distributions are estimated with kernel density estimators.
5. For more information about the methodology behind the KL statistic, see Filardo and Guinigundo (2008).
6. The basic thrust of the results using the aggregated IT dummies is obtained using the aggregated price stability and the monetary policy independence

variables described earlier in the chapter, but with somewhat less statistical support; these variables are highly correlated with the inflation targeting dummy variables. The results using the full sample of months from Consensus Economics are also consistent with the results from the January sample.

7. The general narrowing of the forecast distributions could also correspond with biases among professional forecasters towards the benefits of formal inflation targeting, and hence the surveys could yield overly conservative dispersions of inflation forecasts. While this is possible, we also find some evidence in our sample that the reduction in dispersion is accompanied by an increased precision of forecasting accuracy, after correcting for the size of nominal shocks.

8. In some respects, this motivation is one justification for central banks to take on the responsibility of lender of last resort. Recent central bank behaviour raises the practical question, though, of whether the central bank should be lender of first resort, or somewhere in between.

REFERENCES

Ashan, W., M. Skully and J. Wickramanayake (2008). 'Does central bank independence and governance matter in Asia Pacific?' Research Paper no. 2008–27. Milan: Centro Paolo Baffi, Università Bocconi.

Ball, L., and N. Sheridan (2005). 'Does inflation targeting matter?', in B. Bernanke and M. Woodford (eds.). *The Inflation-Targeting Debate*: 249–82. Chicago: University of Chicago Press.

CGFS (2009). 'Capital flows and emerging market economies'. CGFS Paper no. 33. Basel: CGFS, BIS.

Cukierman, A., S. Webb and B. Neyaptı (1992). 'Measuring the independence of central banks and its effect on policy outcomes', *World Bank Economic Review*, 6(3): 353–98.

Dincer, N., and B. Eichengreen (2007). 'Central bank transparency: where, why, and with what effects?' Working Paper no. 13003. Cambridge, MA: NBER.

Disyatat, P. (2005). 'Inflation targeting, asset prices and financial imbalances: conceptualising the debate'. Working Paper no. 168. Basel: BIS.

Eijffinger, S., and P. Geraats (2006). 'How transparent are central banks?', *European Journal of Political Economy*, 22(1): 1–21.

Filardo, A (2009). 'Household debt, monetary policy and financial stability: still searching for a unifying model', in BIS. *Household Debt: Implications for Monetary Policy and Financial Stability*: 31–50. BIS Paper no. 46. Basel: BIS.

Filardo, A., and D. Guinigundo (2008). 'Transparency and communication in monetary policy: a survey of Asian central banks'. Mimeo. Basel: BIS.

Fischer, S. (2008). 'The Phillips curve and Israeli monetary policy'. Presentation at the conference 'Understanding inflation and the implications for monetary policy: a Phillips curve retrospective', sponsored by the Federal Reserve Bank of Boston. Cape Cod, MA, 11 June.

Fry, M. (1996). 'Governance at the macro level: assessing central bank independence in Pacific Asia and other developing areas'. Discussion Paper no. 96–27. Birmingham: Department of Economics, University of Birmingham.

Garcia-Herrero, A., and E. Remolona (2008). 'Managing expectations by words and deeds: monetary policy in Asia and the Pacific'. Mimeo. Bilbao: Banco Bilbao Vizcaya Argentaria.

Genberg, H., and D. He (2009). 'Monetary and financial cooperation among central banks in East Asia and the Pacific', in R. Rajan, S. Thangavelu and R. Parinduri (eds.). *Exchange Rate, Monetary and Financial Issues and Policies in Asia*: 247–70. Singapore: World Scientific Publishing.

Mishkin, F., and K. Schmidt-Hebbel (2007). 'Does inflation targeting make a difference?', in F. Mishkin and K. Schmidt-Hebbel (eds.). *Monetary Policy under Inflation Targeting*: 291–372. Santiago: Banco Central de Chile.

Stock, J., and M. Watson (2007). 'Why has US inflation become harder to forecast?', *Journal of Money, Credit and Banking*, 39(supplement 1): 3–33.

Svensson, L. (2003). 'Monetary policy and real stabilization', in Federal Reserve Bank of Kansas City. *Rethinking Stabilization Policy*: 261–312. Kansas City: Federal Reserve Bank of Kansas City.

Woodford, M. (2003). *Interest and Prices: Foundations of a Theory of Monetary Policy*. Princeton, NJ: Princeton University Press.

9 Inflation targeting and asset prices

Christopher Allsopp

9.1 Introduction

The framework of (flexible) inflation targeting has been widely credited with facilitating, or even causing, the 'Great Moderation'. In public perception, hubris has now been followed by nemesis – and the inflation-targeting framework is increasingly being blamed for the current financial crisis and the world recession. Many argue that the basis of monetary policy has to change – especially in the direction of giving more weight to asset prices in setting interest rates (see, for example, Wolf 2009). Common suggestions include the idea that the interest-rate-setting authorities should 'lean against the wind' of asset price movements, especially in the expansionary phase of a boom (Wadhwani 2008), or that the authorities should adopt a sufficiently long horizon that they can take asset prices into account within their mandate (see, for example, Bean 2003). Others call for a much more radical recasting of the objectives and procedures of monetary policy.

This chapter argues that the debate is in serious danger of going off track. The hubris, if hubris there was, arose not in thinking that interest-rate-setting policy was vastly improved, but in believing that flexible inflation targeting was (in macroeconomic policy terms) all that was needed – that other aspects of macroeconomic and prudential policy could be neglected. Clearly, the success of inflation targeting allowed the fiscal authorities to disengage from the traditional macroeconomic concerns of inflation control and stabilisation. It also allowed the regulators to concentrate on micro-regulation (as the macroeconomic consequences of regulatory failure seemed to be someone else's responsibility). However, it would be odd to blame the successes of the monetary framework for inadequacies elsewhere.

Of course, given what happened, the system was at fault. With systematic failure, it is particularly important to focus on what went wrong before prescribing wholesale change. For example, it has long been taken for granted that a macroeconomic management system, such as flexible inflation targeting, could not be expected to work with fiscal policy pulling in the opposite direction or out of control (see, for example, Dodge 2002). Similarly, regulation, including regulation to address externalities and other market failures within the banking and financial sector, is an essential part of the system, without which a regime of inflation targeting could not be expected to function well. To state the obvious, if the system needs to be fixed, a key question is: what parts of it need to be redesigned, and what parts do not?

This means that the debate over the future of inflation targeting involves at least three areas of policy: broadly speaking, interest rate policy, fiscal policy and financial regulation. A key question is about *assignment* – the assignment of responsibilities, objectives and policy instruments to various institutions. A second question is about policy design within each area of responsibility or competence. A third question is about coordination between the three areas. This chapter concentrates largely on the assignment issues and the role of interest rate policy.

9.2 What is inflation targeting? Why was it a vast improvement?

A key problem in macroeconomic policy, arguably the key problem, is the reconciliation of two competing aims – the credible control of the price level/inflation in the medium term and the stabilisation of output and prices, especially output. The search for a stable financial framework that would deliver this complex set of objectives has been subject to a bewildering series of twists and turns (including U-turns) over the past decades. Cutting a very long story short, flexible inflation targeting eventually emerged as the preferred solution to the complex political and economic issues involved.[1]

What is now known as flexible inflation targeting evolved in different ways. In the United States, after the 'Great Inflation' of the 1970s, it was essentially established as a set of behavioural reactions that came to be understood by financial markets. Famously, the Taylor rule (Taylor 1993) was originally put forward as a description of Federal Reserve behaviour. Even now, the Fed has not, formally speaking, adopted inflation targeting – though it is commonly taken as a model by many countries that have. By contrast, in many other countries, such as New Zealand and the United Kingdom, inflation targeting involved institutional change – regime change by design. By and large, the experience of inflation targeting has, until recently, been extremely positive.

There is, or was, an emerging consensus on what might be termed 'best practice' inflation targeting. It normally involves the delegation of responsibility for medium-term control over inflation (or price stability) to an independent central bank using interest rates as its primary instrument to influence inflationary pressure (for a more extended account, see, for example, Allsopp 2002). In practice, the interest rate policy reaction function is embedded in an institution that operates with 'constrained discretion'. Formal mandates, such as those of the ECB and the Bank of England, are – usually – hierarchical or lexicographical with the primary objective being price stability, and *subject to that* (or *without prejudice to that*), a responsibility for stabilisation.

Theory played a role. At its simplest, the system can be represented by just three equations: an IS relationship, a Phillips-type relationship and the interest rate policy reaction function. The reaction function needs to have certain properties – such as the Taylor principle.[2] Variants abound, ranging from simple rules, such as the Taylor rule, via set-ups involving assumed loss functions to fully micro-founded forward-looking approaches. The connection between theory and practice is close enough to be highly productive, but it is not exact. Given the importance of expectations, it is widely argued that central bank behaviour should be 'rule-like' in the sense of Taylor (1993) and 'predictable' in the sense of Woodford (2003). Both of these require credibility and transparency.

I want to make a few points before addressing the problems posed by imbalances, by asset price movements and the recent crisis. The first is about the system of flexible inflation targeting. At a high level of generality, flexible inflation targeting is about the management of demand to meet the twin objectives of price stability and stabilisation. There is nothing in this that requires that the instrument of policy should be the short-term interest rate or that the agent should be the central bank (or part of it). Both these are pragmatic choices – though sensible ones. In principle, different control instruments could be used within a similar framework – for example, a fiscal instrument, or multiple instruments. In principle, other institutions could be assigned responsibility for the complex trade-offs in achieving inflation control and as much stabilisation as is compatible with it. To illustrate, Singapore uses the exchange rate, in effect, as an instrument within an inflation-targeting framework;[3] fiscal policy committees have been proposed for countries within EMU (Wyplosz 2002), and these would, of course, not be part of the central bank. A broad perspective on what constitutes an inflation-targeting framework is needed, given that many central banks are now using quantitative easing as an additional instrument and that, with nominal interest rates close to or at the 'lower bound' of zero, fiscal instruments are being used to counter deflationary forces. I return to these issues below.

The second point can be expressed as a question: what accounts for the apparent success of flexible inflation targeting and – by revealed preference – its popularity? The story, as so often, is different for the United States from what it is for most other countries. In the United States, the central bank was already 'independent' and already effectively responsible for managing the complex trade-offs between inflation control and stabilisation that we are concerned with (its mandate includes price stability and economic growth as well as financial stability).[4] After some unsuccessful experiments with monetary targets, policy moved fairly naturally into a system that gave overriding priority to inflation control over the medium term (implied by natural-rate versions of the Phillips curve) while delivering as much stabilisation as possible. This is a story of better policy supported by better theory and better empirical analysis (though for some time theory appeared to lag behind policy practice).

For most other countries, I would argue that the *assignment* problem was key. One of the problems historically was that different arms of government frequently appeared to pull against each other, and, even when Treasuries were in overall charge, the tensions were unresolved. Given the increasing commitment to non-accommodating policies against inflation, and the failure of both monetary targeting and exchange rate targeting (which, with hindsight, look like particularly badly designed interest rate policy reaction functions), the time was – how shall I put it? – ripe for the delegation of these important aspects of macroeconomic policy to independent entities with clear mandates. There was also a powerful push from theory in the direction of delegation as a way of increasing credibility.[5] In the 'new consensus macroeconomics', the assignment is also particularly simple: the delegation of responsibility for inflation control (and, subject to that, stabilisation) to an independent institution, with a single instrument of control: the policy interest rate. It is so simple that, given the mandate and a modicum of transparency, the (conditional) policy reaction function is easily discernible, and came to be anticipated by financial markets and the public.

The other important aspect of this assignment is that the inflation-targeting authority *does not have* responsibility for other important economic variables, such as the current account deficit, household indebtedness, asset prices or – for the purist – financial stability. Of course, central banks typically have multiple responsibilities; but the inflation-targeting arm needs to be effectively separate, even though it would obviously take into account what the other arm was doing. (In the UK system, for example, it is the Monetary Policy Committee (MPC) that is independent; and, in UK practice, the MPC – *qua* MPC – does not comment on fiscal policy.)

The contention here is that this clear and simple assignment of roles and responsibilities, which was hard won, is the thing that is most at risk in the political/economic debates over the future role of monetary (and, specifically, interest rate) policy.

9.3   Monetary and other policies in the new consensus assignment

In the consensus, it is the job of the interest-rate-setting arm of the central bank (the MPC in the case of the United Kingdom, the FOMC in the United States) to take everything into account. This includes international shocks, the exchange rate, real estate prices, oil and other commodity price movements, regulatory changes and fiscal policy. (Practice may be faulty, but the principle is clear.) In the case of fiscal policy, this means that fiscal actions are 'internalised' by the monetary policy reaction function (Allsopp and Vines 2005). In the United Kingdom, the relationship between fiscal and monetary policy has been described as akin to 'Stackleberg leadership' by Bean (1998b) (see also Balls and O'Donnell 2001 for an 'official' view of the interaction). Before the recent crisis, the coordination between fiscal and monetary policy was described by the Treasury as particularly good – and as functioning much better than in earlier decades.

The adoption of inflation targeting implied, as far as the fiscal authorities were concerned, delegating the responsibility for the inflation control/stabilisation trade-off to the interest-rate-setting authorities. In many cases, this was greeted with relief. Treasuries could concentrate on 'good housekeeping', and on the traditional distributional and resource allocation functions of the fiscal system.[6] Under the new assignment, fiscal policy did not appear to 'matter very much' (Allsopp and Vines 2005: 486) for the traditional macroeconomic concerns of inflation control and stabilisation.

The assignment, or set-up, did imply, however, that the fiscal authorities were constrained by the monetary policy reaction function. For example, a fiscal expansion would, predictably, lead to higher interest rates (and a higher exchange rate) than otherwise. Therefore, to the extent that the time inconsistency problem of monetary policy was solved by delegation (see Bean 1998a and Vickers 1998), the fiscal authorities were similarly constrained.

By the same mechanism, it was also the case that it was the fiscal stance that determined the medium-term level of interest rates (the 'neutral rate') and therefore, in an open economy, the exchange rate. Thus, any concern over an external imbalance was essentially the responsibility

of the Treasury, not of the monetary authorities. In practice, this responsibility, built into the assignment, was rarely admitted.[7]

In principle, too, the fiscal authorities could intervene fiscally to offset shocks to the economy – e.g. to offset a savings shock, or to affect
asset prices. There are certainly cases in which a fiscal intervention might
be preferred to an interest rate change, and, under the new consensus
assignment, this would be a decision for the fiscal authorities. Such fiscal interventions would be taken into account (or 'internalised') by the
monetary authorities, however.[8]

Similar considerations apply to the assignment of responsibility for
financial regulation – for which there is, however, great diversity in
practice.[9] The regulatory system is not the responsibility of the interest-
rate-setting authorities, but the institution charged with inflation control
and macro-stabilisation does, of course, need to take the regulatory system and changes in it into account in setting interest rates. Thus, if
financial regulation is procyclical, this should affect interest-rate-setting
behaviour; and interventions by the regulator would be treated by the
inflation-targeting institution in much the same way as fiscal policy
changes (or other shocks) are treated.

From the assignment perspective, most of the suggestions for changes
to the inflation-targeting system involve expanding the role of the interest-
rate-setting authorities – giving them more instruments, more responsibilities and more objectives. The danger is that the perceived institutional
reaction function becomes less 'rule-like' and less 'predictable'.

9.4   Does the framework of monetary policy need to change?

It may seem complacent to suggest that the answer is 'no'. For the main,
though, that is what I want to argue – with some important qualifications
and caveats below.

Could monetary policy have been better?

A first point to get out of the way is that policy practice could, I am sure,
have been better (especially with the benefit of hindsight). I take that for
granted – as well as the point that monetary policymakers need to learn
from the past. That is not an argument for regime change, however –
simply an argument for doing things better if one can. As an illustration,
Taylor (2009) has argued forcefully that a departure from his rule by
the United States was a major cause of the financial crisis. He may be
right – or not. Either way, it is not an argument for changing the basis of
inflation targeting.

An older argument, that US monetary policy was too expansionary during the dot.com boom (given that Greenspan himself had considered restraining it by margin requirements), is also not really relevant to the broader questions of inflation targeting. Regulatory restraint may indeed have been a good idea. If it had been applied, it would have been applied mainly by the regulatory arm of the Fed – and would, presumably, have been taken into account by the interest-rate-setting machinery. It is not the same as an argument that interest rate setters, within a flexible inflation-targeting framework, should 'lean against the wind of asset price rises' (see below). The latter would be a change in the interest rate 'reaction function'; the former would not be.

Three related issues for inflation targeting

Broadly, there are three suggestions for change in the inflation-targeting framework that would constitute a significant change in the 'reaction function': first, that interest rate policy should react to developing imbalances; second, that interest rate policy should 'lean against the wind' of asset price rises; and, third, that interest rate setters should act to offset or quell boom-bust-type scenarios, including asset price drifts and 'bubbles'. None of these is new – but all have increased salience in the light of the credit crisis.

Economic imbalances

Concern over economic imbalances and 'sustainability' is certainly not new – but could or should an inflation-targeting regime seek to do anything about them? Generally speaking, the conventional answer is a resounding 'no'. This follows directly from the limited mandate (and the limited number of policy instruments) in a flexible inflation-targeting regime. Using the example of an external balance of payments deficit (presumed large enough to be problematic), a diversion of policy away from a proper concern with inflation and stabilisation would simply destroy the regime and its credibility.[10] It is not clear that the interest rate would be an appropriate instrument for dealing with a current account imbalance, and, even if it were, the costs to the other parts of the system would be great. A reaction to the build-up of, say, household indebtedness would appear equally inappropriate.

This is not to imply that imbalances do not matter. The argument is that, if they do matter, then it should be the responsibility of other parts of the system to react. For example, a first best response might involve fiscal policy being used to affect the balance of payments – directly and indirectly via the (predictable) interest rate responses of the inflation-targeting institution. In the case of housing, there are many ways the market could be affected other than by interest rate policy. We are back to the assignment problem.

That said, much of the practical concern with imbalances (which are not easy to define) is that they are harbingers of a major, destabilising future correction. To make the obvious point, the possibility or probability of boom and bust is of central concern to an inflation-targeting institution. This issue, the most difficult one in practice and in theory, is discussed below.

Asset prices and leaning against the wind

In many ways, the issue of asset prices is dual to the issue of imbalances. The big issue is about booms and busts, how to moderate them and how to formulate policy taking them into account.

The prevailing central bank consensus was well set out by Vickers (1999). He argues (i) that asset prices should not be part of the definition of the inflation target or of the loss function of the authorities; (ii) that asset prices do contain considerable information relevant to forecasting the future state of the economy; and (iii) that, in an inflation-forecast-targeting regime, 'it is neither necessary nor desirable for monetary policy to respond to changes in asset prices, *except to the extent that they help to forecast inflationary or deflationary pressures*' (Bernanke and Gertler 1999: 115; emphasis added by Vickers). More recently, Bean (2003) reiterates the view that, since the inflation-targeting central bank is not targeting asset prices, and since it is its duty to take everything relevant into account, there can be no special place for asset prices in the procedures.

Nonetheless, there is a literature suggesting that inflation-targeting institutions should take asset prices into account by 'leaning against the wind' (Cecchetti *et al.* 2000; Cechetti, Genberg and Wadhwani 2002; Wadhwani 2008). Wadhwani (2008) quotes, in support of his view, a newspaper article by Lars Heikensten (2008), the deputy governor of the Swedish central bank, the Riksbank, stating that such a policy had been followed in Sweden in 2004–5. A recent speech by the vice-president of the ECB, Lucas Papademos (2009), also suggests that some ECB policymakers find the idea of leaning against the wind attractive (although he insists that such a policy could not be followed mechanically).

In his recent paper, Wadhwani (2008) revisits the debate. He accepts the theoretical case made by Bean (2003) that an optimising central bank would be taking everything into account, including asset prices. Essentially, the core of the argument for 'leaning against the wind' is pragmatic: that imperfect procedures, limited time horizons and 'rules of thumb' give too little weight to asset prices and asset price dynamics and that performance would be improved by 'leaning against the wind'. The purist would reply that if that were the best policy the inflation-targeting institution would be doing that anyway.[11] Moreover, as argued by Bean (2003), comparing one simplified rule, including 'leaning against the wind', with other simple rules or procedures – such as a Taylor rule, or inflation-forecast-targeting based on a two-year horizon – is, arguably, not very helpful.[12]

The debate will no doubt continue. There are some obvious and well-known difficulties, however, with any formal procedure for tying the interest rate decision to asset prices in a particular way (applying a 'tilt'). A general objection is that it does appear to violate the *raison d'être* of the institutional set-up – which is to assign responsibility for managing the trade-off between the nominal anchor function of monetary policy and stabilisation to a particular institution (which operates with constrained discretion). The suggestion is that the authorities' discretion should be used in a particular way. Similar objections apply to other suggestions – for example that central banks should operate according to a Taylor rule. If it were as simple as that, there would not be much point in seeking an institutional solution in the first place; central banks or monetary policy committees could be replaced by an automaton, with considerable savings on costs.

The argument for institutional discretion, in this area as in others, is that not all asset price movements have the same significance; it depends on what gave rise to them and the circumstances of the economy. The dynamic processes vary a lot. It is not easy to generalise. Moreover, why should the debate be confined to asset prices? Why not have 'tilts' applying to imbalances, or to investment or to other variables that display cumulative processes?

The discussion here has considered only parts of the argument for 'leaning against the wind'. The bigger question is whether the monetary authorities should use their discretion over interest rates to head off boom-bust cycles.

Booms and busts

There is a considerable literature on the importance of booms and busts, and the implications for stability (see, for example, Bordo and Jeanne 2002, Borio and Lowe 2002, Borio, English and Filardo 2003 and Borio and White 2004). As noted by Wadhwani, the World Bank suggests that the average stock market bust lasts for about two and a half years and is associated with a 4 per cent decline in GDP, while financial/housing crises last about twice as long with twice the effect on GDP. Prominent among the stories that condition debate are the 'great crash' of the interwar period and the ending of the late 1980s bubble in Japan, which was followed by deflation and slow growth. Housing market booms and busts were a feature of the financial crises in Scandinavia in the late 1980s, and in the United Kingdom. In addition, of course, it is the current crisis that has brought the framework of monetary policy to the top of the economic policy agenda. The stylised facts are well known.

The key questions for the monetary authorities are how they should react in the face of boom-bust scenarios and whether they should use interest rates to moderate booms and busts (including by leaning against the wind) or to make them less likely to occur. There is a further question, which I postpone for the moment, as to whether successful inflation targeting makes asset price bubbles and other boom-bust phenomena more likely: does inflation targeting contain the seeds of its own destruction?

On the first, there is no doubt that cumulative processes, which appear likely to go into reverse later, pose problems for decision-makers. Wadhwani (2008) suggests that inconsistencies in approach are likely to arise, citing varying attitudes within the MPC to issues of this kind. For example, the overvaluation of sterling could be used to suggest heightened inflation risk (if there were a substantial fall) and thus higher interest rates. Such a policy could risk worsening or prolonging the overvaluation, however. Alternatively, 'overvaluations' could be used to suggest lower interest rates to curb the overvaluation (the LATW strategy) in order to head off the prospect of future falls. The problems with asset prices, in housing or the stock market, are similar. Should interest rates be raised to choke off a house price boom, or should they be lowered to counter the downward skew to inflation prospects? To me, these dilemmas are inherent in the situation. Booms and potential busts pose real difficulties for policymakers, especially when the size of the boom and the timing of any bust are endogenous to the interest rate decision (and to anticipated future interest rate decisions).

Not surprisingly, the difficulties in reliably identifying bubbles and other persistent departures from 'the fundamentals' led to a degree of consensus amongst central bankers that the risks involved in an offsetting strategy were considerable (see, for example, Greenspan 2002) and that a sensible strategy was to react aggressively when or if a bust occurred. It is this consensus that is increasingly being questioned.

Suppose we think of the problem, in stripped-down terms, as involving the anticipation of a large positive shock followed by a large negative shock, with the negative shock roughly balancing the positive shock – so that the negative shock is larger the larger the preceding positive shock is. (Such a pattern could result, for example, from some stock flow processes, or from bubble-type phenomena.) The conventional position is that the consequences would be taken into account in the forward-looking procedures of the monetary authority and that the consequences for output and price instability would be minimised in terms of some 'loss function'. That is the end of the story as far as interest rates are concerned.

Clearly, however, if there were some other policy instrument capable of lowering the first shock (and therefore the second shock as well) it is desirable that that instrument should be used. The task of the monetary authorities would then be eased and, short of completely successful off-sets by the monetary authority, the instability of the economy would be reduced and economic welfare increased. The first best response – which, of course, might be unrealistic or costly for other reasons – is that the causes of instability should be tackled at source, removing or attenuating the magnitude of the negatively correlated shocks themselves. There are many examples of interventions of this type that have been suggested as ways of moderating boom-bust cycles, or other persistent, but unsustainable, processes. These include regulatory actions of various kinds, or fiscal interventions – e.g. to slow house price rises.

In this first best case, in which it is the responsibility of other institutions to check the destabilising processes behind booms and busts, the role of the interest-rate-setting authorities would be unaffected. Inevitably, in fulfilling their mandate, they would take into account the effects of the actions by the fiscal authorities or the regulators; but that is already built into the system. In the same way that fiscal actions are 'internalised' by the interest-rate-setting authority, regulatory actions (e.g. to rein in a credit boom) would also be taken into account. In principle, moreover, from the point of view of the interest-rate-setting authority, no further coordination would be needed.[13]

From an inflation-targeting perspective, however, the interesting question is what should be done in the *absence* of alternative policies. This situation would arise if there were no other feasible policy instruments, or if it were known that other instruments would, in fact, not be used. As second best, should interest rate policy then be diverted from its normal role, not to target an asset price, but to check some cumulative process early on – in effect, to lower the magnitude of the correlated shocks under discussion? The argument for so doing would be that the variances of inflation and output would thereby be reduced – which is perfectly consistent with standard interpretations of the loss function. However, there is a trade-off involved (Bordo and Jeanne 2002). The reduction in the 'shocks' takes the monetary authorities closer to their objective; but the diversion of the instrument from its normal role takes them further away (effectively imposing additional variability). The benefit from the first needs to be greater than the loss from the second.

Essentially, what is going on here is that the monetary authorities are using interest rates for two different purposes. The first is to carry out, as far as possible, their inflation-targeting role. The second is to alter the shock structure hitting the economy (including, in particular, the extent and nature of endogenously generated shocks) to make their task easier. If asset price bubbles and other cumulative and persistent processes are, potentially, very adverse, then policy would swing towards mitigating the shock structure. Furthermore, the more effective interest rates are in checking cumulative processes, the more likely they are to be used for this purpose – since the costs of diverting policy from its normal role are smaller.

It is not surprising that much of the discussion in favour of central banks using *interest rates* in this way is conducted in terms of heading off bubble-type phenomena. There is an easy-to-make assumption that a timely, small and temporary upward movement in interest rates would prick the bubble, with large effects on both the upward and downward shocks to the economy. This is exactly the case when the cost–benefit ratio in favour of this type of policy would be greatest. Opponents, such as Nickell (2005), suggest (in the context of the UK housing boom) that the costs would be large. A recent empirical study by Assenmacher-Wesche and Gerlach (2008) suggests that using monetary policy to offset asset price movements would have substantial effects on activity – implying that the use of such policies within an inflation-targeting framework would be costly. Others have suggested much smaller costs. So far there seems little empirical consensus, but the issues are clear enough.

Obviously, within this kind of cost–benefit framework, there is scope for interest rates to be used in moderating asset price and other cumulative processes. 'Leaning against the wind' may be consistent with the inflation-targeting framework as commonly understood. It is not just a case of taking asset price movements and processes into account in forecasting and assessment. There may indeed be scope to improve performance by moderating the processes themselves. To a purist, the ultimate objectives of the interest-rate-setting authority would not be changed; but what is normally thought of as the policymaker's reaction function would be.

Recently, the 'credit crisis' has markedly altered the perception of the trade-offs involved. The cost of not heading off booms and busts now appears very much larger than previously thought, leading inevitably to calls for greater weight to be given to financial stability concerns in the setting of interest rates.

Is this 'cost–benefit' way of looking at the issues (in terms of the authorities' 'loss function') the right way of framing the problem, however? I would suggest that it is not. Going back to the institutional framework of flexible inflation targeting, it is important that the behaviour of the inflation-targeting institution is rule-like and predictable. A policy of acting against asset price movements, even if directed towards meeting the mandate, may be hard to communicate. There may be a cost to the credibility and transparency of the system, which needs to be weighed in the balance. The essential purpose of the institutional framework – to reconcile the tensions between the commitment to price stability and the objective of delivering as much stabilisation as possible – could be threatened. Put another way, it would be a challenge to policymakers to convince the public that the system had not changed while policy was redirected (in part) towards asset prices and the heading off of bubble-type phenomena.[14]

9.5   Further discussion

This section does four things. First, the question of whether the success of inflation targeting is to blame for asset price booms and busts is briefly discussed. Second, the question of whether the monetary authorities could effectively split their reaction function into two is raised. Third, I look very briefly at the credit crisis in the light of the foregoing. Finally, it is suggested that the real challenge for policy – including monetary policy – has been (and may well be again) low real interest rates, required by the global savings 'glut' (Bernanke 2005, 2007).

Does successful inflation targeting contain the seeds of its own destruction?

Borio and White (2004) give a comprehensive account of much of the history of boom-bust cycles. Many of them occurred in non-inflationary circumstances. Any idea that the adoption of inflation targeting would solve all economic problems, including financial stability, is falsified by experience. The asset boom in Japan, for example, occurred without strong inflationary consequences. This is what is to be expected. There is no obvious reason why successful inflation targeting should stop bubbles and other persistent processes. (Of course, inflation may cause financial instability, but for different reasons, surely.)

Inflation targeting and asset prices

Inflation targeting and asset prices

Inflation targeting and asset prices

Inflation targeting and asset prices

Inflation targeting and asset prices

Inflation targeting and asset prices

Inflation targeting and asset prices

185
Inflation targeting and asset prices185
The more interesting question is whether successful inflation targeting facilitates or encourages asset price misalignments and bubbles. There are many reasons why it might. The principal one is that, if interest rates are assigned to inflation control, they are not available to head off bubble-type phenomena, and market participants know this; and a common argument for 'leaning against the wind' is that asset price misalignments might thereby be discouraged – see Wadhwani (2008), for example. There is a further reason. A predictable response by an inflation-targeting regime to the consequences of the bust provides 'insurance' and lowers risk – possibly prolonging the period of misalignment.[15]

The obvious 'first best' response to the possibility of additional asset price instability is to address the source of the problem: to address the market failures in the financial system by enhanced regulation or other means. That said, low interest rates internationally (lower than real growth rates) may be the root of the problem – and are not easily addressed either by the national monetary authorities or by regulation.

Could the authorities develop a two-part reaction function?

The possible need for the monetary authority to trade off financial stability (lower shocks) for the purity of an inflation-targeting regime has been discussed above. What is really needed, however, is two different policy reaction functions – hence the attractiveness of the first best solution of assigning responsibility to two different institutions using two different instruments. The inflation-targeting reaction function needs to be predictable, but it is also strategic. There is a commitment that policy will do whatever turns out to be necessary to keep inflation under control. The credible commitment affects expectations. Ideally, the authorities, it might be argued, need also a 'threat strategy' against asset price misalignments and bubble-type phenomena. With a highly credible inflation-targeting institution it is not impossible to think that a mixed strategy of inflation targeting in normal times could be combined with occasional punishments to 'speculators'. Not an easy trick to carry off, perhaps – but some central banks have tried something like it in the past. In his recent speech, Papademos (2009) suggests that the use of interest rates to counter asset price movements (though not in a mechanical way) could be consistent with the ECB's mandate.

On a more practical note, Borio and White (2004) suggest that indicators of imbalance and stress are good predictors of future busts. Triggers, such as leverage ratios above some reference level, could be used to improve forecasting and assessment. If publicly known, such trigger points could perhaps lead to changed perceptions about likely future interest rate policy. It is not fully clear how this would work in practice, however, without a major change in the policy regime.

It is important to come back to the main point, though. Why should the single instrument of the short-term interest rate be used for two different jobs? Surely this would be sensible only if there is no feasible alternative. Usually there are alternatives, however – such as regulatory action. Moreover, it is often argued that the short-term rate of interest is a blunt and possibly inappropriate instrument for dealing with financial market failures and their consequences – further strengthening the argument for finding alternative ways of intervening to head off cumulative and reversible processes.

The credit crunch and its aftermath

One way of accounting for the change in mood towards giving greater weight to asset prices is simply that the perceived cost–benefit ratio has changed as a result of the crisis. The consequences of failing to control asset prices now seem very much worse than they did before; but to go down that route would be a mistake. The key failure has been regulatory failure – along with the behaviour of the banks. Tempting as it may be to change the monetary policy regime, this is a classic case in which the first best solution – dealing with regulatory failure – is the right one. The question of what institutions should ideally be in charge of regulatory policy is not discussed here. I subscribe to the conventional view that macro-prudential policy must be made anticyclical and that market failures within the financial sector, leading to positive feedback loops, must be addressed (on the need for regulatory changes, see Brunnermeier *et al.* 2009, and, for an eclectic view on the issues, see Haldane 2009).

On asset prices and the build-up of imbalances, the first best response is still for a combination of regulatory and fiscal policy to take responsibility, leaving the role of the inflation-targeting regime much as before.

A more tricky question concerns quantitative easing and the use of fiscal policy to support demand. In a crisis, a change in policy regime and a move to coordinated policies is to be expected. Clearly, however, the independence of central banks is much compromised during a crisis, since the fiscal authorities are inevitably involved. Looking beyond the crisis, with quantitative easing unwound, there is little reason to change the underlying basis of inflation targeting.

International imbalances and the savings–investment balance

Finally, I turn to the question of whether central banks should have had higher interest rates during the boom, as the inflation-targeting system is widely blamed for the asset price rises that occurred. Real interest rates were well below growth rates – an invitation to speculation and excess.

The difficulty here is that it is hard to discern what other policies could have been followed. Higher interest rates would have tended to lead to low growth and falling inflation unless balanced by larger fiscal injections. The simple fact is that, with very high world savings (reflected in the world imbalances) interest rates may have to be dangerously low, or fiscal deficits may have to be dangerously large. The situation is all too likely to recur as the world returns to normality. There seems to be no easy solution to this, short of major changes in Asian savings and international rebalancing (including in China). This is the real challenge to policymakers, which goes far beyond the narrow question of whether central banks should pay more attention in their procedures to asset prices. There is a real danger that misdiagnosis of the underlying problem may lead to damaging changes in a monetary policy framework that does not need fixing.

9.6   Conclusions

This chapter has suggested that a key virtue of the flexible inflation-targeting system adopted by many countries was the assignment of the task of reconciling the complex trade-off between inflation control and stabilisation to a single institution charged with managing that trade-off as well as possible. The success of that framework was not, however, the end of history, or the end of macroeconomics. There remain extremely important roles for fiscal policy (e.g. in determining the 'mix' and addressing imbalances that threaten sustainability) and for regulatory policy, especially in the areas of macro-prudential regulation and in dealing with the market processes that lead to instability.

Arguments for changing the framework of monetary policy come in several guises. One is that mistakes were made that contributed to the recent crisis. This is not an argument for changing the framework, but for improving it.

The chief danger for monetary policy is that the interest rate policy instrument – assigned under flexible inflation targeting to the control of inflation – will be asked to do too much, weakening the credibility and predictability of the inflation-targeting system.

Of course, other aspects of 'monetary' policy, more broadly defined, do need to change. Regulatory reforms, including the development of systems of macro-prudential regulation, are urgently required. The contentious question of what institution (or institutions) should be assigned the responsibility for designing and using the new regulatory instruments has not been discussed here. In principle, the task could be assigned to the (regulatory arm of the) central bank, to a regulatory authority or, for that matter, to the finance ministry or Treasury. The choice is essentially pragmatic: what system would work best? The inflation-targeting institution would then take regulatory changes or interventions into account in fulfilling its mandate.

One reason for the build-up of unsustainable imbalances and financial fragility has been the prevalence of interest rates well below growth rates in the global economy. It would be a mistake to see low interest rates as arising from a failure of inflation targeting. The lesson instead is that global imbalances need to be addressed, which raises issues that go far beyond the design of monetary-policymaking institutions.

NOTES

1. Most policy intervention needs to be justified on the basis of some market failure. The need for policy to provide a nominal anchor is more fundamental than that: without a nominal anchor, the price level and the rate of inflation are, in the standard paradigm, indeterminate.
2. The Taylor principle captures the idea that, for stability, real interest rates must rise as inflation goes up.
3. It is quite sensible for a very open economy to see policy as working through the real exchange rate. Of course, interest rates are the most important way of influencing the exchange rate.
4. A major reason for this assignment is not the virtues of the Federal Reserve but the deficiencies of the fiscal system in the United States.
5. One strand of this was the idea of reducing the inflation bias by delegation to a 'conservative' central banker (Rogoff 1985). In practical terms, the idea of delegation to a technocratic committee with no incentive or desire to induce 'surprise inflation' in the first place was probably more influential (Bean 1998a; Vickers 1998).
6. In the United Kingdom, fiscal prudence and sustainability were supposedly ensured by adherence to the fiscal rules – especially the 'debt sustainability rule', that net debt should not exceed 40 per cent of GDP. In the European context, under the 'Maastricht Assignment' in EMU (Issing 2002), fiscal policy was the responsibility of the national authorities, but subject to the Stability and Growth Pact (SGP). Alesina *et al.* (2001) describe the role of the fiscal authorities in EMU as being 'to keep their houses in order' – i.e. by conforming to the SGP.
7. In discussions about potential EMU entry, however, the point was freely admitted: it was widely appreciated that fiscal policy might need to alter to bring about an appropriate entry rate for sterling – were the United Kingdom to join the arrangements.
8. Interestingly, suggestions that the monetary authorities should be given an additional (short-term) fiscal instrument to improve their armoury (see,

for example, Wren-Lewis 2000) did not imply a change in the assignment of responsibilities. Clearly, however, with more than one instrument, the monetary authorities' reaction function would become more complicated and less predictable – since they could use alternative instruments. In pragmatic terms, moreover, there would be ambiguity over which institution was responsible for the (longer-term) fiscal/monetary mix.

9. In the United Kingdom, responsibility for financial stability is split between the Financial Services Authority and the central bank (the stability wing), with the whole being subject to a tripartite agreement between the Treasury, the Bank of England and the Financial Services Authority. The system did not work well in the crisis.

10. There are endless examples from the past of policy swinging about between internal and external objectives, with a loss of overall policy credibility.

11. There are two aspects to how an inflation-targeting institution takes asset prices into account. The first is in terms of forecasting (or, more generally, assessment). There is no disagreement that asset prices (and their dynamics) are relevant to this process. The second is concerned with the reconciliation of the trade-offs between the nominal anchor function of the system and the stabilisation function. Asset prices per se are not relevant to this.

12. There is, however, a perfectly respectable argument, used by Wadhwani, that simple communicable rules have great advantages and are 'good enough'. The best may then be the enemy of the good.

13. Of course, the interest-rate-setting institution would need to be informed – as it typically is about likely fiscal actions. It might seem 'odd' that regulatory restraint on credit would be followed (*ceteris paribus*) by lower interest rates – which would be the case if the action on credit lowered aggregate demand. In fact, though, this implication is no more controversial than the accepted proposition that fiscal tightening would normally lead through to lower interest rates via the monetary policy reaction function.

14. A point often made in practical discussions is that a policy of heading off the risk of an asset price boom and bust may be particularly difficult to justify to the public if it is successful. *Ex post*, the costs (e.g. of unemployment and an undershoot of inflation) could well appear unnecessary.

15. It was often suggested that the dot.com boom in the United States was prolonged by the perception that interest rates would be cut if a bust were to occur – sometimes described as the 'Greenspan put'. The presumed conditional behaviour of the FOMC undoubtedly lowered perceptions of risk.

REFERENCES

Alesina, A., O. Blanchard, J. Galí, F. Giavazzi and H. Uhlig (2001). *Defining a Macroeconomic Framework for the Euro Area*. London: Centre for Economic Policy Research [CEPR].

Allsopp, C. (2002). 'Macroeconomic policy rules in theory and practice', *Bank of England Quarterly Bulletin*, 42(4): 485–504.

Allsopp, C., and D. Vines (2005). 'The macroeconomic role of fiscal policy', *Oxford Review of Economic Policy*, 21(4): 485–508.

Assenmacher-Wesche, K., and S. Gerlach (2008). 'Ensuring financial stability: financial structure and the impact of monetary policy on asset prices'. Working Paper no. 361. Zurich: Institute for Empirical Research in Economics, University of Zurich.

Balls, E., and G. O'Donnell (eds.) (2001). *Reforming Britain's Economic and Financial Policy*. London: Palgrave.

Bean, C. (1998a). 'The new monetary arrangements: a view from the literature', *Economic Journal*, 108: 1795–809.

(1998b). 'Monetary policy under EMU', *Oxford Review of Economic Policy*, 14(3): 41–53.

(2003). 'Asset prices, financial imbalances and monetary policy: are inflation targets enough?'. Working Paper no. 140. Basel: BIS.

Bernanke, B.(2005). 'The global savings glut and the US current account deficit'. Remarks at the Sandridge Lecture to the Virginia Association of Eonomics. Richmond, VA, 10 March.

(2007). 'Global imbalances: recent developments and prospects'. Speech at the Bundesbank Lecture. Berlin, 11 September.

Bernanke, B., and M. Gertler (1999). 'Monetary policy and asset price volatility', in Federal Reserve Bank of Kansas City. *New Challenges for Monetary Policy*: 77–128. Federal Reserve Bank of Kansas City.

Bordo, M., and O. Jeanne (2002). 'Boom-busts in asset prices, economic instability and monetary policy'. Discussion Paper no. 3398. London: CEPR.

Borio, C., B. English and A. Filardo (2003). 'A tale of two perspectives: old or new challenges for monetary policy?'. Working Paper no. 127. Basel: BIS.

Borio, C., and P. Lowe (2002). 'Asset prices, financial and monetary stability: exploring the nexus'. Working Paper no. 114. Basel: BIS.

Borio, C., and W. White (2004). 'Whither monetary and financial stability? The implications of evolving monetary policy regimes'. Working Paper no. 147. Basel: BIS.

Brunnermeier, M., A. Crockett, C. Goodhart, A. Persaud and H. Shin (2009). *The Fundamental Principles of Financial Regulation*. Geneva: CIMB.

Cecchetti, S., H. Genberg, J. Lipsky and S. Wadhwani (2000). *Asset Prices and Central Bank Policy*. Geneva: CIMB.

Cecchetti, S., H. Genberg and S. Wadhwani (2002). 'Asset prices in a flexible inflation targeting framework'. Working Paper no. 8970. Cambridge, MA: NBER.

Dodge, D. (2002). 'The interaction between monetary and fiscal policies'. Donald Gow Lecture at School of Policy Studies, Queens University. Kingston, ON, 26 April.

Greenspan, A. (2002). 'Economic volatility'. Speech given at the Federal Reserve Bank of Kansas City symposium 'Rethinking stabilisation policy'. Jackson Hole, WY, 29 August.

Haldane, A. (2009). 'Rethinking the financial network'. Speech to the Financial Student Association at the University of Amsterdam. Amsterdam, 28 April. Available at www.bankofengland.co.uk/publications/speeches/2009/speech386.pdf.

Heikensten, L. (2008). 'More to it than just leaning against the wind', *Financial Times*, 5 June.

Issing, O. (2002). 'On macroeconomic policy coordination in EMU', *Journal of Common Market Studies*, 40(2): 345–58.

Nickell, S. (2005). 'Practical issues in UK monetary policy, 2000–2005'. British Academy Keynes Lecture. London, 20 September. Available at www.bankofengland.co.uk/publications/speeches/2005/speech255.pdf.

Papademos, L. (2009). 'Monetary policy and the great crisis: lessons and challenges'. Speech at the Oesterreichishe Nationalbank's thirty-seventh economic conference, 'Beyond the crisis: economic policy in a new macroeconomic environment'. Vienna, 14 May. Available at www.ecb.int/press/key/date/2009/html/sp090514.en.html.

Rogoff, K. (1985). 'The optimal degree of commitment to an intermediate monetary target', *Quarterly Journal of Economics*, 100(4): 1169–89.

Taylor, J. (1993). 'Discretion versus policy rules in practice', *Carnegie-Rochester Conference Series on Public Policy*, 39(1): 195–214.

(2009). 'The financial crisis and the policy responses: an empirical analysis of what went wrong'. Working Paper no. 14641. Cambridge, MA: NBER.

Vickers, J. (1998). 'Inflation targeting in practice: the UK experience', *Bank of England Quarterly Bulletin*, 38(4): 368–75.

(1999). 'Monetary policy and asset prices', *Bank of England Quarterly Bulletin*, 39(4): 428–35.

Wadhwani, S. (2008). 'Should monetary policy respond to asset price bubbles? Revisiting the debate', *National Institute Economic Review*, 206(1): 25–34.

Wolf, M. (2009). 'Central banks must target more than just inflation', *Financial Times*, 5 May.

Woodford, M. (2003). *Interest and Prices: Foundations of a Theory of Monetary Policy*. Princeton, NJ: Princeton University Press.

Wren-Lewis, S. (2000). 'The limits to discretionary stabilisation policy', *Oxford Review of Economic Policy*, 16(4): 92–105.

Wyplosz, C. (2002). 'Fiscal policy: institutions versus rules'. Discussion Paper no. 3238. London: CEPR.

10 The optimal monetary policy instrument, inflation versus asset price targeting, and financial stability

Charles Goodhart, Carolina Osorio and Dimitrios Tsomocos[1]

10.1 Introduction

Over the last couple of years the global financial system has undergone a period of unprecedented turmoil initiated by problems in the US mortgage market, which then spread to securitised products and a wide range of credit markets. Interbank markets have struggled to provide liquidity across the banking sector, thereby failing to act as a conduit for monetary policy, and systemically important financial institutions have collapsed, calling for public intervention on a scale not seen for decades. We believe that this crisis is a reflection of an overly expansionary monetary policy, carried out through an inflation-targeting regime, which induced excessive growth in credit and asset prices, as well as the inability of regulators to predict and deal with the distortions generated by financial innovations.

Inflation targeting has been successful in keeping inflation low and stable, but its proliferation is threatened by the fact that it accords overriding importance to price stability while central banks remain responsible for promoting financial stability. Since these two objectives reinforce each other in the long run, the conventional central banker's wisdom has been sceptical about the existence of a trade-off between price and financial stability. However, the current crisis has demonstrated that there are situations of short-term conflict; in the recent past, low interest rates and the success of central banks in achieving low inflation gave market participants a false sense of security, which contributed to the mispricing of risks and made the financial system more vulnerable.

We explain the current US financial crisis by modelling a contagion phenomenon that commences with increased default in the mortgage sector and then spreads to the rest of the nominal sector of the economy;

we argue that the current crisis is a bona fide general equilibrium example, whereby various interacting channels in the financial markets affect and are affected by the real economy. In addition, we assess the choice of policy instruments and whether central banks should target consumer and asset prices to maintain financial stability. Our results suggest that in times of financial distress the interest rate is more effective than the money supply instrument, because the central bank automatically satisfies the increased demand for money. Furthermore, to achieve financial and price stability, we propose two policy prescriptions; on the one hand, to widen the targeted inflation rate to include an appropriate measure of housing price movements; and, on the other hand, to use regulatory policies that induce systemic financial institutions to behave more prudently *ex ante*. We favour the latter, since ensuring price and financial stability requires more instruments than the short-term interest rate.

We construct a two-period, rational expectations, monetary general equilibrium model with commercial banks, default, and collateral along the lines of Goodhart, Tsomocos and Vardoulakis (2009). We extend this framework, however, by introducing an investment bank and a hedge fund, allowing mortgage debt to be securitised, and separating the inter-bank from the repo market. By doing this we succeed in focusing more closely on the transmission mechanism of monetary policy – i.e. credit expansion through securitisation – and, consequently, its impact on financial stability. Moreover, we model two types of default; in the mortgage market, default is highly discontinuous, as modelled by Geanakoplos and Zame (2002) and Geanakoplos (2003), whereas in credit markets, in which financial institutions interact with each other, default is modelled as a continuous phenomenon (see Shubik and Wilson 1977 and Dubey, Geanakoplos and Shubik 2005). Unlike Goodhart, Sunirand and Tsomocos (2006), we abstract from modelling capital adequacy requirements explicitly as we are not considering a wide range of asset markets.

Although dynamic stochastic general equilibrium models have gained popularity as tools for policy discussion and analysis among academics and central banks in recent years, they are inappropriate, at best, for financial stability analysis. The benchmark DSGE model is a fully micro-founded representative agent model with real and nominal rigidities that incorporates elements of the real business cycle approach and the New Keynesian paradigm. The latter has its cornerstone in the work of Woodford (2003), which explains why his neo-Wicksellian theory of monetary policy, whereby an interest rate rule-based approach is the optimal policy to stabilise the rate of inflation, is used by most central banks operating in an inflation-targeting regime, rather than the quantity theory of money approach favoured by Irving Fisher.

To explore contagious financial crises, a model of heterogeneous banks with different portfolios is needed to allow for the existence of an inter-bank market and contagion. A framework that allows for liquidity and default is also required; otherwise there would be no crises. Further-more, money, banks and interest rates must play an essential role, since we are concerned with financial crises. Finally, financial markets cannot be complete, otherwise all eventualities could be hedged and equilibrium outcomes would be constrained efficient, thus limiting the scope for welfare-improving economic policy (Barsden, Linduist and Tsomocos 2008).

The framework presented here incorporates all these elements. More-over, in this model monetary policy is non-neutral, a non-trivial quantity theory of money holds, the term structure of interest rates depends on aggregate liquidity and default risk in the economy, and the Fisher effect, whereby nominal rates are a function of real rates and inflation expec-tations, holds. Additionally, financial fragility arises as an equilibrium outcome.

Owing to the non-linearity of the system and its large size, we have solved the model numerically. In the initial equilibrium, the economy experiences an initial adverse productivity shock, which leads to inflation in terms of goods prices and deflation in the housing market, thereby creating a policy trade-off between price and financial stability; further, the central bank reacts to this shock by changing its monetary policy stance. Both shocks lead to increased default in the mortgage market, thus affecting the financial system as a whole through the derivatives markets. This set-up embodies the key features of the US experience from 2004 to 2008.

The chapter proceeds as follows. Section 10.2 presents the model. In section 10.3 the equilibrium of the model is defined, its properties are derived and the benchmark equilibrium outcome is discussed. The comparative statics results are reported in section 10.4, and section 10.5 presents the implications for inflation targeting based on the model's results. Finally, section 10.6 concludes. A complete description of the model and proofs of all the propositions, as well as additional comparative statics, are provided by Goodhart, Osorio and Tsomocos (2009).

10.2   The baseline model

The economy

Consider a canonical general equilibrium with incomplete markets (GEI) model in which time extends over two periods ($t \in T = \{0, 1\}$). The first period consists of a single initial state and the second period consists of

S possible states. In the initial period, households, commercial banks, financial institutions and the authorities make their decisions expecting (rationally) the realisation of any of the possible states in the next period. In the second period, one of the S states occurs and agents make their choices accordingly. Suppose there are two possible states of the world in the second period ($s \in S = \{1, 2\}$), and let the set of all states be denoted by $s^* \in S^* = \{0\} \cup S = \{0, 1, 2\}$.

The (endowment) economy has two goods, a basket of consumption goods and housing, which are denoted by subscripts 1 and 2, respectively. Housing is a durable good, which provides utility in every period after its purchase, and for tractability purposes it is assumed to be infinitely divisible. There are two households $h \in H = \{\alpha, \theta\}$, two commercial banks $j \in \mathcal{J} = \{\gamma, \delta\}$, an investment bank ($\psi$) and a hedge fund ($\phi$). The economy has three other players: a central bank that can inject (withdraw) money into (from) the system through open market operations (OMOs); the government, which can increase or decrease the level of private monetary or commodity endowments; and a financial supervisory agency (FSA), which imposes penalties on defaults. We do not seek to model the actions of these official players, which is why they operate as strategic dummies. There are ten active markets in this economy: the goods, housing, mortgage, short-term loans, consumer deposit, repo, interbank, mortgage-backed securities (MBSs), collateralised debt obligations (CDOs) and wholesale money markets.

Households are risk-averse agents that maximise their expected utility over their consumption stream of housing and goods. We use a constant relative risk aversion (CRRA) utility function for $h \in H$ to capture the wealth effects of price and interest rate movements. Households are heterogeneous in their endowments of goods and money; α is endowed with goods at all states and with a small amount of money in the initial period, whereas θ is endowed with housing only at $t = 0$ and with a large amount of cash in the first period.

Commercial banks are also risk-averse agents that maximise their expected second-period profits. We suppose commercial banks have quadratic preferences over their profits (a constant absolute risk aversion (CARA) utility function), which implies that they face a portfolio allocation problem whereby they try to diversify idiosyncratic risks. Commercial banks are heterogeneous in their endowments of capital; while bank γ has a large endowment of capital in the initial period, bank δ is poorly capitalised in all states.

Following Goodhart, Sunirand and Tsomocos (2004, 2006), an important friction is introduced in the short-term consumer credit markets. Individual borrowers are assigned, by history or by informational constraints, to a single bank over the two periods of the model.[2] By assumption, households cannot default on short-term loans; hence, without loss of generality, let α borrow from bank γ, and θ borrow from bank δ, in the short-term credit market.

In the case of inter-period loans and deposits, we assume that households make transactions with the bank offering the best rate, which is the highly capitalised bank (γ). Since α is poor and θ is rich in monetary endowments, the former takes out a mortgage with bank γ, while the latter makes a long-term deposit in that bank.

In contrast to commercial banks, the investment bank and the hedge fund are assumed to have linear preferences over their expected second-period profits, which implies that these agents are risk-neutral and do not seek to accumulate profits.

Money

Money is introduced by a cash-in-advance constraint, whereby all commodities and assets can be traded only for money, and all asset deliveries are paid for in money. Cash-in-advance models aim to illustrate the importance of liquidity for transactions. There are many versions of cash-in-advance models in the monetary theory literature (see, for example, Lucas and Stokey 1983, 1987, Svensson 1985 and Bloise, Drèze and Polemarchakis 2005); we follow the model developed by Dubey and Geanakoplos (1992), in which multiple facets of money are captured. Money is fiat and is the stipulated medium of exchange; it doesn't give utility to agents; it cannot be privately produced; and it is perfectly durable. Moreover, money enters the system as outside or inside money.

Outside money enters the system free and clear of any offsetting obligations – i.e. as private sector aggregate monetary endowments – which can be interpreted as a government transfer or as an inheritance from the (unmodelled) past. Inside money enters the system accompanied by an offsetting obligation; it is the stock of money supplied by the central bank that is matched by individual borrowers' debt obligation to commercial banks. Since money is fiat, it must exit the system at the final period. As a result, inside and outside money exit the economy via loan repayments by households/investors to commercial banks, via loan repayments by commercial banks to the central bank or through the central bank's liquidation of commercial banks.

Default and collateral

The model incorporates two types of (endogenous) default. In the mortgage market, default is highly discontinuous, as agents default on their mortgage when the endogenous value of collateral is lower than the amount due on the mortgage. In this case, the bank seizes the amount of housing pledged as collateral and offers it for sale in the next period; the proceeds from this sale determine the effective mortgage rate (or, equivalently, the mortgage repayment rate) (Geanakoplos 2003; Geanakoplos and Zame 2002).

By assumption, in addition to mortgages, only interbank and wholesale money market loans are defaultable. These loans are unsecured, however, which is why we model default in these markets as a continuous phenomenon, following Shubik and Wilson (1977) and Dubey, Geanakoplos and Shubik (2005). In this case, the fraction of (defaultable) loans that agents repay is a choice variable. By defaulting, agents face a penalty that reduces their utility by a scalar $\bar{\tau}_s^k$, $s = \{1, 2\}$, $k = \{\delta, \psi, \phi\}$, per monetary unit of account not repaid. In equilibrium, agents will equalise the marginal utility of defaulting with the marginal disutility of the bankruptcy penalty.[3] The vector $\{\bar{\tau}_s^k\}$ represents the default penalties set by the FSA.

Since rational expectations are assumed throughout, in equilibrium, expected rates of delivery for mortgage, interbank and wholesale money market loans are equal to actual rates of delivery. For this reason, default can be established as an equilibrium outcome without destroying the orderly functioning of the financial system. This result contrasts with the multitude of papers following the work of Bryant (1982) and Diamond and Dybvig (1983), in which financial instability is rationalised by modelling bank runs and panics based on some type of coordination failure. Tsomocos (2003) shows that bank runs are a particular case of the monetary general equilibrium model with commercial banks and default, which arises when commercial banks are homogeneous.

Securitisation

Geanakoplos and Zame (2002) argue that a reliance on collateral to secure loans can distort households' consumption plans, because collateral is scarce. One way of stretching collateral is by allowing the same physical collateral to be used many times, which motivates the existence and growth of securitisation and derivatives markets. In this framework, the mortgage's collateral is securitised twice: first, in the MBS market, when the investment bank purchases the mortgage asset from the commercial bank that extended the loan; and, second, in the CDO market. Thus, through securitisation, credit expansion is increased.

The investment bank (ψ) buys the mortgage asset from bank γ at a price p^α. Then it structures a CDO by attaching a credit default swap to the MBS. The CDS protects the CDO buyer (ϕ) against default in the mortgage market, in which case ϕ delivers the mortgage's collateral to ψ, and ψ reimburses ϕ with the amount of cash it invested. $\tilde{q}^{\alpha}$ is the price of the CDO, which is higher than the MBS's price because it includes the CDS's cost of insurance.

Assume that α honours his mortgage if $s = 1$ and defaults if $s = 2$. The mortgage can therefore be regarded as an asset with the following vector of pay-offs across states:

$$R^{\alpha} = \begin{bmatrix} 1 + \bar{r}^{\gamma\alpha} \\ 1 + \bar{r}_s^{\gamma\alpha} \end{bmatrix}$$

where $\bar{r}^{\gamma\alpha}$ is the interest rate offered by γ at the initiation of the mortgage contract and $\bar{r}_s^{\gamma\alpha}$ is the effective mortgage rate in case of default. This implies that the CDO has the following pay-offs:

$$R^{CDO} = \begin{bmatrix} (1 + \bar{r}^{\gamma\alpha})/\tilde{q}^{\alpha} \\ 1 \end{bmatrix}$$

In the bad states of the world ψ pays ϕ the total amount of cash it invested in the CDO, whereas in the good states ϕ earns the monetary pay-off of the mortgage asset net of the premium paid to ψ.

Time structure of markets

Initially, commercial banks $j \in \mathcal{J}$ organise a short-term credit market with the central bank, which operates as a strategic dummy in the repo market at $t \in T$ by providing liquidity through OMOs (M_{s*}^{CB}), or by entering into (reverse) repurchase agreements with commercial banks.[4] Since bank γ is assumed to be highly capitalised, it enters into a reverse repurchase agreement with the central bank (makes a deposit), while δ, the poor bank, enters into a repurchase agreement (borrows).

Long-term credit markets meet in the initial period after short-term consumer credit and repo markets close. α and θ take out short-term loans at $s^* \in S^*$ because cash-in-advance is needed for all market transactions. Then α takes out a mortgage with bank γ, while θ makes a long-term deposit at that bank. In addition, given that bank δ is poorly capitalised, it must borrow from bank γ in the interbank market before extending credit to investors.

The investment bank (ψ) buys the mortgage asset from γ in the MBS market, and securitises it into a CDO containing the mortgage-backed security and CDS. Since ϕ has no capital and ψ has a small endowment of capital, both borrow from bank δ in the wholesale money market before making their respective investments in the derivatives markets. At

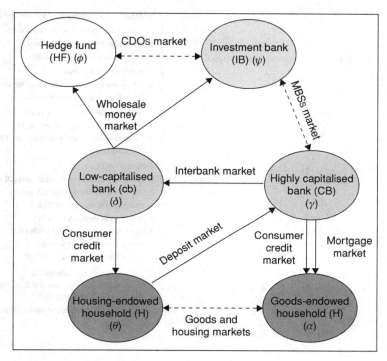

Figure 10.1 Nominal flows in the economy

Note: The straight lines and their direction represent lending flows; the dashed lines indicate trade.

the end of the first period the consumption and settlement of one-period loans take place.

In the second period the repo and consumer short-term credit markets meet before settlement and defaults take place in the mortgage, MBS, CDO, interbank and wholesale money markets. At the end of this period the consumption and settlement of one-period loans take place, and the central bank liquidates commercial banks by taking over their profits. Figures 10.1 and 10.2 provide diagrams of the economy's nominal flows and its time structure.

Household α's optimisation problem

Consumer α maximises his utility, which depends on his consumption of goods and housing. He is endowed with goods and money in every state, and takes out a short-term loan and a mortgage with bank γ to

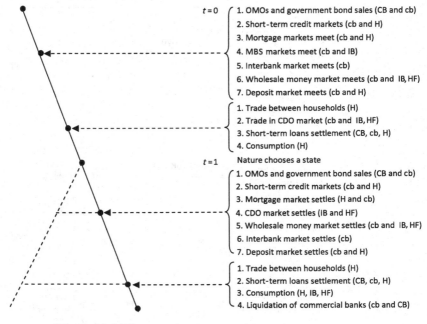

Figure 10.2 Time structure

purchase housing in the first period. At $t = 0$, α uses the cash obtained from the mortgage loan, the short-term loan and his monetary endowment to buy housing units, and he pledges these as collateral to the mortgage.

If a good state is realised in the second period, he takes out a short-term loan to buy more housing and pay back his mortgage. In the bad states of the world, α defaults on his mortgage and his house is seized by bank γ. Nevertheless, α still needs housing services; therefore he takes out a short-term loan to purchase housing in the second period. At the end of each period, consumer α repays his short-term obligations with the proceeds of goods sales.

Denote by $S_1^\alpha \subset S$ the set of states in which α honours his mortgage:

$$S_1^\alpha = \left\{ s \in S : \frac{b_{02}}{p_{02}} p_{s2} \geq \bar{\mu}^\alpha \right\}$$

where (b_{02}/p_{02}) is the amount of housing purchased at $t = 0$, p_{s2} is the price of housing at $s \in S_1^\alpha$ in the second period and $\bar{\mu}^\alpha$ is the value of outstanding mortgage debt. The maximisation problem is as follows:

$$\max_{q_{s*1}, b_{s*2}, \mu_{s*}, \bar{\mu}} U^{\alpha} = u\left(e_{01}^{\alpha} - q_{01}^{\alpha}\right) + u\left(\frac{b_{02}^{\alpha}}{p_{02}}\right) + \sum_{s \in S} \varpi_s u\left(e_{s1}^{\alpha} - q_{s1}^{\alpha}\right)$$

$$+ \sum_{s \in S^1} \varpi_s u\left(\frac{b_{02}^{\alpha}}{p_{02}} + \frac{b_{s2}^{\alpha}}{p_{s2}}\right) + \sum_{s \notin S^1} \varpi_s u\left(\frac{b_{s2}^{\alpha}}{p_{s2}}\right)$$

$$\tag{10.1}$$

$$s.t. \ b_{02}^{\alpha} \leq \frac{\bar{\mu}^{\alpha}}{1 + \bar{r}^{\gamma\alpha}} + \frac{\mu_0^{\alpha}}{1 + r_0^{\gamma}} + e_{m,0}^{\alpha} \tag{10.2}$$

$$\mu_0^{\alpha} \leq p_{01} q_{01}^{\alpha} \tag{10.3}$$

$$b_{s2}^{\alpha} + \bar{\mu}^{\alpha} \leq \frac{\mu_s^{\alpha}}{1 + r_s^{\gamma}} + e_{m,s}^{\alpha} \quad for \quad s \in S_1^{\alpha} \tag{10.4}$$

$$b_{s2}^{\alpha} \leq \frac{\mu_s^{\alpha}}{1 + r_s} + e_{m,s}^{\alpha} \quad for \quad s \notin S_1^{\alpha} \tag{10.5}$$

$$\mu_s^{\alpha} \leq p_{s1} q_{s1}^{\alpha} \quad for \quad s \in S \tag{10.6}$$

$$q_{s*1}^{\alpha} \leq e_{s*1}^{\alpha} \tag{10.7}$$

where:

$b_{s*2}^{\alpha} \equiv$ fiat money spent by α to trade in the housing market in $s*$;

$q_{s*1}^{\alpha} \equiv$ goods offered for sale by α in $s*$;

$\bar{\mu}^{\alpha} \equiv$ repayment value of the mortgage credit that γ extends to α;

$\bar{r}^{\gamma\alpha} \equiv$ mortgage rate offered to α by bank γ;

$r_{s*}^{\gamma} \equiv$ short-term rate offered to α by bank γ in $s*$;

$\mu_{s*}^{\alpha} \equiv$ short-term loan γ extends to α in $s*$;

$p_{s*2} \equiv$ price of housing in state $s*$;

$p_{s*1} \equiv$ price of goods in state $s*$;

$e_{s*1}^{\alpha} \equiv$ endowment of goods of α in state $s*$;

$e_{m,s*}^{h} \equiv$ monetary endowment (outside money) of $h \in (\alpha, \theta)$ in state $s*$; and

$\varpi_s \equiv$ probability of state s.

$u(x) = x^{1-c^h}/(1 - c^h)$ for $h \in H = \{\alpha, \theta\}$.

Household θ's optimisation problem

θ is endowed with money in every state and with a large amount of housing at $t = 0$. He sells houses and buys goods in both periods. At the beginning of the first period θ uses his cash inflows (monetary endowment and a short-term loan) to buy goods and to make a long-term deposit in bank γ. In the second period θ uses the gross return of his deposit, his monetary endowment and a short-term loan to purchase consumption goods.

Finally, θ repays his short-term obligations with the proceeds from housing sales at the end of each period. The maximisation problem is as follows:

$$\max_{q_{s*2}, b_{s*1}, \mu_{s*}, \bar{d}} U^\theta = u\left(\frac{b_{01}^\theta}{p_{01}}\right) + u\left(e_{02}^\theta - q_{02}^\theta\right) + \sum_{s \in S} \varpi_s u\left(\frac{b_{s1}^\theta}{p_{s1}}\right)$$

$$+ \sum_{s \in S} \varpi_s u\left(e_{02}^\theta - q_{02}^\theta - q_{s2}^\theta\right) \tag{10.8}$$

$$s.t. \; b_{01}^\theta + \bar{d}^\theta \leq \frac{\mu_0^\theta}{1 + r_0^\delta} + e_{m,0}^\theta \tag{10.9}$$

$$\mu_0^\theta \leq p_{02} q_{02}^\theta \tag{10.10}$$

$$b_{s1}^\theta \leq e_{m,s}^\theta + \frac{\mu_s^\theta}{1 + r_s^\delta} + \bar{d}^\theta\left(1 + \bar{r}_d^\gamma\right) \tag{10.11}$$

$$\mu_s^\theta \leq p_{s2} q_{s2}^\theta \tag{10.12}$$

$$q_{s2}^\theta \leq e_{02}^\theta - q_{02}^\theta \tag{10.13}$$

where:

$b_{s*1}^\theta \equiv$ fiat money spent by θ to trade in the goods market in $s*$;
$q_{s*2}^\theta \equiv$ housing offered for sale by α in $s*$;
$\bar{d}^\theta \equiv$ deposits by θ in bank γ;
$\mu_{s*}^\theta \equiv$ short-term loan δ extends to θ in $s*$;
$r_{s*}^\delta \equiv$ short-term interest rate offered by δ to θ in $s*$;
$\bar{r}_d^\gamma \equiv$ deposit rate on $\bar{d}^\theta$; and
$e_{s*2} \equiv \theta$'s endowment of housing.

Bank γ's optimisation problem

Bank γ is a risk-averse agent that maximises the utility of its second-period expected profits, after which it is liquidated by the central bank. γ has quadratic preferences over its expected profits, and a high level of capital endowments in the first period. Initially, γ interacts with the central bank in the repo market by entering into a reverse repurchase agreement; it also makes a short-term loan and a mortgage extension to α. Then it sells its mortgage asset to ψ, receives a deposit from θ and makes a deposit in the long-term interbank market.

In the second period γ uses the profits accumulated from the first period and the repayment of the interbank deposit to extend a short-term loan to α, make a deposit in the repo market and pay back its depositor (θ). γ's second-period profits are the sum of the reverse repurchase agreement gross returns and α's repayment on the short-term loan. The maximisation problem is as follows:

$$\max_{m_s*,\bar{m},d_s^{G\gamma},\bar{d},d_d,\pi_s*1} \prod\gamma = \sum_{s\in S} \varpi_s \left(\pi_s^\gamma - c^\gamma \left(\pi_s^\gamma\right)^2\right) \tag{10.14}$$

$$s.t.\ d_0^{G\gamma} + m_0^\gamma + \bar{m}^\alpha + \bar{d}^\gamma \le e_0^\gamma + \frac{\bar{\mu}_d^\gamma}{1+\bar{r}_d^\gamma} \tag{10.15}$$

$$m_s^\gamma + d_s^{G\gamma} + \bar{\mu}_d^\gamma \le e_s^\gamma + \pi_0^\gamma + \bar{R}_s^\delta \bar{d}^\gamma \left(1+\bar{\rho}\right) \tag{10.16}$$

$$\pi_0^\gamma = m_0^\gamma \left(1+r_0^\gamma\right) + d_0^{G\gamma} \left(1+\rho_0^{CB}\right) + p^\alpha \bar{m}^\alpha \tag{10.17}$$

$$\pi_s^\gamma = m_s^\gamma \left(1+r_s^\gamma\right) + d_s^\gamma \left(1+\rho_s^{CB}\right) \tag{10.18}$$

where:

$\pi_{s*}^\gamma \equiv$ bank γ's profits at state $s*$;

$\bar{m}^\alpha \equiv$ mortgage extension to α;

$m_s^\gamma \equiv$ short-term credit extension to α in state $s*$;

$\bar{d}^\gamma \equiv$ long-term deposits in the interbank market by bank γ in $s*$;

$d_{s*}^{Gj} \equiv$ cash sent by bank $j \in \mathcal{J}$ to enter a reverse repurchase agreement in state $s*$;

$\bar{\mu}_d^\gamma \equiv$ long-term borrowing by γ from household θ;

$\bar{\rho} \equiv$ long-term interbank market rate;

$\rho_{s*}^{CB} \equiv$ short-term interest rate on government bonds in state $s*$;

$e_{s*}^j \equiv$ capital endowment of bank $j \in \mathcal{J}$ in state $s*$;

$p^\alpha \equiv$ price of MBS sold to ψ; and

$\bar{R}_s^\delta \equiv$ delivery rate on the inter-period interbank deposit that γ made in bank δ.

Bank δ's optimisation problem

δ is also a risk-averse bank with quadratic preferences that maximises the utility provided by its second-period expected profits. At the end of the second period the bank is liquidated by the central bank.

At every $s* \in S*$, δ enters into a repurchase agreement with the central bank and uses θ's short-term credit repayment to meet its repo market obligation. In the first period δ borrows money in the long-term interbank market, and extends long-term credit to ψ and ϕ in the wholesale money market. In the second period it uses wholesale money market repayments to meet its obligation in the interbank market. Its second-period profits are given by θ's short-term loan repayment less the amount due in the repo market. The maximisation problem is as follows:

$$\max_{m_{s*},\,\mu_{s*}^{G\delta},\,\bar{m},\,\bar{\mu}_s^\delta,\,\mu_s^\delta,\,\bar{v}_s^\delta,\,\pi_s} \sum_{s\in S} \varpi_s \left(\pi_s^\delta - c^\delta \left(\pi_s^\delta\right)^2\right) - \sum_{s\in S} \varpi_s \bar{\tau}_s^\delta \left[\bar{D}_s^\delta\right]^+$$

(10.19)

$$s.t.\ m_0^\delta + \bar{m} \le e_0^\delta + \frac{\mu_0^{G\delta}}{\left(1 + \rho_0^{CB}\right)} + \frac{\bar{\mu}^\delta}{\left(1 + \bar{\rho}\right)}$$

(10.20)

$$\mu_0^{G\delta} \le m_0^\delta \left(1 + r_0^\delta\right)$$

(10.21)

$$m_s^\delta + \bar{v}_s^\delta \bar{\mu}^\delta \le e_s^\delta + \frac{\mu_s^{G\delta}}{\left(1 + \rho_s^{CB}\right)} + \bar{R}_s \bar{m} \left(1 + \bar{r}\right)$$

(10.22)

$$\pi_s^\delta = m_s^\delta \left(1 + r_s^\delta\right) - \mu_s^{G\delta}$$

(10.23)

where:

$\pi_s^\delta \equiv$ bank δ's profits in state s;

$m_{s*}^\delta \equiv$ short-term credit extended by δ to θ in state $s*$;

$\bar{m} \equiv$ overall long-term credit extension to financial institutions $\{\psi,\phi\}$;

$\mu_{s*}^{Gj} \equiv$ amount due by bank $j \in \mathcal{J}$ in the repo market in state $s*$;

$\bar{\mu}^\delta \equiv$ long-term borrowing by δ in the interbank market;

$\bar{v}_s^\delta \equiv$ repayment rate to γ on long-term interbank loans;

$\bar{R}_s \equiv$ delivery rate on the wholesale money market credit extension;

$\bar{\tau}_s^\delta \equiv$ marginal disutility to δ for defaulting on the interbank loan in states; and

$\bar{D}_s^\delta = \left(1 - \bar{v}_s^\delta\right) \bar{\mu}^\delta \equiv \delta$'s nominal value of long-term interbank debt due to default in state s.

Investment bank ψ's optimisation problem

ψ has risk-neutral preferences over its expected second-period profits. It buys mortgage assets from γ and securitises them as explained in the subsection, 'Securitisation'. Then it sells the structured asset (CDO) to ϕ. ψ finances the purchase of mortgage assets with an inter-period loan from δ. In the second period ψ repays δ after the CDO market has settled. In the bad state of the world ψ ends up owning the mortgage's collateral and selling it in the housing market.[5] Moreover, the CDS leg of the CDO contract forces ψ to return to ϕ its initial CDO investment.[6] The maximisation problem is as follows:

$$\max_{\tilde{m},\bar{\mu}^{\psi},\bar{v}^{\psi}_s} \overset{\psi}{\prod} = \sum_{s \in S} \varpi_s \pi^{\psi}_s - \sum_{s \in S} \varpi_s \bar{\tau}^{\psi}_s \left[\bar{D}^{\psi}_s \right]^+ \tag{10.24}$$

$$s.t. \; \tilde{m}^{\alpha} \le e^{\psi}_0 + \frac{\bar{\mu}^{\psi}}{(1+\bar{r})} \tag{10.25}$$

$$\bar{v}^{\psi}_s \bar{\mu}^{\psi} \le \frac{\tilde{m}^{\alpha}}{p^{\alpha}} \tilde{q}^{\alpha} + e^{\psi}_s \quad for \quad s \in S^{\alpha}_1 \tag{10.26}$$

$$\tilde{m}^{\alpha} \tilde{q}^{\alpha} + \bar{v}^{\psi}_s \bar{\mu}^{\psi}$$

$$\le e^{\psi}_s + \left(\tilde{q}^{\alpha} + \frac{b^{\alpha}_{02} p_{22}}{\tilde{m}^{\alpha} p_{02}} \right) \frac{\tilde{m}^{\alpha}}{p^{\alpha}} \quad for \quad s \notin S^{\alpha}_1 \tag{10.27}$$

$$\pi^{\psi}_s = \frac{\tilde{m}^{\alpha}}{p^{\alpha}} \tilde{q}^{\alpha} + e^{\psi}_s - \bar{v}^{\psi}_s \bar{\mu}^{\psi} \quad for \quad s \in S^{\alpha}_1 \tag{10.28}$$

$$\pi^{\psi}_s = e^{\psi}_s + \left(\tilde{q}^{\alpha} + \frac{b^{\alpha}_{02} p_{22}}{\tilde{m}^{\alpha} p_{02}} \right) \frac{\tilde{m}^{\alpha}}{p^{\alpha}}$$

$$- \tilde{m}^{\alpha} \tilde{q}^{\alpha} - \bar{v}^{\psi}_s \bar{\mu}^{\psi} \quad for \quad s \notin S^{\alpha}_1 \tag{10.29}$$

where:

$\pi^{\psi}_s \equiv$ bank ψ's profits at state s;

$\tilde{m}^{\alpha} \equiv$ money sent by ψ to purchase mortgage assets from γ;

$\bar{\mu}^{\psi} \equiv$ inter-period borrowing from δ;

$\bar{r} \equiv$ interest rate offered by δ on the inter-period loan;

$\bar{v}^{\psi}_s \equiv$ ψ's repayment rate on the loan extended by δ in state s;

$\tilde{q}^{\alpha} \equiv$ price of CDO;

$\bar{\tau}^{\psi}_s \equiv$ marginal disutility to ψ for defaulting on the long-term loan with δ in state s;

$\bar{D}^{\psi}_s = \left(1 - \bar{v}^{\psi}_s \right) \bar{\mu}^{\psi} \equiv$ ψ's nominal value of wholesale debt due to default in state s; and

$\left(1 + \bar{r}^{\gamma\alpha}_s \right) = \frac{p_{22} b^{\alpha}_{02}}{p_{02}} (\tilde{m}^{\alpha})^{-1} \equiv$ effective mortgage rate in state $s \notin S^{\alpha}_1$.

Hedge fund ϕ's optimisation problem

ϕ also has risk-neutral preferences over its expected second-period profits. It buys CDOs from ψ and finances this purchase with an inter-period loan from δ in the wholesale money market. After the state of the world is realised in the second period, ϕ repays δ with the gross returns of its CDO investment. The maximisation problem is as follows:

$$\max_{\bar{\mu}^\phi, \hat{m}, \bar{v}_{s*}^\phi} \prod^\phi = \sum_{s \in S} \varpi_s \pi_s^\phi - \sum_{s \in S} \varpi_s \bar{\tau}_s^\phi \left[\bar{D}_s^\phi\right]^+ \tag{10.30}$$

$$s.t. \ \hat{m}^\alpha \leq \frac{\bar{\mu}^\phi}{(1 + \bar{r})} \tag{10.31}$$

$$\bar{v}_s^\phi \bar{\mu}^\phi \leq \frac{\hat{m}^\alpha}{\tilde{q}^\alpha}(1 + \bar{r}^{\gamma\alpha}) \quad for \quad s \in S_1^\alpha \tag{10.32}$$

$$\bar{v}_s^\phi \bar{\mu}^\phi \leq \hat{m}^\alpha \quad for \quad s \notin S_1^\alpha \tag{10.33}$$

$$\pi_s^\phi = \frac{\hat{m}^\alpha}{\tilde{q}^\alpha}(1 + \bar{r}^{\gamma\alpha}) - \bar{v}_s^\phi \bar{\mu}^\phi \quad for \quad s \in S_1^\alpha \tag{10.34}$$

$$\pi_s^\phi = \hat{m}^\alpha - \bar{v}_s^\phi \bar{\mu}^\phi \quad for \quad s \notin S_1^\alpha \tag{10.35}$$

where:

$\pi_s^\phi \equiv$ bank ϕ's profits at state s;

$\hat{m}^\alpha \equiv$ money sent by ϕ to purchase CDOs from ψ;

$\bar{\mu}^\phi \equiv$ inter-period borrowing from δ;

$\bar{v}_s^\phi \equiv \phi$'s repayment rate on the loan extended by δ;

$\bar{\tau}_s^\phi \equiv$ marginal disutility to ϕ for defaulting on the long-term loan with δ in state s; and

$\bar{D}_s^\phi = (1 - \bar{v}_s^\phi)\bar{\mu}^\phi \equiv \phi$'s nominal value of long-term interbank debt in state s.

Market-clearing conditions

There are ten markets in the economy: the goods, housing, mortgage, short-term loans, consumer deposit, wholesale money, repo, interbank, MBS and CDO markets. In each of these markets the price equating demand and supply is determined. The price formation mechanism is identical to the offer-for-sale mechanism given by Dubey and Shubik (1978). The denominator of each of the expressions (10.36) to (10.50) represents the supply side, whereas the numerator divided by the price corresponds to the demand.

Goods market In every state-period, the goods market clears when the amount of money offered for goods is exchanged for the quantity of goods offered for sale.

$$p_{01} = \frac{b_{01}^{\theta}}{q_{01}^{\alpha}} \tag{10.36}$$

$$p_{s1} = \frac{b_{s1}^{\theta}}{q_{s1}^{\alpha}} \quad for \quad s \in S \tag{10.37}$$

Housing market In every state-period, the housing market clears when the amount of money offered for housing is exchanged for the quantity of housing offered for sale. In every $s \notin S_1^{\alpha}$, since agent α defaults on his mortgage, the amount of housing he pledged as collateral in the previous period is also offered for sale by the investment bank.

$$p_{02} = \frac{b_{02}^{\alpha}}{q_{02}^{\theta}} \tag{10.38}$$

$$p_{s2} = \frac{b_{s2}^{\alpha}}{q_{s2}^{\theta}} \quad for \quad s \in S_1^{\alpha} \tag{10.39}$$

$$p_{s2} = \frac{b_{s2}^{\alpha}}{q_{s2}^{\theta} + b_{02}^{\alpha}/p_{02}} \quad for \quad s \notin S_1^{\alpha} \tag{10.40}$$

Mortgage market The mortgage market clears when the amount offered to be repaid in the second period is exchanged for the mortgage extension offered in the first period.

$$\left(1 + \bar{r}^{\gamma\alpha}\right) = \frac{\bar{\mu}^{\alpha}}{\bar{m}^{\alpha}} \tag{10.41}$$

The effective return on the mortgage at any state in the second period is given by

$$\left(1 + \bar{r}_s^{\gamma\alpha}\right) = \frac{\min\{value\ of\ collateral,\ mortgage\ amount\ due\}}{initial\ mortgage\ extension}$$

$$= \frac{\min\{p_{22}\left(b_{02}^{\alpha}/p_{02}\right),\ \bar{\mu}^{\alpha}\}}{\bar{m}^{\alpha}}$$

Therefore, the clearing conditions for effective returns on mortgages are given by

$$\left(1 + \bar{r}_s^{\gamma\alpha}\right) = \begin{cases} \left(1 + \bar{r}^{\gamma\alpha}\right) & for\ s \in S_1^{\alpha} \\ \frac{p_{22}b_{02}^{\alpha}}{p_{02}}\left(\frac{\bar{\mu}^{\alpha}}{1+\bar{r}^{\gamma\alpha}}\right)^{-1} & for\ s \notin S_1^{\alpha} \end{cases} \tag{10.42}$$

Short-term consumer credit markets   For any state-period, short-term consumer credit markets clear when the amount offered to be repaid at the end of the period is exchanged for the short-term credit extension offered at the beginning of that period.

$$\left(1 + r_{s*}^{\gamma}\right) = \frac{\mu_{s*}^{\alpha}}{m_{s*}^{\gamma}} \tag{10.43}$$

$$\left(1 + r_{s*}^{\delta}\right) = \frac{\mu_{s*}^{\theta}}{m_{s*}^{\delta}} \tag{10.44}$$

Consumer deposit market   The consumer deposit market clears when the amount commercial banks offer to repay to households in the second period is exchanged for the amount of savings offered for deposit in the first period.

$$\left(1 + \bar{r}_{d}^{\gamma}\right) = \frac{\bar{\mu}_{d}^{\gamma}}{\bar{d}^{\theta}} \tag{10.45}$$

Wholesale money market   The wholesale money market clears when the amount offered to be repaid in the second period is exchanged for the long-term credit extension offered in the first period.

$$(1 + \bar{r}) = \frac{\bar{\mu}^{\psi} + \bar{\mu}^{\phi}}{\bar{m}} \tag{10.46}$$

Repo market   In every state-period, the repo market clears when the amount offered to be repaid at the end of the period is exchanged for the short-term credit extension and the liquidity provided by the central bank (through OMOs) at the beginning of the period.

$$\left(1 + \rho_{s*}^{CB}\right) = \frac{\mu_{s*}^{G\delta}}{M_{s*}^{CB} + d_{s*}^{G\gamma}} \tag{10.47}$$

Interbank market   The interbank market clears when the amount offered to be repaid in the second period is exchanged for the long-term credit extension in the first period.

$$(1 + \bar{\rho}) = \frac{\bar{\mu}^{\delta}}{\bar{d}^{\gamma}} \tag{10.48}$$

MBS market The MBS market clears when the amount of money offered for these securities is exchanged for the quantity of MBSs offered for sale.

$$p^\alpha = \frac{\tilde{m}^\alpha}{\overline{m}^\alpha} \tag{10.49}$$

CDO market The CDO market clears when the amount of money offered for these securities is exchanged for the quantity of CDOs offered for sale.

$$\tilde{q}^\alpha = \frac{\hat{m}^\alpha}{\tilde{m}^\alpha / p^\alpha} \tag{10.50}$$

Conditions on expected delivery rates (rational expectations) Rational expectations conditions imply that commercial banks are correct in their expectations about the fraction of loans that will be repaid to them.

Wholesale money market δ's expected rate of wholesale money market loan delivery is given by

$$\bar{R}_s = \begin{cases} \frac{\bar{v}_s^\psi \bar{\mu}^\psi + \bar{v}_s^\phi \bar{\mu}^\phi}{\bar{\mu}^\psi + \bar{\mu}^\phi} & if \quad \bar{\mu}_s^\psi + \bar{\mu}_s^\phi > 0 \\ arbitrary & if \quad \bar{\mu}_s^\psi + \bar{\mu}_s^\phi = 0 \end{cases} \quad \forall s \in S \tag{10.51}$$

Interbank markets γ's expected rate of interbank loan delivery is given by

$$\bar{R}_s^\delta = \begin{cases} \frac{\bar{v}_s^\delta \bar{\mu}^\delta}{\bar{\mu}^\delta} = \bar{v}_s^\delta & if \quad \bar{\mu}^\delta > 0 \\ arbitrary & if \quad \bar{\mu}^\delta = 0 \end{cases} \quad \forall s \in S \tag{10.52}$$

10.3   Equilibrium

Definition

Let

$$\sigma^\alpha = \left(q_{s1}^\alpha, b_{s2}^\alpha, \mu_s^\alpha, \bar{\mu}^\alpha\right) \in \Re^{s+1} \times \Re^{s+1} \times \Re^{s+1} \times \Re$$
$$\sigma^\theta = \left(q_{s2}^\theta, b_{s1}^\theta, \mu_s^\theta, \bar{d}^\theta\right) \in \Re^{s+1} \times \Re^{s+1} \times \Re^{s+1} \times \Re$$
$$\sigma^\gamma = \left(\pi_s^\gamma, m_s^\gamma, d_s^{G\gamma}, \bar{m}^\alpha, \bar{\mu}_d^\gamma, \bar{d}^\gamma\right) \in \Re^s \times \Re^{s+1} \times \Re^{s+1}$$
$$\times \Re \times \Re \times \Re$$

$$\sigma^\delta = \left(\pi_s^\delta, m_s^\delta, \mu_s^{G\gamma}, \bar{v}_s^\delta, \bar{m}, \bar{\mu}^\delta\right) \in \Re^s \times \Re^{s+1} \times \Re^{s+1}$$
$$\times \Re^s \times \Re \times \Re$$
$$\sigma^\psi = \left(\bar{v}_s^\psi, \bar{\mu}^\psi, \hat{m}^\alpha\right) \in \Re^s \times \Re \times \Re$$
$$\sigma^\phi = \left(\bar{v}_s^\phi, \bar{\mu}^\phi, \hat{m}^\alpha\right) \in \Re^s \times \Re \times \Re$$

In addition, let the vector of macroeconomic variables be represented by

$$\eta = \left(p_{s1}, p_{s2}, \rho_s^{CB}, r_s^\gamma, r_s^\delta, \bar{r}^{\gamma\alpha}, \bar{r}_d^\gamma, \bar{r}, \bar{\rho}, p^\alpha, \tilde{q}^\alpha\right) \in \Re^{s+1}$$
$$\times \Re^{s+1} \times \Re^{s+1} \times \Re^{s+1} \times \Re^{s+1} \times \Re \times \Re \times \Re \times \Re \times \Re \times \Re$$

and the budget set of all agents be denoted by

$$B^\alpha(\eta) = \{\sigma^\alpha : (2) - (7) \ hold\}, \ B^\theta(\eta) = \{\sigma^\theta : (9) - (13) \ hold\}$$
$$B^\gamma(\eta) = \{\sigma^\gamma : (15) - (16) \ hold\}, \ B^\delta(\eta) = \{\sigma^\delta : (20) - (22) \ hold\}$$
$$B^\psi(\eta) = \{\sigma^\psi : (25) - (27) \ hold\}, \ B^\phi(\eta) = \{\sigma^\phi : (31) - (33) \ hold\}$$

Then $(\sigma^\alpha, \sigma^\theta, \sigma^\gamma, \sigma^\delta, \sigma^\psi, \sigma^\phi, \eta)$ is a monetary equilibrium with commercial banks, collateral, securitisation and default (MEBCSD) if and only if (iff):

(i) all agents optimise given their budget sets:
   (a) $\sigma^h \in \arg\max_{\sigma^h \in B^h(\eta)} U^h\left(\chi_{s^*}^h\right), \ h \in H = \{\alpha, \theta\}, \ s^* \in S^*$
   (b) $\sigma^j \in \arg\max_{\sigma^j \in B^j(\eta)} \Pi^j\left(\pi_s^j\right), \ j \in \mathcal{J} = \{\gamma, \delta\}, \ s \in S$
   (c) $\sigma^k \in \arg\max_{\sigma^k \in B^k(\eta)} \Pi^k\left(\pi_s^k\right), \ k = \{\psi, \phi\}, \ s \in S$
   where $\chi_{s^*}^h$ is the vector of quantities of housing and goods consumed by agent h at state $s^* \in S^*$, $U^h(\cdot)$ is households' utility function over consumption streams of goods and houses, and $\Pi(\cdot)$ is the commercial banks and investors' utility function over their second-period profits;

(ii) all markets clear – hence, equations (10.36) to (10.50) hold; and

(iii) expectations are rational – thus conditions (10.51) to (10.52) are satisfied.

Properties of the MEBCSD

At each market meeting, money is exchanged for another commodity or security. Accordingly, the traditional transaction motive for holding money and the standard Hicksian IS/LM determinants of money demand, namely interest rates and income, are at work in this model.

*The transmission mechanism of monetary policy, credit spreads
and the term structure of interest rates proposition*

At all states, monetary policy is transmitted to the economy through
the repo market via credit extension by commercial banks in the short-
term credit markets; in the first period, however, long-term credit markets create an additional channel for the transmission of monetary
policy.

As a result, banks' portfolio decisions and default in the mortgage,
interbank, short-term credit, repo and wholesale money markets determine the money multiplier in the economy, as well as credit spreads
between lending and borrowing interest rates. The model can encom-
pass monetary propositions about credit spreads that hold because
ex ante interest rates are considered, and these do not incorporate
default premiums. Therefore, in the presence of default, borrowing
rates have to be at least as high as lending rates to preclude arbitrage
opportunities.

Proposition 1 *At any MEBCSD, $r_{s*}^\delta, \rho_{s*}^{CB} \geq 0$ and, since household θ cannot default on short-term credit loans, $r_{s*}^\delta = \rho_{s*}^{CB} \forall s^* \in S^*$.*

Proposition 2 *At any MEBCSD, $r_{s*}^\gamma, \rho_{s*}^{CB} \geq 0$ and, since household α cannot default on short-term credit loans, $r_{s*}^\gamma = \rho_{s*}^{CB} \forall s^* \in S^*$.*

Proposition 3 *At any MEBCSD, $\rho_0^{CB}, \bar{r}_d^\gamma \geq 0$ and, since bank γ cannot
default on consumer deposits, $\rho_0^{CB} = \bar{r}_d^\gamma$.*

Proposition 4 *At any MEBCSD, $\rho_0^{CB}, p^\alpha \geq 0$ and $p^\alpha = 1 + \rho_0^{CB}$.*

Proposition 5 *At any MEBCSD, $\bar{r}, \bar{\rho}, \bar{r}_d^\gamma \geq 0$ and $\bar{r} \geq \bar{\rho} \geq \bar{r}_d^\gamma \geq 0$.*

The term structure of interest rates is affected by both liquidity provision by banks and default by households, investors and banks. Moreover,
default emerges as an equilibrium phenomenon that affects interest rates
because these price in anticipated default rates (default premiums).

Put formally, $\forall s \in S$ aggregate *ex post* interest payments to commercial banks adjusted by default equal the economy's total amount
of outside money plus interest payments of commercial banks' accumulated profits. This is not the case in the first period, when uncertainty induces commercial banks to accumulate profits and/or make
indirect investments in the derivatives markets; thus aggregate interest payments will be less than or equal to aggregate initial monetary
endowments.

212 Goodhart, Osorio and Tsomocos

Proposition 6 *At any MEBCSD for* $s \in S_1^\alpha$,

$$\sum_{j \in \mathcal{J}} \left(m_0^j r_0^j \right) + \rho_0^{CB} \bar{m}^\alpha + \sum_{j \in \mathcal{J}} \left(\pi_s^j \right) + \rho_s^{CB} M_s^{CB} + \rho_0^{CB} \bar{m}^\alpha \bar{r}^{\gamma \alpha}$$

$$= \sum_{h \in H} \left(e_{m,o}^h + e_{m,s}^h \right) + \sum_{\tilde{k} = \{\gamma, \delta, \psi\}} \left(e_o^k + e_s^k \right) + \frac{r_0^\gamma}{1 + r_0^\gamma} \pi_0^\gamma$$

For $s \notin S_1^\alpha$

$$\sum_{j \in \mathcal{J}} \left(m_0^j r_0^j \right) + \rho_0^{CB} \bar{m}^\alpha + \sum_{j \in \mathcal{J}} \left(\pi_s^j \right) + \rho_s^{CB} M_s^{CB}$$

$$+ \rho_0^{CB} \bar{m}^\alpha \left(\tilde{q}^\alpha - (1 + \bar{r}_s^{\gamma \alpha}) \right)$$

$$= \sum_{h \in H} \left(e_{m,o}^h + e_{m,s}^h \right) + \sum_{\tilde{k} = \{\gamma, \delta, \psi\}} \left(e_o^k + e_s^k \right) + \frac{r_0^\gamma}{1 + r_0^\gamma} \pi_0^\gamma$$

For $t = 0$[7]

$$\sum_{j \in \mathcal{J}} \left(m_0^j r_0^j \right) < \sum_{h \in H} \left(e_{m,o}^h \right) + \sum_{\tilde{k} = \{\gamma, \delta, \psi\}} \left(e_o^k \right)$$

Monetary policy non-neutrality proposition

We have introduced two nominal frictions to the model, private monetary endowments and default on credit markets, which ensure positive nominal interest rates by pinning down the price of money (Shubik and Wilson 1977; Dubey and Geanakoplos 1992; Shubik and Tsomocos 1992; Espinoza, Goodhart and Tsomocos 2008).

Proposition 7 *Assume agent h borrows from bank j in the short-term credit market. Furthermore, let* $\{\chi_{s^*,l}^h, \chi_{s^*,m}^h\}$ *denote traded quantities of two distinct goods* $\{l, m\}$, *and suppose that h purchases good l, and sells and has an endowment* $\left(e_{s^*,m}^h \right)$ *of good m at* $s^* \in S^*$. *If* $r_{s^*}^j > 0$, *then*

$$\frac{p_{s^*l}(1 + r_{s^*}^j)}{p_{s^*m}} = \frac{u'\left(\chi_{s^*,l}^h\right)}{u'\left(e_{s^*,m}^h - \chi_{s^*,m}^h\right)}$$

i.e. there is a wedge between selling and purchasing prices.

Proposition 8 *If nominal interest rates are positive, then monetary policy is non-neutral.*

The quantity theory of money proposition

The model has a non-trivial quantity theory of money. An agent will not hold idle cash he does not want to spend; instead, he will lend it out to someone who is willing to use it. It follows that, if all the interest rates are positive, then in equilibrium the quantity theory of money holds with money velocity equal to one. Moreover, since quantities supplied in the markets are chosen by agents (unlike the representative agent model's sell-all assumption), the real velocity of money is endogenous. Consequently, nominal changes affect both prices and quantities.

At each state in the second period, nominal income equals the stock of money, because all the liquidity available in the economy is channelled to commodity markets. However, at $t = 0$ uncertainty and the inability of agents to complete the asset span will induce commercial banks to accumulate profits and/or make indirect investments in the derivatives markets (through credit extensions in the interbank and wholesale money markets).

Proposition 9 *In an MEBCSD, if $\rho_{s^*}^{CB} > 0$ for some $s^* \in S^*$, then aggregate income at $s \in S_1^\alpha$ is equal to the stock of money at that period, namely the total amount of outside and inside money, plus commercial banks' accumulated profits from the previous period plus the banking financial sector's net pay-offs from its indirect investments in the derivatives markets. When there is no default in the mortgage market, the mortgage's repayment is forgone income to commercial banks and is used by the hedge fund to repay its wholesale money market obligation.*

$$\sum_{h\in H, l=\{1,2\}} \left(p_{sl}q_{sl}^h\right)$$
$$= \sum_{h\in H} e_{m,s}^h + \sum_{j\in \mathcal{J}} e_s^h + M_s^{CB} + \pi_o^\gamma + \bar{R}_s\bar{m}(1+\bar{r}) - \bar{m}^\alpha(1+\bar{r}^{\gamma\alpha})$$

For $s \notin S_1^\alpha$, the quantity theory of money holds as above, except that the banking financial sector's loss due to default on the mortgage and derivatives markets is embedded in the expected repayment rates of wholesale money market loans.

$$\sum_{h\in H, l\in\{1,2\}} \left(p_{sl}q_{sl}^h\right) = \sum_{h\in H} e_{m,s}^h + \sum_{j\in \mathcal{J}} e_s^h + M_s^{CB} + \pi_o^\gamma + \bar{R}_s\bar{m}(1+\bar{r})$$

For $s = 0$, national income is equal to the stock of money in the economy less indirect expenditures by commercial banks in the derivatives markets.

$$\sum_{h\in H, l\in\{1,2\}} \left(p_{0l}q_{0l}^h\right) = \sum_{h\in H} e_{m,0}^h + \sum_{j\in \mathcal{J}} e_0^h + M_0^{CB} - \bar{m}$$

The Fisher effect proposition

The model has an integral monetary sector in which equilibrium interest rates are determined in nominal terms. As a result, long-term nominal interest rates equal their corresponding real interest rate plus the expected rate of inflation and a risk premium.

Proposition 10 *Suppose agent α chooses b_{02}^α, $b_{12}^\alpha > 0$, and has money left over when the mortgage loan comes due, then in an MEBCSD the following equation must hold:*

$$(1 + \bar{r}^{\gamma\alpha}) = \left(1 + \frac{u'\left(\chi_{02}^\alpha\right)}{\varpi_1 u'\left(\chi_{02}^\alpha + \chi_{12}^\alpha\right)}\right)\left(\frac{p_{12}}{p_{02}}\right) \Leftrightarrow \bar{r}^{\gamma\alpha}$$

$$\approx \frac{u'\left(\chi_{02}^\alpha\right)}{\varpi_1 u'\left(\chi_{02}^\alpha + \chi_{12}^\alpha\right)} + \Pi_{12}$$

where $\Pi_{12} = (p_{12} - p_{02})/p_{02}$ represents housing inflation at state 1. Similarly, assume agent θ chooses $b_{s*2}^\theta > 0 \, \forall \, s^* \in S^*$ and has money left over when the consumer deposit market meets, then at an MEBCSD

$$(1 + \bar{r}_d^\gamma) = \frac{u'\left(\chi_{01}^\theta\right)/p_{01}}{E_s\left\{u'\left(\chi_{s1}^\theta\right)/p_{s1}\right\}} = \left(\frac{u'\left(\chi_{01}^\theta\right)/p_{01}}{u'\left(\chi_{s1}^\theta\right)/p_{s1}}\right)\frac{\lambda_s}{\varpi_s} \quad for \quad s \in S$$

where $\Pi_{s1} = (p_{s1} - p_{01})/p_{01}$ represents goods inflation at state $s \in S$ and λ_s are the risk-neutral probabilities.

Thus, nominal long-term interest rates are approximately equal to real interest rates (which are linear in the intertemporal marginal rates of substitution) plus expected inflation and a risk premium.

Discussion of equilibrium

Hereafter, we analyse a parameterised version of the model, in which the chosen vector of parameter values allows for an illustration of how default in the mortgage market hinges upon the nominal sector of the economy (see Tables 10.1 and 10.2). We have assumed two possible states of nature in the second period, and that a state 1 realisation is more likely than a state 2 realisation. In the first period agent θ is somewhat richer than α in monetary endowments; at all states bank γ is more capitalised than bank δ, the investment bank (ψ) has a very small amount of capital and the hedge fund (ϕ) has no capital.

The economy experiences an adverse productivity shock in the goods sector that is moderate in the first state and severe in the second state. Moreover, the central bank reacts by loosening monetary policy in state

Table 10.1 *Exogenous variables: selected parameters*

Risk aversion coefficients		Commodity endowments		Monetary endowments		Default penalties		Money supply and state probabilities	
		Goods	Housing						
c^α	1.30	e^α_{01} 30	e^θ_{02} 20	m^α_0	10	$\bar\tau^\delta_1$	1.00	M^{CB}_0	25.0
c^θ	1.30	e^α_{11} 20		m^α_1	1	$\bar\tau^\delta_2$	0.05	M^{CB}_1	28.0
c^γ	0.03	e^α_{21} 4		m^α_2	1	$\bar\tau^\psi_1$	2.00	M^{CB}_2	0.1
c^δ	0.03			m^θ_0	60	$\bar\tau^\psi_2$	0.00001	ϖ_1	0.85
				m^θ_1	1	$\bar\tau^\phi_1$	0.10	ϖ_2	0.15
				m^θ_2	1	$\bar\tau^\phi_2$	0.00005		
				e^γ_0	60				
				e^γ_1	1				
				e^γ_2	1				
				e^δ_0	1.0				
				e^δ_1	0.1				
				e^δ_2	0.1				
				e^ψ_0	0.00001				
				e^ψ_1	0.00001				
				e^ψ_2	0.00001				

1 and by tightening it in state 2; hence, relative to the first period, the repo rate is lower at $s = 1$ and higher at $s = 2$. The latter illustrates the policy trade-off between price and financial stability, as well as the consequences of disregarding financial imbalances in the pursuit of low and stable inflation.

Repo rates equal short-term interest rates at all states, and in the first period the deposit rate equals the repo rate (as the no-arbitrage conditions for default-free loans hold). Furthermore, the wholesale money market rate is higher than the interbank rate, which in turn is higher than the deposit rate, thus confirming that the no-arbitrage conditions for long-term defaultable loans are maintained.

In the benchmark equilibrium, house and goods prices move in opposite directions; the relative price of houses drops from the first to the second period, and is lower in state 2 than in state 1. This is a consequence of the negative supply shock in the goods market. Intuitively, agent α defaults on his mortgage when the value of his house is low, and house prices fall when goods endowments are scarce because α is forced to demand less housing on account of lower goods sales revenues. As a

Table 10.2 *Initial equilibrium*

Prices		Households' lending, borrowing		Financial sector lending, borrowing		Repayment rates		Trade and spending				Derivatives	
								Goods		Housing			
p_{01}	3.23	μ_0^α	53.43	$d_0^{G\gamma}$	14.62	$\bar{v}_1^\alpha$	100.0%	q_{01}^α	16.53	q_{02}^θ	4.47	$\tilde{m}^\alpha$	14.10
p_{11}	11.46	μ_1^α	6.46	$d_1^{G\gamma}$	8.18	$\bar{v}_2^\alpha$	85.3%	q_{11}^α	9.29	q_{12}^θ	4.34	$\hat{m}^\alpha$	31.51
p_{21}	53.59	μ_2^α	85.70	$d_2^{G\gamma}$	7.64	$\bar{v}_1^\delta$	98.5%	q_{21}^α	1.60	q_{22}^θ	4.30		
p_{02}	12.75	$\bar{\mu}^\alpha$	34.07	m_0^γ	37.16	$\bar{v}_2^\delta$	58.6%	b_{01}^θ	53.43	b_{02}^α	56.96		
p_{12}	11.53	μ_0^θ	56.96	m_1^γ	83.09	$\bar{v}_1^\psi$	100.0%	b_{11}^θ	106.46	b_{12}^θ	50.02		
p_{22}	6.50	μ_1^θ	50.02	m_2^γ	56.02	$\bar{v}_2^\psi$	88.8%	b_{21}^θ	85.70	b_{22}^α	57.02		
r_0^γ	0.44	μ_2^θ	27.96	$\bar{m}^\alpha$	9.81	$\bar{v}_1^\phi$	100.0%						
r_1^γ	0.28	$\bar{d}^\theta$	46.19	$\bar{\mu}_d^\gamma$	66.42	$\bar{v}_2^\phi$	64.3%						
r_2^γ	0.53			$\bar{d}^\gamma$	44.61								
r_0^δ	0.44			$\mu_0^{G\delta}$	56.96								
r_1^δ	0.28			$\mu_1^{G\delta}$	46.36								
r_2^δ	0.53			$\mu_2^{G\delta}$	11.84								
$\bar{r}_d^\gamma$	0.44			m_0^δ	39.62								
$\bar{r}^{\gamma\alpha}$	2.47			m_1^δ	39.04								
ρ_0^{CB}	0.55			m_2^δ	18.28								
ρ_1^{CB}	0.44			$\bar{m}$	45.61								
ρ_2^{CB}	0.28			$\bar{\mu}^\delta$	69.17								
$\bar{\rho}$	0.53			$\bar{\mu}^\psi$	21.92								
$\bar{r}$	0.55			$\bar{\mu}^\phi$	48.98								
p^α	1.44												
$\bar{q}^\alpha$	2.23												

result, lower demand in the housing market reduces house prices, while lower supply in the goods market raises the price of goods.

Moreover, as the relative price of houses drops across time, consumer α's marginal rate of substitution of housing over goods consumption decreases (proposition 7); accordingly, the volume of trade in the housing market is lower in the second period, since he retains more of his goods endowment. Similarly, as the Fisher effect proposition holds, positive inflation rates of goods in both states of the second period imply that household θ's marginal utility of goods consumption is higher at $t = 1$, or, equivalently, that the quantity of traded goods is higher at $t = 0$ than at either state of the second period.

Consumer α is rich in the endowment of goods at the first period; thus he can finance a large percentage of his desired housing expenditure with sales revenues, and he is not required to have a large loan-to-value mortgage. Because of falling house prices, however, α defaults on his mortgage in state 2; consequently, the effective return on the mortgage decreases, and default rates in the wholesale and interbank markets increase in that state. Since rational expectations are assumed throughout, this induces bank γ to offer a very high mortgage rate in the first period.

In state 1 there is no default in the wholesale money market, because α honours his mortgage obligation, which is the underlying asset for MBS and CDO securities; ψ and ϕ repay their wholesale money market obligations fully with the proceeds from the securitisation premium and the pay-off on the mortgage, respectively. However, bank δ defaults on a small percentage of its interbank liability, because this is the repayment rate that equates its marginal utility of default to the default penalty.

In contrast, in state 2 default in the mortgage market creates significant losses in the non-banking financial sector. The CDS contract forces the hedge fund to deliver the mortgage's collateral to ψ, and in return ϕ receives the total amount of its investment. ψ assumes a write-down loss because it sells the collateral, which lowers house prices further. Although ϕ and ψ have undertaken hedging strategies and have no incentives to accumulate profits, their overall revenues are not enough to cover their obligations with bank δ. Thus default increases in the wholesale money market, which reduces bank δ's revenues and forces it to default significantly on its interbank loan.

We hasten to emphasise that, since monetary policy is non-neutral and a non-trivial quantity theory of money holds, expansionary monetary policy in state 1 offsets partially the adverse effects of the productivity shock on trade, while tighter monetary policy in state 2 exacerbates them.

Remarks on welfare

There are two states and two assets (the MBS or mortgage and the CDO). Markets are not complete, however, because there is default in the mortgage, interbank and wholesale money markets as well as limited participation of agents in the derivatives, repo, interbank, short-term credit, consumer deposit and wholesale money markets. These restrictions prevent each agent from completing the asset span, which implies that financial markets are incomplete and that any MEBCSD is constrained inefficient. Therefore there is scope for welfare-improving economic policy, both regulatory and monetary (Geanakoplos and Polemarchakis 1986).

10.4   Comparative statics

In this section we describe how endogenous variables react to shocks by analysing their directional response to changes in the vector of exogenous variables. We conducted several experiments, but we report only those we reckon more interesting: expansionary policy, government subsidies and tighter default penalties for investment banks.

The purpose of these exercises is to show how certain measures contribute to financial fragility and to assess the efficiency of different policies for crisis management. Hereafter, we will use the Aspachs *et al.* (2006) measure[8] to determine whether a policy promotes financial stability or not.

Policies that contribute to financial fragility

Expansionary monetary policy in the first period[9]   Let the central bank engage in expansionary monetary policy by increasing the money supply in the initial period (see column 1 of Table 10.3). This lowers the repo rate, which induces bank δ to borrow more from the repo market, and bank γ to deposit less in it. Both commercial banks increase their supply of short-term loans, which reduces r_0^γ and r_0^δ. Thus households borrow and spend more in the goods and housing markets. This increases prices and the aggregate quantity of trade in the first period, as predicted by the quantity theory of money proposition.

Household θ uses the additional liquidity to increase his deposits with bank γ, thereby reducing the deposit rate. Consequently, bank γ admits additional deposits, which lowers the deposit rate.

In turn, this allows bank γ to extend more credit in the interbank and mortgage markets, thus reducing their corresponding interest rates and the price of MBSs. A lower interbank rate induces bank δ to borrow more

Table 10.3. *Expansionary monetary policy*

	Increase money supply $t=0$	Increase money supply $s=2$	Decrease repo rate $s=2$		Increase money supply $t=0$	Increase money supply $s=2$	Decrease repo rate $s=2$
p_{01}	+	+	+	$\bar{d}^\theta$	+	−	−
p_{11}	−	−	−	$\bar{m}^\alpha$	+	−	+
p_{21}	−	+	+	$d_0^{G\gamma}$	−	−	−
p_{02}	+	+	+	$d_1^{G\gamma}$	−	+	−
p_{12}	−	−	−	$d_2^{G\gamma}$	−	−	−
p_{22}	−	+	+	$\bar{d}^\gamma$	+	−	+
$\bar{r}^{\gamma\alpha}$	−	−	−	m_0^γ	+	+	+
r_0^γ	−	≈	≈	m_1^γ	+	−	−
r_1^γ	−	≈	≈	m_2^γ	−	+	+
r_2^γ	+	−	−	$\bar{\mu}_d^\gamma$	+	−	−
r_0^δ	−	≈	≈	$\bar{m}$	+	−	+
r_1^δ	−	≈	≈	$\mu_0^{G\delta}$	+	+	+
r_2^δ	+	−	−	$\mu_1^{G\delta}$	−	+	−
ρ_0^{CB}, M_0^{CB}	−	≈	+	$\mu_2^{G\delta}$	−	+	+
ρ_1^{CB}, M_1^{CB}	−	≈	+	m_0^δ	+	+	+
ρ_2^{CB}, M_2^{CB}	+	−	+	m_1^δ	−	+	−
$\bar{r}_d^\gamma$	−	≈	≈	m_2^δ	−	+	+
r	−	≈	≈	$\bar{\mu}^\delta$	+	−	−
$\bar{\rho}$	−	≈	≈	$\bar{v}_1^\delta$	+	−	−
p^α	−	≈	≈	$\bar{v}_2^\delta$	≈	+	+
$\tilde{q}^\alpha$	−	−	−	$\tilde{m}^\alpha$	+	−	−
q_{01}^α	−	+	+	$\bar{\mu}^\psi$	+	−	−
q_{11}^α	+	≈	+	$\bar{v}_1^\psi$	≈	≈	≈
q_{21}^α	+	−	−	$\bar{v}_2^\psi$	−	+	+
b_{02}^α	+	+	−	$\tilde{m}^\alpha$	+	−	−
b_{12}^α	−	+	+	$\bar{\mu}^\phi$	+	−	−
b_{22}^α	−	+	+	$\bar{v}_1^\phi$	≈	≈	≈
$\bar{\mu}^\alpha$	+	−	−	$\bar{v}_2^\phi$	+	+	+
μ_0^α	+	+	+	U^α	+	≈	≈
μ_1^α	−	−	−	U^θ	+	−	+
μ_2^α	−	+	+	U_0^α	+	−	−
b_{01}^θ	+	+	+	U_1^α	−	−	−
b_{11}^θ	−	−	−	U_2^α	−	+	+
b_{21}^θ	−	+	+	U_0^θ	−	+	+
q_{02}^θ	+	−	−	U_1^θ	+	+	+

(cont.)

Table 10.3. (*cont.*)

	Increase money supply $t = 0$	Increase money supply $s = 2$	Decrease repo rate $s = 2$		Increase money supply $t = 0$	Increase money supply $s = 2$	Decrease repo rate $s = 2$
q_{12}^θ	−	+	+	U_2^θ	+	−	−
q_{22}^θ	−	+	+	π_1^γ	−	−	−
μ_0^θ	+	+	+	π_2^γ	−	−	−
μ_1^θ	−	+	−	π_1^δ	−	+	≈
μ_2^θ	−	+	+	π_2^δ	+	−	−

from γ. Therefore δ extends more credit in the wholesale money market, thereby reducing its interest rate. This provides incentives to ψ and ϕ to increase their leverage and spend more in the MBS and CDO markets.

In the first period the purchasing price of houses increases relative to the selling price of goods; this leaves α with a suboptimally low marginal rate of substitution (MRS) of housing over goods consumption, which induces him to reduce the supply of goods. The opposite is true for θ.

By the term structure of interest rates proposition, short-term rates fall in state 1 and increase in state 2. In the second state, higher short-term interest rates increase the purchasing price of houses and goods, leaving both α and θ with lower marginal rates of substitution. Thus households reduce their spending in the goods and housing markets (by proposition 7), which decreases their respective prices, p_{21} and p_{22}. Lower house prices in this state intensify the housing crisis.

Expansionary monetary policy in the initial period induces households to smooth consumption across time, as their overall consumption stream rises. This policy contributes to financial fragility, however, because in the bad states of nature the poor household and the investment bank default more, and the rich bank's profits decrease.

Government subsidies (the transfer paradox)   Let the government engage in an initiative to promote home ownership by increasing the endowment of houses in the economy (see column 1 of Table 10.4). Such a policy leaves θ with a high MRS of goods over housing consumption, which induces him to increase the supply of houses at all states, thereby reducing their price. This allows household α to spend less while still purchasing a larger amount of housing. Consequently, θ makes fewer deposits, borrows less and reduces his consumption of goods at all states

Table 10.4 *Government subsidies and regulatory policies*

	Increase θ's housing endowment $t = 0$	Increase ψ's default penalty $s = 2$	Increase Y's risk aversion		Increase θ's housing endowment $t = 0$	Increase ψ's default penalty $s = 2$	Increase Y's risk aversion
p_{01}	+	≈	+	$\bar{d}^\theta$	−	+	+
p_{11}	+	+	+	$\bar{m}^\alpha$	+	−	−
p_{21}	+	+	+	$d_0^{G\gamma}$	−	+	+
p_{02}	−	+	+	$d_1^{G\gamma}$	+	−	+
p_{12}	−	+	+	$d_2^{G\gamma}$	−	+	+
p_{22}	−	+	+	$\bar{d}^\gamma$	+	−	−
$\bar{r}^{\gamma\alpha}$	+	≈	−	m_0^γ	−	+	+
r_0^γ	+	−	−	m_1^γ	+	−	−
r_1^γ	−	≈	≈	m_2^γ	−	+	+
r_2^γ	+	≈	−	$\bar{\mu}_d^\gamma$	+	−	−
r_0^δ	+	−	−	$\bar{m}$	+	−	−
r_1^δ	−	≈	≈	$\mu_0^{G\delta}$	−	+	+
r_2^δ	+	≈	−	$\mu_1^{G\delta}$	−	−	+
ρ_0^{CB}, M_0^{CB}	+	−	−	$\mu_2^{G\delta}$	−	+	+
ρ_1^{CB}, M_1^{CB}	−	≈	≈	m_0^δ	−	+	+
ρ_2^{CB}, M_2^{CB}	+	≈	−	m_1^δ	−	−	+
$\bar{r}_d^\gamma$	+	−	−	m_2^δ	−	+	+
r	+	−	+	$\bar{\mu}^\delta$	+	−	−
$\bar{\rho}$	+	≈	+	$\bar{v}_1^\delta$	+	≈	≈
p^α	+	−	−	$\bar{v}_2^\delta$	−	≈	+
$\tilde{q}^\alpha$	+	+	−	$\hat{m}^\alpha$	+	−	−
q_{01}^α	−	+	+	$\bar{\mu}^\psi$	+	−	−
q_{11}^α	−	−	−	$\bar{v}_1^\psi$	≈	≈	≈
q_{21}^α	−	≈	≈	$\bar{v}_2^\psi$	−	+	+
b_{02}^α	−	+	+	$\hat{m}^\alpha$	+	+	−
b_{12}^α	−	+	+	$\bar{\mu}^\phi$	+	−	−
b_{22}^α	−	+	+	$\bar{v}_1^\phi$	≈	≈	≈
$\bar{\mu}^\alpha$	+	−	−	$\bar{v}_2^\phi$	−	+	≈
μ_0^α	−	+	+	U^α	+	≈	+
μ_1^α	+	−	−	U^θ	−	≈	≈
μ_2^α	−	+	+	U_0^α	+	−	+
b_{01}^θ	−	+	+	U_1^α	+	+	+
b_{11}^θ	+	−	−	U_2^α	+	+	+
b_{21}^θ	−	+	+	U_0^θ	−	+	+
q_{02}^θ	+	≈	+	U_1^θ	−	−	−

(cont.)

Table 10.4 (*cont.*)

	Increase θ's housing endowment $t = 0$	Increase ψ's default penalty $s = 2$	Increase Y's risk aversion		Increase θ's housing endowment $t = 0$	Increase ψ's default penalty $s = 2$	Increase Y's risk aversion
q_{12}^θ	+	≈	≈	U_2^θ	−	−	−
q_{22}^θ	+	+	+	π_1^γ	+	−	+
μ_0^θ	−	+	+	π_2^γ	−	+	+
μ_1^θ	−	+	+	π_1^δ	−	+	+
μ_2^θ	−	+	+	π_2^δ	+	≈	−

except for $s = 1$, in which interest rates are low and allow him to finance his goods purchases with short-term loans.

As household θ deposits less, the deposit rate rises. Hence bank γ reallocates its first-period portfolio, by reducing its deposits in the repo and short-term credit markets. Similarly, bank δ borrows less in the repo market and reduces its short-term credit assets until $r_0^\delta = \rho_0^{CB}$.

Higher short-term interest rates in the initial period induce α to substitute short-term for mortgage borrowing, which increases the mortgage rate. As mortgage lending and the price of MBSs rise, derivatives become expensive and induce ψ and ϕ to increase their leverage. Higher mortgage rates and house price deflation in the bad state reduce the effective mortgage repayment and the value of the collateral; as a consequence, earnings in the shadow banking system decrease dramatically, thereby increasing default and interest rates in the wholesale money market.

This policy improves α's welfare at the expense of household θ, because the relative price of houses falls significantly at all states; therefore household α's capacity to finance house purchases with goods sales improves, while θ's capacity to finance goods purchases with housing sales deteriorates. This result provides an example of the so-called transfer paradox (see Leontief 1936 and Mas-Collel, Whinston and Green 1995).[10]

Furthermore, this measure promotes financial instability, because in the bad states of nature default increases in the mortgage, interbank and wholesale money markets and the rich bank's profit decreases. Bank γ is worse off as it assumes large losses due to increased default in the interbank market, a narrower interbank deposit spread and lower short-term credit demand in the bad states of nature. On the other hand, bank δ's profits increase marginally, because under the prevailing bankruptcy code the bank is better off by accumulating profits than by defaulting less on its interbank obligation. However, a stricter bankruptcy penalty would affect adversely its profits as well.

Policies for crisis management and prevention

Expansionary monetary policy in the bad states of nature The choice between adopting either the monetary base or the repo rate as policy instrument may have implications for the central bank's ability to maintain financial stability.

Monetary base instrument (localised liquidity trap) Let the central bank engage in expansionary monetary policy in state 2 in the second period by increasing the monetary base and letting the repo rate clear the market (see column 2 of Table 10.3). This policy reduces the repo rate in $s = 2$, thus inducing bank δ to borrow more and bank γ to deposit less in that market. Consequently, both commercial banks increase their supply of short-term loans in order to preclude arbitrage opportunities; this reduces r_2^γ and r_2^δ until they equal the repo rate. Lower short-term interest rates provide incentives to households to borrow and spend more in the goods and housing markets. Hence prices and the aggregate quantity of trade increase in state 2, as predicted by the quantity theory of money proposition.

Higher spending and inflation in the goods market in $s = 2$ leave θ with a suboptimally high MRS. As a result, θ increases his expenditure in the goods market in the initial period (Fisher effect proposition), for which he needs to make fewer deposits in bank γ and to borrow more in the short-term credit market. Higher spending in the goods market at $t = 0$ increases the price of goods and induces θ to reduce the supply of houses, thus increasing p_{02}. Similarly, α responds to higher goods prices by increasing his spending in the goods market at $t = 0$, and then, as house prices rise, he reduces the supply of goods.

α's revenues improve in the first period and induce him to substitute mortgage for short-term borrowing, which reduces the mortgage rate and raises the value of the collateral and the effective mortgage rate at $s = 2$. Therefore ψ and ϕ default less on their respective wholesale money market obligations, which reduces the interbank and wholesale money market interest rates (by proposition 5).

Nonetheless, these interest rates rise back to their original levels. As θ makes fewer deposits, the deposit rate increases significantly. This represents a shortage of long-term funds for bank γ, and hence for bank δ, which limits commercial banks' capacity to lend in the second period. Thus default in the interbank market increases, inducing γ to take fewer deposits and switch from risky assets (mortgage and interbank lending) to short-term credit assets.

Since the credit spread between the interbank and repo interest rates remains unchanged, however, δ demands even more credit in the repo market, thus raising the repo rate back to its initial value. Therefore δ provides less short-term credit to household θ, thereby raising r_0^δ to its original level.

Anticipated expansionary policy in the bad states of nature fails to improve households' welfare; household θ is worst off because he is credit constrained. Furthermore, this policy is unsuccessful in promoting financial stability, because commercial banks' profitability falls in the bad states of nature. Thus, once a crisis unravels, the economy falls into a *localised* liquidity trap:[11] the transmission mechanism of monetary policy is distorted as commercial banks restructure their portfolios away from risky assets into default-free assets. Although liquidity is channelled to consumer credit markets, interest rates remain unchanged and households are subject to credit rationing.

Repo rate instrument   Let the central bank engage in expansionary monetary policy in state 2 (see column 3 of Table 10.3). The effects are broadly the same as they are for a money supply expansion, but the crucial differences lie in the better functioning of the transmission mechanism of monetary policy, which has *important* implications for financial stability.

Bank γ is subject to a shortage of long-term funds after the deposit rate increases significantly; when the central bank fixes the repo rate at a lower level in $s = 2$, however, these additional funds are quasi-automatically (see Steiger 2006 and Goodhart, Sunirand and Tsomocos 2008) supplied to commercial banks, because their lending capacity in the second period is less affected. Consequently, and in contrast to the money supply setting, bank γ reallocates its portfolio away from repo market deposits and into short-term consumer, mortgage and interbank lending. This reduces the interbank rate, and pushes the mortgage rate down further, thereby improving the wholesale and interbank market repayment rates for the bad states of nature.

A lower interbank rate allows bank δ to borrow more long-term funds and extend more credit in the second period to the consumer credit and wholesale money markets. Note that, in contrast to the money supply expansion case, the interbank–repo and wholesale–repo credit spreads narrow.

A reduction of the repo rate in the bad states of nature does not improve financial stability fully either; default rates fall in the mortgage, interbank and wholesale money markets, but the banking sector's profits drop as credit conditions between financial institutions do not ease enough. However, households' welfare improves, because they are able to substitute consumption across time and goods efficiently as short-term consumer and mortgage lending increase.

Comparison of expansionary monetary policies in the bad states   Our results suggest that the repo rate is preferable to the monetary base as a policy instrument. In times of financial distress agents lose confidence in the banking system, which increases significantly the demand for safe and liquid assets. With the repo rate instrument, all price effects from the interbank market are eliminated, whereas, if the monetary base is controlled, the central bank creates a deadweight loss due to households' lower access to credit.

Tighter default penalties in the bad states of nature   In this subsection we describe the effects of increasing default penalties to the investment bank (see also Steiger 2006 and Goodhart, Sunirand and Tsomocos 2008).[12]

Let the FSA set a stricter bankruptcy code that affects the investment bank by increasing its default penalty in the bad states of the world – i.e. $\bar{\tau}_2^\psi$ rises (see column 2 of Table 10.4). This policy induces ψ to default less in that state by reducing its leverage and spending in the MBS market. Consequently, the price of MBSs drops while the price of CDOs increases. By proposition 5, the wholesale money market rate drops. This allows the hedge fund to make a larger CDO investment while still reducing its leverage, which induces bank δ to extend less credit in that market and borrow less in the interbank market.

As the price of MBSs and the interbank rate fall, bank γ substitutes long- for short-term assets at $t = 0$; thus ρ_0^{CB} and r_0^γ decrease and the mortgage rate increases. Since γ requires fewer deposits from θ, the deposit rate falls. Similarly, bank δ increases its borrowing in the repo market and extends more short-term credit to households in the initial period.

Even though short-term interest rates drop in the initial period, credit extension rises, thereby leaving aggregate interest payments unchanged. Therefore, by the term structure of interest rates proposition, short-term interest rates in both states of the second period, as well as the mortgage rate, remain unchanged.

Households increase their goods and housing expenditure. However, lower interest rates in the initial period induce agents to spend more in the goods and housing markets. Since house prices increase in $s = 2$, the value of the collateral and the effective mortgage rate in the bad states of nature rise, allowing ψ and ϕ to increase further their wholesale money market repayment rates.

This policy improves households' welfare and financial stability, because agents are able to substitute consumption efficiently across time, and commercial banks' profits in the bad states of nature increase as default in the interbank and wholesale money markets falls.

10.5   Implications for inflation targeting

Central banks around the world operate under an inflation-targeting regime, whereby the short-term interest rate is set to control and stabilise inflation over the medium term. In most cases, price stability would foster financial stability in the long run, which is why central bankers' accepted wisdom is that it is prudent to be sceptical about the existence of a trade-off between price and financial stability. The intuition is that excess liquidity provided by the central bank can create an environment of accelerated economic growth and high inflation; generally, these factors lead to real overinvestment and excessive credit and asset price growth, which increase the vulnerability of the financial system.

However, the current financial crisis has reminded us all that, in the short term, price and financial stability objectives may often conflict. Our model portrays this disjuncture. We have chosen a parameterisation for the model's benchmark equilibrium that allows the central bank to follow actions consistent with a strict inflation-targeting strategy. Goods have a positive inflation rate while house prices fall, and the central bank tightens monetary policy when goods inflation is very high. Nevertheless, in those states of nature, default rates in the mortgage, interbank and wholesale money markets also reach their highest levels.

Although the initial equilibrium is driven by demand and supply shocks, it is possible to assess the contribution of monetary policy to financial instability through the comparative statics exercises. Our simulations show that expansionary monetary policy in the first period promotes financial instability by increasing aggregate default and reducing commercial banks' profits, whereas, in the bad states of nature of the second period, expansionary monetary policy (if effective) reduces default in the mortgage, interbank and wholesale money markets. Thus the short-term policy conflict is evident, and it refers to the fact that it is optimal to deviate from the 'desired' rate of inflation in the short run in order to maintain price as well as financial stability best in the longer run.

Along these lines, many economists have proposed policy prescriptions that induce central banks to 'lean against the wind' of financial imbalances or asset price misalignments (such as Cechetti *et al.* 2000). However, such policies pose yet another trade-off between optimal short-term deviations from the target rate of inflation and the central bank's credibility, which is essential for the good practice of inflation targeting. If optimal monetary policy leads to prolonged deviations from the announced target rate of inflation, the central bank could lose credibility, thereby undermining the effectiveness of monetary policy. On the other hand, reputation can also be threatened if agents perceive that the central bank ignores its financial stability objective.

We argue that one way to balance these policy conflicts is to widen the targeted consumer price index to include an appropriate measure of housing prices, as suggested by Goodhart (2001), given that the most severe financial crises spring from housing market bubbles. This would allow the central bank to take asset price movements into account when conducting monetary policy.

Nevertheless, one of the reasons why central banks fail to manage the trade-off between price and financial stability is that they have only one instrument, the short-term interest rate, at their disposal. With one instrument, only one independent goal can be achieved, which is price stability. The objective of financial stability could be achieved better, therefore, by the development and application of separate instruments designed for that purpose. Brunnermeier *et al.* (2009) develop a detailed proposal along these lines and stress the importance of designing a *counter-cyclical* regulatory mechanism aimed at reducing the systemic risks that threaten financial stability.

In a similar vein, our results show that the regulation of systemic financial institutions is more effective than monetary policy in promoting financial stability; the implementation of measures that induce investment banks to behave more prudently *ex ante* reduces default and improves the banking sector's profitability without reducing households' welfare.

10.6   Concluding remarks

This model overcomes some of the limitations that DSGE models have for undertaking financial stability analyses. We present a framework that incorporates heterogeneous agents, endogenous default, an essential role for money, and incomplete financial markets; these elements ensure that financial fragility arises as an equilibrium outcome, thereby justifying the role of economic policy. Moreover, to understand and explore policy issues related to the current financial crisis, we have introduced collateralisation and securitisation to the model, because these elements capture financial markets' innovations in the recent past.

Regarding policy analysis, our results suggest that government subsidies and expansionary monetary policy in the first period are crisis catalysts. This result is consistent with the United States' recent experience: on the one hand, extremely accommodative monetary policy in a world in which regulation could not keep up with emerging financial innovations was a major contributor to the emergence of the current financial crisis; on the other hand, the US government subsidised home ownership in ways that rewarded mortgage leverage, thus promoting financial fragility.

The comparative statics exercises also show that, in times of financial distress, expansionary monetary policy implemented by means of the money supply is ineffective. This is due to the fact that, once a crisis unravels, the transmission mechanism of monetary policy is distorted and the economy falls into a localised liquidity trap. When the interest rate is used as the monetary policy instrument, however, the central bank automatically satisfies the additional demand for money that arises in times of crisis, thus easing credit conditions between financial institutions and allowing households to have more access to credit.

Finally, we suggest that central banks operating in an inflation-targeting regime should take into account the behaviour of housing prices by including them in the targeted price index. This enables them to balance better the trade-off between price and financial stability without jeopardising their credibility. However, our results show that the financial stability objective should be achieved primarily by regulatory measures, which are implemented by means of policy instruments different from those used to achieve price stability. Because of agent heterogeneity, the effects of these policies depend on the particular agent or part of the economy on which they fall. This is why tighter default penalties work better when imposed on the investment bank, because this agent bears the risk of mortgages and CDSs, which are the riskiest assets in the economy.

NOTES

1. The authors are grateful to the seminar participants for their helpful comments at the Sixth Norges Bank Monetary Policy Conference, and to Udara Peiris, Alexandros Vardoulakis, Mike Wickens and the editors of this volume.
2. Restricted participation can also arise as an outcome of banks aiming to outperform each other by introducing a relative performance criterion into their objective functions (see Bhattacharya *et al.* 2007).
3. In the literature, this requirement is known as the 'on-the-verge' condition: see Dubey, Geanakoplos and Shubik (2005).

4. In practice, these repurchase agreements are very short-term collateralised loans, in which the collateral is a very liquid and safe asset that is exchanged for cash when the loan is acquired and when it is repaid. We abstract from this collateralisation feature for simplicity.

5. This will help us capture the underwriting effects that have affected financial institutions in the current crisis.

6. For simplicity, we have abstracted from allowing the investment bank to default on its CDS obligation, which would capture counterparty risk in the derivatives markets.

7. This condition holds with strict inequality when the system has an interior solution and with weak inequality otherwise.

8. According to these authors, an economy is financially unstable whenever substantial default of a 'number' of households and banks occurs, and the aggregate profitability of the banking sector decreases significantly.

9. We refrain from reporting the results of an anticipated expansionary monetary policy shock in the good states of nature, because its effects are very similar to those of a monetary expansion in the first period.

10. Initially, it was demonstrated that in a two-agent, two-good economy this transfer paradox could occur only at Walrasian unstable equilibria (see Samuelson 1947, 1952, and Balasko 1978). Geanakoplos and Heal (1983) showed that it could occur in a globally stable Walrasian equilibrium for a three-agent, two-good economy.

11. The well-known liquidity trap is an extreme case of financial instability, whereby the latter is coupled with monetary policy ineffectiveness. Various authors provide formalisations of the liquidity trap based on non-rational expectations (Grandmont and Laroque 1975; Hool 1976; Tobin 1982). In this model, however, this phenomenon is related to the explanation proposed by Dubey and Geanakoplos (2003) and Tsomocos (2003), whereby a liquidity trap occurs because of the incompleteness of asset markets, and it manifests itself when the government employs an expansionary monetary policy and commercial banks channel the increased liquidity not to the consumer credit markets but to the asset market. The proof of a liquidity trap proposition for this model is quite technical and beyond the scope of this chapter. Nonetheless, the comparative statics exercise shows that a localised version of this phenomenon is at work in this model, because expansionary monetary policy fails to ease credit transactions between financial institutions.

12. We have also analysed the effects of tighter bankruptcy code policies affecting the less capitalised commercial bank and the hedge fund; however, these were not as effective as the policy affecting the investment bank, as they failed to improve households' welfare and financial stability.

REFERENCES

Aspachs, O., C. Goodhart, D. Tsomocos and L. Zicchino (2006). 'Towards a measure of financial fragility', *Annals of Finance*, 3(1): 37–74.

Balasko, Y. (1978). 'The transfer problem and the theory of regular economies', *International Economic Review*, 19(3): 687–94.

Barsden, G., K. Linduist and D. Tsomocos (2008). 'Evaluation of macroeconomic models for financial stability analysis'. Working Paper no. 2006/1. Oslo: Norges Bank.

Bhattacharya, S., C. Goodhart, P. Sunirand and D. Tsomocos (2007). 'Banks, relative performance, and sequential contagion', *Economic Theory*, 32(2): 381–98.

Bloise, G., J. Drèze and H. Polemarchakis (2005). 'Monetary economy over infinite horizon', *Journal of Economic Theory*, 25(1): 51–74.

Bryant, J. (1982). 'A model of reserves, bank runs, and deposit insurance', *Journal of Banking and Finance*, 4(4): 335–44.

Brunnermeier, M., A. Crockett, C. Goodhart, A. Persaud and H. Shin (2009). *Fundamental Principles of Financial Regulation*. Geneva: CIMB.

Cecchetti, S., H. Genberg, J. Lipsky and S. Wadhwani (2000). *Asset Prices and Central Bank Policy*. Geneva: CIMB.

Diamond, D., and P. Dybvig (1983). 'Bank runs', *Journal of Political Economy*, 91(3): 401–19.

Dubey, P., and J. Geanakoplos (1992). 'The value of money in a finite-horizon economy: a role for banks', in P. Dasgupta, D. Gale, O. Hart and E. Maskin (eds.). *Economic Analysis of Markets and Games: Essays in Honor of Frank Hahn*: 407–44. Cambridge, MA: MIT Press.

  (2003). 'Monetary equilibrium with missing markets', *Journal of Mathematical Economics*, 39(5): 585–618.

Dubey, P., J. Geanakoplos and M. Shubik (2005). 'Default and punishment in general equilibrium', *Econometrica*, 73(1): 1–37.

Dubey, P., and M. Shubik (1978). 'The non-cooperative equilibria of a closed trading economy with market supply and bidding strategies', *Journal of Economic Theory*, 17(1): 1–20.

Espinoza, R., C. Goodhart and D. Tsomocos (2008). 'State prices, liquidity and default', *Economic Theory*, 39(2): 174–99.

Geanakoplos, J. (2003). 'Liquidity, default, and crashes: endogenous contracts in general equilibrium', in M. Dewatripont, L. Hansen and S. Turnovsky (eds.). *Advances in Economics and Econometrics: Theory and Applications*, vol. II: 170–205. Cambridge: Cambridge University Press.

Geanakoplos, J., and G. Heal (1983). 'A geometric explanation of the transfer paradox in a stable economy', *Journal of Development Economics*, 13(1–2): 223–36.

Geanakoplos, J., and H. Polemarchakis (1986). 'Existence, regularity and constrained suboptimality of competitive allocations when the asset market is incomplete', in W. Heller and D. Starret (eds.). *Essays in Honor of Kenneth J. Arrow*, vol. III: 65–95. Cambridge: Cambridge University Press.

Geanakoplos, J., and W. Zame (2002). 'Collateral and the enforcement of intertemporal contracts'. Working paper. New Haven, CT: Yale University.

Goodhart, C. (2001). 'What weight should be given to asset prices in the measurement of inflation?', *Economic Journal*, 111: 335–56.

Goodhart, C., C. Osorio and D. Tsomocos (2009). 'Asset price targeting, financial Stability, and the 2007–2009 Credit Crunch'. Working paper. Oxford: OFRC, University of Oxford.

Goodhart, C., P. Sunirand and D. Tsomocos (2004). 'A model to analyse financial fragility: applications', *Journal of Financial Stability*, 1(1): 1–30.

(2006). 'A model to analyse financial fragility', *Economic Theory*, 27(1): 107–42.

(2008). 'The optimal monetary instrument for prudential purposes'. Working paper. Oxford: Oxford Financial Research Centre [OFRC], University of Oxford.

Goodhart, C., D. Tsomocos and A. Vardoulakis (2009). 'Modelling a housing and mortgage crisis'. Working paper. Oxford: OFRC, University of Oxford.

Grandmont, J., and G. Laroque (1975). 'On money and banking', *Review of Economic Studies*, 42(2): 207–36.

Hool, R. (1976). 'Money, expectations and the existence of a temporary equilibrium', *Review of Economic Studies*, 43(3): 439–45.

Leontief, W. (1936). 'Note on the pure theory of capital transfers', in F. Taussig (ed.). *Explorations in Economics: Notes and Essays Contributed in Honor of F. W. Taussig*: 84–91. New York: McGraw-Hill.

Lucas, R., and N. Stokey (1983). 'Optimal fiscal and monetary policy in an economy without capital', *Journal of Monetary Economics*, 12(1): 55–93.

(1987). 'Money and interest in a cash-in-advance economy', *Econometrica*, 55(3): 491–513.

Mas-Colell, A., M. Whinston and J. Green (1995). *Microeconomic Theory*. Oxford: Oxford University Press.

Samuelson, P. (1947). *Foundations of Economic Analysis*. Cambridge, MA: Harvard University Press.

(1952). 'The transfer problem and transport costs: the terms of trade when impediments are absent' *Economic Journal*, 62: 278–304.

Shubik, M., and D. Tsomocos (1992). 'A strategic market game with a mutual bank with fractional reserves and redemption in gold (a continuum of traders)', *Journal of Economics*, 55(2): 123–50.

Shubik, M., and C. Wilson (1977). 'The optimal bankruptcy rule in a trading economy using fiat money', *Journal of Economics*, 37(3–4): 337–54.

Steiger, O. (2006). 'The endogeneity of money and the Eurosystem: a contribution to the theory of central banking', in M. Setterfield (ed.). *Complexity, Endogenous Money and Macroeconomic Theory: Essays in Honour of Basil J. Moore*: 150–69. Cheltenham: Edward Elgar.

Svensson, L. (1985). 'Money and asset prices in a cash-in-advance economy', *Journal of Political Economy*, 93(5): 919–44.

Tobin, J. (1982). 'The commercial banking firm: a simple model', *Scandinavian Journal of Economics*, 84(4): 495–530.

Tsomocos, D. (2003). 'Equilibrium analysis, banking and financial instability', *Journal of Mathematical Economics*, 39(5): 619–55.

Woodford, M. (2003). *Interest and Prices: Foundations of a Theory of Monetary Policy*. Princeton, NJ: Princeton University Press.

11 Expectations, deflation traps and macroeconomic policy

George W. Evans and Seppo Honkapohja[1]

11.1 Introduction

Following the introduction of inflation targeting and related monetary strategies, target inflation seems to have fallen to relatively low rates, about 2 to 3 per cent in many countries. This implies that large adverse shocks might push the economy into periods of deflation. This was clearly a major concern in the United States during the 2001 recession. The experiences of 2008 and 2009, as well as the earlier experience of Japan since the 1990s, have underlined these concerns and created a situation in which the monetary policy response is constrained by the zero lower bound on nominal interest rates – a phenomenon sometimes called a 'liquidity trap'. Furthermore, in a liquidity trap there is the potential for the economy to get stuck in a deflationary situation with declining or persistently low levels of output.

The theoretical plausibility of the economy becoming trapped in a deflationary state, and the macroeconomic policies that might be able to avoid or extricate the economy from a liquidity trap, have been examined predominantly from the rational expectations (RE) perspective. One central feature of this literature emphasises the role of commitment. For example, Krugman (1998) and Eggertsson and Woodford (2003) argue that, if the economy encounters a liquidity trap, monetary policy should be committed to being expansionary for a considerable period of time, by keeping interest rates near zero even after the economy has emerged from deflation. Another issue concerns the possibility of permanent deflation. Under RE, this hinges on the precise form of fiscal policy in the deflationary steady state and on whether this is consistent with the household's transversality condition (see Benhabib, Schmitt-Grohe and Uribe 2001, 2002, and Eggertsson and Woodford 2003). A further issue is the impact of the interest rate zero lower bound on the performance of policies during the transition back to the inflation target (see Adam and Billi 2007 and Coenen, Orphanides and Wieland 2004 for representative recent analyses and further references).

In our opinion, the RE assumption is questionable in an episode of deflation, which is far away from the inflation target and the normal state of the economy, and presents a new environment for economic agents. Our own view, as presented by Evans and Honkapohja (2005) and Evans, Guse and Honkapohja (2008), is that the evolution of expectations plays a key role in the dynamics of the economy and that the tools from learning theory are needed for a realistic analysis of these issues. As we will see, there is the possibility of a self-reinforcing feedback loop, in which sufficiently pessimistic expectations result in low output and deflation, leading to high real interest rates because of the zero lower bound, which in turn results in a downward revision of expectations, strengthening the downward pressure on output and deflation.

More specifically, under learning, private agents are assumed to form expectations using an adaptive forecasting rule, which they update over time in accordance with standard statistical procedures. The analysis by Evans, Guse and Honkapohja (2008) was conducted in a standard New Keynesian model with sticky prices, using the assumption that the decisions of private agents are based on short-horizon rules. These rules are based on the agents' Euler equations, specifying the optimal trade-off between current and anticipated next-period decisions. These anticipations are in turn formed using subjective expectations based on forecasting models that are updated over time using recursive estimation procedures. This framework, often called 'Euler equation learning', yielded important results about formulating robust policies to combat deflationary outcomes. However, its short decision horizon means that one cannot study the implications for current behaviour of an explicit commitment to future policies. In particular, this learning framework cannot be used to assess the conventional wisdom of the RE literature that an appropriate policy to combat a deflation episode is a commitment to low interest rates for a sustained period in the future.

In this chapter we replace Euler equation learning with the assumption that agents have infinite-horizon decision rules derived from intertemporal optimisation under given paths of expectations of aggregate economic variables. This type of formulation is often called 'infinite-horizon learning', and it has been emphasised recently by Preston (2005, 2006).[2] In general, in this setting the individual consumers need to forecast interest rates, inflation, income and taxes over the infinite future. As a benchmark, we assume in this chapter that the consumers are fully Ricardian and incorporate the government's intertemporal budget constraint into their own lifetime budget constraint. This last assumption means that the consumption function depends on expected future real interest rates and incomes net of government spending. In this formulation, the mix of government financing does not influence private consumption behaviour.

The possibility of deflation traps under a standard forward-looking global Taylor rule emerges as a serious concern. Although the targeted steady state is locally stable under learning, a large pessimistic shock to expectations can result, under learning, in a self-reinforcing deflationary process accompanied by declining output. Our results under learning are in stark contrast to what is possible under RE. Benhabib, Schmitt-Grohe and Uribe (2001) show that under perfect foresight, in addition to the targeted steady state, there are non-linear paths that converge to an unintended low-inflation steady state.[3] The learning dynamics under standard monetary and fiscal policy are even more disturbing, therefore, than those under RE.

We next consider monetary and fiscal policies that have been suggested to combat the possibility of deflation. One case is aggressive monetary easing in which the Taylor rule is overridden by dropping the interest rate to (very near) zero whenever expected inflation falls below a specified threshold. In our infinite-horizon set-up, agents are assumed to understand that this aggressive policy will be in place throughout the future. Strikingly, this policy, although it does offer some protection, is not sufficient to eliminate the possibility of deflation traps if the negative expectations shock is very large. In fact, even if the monetary authorities commit to zero interest rates for ever, regardless of the state of the economy, the possibility of a deflation trap remains (although the likelihood is reduced).

These results raise the question of whether there exists a policy that ensures that the economy will never get trapped in a deflationary process and will converge to the targeted steady state. We focus on the policy recommended by Evans, Guse and Honkapohja (2008). Under this policy, aggressive monetary easing is augmented by aggressive fiscal easing when required to keep inflation at or above the threshold. This policy always eliminates the possibility of deflationary spirals and ensures the global stability of the targeted steady state.

11.2   The model

We start with the same economic framework as that of Evans, Guse and Honkapohja (2008). There is a continuum of household firms, which produce a differentiated consumption good under monopolistic competition and price adjustment costs. There is also a government that uses both monetary and fiscal policy and can issue public debt, as described below.

The objective for agent s is to maximise expected, discounted utility subject to a standard flow budget constraint:

$$MaxE_0 \sum_{t=0}^{\infty} \beta^t U_{t,s} \left(c_{t,s}, \frac{M_{t-1,s}}{P_t}, h_{t,s}, \frac{P_{t,s}}{P_{t-1,s}} - 1 \right) \qquad (11.1)$$

$$s.t. \ c_{t,s} + m_{t,s} + b_{t,s} + \Upsilon_{t,s} = m_{t-1,s}\pi_t^{-1} + R_{t-1}\pi_t^{-1}b_{t-1,s} + \frac{P_{t,s}}{P_t}y_{t,s} \qquad (11.2)$$

where $c_{t,s}$ is the Dixit–Stiglitz consumption aggregator, $M_{t,s}$ and $m_{t,s}$ denote nominal and real money balances, $h_{t,s}$ is the labour input into production, $b_{t,s}$ denotes the real quantity of risk-free one-period nominal bonds held by the agent at the end of period t, $\Upsilon_{t,s}$ is the lump sum tax collected by the government, R_{t-1} is the nominal interest rate factor between periods $t-1$ and t, $P_{t,s}$ is the price of consumption good s, $y_{t,s}$ is output of good s, P_t is the aggregate price level and the inflation rate is $\pi_t = P_t/P_{t-1}$. The subjective discount factor is denoted by β. The utility function has the parametric form

$$U_{t,s} = \frac{c_{t,s}^{1-\sigma_1}}{1-\sigma_1} + \frac{\chi}{1-\sigma_2} \left(\frac{M_{t-1,s}}{P_t} \right)^{1-\sigma_2} - \frac{h_{t,s}^{1+\varepsilon}}{1+\varepsilon} - \frac{\gamma}{2} \left(\frac{P_{t,s}}{P_{t-1,s}} - 1 \right)^2$$

where $\sigma_1, \sigma_2, \varepsilon, \gamma > 0$. The final term parameterises the cost of adjusting prices in the spirit of Rotemberg (1982).[4] The household decision problem is also subject to the usual 'no Ponzi game' (NPG) condition.

The production function for good s is given by

$$y_{t,s} = h_{t,s}^{\alpha}$$

where $0 < \alpha < 1$. Output is differentiated and firms operate under monopolistic competition. Each firm faces a downward-sloping demand curve, given by

$$P_{t,s} = \left(\frac{y_{t,s}}{Y_t} \right)^{-1/v} P_t \qquad (11.3)$$

where $P_{t,s}$ is the profit-maximising price set by firm s consistent with its production $y_{t,s}$. The parameter v is the elasticity of substitution between two goods and is assumed to be greater than one. Y_t is aggregate output, which is exogenous to the firm.

The government's flow budget constraint is

$$b_t + m_t + \Upsilon_t = g_t + m_{t-1}\pi_t^{-1} + R_{t-1}\pi_t^{-1}b_{t-1} \tag{11.4}$$

where g_t denotes government consumption of the aggregate good, b_t is the real quantity of government debt and Υ_t is the real lump sum tax collected. We assume that fiscal policy follows a linear tax rule for lump sum taxes as given by Leeper (1991):

$$\Upsilon_t = \kappa_0 + \kappa b_{t-1} + \eta_t \tag{11.5}$$

where η_t is a white noise shock and $\beta^{-1} - 1 < \kappa < 1$. The restriction on κ means that fiscal policy is 'passive', in the terminology of Leeper (1991), and implies that an increase in real government debt leads to an increase in taxes sufficient to cover the increased interest and at least some fraction of the increased principal. In a companion study we plan to investigate the implications of 'active' fiscal policy, in which $0 \leq \kappa < \beta^{-1} - 1$.

We assume that g_t is stochastic:

$$g_t = \bar{g} + u_t \tag{11.6}$$

where u_t is an observable, stationary, AR(1) mean zero shock. From market clearing we have

$$c_t + g_t = y_t \tag{11.7}$$

Monetary policy is assumed to follow a global interest rate rule:

$$R_t - 1 = \theta_t f\left(\pi_{t+1}^e\right) \tag{11.8}$$

The function $f(\pi)$ is taken to be positive and non-decreasing, while θ_t is an exogenous, observable, stationary, AR(1) positive random shock with a mean of one representing random shifts in the behaviour of the monetary policymaker. The rule (11.8) is a non-linear forward-looking Taylor rule, in which dependence on output expectations is suppressed for simplicity.[5] We assume the existence of π^*, R^* such that $R^* = \beta^{-1}\pi^*$ and $f(\pi^*) = R^* - 1$. π^* can be viewed as the inflation target of the central bank, and we assume that $\pi^* \geq 1$. In the numerical analysis we use the functional form

$$f(\pi) = (R^* - 1)\left(\frac{\pi}{\pi^*}\right)^{AR^*/(R^*-1)}$$

which implies the existence of a non-stochastic steady state at π^*. Note that $f'(\pi^*) = AR^*$, which we assume is bigger than β^{-1}. Equations (11.4), (11.5) and (11.8) constitute 'normal policy'.

Optimal decisions for the private sector

As with Evans, Guse and Honkapohja (2008), the first-order conditions for an optimum yield

$$0 = -h_{t,s}^\varepsilon + \frac{\alpha\gamma}{v}(\pi_{t,s} - 1)\pi_{t,s}\frac{1}{h_{t,s}} \tag{11.9}$$

$$+ \alpha\left(1 - \frac{1}{v}\right)Y_t^{1/v}\frac{y_{t,s}^{(1--1/v)}}{h_{t,s}}c_{t,s}^{-\sigma_1} - \frac{\alpha\gamma\beta}{v}\frac{1}{h_{t,s}}E_{t,s}(\pi_{t+1,s} - 1)\pi_{t+1,s}$$

$$c_{t,s}^{-\sigma_1} = \beta R_t E_{t,s}\left(\pi_{t+1}^{-1}c_{t+1,s}^{-\sigma_1}\right)$$

and

$$m_{t,s} = (\chi\beta)^{1/\sigma_2}\left(\frac{\left(1 - R_t^{-1}\right)c_{t,s}^{-\sigma_1}}{E_{t,s}\pi_{t+1}^{\sigma_2-1}}\right)^{-1/\sigma_2}$$

where $\pi_{t+1,s} = P_{t+1,s}/P_{t,s}$. We now make use of the representative agent assumption. In the representative agent economy, all agents s have the same utility functions, initial money and debt holdings and prices. We also assume that they make the same forecasts $E_{t,s}c_{t+1,s}$, $E_{t,s}\pi_{t+1,s}$, $E_{t,s}\pi_{t+1}$, as well as forecasts of other variables that will become relevant below. Under these assumptions, all agents make the same decisions at each point in time, so that $h_{t,s} = h_t$, $y_{t,s} = y_t$, $c_{t,s} = c_t$ and $\pi_{t,s} = \pi_t$, and all agents make the same forecasts. Imposing also the equilibrium condition $Y_t = y_t = h_t^\alpha$, one obtains the equations

$$\frac{\alpha\gamma}{v}(\pi_t - 1)\pi_t = h_t\left(h_t^\varepsilon - \alpha\left(1 - \frac{1}{v}\right)h_t^{\alpha-1}c_t^{-\sigma_1}\right)$$

$$+ \beta\frac{\alpha\gamma}{v}E_t\left[(\pi_{t+1} - 1)\pi_{t+1}\right]$$

$$c_t^{-\sigma_1} = \beta R_t E_t\left(\pi_{t+1}^{-1}c_{t+1}^{-\sigma_1}\right)$$

$$m_t = (\chi\beta)^{1/\sigma_2}\left(\frac{\left(1 - R_t^{-1}\right)c_t^{-\sigma_1}}{E_t\pi_{t+1}^{\sigma_2-1}}\right)^{-1/\sigma_2}$$

For convenience, we make the assumptions $\sigma_1 = \sigma_2 = 1$ – i.e. that the utility of consumption and of money is logarithmic. It is also assumed that agents have point expectations, so that their decisions depend only on the mean of their subjective forecasts. This is a satisfactory assumption provided the shocks are sufficiently small. This allows us to write the system as

$$m_t = \chi\beta \left(1 - R_t^{-1}\right)^{-1} c_t \tag{11.10}$$

$$c_t^{-1} = \beta r_{t+1}^e \left(c_{t+1}^e\right)^{-1} \tag{11.11}$$

where $r_{t+1}^e = R_t / \pi_{t+1}^e$, and

$$\frac{\alpha\gamma}{\nu} (\pi_t - 1) \pi_t = h_t \left(h_t^\varepsilon - \alpha \left(1 - \frac{1}{\nu}\right) h_t^{\alpha-1} c_t^{-1} \right)$$
$$+ \beta \frac{\alpha\gamma}{\nu} \left[\left(\pi_{t+1}^e - 1\right) \pi_{t+1}^e \right] \tag{11.12}$$

Equation (11.12) is the non-linear New Keynesian Phillips curve, which describes the optimal price setting by firms. The term $(\pi_t - 1) \pi_t$ arises from the quadratic form of the adjustment costs, and this expression is increasing in π_t over the allowable range $\pi_t \geq 1/2$. To interpret this equation, note that the bracketed expression in the first term on the right-hand side is the difference between the marginal disutility of labour and the product of the marginal revenue from an extra unit of labour with the marginal utility of consumption. The terms involving current and future inflation arise from the price adjustment costs resulting from marginal variations in labour supply. Equation (11.11) is the standard Euler equation giving the intertemporal first-order condition for the consumption path. Equation (11.10) is the money demand function resulting from the presence of real balances in the utility function. Note that, for our parameterisation, the demand for real balances becomes infinite as $R_t \to 1$.

We now proceed to rewrite the decision rules for c_t and π_t so that they depend on forecasts of key variables over the infinite horizon.

The infinite-horizon Phillips curve

We start with an infinite-horizon version of the Phillips curve (11.12). Let

$$Q_t = (\pi_t - 1) \pi_t \tag{11.13}$$

The appropriate root for given Q is $\pi \geq \frac{1}{2}$, and so we need to impose $Q \geq -\frac{1}{4}$ to have a meaningful model. Making use of the aggregate relationships $h_t = y_t^{1/\alpha}$ and $c_t = y_t - g_t$ we can rewrite (11.12) as

$$Q_t = \frac{\nu}{\alpha\gamma} y_t^{(1+\varepsilon)/\alpha} - \frac{\nu-1}{\gamma} y_t^\alpha (y_t - g_t)^{-1} + \beta Q_{t+1}^e$$

Solving this forward we obtain

$$Q_t = \frac{\nu}{\gamma} \sum_{j=0}^{\infty} \alpha^{-1} \beta^j \left(y_{t+j}^e\right)^{(1+\varepsilon)/\alpha} - \frac{\nu-1}{\gamma} \sum_{j=0}^{\infty} \beta^j \left(\frac{y_{t+j}^e}{x_{t+j}^e}\right) \quad (11.14)$$

Here x_{t+j}^e denotes expected net output, which equals expectations of $y_{t+j} - g_{t+j}$. The expectations are formed at time t, and the variables at time t are assumed to be in the information set of the agents. We will treat (11.14), together with (11.13), as the temporary equilibrium equations that determine π_t, given expectations $\{y_{t+j}^e, x_{t+j}^e\}_{j=1}^{\infty}$.

In the Phillips curve relationship (11.14), one might wonder why inflation does not also depend directly on the expected future aggregate inflation rate.[6] Equation (11.9) is obtained from the first-order conditions using (11.3) to eliminate relative prices. Because of the representative agent assumption, each firm's output equals average output in every period. Since firms can be assumed to have learned that this is the case, we obtain (11.14). An alternative procedure would be to start from (11.9), iterate it forward and use the demand function to write the third term on the right-hand side of (11.9) in terms of the relative price. This would lead to a modification of (11.14) in which future relative prices also appear, but, given the representative agent assumption, the relative price term would drop out.

The consumption function

To derive the consumption function from (11.11) we use the flow budget constraint and the NPG condition to obtain an intertemporal budget constraint:

$$b_t = r_t b_{t-1} + \Phi_t$$

where $r_t = R_{t-1}/\pi_t$ and

$$\Phi_t = y_t + m_{t-1}\pi_t^{-1} - c_t - m_t - \Upsilon_t \quad (11.15)$$

Note that we assume $(P_{jt}/P_t)y_{jt} = y_t$ – i.e. the representative agent assumption is being invoked. Iterating (11.15) forward and imposing

$$\lim_{j \to \infty} \left(D_{t,t+j}^e\right)^{-1} b_{t+j} = 0 \quad (11.16)$$

we obtain the lifetime budget constraint of the household

$$0 = r_t b_{t-1} + \Phi_t + \sum_{j=1}^{\infty} \left(D_{t,t+j}^e\right)^{-1} \Phi_{t+j}^e \quad (11.17)$$

where $D^e_{t,t+j} = \prod_{i=1}^{j} r^e_{t+i}$, with $r^e_{t+j} = R_{t+j-1}/\pi^e_{t+j}$ and

$$\Phi^e_{t+j} = y^e_{t+j} + m^e_{t+j-1}\left(\pi^e_{t+j}\right)^{-1} - c^e_{t+j} - m^e_{t+j} - \Upsilon^e_{t+j} \qquad (11.18)$$

Here all expectations are formed in period t, which is indicated in the notation for $D^e_{t,t+j}$ but is omitted from the other expectational variables.

The consumption Euler equation (11.11) implies that

$$c^e_{t+j} = c_t \beta^j D^e_{t,t+j}$$

Substituting this expression for c^e_{t+j} in (11.18), it follows that

$$0 = r_t b_{t-1} - \sum_{j=0}^{\infty} c_t \beta^j + \phi_t + \sum_{j=1}^{\infty} \left(D^e_{t,t+j}\right)^{-1} \phi^e_{t+j} \qquad (11.19)$$

where

$$\phi_t = y_t + m_{t-1}\pi_t^{-1} - m_t - \Upsilon_t$$

and

$$\phi^e_{t+j} = y^e_{t+j} + m^e_{t+j-1}\left(\pi^e_{t+j}\right)^{-1} - m^e_{t+j} - \Upsilon^e_{t+j}$$

A crucial issue is how households form expectations of future taxes. In this chapter we make the strong Ricardian equivalence assumption that households understand that the government's intertemporal budget constraint will be satisfied.[7] First we write down the latter constraint. From (11.4) one has

$$b_t + m_t + \Upsilon_t = g_t + m_{t-1}\pi_t^{-1} + r_t b_{t-1}$$

or

$$b_t = \Delta_t + r_t b_{t-1}$$

where

$$\Delta_t = g_t - \Upsilon_t - m_t + m_{t-1}\pi_t^{-1}$$

By forward substitution, and assuming $\lim_{T\to\infty} D_{t,t+T} b_{t+T} = 0$,

$$0 = r_t b_{t-1} + \Delta_t + \sum_{j=1}^{\infty} D^{-1}_{t,t+j} \Delta_{t+j} \qquad (11.20)$$

Note that Δ_{t+j} is the primary government deficit in $t + j$, measured as government purchases less lump sum taxes and less seigniorage. Under the Ricardian equivalence assumption, we assume that agents at each time t expect this constraint to be satisfied – i.e.

$$0 = r_t b_{t-1} + \Delta_t + \sum_{j=1}^{\infty} \left(D_{t,t+j}^e \right)^{-1} \Delta_{t+j}^e$$

where

$$\Delta_{t+j}^e = g_{t+j}^e - \Upsilon_{t+j}^e - m_{t+j}^e + m_{t+j-1}^e \left(\pi_{t+j}^e \right)^{-1} \text{ for } j = 1, 2, 3, \ldots$$

Substituting out $r_t b_{t-1}$ from (11.19) and rearranging, we get

$$(1 - \beta)^{-1} c_t = (\phi_t - \Delta_t) + \sum_{j=1}^{\infty} \left(D_{t,t+j}^e \right)^{-1} \left(\phi_{t+j}^e - \Delta_{t+j}^e \right)$$

or

$$c_t = (1 - \beta) \left(y_t - g_t + \sum_{j=1}^{\infty} \left(D_{t,t+j}^e \right)^{-1} x_{t+j}^e \right) \tag{11.21}$$

Equation (11.21) is viewed as the temporary equilibrium equation that, under Ricardian equivalence, determines consumption, given expectations. In the inflation equation (11.14) it is assumed that households form $\{x_{t+j}^e\}_{j=1}^{\infty}$ and $\{y_{t+j}^e\}_{j=1}^{\infty}$ using an adaptive learning rule that treats these aggregates as an exogenously given process. For the consumption function (11.21) one needs also to specify how private agents form the discount factors $D_{t,t+j}^e = \prod_{i=1}^{j} r_{t+i}^e$. Various assumptions are natural, but we focus on the assumption that r_{t+i}^e is obtained from separate forecasts of inflation and interest rates, making use of the monetary policy rule to forecast the latter. Thus, monetary policy is both transparent and credible, in that agents incorporate the interest rate rule in their expectations formation for all future periods.[8] In this case, combining $r_{t+j}^e(t) = R_{t+j-1}^e / \pi_{t+j}^e$ and $R_t = 1 + f\left(\pi_{t+1}^e \right)$, one obtains

$$D_{t,t+j}^e = \prod_{i=1}^{j} \left(1 + f\left(\pi_{t+j}^e \right) \right) / \pi_{t+j}^e \tag{11.22}$$

We remark that our consumption function (11.21) exhibits Ricardian equivalence in the following sense.

Proposition 1 *Household consumption depends on the sequence of expected government spending but not in any way on how it is financed.*

This temporary equilibrium result for arbitrary subjective expectations generalises the results of Wallace (1981) and Eggertsson and Woodford

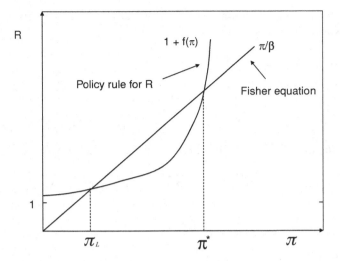

Figure 11.1 Multiple steady states under normal policy

(2003), which presume that the RE hypothesis holds. The assumption of Ricardian consumers has, in particular, the implication that an open market operation altering the initial composition of wealth between money and bonds has no effect on consumption, given subsequent interest rate policy and the sequence of government spending. In addition, the standard result about the neutrality of changes in lump sum taxes holds in our setting.

11.3   Learning and stability of steady states

Consider first the steady states of the model. These are found by setting the random shocks to zero and setting $\pi_{t+j}^e = \pi_t = \pi$, $y_{t+j}^e = y_t = y$ and $x_{t+j}^e = y_{t+j}^e - \bar{g} = y - \bar{g}$. For any steady state π, equation (11.11) implies that the nominal interest rate factor satisfies the Fisher equation

$$R = \beta^{-1}\pi \tag{11.23}$$

As emphasised by Benhabib, Schmitt-Grohe and Uribe (2001), because $f(\cdot)$ is non-negative, continuous (and differentiable) and has a steady state π^* with $f'(\pi^*) > \beta^{-1}$, there must be a second steady state $\pi_L < \pi^*$ with $f'(\pi_L) < \beta^{-1}$. For our parameterisation of $f(\cdot)$, there are no steady states other than the intended steady state π^* and the unintended low-inflation steady state π_L. Figure 11.1 illustrates the two steady states resulting from the global Taylor rule subject to the zero lower bound on net interest rates.[9]

The other steady-state equations are given by

$$c = h^\alpha - \bar{g} \tag{11.24}$$

$$-h^{1+\varepsilon} + \frac{\alpha\gamma}{\nu}(1-\beta)(\pi-1)\pi + \alpha\left(1-\frac{1}{\nu}\right)h^\alpha c^{-1} = 0 \tag{11.25}$$

and a steady-state version of (11.10). It is shown by Evans, Guse and Honkapohja (2008: appendix) that in most cases there is a corresponding unique interior steady state $c > 0$ and $h > 0$.

The starting point in the learning approach to expectations formation is that economic agents have very limited knowledge about the structure of the economy, so that they do not have RE and instead make inferences about the relevant parts of the economy that they need for forecasting. The agents make forecasts using a reduced-form econometric model of the relevant variables and using parameters that are estimated using past data. The forecasts are input to agents' decision rules, and in each period the economy attains a temporary equilibrium – i.e. an equilibrium for the current period variables given the forecasts of the agents (see, for example, Evans and Honkapohja 2001, 2009, and Sargent 2008 for general discussions of adaptive learning).

The temporary equilibrium provides a new data point, which in the next period leads to a re-estimation of the parameters and an updating of the forecasts and, in turn, to a new temporary equilibrium. The sequence of temporary equilibria may generate parameter estimates that converge to a fixed point corresponding to an RE equilibrium for the economy. When the convergence takes place, we say that the RE equilibrium is stable under learning. In the general formulation of the model given above, it was assumed that the economy is subject to stationary autoregressive random shocks. If these exogenous shocks are observable then agents would naturally include them in their forecasting model, and the coefficients of the model would be estimated and updated by an econometric technique such as recursive least squares. If the exogenous shocks are independent and identically distributed (*i i d.*) then they provide no information about their future values, and thus would be excluded from the forecasting model. In this case agents would simply estimate the intercept for each variable. If these estimates converge over time to fixed values, the limit corresponds to an RE stochastic steady state. In the current model there are two possible RE stochastic steady states. When the random shocks are small these are close to the non-stochastic steady states discussed above.

The simple set-up just described, in which only intercepts are estimated, is referred to as 'steady-state learning'. More specifically, steady-state learning with point expectations is formalised as

$$y^e_{t+j} = y^e_t \quad \text{and} \quad \pi^e_{t+j} = \pi^e_t \quad \text{for all } j \geq 1$$

and

$$z^e_t = z^e_{t-1} + \omega_t \left(z_{t-1} - z^e_{t-1}\right) \tag{11.26}$$

for $z = y, \pi$. Here ω_t is called the 'gain sequence', and measures the extent of adjustment of estimates to the most recent forecast error. In stochastic systems one often sets $\omega_t = t^{-1}$, and this 'decreasing gain' learning corresponds to least-squares updating. Also widely used is the case $\omega_t = \omega$, for $0 < \omega \leq 1$, called 'constant gain' learning. In this case it is usually assumed that ω is small. Stability of the steady states is examined below using the simple learning rules just described. The exogenous random shocks are therefore assumed to be *iid*. This is merely a simplification, since it can be shown that the stability of the steady states is governed by the stability of the estimates of the intercepts. Furthermore, it can also be shown that, provided the *iid* shocks are sufficiently small, the stability properties of steady states are the same as for the corresponding non-stochastic system. Thus, for simplicity, in what follows the exogenous shocks θ_t, u_t, η_t are assumed to be constants, equal to their respective mean values, and we study steady-state learning within the non-stochastic system.

Temporary equilibrium

If we collect together the preceding points, the following equations define the temporary equilibrium under normal policy.
(1) Phillips curve:

$$Q_t = \frac{\nu}{\gamma} \sum_{j=0}^{\infty} \alpha^{-1} \beta^j \left(y^e_{t+j}\right)^{(1+\varepsilon)/\alpha} - \frac{\nu - 1}{\gamma} \sum_{j=0}^{\infty} \beta^j \left(\frac{y^e_{t+j}}{y^e_{t+j} - \bar{g}}\right)$$

$$Q_t = (\pi_t - 1)\pi_t$$

(2) Consumption function:

$$c_t = (1 - \beta)\left(y_t - g_t + \sum_{j=1}^{\infty} \left(D^e_{t,t+j}\right)^{-1} \left(y^e_{t+j} - \bar{g}\right)\right)$$

$$D^e_{t,t+j} = \prod_{i=1}^{j}(1 + f(\pi^e_{t+i}))/\pi^e_{t+i}$$

(3) Money demand:

$$m_t = \chi\beta \left(1 - R_t^{-1}\right)^{-1} c_t$$

(4) Government budget constraint:

$$b_t + m_t + \kappa_0 + \kappa b_{t-1} = \bar{g} + m_{t-1}\pi_t^{-1} + R_{t-1}\pi_t^{-1}b_{t-1}$$

(5) Interest rate rule:

$$R_t - 1 = f\left(\pi_{t+1}^e\right)$$

where

$$f(\pi) = (R^* - 1)\left(\frac{\pi}{\pi^*}\right)^{AR^*/(R^*-1)}$$

(6) Market clearing:

$$y_t = c_t + \bar{g}$$

Given expectations $\{y_{t+j}^e, \pi_{t+j}^e\}_{j=1}^{\infty}$, the above six equations define the temporary equilibrium in $c_t, \pi_t, y_t, R_t, m_t, b_t$. The model dynamics are then completed by specifying the evolution of expectations over time in accordance with the learning rules described above. The dynamics under learning can be conveniently described by using the close connection between the possible convergence of least-squares learning to an RE equilibrium and a stability condition, known as E-stability. E-stability of an equilibrium is based on a mapping from the perceived law of motion that private agents are estimating and using to make forecasts to the implied actual law of motion generating the data (i.e. the temporary equilibrium) under these perceptions. E-stability is defined in terms of local stability, at an RE equilibrium, of a differential equation based on this map (for a general discussion of adaptive learning and the E-stability principle, see Evans and Honkapohja 2001).

Before turning to the E-stability results, we briefly discuss the issue of the transversality conditions in our temporary equilibrium set-up. Under steady-state learning, $\pi_{t+j}^e = \pi_t^e$ for all $j \geq 1$ implies

$$D_{t,t+j}^e = \left((1 + f(\pi_t^e))/\pi_t^e\right)^j = (r_t^e)^j$$

where $r_t^e = (1 + f(\pi_t^e))/\pi_t^e$ is the expected real interest factor, and the consumption function takes the form

$$c_t = (1 - \beta)\left(y_t - \bar{g} + \frac{1}{r_t^e - 1}(y_t^e - \bar{g})\right) \qquad (11.27)$$

provided $r_t^e > 1$ (see the discussion below for our treatment of the case in which $r_t^e \leq 1$). The consumption function gives the time t choice of consumption based on information and forecasts at time t, and can be viewed as the first step of an infinite-horizon dynamic plan. From the consumption Euler equation it follows that the expected path of future consumption (with $\sigma_1 = 1$) is given by

$$c_{t+j}^{-1} = (r_t^e)^{-j} \beta^{-j} c_t^{-1} \text{ for } j = 1, 2, 3, \ldots$$

where c_{t+j}^{-1} is the expected marginal utility of money at $t + j$. The relevant transversality condition for the household is that

$$\lim_{j \to \infty} c_{t+j}^{-1} \beta^j b_{t+j} = 0 \tag{11.28}$$

holds along the planned path of consumption and bonds. Because the consumption function is derived using the intertemporal budget constraint obtained on the basis of the NPG condition, we know that the condition

$$\lim_{j \to \infty} \left(D_{t,t+j}^e\right)^{-1} b_{t+j} = \lim_{j \to \infty} (r_t^e)^{-j} b_{t+j} = 0$$

is satisfied. Since, using the consumption Euler equation, we have $c_{t+j}^{-1} \beta^j b_{t+j} = (r_t^e)^{-j} c_t^{-1} b_{t+j}$, it follows that (11.28) is satisfied along the planned path.[10] Thus, at each point in time, the transversality condition is met for the household's planned path of consumption and wealth.

E-stability

The theoretical results for learning below are based on E-stability analysis of the system under the learning rules (11.26). It can be shown that a steady state is locally stable under learning for decreasing or small constant gains if and only if it is E-stable.[11] The definition of E-stability for the case at hand is given below.

We now proceed to the analysis of E-stability of the two possible steady states when the global interest rate rule (11.8) describes monetary policy. Using (11.27) and market clearing,

$$y_t = \bar{g} + (\beta^{-1} - 1)(y_t^e - \bar{g}) \left(\frac{\pi_t^e}{1 + f(\pi_t^e) - \pi_t^e} \right) \tag{11.29}$$

$$\equiv G_1(y_t^e, \pi_t^e)$$

Temporary equilibrium is given by equations (11.29) and

$$\pi_t = Q^{-1}[K(G_1(y_t^e, \pi_t^e), y_t^e)] \equiv G_2(y_t^e, \pi_t^e)$$

where

$$Q(\pi_t) \equiv (\pi_t - 1)\pi_t \qquad\qquad (11.30)$$

and

$$K(y_t, y_t^e) \equiv \frac{\nu}{\gamma}\left(\alpha^{-1}y_t^{(1+\varepsilon)/\alpha} - (1 - \nu^{-1})\frac{y_t}{(y_t - \bar{g})}\right) \qquad (11.31)$$

$$+ \frac{\nu}{\gamma}\left(\beta(1-\beta)^{-1}\left(\alpha^{-1}(y_t^e)^{(1+\varepsilon)/\alpha}\right.\right.$$

$$\left.\left. - (1 - \nu^{-1})\frac{y_t^e}{(y_t^e - \bar{g})}\right)\right)$$

The E-stability equations are

$$\frac{dy^e}{d\tau} = G_1(y^e, \pi^e) - y^e \qquad\qquad (11.32)$$

$$\frac{d\pi^e}{d\tau} = G_2(y^e, \pi^e) - \pi^e$$

By construction, the steady states are the fixed points of this system of differential equations. A steady state is said to be E-stable if it is locally stable under (11.32). The differential equations operate in 'notional' or 'virtual' time. It can be shown that, for large values of the (discrete) real time t, the continuous time paths $(y^e(\tau), \pi^e(\tau))$ of (11.32) are approximately related to the discrete-time trajectories (y_t^e, π_t^e) of (11.26) at specific points of real time:

$$(y^e(t_n), \pi^e(t_n)) \approx (y_n^e, \pi_n^e) \text{ for } t_n = \sum_{i=1}^{n}\omega_i$$

To examine the local stability of a steady state $(\bar{\pi}, \bar{y})$, one calculates the Jacobian

$$DGI = \begin{pmatrix} D_{y^e}G_1 - 1 & D_{\pi^e}G_1 \\ D_{y^e}G_2 & D_{\pi^e}G_2 - 1 \end{pmatrix}$$

Starting with function G_2, one takes differentials

$$D_{y^e}G_2 = (Q^{-1})'(K_yD_{y^e}G_1 + K_{y^e}) > 0$$
$$D_{\pi^e}G_2 = (Q^{-1})'K_yD_{\pi^e}G_1$$

The various derivatives at a steady state are

$$(Q^{-1})' = \frac{1}{2\bar{\pi} - 1} > 0$$

$$K_y = \frac{\nu}{\gamma}\left((1+\varepsilon)y^{\frac{1+\varepsilon+\alpha}{\alpha}} + (1-\nu^{-1})\frac{\bar{g}}{(y-\bar{g})^2}\right) > 0$$

$$K_{y^e} = \frac{\nu}{\gamma}\frac{\beta}{1-\beta}\left((1+\varepsilon)y^{\frac{1+\varepsilon+\alpha}{\alpha}} + (1-\nu^{-1})\frac{\bar{g}}{(y-\bar{g})^2}\right) > 0$$

One also needs to compute the following partial derivatives at a steady state:

$$D_{y^e}G_1 = (\beta^{-1} - 1)\left(\frac{\bar{\pi}}{1 + f(\bar{\pi}) - \bar{\pi}}\right) = 1$$

$$D_{\pi^e}G_1 = (\beta^{-1} - 1)(\bar{y} - \bar{g})\left(\frac{1 + f(\bar{\pi}) - \bar{\pi}f'(\bar{\pi})}{(1 + f(\bar{\pi}) - \bar{\pi})^2}\right)$$

Here $1 + f(\bar{\pi}) - \bar{\pi}f'(\bar{\pi}) = (\beta^{-1} - f'(\bar{\pi}))\bar{\pi}$, which is negative at π^* and positive at π_L. Thus

$$D_{\pi^e}G_1 < 0 \text{ at } \pi^* \quad \text{and} \quad > 0 \text{ at } \pi_L$$

For the sign of $D_{\pi^e}G_2$ we have

$$sgn[D_{\pi^e}G_2] = sgn[D_{\pi^e}G_1]$$

It follows that the Jacobian at the normal steady state π^* is

$$DGI = \begin{pmatrix} 0 & - \\ + & - \end{pmatrix}$$

implying E-stability of π^*. At the low-inflation steady state π_L, the Jacobian is

$$DGI = \begin{pmatrix} 0 & + \\ + & ? \end{pmatrix}$$

The (2, 2) element is $D_{\pi^e}G_2 - 1$ and for sufficiently small γ $D_{\pi^e}G_2$ becomes large (see the expression for K_y), so the element is positive for small γ, which implies the E-instability of π_L.

Collecting the results gives the following.

Proposition 2 *The model with normal policy has two steady states π^* and π_L. Under infinite-horizon decision rules with learning, the targeted steady state π^* is locally stable under learning. For γ sufficiently small, the low-inflation steady state is locally unstable and takes the form of a saddle point.*

For global results we turn to numerical analysis. One technical issue has to be taken care of in connection with steady-state learning by households. With an arbitrary value of inflation expectations, there are regions of the space of expectations in which the expected real interest rate and thus $1 + f(\pi_t^e) - \pi_t^e$ can be negative. This would imply infinite consumption in the preceding formula for the consumption function. To avoid this difficulty, we truncate the steady-state expectations of the household at some long but finite horizon T and postulate that, beyond the horizon, agents just assume that the real rate of interest has reached its steady-state value β^{-1}. With this assumption, the consumption function becomes

$$c_t = (1-\beta)\left[y_t - \bar{g} + (y_t^e - \bar{g})\left[\frac{\pi_t^e\left(1 - \left(\frac{\pi_t^e}{1+f(\pi_t^e)}\right)^T\right)}{1 + f(\pi_t^e) - \pi_t^e} + \frac{\beta^T}{\beta^{-1} - 1}\right]\right]$$

and so

$$y_t = \bar{g} + (\beta^{-1} - 1)(y_t^e - \bar{g})\left[\frac{\pi_t^e\left(1 - \left(\frac{\pi_t^e}{1+f(\pi_t^e)}\right)^T\right)}{1 + f(\pi_t^e) - \pi_t^e} + \frac{\beta^T}{\beta^{-1} - 1}\right]$$

In the global analysis one must also make sure that $\pi \geq 1/2$. This is achieved in the numerics by setting $\pi = 1/2$ if the other temporary equilibrium equations would imply $Q < -\frac{1}{4}$.

Figure 11.2 illustrates the theoretical results in proposition 2. The parameter values $A = 2.5$, $\pi^* = 1.02$, $\beta = 0.99$, $\alpha = 0.75$, $\beta = 20$, $\nu = 1.5$, $\varepsilon = 1$, $R^* = \pi^*/\beta$, $\bar{g} = 0.1$ and $T = 50$ are used. The figure shows the phase diagram of the system (11.32) for the evolution of expectations under learning. Given expectations dynamics, it is easy to compute the trajectories of actual inflation and output.

Figure 11.2 shows the global E-stability dynamics that provide an approximation to the real-time dynamics of learning. On examining the aggregate demand equation (11.29), it is seen that the locus consisting of the two vertical lines gives values for (π^e, y^e) at which $\frac{dy^e}{d\tau} = 0$, while the upward-sloping curve gives values for (π^e, y^e) at which $\frac{d\pi^e}{d\tau} = 0$. The targeted steady state at $\pi^* = 1.02$ is locally stable under E-stability dynamics and convergence towards it is cyclical. The low steady state $\pi_L = 0.993092$, $y_L = 0.633614$ is a saddle point and, most importantly, there is a region of initial expectations implying unstable trajectories with falling inflation expectations and, eventually, falling output

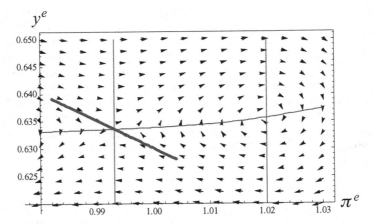

Figure 11.2 E-stability dynamics under a global Taylor rule

expectations. The same holds true for actual inflation and output. We call these paths 'deflationary spirals' and this region the 'deflationary trap'. The downward-sloping line through the low steady state gives the local linear approximation of the stable manifold separating the basin of attraction of the targeted steady state from the deflationary region.

Figure 11.2 shows that the problem of deflationary traps for sufficiently pessimistic expectations, discovered by Evans, Guse and Honkapohja (2008) for Euler equation learning, continues to arise under infinite-horizon learning, in which consumption, output and inflation are determined as the first-period decisions of the solution to the infinite-horizon optimisation problem under subjective expectations based on our learning rule. The intuition for the unstable trajectories is that sufficiently pessimistic expectations π_t^e, y_t^e lead to high expected real interest rates, because of the zero lower bound on net nominal interest rates. High expected real interest rates, and low expected incomes, imply lower inflation and output through the consumption function and the infinite-horizon Phillips curve. The learning rule can then lead to a downward revision of expectations over time, pushing the economy further along an unstable trajectory. Of course, along an unstable path one would expect either private agents or policymakers eventually to alter their actions, but our results nonetheless indicate the potential for major disruptions to the economy resulting from large negative shocks to expectations. We now turn to possible policy changes that can avoid these undesirable outcomes.

11.4   Alternative monetary and fiscal policies

Monetary policy committed to low interest rates

In earlier work with Guse (Evans, Guse and Honkapohja 2008), we considered the implications of aggressive monetary easing triggered by inflation rates below some threshold $\tilde{\pi}$, where $\pi_L < \tilde{\pi} < \pi^*$. That study looked at Euler equation learning in which agents have short horizons, and it was found that this type of policy did not provide a foolproof way to avoid deflationary spirals. In the current framework, agents have long horizons in their decision-making, with the result that there appears to be more scope for aggressive monetary policy to eliminate these unstable trajectories. Moreover, in models with RE, a commitment to long periods of low interest rates has been advocated as a way of avoiding the consequences of liquidity traps (see, for example, Krugman 1998, Eggertsson and Woodford 2003 and Svensson 2003).

We modify the interest rate rule to include aggressive monetary easing if expected inflation gets too low. This idea is formalised by introducing a lower threshold for inflation, so that the interest rate R_t is cut to a low level $\hat{R}$ very close to one. To maintain continuity of the interest rate rule, one introduces two threshold values $\pi_L < \tilde{\pi}_1 < \tilde{\pi}_2 < \pi^*$ with $\tilde{\pi}_1 \approx \tilde{\pi}_2$ and

$$\tilde{f}(\pi^e) = R - 1 = \begin{cases} f(\pi^e) & \text{if } \pi^e > \tilde{\pi}_2 \\ \hat{R} + (\pi^e - \tilde{\pi}_1)\dfrac{f(\tilde{\pi}_2) - \hat{R}}{\tilde{\pi}_2 - \tilde{\pi}_1} & \text{if } \tilde{\pi}_1 \leq \pi^e \leq \tilde{\pi}_2 \\ \hat{R} & \text{if } \pi^e < \tilde{\pi}_1 \end{cases}$$

(11.33)

so that $f(\pi^e)$ in the earlier rule (11.8) is replaced by $\tilde{f}(\pi^e)$.

Figure 11.3 illustrates the expectation dynamics with aggressive monetary easing. The numerics set $\tilde{\pi}_1 = 1.009$ and $\tilde{\pi}_2 = 1.01$, so the interest rate is adjusted linearly down to $R = 1.001 \equiv \hat{R}$. The other parameter values are unchanged. It is evident that the possibility of deflationary spirals remains. The new policy does help to a limited extent, because it shifts the unstable region to the south-west, as is evident from comparing Figures 11.2 and 11.3. The constrained low steady-state values in Figure 11.3 are $\pi_L = 0.99099$, $y_L = 0.633459$, which are lower than the values of the low-inflation steady state in Figure 11.2. Our main conclusion is that adding aggressive monetary easing at low (expected) inflation rates is not sufficient to eliminate the region of deflation traps.

In Figure 11.3 it is assumed that agents have incorporated the interest rate rule in their consumption function, and thus they are assumed to

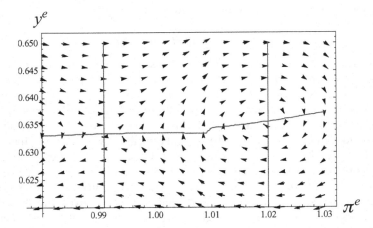

Figure 11.3 Global expectations dynamics with aggressive monetary easing

know that aggressive monetary easing will be continued as long as inflation expectations remain low. We now take up the possibility that the central bank commits itself to zero interest rates for an extended period of time that continues even if inflation expectations increase towards the targeted value. This is investigated in our learning set-up by considering the limit case, in which policymakers respond to low inflation by committing themselves to the zero interest rate policy for ever. Surprisingly, the possibility of deflation traps remains even in this extreme case of monetary easing for all future time. This result is illustrated in Figure 11.4.

It can be seen that, for sufficiently pessimistic expectations, the region of deflation traps continues to exist. This policy reduces the deflationary region somewhat but at the great cost of converting the previous region of stability into a regime in which inflation would increase without bound.

Combined monetary and fiscal easing

We now add aggressive fiscal policy to the preceding monetary easing policy, following Evans, Guse and Honkapohja (2008). The key idea is to increase government spending temporarily in order to ensure that inflation never falls below a suitable threshold. With changes in government spending, agents now have to forecast both gross and net output, which implies that the expectation dynamics become three-dimensional,

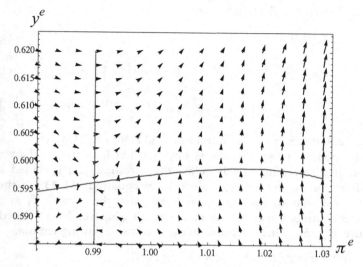

Figure 11.4 Dynamics with aggressive monetary easing for ever

and phase diagrams are no longer convenient for illustrating the dynamics. Instead, selected time paths of central variables are plotted in the final two figures. The formal changes to the model are as follows.

First, we assume that expectations of net output are determined by steady-state learning, as was done earlier with regard to output and inflation. Thus, in addition to (11.26), the expectation dynamics for x_t^e are given by

$$x_t^e = x_{t-1}^e + \omega_t(x_{t-1} - x_{t-1}^e)$$

The temporary equilibrium equations are now given by the following. Gross output is[12]

$$y_t = g_t + (\beta^{-1} - 1)x_t^e \sum_{j=1}^{\infty} \left(D_{t,t+j}^e\right)^{-1} \tag{11.34}$$

$$D_{t,t+j}^e = [(1 + \tilde{f}\left(\pi_t^e\right))/\pi_t^e]^j \tag{11.35}$$

Net output is given by

$$x_t = y_t - g_t \tag{11.36}$$

Evidently, for given expectations, net output is independent of g_t, with the result that in temporary equilibrium the government spending multiplier is one. Inflation is determined by

$$Q(\pi_t) \equiv (\pi_t - 1)\,\pi_t \tag{11.37}$$

$$Q(\pi_t) = \frac{\nu}{\gamma}\left(\alpha^{-1}y_t^{(1+\varepsilon)/\alpha} - \left(1 - \nu^{-1}\right)\frac{y_t}{x_t}\right) \tag{11.38}$$

$$+ \frac{\nu}{\gamma}\left(\beta(1-\beta)^{-1}\left(\alpha^{-1}(y_t^e)^{(1+\varepsilon)/\alpha} - \left(1-\nu^{-1}\right)\frac{y_t^e}{x_t^e}\right)\right)$$

These equations are a generalisation of (11.30) to (11.31).[13]

The policy of fiscal easing is begun when it is triggered by actual inflation threatening to fall below the threshold $\tilde{\pi}_1$, specified in the modification to the interest rate rule in equation (11.33) in the preceding subsection. Specifically, it is assumed that if $\pi_t < \tilde{\pi}_1$ at $g_t = \bar{g}$ then government spending is increased to whatever level is needed to ensure $\pi_t = \tilde{\pi}_1$. This is feasible because of the following lemma.

Lemma 1 *For given expectations* π_t^e, y_t^e, x_t^e,

$$\frac{d\pi_t}{dg_t} \geq k$$

for some $k > 0$ and g_t sufficiently large.

Proof As net output is constant, we have $\frac{dy_t}{dg_t} = 1$. Then it is seen from equations (11.37) to (11.38) that $\frac{\partial Q}{\partial y_t}$ is bounded above zero for y_t sufficiently large, and so the same holds for $\frac{\partial \pi_t}{\partial y_t}$. ∎

Lemma 1 implies that, under our policy of combined fiscal and monetary easing triggered by the inflation threshold, inflation will never fall below $\tilde{\pi}_1$. We remark that this result holds regardless of the elasticity of labour supply, which is parameterised by $\varepsilon > 0$. If ε is large, so that labour supply is highly inelastic, then the sensitivity of inflation to output in the Phillips curve is correspondingly higher.

The lemma implies the following global uniqueness result.

Proposition 3 *Consider the temporary equilibrium system (11.33), (11.34), (11.35), (11.36), (11.37) and (11.38) with fiscal easing triggered by the threshold $\tilde{\pi}_1$. There is a unique steady state with inflation at π^* and a corresponding value for output, with $g_t = \bar{g}$. The targeted steady state is locally stable under learning.*

Proof From (11.34) to (11.35) in a steady state we obtain the Fisher equation $R = \beta^{-1}\pi$. The interest rate rule provides a second steady-state relationship, $R = 1 + \tilde{f}(\pi)$. These equations have a unique solution at π^*

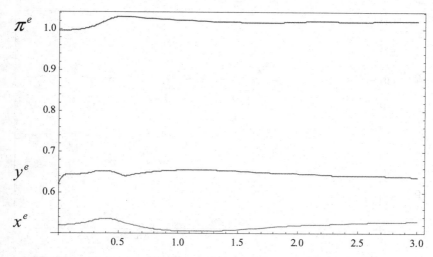

Figure 11.5 Inflation, output and net output expectations over time, with combined monetary and fiscal easing in response to a large pessimistic shock

under the specified policy, since the policy implies the restriction $\pi \geq \tilde{\pi}_1$. Local stability under learning follows from proposition 2.   ∎

The numerical results indicate that the steady state is globally stable under learning.

The results are illustrated in Figures 11.5 and 11.6. Let us consider a starting point $\pi^e = 0.995$, $y^e = 0.62$ and $x^e = 0.52$, which is picked from the deflationary region in Figure 11.3. Figure 11.5 shows the time paths for expectations of inflation, output and net output. The ordering of the time paths from top to bottom is π^e, y^e and x^e. While there are initial fluctuations in these expectations, the time paths converge to the targeted steady state over time. Figure 11.6 shows the corresponding dynamics of actual inflation, output and government spending. The ordering of curves from top down is π, y and g. It is seen that the actual values of inflation and the output variables also converge to their steady-state values after initial fluctuations. We note that the time variable plotted here is notional time τ, corresponding to the E-stability differential equation. For constant gains, the link to real time t depends on the 'gain' ω of the learning rule according to $\tau = \omega t$. Thus, if $\omega = 0.10$ per quarter, then $\tau = 2$ corresponds to $t = 20$ quarters.

It is evident that there is convergence to the unique steady state, and this result appears to be robust numerically. This policy therefore appears

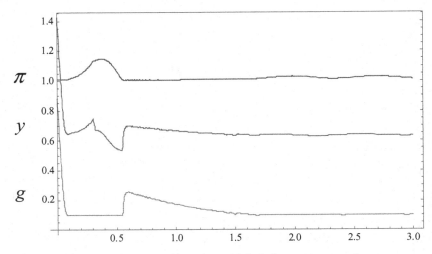

Figure 11.6 Time paths of actual inflation, output and government spending, with combined monetary and fiscal easing in response to a large pessimistic shock

to provide a robust way of avoiding a liquidity trap and the associated deflationary dynamics that arise with learning under the basic interest rate policy. The mechanism is that, by stabilising prices through expansionary government spending, low nominal interest rates yield low expected real interest rates, which leads to a recovery of private spending.

Although our recommended policy does successfully insulate the economy from the deflation trap, the resulting path is cyclical and exhibits some overshooting of the inflation target after the economy has been pushed out of the deflationary region. There are big fluctuations in inflation, output and government spending in the initial stages of the dynamics – a feature that was not seen in the short-horizon learning examined by Evans, Guse and Honkapohja (2008). The reason for the large fluctuations is as follows. The combined monetary and fiscal easing during the initial period of pessimistic expectations leads to high levels of government spending and output, which in turn increases y^e substantially. When the initial period of easing ends, at around $\tau = 0.1$, π^e is near the threshold value $\tilde{\pi}_1$, but y^e is above the value corresponding to the targeted steady state. For a period of time g_t remains at the normal value $\bar{g}$ and Figure 11.2 applies. It can be seen that the economy is in a region north-west of the targeted steady state, implying that π^e and y^e increase. Eventually the economy enters a region north-east of the π^* steady state, with increasing π^e and decreasing y^e. The next phase is in the region south-east of the π^* steady state, with decreasing π^e and y^e. This is followed by a phase in the region south-west of the π^* steady state, and a second time interval during which aggressive fiscal policy is followed before gradual convergence to the targeted steady state is achieved. This particular simulation shows that the cyclical adjustment path to the targeted steady state can entail more than one time interval during which the thresholds for aggressive policy are binding.

These numerical results raise the question of whether alternative versions of our combined policy of monetary and fiscal easing can insulate the economy from deflation traps with smaller fluctuations in output and inflation. In the study conducted by Evans, Guse and Honkapohja (2008), interest rates reacted to current rather than expected inflation, and it is possible that this response would improve performance under infinite-horizon learning. One related issue to examine is the performance of interest rate rules that additionally depend on actual or expected output (or net output). Based on the steady-state relationship between output and inflation, these more general Taylor rules are unlikely to change the number of steady states, and hence will not eliminate deflation traps, but they may improve the cyclical performance of the economy. Other possible modifications of policy include fiscal responses that are smoother and that respond counter-cyclically to high expected output and inflation, and explicit commitments to temporary increases in government spending with a suitable time profile.

The time path of public debt is an important feature not shown in Figures 11.5 and 11.6. The large increases in government spending in the early periods obviously lead to a substantial increase in public debt. Because g_t eventually converges to $\bar{g}$ and because the tax rule (11.5) is passive in the sense of Leeper (1991), however, the debt level eventually returns to the normal steady-state value. In the case of Euler equation learning, this was illustrated in the numerical simulations carried out by Evans, Guse and Honkapohja (2008). An implication of the result that the debt level stabilises in the long run is that the transversality condition holds *ex post* as well as *ex ante*.

Noting the critical role of fiscal policy in stabilising inflation, one might ask whether we could dispense entirely with aggressive monetary policy and simply resort to aggressive fiscal policy whenever π_t threatens to fall below $\tilde{\pi}_1$. Although the answer is 'Yes', we think our combined policy is clearly preferable, because there are good reasons to treat monetary policy as the primary tool for counter-cyclical macroeconomic policy. If extensive government spending is used to guarantee the inflation threshold then it is likely that much of the spending will be wasteful, in the sense that private consumption would be more highly valued. We therefore prefer to use fiscal policy as a policy of last resort to ensure the inflation threshold.

11.5   Conclusions

When monetary policy is conducted using a standard Taylor rule, the intended steady state is locally stable under learning. The economy is not globally stable under learning, however, and this remains true even if agents make decisions based on infinite-horizon optimisation problems. A large exogenous negative shock to expectations can lead to a deflation trap in which expected deflation and low output are reinforced under learning and the economy fails to return to the intended equilibrium. Deflation traps can be avoided by a policy of aggressive monetary and fiscal easing if inflation falls below a suitable threshold, such as zero net inflation. Interestingly, current monetary and fiscal policies to combat the ongoing global economic crisis are qualitatively in line with the aggressive policies discussed in this chapter.

The policy of combined monetary and fiscal easing is effective in avoiding deflation even though households are assumed to make consumption decisions using a perceived lifetime budget constraint that incorporates Ricardian equivalence. Although our suggested policy successfully insulates the economy against deflation traps, in some cases there are substantial fluctuations in output and inflation along the transition back to the intended steady state. As briefly discussed above, finding simple policies that can reduce the fluctuations in output and inflation, during this transition, is a high priority for future research.

NOTES

1. Early versions of this chapter were presented at the Sixth Norges Bank Monetary Policy Conference, at the conference in honour of Roger Guesnerie held at the Paris-Jourdan Sciences Economiques Research Centre in June 2009 and at the San Francisco Federal Reserve Bank. The authors are particularly indebted for comments received from Jess Benhabib, Krisztina Molnar, John Williams, Mike Woodford and the editors of this volume.
2. The formulation was used earlier by Marcet and Sargent (1989) and Evans, Honkapohja and Romer (1998). Other recent studies include those by Evans, Honkapohja and Mitra (2007) and Eusepi and Preston (2007).
3. The low steady state can be one of either low positive inflation or deflation, depending on the details of the interest rate rule.
4. We use the Rotemberg formulation in preference to the Calvo model of price stickiness because it enables us to study global dynamics in a non-linear system. The linearisations at the targeted steady state are identical for the two approaches.

5. The main results below would also hold in the case of a contemporaneous-data Taylor rule, which is used by Evans, Guse and Honkapohja (2008).
6. There is an indirect effect of expected inflation on current inflation via current output.
7. Relaxing this assumption would be of interest. This would require agents to forecast future taxes and the evolution of public debt. For a simple example of this approach, see Evans, Honkapohja and Mitra (2007).
8. Alternatively, if the policy rule is not known to the agents, one could assume that agents forecast future real interest rates directly using an adaptive learning rule. The local stability results given below would continue to hold.
9. We note that it follows from Benhabib, Schmitt-Grohe and Uribe (2001) and Evans, Guse and Honkapohja (2008) that π^* is locally determinate and π_L is locally indeterminate under RE.
10. Using the money demand equation it follows that $\lim_{j \to \infty} m_{t+j}^{-1} \beta^j b_{t+j} = 0$ also holds along the planned path.
11. See Evans and Honkapohja (2001, 2009) for general discussions of E-stability. Evans and Honkapohja (2001: sections 3.3–3.4, 7.2 and chap. 11) discuss the special case of steady-state learning.
12. It should be noted that this equation holds only if $(1 + \tilde{f}(\pi_t^e))/\pi_t^e > 1$, and this issue was dealt with by the truncation of the consumption function in the numerical analysis, as explained earlier.
13. As mentioned earlier, these equations hold provided that $Q(\pi_t) > -\frac{1}{4}$, and in this case π_t is taken as the upper root of the quadratic. For $Q(\pi_t) \leq -\frac{1}{4}$ we set $\pi_t = \frac{1}{2}$.

REFERENCES

Adam, K., and R. Billi (2007). 'Discretionary monetary policy and the zero lower bound on nominal interest rates', *Journal of Monetary Economics*, 54(3): 728–52.

Benhabib, J., S. Schmitt-Grohe and M. Uribe (2001). 'The perils of Taylor rules', *Journal of Economic Theory*, 96(1–2): 40–69.

    (2002). 'Avoiding liquidity traps', *Journal of Political Economy*, 110(3): 535–63.

Coenen, G., A. Orphanides and V. Wieland (2004). 'Price stability and monetary policy effectiveness when nominal interest rates are bounded at zero', *B. E. Journal of Macroeconomics*, 4: article 1.

Eggertsson, G., and M. Woodford (2003). 'The zero bound on interest rates and optimal monetary policy', *Brookings Papers on Economic Activity*, 1: 139–211.

Eusepi, S., and B. Preston (2007). 'Central bank communication and expectations stabilization'. Working Paper no. 13259. Cambridge, MA: NBER.

Evans, G., E. Guse and S. Honkapohja (2008). 'Liquidity traps, learning and stagnation', *European Economic Review*, 52(8): 1438–63.

Evans, G., and S. Honkapohja (2001). *Learning and Expectations in Macroeconomics*. Princeton, NJ: Princeton University Press.

    (2005). 'Policy interaction, expectations and the liquidity trap', *Review of Economic Dynamics*, 8(2): 303–23.

(2009). 'Learning and macroeconomics', *Annual Review of Economics*, 1: 421–51.

Evans, G., S. Honkapohja and K. Mitra (2007). 'Anticipated fiscal policy and adaptive learning'. Working Paper no. 0717. Fife: Centre for Dynamic Macroeconomic Analysis, University of St Andrews.

Evans, G., S. Honkapohja and P. Romer (1998). 'Growth cycles', *American Economic Review*, 88(3): 495–515.

Krugman, P. (1998). 'It's baaack: Japan's slump and the return of the liquidity trap', *Brookings Papers on Economic Activity*, 2: 137–205.

Leeper, E. (1991). 'Equilibria under "active" and "passive" monetary and fiscal policies', *Journal of Monetary Economics*, 27(1): 129–47.

Marcet, A., and T. Sargent (1989). 'Convergence of least-squares learning mechanisms in self-referential linear stochastic models', *Journal of Economic Theory*, 48(2): 337–68.

Preston, B. (2005). 'Learning about monetary policy rules when long-horizon expectations matter', *International Journal of Central Banking*, 1(2): 81–126.

(2006). 'Adaptive learning, forecast-based instrument rules and monetary policy', *Journal of Monetary Economics*, 53(3): 507–35.

Rotemberg, J. (1982). 'Sticky prices in the United States', *Journal of Political Economy*, 90(6): 1187–211.

Sargent, T. (2008). 'Evolution and intelligent design', *American Economic Review*, 98(1): 5–37.

Svensson, L. (2003). 'Escaping from a liquidity trap and deflation: the foolproof way and others', *Journal of Economic Perspectives*, 17(4): 145–66.

Wallace, N. (1981). 'A Modigliani–Miller theorem for open-market operations', *American Economic Review*, 71(3): 267–74.

12 Heterogeneous expectations, learning and European inflation dynamics

Anke Weber[1]

12.1 Introduction

Most central banks nowadays gear monetary policy directly towards maintaining a low and stable rate of inflation (IMF 2005: chap. 4). There are, of course, important differences between central banks. While some are explicit inflation targeters, others, such as the European Central Bank, have a numerical definition of price stability as the overriding objective of monetary policy (Gerlach and Schnabel 2000). In either case, however, an understanding of how the public forms inflation expectations is of crucial importance for policymakers.

From the 1970s onwards the idea that expectations are rational has dominated much of the literature. Lately a new view on expectations has emerged, which views economic agents as econometricians when forecasting (an extensive overview of this literature is provided by Evans and Honkapohja 2001). This approach, referred to as adaptive learning, assumes that economic agents are boundedly rational but employ statistical forecasting techniques, which allows for the possibility of a rational expectations equilibrium to be learnt in the long run. One important insight from the adaptive learning literature is that policies that may be optimal under rational expectations are not optimal when individuals use a learning process. Orphanides and Williams (2005) show that the optimal monetary policy under a learning process should respond more aggressively to inflation and become more focused on inflation stability than if expectations were rational, since tight inflation control can facilitate learning and provide better guidance for the formation of inflation expectations.

The contribution of this chapter is twofold. First, it investigates whether learning by economic agents is a plausible assumption for the euro area. Second, it analyses whether the learning process of economic agents converges towards equilibrium and, specifically, whether households and professional forecasters are able to learn the inflation objective of the European Central Bank, which is to maintain inflation close to but below 2 per cent in the medium term. The chapter accordingly focuses on expectations in the euro area. One reason this is interesting is that there are several member countries and, thus, different sets of inflation expectations. As a result, it is possible to investigate whether there are differences in inflation expectations between countries and between households and professional forecasters. Thereby the extent to which the learning behaviour of economic agents is determined by past inflation rates is also examined.

In order to analyse whether expectations result from a learning process, the performance of different forecasting models with time-varying parameters in terms of their ability to fit actual data on inflation and inflation expectations is assessed. Data on household and expert expectations for Germany, Spain, France, Italy and the Netherlands are used. The chapter finds evidence that inflation expectations result from a learning process and that a simple constant-gain algorithm, which is used widely in the learning literature, performs best in fitting data on inflation and inflation expectations. These findings for the euro area confirm the results by Branch and Evans (2006) for the United States. Branch and Evans show that a simple recursive forecasting model with constant-gain learning forecasts well out of sample and also provides the best fit with the Survey of Professional Forecasters.

The results show, furthermore, that professional forecasters use higher constant-gain parameters than households. They therefore update their information sets more frequently and are able to pick up structural changes more quickly. A possible explanation is that households find it more costly to update their information sets than professional forecasters. This empirical finding is related to Carroll's (2003a, 2003b) theoretical model, which assumes that households update their information sets only sporadically by reading newspapers, learning in this way from professional forecasters. This model is supported by the literature on sticky information, which emphasises that agents only intermittently update their information sets and that they incur a cost in doing so (Mankiw and Reis 2007). This chapter also shows that economic agents update their information sets more frequently in countries with higher inflation. A possible explanation is provided by Sims' theory of 'rational inattention'. Sims (2003, 2006) models economic agents as having a limited capacity to absorb information. They therefore need to decide how much attention to pay and which pieces of news to look at. Sims argues that, when inflation is high, agents will pay more attention to new information, as their opportunity cost of being inattentive is significantly greater during these periods.

It is also crucial to investigate whether the learning process converges to equilibrium and whether expectations are anchored at the inflation objective of the ECB. It has often been argued that economic agents should understand the implications of monetary union and hence conclude that inflation differentials cannot last in the medium to long run (ECB 2003). Empirical evidence typically finds large persistent inflation differentials between European countries (see Rogers 2001, Berk and Swank 2002 and Ortega 2003). Angeloni and Ehrmann (2007) show that, after converging sharply in the 1990s, national inflation rates started to diverge again around 1999. They find that, although the differentials have closed somewhat recently, inflation differentials in the euro area are larger and more persistent than, for example, in the United States. However, if actual inflation rates are influenced by inflation expectations through wage- and price-setting behaviour, then convergence in inflation expectations should ultimately lead to convergence in inflation rates across countries. Analysing the convergence of inflation expectations of households and professional forecasters therefore gives us some indication of the likely convergence of future inflation rates. The results show that professional forecasters are more inclined to incorporate the implications of monetary union into their expectations than households. These findings correspond to those of Arnold and Lemmen (2006), who use a growth theory type of model and also find that the expectations of professional forecasters demonstrate more convergence than exists among the public.

The remainder of the chapter is organised as follows. Section 12.2 gives an overview of the data. Section 12.3 discusses the general model. Section 12.4 analyses the fit of simple learning rules with euro area data. Section 12.5 tests for the convergence of expectations to equilibrium and section 12.6 concludes.

12.2   Data

Data sources

The chapter uses data on household inflation expectations derived from the European Commission's (EC's) Consumer Survey as well as expectations of professional forecasters extracted from Consensus Economics, a London-based firm. Data for France, Germany, Italy, the Netherlands and Spain are used. The chapter also uses euro area inflation and inflation expectations. These data are compiled by aggregating the individual country data using weights based on each country's share in total euro area private domestic consumption expenditure.[2]

The EC Consumer Survey asks approximately 20,000 consumers in the euro area for information regarding their expectations of future and past price developments. The survey is conducted on a monthly basis and

Table 12.1 *The EC Consumer Survey*

Q1: How do you think that consumer prices have developed over the last twelve months? They have ...	Q2: By comparison with the past twelve months, how do you expect consumer prices to develop over the next twelve months? They will ...
Fallen	Fall
Stayed about the same	Stay about the same
Risen slightly	Increase at a slower rate
Risen moderately	Increase at the same rate
Risen a lot	Increase more rapidly
Don't know	Don't know

Source: Adapted from Gerberding (2006).

consumers are asked about their expectations of inflation twelve months ahead. Questions and response categories of the survey are shown in Table 12.1.

The data are derived from the EC Consumer Survey, and they are therefore qualitative in nature and need to be quantified. This chapter uses data that have been quantified by Gerberding (2006). Gerberding follows the probability method of Carlson and Parkin (1975), which was extended to the five-category case by Batchelor and Orr (1988). Because of the wording of question 2 (see Table 12.1), the procedure requires the specification of a variable that captures the perception of respondents of the rate of inflation over the past twelve months. Gerberding (2006) follows Berk (1999) in estimating the perceived rate of inflation on the basis of the results from the question on price developments in the past twelve months in the EC Consumer Survey (question 1 in Table 12.1) (a detailed overview of the method used to quantify the qualitative data in this chapter is provided by Gerberding 2001, 2006 and Nielsen 2003).

The data on experts' expectations are provided by Consensus Economics. Every quarter more than 700 professional forecasters from major banks, economic research institutes and investment firms are asked to provide quantitative forecasts on key macro-variables, including consumer prices. These forecasts are available for each of the following six quarters. Simple arithmetic means of these quarterly forecasts are then published for each country. In order for expert expectations to be comparable to the inflation expectations of households derived from the EC Consumer Survey, this chapter uses expectations of professional forecasters on consumer prices for four quarters ahead.

Further details on the data sources, including those sources used to construct time series of actual inflation, can be found in Table 12A.1 in Appendix 12A.

It has to be emphasised that there are limits to the compatibility of the data in this chapter. First, observations for households are monthly, while the data on expectations of professional forecasters are quarterly. Second, household expectations have to be quantified while expert expectations are an average of quantitative forecasts. In addition, there are limitations to the probability method. These include the rather strict assumption of normality for the underlying aggregate distribution function. This assumption has been criticised by Carlson (1975) and Pesaran (1987), who find non-normal features of the aggregate distribution function. As noted by Berk (1999), and Nielsen (2003), however, alternatives to the normal distribution make little difference to the derived expectations series.

The probability approach is widely used in the literature, and an important advantage of this approach is that it does not impose unbiasedness as an a priori property of the measure of future expectations of inflation. This is crucial, as this chapter tests whether households are boundedly rational. Nevertheless, the limitations of the probability approach have to be taken into account when evaluating the results. In particular, it should be noted that survey data, and therefore the quantified proxies constructed from them, are only an approximation of unknown economic agents' expectations (Nardo 2003). Thus survey data approximations of unobservable expectations necessarily entail a measurement error. This error can be due both to sampling and aggregation error and to the general uncertainty attached to survey figures. Depending on the quality of the approximation, the performance of the quantified proxy in fitting true inflation might be poor even if economic agents were perfectly rational. The findings that economic agents are boundedly rational and use adaptive learning to form expectations might therefore be severely affected. In this light, the chapter also computes quarterly averages of the constructed series for household inflation expectations and assesses the robustness of the key results. If the measurement error is unbiased then using quarterly household inflation expectations data helps to average out this error.

So far, it has been explained how the data are obtained, and some of the shortcomings of the probability method have been pointed out. The next subsection provides a more detailed analysis of the data. It examines whether monthly household expectations and quarterly averages of these expectations differ, and thereby assesses the extent to which the measurement error that is likely to be present in the quantified

Table 12.2 *Mean and mean squared forecast errors, households*

	Monthly data		, Quarterly averages	
	ME HH	MSE HH	ME HH	MSE HH
France	0.3941	0.8140	0.3576	0.6910
Germany	0.2166	1.1565	0.3280	1.6106
Italy	−0.1008	1.3209	−0.1070	1.1650
Netherlands	0.6052	1.1442	0.4962	1.0975
Spain	0.7776	3.3285	0.7130	2.9854

Notes: ME = mean forecast error; MSE = mean squared forecast error; HH = household inflation expectations. Monthly data for inflation and household expectations from 1990M1 to 2006M9 are used. Quarterly data for inflation and averaged household expectations from 1990Q1 to 2006Q3 are used.

household expectations data might affect the analysis in this chapter. Rationality tests are also conducted for household and expert inflation expectations.

A preliminary look at the data

Figure 12A.1 in Appendix 12A shows monthly data for actual inflation as well as household expectations from 1990 to 2006 for the different countries investigated in this chapter.[3] Consensus Economics forecasts and actual inflation are also plotted for 1990 to 2006. These series are shown in Figure 12A.2. The expectations series are dated back twelve months for households and four quarters for experts. As a result, the vertical differences between the series in each figure measure the forecast errors of households and professional forecasters.

For household expectations data, the mean forecast errors and mean squared forecast errors are shown in Table 12.2, for both monthly data and the quarterly averages.

The mean squared forecast errors of households differ depending on whether monthly data or quarterly averages of household inflation expectations are used. These differences might be due in part to the measurement error that arises when quantifying the qualitative household expectations data. However, they will also reflect differences between quarterly and monthly measures of inflation.

In order to compare the mean squared forecast errors of expert and household expectations, quarterly averages of household expectations are used.[4] The mean forecast errors and mean squared forecast errors of the averaged household inflation expectations and expert expectations are

Table 12.3 *Mean and mean squared forecast errors and modified Diebold–Mariano tests*

	ME HH	ME Exp.	MSE HH	MSE Exp.	DM	Std. error	*p*-value
France	0.3102	−0.1531	0.6335	0.4446	0.1888	0.173606	0.2809
Germany	0.3376	0.0537	1.6105	0.7604	0.8501	0.450979	0.0640
Italy	−0.1340	0.1120	1.1950	0.6921	0.5029	0.291471	0.0894
Netherlands	0.1730	0.0799	0.8899	0.3684	0.5215	0.303481	0.0929
Spain	0.0341	0.2594	2.0311	0.8659	1.1654	0.764674	0.1350

Notes: Exp. = expert expectations; DM = modified Diebold–Mariano test statistic; Std. error = standard errors. For expert expectations in Spain and the Netherlands, data are available for 1995Q4 to 2006Q3. For the other countries, data for 1990Q4 to 2006Q3 are available.

shown in Table 12.3. The results illustrate that the mean squared forecast errors are larger for households than for professional forecasters. It is possible to test whether these differences in mean squared errors are significant. Equal forecast accuracy can be tested using the method proposed by Diebold and Mariano (1995), with the small-sample correction for the Diebold–Mariano statistic as introduced by Harvey, Leybourne and Newbold (1997). The Diebold–Mariano test results are also shown in Table 12.3.

Table 12.3 shows that, with the exceptions of France and Spain, the differences between the mean squared errors of professional forecasters and households are significant at the 10 per cent level. Thus there is evidence that professional forecasters are, on average, better at forecasting inflation than households.

Several studies have investigated whether expectations of households and professional forecasters are unbiased. This chapter follows the procedure of Forsells and Kenny (2004) and investigates the rationality of monthly household and quarterly expert expectations by running the following regression:

$$\pi_t = \alpha + \beta \pi_t^e + \varepsilon_t \tag{12.1}$$

where π_t denotes the actual inflation rate in period t and π_t^e denotes the expected inflation rate formed in $t-12$ by households and $t-4$ by professional forecasters for which the data frequency is monthly and quarterly, respectively. If the joint null hypothesis $H_0 : (\alpha, \beta) = (0, 1)$ cannot be rejected and ε_t exhibits no evidence of autocorrelation then it follows that expectations are unbiased in a statistical sense. The above rationality tests are conducted for both data on household and expert inflation expectations by ordinary least squares using covariance matrix corrections suggested by Newey and West (1987). Tables 12A.2 and 12A.3 show the estimation results for households and professional forecasters, respectively. The results illustrate that, for household expectations, the null hypothesis $H_0 : (\alpha, \beta) = (0, 1)$ can be rejected at the 1 per cent and 5 per cent levels for each country and the euro area as a whole. For expert expectations, the null hypothesis can be rejected at the 1 per cent and 5 per cent levels for most countries and for the euro area, with the exception of Germany and the Netherlands. However, the Durbin–Watson (DW) statistic shows evidence of significant autocorrelation for households and experts alike and in each country, which is inconsistent with rationality.

As Holden and Peel (1990) have shown, if the null hypothesis in equation (12.1) cannot be rejected this is sufficient for rationality but not necessary. Holden and Peel suggest regressing the forecast error on a constant instead and testing whether the constant is significantly different from zero:

$$\pi_t - \pi_t^e = \alpha + \varepsilon_t \tag{12.2}$$

If ε_t is *iid* then it can be shown that the condition $\alpha = 0$ is both necessary and sufficient for rationality. The test is conducted for household and expert expectations. Table 12A.4 shows the estimation results for households and professional forecasters following Holden and Peel. For households, the null hypothesis, $H_0 : \alpha = 0$, can be rejected at the 1 per cent and 5 per cent levels for each country and the euro area, with the exception of Italy. For experts, the null hypothesis can be rejected for Italy, Spain and the euro area as a whole at the 1 per cent and 5 per cent levels. Again, the Durbin–Watson statistic shows evidence of significant autocorrelation for both households and experts and each country. This is inconsistent with rationality.[5]

So far it has been illustrated that there is little evidence that the inflation expectations of households and professional forecasters are rational. This raises the question of whether expectations can be explained better with theories of adaptive learning. The next section introduces a general model that is used to examine the fit of simple recursive forecasting rules with data on actual inflation and inflation expectations.

12.3   The model

This section follows the examples set by Basdevant (2005) and Branch and Evans (2006) and outlines a general state-space forecasting model that nests alternative models.

Let π_t denote inflation in period t. It is assumed that the reduced form that economic agents use in order to form expectations of inflation is given by

$$\pi_t = \mathbf{b}'_t \mathbf{x}_t + \varepsilon_t \qquad (12.3)$$

where $\mathbf{b}_t = (b_{1t}, b_{2t}, b_{3t}, \ldots, b_{(n+1)t})'$ and $\mathbf{x}_t = (1, \mathbf{y}_{t-1})'$. Furthermore ε_t is a serially uncorrelated disturbance with mean zero and variance H_t – that is, $E(\varepsilon_t) = 0$ and $Var(\varepsilon_t) = H_t$.

Let $\mathbf{y}_t$ with dimension $n\mathrm{x}1$ denote a vector of variables of interest. Thus n is the number of independent variables in our model. These could be lagged values of inflation, output growth or changes in interest rates, for example. It is therefore assumed that economic agents view inflation in period t as a function of a constant and lagged variables of general interest. Moreover, economic agents are seen as forming their expectations for inflation for the next period using the current values of variables of interest such as inflation and output growth.

Together with the assumption that

$$\mathbf{b}_t = \mathbf{b}_{t-1} + \eta_t \qquad (12.4)$$

where $E(\eta_t) = 0$ and $E(\eta_t \eta'_t) = \mathbf{Q}_t$, the above corresponds to a general state-space model with $\mathbf{b}_t$ being the state.

Conditional forecasts of π_t are given by $\widehat{\pi}_{t|t-1} = \widehat{\mathbf{b}}'_{t-1} \mathbf{x}_t$.

The parameter vector $\mathbf{b}_t$ can be estimated using the Kalman filter (for an explanation of the basic Kalman-filtering procedure, see Hamilton 1994).

The recursion can be written as follows:

$$\widehat{\mathbf{b}}_t = \widehat{\mathbf{b}}_{t-1} + \mathbf{k}_t (\pi_t - \widehat{\mathbf{b}}'_{t-1} \mathbf{x}_t) \qquad (12.5)$$

where the Kalman gain, $\mathbf{k}_t$, is given by

$$\mathbf{k}_t = \frac{(\mathbf{P}_{t-1} + \mathbf{Q}_t)\, \mathbf{x}_t}{H_t + \mathbf{x}'_t (\mathbf{P}_{t-1} + \mathbf{Q}_t)\mathbf{x}_t} \qquad (12.6)$$

and

$$\mathbf{P}_t = \mathbf{P}_{t-1} - \frac{(\mathbf{P}_{t-1} + \mathbf{Q}_t)\, \mathbf{x}_t \mathbf{x}'_t\, (\mathbf{P}_{t-1} + \mathbf{Q}_t)}{H_t + \mathbf{x}'_t\, (\mathbf{P}_{t-1} + \mathbf{Q}_t)\, \mathbf{x}_t} + \mathbf{Q}_t \qquad (12.7)$$

where $\mathbf{P}_t = E(\mathbf{b}_t - \widehat{\mathbf{b}}_t)(\mathbf{b}_t - \widehat{\mathbf{b}}_t)'$.

As shown by Marcet and Sargent (1989a, 1989b), the learning process converges to equilibrium only when the law of motion of the parameters is time-invariant.[6] In other words, convergence requires $\mathbf{Q}_t = 0$. Within the Kalman filter framework it is thus possible to test whether learning is perpetual or whether it converges to equilibrium by examining whether the variance of the state variables is significantly different from zero.

If $\mathbf{Q}_t = 0$ and $H_t = 1$, the Kalman filter recursions, equations (12.5) to (12.7), become equivalent to recursive least squares (RLS), as shown by Sargent (1999). The system can then be written as

$$\widehat{\mathbf{b}}_t = \widehat{\mathbf{b}}_{t-1} + \gamma_t \mathbf{R}_t^{-1} \mathbf{x}_t (\pi_t - \widehat{\mathbf{b}}_{t-1}' \mathbf{x}_t) \tag{12.8}$$

$$\mathbf{R}_t = \mathbf{R}_{t-1} + \gamma_t (\mathbf{x}_t \mathbf{x}_t' - \mathbf{R}_{t-1}) \tag{12.9}$$

where $\gamma_t = t^{-1}$ and $\mathbf{R}_t$ is the matrix of second moments of $\mathbf{x}_t$. The gain, γ_t, will approach zero as $t \to \infty$. The above algorithm therefore corresponds to the recursive formulation of ordinary least squares. As shown by Evans and Honkapohja (2001), when economic agents use recursive least squares to update their parameter estimates, these estimates will eventually converge to their rational expectations values.

If $\mathbf{Q}_t = \frac{\gamma}{1-\gamma} \mathbf{P}_{t-1}$ and $H_t = 1 - \gamma$, the system becomes equivalent to the constant-gain version of RLS (Sargent 1999), so that $\gamma_t = \gamma$ in equations (12.8) and (12.9). Using a constant-gain algorithm implies that more weight is placed on recent observations. This algorithm is equivalent to applying weighted least squares, whereby the weights decline geometrically with the distance in time between the observation being weighted and the most recent observation. Thus the constant-gain learning algorithm resembles estimation by ordinary least squares, but with a rolling window of data in which the sample size is approximately $\frac{1}{\gamma}$. Past observations are discounted at a geometric rate of $1 - \gamma$. Hence constant-gain least squares (CGLS) learning is more robust to structural change than recursive least squares learning. Evans and Honkapohja (2001) provide a more detailed explanation of both learning algorithms.

12.4   Simple learning rules

This section compares the performance of alternative recursive forecasting models. It assesses the ability of different simple learning models to fit data on actual inflation and inflation expectations. It is thereby examined whether learning is a plausible description of household and professional forecaster behaviour. The section also investigates the extent to which RLS and CGLS, which are the two most commonly used learning mechanisms described in the theoretical literature, provide a good description of forecaster behaviour. Estimates of the constant-gain parameters are provided for each country and an analysis is carried out to establish whether there is country heterogeneity with respect to learning. Heterogeneity between households and professional forecasters is also examined. An assessment is then made of the extent to which the results are plausible, and specifically whether they agree with other economic theories, such as Sims' theory of 'rational inattention'.

Estimation procedure

In line with Branch and Evans (2006), this chapter divides the sample for each country into three parts: a pre-forecasting period, in which prior beliefs are formed by estimating (12.3); an in-sample period, in which optimal-gain parameters are determined for the case of constant-gain least squares, while for recursive least squares learning the gain sequence continues to be updated as t^{-1}; and, finally, an out-of-sample forecasting period.

For household expectations, a fairly long pre-forecasting period, 1981M1 to 1989M12, is chosen in order to avoid over-sensitivity in respect of the initial estimates. The in-sample period is 1990M1 to 1998M4. The out-of-sample period is hence 1998M5 to 2006M9.[7] Given the monthly frequency of the data, the independent variable vector $\mathbf{x}_t$ is defined as $(1, \mathbf{y}_{t-12})'$. The inflation expectation by households in period $t-12$ for period t is thus given by

$$\pi_{t|t-12} = \widehat{\mathbf{b}}'_{t-12}\mathbf{x}_t \tag{12.10}$$

When economic agents form expectations, the best estimate of the coefficients in period $t-12$ is used. As new data become available agents update their estimates according to either CGLS or RLS learning. The formulae for this updating process under RLS learning are given by equations (12.8) and (12.9). Under CGLS learning, γ_t in these recursions is replaced by the constant gain, γ. It should be noted that, in order to form inflation expectations in period $t-12$ for period t, π_{t-12} is used as an explanatory variable. As a result, the forecast error, $\pi_t - \pi_{t|t-12}$, is serially correlated due to overlapping forecast errors. If the exact nature of this serial correlation is known, in principle, the serial correlation can be incorporated into the Kalman-filtering framework by specifying additional measurement and state equations. In our simple learning models, this means that, when forming expectations of inflation and updating the coefficients $\widehat{\mathbf{b}}_t$, economic agents could make use of these past forecast errors. Following the analysis of Branch and Evans (2006), this chapter does not incorporate the serial correlation into the Kalman-filtering framework or the updating process of coefficients under learning. Instead, a very simple model is used in which individuals predict inflation using relevant explanatory variables, such as inflation and output growth. This means that the results of this chapter may understate the case for learning, as using past values of forecast errors could improve the coefficient estimates and thus improve the fit of the simulated inflation expectations with the true inflation expectations by households.

To calculate the optimal in-sample constant-gain parameters, the in-sample mean square forecast error

$$MSE_{IN}(\pi) = \frac{1}{T} \sum_{t=t_0}^{T} (\pi_t - \widehat{\pi}_t)^2$$

is minimised by searching over all $\gamma \in (0, 1)$ with $t_0 =$1990M1 and $T =$1998M4. The distances between grids are set at 0.0001. $\widehat{\pi}_t$ denotes the forecast made in period $t-12$ for t. This forecast is generated by starting the recursions, equations (12.8) and (12.9), with $\gamma_t = \gamma$, the initial values having been calculated from the pre-sample period, and then using these recursive equations to calculate $\widehat{\mathbf{b}}_t$. The fact that $\widehat{\pi}_t = \widehat{\mathbf{b}}'_{t-12}\mathbf{x}_t$ is then used to generate values for $\widehat{\pi}_t$. When using recursive least squares to update estimates of $\widehat{\mathbf{b}}_t$ there is no need to compute an optimal-gain parameter as $\gamma = t^{-1}$. However, the mean square errors can be computed by updating the sequence for $\widehat{\mathbf{b}}_t$ with t^{-1} and then using the fact that $\widehat{\pi}_t = \widehat{\mathbf{b}}'_{t-12}\mathbf{x}_t$ to generate values for $\widehat{\pi}_t$. These values can then be used as before in order to calculate in-sample mean square errors.

Having determined the optimal in-sample values of the constant gain, out-of-sample MSEs can be computed for each country as

$$MSE_{OUT}(\pi) = \frac{1}{T} \sum_{t=1}^{T} (\pi_t - \widehat{\pi}_t)^2$$

where t ranges from 1998M5 to 2006M9.

It is also possible to find the best-fitting constant-gain parameters for households. These are computed by minimising the in-sample mean square comparison error (MSCE),

$$MSCE_{IN}(\pi) = \frac{1}{T} \sum_{t=t_0}^{T} (\pi_t^F - \widehat{\pi}_t)^2$$

by searching over all $\gamma \in (0, 1)$ with $t_0 =$1990M1 and $T =$1998M4. π_t^F denotes household expectations for period t. The distances between grids are set at 0.0001. The best-fitting constant-gain parameters are computed to determine whether the best-fitting gains that are needed to fit household expectations are equivalent to those needed to fit actual data on inflation in the in-sample period. This is important to investigate, as Branch and Evans (2006) find that, for explaining the forecasts of professional forecasters in the United States, the best-fitting gain is substantially below the optimal gain for fitting data on actual inflation. As before, using the best-fitting gains for household expectations, the out-of-sample mean square comparison forecast error is determined. This is given by

$$MSCE_{OUT}(\pi) = \frac{1}{T} \sum_{t=1}^{T} (\pi_t^F - \widehat{\pi}_t)^2$$

where t ranges from 1998M5 to 2006M9.

For RLS learning, the in-sample and out-of sample MSCEs are calculated as above. The recursive equations (12.8) and (12.9) are updated with t^{-1}.

In addition to absolute mean square comparison errors, relative MSCEs for each country for the model that yields the smallest mean square comparison forecast error are also calculated. These are computed on an out-of-sample basis relative to the variance of the series that the chapter is trying to predict – i.e. household inflation expectations. This follows the procedure used by Forni, Hallin and Reichlin (2003) and Schumacher (2007). Computing relative MSCEs is related to the concept of the predictability of a series (see, for example, Diebold and Kilian 2001). It could be the case that household expectations are more predictable in some countries, which results in lower MSCEs for those countries. Computing the variances of these series gives us some indication about how predictable the different series are.

For professional forecasters, the method is identical to that described above, with the exception that the data are quarterly. Forecasts of experts for four quarters ahead are used in order to make the results comparable between households and professional forecasters.[8] The sample is divided as follows. Data on inflation from 1961Q1 to 1975Q4 are used as the pre-sample period. The in-sample period consists of data from 1976Q1 to 1990Q3. The out-of-sample period was chosen so that it corresponds to the sample of professional forecasters: 1990Q4 to 2006Q3. Given the quarterly frequency of the data, the independent variable vector $\mathbf{x}_t$ is now defined as $(1, \mathbf{y}_{t-4})'$. The inflation expectation by professional forecasters in period $t-4$ for period t is hence given by

$$\pi_{t|t-4} = \widehat{\mathbf{b}}'_{t-4} \mathbf{x}_t \tag{12.11}$$

It should be noted that, because there are relatively few observations for expert expectations, it is possible to determine only in-sample best-fitting gains and in-sample mean square comparison errors for quarterly data.

Four different models are estimated. Model 1 is a simple AR(1) model in which the independent variables are a constant and the lagged value of inflation. Model 2 is a simple AR(2) model with a constant and lagged values of inflation.[9] Model 3 includes a constant, lagged inflation and lagged output growth, which is approximated by growth in industrial production.[10] Model 4 includes changes in interest rates in addition to the variables in model 3. Models 1 to 4 for households can thus be written as follows:

$$\pi_{t+12|t} = b_{1t} + b_{2t}\pi_t + \varepsilon_t \qquad \text{(model 1)}$$

$$\pi_{t+12|t} = b_{1t} + b_{2t}\pi_t + b_{3t}\pi_{t-1} + \varepsilon_t \qquad \text{(model 2)}$$

$$\pi_{t+12|t} = b_{1t} + b_{2t}\pi_t + b_{3t}z_t + \varepsilon_t \qquad \text{(model 3)}$$

$$\pi_{t+12|t} = b_{1t} + b_{2t}\pi_t + b_{3t}z_t + b_{4t}w_t + \varepsilon_t \qquad \text{(model 4)}$$

where z_t denotes industrial production growth and w_t denotes changes in interest rates. The interest rate used in the models is the three-month interbank lending rate. Since the introduction of the European single currency, this rate is known as EURIBOR (Euro Interbank Offered Rate). For quarterly data, models 1 to 4 are identical apart from the fact that the dependent variable is now denoted as $\pi_{t+4|t}$. In addition, for quarterly data, data on GDP are available and so it is not necessary to approximate output growth by industrial production.

Results

'*Households: learning matters*' This subsection examines the ability of simple linear recursive forecasting rules to explain actual data on inflation and inflation expectations. It also examines whether there is heterogeneity between households in different countries.

In order to assess whether it is possible to fit actual inflation with a learning model, the optimal constant gains that minimise the MSE for the in-sample period are first computed for different countries. These are shown in Table 12.4.

These optimal constant-gain parameters are significantly higher than those typically found for the United States. For the United States, Orphanides and Williams (2007) suggest estimates of around 0.01 to 0.04, Branch and Evans (2006) find values of the gain of around 0.06 and Milani (2007) finds values between 0.02 and 0.12 using quarterly data and depending on the time period used.[11] A higher gain coefficient for the euro area implies that agents should optimally use fewer years of data to form a prediction of inflation. A possible explanation for this might be that inflation in European countries was subject to

Table 12.4 *Optimal constant-gain parameters, monthly data*

1990M1–1998M4		γ		
	Model 1	Model 2	Model 3	Model 4
France	0.1870	0.1280	0.1700	0.1360
Germany	0.1400	0.0960	0.1740	0.1300
Italy	0.1790	0.1490	0.0950	0.0670
Netherlands	0.2410	0.1580	0.1420	0.1150
Spain	0.1750	0.1480	0.1752	0.1090

Table 12.5 *Mean square forecast errors, monthly data*

	Out-of-sample period: 1998M5–2006M9							
	RLS				CGLS			
	Model 1	Model 2	Model 3	Model 4	Model 1	Model 2	Model 3	Model 4
France	0.3269	0.3200	0.3217	0.3520	0.0457	0.0613	0.1648	**0.0430**
Germany	0.4929	0.4859	0.4864	0.5350	**0.0720**	0.0879	0.1220	0.4129
Italy	0.2153	0.2243	0.2147	0.2170	**0.0198**	0.0260	0.0535	0.0346
Netherlands	0.7602	0.4580	0.7584	0.4349	**0.0440**	0.0784	0.0806	0.0670
Spain	0.7727	0.7680	0.7631	0.8599	0.0664	**0.0611**	0.1397	0.0688

Note: Bold entries correspond to the model that yields the smallest MSE.

more frequent structural breaks. Constant-gain least squares learning discounts past observations geometrically, and hence, if there are more structural breaks, fewer years of data should optimally be used to generate forecasts.

The ability of different models to fit inflation is also assessed, and this makes it possible to examine whether RLS or CGLS generates better predictions of actual inflation. Table 12.5 shows out-of-sample mean square forecast errors using both constant-gain and recursive least squares learning.

It can be seen that constant-gain clearly dominates recursive least squares learning in terms of forecast accuracy.[12] No single model fits best for all countries, though, but the simple model with constant-gain learning and just lagged inflation and a constant as the independent variables does well for all countries. Figure 12A.3 shows actual inflation together with forecasts generated using the optimal gain and model for the different economies. This figure highlights the fact that CGLS learning performs well in fitting actual inflation.

Table 12.6 *Best-fitting constant-gain parameters, households, monthly data*

1990M1–1998M4			γ	
	Model 1	Model 2	Model 3	Model 4
France	0.0002	0.0082	0.0001	0.0051
Germany	0.0010	0.0020	0.0010	0.0010
Italy	0.0270	0.0280	0.0260	0.0240
Netherlands	0.0010	0.0010	0.0210	0.0010
Spain	0.0530	0.0510	0.0640	0.0460

It is also important to analyse which model can best explain data on inflation expectations. The best-fitting gains are computed by minimising the in-sample mean square comparison errors. It is thereby possible to assess whether there is heterogeneity regarding the best-fitting constant-gain parameters between countries. These gains are shown in Table 12.6 for each country and model.

From Table 12.6, it can be seen that the best-fitting gains are much smaller than the optimal constant gains. The best-fitting gains for the European economies in our sample range from 0.0001 to 0.064. These results roughly correspond with results found for the United States (Pfaj-far and Santoro 2006 find the best-fitting constant gains between 0.0008 and 0.001 for monthly data). The fact that the best-fitting constant gains are well below optimal constant gains might imply that households are possibly unaware of some of the structural breaks in the data and use a larger number of past observations to form an expectation of inflation than would be optimal.

The results from Table 12.6 suggest that households in 'high-inflation' countries, such as Spain and Italy, use higher constant gains than those in 'low-inflation' countries and hence detect structural changes more rapidly. A possible explanation as to why households in 'high-inflation' countries 'learn more rapidly' is provided by Sims (2003, 2006), who argues that economic agents will pay more attention to new information becoming available as their cost of being inattentive is significantly higher during periods of high inflation. It is also found that higher constant gains are needed to explain the data on the inflation expectations of professional forecasters than those of households. This could be caused by a greater awareness of the presence of structural breaks by professional forecasters, but it could also be the case that professional forecasters are more willing to incur the costs of updating their information sets than households, which update their information sets less frequently (Carroll 2003a, 2003b; Döpke *et al.* 2006).[13] Theories of sticky information also emphasise that households update their information sets infrequently because of the substantial costs incurred in this updating process (Mankiw and Reis 2007).

Table 12.6 also shows that the average best-fitting constant gains for monthly data across the four models for Germany and Spain equal 0.00125 and 0.054, respectively. This implies that, for Germany, if an observation in September 2006 gets a weight of 1, we have to go back as far as July 1960 before seeing an observation that receives a weight of 1/2.[14] The unconditional inflation expectation of German households is thus based on a long history of inflation. In the case of Spain, in order to get the same result we need to go back only about one year. A sensible interpretation of this finding lies in the potential consequences of the introduction of the European Monetary Union. There was a major change towards lower and more stable rates of inflation in Spain and Italy, whereas the changes in inflation observed in Germany and the Netherlands were much smaller. In particular, the inflation process itself in Spain and Italy evolved more sharply over time. The constant-gain learning algorithm is robust to these structural changes. When structural breaks are present, a higher constant gain (and thus fewer years of data), is used to form expectations of inflation. The higher constant gains that are observed in Italy and Spain compared to Germany and the Netherlands may therefore be a result of these structural changes and not of the high rates of inflation that were observed in those countries per se. As a consequence, the results are not easily comparable between countries, and one has to be careful in interpreting the differences in constant gains between 'low-inflation' countries and 'high-inflation' countries as evidence for Sims' theory of rational inattention. Ideally, with longer data series on household expectations, one could evaluate whether the constant gain that households use to form expectations in a particular country is larger in periods in which there is a high rate of inflation.

Mean square comparison forecast errors are then computed for household expectations using data generated with the RLS algorithm as well as data generated using the CGLS algorithm with the best-fitting constant gains. Hence it is possible to examine whether learning matters for the inflation expectations formation of households and which dependent variables households use when predicting inflation. We can also assess whether recursive least squares or constant-gain learning provides a better description of household behaviour and whether there is country heterogeneity with respect to learning. The results are found in Table 12.7.

Table 12.7 *Mean square comparison errors, households, monthly data*

	RLS				CGLS			
	\multicolumn{8}{c}{Out-of-sample period: 1998M5–2006M9}							
	RLS				CGLS			
	Model 1	Model 2	Model 3	Model 4	Model 1	Model 2	Model 3	Model 4
France	0.3226	0.3096	0.3229	0.3549	0.4491	0.3532	0.3812	**0.2958**
Germany	0.5589	0.5508	0.5609	0.6502	**0.5349**	0.5631	0.5360	0.6858
Italy	0.3781	0.3785	0.3805	0.3229	0.3095	0.2991	0.3082	**0.2402**
Netherlands	0.5278	0.3320	0.5325	0.3657	0.4500	0.5753	0.6906	**0.2774**
Spain	1.7622	**1.7565**	1.7661	1.9075	1.9083	1.9885	2.0407	2.1847

Note: Bold entries correspond to the model that yields the smallest MSCE.

Table 12.7 shows that expectations in France, the Netherlands and Italy can be fitted better with our simple models than expectations in Germany and Spain. Specifically, model 4 seems to perform well in these countries, which suggests that agents use more complicated models than those simply including lagged inflation. In the case of Spain, however, given the large forecast errors, there is little evidence that agents are using any of the simple linear forecasting models employed by this chapter. Furthermore, it can be seen that, with the exception of Spain, constant-gain dominates recursive least squares learning in terms of forecast accuracy.

The relative MSCEs for the model that yields the smallest mean square comparison error are also computed for each country, and they are shown in Table 12.8. In order to compute relative MSCEs, the out-of-sample mean square comparison errors are divided by the variance of the household expectations series. It could be the case that household expectations are more predictable in some countries, which results in lower MSCEs. Computing the variances of these series gives us some indication as to how predictable the different series are.

The relative MSCE is still the smallest for Italy, meaning that the model is able to fit expectations in Italy best. The difference between the relative MSCE for the best-fitting model for Italy and the relative MSCE corresponding to the best-fitting models for France and the Netherlands is now larger than was the case with absolute MSCEs. There is evidence, therefore, that our simple learning model does significantly better in predicting household expectations in Italy than in predicting expectations in other countries.

Figure 12A.4 shows actual household inflation expectations and the generated series for expectations of inflation using the optimal model and

Table 12.8 *Relative mean square comparison errors, households, monthly data*

Out-of-sample period: 1998M5–2006M9	
	Relative MSCE
France	0.5096
Germany	0.7865
Italy	0.0619
Netherlands	0.5660
Spain	0.9494

best-fitting constant gain for each country. While the direction of inflation expectations can be predicted well (even for Spain), expectations are somewhat more volatile than our generated series. A possible explanation may be that, although households use simple linear forecasting models, there are certain stochastic shocks and events to which households react and which also influence their expectations.

So far, it has been demonstrated that constant-gain least squares learning performs well in explaining actual inflation and monthly household inflation expectations. Moreover, households in 'high-inflation' countries use higher constant-gain parameters than households in 'low-inflation' countries. This raises the issue of whether the same is true for experts and for quarterly averages of household expectations, which I turn to next.

'Professional forecasters use higher constant-gain parameters than households' This subsection assesses the extent to which simple learning rules can explain survey data on inflation expectations by professional forecasters, and investigates whether there exists heterogeneity between experts and households.

The first assessment is whether a simple learning model can fit actual data on inflation. Optimal gains for each model are shown in Table 12.9. Results are shown for only three countries, because there are data constraints for the Netherlands and Spain.[15]

As was the case in the previous subsection, optimal constant gains are higher than those found by empirical studies for the United States.

The out-of-sample forecast errors for actual inflation are shown in Table 12.10. It can be seen that CGLS learning again dominates RLS learning and that the simplest model does well in explaining actual inflation.[16] This is illustrated in Figure 12A.5, which shows actual and

Table 12.9 *Optimal constant-gain parameters, quarterly data*

1976Q1–1990Q3	γ			
	Model 1	Model 2	Model 3	Model 4
France	0.2160	0.1050	0.1230	0.1020
Germany	0.1380	0.1120	0.1780	0.1110
Italy	0.3000	0.2000	0.1570	N/A

Table 12.10 *Mean square forecast errors, quarterly data*

	Out-of-sample period: 1990Q4–2006Q3							
	RLS				CGLS			
	Model 1	Model 2	Model 3	Model 4	Model 1	Model 2	Model 3	Model 4
France	0.2986	0.3226	0.3043	0.4526	**0.0721**	0.1203	0.1742	0.2296
Germany	0.9801	1.0137	0.8508	0.8734	0.2356	0.3864	**0.2142**	0.3888
Italy	1.1611	1.3113	0.9977	N/A	**0.0658**	0.1011	0.2647	N/A

Note: Bold entries correspond to the model that yields the smallest MSE.

predicted inflation using the optimal model and gain parameter for each country.

Table 12.11 shows the best-fitting constant gains, which can be used to examine whether there is heterogeneity between professional forecasters and households. As already indicated, data on household expectations, which have a monthly frequency, are averaged to convert them into quarterly data, and then the same estimations are performed with household expectations as with expert expectations in order to produce a direct comparison between the expectations of households and professional forecasters.

Tables 12.12 and 12.13 show mean square comparison errors for households and experts. These suggest that there is no single model that fits best across all three countries. There is some evidence that households are more inclined to use simpler models with just lagged values of inflation compared to professional forecasters, who use a larger variety of variables to predict inflation. This does not correspond to the findings for the monthly data, however. This apparent contradiction between

Table 12.11 *Best-fitting constant-gain parameters, households and experts, quarterly data*

	In-sample period: 1990Q4–2006Q3							
	γ							
	Model 1		Model 2		Model 3		Model 4	
	Experts	Households	Experts	Households	Experts	Households	Experts	Households
France	0.0200	0.0080	0.0240	0.0142	0.0130	0.0060	0.0410	0.0070
Germany	0.1380	0.0018	0.1000	0.0010	0.1080	0.0010	0.0460	0.0012
Italy	0.1780	0.0720	0.1380	0.0720	0.1370	0.0930	N/A	N/A

Table 12.12 *Mean square comparison errors, experts, quarterly data*

	In-sample period: 1990Q4–2006Q3							
	RLS				CGLS			
	Model 1	Model 2	Model 3	Model 4	Model 1	Model 2	Model 3	Model 4
France	0.2752	0.2910	0.2765	0.4613	0.2780	0.2439	0.2707	**0.2194**
Germany	0.3419	0.4805	0.2930	0.3704	0.4068	0.2268	**0.2046**	0.2664
Italy	0.8475	1.0138	0.8242	N/A	**0.4300**	0.4865	0.4926	N/A

Note: Bold entries correspond to the model that yields the smallest MSCE.

Table 12.13 *Mean square comparison errors, households, quarterly data*

	In-sample period: 1990Q4–2006Q3							
	RLS				CGLS			
	Model 1	Model 2	Model 3	Model 4	Model 1	Model 2	Model 3	Model 4
France	0.7233	0.7918	0.7439	0.9859	**0.3897**	0.6250	0.5403	0.4757
Germany	0.7816	0.9610	0.7913	0.9064	0.7197	**0.6912**	0.7113	0.9762
Italy	0.8662	0.9625	0.9711	N/A	0.6062	**0.5811**	0.8091	N/A

Note: Bold entries correspond to the model that yields the smallest MSCE.

282 *Weber*

Table 12.14 *Relative mean square forecast comparison errors, households and experts, quarterly data*

In-sample period: 1990Q4–2006Q3	Relative MSCEs	
	Households	Experts
France	0.6938	0.4705
Germany	1.0710	0.2794
Italy	0.1510	0.1679

Table 12.15 *Modified Diebold–Mariano tests for equal forecast accuracy of households and experts, quarterly data*

	Mod. DM statistic	*p*-value
France	1.3768	0.1906
Germany	2.0921	0.0487
Italy	1.1567	0.2706

the results for household expectations for monthly data and quarterly data could be attributable to the fact that using quarterly averages of household data helps to average out the measurement error in monthly expectations, and this could affect the results.

Again, it is possible to compute relative mean square comparison forecast errors. The best-fitting model is used for each country. Relative MSCEs for households and experts are shown in Table 12.14.

From Table 12.14 it can be seen that, according to the relative MSCEs, the simple recursive forecasting model is able to fit expectations in Italy best. This is different from the conclusions drawn from Tables 12.12 and 12.13. It highlights the fact that expectations in Germany and France may be more predictable than in Italy.

It seems to be the case that our simple models fit expectations of professional forecasters somewhat better than those of households. It can be tested whether the differences in mean squared comparison errors are significant by using a modified Diebold–Mariano (1995) test with the small sample correction proposed by Harvey, Leybourne and Newbold (1997). It is possible to compare the MSCEs of the optimal model for each country – i.e the model that yields the smallest absolute MSCE. For example, for Germany, model 3 is used for experts and model 2 for households. The results of the modified Diebold–Mariano tests are shown in Table 12.15.

With the exception of Germany, the null hypothesis of equal forecast accuracy cannot be rejected at the 1 per cent and 5 per cent levels. There is therefore evidence that, for France and Italy, the model is able to predict expectations of households and experts equally well. Figure 12A.6 shows expert expectations and the generated series for inflation forecasts. It can be seen that the general direction of expectations can be predicted well with the model. This is also the case for fitting household expectations, which Figure 12A.7 illustrates.

The findings of this subsection can therefore be seen to provide support for adaptive learning as a description of actual forecaster behaviour. This raises the issue of whether the learning processes of households and professional forecasters converge to equilibrium, which I turn to next.

12.5 Testing for convergence

Estimation procedure

This section investigates whether expectations converge to equilibrium and whether agents are able to learn the inflation objective of the ECB, which is to maintain inflation close to but below 2 per cent in the medium term. As explained above this can be tested within a Kalman-filtering framework by investigating whether the variance of the hyper-parameters is significantly different from zero. Time-varying parameters are estimated using the model outlined in equations (12.3) to (12.7). Given that the simplest model of inflation performs quite well for all countries, it is assumed that inflation expectations are derived from the following rules:

$$\pi_{t+12|t} = b_{1t} + b_{2t}\pi_t + \varepsilon_t \tag{12.12}$$

for households and

$$\pi_{t+4|t} = b_{1t} + b_{2t}\pi_t + \varepsilon_t \tag{12.13}$$

for professional forecasters. Furthermore, the following assumptions are made:

$$b_{i,t} = b_{i,t-1} + \eta_{i,t} \tag{12.14}$$

and

$$\varepsilon_t \sim N(0, \sigma^2) \quad \text{and} \quad \eta_{i,t} \sim N\big(0, (Q_t^i)^2\big)$$

It is hence assumed that the variance on the measurement equation is constant while the variance of the hyper-parameters may be time-dependent. The variance of the measurement equation is assumed to be constant in order to restrict the number of free parameters that have to be estimated within the Kalman filter. To test for convergence, it is investigated whether the variance of the state decreases over time, which would imply that the learning process is converging towards least squares estimates. Following Basdevant (2005), who uses the methods discussed by Hall, Robertson and Wickens (1997) to test for convergence, Q_t is modelled as follows:

$$Q_{i,t} = \lambda^2 Q_{i,t-1} \tag{12.15}$$

for $i = 1, 2$.

As shown by Hall and St Aubyn (1995) and Hall, Robertson and Wickens (1997), if $0 \leq \lambda < 1$ convergence in expectations holds. The null hypothesis $H_0 : \lambda = 1$ is tested against the alternative $H_1 : \lambda < 1$. In order to obtain the distribution of some function of λ under the null, this chapter follows Basdevant (2005) in constructing the test statistic proposed by Hall and St Aubyn (HSA) (1995) and St Aubyn (1999). This is given by

$$HSA = \frac{\widehat{\lambda} - 1}{\widehat{\sigma}(\widehat{\lambda})}$$

where $\widehat{\sigma}(\widehat{\lambda})$ is the estimated standard error of λ. Hall and St Aubyn (1995) and St Aubyn (1999) calculate critical values for the HSA statistic. These are -3.479 at the 1 per cent level, -2.479 at the 5 per cent level and -1.970 at the 10 per cent level.

To test for convergence, EViews is used in order to set up a state-space model. As EViews cannot estimate equation (12.15) in its present form, the equation is rewritten as $Q_{i,t} = \lambda^{2t} Q_{i,0}$, where t is a time trend. In order to impose values for $Q_{i,0}$, equations (12.12) and (12.13) are estimated using OLS and the squared standard deviations of the coefficients are used as estimates of the initial variances. For household expectations, initial values of the variances are determined using data for 1981M1 to 1989M12, and, for experts, initial values are determined using data for 1961Q1 to 1990Q3.

Results

Household expectations   The results are shown in Tables 12.16 and 12.17.

Table 12.16 *Households: testing for convergence*

	λ	Std. error	HSA
France	0.998199	0.000525	−3.4302*
Germany	0.996640	0.000387	−8.6820***
Italy	0.995096	0.000667	−7.3522***
Netherlands	0.998652	0.000579	−2.3274*
Spain	0.998010	0.000505	−3.9406***
Euro area	0.991442	0.000543	−15.7510***

Notes: * = 'no convergence' rejected at 10 per cent confidence level;
*** = 'no convergence' rejected at 1 per cent confidence level.

Table 12.17 *Households: testing for convergence, final state estimates*

		Final state	Root MSE	p-value
France	$\widehat{b}_1$	2.3013	0.4103	0.0000
	$\widehat{b}_2$	0.2106	0.1934	0.2759
Germany	$\widehat{b}_1$	1.4536	0.3550	0.0000
	$\widehat{b}_2$	−0.0584	0.2934	0.8422
Italy	$\widehat{b}_1$	3.0022	0.734328	0.0000
	$\widehat{b}_2$	−0.7352	0.3493	0.0353
Netherlands	$\widehat{b}_1$	1.1782	0.4746	0.0131
	$\widehat{b}_2$	0.1214	0.1172	0.3002
Spain	$\widehat{b}_1$	4.4108	1.2780	0.0006
	$\widehat{b}_2$	−0.1406	0.2512	0.5755
Euro area	$\widehat{b}_1$	1.7892	0.3176	0.0000
	$\widehat{b}_2$	0.2662	0.1455	0.0673

There is evidence of convergence to equilibrium for all countries. The values found for λ are extremely close to one, however, and hence convergence is very slow. From equation (12.12), the steady-state rate of inflation is given by $\frac{b_{1t}}{1-b_{2t}}$. It can be seen that the weights on lagged inflation converge to zero in Germany, France, the Netherlands and Spain. In the euro area and Italy they remain significant at the 5 per cent level. This suggests that inflation expectations are becoming more anchored. The coefficients on the constant in equation (12.12) do not converge to just below two, however, which would imply that economic agents have learned the inflation goal of the ECB correctly. Instead, households in Spain consistently overestimate the inflation goal and households in Germany consistently underestimate the inflation goal. For the euro area as a whole, the steady-state rate of inflation is more in line with the goal of the ECB. Thus household expectations in European economies do not seem to have converged to the inflation goal of the ECB. If there is a link between actual inflation and expected rates of inflation, via a New Keynesian Phillips curve relationship, for example, this implies that it is likely that there will remain persistent differences in inflation rates between euro area countries even though the average inflation rate will be on target.

In an integrated market such as the euro area, inflation differentials between countries arise as a part of the catching-up and adjustment mechanisms to shocks. At least part of the difference in inflation rates reflects different rates of productivity between countries, with the process of convergence driving up wages and, hence, the prices of non-traded goods and services. This is just the Balassa–Samuelson effect at work (Rogers 2001). If the inflation differentials between countries are more than just temporary deviations from the euro area average, however, they could be harmful in a monetary union. As Angeloni and Ehrmann (2007) argue, in a monetary union countries share the same nominal interest rates, and therefore a high-inflation country tends to have a lower real interest rate. A lower real interest rate discourages saving and stimulates consumption and investment, thereby amplifying the inflation differentials. This effect may be further strengthened by wealth effects, as low real interest rates may inflate share and real estate prices. Although a high-inflation country tends to lose price competitiveness within the currency area, something that dampens demand and output at home and thus inflation, this effect is likely to operate only at a slow pace (Arnold and Lemmen 2006).

Figures 12A.8 and 12A.9 show smoothed state estimates. The estimates for the constant in equation (12.12) rise substantially around 2002 and then fall again in Germany and the Netherlands but stay at elevated levels in Italy and Spain. In 2002 there was the cash changeover, when euro notes and coins came into circulation, and this had a large effect on the perceived inflation rate of households. Berk and Hebbink (2006) also conclude that this event had a significant effect on perceived inflation. They argue that this effect is due to a relative price increase of the most visible expenditure items in the period before the cash changeover. The fact that household expectations are affected so substantially means that one has to be cautious in interpreting the results in Tables 12.16 and 12.17. Even though the final state estimates for the constant in Table 12.17 are highly significant, it could be the case that, as a result of the developments in 2002, these estimates for the coefficients may not have

Table 12.18 *Experts: testing for convergence*

	λ	Std. error	HSA
France	0.998787	0.000341	−3.5580***
Germany	0.998366	0.000199	−8.2094***
Italy	0.994084	0.000368	−16.0773***
Netherlands	0.996944	0.000314	−9.7319***
Spain	0.998939	0.000394	−2.6927**
Euro area	0.992691	0.000515	−14.1916***

Notes: ** = 'no convergence' rejected at 5 per cent confidence level;
*** = 'no convergence' rejected at 1 per cent confidence level.

Table 12.19 *Experts: testing for convergence, final state estimates*

		Final state	Root MSE	p-value
France	$\widehat{b}_1$	1.7068	0.1753	0.0000
	$\widehat{b}_2$	−0.0021	0.0510	0.9716
Germany	$\widehat{b}_1$	1.6322	0.2622	0.0000
	$\widehat{b}_2$	0.3248	0.1644	0.0482
Italy	$\widehat{b}_1$	1.6705	0.1825	0.0000
	$\widehat{b}_2$	0.0591	0.0872	0.4980
Netherlands	$\widehat{b}_1$	1.7160	0.1622	0.0000
	$\widehat{b}_2$	−0.0050	0.0534	0.9260
Spain	$\widehat{b}_1$	2.9048	0.3512	0.0000
	$\widehat{b}_2$	0.1007	0.0455	0.0270
Euro area	$\widehat{b}_1$	1.7463	0.2636	0.0000
	$\widehat{b}_2$	0.1548	0.1156	0.1806

converged to their final values. A longer data period after the events of 2002 would make it possible to be more confident in the conclusions drawn from Tables 12.16 and 12.17.

Expectations of professional forecasters It is also possible to investigate whether the expectations of professional forecasters converge towards equilibrium. Tables 12.18 and 12.19 show the results of convergence tests for the expectations of professional forecasters for the period 1990Q4 to 2006Q3.

The results indicate that the null hypothesis of 'no convergence' can be rejected at the 5 per cent level of significance for all countries in our sample. λ is very close to one, however, which implies that convergence takes a long time. It is again interesting to note that, with the exceptions of Spain and Germany, the weight on lagged inflation converges to zero and expectations become anchored to a constant. The coefficients on this constant seem to be more in line with the goal of the ECB. This contrasts with the findings for the inflation expectations of households. Only professional forecasters' expectations for Spain now somewhat overestimate inflation. Professional forecasters' expectations of inflation therefore seem to be more anchored to the inflation goal of the ECB than inflation expectations of households. Figure 12A.9 shows smoothed state estimates for the constant and lagged inflation and suggests that expectations have not been affected by the introduction of the euro. The graphs give further evidence that coefficients have converged to the values given in Tables 12.18 and 12.19.

The results suggest that professional forecasters are more inclined to incorporate the implications of monetary union for convergence in inflation rates into their expectations than ordinary consumers. Unfortunately, given that the EC Consumer Survey asks households only for expectations of inflation twelve months ahead, it is not possible to test whether these results hold for longer-expectation horizons (for instance, expectations two years ahead). It should be noted that these findings correspond to those obtained by Arnold and Lemmen (2006), who use a growth theory type of model to test for convergence and also find that Consensus Economics data on the inflation expectations of professional forecasters demonstrate more convergence than exists among the public.

The chapter illustrates that there is heterogeneity between households and professional forecasters. Professional forecasters use higher constant gains than households and thus seem to be more aware of structural changes. Their expectations also display more evidence of convergence. This raises the issue of which type of agent might matter more for the process of setting wages and prices. If household expectations have a stronger impact on wage and price setting then the results of this chapter provide some explanation for the empirical finding that there are sizeable and persistent inflation differentials between euro area countries. Analysing whose expectations are more important thus represents an interesting direction for future research.

12.6   Conclusions

It is of crucial importance for central banks to understand how inflation expectations are formed. This is true for all central banks that gear monetary policy directly towards maintaining a low and stable rate of inflation. Against this background, this chapter provides a first attempt to assess whether adaptive learning behaviour on the part of economic agents is a reasonable assumption for the euro area.

Overall, the chapter provides further support for constant-gain algorithms as a description of actual forecaster behaviour. Heterogeneity in expectations is found between different euro area economies and between households and professional forecasters. Households in so-called 'high-inflation' countries use higher constant-gain parameters and hence update their information sets more frequently than households in 'low-inflation' countries. Professional forecasters update their information sets more frequently than households. Furthermore, it is shown that the inflation expectations of households and experts converge to equilibrium but at a slow rate. Household expectations have not converged to the inflation objective of the ECB, which contrasts with the findings for professional forecasters, which are more inclined to incorporate the implications of monetary union into their expectations.

Some useful directions for further research should be noted. First, it would be interesting to evaluate more complicated forecasting models. Data on expectations of output are available for professional forecasters, and with these data it would be possible to use vector autoregressive forecasting models in order to predict inflation–output vectors. Recently, there has been a growing literature on estimating DSGE models under learning, particularly for the United States (see, for example, Milani 2007 and Slobodyan and Wouters 2009). Assessing the extent to which these models can be used to explain survey-based expectations would be an area of research worth pursuing, as in these models, rather than taking inflation as given, households can affect the dynamics of inflation. Moreover, the inflation dynamics of more countries could be assessed. The United Kingdom would be an interesting example, as it is not part of the monetary union and has had an independent central bank since 1997 with an explicit inflation target. One could then investigate whether different institutional set-ups for central banks affect the learning behaviour of agents.

Once longer data sets on expectations are available it would be possible to test whether optimal gains stay constant over time and to analyse whether learning is faster in periods of high inflation than in periods of low inflation – a finding that would give further support to theories of rational inattention. Additionally, with longer data sets, it would be possible to test whether agents exhibit switching behaviour, as outlined by Marcet and Nicolini (2003), in which they switch between constant-gain least squares and recursive least squares learning. It would be interesting to investigate whether RLS learning outperforms CGLS learning in periods with very stable inflation, such as have been observed during the past decade. These questions are left to be explored in future research.

Appendix 12A   Supporting data

Table 12A.1 *Data sources*

Variable	Source	Frequency	Data period
Household expectations for inflation in $t + 12$	EC Consumer Survey	Monthly	1990M1–2006M9
Professional experts' expectations for inflation in $t + 4$	Consensus Economics	Quarterly	1990Q1–2006Q3
Consumer price index (HICP)	Eurostat – indices of consumer prices	Monthly	1981M1–2006M9
Consumer price index – all items	OECD – *Main Economic Indicators*	Quarterly	1961Q1–2006Q3
Industrial production – all items, seasonally adjusted	BIS	Monthly	1981M1–2006M9
GDP in real terms, seasonally adjusted	BIS	Quarterly	1961Q1–2006Q3
Three-month interbank interest rate	BIS and ECB	Monthly	1981M1–2006M9
Three-month interbank interest rate	BIS and ECB	Quarterly	1961Q1–2006Q3

Table 12A.2 *Tests for unbiasedness, households*

	α	β	r^2	χ^2 for H_0	DW
France	1.1943 (0.2115)	0.4669 (0.1317)	0.2022	35.754 [0.0000]	0.1852
Germany	1.2275 (0.2535)	0.4349 (0.1530)	0.1228	24.142 [0.0000]	0.0991
Italy	1.1347 (0.1872)	0.6430 (0.0569)	0.6224	43.485 [0.0000]	0.2464
Netherlands	1.9934 (0.2742)	0.2511 (0.1425)	0.0352	61.891 [0.0000]	0.1180
Spain	2.8414 (0.4807)	0.3343 (0.1609)	0.0960	43.418 [0.0000]	0.0696
Euro area	−0.1384 (0.3448)	1.2290 (0.1717)	0.4528	11.509 [0.0032]	0.1509

Notes: Figures in parentheses are standard errors. Figures in brackets are *p*-values. Chi-squared statistics pertain to null hypothesis $H_0 : (\alpha, \beta) = (0, 1)$ where $\pi_t = \alpha + \beta\pi_t^e + \varepsilon_t$. DW denotes the Durbin–Watson statistic. 5 per cent significance points of the lower and upper values, dL and dU, are 1.65 and 1.69 (>100 observations), respectively. Equations are estimated by OLS using covariance matrix corrections suggested by Newey and West (1987).

Table 12A.3 *Tests for unbiasedness, experts*

	α	β	r^2	χ^2 for H_0	DW
France	0.7303 (0.3993)	0.5497 (0.1865)	0.2971	7.7406 [0.0209]	0.3226
Germany	−0.4072 (0.4801)	1.2129 (0.2351)	0.5970	0.8689 [0.6476]	0.3641
Italy	0.7366 (0.2856)	0.8052 (0.0913)	0.7368	6.6533 [0.0359]	0.2873
Netherlands	0.1197 (0.4922)	0.9815 (0.2724)	0.4776	0.5463 [0.7610]	0.4135
Spain	2.2672 (0.5824)	0.2717 (0.1736)	0.0583	17.683 [0.0001]	0.4552
Euro area	1.7781 (0.3706)	0.2655 (0.2226)	0.0275	83.607 [0.0000]	1.3329

Notes: Figures in parentheses are standard errors. Figures in brackets are p-values. Chi-squared statistics pertain to null hypothesis $H_0 : (\alpha, \beta) = (0, 1)$, where $\pi_t = \alpha + \beta \pi_t^e + \varepsilon_t$. DW denotes the Durbin–Watson statistic. 5 per cent significance points of the lower and upper values, dL and dU, are 1.55 and 1.62 ($\approx$ 60 observations), respectively. Equations are estimated by OLS using covariance matrix corrections suggested by Newey and West (1987).

Table 12A.4 *Tests for unbiasedness, following Holden and Peel (1990)*

	Households			Experts		
	α	t-statistic	DW	α	t-statistic	DW
France	0.4062 (0.1111)	3.6573 [0.0003]	0.2531	−0.1531 (0.1509)	−1.0151 [0.3140]	0.2942
Germany	0.2173 (0.1567)	1.3870 [0.1670]	0.1791	0.0537 (0.1926)	0.2786 [0.7814]	0.3359
Italy	−0.1208 (0.1631)	−0.7403 [0.4600]	0.3741	0.3675 (0.1006)	3.6520 [0.0005]	0.5652
Netherlands	0.6116 (0.1294)	4.7273 [0.0000]	0.1861	0.0799 (0.1578)	0.5065 [0.6151]	0.4189
Spain	0.7823 (0.2380)	3.2869 [0.0012]	0.2028	0.3710 (0.1348)	2.7511 [0.0084]	0.7135
Euro area	0.3818 (0.1170)	3.2634 [0.0013]	0.1163	0.4939 (0.0618)	9.7549 [0.0000]	1.6063

Notes: Figures in parentheses are standard errors. Figures in brackets are p-values. t-statistics pertain to null hypothesis $H_0 : \alpha = 0$, where $\pi_t - \pi_t^e = \alpha + \varepsilon_t$. DW denotes the Durbin–Watson statistic. Equations are estimated by OLS using covariance matrix corrections suggested by Newey and West (1987).

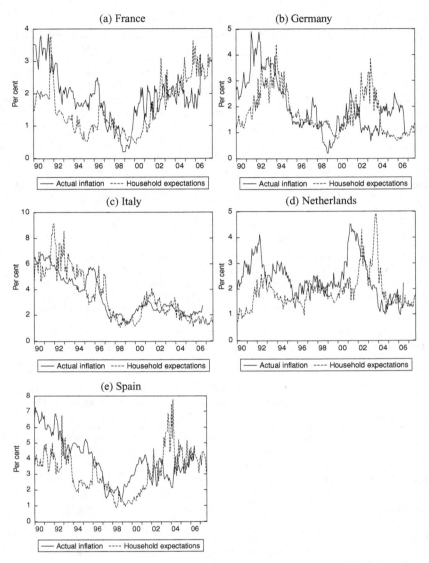

Figure 12A.1 Actual inflation and household expected inflation from $t - 12$ for t

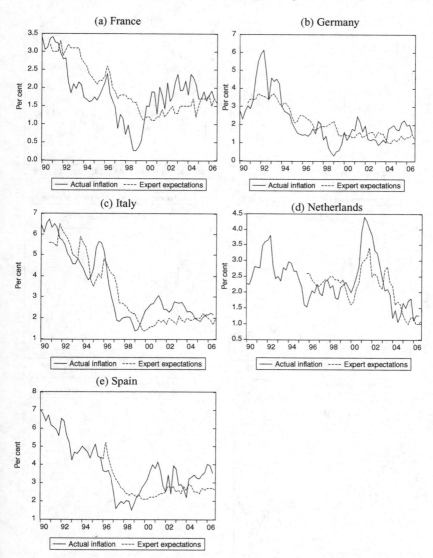

Figure 12A.2 Actual inflation and Consensus Economics forecasts from $t - 4$ for t

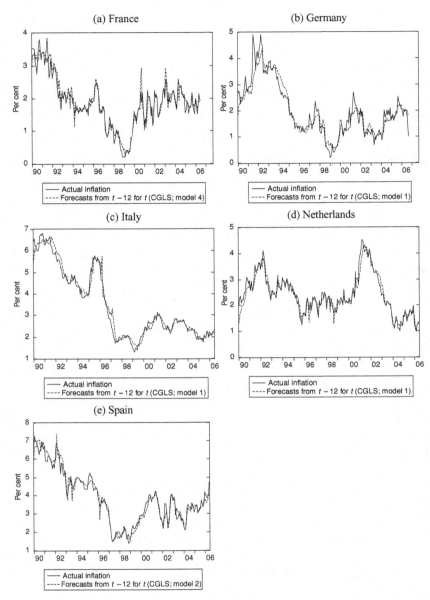

Figure 12A.3 Actual inflation and generated forecasts from $t - 12$ for t using the optimal constant gain and model

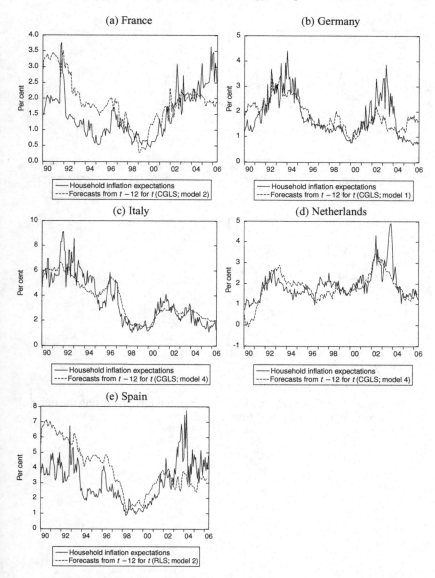

Figure 12A.4 Household expectations from $t - 12$ for t and generated forecasts using the best-fitting constant gain and model

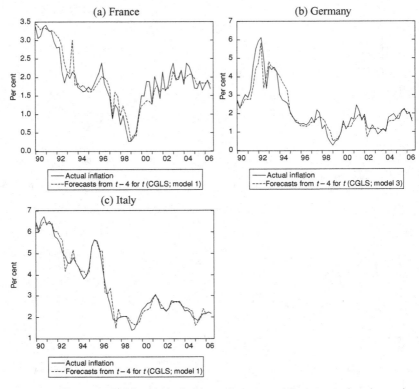

Figure 12A.5 Actual inflation and generated forecasts using the optimal constant gain and model from $t-4$ for t

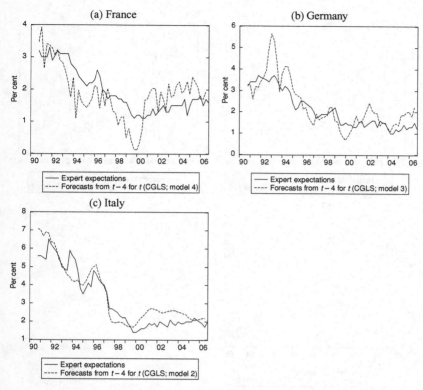

Figure 12A.6 Consensus Economics forecasts from $t - 4$ for t and generated forecasts using the best-fitting constant gain and model

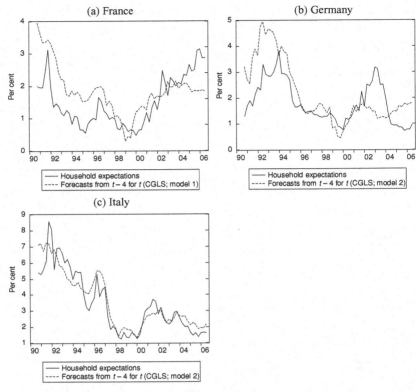

Figure 12A.7 Household expectations from $t - 4$ for t and generated forecasts using the best-fitting constant gain and model

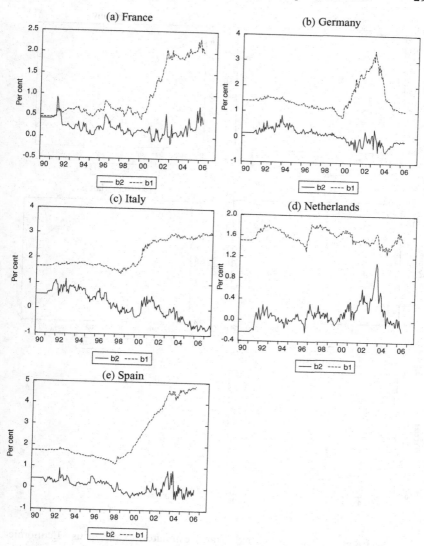

Figure 12A.8 Smoothed state estimates, household expectations

300   *Weber*

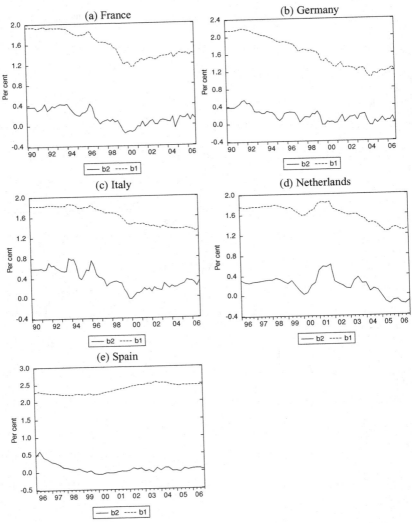

Figure 12A.9 Smoothed state estimates, Consensus Economics forecasts

NOTES

1. The author is particularly grateful to Sandra Eickmeier, Christina Gerberding and Chryssi Giannitsarou for many helpful discussions. The author also thanks Olivier Basdevant, Petra Geraats, Stefan Gerlach, Seppo Honkapohja, Christopher Kent, Albert Marcet, Demosthenes Tambakis, participants at the Sixth Norges Bank Monetary Policy Conference, seminar participants at the 2009 Cambridge Macroeconomics Workshop, the Deutsche Bundesbank, the Swedish Riksbank and the Oesterreichische Nationalbank for helpful comments. This study was written prior to the author becoming an economist at the International Monetary Fund, when the author was visiting the Deutsche Bundesbank; the views expressed in this chapter are the author's and do not necessarily represent those of the IMF or IMF policy.
2. The most recent weights that are assigned to each country are published by Eurostat with the release of the January data each year under Harmonised Index of Consumer Prices (HICP) country weights; see http://sdw.ecb.int/reports.do?currentNodeId=100000298.
3. There were some missing observations in the quantified consumer expectations series, which reflects the fact that the quantification method breaks down when the share of respondents in one category is equal to zero (Berk 1999). To deal with these gaps, the consumer expectations series were interpolated using the cubic spline function in Matlab. This was needed for some of the computations conducted in this chapter.
4. In order to test for equal forecast accuracy between households and professional forecasters, both series need to have the same frequency and number of observations. Data for the expectations of professional forecasters are available from 1990Q4 to 2006Q3 for France, Germany and Italy and from 1995Q4 to 2006Q3 for the Netherlands and Spain.
5. In order to test the robustness of the results for the monthly household inflation expectations, both rationality tests are also conducted for quarterly averages. The results generally confirm the findings for monthly expectations. The only exception is Germany, for which the null hypothesis, $H_0 : \alpha = 0$ in equation (12.2), cannot be rejected at the 5 per cent level. For all countries, however, there is evidence of significant autocorrelation, which is inconsistent with rationality. Test statistics and the results of key diagnostic tests are available from the author upon request.
6. According to Basdevant (2005), the Kalman filter framework allows one to test whether expectations converge towards the rational expectations equilibrium. However, this assumes that agents use the correct model of the economy. If the model used for forecasting is incorrect, expectations may converge towards a so-called 'restricted perceptions equilibrium' (Evans and Honkapohja 2001).
7. This sample period was chosen so that the in- and out-of-sample periods correspond to the period for which household expectations are available. The period from 1990M1 to 2006M9 was then split in half to generate the in- and out-of-sample periods.
8. Household expectations are averaged so that, rather than having monthly data, we get quarterly data for household expectations as well. Results for

households are derived using the same methods as for experts. They are provided together with the results for professional forecasters for direct comparison purposes.

9. Results for higher-order AR models were also computed but it was found that the AR(1) and AR(2) models outperformed higher-order models. The AR(1) and AR(2) models led to both smaller out-of-sample MSEs and smaller out-of-sample MSCEs for each country. This is true for households and professional forecasters alike.

10. This chapter follows Branch and Evans (2006) in using output growth as one of the explanatory variables. Conventional New Keynesian Phillips curve estimations typically use the output gap instead. Results using the output gap (defined as $y = \ln(Y) - \ln(Y^*)$, where Y is GDP seasonally adjusted and Y^* is potential output estimated as the HP-filtered Y) instead of output growth were also computed, and they were found to be very similar.

11. If the gain is denoted by γ then this gain implies that agents use $(1/\gamma)/f$ years of data, where f denotes the data frequency: $f = 1$ for yearly data, $f = 4$ for quarterly data and $f = 12$ for monthly data.

12. Modified Diebold–Mariano tests with the null hypothesis of equal forecast accuracy were performed to test whether the differences in MSEs between RLS and CGLS are significant, and whether the difference between the largest MSE under CGLS and the smallest MSE under RLS is significant. It is found that the null hypothesis of equal forecast accuracy can be rejected at the 5 per cent level of significance for each country. P-values and modified Diebold–Mariano statistics can be provided by the author upon request.

13. Studies by Carroll (2003a, 2003b) and Döpke *et al.* (2006) are based on a model in which households update their information sets only sporadically, when they read newspapers and thereby learn what professional forecasters are saying. Unfortunately, the data sample is too short to test for such behaviour in this chapter.

14. The time (in months) it takes for the weight given to an observation to fall to 1/2 is given by the following formula: $t_{half} = \frac{\ln 2}{\gamma}$.

15. Data on expert expectations for the Netherlands and Spain are available for 1995Q4 to 2006Q3. Data on output growth are available from 1977Q2 for the Netherlands and from 1970Q2 for Spain. Data on interest rates are available from 1986Q2 for the Netherlands and 1977Q2 for Spain. These series would have been too short for present purposes. The ability of the simple recursive forecasting model to fit averaged household expectations in the Netherlands and Spain could have been tested but, given that the purpose of this subsection is a comparison between households and experts, these results are not reported here.

16. Modified Diebold–Mariano tests were computed to test the null hypothesis of equal forecast accuracy between the model yielding the largest MSE under CGLS and the model yielding the smallest MSE under RLS. The null hypothesis of equal forecast accuracy can be rejected at the 5 per cent level of significance for each country. Test statistics and p-values are available from the author upon request.

REFERENCES

Angeloni, I., and M. Ehrmann (2007). 'Euro area inflation differentials', *B. E. Journal of Macroeconomics*, 7: article 24.

Arnold, I., and J. Lemmen (2006). 'Inflation expectations and inflation uncertainty in the Eurozone: evidence from survey data'. Working Paper no. 1667. Munich: CESifo.

Basdevant, O. (2005). 'Learning process and rational expectations: an analysis using a small macroeconomic model for New Zealand', *Economic Modelling*, 22(6): 1074–89.

Batchelor, R., and A. Orr (1988). 'Inflation expectations revisited', *Economica*, 55: 317–31.

Berk, J. (1999). 'Measuring inflation expectations: a survey data approach', *Applied Economics*, 31(11): 1467–80.

Berk, J., and G. Hebbink (2006). 'The anchoring of European inflation expectations'. Working Paper no. 116. Amsterdam: De Nederlandsche Bank.

Berk, J., and J. Swank (2002). 'Regional price adjustment in a monetary union: the case of EMU'. MEB Paper no. 2002-7. Amsterdam: De Nederlandsche Bank.

Branch, W., and G. Evans (2006). 'A simple recursive forecasting model', *Economics Letters*, 91(2): 158–66.

Carlson, J. (1975). 'Are price expectations normally distributed?', *Journal of the American Statistical Association*, 70: 749–54.

Carlson, J., and M. Parkin (1975). 'Inflation expectations', *Economica*, 42: 123–38.

Carroll, C. (2003a). 'Macroeconomic expectations of households and professional forecasters', *Quarterly Journal of Economics*, 118(1): 268–98.

(2003b). 'The epidemiology of macroeconomic expectations'. Mimeo. Baltimore: John Hopkins University.

Diebold, F., and L. Kilian (2001). 'Measuring predictability: theory and macroeconomic applications', *Journal of Applied Econometrics*, 16(6): 657–69.

Diebold, F., and R. Mariano (1995). 'Comparing predictive accuracy', *Journal of Business and Economic Statistics*, 13(3): 253–63.

Döpke, J., J. Dovern, U. Fritsche and J. Slacalek (2006). 'The dynamics of European inflation expectations'. Macroeconomies and Finance Working Paper no. 200603. Hamburg: Universität Hamburg.

ECB (2003). *Inflation Differentials in the Euro Area: Potential Causes and Policy Implications*. Frankfurt: ECB.

Evans, G., and S. Honkapohja (2001). *Learning and Expectations in Macroeconomics*. Princeton, NJ: Princeton University Press.

Forni, M., M. Hallin and L. Reichlin (2003). 'Do financial variables help forecasting inflation and real activity in the euro area?', *Journal of Monetary Economics*, 50(6): 1243–55.

Forsells, M., and G. Kenny (2004). 'Survey expectations, rationality and the dynamics of euro area inflation', *Journal of Business Cycle Measurement and Analysis*, 1(1): 13–41.

Gerberding, C. (2001). 'The information content of survey data on expected price developments for monetary policy'. Discussion Paper no. 9/01. Berlin: Deutsche Bundesbank.

  (2006). 'Household versus expert forecasts of inflation: new evidence from European survey data'. Mimeo. Berlin: Deutsche Bundesbank.

Gerlach, S., and G. Schnabel (2000). 'The Taylor rule and interest rates in the EMU area', *Economics Letters*, 67(2): 165–71.

Hall, S., D. Robertson and M. Wickens (1997). 'Measuring economic convergence', *International Journal of Finance and Economics*, 2(2): 131–43.

Hall, S., and M. St Aubyn (1995). 'Using the Kalman filter to test for convergence: a comparison to other methods using artificial data'. Working Paper no. 11/95. Lisbon: Instituto Superior de Economia e Gestâo.

Hamilton, J. (1994). *Time Series Analysis*. Princeton, NJ: Princeton University Press.

Harvey, D., S. Leybourne and P. Newbold (1997). 'Testing the equality of prediction mean square errors', *International Journal of Forecasting*, 13(2): 273–81.

Holden, K., and D. Peel (1990). 'On testing for unbiasedness and efficiency of forecasts', *The Manchester School*, 58(2): 120–7.

IMF (2005). *World Economic Outlook, September 2005: Building Institutions*. Washington, DC: IMF.

Mankiw, N., and R. Reis (2007). 'Sticky information in general equilibrium', *Journal of the European Economic Association*, 5(2–3): 603–13.

Marcet, A., and J. Nicolini (2003). 'Recurrent hyperinflations and learning', *American Economic Review*, 93(5): 1476–98.

Marcet, A., and T. Sargent (1989a). 'Convergence of least-squares learning mechanisms in self-referential linear stochastic models', *Journal of Economic Theory*, 48(2): 337–68.

  (1989b). 'Convergence of least-squares learning in environments with hidden state variables and private information', *Journal of Political Economy*, 97(6): 1306–22.

Milani, F. (2007). 'Expectations, learning and macroeconomic persistence', *Journal of Monetary Economics*, 54(7): 2065–82.

Nardo, M. (2003). 'The quantification of qualitative survey data: a critical assessment', *Journal of Economic Surveys*, 17(5): 645–68.

Newey, W., and K. West (1987). 'A simple, positive semi-definite, heteroskedasticity and autocorrelation consistent covariance matrix', *Econometrica*, 55(3): 703–8.

Nielsen, H. (2003). 'Inflation expectations in the EU: results from survey data'. Discussion Paper no. 13/2003. Berlin: Humboldt Universität.

Orphanides, A., and J. Williams (2005). 'Imperfect knowledge, inflation expectations, and monetary policy', in B. Bernanke and M. Woodford (eds.). *The Inflation-Targeting Debate*: 201–34. Chicago: University of Chicago Press.

  (2007). 'Robust monetary policy with imperfect knowledge', *Journal of Monetary Economics*, 54(5): 1406–35.

Ortega, E. (2003). 'Persistent inflation differentials in Europe'. Working Paper no. 0305. Madrid: Banco de España.

Pesaran, M. (1987). *The Limits to Rational Expectations*. Oxford: Basil Blackwell.

Pfajfar, D., and E. Santoro (2006). 'Heterogeneity and learning in inflation expectation formation: an empirical assessment'. Mimeo. Cambridge: University of Cambridge.

Rogers, J. (2001). 'Price level convergence, relative prices, and inflation in Europe'. International Finance Discussion Paper no. 699. Washington, DC: Federal Reserve.

Sargent, T. (1999). *The Conquest of American Inflation*. Princeton, NJ: Princeton University Press.

Schumacher, C. (2007). 'Forecasting German GDP using alternative factor models based on large datasets', *Journal of Forecasting*, 26(4): 271–302.

Sims, C. (2003). 'Implications of rational inattention', *Journal of Monetary Economics*, 50(3): 665–90

(2006). 'Rational inattention: a research agenda'. Mimeo. Princeton, NJ: University of Princeton.

Slobodyan, S., and R. Wouters (2009). 'Learning in an estimated medium-scale DSGE model'. Working Paper no. 396. Prague: Economic Institute, Center for Economic Research and Graduate Education.

St Aubyn, M. (1999). 'Convergence across industrialised countries (1890–1989): new results using time series methods', *Empirical Economics*, 24(1): 23–44.

13   Inflation targeting and private sector forecasts

Stephen G. Cecchetti and Craig S. Hakkio[1]

13.1   Introduction

Transparency is one of the biggest innovations in central bank policy of the past quarter-century. Modern central bankers believe that they should be as clear about their objectives and actions as possible. This notion arises from the view that policymakers should be a source of stability, not a source of noise, with the economy and markets responding to data and not to the policymakers themselves.

Inflation targeting is one of the first and most comprehensive implementations derived from this view. As a framework for monetary policy, inflation targeting involves 'the public announcement of medium-term numerical targets for inflation [and] increased transparency of the monetary policy strategy through communication with the public and the markets about plans, objectives, and decisions of the monetary authority' (Mishkin 2002: 361). The result is not just clearly understood and published numerical targets, but also inflation reports that explain past and likely future actions. Most economists believe that greater transparency is beneficial (see, for example, the surveys by Geraats 2002, Carpenter 2004, Dincer and Eichengreen 2007 and Walsh 2007). Transparency is not nudity, however. Understanding policymakers' contingency plans does not mean laying the policymaking process bare for all to see. Monetary policymakers should not put cameras in the meeting room. There are clear limits. What are they?

Recent theoretical work has put this question into a new perspective. In their pioneering work, Morris and Shin (2002, 2005) show that, when private agents have diverse sources of information, public information can cause them to overreact to the signals from the central bank, which makes the economy too sensitive to common forecast errors. The reason for this is that individuals care not only about accurately estimating the state of the economy, but also about having an estimate that is not too different from that of others. The implication is that more transparency may in fact be destabilising, so policymakers should think long and hard

306

before changing their disclosure policies in ways that publicise more information.

Woodford (2005) and Svensson (2006) both suggest that the Morris and Shin result is likely to be a theoretical curiosum rather than anything policymakers should worry about. In other words, the circumstance under which additional information is welfare-reducing is extremely unlikely to occur in the real world. As Svensson shows, Morris and Shin's own conclusion holds only when the noise in policymakers' publicly announced information is at least eight times that in the private information that agents have obtained on their own – that is, public officials must be far worse in their evaluations of the economic environment than private agents. Evidence, such as that produced by Romer and Romer (2000), suggests that central bank staff forecasts are at least as good as, if not better than, those of market economists.

Woodford's critique is based on the Morris and Shin choice of how to aggregate the quadratic loss functions of the individual agents. In their original study, Morris and Shin assume that policymakers seek to minimise a social loss function that is based on the average squared error of individual estimates of the state of the economy. By contrast, if the social welfare function includes losses associated with the dispersion of agents' estimates of the state – something Morris and Shin assume the agents themselves care about – then more information is unambiguously a good thing.

Regardless of these two coherent and largely convincing criticisms, the Morris and Shin argument retains intuitive appeal. In particular, policymakers worry that releasing more information might cause private agents to coordinate expectations, leaving the economy more exposed to common shocks. In the end, however, we are left with an empirical question: does increased transparency lead to lower dispersion in private forecasts? If the answer is 'No' then there is little to worry about. If the answer is 'Yes', however, we cannot necessarily conclude that greater transparency – in the form of adopting an inflation target – is harmful. The reason is that greater transparency about the fundamentals and the long-run inflation objective should also lead to a smaller dispersion of inflation forecasts, which is beneficial. A smaller dispersion of private forecasts could therefore reflect the beneficial effects of greater transparency and not the harmful effects described by Morris and Shin.

In this chapter we study the degree to which increased information about monetary policy might lead to a reduction in the dispersion of inflation forecasts. By combining information about whether a country

targets inflation with the dispersion of private sector forecasts of inflation, we seek to understand how inflation targeting affects private sector
behaviour. In particular, does inflation targeting lead to a smaller or possibly larger dispersion of private sector inflation forecasts? If it leads to
a larger dispersion then there is no need to worry about the harmful
effects of greater transparency discussed by Morris and Shin. However,
if inflation targeting leads to a smaller dispersion then there is at least
some evidence that increased information could be harmful, because it
leads individuals to coordinate their forecasts *à la* Morris and Shin, or
could be beneficial, because of additional information about central bank
objectives and fundamentals.

In order to examine this, we estimate a series of simple models designed
to measure the impact of inflation targeting on the dispersion of private
sector forecasts of inflation. Using a panel data set that includes fifteen
countries over twenty years, we find no convincing evidence that adopting
an inflation-targeting regime leads to a reduction in the dispersion of
private sector forecasts of inflation. While for some specifications the
adoption of an inflation target does seem to reduce the standard deviation
of inflation forecasts, in others it does not. Moreover, the precision of the
estimates is rarely very high. The bulk of our evidence does not support
the view that a shift to inflation targeting has resulted in a significant
decline in the cross-sectional standard deviation of inflation forecasts
across survey respondents.

Before proceeding, it is useful to note that our work is distinct from, but
related to, two earlier pieces of research. First, Mankiw, Reis and Wolfers
(2004) examine the dispersion of inflation expectations in survey data and
find that inflation expectations have become more concentrated around
the mean as the rate of inflation has fallen. At first glance this may seem
as if it is a result that is more positive than ours; but, given that Mankiw,
Reis and Wolfers study only US data, it is not possible to disentangle
the impact of disinflation from increased Federal Reserve transparency.
Second, Levin, Natalucci and Piger (2004) investigate how well the mean
of inflation expectations has been anchored, also from survey data. They
provide evidence on how inflation targeting has changed the dynamics of
inflation. Their results suggest that the adoption of an explicit inflation
target reduces the correlation of long-run inflation expectations with
short-run movements in inflation, largely eliminating the link between
expectations and realised inflation. Furthermore, Levin, Natalucci and
Piger find that the adoption of an inflation-targeting framework lowers
the persistence of inflation, so that inflation behaves more like a random
walk.

The remainder of this chapter is organised in five sections. Section 13.2 provides a description of the data we use. This is followed in section 13.3 with a simple statistical analysis, and in section 13.4 with the results of more sophisticated regressions. Section 13.5 discusses some possible extensions and provides evidence on the robustness of the results. Section 13.6 provides a conclusion.

13.2   Description of the data

We study the dispersion of monthly survey-based inflation expectations for a number of countries from October 1989 to April 2009. The data are collected by Consensus Economics. Each month the firm surveys a large cross-section of professional forecasters – currently more than 700 worldwide – asking them for their current and next calendar years' predictions for growth, inflation, unemployment and short- and long-term interest rates in the countries that they follow. For each month, for each variable, Consensus Economics reports the high, low and median forecast, as well as the standard deviation of survey responses. Although Consensus Economics supplies forecast information for more than seventy countries, we restrict ourselves to the following fifteen: Australia, Canada, the euro area, France, Germany, Italy, Japan, the Netherlands, New Zealand, Norway, Spain, Sweden, Switzerland, the United Kingdom and the United States (see Table 13.1). For many of the results we ignore the euro area, because the data are available only from December 2002.

This sample is sufficiently diverse to allow us to study the impact of inflation targeting, as two countries (New Zealand and Sweden) targeted inflation over the entire period, six (Australia, Canada, Norway, Spain, Switzerland and the United Kingdom) adopted inflation targeting at some point during the sample and the remaining seven have never adopted an explicit inflation target. For the second group, the six that adopted an inflation target during the 1990s, we need to choose a date for the adoption. It is perhaps surprising that there is disagreement on this timing. Ball and Sheridan (2005), Mishkin and Schmidt-Hebbel (2007) and Truman (2003), among others, all choose slightly different dates. For the most part, we adopt the dating of Mishkin and Schmidt-Hebbel (2007: appendix A).

Clearly, some notation is required. We use the general form $S_{it}(.,.)$ to denote the standard deviation of private sector forecasts for country i made on date t. Next, we specify the variable being forecast as π for CPI inflation and y for GDP growth, and whether the forecast is for the

Table 13.1 *Dates for which inflation forecast data are available*

	Inflation-targeting regime	Non-inflation-targeting regime
Australia	June 1993 to April 2009	November 1990 to May 1993
Canada	February 1991 to April 2009	October 1989 to January 1991
Euro area		December 2002 to April 2009
France		October 1989 to April 2009
Germany		October 1989 to April 2009
Italy		October 1989 to April 2009
Japan		October 1989 to April 2009
Netherlands		January 1995 to April 2009
New Zealand	December 1994 to April 2009	
Norway	March 2001 to April 2009	June 1998 to February 2001
Spain	January 1995 to June 1998	July 1998 to April 2009
Sweden	January 1995 to April 2009	
Switzerland	January 2000 to April 2009	June 1998 to December 1999
United Kingdom	October 1992 to April 2009	October 1989 to September 1992
United States		October 1989 to April 2009

Notes: For the 'Inflation-targeting regime' countries, the dates shown are either the first date of inflation targeting or the first date for which data are available; as a result, they do not necessarily correspond to the dates at which a country adopted an inflation target. For the 'Non-inflation-targeting regime' countries, the dates shown correspond to the dates for which the dispersion of inflation and GDP forecasts are available.

Source: Mishkin and Schmidt-Hebbel (2007: appendix A); Norges Bank Regulation on Monetary Policy, March 29, 2001. Contrary to the date given by Mishkin and Schmidt-Hebbel (2007), the start date of inflation targeting for Australia is June 1993, based on data from the Reserve Bank of Australia.

current year, which we denote by c, or for the next year, which we denote by n. Using this notation, $S_{it}(\pi, c)$ is the standard deviation of private sector forecasts for CPI inflation made at date t for the current year (the year containing t). Analogously, $S_{it}(\pi, n)$ is the standard deviation of private sector forecasts for CPI inflation also made at date t but for the next year (the year containing $t+1$), and $S_{it}(y, c)$ and $S_{it}(y, n)$ are the standard deviations of private sector forecasts for GDP growth for the current and next year, respectively.

To provide a sense of the time series properties of the data, Figures 13.1 and 13.2 plot the standard deviation of the current and next year's forecasts of inflation, $S_{it}(\pi, c)$ and $S_{it}(\pi, n)$, for all the countries in our sample. Simple inspection reveals that the standard deviation of forecasts for the current year, $S_{it}(\pi, c)$ plotted in Figure 13.1, has significant seasonality, while $S_{it}(\pi, n)$ has less seasonality. Focusing on $S_{it}(\pi, c)$, a closer look shows that the standard deviation is highest in January and

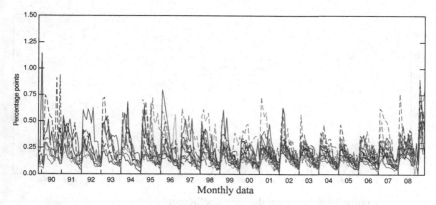

Figure 13.1 Standard deviation of current year's inflation forecasts, $S_{it}(\pi, c)$

Source: Consensus Economics.

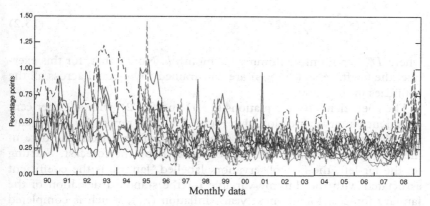

Figure 13.2 Standard deviation of next year's inflation forecasts, $S_{it}(\pi, n)$

Source: Consensus Economics.

falls throughout the year. This is not at all surprising, since, as a particular year progresses, inflation during that year increasingly becomes an historical fact that need not be estimated.

To assess the seasonality in these series, we assume they are deterministic and estimate the following regressions:

$$S_{it}(\pi, c) = \sum_{k=1}^{12} \beta_k^c D_{kt}^m + \varepsilon_{it} \qquad (13.1)$$

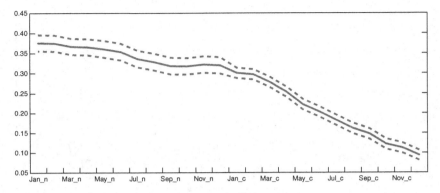

Figure 13.3 Seasonal dummy coefficients

Source: Author's calculations based on equations (13.1) and (13.2).

and

$$S_{it}(\pi, n) = \sum_{k=1}^{12} \beta_k^n D_{kt}^m + \varepsilon_{it} \tag{13.2}$$

where D_{kt}^m is a monthly dummy for month k. Notice that, for this exercise, the coefficients (the β_ks) are constrained to be equal across all the countries in the sample.

The coefficients from equations (13.1) and (13.2), with a 95 per cent confidence interval, are plotted in Figure 13.3. We report the coefficients from left to right depending on the amount of time from the date of the survey to the end of the period covered by the forecast. Starting on the far left, the first observation, labelled 'Jan_n', is the coefficient associated with the dummy variable for the standard deviation of the January forecast for the next year's inflation (β_1^n), which is completed twenty-four months in the future. By contrast, the far right of the figure plots the coefficient associated with the standard deviation of inflation in December of the current year (β_{12}^c), which is completed in only one month. While the relationship is not linear, it is clearly declining. A regression of $\{\beta_1^n, \beta_2^n, \ldots, \beta_{11}^c, \beta_{12}^c\}$ against $\{1, 2, \ldots, 23, 24\}$ yields a slope coefficient of −0.012 and a t-statistic of 16.2.[2] This means that the marginal effect of an additional month of data reduces the standard deviation of private inflation forecasts by 0.012. The average value of $S_{it}(\pi, n)$ in January (the standard deviation of private sector forecasts for 'next' year in January of 'this' year) is 0.377 percentage points and the average value of $S_{it}(\pi, c)$ in December is 0.094 p.p. Each additional month of data therefore tightens the spread of private sector inflation forecasts (reduces the standard deviation) by 3.2 per cent (0.012 / 0.377). The implication of all this is that it is important that further analysis account for the pronounced seasonality in the data.

13.3   Simple statistical tests

We now turn to the key question of this chapter: is the spread (standard deviation) of inflation forecasts by survey participants lower in countries that adopt an explicit inflation target? To examine this, we start with some very simple statistics designed to measure whether the spreads $S_{it}(\pi, c)$ and $S_{it}(\pi, n)$ are lower when a country's policymakers employ an inflation target. For clarity, we do this with a series of regressions. In the first one we estimate the following regression for each country separately:

$$S_{it}(\pi, c) = \alpha + \sum_{k=2}^{12} \beta_k D_{kt}^m + \gamma \, Target_{it} + u_{it}^c \qquad (13.3)$$

and similarly for $S_{it}(\pi, n)$. Of course, the variable 'Target' is included only if the country was both an ITer and a non-ITer during the sample period. In addition, since the available data are different for different countries, each equation is estimated with a different number of observations.

The results are shown in detail in Appendix 13A in Tables 13A.1 and 13A.2, and they are summarised here in Table 13.2. Note that there are only six countries that switched regimes during the sample period. For these countries, the average standard deviation for the non-inflation-targeting regime is α, the average standard deviation for the inflation-targeting regime is $\alpha + \gamma$, and γ is the difference. If the dispersion is smaller for inflation-targeting regimes, we would expect to see $\gamma < 0$.

These results allow us to conclude that, for those countries that adopted inflation targeting during the period 1990 to 2009, the standard deviation of private sector forecasts for CPI inflation sometimes falls and sometimes rises. Specifically, the standard deviation of inflation forecasts falls when Australia, Canada and the United Kingdom adopt inflation targets; but it increases when Norway adopts an inflation target. Spain and Switzerland are somewhere in between, depending on whether you are looking at the dispersion of current-year forecasts or next-year forecasts.

A next step is to estimate the equations jointly using Zellner's seemingly unrelated regression (SUR) approach. Since the model is estimated as a set of equations, we need the same number of observations for all countries. There are, basically, three different start dates that

Table 13.2 *Comparing the standard deviations of inflation forecasts for countries that switch regime*

γ	Standard deviation of current year's inflation forecast, $S_{it}(\pi, c)$	Standard deviation of next year's inflation forecast, $S_{it}(\pi, n)$
Negative, significant at 5 per cent	Australia, United Kingdom	Australia, Canada, United Kingdom
Negative, insignificant at 5 per cent	Spain, Switzerland	
Positive, insignificant at 5 per cent	Canada	Switzerland
Positive, significant at 5 per cent	Norway	Norway, Spain

Source: Authors' calculations based on country-by-country estimation of equation (13.3).

Table 13.3 *Inflation regime status for various start dates*

Start date	Switched	Non-targeter	Targeter only
November 1990 ($T = 222, N = 8$)	Australia, Canada, United Kingdom	France, Germany, Italy, Japan, United States	
January 1995 ($T = 172, N = 12$)	Spain	France, Germany, Italy, Japan, Netherlands, United States	Australia, Canada, New Zealand, Sweden, United Kingdom
June 1998 ($T = 131, N = 14$)	Norway, Spain, Switzerland	France, Germany, Italy, Japan, Netherlands, United States	Australia, Canada, New Zealand, Sweden, United Kingdom

Source: Table 13.1.

could be used: November 1990, January 1995 or June 1998. Depending on the start date, the number of countries that were both ITers and non-ITers differs, as seen in Table 13.3. There is clearly a trade-off between the sample size, the number of countries and the mix of inflation regimes.

Table 13.4 summarises the results of estimation using Zellner's SUR approach, focusing on the sign and significance of the inflation-targeting variable for countries that were both inflation targeters and non-targeters (additional results are shown in Table 13A.3). In general, the results are similar to the single-equation regressions in Table 13.2: sometimes the

Table 13.4 *Comparing the impact of inflation targeting on the standard deviation of inflation forecasts for inflation-targeting and non-inflation-targeting central banks, using SUR estimation*

γ	Standard deviation of current year's inflation forecast, $S_{it}(\pi, c)$	Standard deviation of next year's inflation forecast, $S_{it}(\pi, n)$
Negative, significant at 5 per cent	Australia, United Kingdom (1990) Spain (1995)	Australia (1990)
Negative, insignificant at 5 per cent	Spain (1998)	United Kingdom (1990) Spain (1998)
Positive, insignificant at 5 per cent	Canada (1990) Switzerland (1998)	Canada (1990)
Positive, significant at 5 per cent	Norway (1998)	Spain (1995) Norway (1998) Switzerland (1998)

Note: The dates in parentheses denote the start dates for the estimation.
Source: Authors' calculations based on SUR estimation of equation (13.3).

coefficient is negative and sometimes it is positive; sometimes it is significantly different from zero at standard levels of statistical significance and sometimes it is not.

So far, the determinants of the dispersion of private sector forecasts are deterministic variables: seasonal dummies and an inflation targeting dummy. There are no economic variables affecting the dispersion of forecasts. For example, the dispersion of inflation forecasts may be greater when overall macroeconomic variability is greater. While we do not have a country-specific measure of macroeconomic variability, we use the dispersion of private sector forecasts of GDP growth. To avoid any simultaneity concerns, we actually use the lagged value of the spread of GDP forecasts, $S_{i,t-1}(y, c)$ and $S_{i,t-1}(y, n)$. In addition, to capture the fact that volatility may have changed over time, reflecting the so-called 'Great Moderation' and then the more recent financial crisis, we include a year variable and two dummy variables to capture the recent financial crisis. The two financial crisis variables are $Crisis_1 = 1$ for September 2007 to September 2008, and $Crisis_2 = 1$ for October 2008 to April 2009. These two variables reflect the fact that the financial crisis is generally thought to have started in August 2007 and then intensified in September 2008. Since the survey respondents presumably did not recognise the start and intensification of the crisis until the next month, the *Crisis* variables

Table 13.5 *SUR estimation*

	Current year's spread			Next year's spread		
	Target	$S_{t,t-1}(\pi, c)$	$S_{t,t-1}(y, c)$	Target	$S_{t,t-1}(\pi, n)$	$S_{t,t-1}(y, n)$
	January 1990–April 2009					
Australia	-0.004 [0.2]	0.460 [7.7]	0.018 [0.3]	0.008 [0.3]	0.745 [16.9]	0.020 [0.5]
Canada	-0.006 [0.2]	0.409 [6.8]	-0.032 [0.7]	-0.008 [0.2]	0.573 [10.7]	-0.033 [0.9]
United Kingdom	0.009 [0.4]	0.407 [8.5]	0.049 [0.8]	0.029 [1.4]	0.811 [23.3]	0.075 [1.6]
	November 1995–April 2009					
Spain	-0.016 [1.0]	0.344 [5.2]	-0.008 [0.1]	-0.014 [0.5]	0.637 [11.6]	0.121 [1.3]
	June 1998–April 2009					
Norway	0.034 [1.4]	0.432 [5.9]	-0.085 [1.7]	0.044 [1.5]	0.395 [5.5]	0.035 [0.7]
Switzerland	0.008 [0.5]	0.483 [7.3]	-0.013 [0.3]	0.029 [1.6]	0.322 [4.3]	0.096 [1.6]

Note: Numbers in brackets are asymptotic t-ratios.
Source: Authors' calculations based on equation (13.4).

are dated one month after the start and the intensification, respectively. In addition, we allow the current inflation dispersion to depend on its own lagged value, $S_{i,t-1}(\pi, c)$ and $S_{i,t-1}(\pi, n)$. In all, we estimate a set of equations of the following form:

$$S_{it}(\pi, c) = \alpha_i^c + \sum_{k=2}^{12} \beta_k^c D_{kt}^m + \gamma^c Target_{it} + \delta^c year_t + \kappa_1^c Crisis_{1it}$$
$$+ \kappa_2^c Crisis_{2it} + \rho_i^c S_{it-1}(\pi, c) + \theta_i^c S_{it-1}(y, c) + u_{it}^c$$

$$(13.4)$$

Since the model is estimated as a set of equations, a *Target* variable can be included only for those countries that switched during the same period.

The results of estimating these equations using Zellner's seemingly unrelated regression approach are summarised in Table 13.5. With three different start dates, the countries that were both ITers and non-ITers differ. We report results only for the countries that change regime, so the coefficient of interest on *Target* can be estimated.

This exercise allows us to draw several conclusions. First, the coefficients on *Target* reported in Table 13.5 are always insignificant. Second, the coefficient on the lagged value of the spread of the inflation forecast (ρ^c and ρ^n) is positive and significant, with the estimated impact in the regression of the dispersion in next year's inflation forecast larger than for the current year's inflation forecast ($\rho^n > \rho^c$). Third, in looking at the full set of regressions not reported in the table, the coefficient on the lagged value of $S(y, \cdot)$ is generally insignificant. When the coefficient is significant it is mostly positive, although there are a couple of cases when the coefficient is negative and significant.

Although these results are interesting, they fail to utilise information from the countries that either never adopted an inflation target or did so prior to the beginning of our sample. We now turn to a more sophisticated analysis designed to account for seasonality, control for general macroeconomic volatility and employ all the data we have available.

13.4 Panel regressions

The various shortcomings mentioned at the end of the previous section can be addressed by estimating a set of equations using a panel regression approach. By estimating various regressions using both fixed effects and random effects (Baum 2006), we show that there is little evidence that inflation-targeting countries have a smaller dispersion of private sector inflation forecasts.

Table 13.6 *Panel estimation using fixed effects*

	Standard deviation of current year's inflation forecasts, $S_{it}(\pi, c)$			Standard deviation of next year's inflation forecasts $S_{it}(\pi, n)$		
	(1)	(2)	(3)	(4)	(5)	(6)
Inflation target (γ)	−0.023 [3.0]	−0.011 [1.4]	−0.009 [1.3]	−0.021 [2.0]	−0.017 [1.6]	−0.009 [1.3]
Lagged $S_{it}(\pi, \cdot)(\rho)$			0.488 [29.1]			0.737 [57.3]
Lagged $S_{it}(y, \cdot)(\theta)$		0.142 [9.1]	0.036 [2.6]		0.103 [6.1]	0.015 [1.3]
$\dfrac{\gamma}{(1-\rho)}$			−0.017 [1.3]			−0.036 [1.3]
R^2	0.36	0.44	0.62	0.24	0.29	0.75
σ_ε	0.084	0.083	0.073	0.119	0.118	0.180
Number of observations	2,895	2,880	2,880	2,895	2,880	2,880

Notes: Asymptotic t-ratios are in brackets. Coefficients on monthly and yearly dummy variables are not shown.
Source: Authors' calculations based on equation (13.5).

Fixed effects

We start by estimating some FE models given the general applicability of this approach. To capture the fact that volatility may have changed over time on account of the Great Moderation and then the more recent financial crisis, several dummy variables are included in the equation. Specifically, year dummy variables are included (*Year$_{1991}$*, ..., *Year$_{2006}$*), where, for example, *Year$_{1991}$* = 1 for 1991. We also define *Year$_{2007}$* = 1 for January to August 2007, *Crisis$_1$* = 1 for September 2007 to September 2008 and *Crisis$_2$* = 1 for October 2008 to April 2009. The results from estimating the following equation (or some variant of it) are reported in Table 13.6 and the time-varying constants (the constant and terms related to time) are shown in Figure 13.4:[3]

$$S_{it}(\pi, c) = \alpha^c + u_i^c + \sum_{k=2}^{12} \beta_{ik}^c D_{kt}^m + \sum_{t=1991}^{2007} \delta_t^c \, Year_t$$
$$+ \kappa_1^c Crisis_{1it} + \kappa_2^c Crisis_{3it} + \gamma_i^c \, Target_{it} + \rho^c S_{1t-1}(\pi, n)$$
$$+ \theta^c S_{1t-1}(y, n) + \varepsilon_{it}^c \tag{13.5}$$

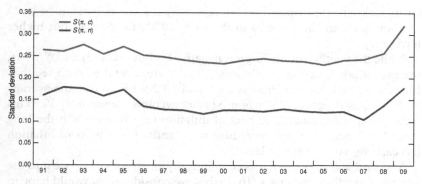

Figure 13.4 Time-varying constant term
Source: Author's calculations.

where the constant α can be thought of as a mixture of the average level in January, the base month, plus the average impact of October 1989 to December 1990, while the u is the country-specific fixed effect. In addition, the table reports the long-run effect of inflation targeting on the dispersion: $\gamma/(1 - \rho)$.

In all cases, the coefficient on *Target* is negative, which suggests that countries with an inflation target have a smaller standard deviation of private sector inflation forecasts. However, the coefficient is significant only for the bare-bones regression (excluding lagged values of $S(\pi, \cdot)$ and $S(y, \cdot)$). In addition, the coefficients on lagged values of $S(\pi, \cdot)$ and $S(y, \cdot)$ are positive and significant. The estimate of ρ is 0.49 for regressions using $S_{it}(\pi, c)$ and 0.74 when looking at $S_{it}(\pi, n)$. This suggests that the persistence of the spread is less for current-year forecasts than for next-year forecasts, but still sizeable. A larger coefficient on the lagged spread for next-year forecasts than for current-year forecasts might suggest that incoming monthly data play a smaller role for next-year forecasts than for current-year forecasts. In addition, to the extent that lagged values of $S(y, \cdot)$ capture overall macroeconomic uncertainty, the positive and significant coefficients suggest that the standard deviation of inflation forecasts depends on macroeconomic uncertainty.

Figure 13.4 shows the effect of time and the financial crisis on the standard deviation of private sector forecasts of current- and next-year inflation made in January. In general, the standard deviation declined from 1991 to 1999, was stable through to 2006 and then rose significantly in 2008 and 2009. This suggests that the Great Moderation did lead to a reduction in the dispersion of private sector forecasts of inflation through the first part of the sample period and that the financial crisis led to an increase in the dispersion. Interestingly, the coefficient on $(\alpha + \delta)$ in 2009 is about the same as in the early 1990s for $S(\pi, n)$ but higher for $S(\pi, c)$.

While the coefficient on *Target* is negative for both $S(\pi, c)$ and $S(\pi, n)$, the magnitude is economically small. There are several ways to see this. First, if we look back at Figures 13.1 and 13.2 we note that the average of $S(\pi, c)$ is roughly 0.20 while $S(\pi, n)$ averages closer to 0.35. This means that the estimated impact of inflation targeting even in the long run (0.017 and 0.036) is to reduce the standard deviation of inflation forecasts by 10 per cent or less.

A second way to see that γ is economically small is to compare it to the impact of the financial crisis. To do this, we consider what would happen to $S(\pi, c)$ if a country were to adopt an inflation target in February 2007 as opposed to adopting it in February 2009. Taking the case of the United States, we use equation (13.2) to calculate the predicted value of $S(\pi, c)$ first with the *Target* = 0 (no inflation target) and then with the *Target* = 1 (assuming the United States had an inflation target). The result is that the predicted dispersion in survey inflation expectations would fall from 0.269 to 0.260 in February 2007, but from 0.663 to 0.654 in February 2009. In other words, while dispersion would be less, the impact of financial turmoil on the dispersion is much larger: –0.394 versus –0.036, or no less than eleven times larger.

Random effects

We next considered estimating the panel regression using an RE estimator. The FE model specifies the country-specific effect as a constant, whereas the RE model specifies the country-specific effect as a random variable that is uncorrelated with the regressors. Breusch and Pagan (1980) have developed a Lagrange multiplier test for $\sigma_u^2 = 0$; the p-value is reported in Table 13.7 in the row labelled '$\sigma_u^2 = 0$ p-value'. If the orthogonality assumption is true then the random effects model is more efficient, because it uses the assumption that u_i is uncorrelated with the regressors. Of course, if this assumption is false then the random effects model is inconsistent. We can then use a Hausman test of the extra orthogonality condition imposed by the RE estimator. The idea of the Hausman test is simple: if the regressors are uncorrelated with u_i, the FE estimator is consistent but inefficient and the RE estimator is consistent and efficient; if the regressors are correlated with u_i, however, the FE estimator is consistent but the RE estimator is inconsistent. Table 13.7 estimates the same models and includes the p-value from the Hausman test in the row labelled 'Hausman'.[4]

Table 13.7 *Panel estimation using random effects*

	Standard deviation of current year's inflation forecasts, $S_{it}(\pi, c)$			Standard deviation of next year's inflation forecasts $S_{it}(\pi, n)$		
Inflation target (γ)	−0.004	0.013	0.022	−0.012	−0.007	0.014
	[0.6]	[2.1]	[7.2]	[1.2]	[0.7]	[4.2]
Lagged $S_{it}(\pi, \cdot)(\rho)$			0.542			0.785
			[33.2]			[66.3]
Lagged $S_{it}(y, \cdot)(\theta)$		0.168	0.082		0.110	0.040
		[11.2]	[7.0]		[6.5]	[4.2]
$\dfrac{\gamma}{(1-\rho)}$			0.047			0.066
			[7.4]			[4.4]
R^2	0.39	0.49	0.65	0.25	0.31	0.76
σ_ε	0.084	0.083	0.073	0.119	0.118	0.080
$\sigma_u^2 = 0$ p-value	0.000	0.000	0.000	0.000	0.000	0.000
Hausman p-value	0.276	0.000	0.000	0.961	0.999	0.000
Number of observations	2,895	2,880	2,880	2,895	2,880	2,880

Notes: Asymptotic t-ratios are in brackets. Coefficients on monthly dummy variables are not shown.
Source: Author's calculations based on equation (13.5).

The results from using random effects to estimate the model are mixed. Sometimes the coefficient on *Target* is negative and insignificant and other times it is positive and significant. Not surprisingly, one can always reject the hypothesis that $\sigma_u^2 = 0$. Unfortunately, one can often reject the hypothesis that the orthogonality condition holds. In general, it appears as though we cannot reject the hypothesis that the orthogonality condition holds for the stripped-down model (which includes only *Target* and year and month dummies) but we can reject the orthogonality condition when we include lagged values of $S(\pi, \cdot)$ and $S(y, \cdot)$. Interestingly, in the bare-bones model (which fails to reject the Hausman test), the coefficient on *Target* is negative but insignificant.

13.5 Robustness and extensions

In this section, we check the robustness of the results by considering six modifications to the baseline model:
• we examine the sensitivity of the results to individual countries;
• we compute the standard errors of the estimated coefficients using alternative techniques;

- we consider the effect of the dating of the introduction of inflation targeting;
- we include various measures of actual inflation;
- we introduce commodity prices into the model; and
- we replace the standard deviation of forecasts with their root mean square error.

In what follows, we discuss results only for the FE panel regression using $S_{it}(\pi, c)$ and $S_{it}(\pi, n)$. Accordingly, each of the six modifications to the baseline model is compared to the results shown in Table 13.6. In general, the conclusions from the previous section are supported.

Sensitivity to individual countries

Since the panel includes fifteen countries, the first robustness check is to see whether some countries are 'influential'. To check this, we estimate the FE panel regression with all countries, and then we exclude one country at a time. So, for example, we re-estimate the model with Australia excluded, we then include Australia but exclude Canada, we then include Australia and Canada but exclude Norway, and so on.

Table 13.8 reports the coefficients and t-statistics on *Target* (γ) for all three panel equations for all countries, corresponding to the columns as labelled in Table 13.6, and then for each excluded country. In looking at the table, the appropriate comparison is between the first row ('None' excluded) and each subsequent row.

The results suggest that Canada and Norway may be influential for $S(\pi, c)$ and that Canada, Italy, the Netherlands, Norway and Spain may be influential for $S(\pi, n)$. First, note that in all but six cases – two for $S(\pi, c)$ and four for $S(\pi, n)$ – the sign remains negative. In the six cases in which the sign changes (Australia and the United Kingdom), the coefficient is small and insignificant. More importantly, Canada and Norway appear to be influential for $S(\pi, c)$ because the coefficient is insignificant in columns 2 and 3 when all countries are included, but it becomes *significant* when Canada and Norway are excluded. This suggests that Canada and Norway are the countries behind the insignificant coefficient when all countries are included. These results may not be too surprising, since the coefficient on *Target* was positive and insignificant for Canada and positive and significant for Norway in Tables 13.2, 13.4 and 13.5. In addition, when looking at the results for $S(\pi, n)$, Canada, Italy, the Netherlands, Norway and Spain are influential in the same way: the coefficient on *Target* becomes significant when these countries are excluded in

Inflation targeting and private sector forecasts

323

Table 13.8 *Are countries influential?*

FE panel estimation of import of inflation targeting (γ^c and γ^h)

Excluded country	Standard deviation of current year's inflation forecasts, $S_{it}(\pi, c)$			Standard deviation of next year's inflation forecasts $S_{it}(\pi, n)$		
	(1)	(2)	(3)	(4)	(5)	(6)
None	−0.023 [2.98]	−0.011 [1.36]	−0.009 [1.30]	−0.021 [1.98]	−0.017 [1.59]	−0.009 [1.28]
Australia	−0.007 [0.80]	0.003 [0.41]	−0.000 [0.06]	0.008 [0.68]	0.011 [0.94]	−0.001 [0.08]
Canada	−0.033 [4.06]	−0.020 [2.40]	−0.014 [1.95]	−0.030 [2.62]	−0.025 [2.17]	−0.012 [1.48]
Norway	−0.058 [6.96]	−0.045 [5.28]	−0.028 [3.77]	−0.053 [4.45]	−0.050 [4.14]	−0.019 [2.28]
Spain	−0.014 [1.60]	−0.001 [0.09]	−0.003 [0.41]	−0.039 [3.14]	−0.035 [2.76]	−0.013 [1.51]
Switzerland	−0.022 [2.69]	−0.008 [0.93]	−0.008 [1.08]	−0.026 [2.22]	−0.020 [1.73]	−0.010 [1.28]
United Kingdom	−0.005 [0.59]	0.005 [0.64]	−0.000 [0.04]	0.006 [0.54]	0.011 [0.99]	−0.003 [0.35]
Euro area	−0.023 [2.96]	−0.011 [1.34]	−0.009 [1.27]	−0.021 [1.96]	−0.017 [1.58]	−0.010 [1.27]
France	−0.020 [2.52]	−0.008 [1.02]	−0.007 [1.05]	−0.014 [1.22]	−0.010 [-0.91]	−0.008 [1.00]
Germany	−0.022 [2.72]	−0.009 [1.11]	−0.008 [1.11]	−0.019 [1.70]	−0.014 [1.27]	−0.008 [1.08]
Italy	−0.018 [2.30]	−0.006 [0.70]	−0.006 [0.84]	−0.027 [2.45]	−0.024 [2.10]	−0.011 [1.49]
Japan	−0.028 [3.62]	−0.013 [1.64]	−0.010 [1.53]	−0.021 [1.96]	−0.016 [1.48]	−0.009 [1.26]
Netherlands	−0.024 [3.13]	−0.013 [1.60]	−0.010 [1.42]	−0.024 [2.28]	−0.022 [2.04]	−0.011 [1.44]
United States	−0.023 [2.91]	−0.011 [1.36]	−0.009 [1.28]	−0.016 [1.48]	−0.012 [1.13]	−0.008 [1.11]
New Zealand	−0.023 [3.19]	−0.013 [1.79]	−0.011 [1.64]	−0.020 [1.87]	−0.017 [1.56]	−0.009 [1.24]
Sweden	−0.021 [2.27]	−0.009 [1.20]	−0.008 [1.20]	−0.022 [2.01]	−0.017 [1.58]	−0.009 [1.26]

Notes: Asymptotic t-ratios are in brackets. The coefficient and t-statistic on inflation target (γ) are reported. Numbers in parentheses at the top of the columns refer to those in Table 13.6.

Table 13.9 *Alternative standard errors*

Panel estimation using FE

	Standard deviation of current year's inflation forecasts, $S_{it}(\pi, c)$			Standard deviation of next year's inflation forecasts, $S_{it}(\pi, n)$		
Inflation target (γ)	−0.023	−0.011	−0.009	−0.021	−0.017	−0.009
	[3.0]	[1.4]	[1.3]	[2.0]	[1.6]	[1.3]
	[0.6]	[0.3]	[0.5]	[0.5]	[0.4]	[0.8]
	[0.6]	[0.3]	[0.4]	[0.4]	[0.4]	[0.6]
Lagged $S_{it}(\pi, \cdot)(\rho)$			0.488			0.737
			[29.1]			[57.3]
			[10.0]			[17.3]
			[12.2]			[15.1]
Lagged $S_{it}(y, \cdot)(\theta)$		0.142	0.036		0.103	0.015
		[9.1]	[2.6]		[6.1]	[1.3]
		[3.8]	[1.9]		[2.0]	[1.3]
		[4.6]	[2.1]		[2.2]	[1.2]
$\dfrac{\gamma}{(1-\rho)}$			−0.017			−0.036
			[1.3]			[0.0]
			[0.5]			[0.8]
			[0.4]			[0.7]
R^2	0.36	0.44	0.62	0.24	0.29	0.75
σ_ε	0.084	0.083	0.073	0.119	0.118	0.080
Number of observations	2,895	2,880	2,880	2,895	2,880	2,880

Notes: Three sets of t-statistics, all in brackets, are provided for each coefficient estimate. The first is the asymptotic t-statistic computed using the conventionally computed standard error. The second is based on a standard error that is robust to heteroscedasticity. The third is computed using a bootstrap. Coefficients on monthly and yearly dummy variables are not shown.
Source: Authors' calculations based on equation (13.5).

columns 5 or 6. As with $S(\pi, c)$, these results are not surprising given the earlier results in Tables 13.2, 13.4 and 13.5.

Alternative measure of standard errors

Given the range of countries included in the panel of countries, the conventional standard errors reported in Table 13.6 may be misleading. Therefore another robustness check involves estimating alternative standard errors. The standard errors reported in Table 13.6 are the typical standard errors for generalised least squares. As a check, Table 13.9

Table 13.10 *Effect of lagging the date for the introduction of inflation targeting*

Panel estimation using FE

	Standard deviation of current year's inflation forecasts, $S_{it}(\pi, c)$			Standard deviation of next year's inflation forecasts, $S_{it}(\pi, n)$		
Lagged (3) inflation target (γ)	−0.029 [3.9]	−0.017 [2.3]	−0.014 [2.1]	−0.030 [2.7]	−0.026 [2.4]	−0.006 [0.8]
Lagged $S_{it}(\pi, \cdot)(\rho)$			0.485 [29.6]			0.737 [57.2]
Lagged $S_{it}(y, \cdot)(\theta)$		0.137 [9.0]	0.033 [2.4]		0.101 [5.9]	0.012 [1.0]
$\dfrac{\gamma}{(1-\rho)}$			−0.027 [2.1]			−0.025 [0.9]
R^2	0.35	0.44	0.63	0.22	0.27	0.75
σ_ε	0.08	0.08	0.07	0.12	0.12	0.08
Number of observations	2,850	2,850	2,850	2,850	2,850	2,850

Notes: Asymptotic t-ratios are in brackets. Coefficients on monthly and yearly dummy variables are not shown.
Source: Authors' calculations based on equation (13.5) with *Target* lagged three months.

reports heteroscedasticity-robust standard errors and bootstrap standard errors.

Not surprisingly, the t-statistics are smaller. In particular, the t-statistic on the 'Inflation target' is now insignificant in all cases when using the robust or bootstrap standard errors. The other coefficients generally remain significant, however (the coefficient on lagged $S_{it}(y, n)$ is insignificant no matter what standard errors are used).

Dating the introduction of inflation targeting

As noted earlier, the dating of the inflation-targeting regime is somewhat ad hoc and different researchers use different dates for the start of the regime. In addition, if survey participants take time to learn about the inflation-targeting regime (for example, enquiring how serious the authorities are), then an alternative dating regime could give different results. To test this hypothesis, the fixed effects panel regressions are re-estimated using the third lag of *Target* rather than the current value of *Target* (from Table 13.1), thus allowing survey participants three months to learn about the new regime. The results are shown in Table 13.10.

In this case, the coefficients on the lagged inflation target variable are somewhat larger (in absolute value) and significant for all three models for $S_{it}(\pi, c)$, compared to only one of the models in Table 13.6. Moreover, the coefficient is significant for two out of three models for $S_{it}(\pi, n)$, compared to only one of the models in Table 13.6. Thus there is some evidence that it takes a couple of months for survey participants to respond to the introduction of an inflation-targeting regime. Stated somewhat differently, it means that the first three months of inflation targeting are influential observations in models 2, 3 and 5, because the coefficient on the inflation-targeting variable is insignificant when these observations are included but the coefficient is significant when these observations are excluded.

Including measures of actual inflation

Turning now to some extensions of the baseline model, we first introduce various measures of actual inflation into the specification. One measure of inflation is the percentage change in the CPI from twelve months ago, and the other measure is the year-average-over-year-average percentage change. Since the survey participants provide estimates of the year-average-over-year-average inflation rate, the percentage change from twelve months ago is not exactly comparable to the inflation rate being forecasted. However, it does provide actual inflation data that survey participants could use in forecasting inflation. The year-average-over-year-average inflation rate is comparable, but is the same for all months in the year. Including the lagged value of either inflation rate does not change the results in any meaningful way: the t-statistic on the inflation rate is always less than 1.0 (to conserve space, the results are not shown).

Another inflation measure turned out to be significant. Since the dependent variable is the dispersion of private sector forecasts, one might expect that the variability of inflation would be a significant explanatory variable. The results in Table 13.6 suggest that the dispersion of private sector forecasts is a significant explanatory variable. We extend these results by including a measure of the variability of actual inflation, measured as the twelve-month rolling standard deviation of month-over-twelve-months-before inflation rates. This variable is significant in all six cases; the t-statistic is between 6.5 and 12.3 in equations for $S(\pi, c)$ and between 4.1 and 10.1 in equations for $S(\pi, n)$. The coefficients and t-statistics on the other variables are fairly similar, however, so the results are not shown (to conserve space).

Table 13.11 *Including volatility of commodity price inflation*

Panel estimation using FE

	Standard deviation of current year's inflation forecasts, $S_{it}(\pi, c)$			Standard deviation of next year's inflation forecasts, $S_{it}(\pi, n)$		
Inflation target (γ)	−0.014 [1.9]	−0.006 [0.8]	−0.004 [0.5]	0.003 [0.3]	0.005 [0.4]	−0.004 [0.5]
Lagged $S_{it}(\pi, \cdot)(\rho)$			0.495 [29.7]			0.725 [54.2]
Lagged $S_{it}(y, \cdot)(\theta)$		0.127 [8.6]	0.032 [2.4]		0.092 [5.5]	0.017 [1.4]
$\dfrac{\gamma}{(1-\rho)}$			−0.007 [0.5]			−0.016 [0.5]
R^2	0.363	0.442	0.660	0.135	0.163	0.726
σ_ε	0.078	0.077	0.067	0.114	0.114	0.079
Number of observations	2,811	2,803	2,803	2,811	2,803	2,803

Notes: Asymptotic t-ratios are in brackets. Coefficients on monthly and yearly dummies are not shown.
Source: Authors' calculations based on equation (13.5) with commodity prices added.

Commodity prices

Given the wide range of countries used in the panel, the effect of having an inflation target may be overwhelmed by other factors. In particular, some countries are more susceptible to commodity price shocks than other countries. In an effort to check this, we extend the results in Table 13.6 by including a measure of the volatility of commodity price inflation. Specifically, we include the lagged value of the rolling twelve-month standard deviation of the percentage change (from the previous month) in a commodity price index; the index used is the Commodity Research Bureau spot raw industrial price index. The same commodity price index is used for all countries, under the assumption that commodity prices are set in world markets. The coefficient on the commodity price variable is allowed to be different for each country, however. The results are shown in Table 13.11. As there are fifteen countries and three equations for $S(\pi, c)$, there are forty-five coefficients for commodity price variability. In order to conserve space, these coefficients are not shown. Briefly, the coefficients on commodity price variability are almost always positive and significant. For the $S(\pi, c)$ equations, thirty-six of the forty-five coefficients are positive and significant, and the other nine coefficients are positive and insignificant. For the $S(\pi, n)$ equations, thirty-five of the coefficients are positive (twenty-four are significant and eleven are insignificant) and ten of the coefficients are negative (two are significant and eight are insignificant). Returning to our primary interest, however, we note that, when we add the commodity price variation measure to the regression, the coefficient on 'Inflation target' is similar in magnitude and significance in the $S(\pi, c)$ equations, but about half the magnitude and significance in the $S(\pi, n)$ equations.

Root mean squared error

Finally, we estimate a model similar to equation (13.4) but using the root mean squared error of the inflation forecast, $RMSE_{it}(\pi, c)$ and $RMSE_{it}(\pi, n)$, rather than using the standard deviation of the current (and next) year's inflation forecast. (Appendix 13B describes the mechanics of how the RMSE is recovered from the data we have available.) Specifically, we estimate the following equation by fixed effects:

$$
\begin{aligned}
RMSE_{it}(\pi, n) = {} & \alpha^n + u_i^n + \sum_{k=2}^{12} \beta_{ik}^n D_{kt}^m + \sum_{t=1991}^{2007} \delta_t^n Year_t \\
& + \kappa_1^n Crisis_{1it} + \kappa_2^n Crisis_{2it} + \gamma_i^n Target_{it} \\
& + \rho^n RMSE_{1t-1}(\pi, n) + \theta^n S_{1t-1}(y, n) + \varepsilon_{it}^n
\end{aligned}
\tag{13.6}
$$

Table 13.12 reports the results of this exercise. These are, clearly, more compelling than what we obtained using the dispersion of private sector forecasts against an inflation-targeting variable. In particular, the coefficient on 'Inflation target' is negative and significant in five of the six equations.

Although it may appear that the RMSE results are stronger than those using the dispersion, we view them with caution, for two reasons. First, while the coefficient on the inflation target variable is larger when using RMSE than when using $S(\pi, \cdot)$, the RMSE itself is also larger than $S(\pi, \cdot)$. For example, the average (across all countries and time) of $S(\pi, c)$ is 0.20 while the average of $RMSE(\pi, c)$ is 0.40; and the average of $S(\pi, n)$ is 0.34 while the average of $RMSE(\pi, c)$ is 0.77. A better way to compare the results using $S(\pi, \cdot)$ and RMSE is to look at the effect of adopting an inflation target relative to the average value of $S(\pi, \cdot)$ and $RMSE(\pi, \cdot)$ as we did above. Here the results are the same: the reduction in $S(\pi, \cdot)$ or $RMSE(\pi, \cdot)$ is small relative to the average size of $S(\pi, \cdot)$ or $RMSE(\pi, \cdot)$ for non-inflation-targeting regimes. The reduction is between 3 per cent and 47 per cent, depending on which model is used and whether we look at current-year or next-year forecasts. Second,

Table 13.12 *Using the root mean square error*

Panel estimation using FE

	Standard deviation of current year's inflation forecasts, $RMSE_{it}(\pi, c)$			Standard deviation of next year's inflation forecasts, $RMSE_{it}(\pi, n)$		
Inflation target (γ)	−0.163	−0.126	−0.019	−0.213	−0.209	−0.043
	[7.0]	[5.3]	[1.3]	[5.9]	[5.7]	[2.3]
Lagged $RMSE_{it}(\pi, \cdot)(\rho)$			0.790			0.859
			[68.1]			[87.6]
Lagged $S_{it}(y, \cdot)(\theta)$		0.350	0.017		0.231	0.034
		[6.9]	[0.5]		[4.0]	[1.1]
$\dfrac{\gamma}{(1-\rho)}$			−0.091			−0.303
			[1.3]			[2.7]
R^2	0.10	0.16	0.79	0.07	0.10	0.84
σ_ε	0.257	0.254	0.156	0.396	0.395	0.203
Number of observations	2,835	2,820	2,820	2,820	2,805	2,805

Notes: Asymptotic t-ratios are in brackets. Coefficients on monthly and yearly dummy variables are not shown.
Source: Authors' calculations based on equation (13.6) with the RMSE as the left-hand-side variable.

the $RMSE(\pi, \cdot)$ is much more volatile than $S(\pi, \cdot)$; and not only is it more volatile, the volatility is more episodic, in that there are some years when $RMSE(\pi, \cdot)$ is three to five times larger than $S(\pi, \cdot)$ and other years when they are about the same magnitude. Part of the reason is that $RMSE(\pi, \cdot)$ is calculated from relative actual inflation measured as the year-average-over-year-average percentage change, and is thus the same for all months in a given year.

13.6   Conclusions

Using survey data on inflation expectations drawn from Consensus Economics, we find little evidence that inflation-targeting countries have a smaller dispersion of private sector forecasts of inflation. While, for some countries, some models and some estimation techniques, we estimate that inflation-targeting countries have a smaller dispersion of private sector inflation forecasts, for other countries, other models and other estimation techniques we find that they do not.

Returning to the question that motivated this analysis – 'Does increased transparency lead to lower dispersion in private forecasts?' – the answer appears to be 'No'. This suggests to us that the Morris and Shin argument that increased transparency could be destabilising is of little practical concern to policymakers. Even in the cases when inflation targeting leads to a lower dispersion of private forecasts, we cannot necessarily conclude that greater transparency is harmful, because the lower dispersion could reflect the beneficial effects from greater transparency rather than the harmful effects from greater coordination. Of course, since the survey we use reports results of forecasts for inflation only in the current year and the next year, our results are unable to shed light on whether the distribution of private sector forecasts of long-run inflation is lower. However, even if the inflation target is for the medium run, one would expect that the dispersion of inflation forecasts for 'next year' may still be somewhat smaller than otherwise.

Appendix 13A Supporting data calculations

Table 13A.1 *Average standard deviation of current year's inflation forecasts*

| | Standard deviation in January | | | |
	Non-inflation-targeting	Inflation-targeting	Difference	Number of observations
Australia	0.513 [17.8]	0.377 [15.9]	−0.136 [6.86]	222
Canada	0.294 [15.8]	0.296 [22.8]	0.002 [0.1]	235
Norway	0.277 [8.2]	0.418 [13.6]	0.141 [7.0]	131
Spain	0.249 [11.8]	0.229 [9.8]	−0.020 [1.4]	172
Switzerland	0.313 [12.3]	0.298 [14.7]	−0.015 [0.9]	131
United Kingdom	0.473 [14.5]	0.322 [11.9]	−0.151 [6.9]	235
Euro area	0.169 [10.9]			77
France	0.227 [17.3]			235
Germany	0.211 [26.2]			235
Italy	0.234 [12.6]			235
Japan	0.281 [11.6]			235
Netherlands	0.254 [12.0]			172
United States	0.339 [18.3]			235
New Zealand		0.467 [12.7]		173
Sweden		0.349 [15.0]		172

Table 13A.2 *Average standard deviation of next year's inflation forecasts*

| | Standard deviation in January | | | |
	Non-inflation-targeting	Inflation-targeting	Difference	Number of observations
Australia	0.791 [14.5]	0.496 [11.0]	−0.295 [7.8]	222
Canada	0.426 [13.8]	0.364 [16.9]	−0.062 [2.5]	235
Norway	0.226 [5.7]	0.354 [9.7]	0.128 [5.3]	131
Spain	0.315 [7.9]	0.416 [9.5]	0.101 [3.7]	172
Switzerland	0.269 [10.1]	0.300 [14.0]	0.031 [1.7]	131
United Kingdom	0.771 [12.0]	0.506 [9.5]	−0.265 [6.2]	235
Euro area	0.231 [9.4]			77
France	0.245 [16.1]			235
Germany	0.318 [17.2]			235
Italy	0.304 [8.9]			235
Japan	0.403 [12.2]			235
Netherlands	0.338 [10.4]			172
United States	0.452 [17.5]			235
New Zealand		0.442 [12.2]		173
Sweden		0.327 [11.0]		172

Table 13A.3 *Coefficients on inflation-targeting dummy variable*

		November 1990– April 2009	January 1995– April 2009	June 1998 – April 2009
Australia	$S(\pi, c)$	−0.109 [5.9]		
	$S(\pi, n)$	−0.182 [6.0]		
Canada	$S(\pi, c)$	0.049 [1.7]		
	$S(\pi, n)$	0.004 [0.1]		
United Kingdom	$S(\pi, c)$	−0.077 [4.3]		
	$S(\pi, n)$	−0.059 [1.9]		
Spain	$S(\pi, c)$		−0.029 [3.0]	−0.075 [1.6]
	$S(\pi, n)$		0.080 [4.5]	−0.015 [0.2]
Norway	$S(\pi, c)$			0.135 [8.3]
	$S(\pi, n)$			0.117 [6.8]
Switzerland	$S(\pi, c)$			0.008 [1.1]
	$S(\pi, n)$			0.040 [2.4]

Appendix 13B   Calculation of the root mean squared error of the inflation forecast

Let $\pi_{jt}^{fi,c}$ = inflation forecast (f) for country i, for the current year, made by forecaster j at time t and π_t^{ai} = actual inflation for country i at time t. Since the forecasts are for year-on-year (rather than month-over-twelve-months-before) inflation, π_t^{ai} is the same for each month in the year corresponding to date t: $\pi_{Jan1990}^{ai} = \pi_{Feb1990}^{ai} = \cdots = \pi_{Dec1990}^{ai}$. Next, let E^j denote the expectations (average) over survey participants j. Then, $E^j(\pi_{jt}^{fi,c}) = \bar{\pi}_t^{fi,c}$ (which no longer has the j subscript) is reported by Consensus Economics – namely the average forecast for inflation in country i for the current year, made at time t. There is obviously a similar variable for next year, replacing c with n. Finally, $S_{it}(\pi, c) = S\pi_t^{fi,c}$ is reported by Consensus Economics – the standard deviation of the private sector forecasts for the current year for country i at date t. We have three observations for each country c at time t: $\bar{\pi}_t^{fi,c}$, $S\pi_t^{fi,c}$ and π_t^{ai}.

We calculate the variance of private sector forecasts $\equiv V_t^{fi,c}$ (across forecasters) $\equiv [S\pi_t^{fi,c}]^2$ as follows:

$$V_t^{fi,c} = E^j \left[\pi_{jt}^{fi,c} - \pi_t^{-fi,c} \right]^2 = E^j \left[\pi_{jt}^{fi,c} \right]^2 - \left[\bar{\pi}_t^{-fi,c} \right]^2$$

We can use this equation to solve for $E^j [\pi_{jt}^{fi,c}]^2$ (since we have all the terms on the right-hand side of the equation):

$$E^j \left[\pi_{jt}^{fi,c} \right]^2 = V_t^{fi,c} + \left[\bar{\pi}_t^{-fi,c} \right]^2$$

We can now calculate the RMSE of the forecast for the 'current' year as follows:

$$\begin{aligned} RMSE_t^{fi,c} &= sqrt \left(E^j \left[\pi_{jt}^{fi,c} - \pi_t^{ai} \right]^2 \right) \\ &= \left(V_t^{fi,c} + \left[\bar{\pi}_t^{-fi,c} \right]^2 + \left[\pi_t^{ai} \right]^2 - 2\bar{\pi}_t^{-fi,c} \pi_t^{ai} \right) \end{aligned}$$

(We again have the terms on the right-hand side of this equation.) We can also calculate the RMSE of the forecast for the 'next' year as follows:

$$RMSE_t^{fi,c} = sqrt \left(V_t^{fi,c} + \left[\bar{\pi}_t^{-fi,n} \right]^2 + \left[\pi_{t+1}^{ai} \right]^2 - 2\bar{\pi}_t^{-fi,n} \pi_{t+1}^{ai} \right)$$

where we use actual inflation at $t + 1$ rather than at t.

NOTES

1. The authors gratefully acknowledge comments from seminar participants at the Federal Reserve Bank of Kansas City and conference participants at the

Sixth Norges Bank Monetary Policy Conference. The views expressed are the authors' and not necessarily those of the BIS, the Federal Reserve Bank of Kansas City or the Federal Reserve System.

2. We also regressed the coefficients against $\{1, 2, \ldots, 12, 0, \ldots, 0\}$ and $\{0, \ldots, 0, 1, 2, \ldots, 12\}$. The slope coefficients (t-statistics) were -0.003 (2.80) and -0.024 (23.1).

3. The chart plots the constant term (α) and coefficient on variables related to January of each year: $Year_t$ (δ_t), $Crisis_{1it}$ (κ_1) and $Crisis_{2it}$ (κ_2). In this way, the chart plots the 'time-varying constant term'. Specifically, the values plotted for the years 1991 to 2007 are $= \alpha + \delta_t$, for 2008 $= \alpha + \kappa_1$ and for 2009 $= \alpha + \kappa_2$.

4. Including a lagged dependent variable in a fixed effects model creates a large-sample bias in the estimate of the coefficient on the lagged dependent variable. Since we are not really interested in this estimate, the concern is somewhat mitigated. In addition, in a simple model, Nickell (1981) shows that, for large values of T, the limit of $(\hat{\rho} - \rho)$ as $N \to \infty$ is approximately $- (1 + \rho)/(T - 1)$. With $\rho = 0.5$ (0.8) and $T = 235$, the bias will be -0.0064 (-0.0077).

REFERENCES

Ball, L., and N. Sheridan (2005). 'Does inflation targeting matter?', in B. Bernanke and M. Woodford (eds.). *The Inflation-Targeting Debate*: 249–82. Chicago: University of Chicago Press.

Baum, C. (2006). *An Introduction to Modern Econometrics Using Stata*. College Station, TX: Stata Press.

Breusch, T., and A. Pagan (1980). 'The Lagrange multiplier test and its applications to model specification in econometrics', *Review of Economic Studies*, 47(1): 239–53.

Carpenter, S. (2004). 'Transparency and monetary policy: what does the academic literature tell policymakers?'. Finance and Economics Discussion Paper no. 2004–35. Washington, DC: Federal Reserve.

Dincer, N., and B. Eichengreen (2007). 'Central bank transparency: where, why, and with what effects?'. Working Paper no. 13003. Cambridge, MA: NBER.

Geraats, P. (2002). 'Central bank transparency', *Economic Journal*, 112: 532–65.

Levin, A., F. Natalucci and J. Piger (2004). 'Explicit inflation objectives and macroeconomic outcomes'. Working Paper no. 383. Frankfurt: ECB.

Mankiw, N., R. Reis and J. Wolfers (2004). 'Disagreement about inflation expectations', in M. Gertler and K. Rogoff (eds.). *NBER Macroeconomics Annual 2003*: 209–70. Cambridge, MA: MIT Press.

Mishkin, F. (2002) 'Inflation targeting', in H. Vane and B. Snowdon (eds.). *Encyclopedia of Macroeconomics*: 361–5. Cheltenham: Edward Elgar.

Mishkin, F., and K. Schmidt-Hebbel (2007). 'One decade of inflation targeting in the world: what do we know and what do we need to know?', in F. Mishkin (ed.). *Monetary Policy Strategy*: 405–64. Cambridge, MA: MIT Press.

Morris, S., and H. Shin (2002). 'Social value of public inflation', *American Economic Review*, 92(5): 1521–34.

  (2005). 'Central bank transparency and the signal value of prices', *Brookings Papers on Economic Activity*, 2: 1–43.

Nickell, S. (1981). 'Biases in dynamic models with fixed effects', *Econometrica*, 49(6): 1417–26.

Romer, C., and D. Romer (2000). 'Federal Reserve information and the behavior of interest rates', *American Economic Review*, 90(3): 429–57.

Svensson, L. (2006). 'Social value of public information: Morris and Shin (2002) is actually pro transparency, not con', *American Economic Review*, 96(1): 448–51.

Truman, E. (2003). *Inflation Targeting in the World Economy*. Washington, DC: IIE.

Walsh, C. (2007). 'Optimal economic transparency', *International Journal of Central Banking*, 3(1): 5–36.

Woodford, M. (2005). 'Central bank communication and policy effectiveness', in Federal Reserve Bank of Kansas City. *The Greenspan Era: Lessons for the Future*: 399–474. Kansas City: Federal Reserve Bank of Kansas City.

14 Inflation targeting, transparency and inflation forecasts: evidence from individual forecasters

Christopher Crowe[1]

[T]he most important distinguishing characteristic of inflation target regimes is the emphasis that they place on transparency and accountability.

Mervyn King (1997: 439)

14.1 Introduction

The consensus view among policymakers and academics alike is that the introduction of inflation targeting increases the transparency of monetary policymaking (King 1997; Bernanke *et al.* 1999; Svensson 1999; Mishkin and Schmidt-Hebbel 2001; Faust and Henderson 2004). Following Geraats (2002), transparency can be thought of as the removal of information asymmetries. Geraats catalogues five areas of monetary policymaking in which transparency could affect outcomes: (i) the central bank's objectives and its institutional relationship with the rest of government; (ii) the publication of data and forecasts; (iii) internal decision-making; (iv) the communication and explanation of policy changes; and (v) details of the implementation of policy.

These in turn give rise to five elements of transparency (political, economic, procedural, policy and operational). The introduction of IT is widely held to increase political transparency, by forcing the central bank to specify both the variable that it is targeting (some measure of consumer price inflation) and a precise numerical target for the targeted variable, as well as – in many cases – delineating more clearly the division of responsibilities between the bank and the political authorities (King 1997; Eijffinger and Geraats 2006). The communication strategy accompanying the targeting regime typically includes enhanced policy analysis, more openness about internal policy deliberations and greater explanation of policy decisions, resulting in enhanced procedural, policy and operational transparency (Berg 2005). Finally, this communication strategy usually involves a more explicit and public discussion of the forecasts underlying policy decisions, including the attendant risks and underlying assumptions, which tends to increase economic transparency (Roger and Stone 2005).[2]

Ultimately, the question of whether IT enhances central bank transparency, and with what effects, is an empirical one. Several studies have attempted to measure the transparency-enhancing effects of IT by focusing on economic outcomes.[3] Gürkaynak, Levin and Swanson (2006) find that IT appears to make long-term inflation expectations less responsive to economic news, suggesting that IT helps to anchor long-term inflation expectations. This effect cannot be ascribed necessarily to greater transparency under IT: enhanced credibility – distinct from but related to transparency – may be the explanation. Corbo, Landerretche and Schmidt-Hebbel (2001) analyse model-derived inflation forecasts for a range of advanced and emerging market economies, and find a drop in forecast errors among countries that adopt IT, although the fall seems to pre-date the adoption of IT in many cases and may reflect other changes to the policy environment. Johnson (2002) tests the credibility and transparency effects of IT in a panel of eleven industrial countries including five inflation targeters. He finds some evidence for the credibility benefits of IT (expected inflation falls more in the ITers than the non-ITers) but no evidence for transparency benefits (neither the forecasts' variability nor their absolute error are reduced by IT). Similarly, Cecchetti and Hakkio (Chapter 13 in this volume) analyse the dispersal of private sector inflation forecasts and find no consistent evidence that the introduction of IT leads forecasters to a reduction in the dispersion of forecasts (although this question is distinct from the question of whether IT adoption improves the quality of public information, as is discussed in the following section).

Other studies use subjective assessments of transparency practices as the benchmark for assessing the impact of IT. Eijffinger and Geraats (2006) analyse the practices of nine major central banks and conclude that 'the most transparent central banks ... are all inflation targeters'. Roger and Stone (2005), who measure transparency according to central banks' adherence to the IMF's Code of Monetary and Financial Policy Transparency, come to the same conclusion. Crowe and Meade (2007) find that transparency increased among central banks that had introduced IT. However, the validity of these results relies on the suitability of the subjective transparency measure employed: as with any subjective index, there is a risk of tautological reasoning biasing the results towards finding an effect. Meanwhile, other work has attempted to match subjective transparency assessments to outcomes. Chortareas, Stasavage and Sterne (2002, 2003) find that greater transparency, in the form of more public prominence for the central bank's forecasts, is associated with lower inflation and lower unemployment costs of disinflation in a diverse cross-section of countries.[4] Crowe and Meade (2008), in contrast to Cecchetti and Hakkio (in Chapter 13), find that greater central bank transparency is associated with private sector forecasters making more use of public information. Swanson (2004) finds that financial market forecasts of policy interest rates in the United States improved markedly over time, in step with transparency-enhancing changes to the Federal Reserve's communications strategy and policymaking.

This chapter assesses the potential transparency-enhancing effects of IT adoption by focusing on individual inflation forecasts. First, it builds on the methodology of Crowe (2010) to analyse whether IT adoption enhances the accuracy of inflation forecasts. It briefly outlines the main results in the earlier study, and offers a number of additional robustness checks. Second, it assesses whether IT adoption affects the rationality of private sector inflation forecasts. Although a number of studies in the forecasting literature have assessed forecast rationality (see, for instance, Swidler and Ketcher 1990, Batchelor and Dua 1991 and Loungani 2001), this is the first study to assess whether the introduction of IT has any impact on rationality. Finally, it contrasts the results from these two exercises and uses them to shed light on the apparently contradictory findings in the current chapter and Cecchetti and Hakkio's.

The use of individual forecasters (rather than averages per country) in the first exercise allows one to test whether the effect of IT differs between forecasters with different characteristics. This is useful, since a simple signal extraction model predicts that IT's impact on forecast accuracy will be conditional on how accurate the forecasts are in the first place. Using individual forecasters as the unit of observation permits the estimation of this conditional effect. A critical issue in assessing the effect of IT is that the assignment of the 'treatment' (in this case, IT adoption in the country in question) is likely to be non-random. To control for endogenous IT adoption, forecasters in IT adoption countries are matched with a control group of forecasters in non-IT adoption countries using propensity score matching. A number of studies in the literature on IT have started to adopt these techniques for dealing with the non-random adoption of IT (Vega and Winkelried 2005; Lin and Ye 2007). However, Crowe (2010) and this chapter are the first to apply these techniques to the question of IT's transparency benefits. A second econometric problem (endogeneity resulting from the inclusion of the initial forecast error, which leads to mean reversion) is dealt with using IV estimation. The effect of IT adoption is then estimated by comparing the behaviour of forecasters' errors in the twelve months leading up to and following the adoption of IT in each country. The results in this chapter build on the baseline results presented by Crowe (2010) and provide some additional robustness checks.

The results of this exercise suggest that IT adoption leads to better private sector forecasts, with the effect strongest for forecasters whose initial forecast accuracy is worst, in line with the model. However, while IT adoption improves forecast accuracy most for the worst forecasters, there is no evidence that the best forecasters are harmed. The results are therefore not supportive of Morris and Shin's (2002) concerns over transparency's potential downsides.[5]

However, the results of the second exercise suggest that IT adoption may have a negative effect on forecaster rationality. In this exercise, forecaster rationality is assessed by regressing each forecaster's forecast error on the difference between the forecast and the common prior (where the latter is proxied by the previous month's consensus forecast). If forecasters are rational then the forecast error should be orthogonal to this difference, and the regression coefficient will be zero; if forecasters over-weight new information relative to the prior, however, then the regression coefficient will be positive. The results suggest that, although forecasters generally appear not to place too much weight on new private information, relative to the optimum, the introduction of IT is associated with forecasters significantly over-weighting new private information. One potential cause for this increased over-weighting of new information could be that forecasters are initially unsure of the time-invariant portion of the new public information that enters into the prior (e.g. the degree of commitment to the numerical inflation target), and under-weight this in their forecasts.[6]

The results from the two exercises offer apparently contradictory perspectives on the effect of IT on forecast accuracy. On the one hand, the worst forecasters appear to benefit from enhanced public information. On the other hand, there is an offsetting effect whereby all forecasters appear to increase their over-weighting of private signals. These offsetting effects may explain why the overall impact of IT adoption on forecast accuracy has generally been found to be insignificant (see, for example, Johnson 2002 and Cecchetti and Hakkio in Chapter 13 of this book). In fact, one can demonstrate that the two results in this chapter (IT leads to reduced forecast errors and to increased over-weighting of new information) and Cecchetti and Hakkio's result (IT does not lead to reduced forecast dispersion) are mutually consistent, in a world in which IT adoption *does* enhance transparency but private sector forecasters do not respond optimally.

The rest of the chapter is organised as follows. Section 14.2 outlines a simple signal extraction model with public and private information to motivate the discussion and provide some predictions. Section 14.3 describes the data used. Section 14.4 outlines the methodology, while sections 14.5 and 14.6 give the respective results for the two exercises. Section 14.7 concludes.

14.2   Theoretical framework

I motivate the empirical analysis via a simple signal extraction model. Agents (forecasters) each produce a forecast f_i of the inflation rate π. They share a common prior π_P, which includes the central bank's public signal (a combination of its public forecasts, statements and analysis, and commitment to the inflation target), and also observe their own private signal π_i.[7] Each signal is noisy:

$$
\begin{aligned}
\pi_P &= \pi + \eta \\
\pi_i &= \pi + \varepsilon_i
\end{aligned}
\tag{14.1}
$$

and the precision of the private signals and the prior are denoted, respectively, as[8]

$$
\begin{aligned}
\beta &= \frac{1}{\sigma_\varepsilon^2} \\
\alpha &= \frac{1}{\sigma_\eta^2}
\end{aligned}
\tag{14.2}
$$

As is well known, the optimal forecast weights the two signals and the prior according to their relative precision:

$$
f_i^* = \frac{\alpha \pi_P + \beta \pi_i}{\alpha + \beta}
\tag{14.3}
$$

By contrast, a forecast that differs from this honest forecast (perhaps due to strategic forecasting behaviour, or because the forecaster does not have the correct information on the signals' relative variance) has the general weights

$$
f_i = \frac{a \pi_P + b \pi_i}{a + b}
\tag{14.4}
$$

One can normalise $b = \beta$ and denote the weight on the public prior as $a = \alpha \phi$. The case in which forecasters put too much weight on private information then corresponds to $\phi < 1$.

The mean forecast error, forecast variance (dispersal of individual forecasters around the consensus) and covariance between the forecast error and the forecast update (with respect to the prior) are then given, respectively, as

$$E\left[(f_i - \pi)^2\right] = \frac{\alpha\phi^2 + \beta}{(\alpha\phi + \beta)^2}$$

$$E\left[(f_i - E\,[f_i])^2\right] = \frac{\beta}{(\alpha\phi + \beta)^2} \qquad (14.5)$$

$$E\left[(f_i - \pi)(f_i - \pi_P)\right] = \frac{\beta\,(1 - \phi)}{(\alpha\phi + \beta)^2}$$

The last covariance term gives a measure of forecast rationality: over- or under-weighting the private information ($\phi \neq 1$) creates a non-zero covariance between the forecast error and the divergence of the posterior forecast from the prior, illustrating how weighting the signals incorrectly produces an inferior forecast.

With honest (or rational or efficient) forecasts, these expressions collapse to

$$E\left[(f_i - \pi)^2\right] = \frac{1}{(\alpha + \beta)}$$

$$E\left[(f_i - E\,[f_i])^2\right] = \frac{\beta}{(\alpha + \beta)^2} \qquad (14.6)$$

$$E\left[(f_i - \pi)(f_i - \pi_P)\right] = 0$$

Hence, in this case, increasing the accuracy of the public information has the following effects:

$$\frac{\partial}{\partial\alpha}E\left[(f_i - \pi)^2\right] = -\frac{1}{(\alpha + \beta)^2} \leq 0$$

$$\frac{\partial}{\partial\alpha}E\left[(f_i - E\,[f_i])^2\right] = -\frac{2\beta}{(\alpha + \beta)^3} \leq 0 \qquad (14.7)$$

$$\frac{\partial}{\partial\alpha}E\left[(f_i - \pi)(f_i - \pi_P)\right] = 0$$

Forecast errors fall (with the effect most pronounced for those whose forecast errors were initially highest); forecasts become less dispersed; and forecasts remain fully rational.

However, consider the case in which forecasts are potentially irrational. In particular, assume that forecasts are initially rational ($\phi = 1$) but that the increase in α is offset by a reduction in ϕ, so that the weight a placed on the public prior remains unchanged.[9] This would correspond to a situation in which forecasters do not adapt their weighting of the prior and their private information to take into account the more accurate public signal, and as a result now over-weight their private signal. In this case, the impact of increasing the accuracy of the public information has rather different effects:

$$\frac{\partial}{\partial \alpha} E\left[(f_i - \pi)^2\right] = -\frac{1}{(\alpha + \beta)^2} \leq 0$$

$$\frac{\partial}{\partial \alpha} E\left[(f_i - E[f_i])^2\right] = 0 \qquad (14.8)$$

$$\frac{\partial}{\partial \alpha} E\left[(f_i - \pi)(f_i - \pi_P)\right] = \frac{\beta}{\alpha(\alpha + \beta)^2} \geq 0$$

The effect of better public information on forecast accuracy is unchanged.[10] However, better public information now has no effect on forecaster dispersal, because the negative effect under rational forecasting is driven entirely by the reweighting of the signals, which is ruled out in this case. Finally, better public information results in forecasts becoming increasingly irrational (so that forecast errors are more positively correlated with the difference between the forecast and the prior). This is because, with the increase in public signal accuracy not being recognised by the individual forecasters, they will increasingly under-weight the public signal relative to its proper weight.

In order to take this stylised model to the data, I introduce some identifying assumptions: (i) that the precision of the private signals is constant, for each forecaster i, over the time period covered in the empirical work (generally twenty-four months); and (ii) that the precision of the public prior depends, over the period, only on some country-specific factor and whether the central bank of country j has adopted inflation targeting ($IT = \{0, 1\}$):

$$\begin{aligned} \alpha_t^j &= \alpha^j(IT) \\ \beta_t^i &= \beta^i \end{aligned} \qquad (14.9)$$

As a result, the statement that IT improves transparency is equivalent to the condition that $\alpha^j(1) > \alpha^j(0)$. The forecast error for a typical forecaster in a non-IT central bank is then given by

$$\left(\tilde{V}^{ij} \mid IT = 0\right) \equiv \tilde{V}_0^{ij} = \frac{1}{(\alpha^j(0) + \beta^i)} \qquad (14.10)$$

and hence (for $\phi = 1$)

$$\frac{\partial}{\partial \alpha^j} \tilde{V}^{ij} = -\frac{1}{\left(\alpha^j(0) + \beta\right)^2} = -\left(\tilde{V}_0^{ij}\right)^2 < 0$$

$$\frac{\partial^2 \tilde{V}^{ij}}{\partial \alpha^j \partial \tilde{V}_0^{ij}} = -2\tilde{V}_0^{ij} < 0 \tag{14.11}$$

Linearising the interaction effect around $\tilde{V}_0^{ij}$ then gives the following approximation for the effect of IT on forecast errors that is taken to the data:

$$\Delta \tilde{V}^{ij} \equiv \tilde{V}_1^{ij} - \tilde{V}_0^{ij} \approx b_0 - b_1 \tilde{V}_0^{ij} - b_1 < 0 \tag{14.12}$$

To assess the effect of IT adoption on forecast rationality, I assume that the previous mean (consensus) forecast summarises all the information available to each forecaster prior to receiving his idiosyncratic private information. Hence, I regress the forecast error on the difference between the current forecast and the most recent prior consensus forecast, and test whether the introduction of IT is associated with a change in the coefficient

$$f_t^{ij}(h) - \pi_t^j = c_0 + c_1 IT_t^j + \left(c_2 + c_3 IT_t^j\right)\left(f_t^{ij}(h) - \bar{f}_t^j(h+1)\right) \tag{14.13}$$

where the forecast horizon (i.e. the number of months until the end of the forecast period) is given by h. In the data, this horizon varies between zero and twenty-three months. A positive coefficient c_2 corresponds to forecasters over-weighing their idiosyncratic private information; a positive coefficient c_3 corresponds to an increase in this over-weighting associated with the introduction of IT.

14.3   Data

I use the Consensus Economics data set, which comprises a panel of private sector current-year and next-year forecasts of several key macroeconomic variables. For this study I focus on the forecasts of inflation, since it is for inflation expectations that IT's transparency benefits are usually held to be strongest. The country coverage expands over time, from a small number of industrial countries at the end of 1989 to a large cross-section of industrial and emerging market economies by 2005. Some countries that adopted IT were not in the sample at the time of adoption (even if they later joined the sample).[11] For each country there is a panel of forecasters, whose composition changes somewhat over time as individual forecasters enter or drop out of the survey. Forecasts are monthly or, for some countries, bimonthly. For our purposes, eleven IT adoption episodes are covered by the data set: four industrial countries (Australia, Canada, Norway and the United Kingdom) and seven emerging markets (Brazil, Chile, Colombia, Mexico, Peru, South Korea and Thailand). I date the adoption of IT to a specific month and year as given by Roger and Stone (2005); this seems, for most countries, to represent a broad consensus view.[12]

For the first exercise, the next-year forecasts are most useful (Johnson 2002, who uses the same data for some of the analysis, makes the same decision: the current-year forecasts tend to vary little between forecasters, particularly towards the end of the year – for obvious reasons).[13] In order to control for composition effects and exploit within-country variation in forecaster quality (to test the interaction effect captured by the parameter b_1), I focus on individual forecasters.[14] I identify a twenty-four-month window spread equally either side of the adoption of IT: it makes sense to focus on a relatively narrow window to exploit the monthly nature of the data and identify more sharply the effect of IT.[15] For the first exercise I use the average (per forecaster) absolute forecast error (the absolute difference between the next-year inflation forecast and actual (annual) inflation next year, taken from the IMF's *International Financial Statistics*) in the before and after portions of the window as proxies for $\tilde{V}_0^{ij}$ and $\tilde{V}_1^{ij}$, respectively. The 139 forecasters for whom there are before and after data in the window around IT adoption, in the eleven countries that have adopted IT, form the treatment group. The second exercise relies on the same data sources; it uses both current-year and next-year forecasts, however, and does not aggregate forecast errors per forecaster.

14.4   Methodology

IT and forecast errors

As is well known from the treatment effect literature, evaluating the effect of a treatment (in this case IT adoption) on the treated is made difficult by the fact that it is not possible to observe the counterfactual (no treatment) for the treated group. One can infer this counterfactual from the behaviour of an untreated group, but only if the treatment is randomly assigned or if one can simulate random assignment by selecting a control group for which the probability of receiving the treatment, conditional on a set of observable variables, matches that of the treated (see Heckman, Ichimura and Todd 1998 for a detailed discussion). I use propensity score

Table 14.1 *Probit estimate of propensity score*

Dependent variable	IT
V_0^{ij}	−0.194***
	(0.0351)
$V_{0,g}^{ij}$	−0.0556*
	(0.0307)
f_0^{ij}	0.0786***
	(0.0159)
$f_{0,g}^{ij}$	0.0678**
	(0.0328)
ΔV_{-1}^{ij}	0.197***
	(0.0318)
$\Delta V_{-1,g}^{ij}$	−0.116***
	(0.0254)
Δf_{-1}^{ij}	−0.159***
	(0.0285)
$\Delta f_{-1,g}^{ij}$	0.0459
	(0.0362)
Observations	2,141
Pseudo-R^2	0.0923
LR $\chi^2(8)$	108.7***

Notes: Constant term included but not reported. Standard errors reported in parentheses. Significance levels denoted as: *** = 1 per cent; ** = 5 per cent; * = 10 per cent.

matching, a form of matching on observables, to select the control group (Rosenbaum and Rubin 1983; Leuven and Sianesi 2003; Smith and Todd 2005). The propensity score (the estimated probability of being selected into the treatment group) is calculated by running a probit regression on a selection of observable characteristics. Since the observation unit in our data set is the individual forecaster, forecasters' characteristics are used to estimate the propensity score.[16]

I use eight variables to calculate the propensity score: mean absolute forecast errors for output and inflation in the twelve-month period up to IT adoption $\{V_{0,g}^{ij}; V_0^{ij}\}$; the change in these variables from the *previous* twelve-month period to this period $\{\Delta V_{-1,g}^{ij}; \Delta V_{-1}^{ij}\}$; and similar variables for the forecast level of these variables $\{f_{0,g}^{ij}; f_0^{ij}; \Delta f_{-1,g}^{ij}; \Delta f_{-1}^{ij}\}$. Table 14.1 reports the probit regression results. The groups of control observations are drawn from the pool of forecasters in countries that did not adopt IT during the same twenty-four-month period (or the following twelve-month period) and that had not adopted IT previously.

The baseline matching method chooses the best available control with replacement (so that a single control can appear multiple times as the best match for several of the treated group). To assess the robustness of the results, two additional matching methods were also applied, yielding very similar results (details on these matching algorithms are available in Appendix 14A). Table 14.2 details the sample (including control observations) for the preferred matching method.

It is important to recognise that V^{ij}, the empirical counterpart for $\tilde{V}^{ij}$, will be contaminated by idiosyncratic time-varying shocks to forecasters' accuracy as well as by classical measurement error. If we capture these shocks by the linear error term e_t^{ij} then the empirical counterpart of equation (14.12) is given by

$$\Delta V^{ij} \equiv V_1^{ij} - V_0^{ij} = \begin{cases} b_0 - b_1^{ij} V_0^{ij} + \Delta e_t^{ij} \mid IT = 1 \\ \Delta e_t^{ij} \mid IT = 0 \end{cases} \quad (14.14)$$

Since these shocks to forecasting accuracy are idiosyncratic, the data will exhibit mean reversion. Among the worst forecasters in period 0 will be those whose forecasts in that period were of particularly poor quality, compared with their average performance, and these forecasters will naturally experience an improvement in their performance in period 1. To test equation (14.14) I therefore estimate the following regression:

$$\Delta V^{ij} = b_0 + b_{0T} D_T^{ij} - V_0^{ij} \left(b_1 + b_{1T} D_T^{ij} \right) + u^{ij} \quad (14.15)$$

where D_T is a dummy variable for the treatment (IT adoption). Due to mean reversion, V_0^{ij} is endogenous ($\text{cov}(V_0^{ij}, u^{ij}) < 0$) and the estimate of the coefficient on V_0^{ij} is therefore negatively biased. However, following Ball and Sheridan (2005), the mean reversion term $-b_1 V_0^{ij}$ should remove any bias from the estimate of the effect of IT itself (captured by the term $-b_{1T} D_T V_0^{ij}$). The model can then be tested via ordinary least squares estimation of equation (14.15).

As a robustness check, this chapter also adopts an instrumental variables approach to dealing with the endogeneity of V_0^{ij}. Potential instruments should be correlated with the fundamental component of forecaster ability but uncorrelated with the transient shocks to forecast accuracy e_0^{ij}. I identify two such instruments. The first instrument, $V_{0,g}^{ij}$, is the average absolute forecast error for GDP growth rather than inflation.[17] Assuming that idiosyncratic shocks to forecast accuracy for

Table 14.2 *Baseline sample composition*

Targeter Date	AUS 4/93	BRA 6/99	CAN 2/91	CHL 9/99	COL 9/99	KOR 1/01	MEX 1/01	NOR 3/01	PER 1/02	THA 5/00	UK 10/92	Total
Total	24	26	30	18	16	21	25	16	22	19	11	228
Treatment	13	14	19	13	10	15	17	10	11	11	6	139
Controls	11	12	11	5	6	6	8	6	11	8	5	89
Argentina		1										1
France	5	3	1					1	3	2		15
Germany	3								4	2		9
Hong Kong								1				1
India		3				2	3	1				9
Italy					1					1	1	3
Japan	3	1					1		1			6
Malaysia				2								2
Netherlands				1					1	1		3
Singapore								1				1
Spain		1										1
United States			10						2	2	4	18
Venezuela		3		2	5	4	4	2				20

Notes: Treatment and control observations shown for each of eleven IT adoption episodes. The control observations are broken down into individual countries' contribution in the last thirteen rows of the table.

inflation and GDP growth are orthogonal but that forecasters' fundamental ability is reflected in the accuracy of both forecasts, this should fulfil the relevancy and exogeneity requirements of a good instrument. The second instrument is based on the observation that higher inflation also tends to be more variable, and hence is likely to be harder to forecast. Specifically, I use the expected inflation rate for the one-year period prior to the IT adoption date, f_0^{ij}.[18] Since the treatment dummy D_T is assumed exogenous (conditional on the matching of a control group of observations with the treatment observations), suitable instruments for $D_T V_0^{ij}$ are $\{D_T V_{0,g}^{ij}, D_T f_0^{ij}\}$.

IT and forecast rationality

To assess forecast rationality, I again use individual forecast data and the same twenty-four-month window around the month of IT adoption to see how forecaster behaviour might change with the adoption of IT. However, since there are no compelling reasons *ex ante* to believe that forecaster rationality is likely to be correlated with the decision to adopt IT, matching a suitable control group of countries with the IT adoption countries is not undertaken. Rather, I use the full group of non-IT countries (within the same time window) as the control. I therefore simply estimate equation (14.16) below:

$$f_t^{ij}(h) - \pi_t^j = \left(c_0 + c_1 T_t^j\right)\left(c_2 + c_3 P_t^j\right)$$
$$+ \left(c_4 + c_5 T_t^j\right)\left(c_6 + c_7 P_t^j\right)\left(f_t^{ij}(h) - \bar{f}_t^j(h+1)\right)$$

$$(14.16)$$

where $T_t^j = \{0, 1\}$ denotes whether country j adopted IT or not and $P_t^j = \{0, 1\}$ denotes whether the observation belongs to the pre-IT adoption or post-IT adoption period. For each of the eleven IT adoption windows in the data, only the IT adoption country in question has $T_t^j = 1$, while all other non-IT countries in the data set for the same period have $T_t^j = 0$. The dummy variable P_t^j is equal to one for all countries in the twelve months following the adoption of IT in the episode in question, and zero for the preceding twelve months. Whether IT adoption has any impact on forecast rationality is therefore signalled by the value of $c_5 c_7$, the coefficient on $T_t^j P_t^j$. In particular, a positive value suggests that IT adoption increases the over-weighting of idiosyncratic private information relative to the optimum.

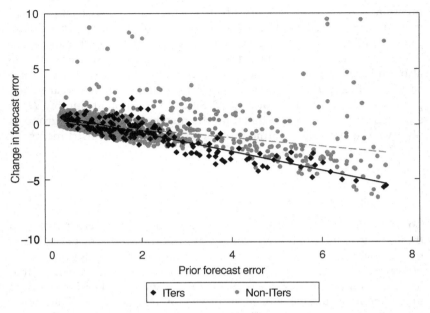

Figure 14.1 Change in forecast performance around IT adoption

Notes: Change in average absolute forecast errors between the twelve months prior to IT adoption and the subsequent twelve months plotted against the average absolute forecast error in the twelve months prior to IT adoption. The sample includes 196 forecasters in IT adoption countries and 2,048 forecasters in non-IT adoption countries. The sample imposes a common support in terms of the prior forecast error between the IT and non-IT adoption groups and has been trimmed to exclude outliers (defined as an absolute change in the forecast error in excess of 10 percentage points).

14.5   IT and forecast errors: results

Graphical results

As a first pass, Figure 14.1 plots the change in the mean absolute inflation forecast error (ΔV^{ij}) against the average prior error (V_0^{ij}) for observations from IT adoption episodes (the treated) and from the full pool of control episodes.[19] The sample of controls includes, for each of the eleven IT adoption episodes, all available forecasters in non-IT adoption countries for the period in which IT was adopted (unlike in the matching exercise below, in which each treated observation is matched with a specific control). The relationship appears to be negative for all forecasters, due to

Table 14.3 *Baseline regression results*

Model	I Levels	II OLS	III 2SLS
IT	−2.42 (1.49)	−1.91 (1.43)	−0.953 (1.12)
$V^{ij}{}_0$		−0.425*** (0.150)	−0.168 (0.259)
$IT \times V_0^{ij}$		−0.626*** (0.217)	−0.836** (0.335)
Advanced	−0.946 (1.38)	−2.77* (1.52)	−1.96* (1.14)
Constant	1.72 (1.87)	4.20** (2.00)	2.85* (1.48)
F-stat	2.34	13.5***	7.17***
R^2	0.086	0.284	0.237
Observations (weighted)	278	278	278
Identification (ID) test (*p*-value)			107.2 (0.000)
Over-ID test (*p*-value)			2.38 (0.304)
Weak ID test (critical value)			25.7 (11.0)

Notes: Standard errors (clustered by episode, country) in parentheses. Significance levels denoted as: *** = 1 per cent; ** = 5 per cent; * = 10 per cent. ID test: Kleibergen–Paap rank Wald statistic. Over-ID test: Hansen J statistic. Weak ID test: Kleibergen–Paap rank Wald F statistic. Critical value is based on 5 per cent maximal IV relative bias.

mean reversion. However, there is also strong evidence of an additional negative effect (conditional on the initial forecast error) due to IT adoption, as predicted by the model (the *p*-value for the test that the slopes are the same is 0.000).

This simple graphical analysis provides some initial evidence that IT adoption has the predicted conditional effect on forecast performance. The next subsection provides a formal econometric analysis of this effect, paying close attention to endogeneity issues.

Matching results

The results of estimating equation (14.15), presented by Crowe (2010), are replicated here in Table 14.3. Column I presents results with the interaction effect suppressed, measuring only the levels (or unconditional) effect of IT adoption on forecast errors. Column II presents estimates for the full equation using OLS; column III presents results using the IV strategy (two-stage least squares, 2SLS).[20] Since advanced as well as emerging market economies are included in the sample, a dummy for advanced countries is included in each specification.[21]

Table 14.3 provides extremely strong evidence for the conditional effect predicted by the model, but little evidence for an unconditional effect. The point estimate derived using 2SLS is higher because the IV strategy succeeds in reducing the evidence of mean reversion present in the OLS results: note that the IV estimate of b_1 is not statistically significant whereas the OLS estimate is positive and highly significant.[22]

Robustness checks

Several robustness checks were undertaken. Table 14.4 replicates the baseline results for the second and third matching algorithms detailed in Appendix 14A. Table 14.5 replicates the baseline results for two 'placebo' data sets; the first three columns use data for IT adoption countries with the adoption window shifted to be twelve months earlier than in reality, and matching controls according to this placebo data using the first algorithm.[23] There is no statistically significant evidence for a conditional or unconditional 'effect' of the placebo IT adoption variable. The last three columns present results for the same exercise shifting the adoption window back twelve months. Again, there is no evidence of an 'effect' from the placebo.

It can be noted that, since the sample size is greater than that for the genuine data in the second placebo experiment, but lower in the first placebo experiment, differences in data coverage seem unlikely to explain the difference between the genuine and the placebo regressions. Table 14.5 therefore provides strong evidence that the results in Table 14.3 are not due to chance or to country-specific factors relating to the treatment (IT adoption) group but, rather, genuinely capture the conditional effect of IT adoption on forecast errors predicted by the model.[24]

Table 14.6 provides additional robustness checks. Despite the use of propensity score matching to ensure broadly similar characteristics in treatment and control observations, the average prior forecast error is somewhat higher in the control group, reflecting a number of particularly high observations (including some that are above the maximum value for this variable in the treatment group). There is no a priori reason why this would bias the results towards finding a (spurious) conditional effect of IT, particularly as greater variation in the control data might have been expected to lead to more pronounced mean reversion for

Table 14.4 *Alternative matching algorithms*

Model	Algorithm 2			Algorithm 3		
	Levels	OLS	2SLS	Levels	OLS	2SLS
IT	−9.81	−1.36	−0.0167	−2.83*	−1.39	0.162
	(1.22)	(1.18)	(0.888)	(1.62)	(1.52)	(1.41)
V_0^{ij}		−0.548***	−0.234		−0.198	0.240
		(0.0831)	(0.213)		(0.292)	(0.533)
$IT \times V_0^{ij}$		−0.439***	−0.710***		−0.825**	−1.18**
		(0.139)	(0.248)		(0.309)	(0.513)
Advanced	0.377	−2.01	−0.900	−1.36	−2.44	−1.13
	(1.12)	(1.28)	(0.919)	(1.48)	(1.56)	(1.25)
Constant	−0.184	3.24*	1.42	2.27	3.50	1.31
	(1.54)	(1.70)	(1.27)	(2.01)	(2.14)	(1.95)
F-stat	2.26	32.3***	14.9***	2.09	12.7***	10.3***
R^2	0.020	0.300	0.227	0.132	0.228	0.138
Observations (weighted)	278	278	278	278	278	278
Clusters	57	57	57	26	26	26
ID test (*p*-value)			92.1			102.8
			(0.000)			(0.000)
Over-ID test (*p*-value)			1.49			1.62
			(0.475)			(0.445)
Weak ID test (critical value)			22.1			24.2
			(11.0)			(11.0)

Notes: Standard errors (clustered by episode, country) in parentheses. Significance levels denoted as: *** =1 per cent; ** =5 per cent; * =10 per cent. ID test: Kleibergen–Paap rank Wald statistic. Over-ID test: Hansen J statistic. Weak ID test: Kleibergen–Paap rank Wald F statistic. Critical value is based on 5 per cent maximal IV relative bias.

these observations and hence bias the results away from finding greater convergence in the treatment group. However, to ensure that this is not driving the results in Table 14.3, Table 14.6 presents results for two trimmed samples in which some potential control observations with high values for V_0^{ij} have been dropped prior to the matching process.

In the first three columns, all controls with values for V_0^{ij} above the maximum value for the treatment group (7.4) are dropped. Eliminating these controls has little substantial effect on the measured conditional effect of IT. The second three columns present results with control observations from Venezuela dropped. This country accounts for the

Table 14.5 *'Placebo' regressions*

Model	Twelve months early			Twelve months late		
	Levels	OLS	2SLS	Levels	OLS	LIML[1]
IT	−0.539	0.303	−0.840	−0.179	0.351	0.333
	(0.645)	(0.764)	(1.10)	(0.403)	(0.538)	(1.48)
V_0^{ij}		−0.066	−0.054		0.042	0.489
		(0.376)	(0.394)		(0.249)	(0.330)
$IT \times V_0^{ij}$		−0.353	0.113		−0.413	−0.330
		(0.389)	(0.382)		(0.533)	(1.24)
Advanced	0.009	−0.531	−0.012	−0.282	−0.223	0.063
	(0.553)	(0.528)	(0.685)	(0.418)	(0.500)	(0.589)
Constant	0.306	0.675	0.461	0.326	0.234	−0.523
	(0.621)	(0.893)	(0.950)	(0.373)	(0.580)	(0.784)
F-stat	0.46	1.19	0.38	0.33	0.66	0.92
R^2	0.013	0.056	0.001	0.009	0.023	
Observations (weighted)	248	248	248	350	350	350
Clusters	49	49	49	65	65	65
ID test			57.4			12.7
(*p*-value)			(0.000)			(0.005)
Over-ID test			4.66			3.81
(*p*-value)			(0.0972)			(0.149)
Weak ID test (critical value)			13.7[2] (11.0)			3.08[3] (2.99)

Notes: Standard errors (clustered by episode, country) in parentheses. Significance levels denoted as: *** = 1 per cent; ** = 5 per cent; * = 10 per cent. ID test: Kleibergen–Paap rank Wald statistic. Over-ID test: Hansen J statistic. Missing R^2: reported R^2 is negative.
[1] IV regression is estimated using limited information maximum likelihood (LIML), which gives more robust results under weak identification.
[2] Kleibergen–Paap rank Wald F statistic. Critical value is based on 5 per cent maximal IV relative bias.
[3] Kleibergen–Paap rank Lagrange Multiplier (LM) statistic. Critical value is based on 20 per cent maximal LIML size.

majority of outliers, both in terms of V_0^{ij} and the dependent variable, ΔV^{ij}. Dropping these observations has a more significant effect: in particular, the main interaction effect is no longer statistically significant when estimated via OLS, although the effect estimated via 2SLS remains statistically significant.

Table 14.7 presents results from a further robustness check, in which the IT adoption window is extended to a forty-eight-month period spread

Table 14.6 *Alternative trimmed samples*

Model	Drop if $V_0^{ij} > 7.4$			Drop Venezuela		
	Levels	OLS	LIML[1]	Levels	OLS	2SLS
IT	−0.612	0.243	3.28*	0.0857	−0.377	0.553
	(0.484)	(0.483)	(1.72)	(0.786)	(0.278)	(0.337)
V_0^{ij}		−0.355	0.851		−0.830***	−0.582***
		(0.228)	(0.641)		(0.0856)	(0.172)
$IT \times V_0^{ij}$		−0.507**	−1.57***		−0.025	−0.429**
		(0.215)	(0.546)		(0.0975)	(0.174)
Advanced	0.620	−0.432	1.65	1.36*	−0.381	−0.042
	(0.426)	(0.384)	(1.35)	(0.786)	(0.280)	(0.302)
Constant	−0.658	0.758	−3.28	−1.5	1.33***	0.600
	(0.453)	(0.632)	(2.35)	(0.964)	(0.353)	(0.411)
F-stat	2.08	76.5***	16.1***	2.51*	75.2***	51.8***
R^2	0.065	0.384		0.157	0.830	0.775
Observations (weighted)	270	270	270	248	248	248
Clusters	53	53	53	41	41	41
ID test (p-value)			11.6 (0.009)			83.9 (0.000)
Over-ID test (p-value)			468 (0.792)			2.37 (0.305)
Weak ID test (critical value)			2.78[2] (2.79)			20.0[3] (11.0)

Notes: Standard errors (clustered by episode, country) in parentheses. Significance levels denoted as: *** = 1 per cent; ** = 5 per cent; * = 10 per cent. ID test: Kleibergen–Paap rank Wald statistic. Over-ID test: Hansen J statistic. Missing R^2: reported R^2 is negative.
[1] IV regression is estimated using LIML, which gives more robust results under weak identification.
[2] Kleibergen–Paap rank LM statistic. Critical value is based on 25 per cent maximal LIML size.
[3] Kleibergen–Paap rank Wald F statistic. Critical value is based on 5 per cent maximal IV relative bias.

symmetrically around the month of IT adoption.[25] Despite the longer window, the results remain qualitatively unchanged.

14.6 IT adoption and forecast rationality: results

As described in section 14.4, the rationality of the individual forecasters is assessed by regressing the forecast error on the difference between the forecast and the prior (the forecast update), where the latter is

Table 14.7 *Extended window*

Model	I Levels	II OLS	III 2SLS
IT	−0.618	−0.081	1.04
	(0.459)	(0.566)	(0.662)
V_0^{ij}		−0.273***	−1.63**
		(0.0886)	(0.0823)
$IT \times V_0^{ij}$		−0.517***	−0.937***
		(0.194)	(0.257)
Advanced	0.730*	−0.695	−0.556
	(0.434)	(0.606)	(0.622)
Constant	−0.578	1.18	0.703
	(0.460)	(0.762)	(0.683)
F-stat	3.53**	6.66***	7.56***
R^2	0.044	0.229	0.188
Observations (weighted)	262	262	262
Clusters	51	51	51
ID test (p-value)			66.9
			(0.000)
Over-ID test (p-value)			1.80
			(0.401)
Weak ID test (critical value)			16.0
			(11.0)

Notes: Standard errors (clustered by episode, country) in parentheses. Significance levels denoted as: *** =1 per cent; ** =5 per cent; * =10 per cent. ID test: Kleibergen–Paap rank Wald statistic. Over-ID test: Hansen J statistic. Weak ID test: Kleibergen–Paap rank Wald F statistic. Critical value is based on 5 per cent maximal IV relative bias.

proxied by the most recent prior consensus (mean) forecast, as in equation (14.16). To provide some initial evidence, Table 14.8 presents simple bivariate correlations between the forecast error and the forecast update, for four subsets of the data: forecasts for the non-IT adoption countries in the twelve-month period prior to the adoption of IT in the episode in question and for the twelve-month period following the adoption of IT in that episode, and for the IT adoption country in the episode in question over the same two sub-periods, pooled across the eleven episodes. The sample is trimmed to include only observations with absolute forecast errors of 5 p.p. or fewer.[26] These initial results suggest that, while the forecasts were approximately rational in non-IT adoption countries and (to a lesser extent) in IT adoption countries prior to the adoption of IT,

Table 14.8 *Rationality correlations*

		IT	
		0	1
After	0	0.046	0.271
	1	0.100	0.518

Notes: This table presents correlation coefficients between forecast errors (forecast minus actual) and forecast updates (forecast minus prior, with the latter proxied by the previous consensus forecast) for the IT adoption episodes described in the text ('IT' = 1 identifies the IT adoption countries; 'After' = 1 identifies the twelve months after the adoption of IT in each episode). Observations with forecast errors > 5 have been dropped.

the forecasts exhibit evidence of significantly increased over-weighting of idiosyncratic private information following the adoption of IT.

Table 14.9 then presents regression results. The first two specifications regress forecast errors on forecast updates in the pre- and post-IT adoption periods for the non-IT and IT adoption groups, respectively.[27] These results confirm those in Table 14.8: there is no significant evidence of correlation in either period in the non-IT adoption countries and only a relatively low correlation in the IT adoption countries prior to the adoption of IT; there is, however, evidence of a significantly increased positive correlation in the latter group after the adoption of IT. The third column provides evidence that this differential effect is significant. The last two columns provide robustness checks, based on alternative trimming criteria. The results remain statistically significant.

14.7   Conclusions

The issue of transparency has become central to discussions of central bank governance in academia and among policymakers. The consensus view of IT as a monetary policy framework is that it delivers enhanced transparency as a significant benefit. This is ultimately an empirical question, however, and little empirical work has, up to now, been conducted on the issue. This chapter outlines a simple signal extraction model for analysing these issues and derives a testable proposition: if IT enhances transparency in the manner assumed in the model then its introduction should promote convergence to lower forecast errors. In other words, forecast errors should decline under IT, proportionately to the

Table 14.9 *Forecast rationality tests*

Sample	(1) Non-IT	(2) IT	(3) Combined	(4) Small errors	(5) Large errors
Forecast update	0.034 (0.022)	0.369** (0.130)	0.034 (0.022)	0.022** (0.010)	0.032 (0.035)
'IT' × forecast update			0.335*** (0.126)	0.188* (0.104)	0.482*** (0.096)
'After' × forecast update	0.095** (0.039)	0.460*** (0.091)	0.095** (0.039)	0.065*** (0.020)	0.043 (0.074)
'IT' × 'after' × forecast update			0.365*** (0.095)	0.234** (0.094)	0.275*** (0.094)
'IT'			0.690*** (0.243)	0.586** (0.277)	0.613** (0.300)
'After'	0.057 (0.065)	−0.397 (0.233)	0.057 (0.065)	0.098** (0.049)	0.032 (0.086)
'IT' × 'After'			−0.454* (0.232)	−0.312 (0.252)	−0.404 (0.266)
Constant	0.402*** (0.073)	1.092*** (0.243)	0.402*** (0.073)	0.110** (0.048)	0.455*** (0.102)
Observations	104,128	6,594	110,722	93,965	116,613
R^2	0.006	0.194	0.020	0.022	0.008

Notes: Standard errors (clustered by country and episode) in parentheses. The observational unit is the individual forecast (for a particular country, year and forecast horizon). Observations with absolute forecast errors in excess of 5 p.p. have been dropped, except for specification (4), (absolute errors in excess of 2 p.p. dropped) and specification (5) (absolute errors in excess of 10 p.p. dropped).

forecasters' initial errors. This conditional result, derived from a microfounded model of rational forecasters, is the correct prediction to take to the data.

I test this proposition using matched difference-in-differences, identifying a window around the adoption of IT in eleven countries and matching forecasters in these countries with their counterparts in similar countries that did not adopt IT, via three different propensity-score-matching strategies. I find that convergence occurs in all countries, due to mean reversion, but that the adoption of IT leads to greater convergence, as predicted by the model. This effect is largely robust to dropping subsets of controls. Moreover, the effect is absent when placebo regressions (with the timing of IT adoption shifted by a year before or after the genuine date) are run. Finally, I am able to eliminate (non-IT-specific) mean reversion by instrumenting for the initial forecast accuracy. However, the estimated conditional effect of IT adoption is not eliminated by adopting this IV strategy: if anything, it is strengthened. I interpret these results as strong evidence that IT does indeed enhance transparency.

The significant conditional effect of IT $(-b_{1T} < 0)$ is in the spirit of Morris and Shin's (2002) argument that better public information is most beneficial for private forecasters whose own information is bad. However, the levels effect b_{0T} is not significantly different from zero (when the interaction effect is included). Hence there is no evidence that IT adoption can lead to higher forecast errors, even for the very best forecasters with initial forecast errors already close to zero. Assuming that IT increases transparency, this finding goes against Morris and Shin's argument that better public information can make private forecasts less accurate, or at least suggests that the rather special conditions – e.g. restrictions on parameter values – necessary for this case to hold are absent for the forecasters in my sample.

This chapter also assesses the impact of IT adoption on forecaster rationality. In other words, does the introduction of IT lead to forecasters making better or worse use of the combined information available to them publicly and privately? While there is no evidence that forecasters in general overreact to new private signals and put too little weight on the public prior (including the central bank's public information), this underweighting of the public information emerges significantly in countries that adopt IT.

One interpretation of this result is that forecasters simply do not recognise the increase in the accuracy of public information that has taken place. Nevertheless, they still benefit from the more accurate signal (and as a result their forecast errors decline). This would explain why Cecchetti and Hakkio (Chapter 13 in this volume) fail to find any consistent impact of IT adoption on forecast dispersal. In countries in which IT adoption increases the accuracy of public information – but forecasters do not take this into account – then there will be no impact on forecast dispersal, whereas forecast irrationality and forecast accuracy will both increase (as is found in this chapter).

Further research could use the same data set and techniques to test whether IT enhances transparency with respect to other variables. A second area of further research is in establishing the dimensions of transparency associated with IT that could account for the apparent effect on forecasters' accuracy. Crowe and Meade (2008) provide some evidence that aspects of transparency associated with the central bank's openness concerning its own data and forecasts (economic and operational transparency) tend to be most strongly associated with the private sector making greater use of public information rather than private signals. However, further work is needed to establish whether these results hold in the specific case of IT adoption. Finally, it would be interesting to investigate in more detail why it is that forecasters in some cases do not appear to react rationally to changes in public signal precision, and whether other elements of central banks' communication strategy can help in this regard.

Appendix 14A   Matching algorithms

For a general discussion of propensity score matching, including a comparison of matching with and without replacement, see Smith and Todd (2005). For all three matching algorithms, the first stage is to estimate the propensity score (*ps*). The relevant sample is drawn, for the eleven IT adoption episodes for which we have data, from (i) the country that adopted IT in the particular episode (the treatment observations) and (ii) all other countries in the data set that did not adopt IT during the twenty-four-month window defining the episode or the subsequent twelve-month period and had not adopted IT prior to this episode (the pool of potential controls). *ps* is then estimated by running a probit regression with the eight right-hand-side variables described in section 14.4 and taking the fitted probability. The total number of observations used to estimate *ps* is 2,141 (see Table 14.1). Matching is undertaken in Stata using the psmatch2 command (Leuven and Sianesi 2003). In all cases (except for the second step in the third algorithm) a common support in terms of *ps* is required (treatment observations with a *ps* value outside the support of *ps* in the control group are dropped).

Algorithm 1: nearest neighbour matching (with replacement)

Observations are ordered randomly. For each treatment observation, the nearest neighbour (the one with least absolute distance in terms of *ps*) drawn from within the same episode group is chosen as the control observation (if there is a tie, the first available observation is chosen). Matching is undertaken with replacement, so that some controls appear as repeated observations in the data set (weighted according to frequency to give an effective data set size of 278).

Algorithm 2: one-to-one matching (without replacement)

As with algorithm 1, except that matching is now undertaken without replacement, so that there is a unique correspondence between the 139 control and 139 treatment observations (once a match has been made, the control observation is removed from the pool of potential controls before the match for the next treatment observation is sought).

Algorithm 3: nearest neighbour matching (with replacement) from the best available country or countries only

Step 1 replicates algorithm 1.

Step 2: pick the best country as that with the highest number of (frequency-weighted) matches in step 1. If there is a tie (as for one

episode in our data), pick both countries. Now repeat the matching algorithm (again, matching with replacement according to *ps*), using only
forecasters from these best countries as the pool of potential controls.

NOTES

1. This work reflects the views of the author alone and does not reflect the
   views of the IMF, its executive board or management. The author would
   like to thank, subject to the usual caveats, the editors of this volume, Petra
   Geraats, Paolo Mauro, Ellen Meade, Scott Roger, Philip Schellekens, Hyun
   Shin and participants at seminars at American University, the IMF and the
   Bank of England, the Royal Economic Society's 2008 annual conference and
   the Sixth Norges Bank Monetary Policy Conference for comments on earlier
   drafts, and Martin Minnoni for excellent research assistance.
2. The theoretical literature on the potential benefits of enhanced central bank
   transparency has, over time, shifted in favour of more transparency, as the
   potential upside from opacity (the ability to deliver monetary surprises) has
   been downplayed and the long-term credibility gains of more transparent
   policymaking have become more salient (see Geraats 2002 and Carpenter
   2004). Morris and Shin (2002) dissent from the emerging consensus, however, arguing that if the private sector attempts to second-guess itself in the
   manner of Keynes' (1936) beauty contest then public information, acting
   as a focal point for beliefs about beliefs, can crowd out high-quality private information and make private sector forecasts more variable, not less.
   Svensson (2006) shows that this result relies on unlikely parameter values;
   in the more general case, the central bank can publish and not be damned.
   Ottaviani and Sørensen (2006) provide a further discussion of the impact
   of strategic forecasting behaviour.
3. The studies cited here focus on transparency-related questions. Others have
   investigated the behaviour of inflation under IT more generally (Kuttner and
   Posen 1999; Petursson 2004; Ball and Sheridan, 2005; Vega and Winkelried
   2005, Lin and Ye 2007) with mixed results.
4. The transparency measure is derived from self-reported information on central bank governance in a wide-ranging survey of central banks (Fry *et al.*
   2000); to this extent it may be less contaminated by tautological reasoning than the transparency indexes employed elsewhere (although additional
   biases may arise from using survey data).
5. See note 2.
6. A second potential cause is that private sector forecasters' incentives to forecast strategically – e.g. to place too much weight on private information in
   order to differentiate their forecast from others' – may be enhanced by IT
   adoption. For instance, with the introduction of a formal inflation target,
   forecasters may perceive that correctly predicting significant deviations from
   target is more important than the overall accuracy of the forecast.
7. The central bank's public information will also typically include a time-
   varying component. However, because a key piece of information under IT
   is the (typically time-invariant) inflation target and because other pieces of

information (e.g. forecasts) are released at relatively long frequencies (e.g. quarterly), assuming that all the public information is subsumed in the prior for a particular time period seems a reasonable approximation to reality.

8. Romer and Romer (2000) analyse whether central bank forecasts (specifically, the Federal Reserve's forecasts, which are published only with a five-year lag) are actually superior to the professional forecasts of the private sector, and they find persuasive evidence that this is the case ($\alpha > \beta$). In fact, the Fed's unpublished forecasts are so good that if the private sector forecasters had access to them they would place no weight on their own forecasts. This is not to say that private sector forecasts are themselves bad: Ang, Bekaert and Wei (2007) find that, in the United States, inflation forecasts from surveys (by both professional and non-professional forecasters) are better predictors of future inflation than model-based forecasts or implied forward inflation from financial market data.

9. The assumption that $\phi = 1$ initially is not necessary for the results; it does simplify the expressions, however. It is also plausible that forecasts are, in general, close to rational.

10. This is an application of the envelope theorem and relies on the assumption that $\phi = 1$. However, with more general assumptions about initial forecaster irrationality the effect remains negative.

11. These include the Czech Republic, Hungary, New Zealand, Poland and Sweden.

12. The dating is extremely clear for some countries; for others there is some controversy as to the precise month that IT was adopted, particularly when a 'soft' version of IT is adopted prior to the adoption of 'fully fledged' IT.

13. The forecasts, although they are collected monthly or bimonthly, refer to calendar years rather than a twelve-month-ahead moving window. As an example, the next-year forecasts from January 1991 through to December 1991 are all for the same twelve-month period ending in December 1992.

14. Forecasters are identified in the survey by their name: there are some minor name changes (some genuine, some apparently due to spelling errors), which complicate attempts to match observations correctly to each individual forecaster. I attempt to overcome this via an algorithm that identifies individual forecasters.

15. Transparency benefits are likely to occur relatively quickly, compared with credibility benefits or effects on actual variables. Annual data may be too coarse to pick up any effects; this could help to explain Johnson's (2002) negative findings. As a robustness check, I extend the window to two years either side of the adoption of IT.

16. As an additional robustness check, I match on country rather than forecaster characteristics (real GDP per capita, trade openness, inflation, GDP growth, exchange rate regime, democracy score and a dummy for industrialised countries). The result is that $-b_{1T} < 0$ is robust to this matching technique. However, only four countries (Argentina, Italy, Japan and the United States) enter into the control group in this exercise.

17. Actual (next-year) GDP growth data are taken from IFS. Some gaps in the data are filled in using data from the IMF's *World Economic Outlook* database. As with the inflation data, final (revised) data for actual growth are used; unrevised (real-time) growth data might be preferable, but since the focus of this chapter is on forecasts of inflation (for which revisions are not a significant issue) this second-best approach is unlikely to have a significant impact on the results.

18. Using expected rather than actual inflation eliminates the impact of unexpected inflationary shocks that are likely to be correlated with the transient component of forecast errors. Since shocks to forecast accuracy should, at least in theory, lead forecasters to over- and underestimate inflation with equal probability, f_0^{ij} should not be correlated with e_0^{ij}.

19. A common support for V_0 is imposed for IT and non-IT adoption episodes. In addition, outliers (defined as those with an absolute change in the inflation forecast error $|\Delta V|$ in excess of 10 per cent) are also dropped. The sample includes 196 observations from IT adoption episodes and 2,048 observations from control episodes. The results are similar if the sample is not truncated to exclude outliers.

20. Bertrand, Duflo and Mullainathan (2004) show that clustering the residuals (allowing arbitrary patterns of correlations within groups) is a simple and effective means of avoiding the problem of overstating the significance level attached to estimated treatment effects that tends to occur when difference-in-difference estimators ignore within-group correlation. Since the observations from the same group (defined over episode and country) are based on forecasts of the same variable, one would expect significant within-group correlation in the current study. All results therefore report clustered standard errors, with forty-nine clusters in the baseline sample. Non-clustered standard error estimates (assuming either *iid* errors or robust estimates) are much lower, as one would expect.

21. For the purposes of this chapter, the advanced countries in the data set are Australia, Canada, France, Germany, Italy, Japan, the Netherlands, Norway, Spain, Switzerland, the United Kingdom and the United States.

22. The IV estimates (with clustered residuals) were undertaken using the ivreg2 Stata program (Baum, Schaffer and Stillman, 2007) and pass tests for instrument relevance (using the Kleibergen and Paap 2006 rank Wald statistic, which generalises the Anderson canonical correlations test statistic for clustered standard errors) and exogeneity (Hansen's J statistic used for the Hansen–Sargan over-identification test). They also pass tests for weak identification based on 2SLS bias and size (the reported Kleibergen–Paap rank Wald F statistic is a generalisation of Stock and Yogo's tests for weak instruments; see Stock, Wright and Yogo 2002 and Stock and Yogo 2002). Test statistics and associated *p*-values or critical values are shown at the bottom of Table 14.3.

23. Note that the first adoption episode (Canada) drops out of the sample because of data constraints.

24. The results from the second placebo exercise additionally suggest that IT adoption involves a one-time transparency gain rather than a gradual process

that delivers additional gains in the period following IT adoption. This also provides some backing for the idea that the effect identified in the data derives from increased transparency rather than credibility, since the latter is likely to accrue over time whereas the former could be instantaneous.

25. Note that, as with the first placebo exercise, the first IT adoption episode in the sample (Canada) is dropped due to data constraints.

26. This corresponds, approximately, to a sample trimmed at around the fifth and ninety-fifth percentiles. A similar pattern is observed with the sample trimmed at an absolute forecast error of 10 p.p. Trimming the sample is necessary to avoid a few outlying control observations (absolute forecast errors in excess of 100 per cent) from dominating the sample. These outliers do not correspond to the kind of forecast errors observed during the adoption of IT, and are not therefore useful controls to include in the sample. In some cases they may also represent coding errors.

27. All the results report standard errors clustered at the country/episode level. In addition, unless otherwise specified, all samples are trimmed to exclude absolute forecast errors in excess of 5 p.p.

REFERENCES

Ang, A., G. Bekaert and M. Wei (2007). 'Do macro variables, asset markets or surveys forecast inflation better?', *Journal of Monetary Economics*, 54(4): 1163–212.

Ball, L., and N. Sheridan (2005). 'Does inflation targeting matter?', in B. Bernanke and M. Woodford (eds.). *The Inflation-Targeting Debate*: 249–82. Chicago: University of Chicago Press.

Batchelor, R., and P. Dua (1991). 'Blue chip rationality tests', *Journal of Money, Credit and Banking*, 23(4): 692–705.

Baum, C., M. Schaffer and S. Stillman (2007). 'Ivreg2: Stata module for extended instrumental variables/2SLS, GMM and AC/HAC, LIML and k-class regression'. Available at http://ideas.repec.org/c/boc/bocode/s425401.html.

Berg, C. (2005). 'Experience of inflation-targeting in 20 countries', *Sveriges Riksbank Economic Review*, 1: 20–47.

Bernanke, B., T. Laubach, F. Mishkin and A. Posen (1999). *Inflation Targeting: Lessons from the International Experience*. Princeton, NJ: Princeton University Press.

Bertrand, M., E. Duflo and S. Mullainathan (2004). 'How much should we trust differences-in-differences estimates?', *Quarterly Journal of Economics*, 119(1): 249–75.

Carpenter, S. (2004). 'Transparency and monetary policy: what does the academic literature tell policymakers?'. Finance and Economics Discussion Paper no. 2004–35. Washington, DC. Federal Reserve.

Chortareas, G., D. Stasavage and G. Sterne (2002). 'Does it pay to be transparent? International evidence from central bank forecasts', *Federal Reserve Bank of St. Louis Review*, 84(4): 99–118.

(2003). 'Does monetary policy transparency reduce disinflation costs?', *The Manchester School*, 71(5): 521–40.

Corbo, V., O. Landerretche and K. Schmidt-Hebbel (2001). 'Assessing inflation targeting after a decade of world experience', *International Journal of Finance and Economics*, 6(4): 343–68.

Crowe, C. (2010). 'Testing the transparency benefits of inflation targeting: evidence from private sector forecasts', *Journal of Monetary Economics*, 57(2): 226–32.

Crowe, C., and E. Meade (2007). 'Evolution of central bank governance around the world', *Journal of Economic Perspectives*, 21(4): 69–90.

(2008). 'Central bank independence and transparency: evolution and effectiveness', *European Journal of Political Economy*, 24(4): 763–77.

Eijffinger, S., and P. Geraats (2006). 'How transparent are central banks?', *European Journal of Political Economy*, 22(1): 1–21.

Faust, J., and D. Henderson (2004). 'Is inflation targeting best-practice monetary policy?', *Federal Reserve Bank of St. Louis Review*, 86(4): 117–44.

Fry, M., D. Julius, L. Mahadeva, S. Roger and G. Sterne (2000). 'Key issues in the choice of monetary policy framework', in L. Mahadeva and G. Sterne (eds.). *Monetary Policy Frameworks in a Global Context*: 1–216. London: Routledge.

Geraats, P. (2002). 'Central bank transparency', *Economic Journal*, 112: 532–65.

Gürkaynak, R., A. Levin and E. Swanson (2006). 'Does inflation targeting anchor long-run inflation expectations? Evidence from long-term bond yields in the US, UK and Sweden'. Working Paper no. 2006–09. San Francisco: Federal Reserve Bank of San Francisco.

Heckman, J., H. Ichimura and E. Todd (1998). 'Matching as an econometric evaluation estimator', *Review of Economic Studies*, 65(2): 261–94.

Johnson, D. (2002). 'The effect of inflation targeting on the behaviour of expected inflation: evidence from an 11 country panel', *Journal of Monetary Economics*, 49(8): 1521–38.

Keynes, J. (1936). *The General Theory of Employment, Interest and Money*. London: Macmillan.

King, M. (1997). 'The inflation target five years on', *Bank of England Quarterly Bulletin*, 37(4): 434–42.

Kleibergen, F., and R. Paap (2006). 'Generalized reduced rank tests using the singular value decomposition', *Journal of Econometrics*, 133(1): 97–126.

Kuttner, K., and A. Posen (1999). 'Does talk matter after all? Inflation targeting and central bank Behavior'. Staff Report no. 88. New York: Federal Reserve Bank of New York.

Leuven, E., and B. Sianesi (2003). 'PSMATCH2: Stata module to perform full Mahalanobis and propensity score matching, common support graphing, and covariate imbalance testing'. Available at http://ideas.repec.org/c/boc/bocode/s432001.html.

Lin, S., and H. Ye (2007). 'Does inflation targeting really make a difference? Evaluating the treatment effect of inflation targeting in seven industrial countries', *Journal of Monetary Economics*, 54(8): 2521–33.

Loungani, P. (2001). 'How accurate are private sector forecasts? Cross-country evidence from consensus forecasts of output growth', *International Journal of Forecasting*, 17(3): 419–32.

Mishkin, F., and K. Schmidt-Hebbel (2001). 'One decade of inflation targeting in the world: what do we know and what do we need to know?'. Working Paper no. 8397. Cambridge, MA: NBER.

Morris, S., and H. Shin (2002). 'Social value of public information', *American Economic Review*, 92(5): 1521–34.

Ottavianni, M., and P. Sørensen (2006). 'The strategy of professional forecasting', *Journal of Financial Economics*, 81(2): 441–66.

Petursson, T. (2004). 'The effects of inflation targeting on macroeconomic performance'. Working Paper no. 23. Reykjavík: Central Bank of Iceland.

Roger, S., and M. Stone (2005). 'On target? The international experience with achieving inflation targets'. Working Paper no. 05/163. Washington, DC: IMF.

Romer, C., and D. Romer (2000). 'Federal Reserve information and the behaviour of interest rates', *American Economic Review*, 90(3): 429–57.

Rosenbaum, R., and B. Rubin (1983). 'The central role of the propensity score in observational studies for causal effects', *Biometrika*, 70(1): 41–55.

Smith, J., and P. Todd (2005). 'Does matching address Lalonde's critique of nonexperimental estimators?', *Journal of Econometrics*, 125(2): 305–53.

Stock, J., J. Wright and M. Yogo (2002). 'A survey of weak instruments and weak identification in generalized method of moments', *Journal of Business and Economic Statistics*, 20(4): 518–29.

Stock, J., and M. Yogo (2002). 'Testing for weak instruments in linear IV regression.' Technical Working Paper no. 284. Cambridge, MA: NBER.

Svensson, L. (1999). 'Inflation targeting as a monetary policy rule', *Journal of Monetary Economics*, 43(3): 607–54.

(2006). 'Social value of public information: Morris and Shin (2002) is actually pro-transparency, not con', *American Economic Review*, 96(1): 448–51.

Swanson, E. (2004). 'Federal Reserve transparency and financial market forecasts of short-term interest rates'. Finance and Economics. Discussion Paper no. 2004–6. Washington, DC: Federal Reserve.

Swidler, S., and D. Ketcher (1990). 'Economic forecasts, rationality, and the processing of new information over time', *Journal of Money, Credit and Banking*, 22(1): 65–76.

Vega, M., and D. Winkelried (2005). 'Inflation targeting and inflation behaviour: a successful story?', *International Journal of Central Banking*, 1(3): 153–75.

15 Gauging the effectiveness of quantitative forward guidance: evidence from three inflation targeters

Magnus Andersson and Boris Hofmann[1]

15.1 Introduction

Over the past decade central banks around the world have gradually moved towards establishing more transparency in their conduct of monetary policy (see Dincer and Eichengreen 2007 and Geraats 2009). In particular, increasing emphasis is being given to effective communication of the prospective future course of monetary policy. The standard practice among central banks is to provide forward guidance via a projection or forecast of their goal variables (mainly inflation and real GDP growth) and other standard channels, such as press conferences, statements and speeches. A few inflation-targeting central banks have gone one step further and give quantitative forward guidance by publishing their own projection or forecast of the future path of policy rates. This practice is currently pursued by four inflation targeters: the Reserve Bank of New Zealand (since 1997), Norges Bank (since 2005),[2] the Swedish Riksbank (since 2007) and the Czech National Bank (since 2008). The vast majority of central banks, in particular the leading non-inflation-targeting central banks, the Federal Reserve, the ECB and the Bank of Japan, but also the Bank of England as one of the leading inflation-targeting central banks,[3] have so far decided against publishing their own interest rate path.

From a theoretical point of view, the main argument brought up in favour of the central bank publishing its own interest rate path is that it would enhance the central bank's ability to manage expectations and thereby facilitate the transmission of monetary policy (Woodford 2005; Svensson 2006, 2009; Rudebusch and Williams 2008). This is also the primary perceived advantage of publishing their own interest rate path from the perspective of central banks that have adopted this tool (Gjedrem 2006; Rosenberg 2007). More specifically, it is held that, by publishing its own interest rate path, a central bank can in principle steer expectations and thereby enhance the effectiveness of monetary policy in a number of ways.

1. By steering market expectations of near-term policy rate decisions, the publication of its own interest rate path by the central bank can enhance the predictability of monetary policy – i.e. helping to avoid policy surprises, and thereby reducing financial market volatility.
2. Publishing a policy rate path may help to signal the central bank's commitment to maintain price stability, and thus lead to a better anchoring of long-term inflation expectations.
3. Announcing a policy path may enhance the central bank's leverage over medium- and longer-term interest rates by enabling it not only to change the current level of policy rates, but also to signal quantitatively changes in the prospective future path of policy rates.

These are, in principle, testable hypotheses. Hypothesis 1 implies that monetary policy surprises – i.e. the deviations between the prior market expectation and the outcome of a policy rate decision – are on average smaller when the central bank publishes an interest rate path. Hypothesis 2 should imply lower responsiveness on the part of longer-term interest rates to incoming macroeconomic news and monetary policy surprises. Finally, hypothesis 3 would imply that the central bank can have a stronger influence on medium- and longer-term yields by being able to shape quantitatively market expectations of the future path of policy rates.

The bulk of the empirical literature on the effects of central bank transparency and communication on monetary policy effectiveness is focused on the world's leading central banks, and only a very few studies address the implications of the publication of the central bank's own interest rate path (for a recent survey, see Blinder *et al.* 2008). For reasons of sample length, these studies exclusively focus on the Reserve Bank of New Zealand and Norges Bank.[4] Some of these studies have also touched upon the issues examined in this chapter, namely quantitative forward guidance and the effect on (i) predictability, (ii) the anchoring of long-term inflation expectations and (iii) potential leverage on the term structure of interest rates. Regarding the effects of quantitative forward guidance on predictability, there is some evidence suggesting that publication of an interest rate path reduces the volatility of short-term interest rates, implying that it may have enhanced predictability (Holmsen *et al.* 2008; Ferrero and Secchi 2009).[5] Concerning the anchoring of inflation expectations, there is only one study on New Zealand (Drew and Karagedikli 2008), which finds that the impact of monetary policy surprises diminishes at longer horizons, which is interpreted as implying that inflation expectations are well anchored. However, it remains open what role the publication of an interest rates path plays in this result.[6]

A number of studies have explored the implications of the RBNZ's quantitative forward guidance on monetary policy leverage over short- to medium-term market interest rates (Archer 2005; Moessner and Nelson 2008; Ferrero and Secchi 2009). The results suggest that the RBNZ's policy path surprises have a positive but weak effect on market interest rates. This evidence is not informative with regard to the question of whether the release of an interest rate path enhances a central bank's leverage over market interest rates, however, as such an assessment would require a comparison with other central banks that do not publish such a path.

This brief review of the existing empirical literature reveals that the incremental impact of central banks publishing their own interest rate path on the three different aspects of policy effectiveness highlighted above has so far not been addressed in a consistent manner. The contribution of this study is to fill this gap by developing a comparative approach for testing all three of the above hypotheses, based on a consistent analytical framework. The main challenge in this regard is to design appropriate comparisons in order to be able to assess the incremental effect of communicating policy intentions by means of an interest rate path. One possible way is to compare two central banks that operate under similar monetary policy frameworks but differ in the sense that one of them publishes a policy rate path and the other does not. Another possible way is to compare the performance of one central bank over two different periods in which the policy framework was similar except that a policy rate path was published in one period but not in the other.

In the following we perform both types of comparison. First, a comparative analysis is conducted for the RBNZ and the Swedish Riksbank over the period from March 1999 (when the RBNZ switched from a framework in which it targeted a monetary conditions index to an operational framework centred on steering the overnight cash rate) to February 2007 (when the Riksbank first published its own interest rate path). Over this sample period the RBNZ regularly published an own interest rate forecast, while the Riksbank published an inflation forecast but not an interest rate forecast. Otherwise, both central banks operated under fairly similar conditions and policy frameworks: both operate in a small open economy environment and have policy frameworks characterised by direct inflation targeting[7] and a high degree of transparency,[8] and their forecasts are released (via their regular publications) on days when monetary policy decisions are also taken. The latter is important for our analysis of hypothesis 3, as we explain in more detail below. The lack of coincidence of the forecast release and monetary policy decisions is also the reason why other leading inflation-targeting central banks, most notably the Bank of England, are excluded from the analysis.

Second, we also perform a comparative analysis for Norges Bank over two different periods, covering the periods from March 2001 to October 2005 and from November 2005 to June 2007. The start and end points of the two samples are determined by Norges Bank's switch from exchange rate to inflation targeting in March 2001,[9] the first publication of its own policy rate forecast (in addition to the inflation forecast) in November 2005 and the outbreak of the global financial turmoil in June 2007. As described in more detail below, we derive monetary policy surprises from money market interest rates. Since the financial market turmoil led to an unprecedented increase in the level and the volatility of risk premia in money market rates from July 2007, these rates became an unreliable gauge of market expectations of future policy rates.

The empirical analysis of the chapter is based on daily data and focuses on monetary policy 'news' or 'surprises' – i.e. the unexpected part of an announced change in the monetary policy stance. The focus on the surprise components is motivated by the insight that financial asset prices are forward-looking and should therefore respond only to unexpected monetary policy (or any other macroeconomic) announcements. Following Gürkaynak, Sack and Swanson (2007), two types of monetary policy surprises are identified: target and path surprises. The former quantifies the extent to which market participants have been able to anticipate the actual outcome of an interest rate decision (based on the change in short-term interest rates surrounding the policy decision) whereas the path surprise gauges the surprise component embedded in the forward-looking guidance (derived from one-year-ahead implied forward rates).

After deriving target and path surprises, we move on to test our three hypotheses. Hypothesis 1 is assessed on the basis of straightforward descriptive analysis. To this end, we compare the magnitude of target and path surprises across the three economies. Hypothesis 2, the anchoring of yield curves, is tested by estimating the effect of monetary policy surprises as well as of a number of key pieces of domestic and global (i.e. US and euro area) macroeconomic news on long-term government bond yields across three maturities: five- and ten-year spot yields and the five-year forward rates expected to prevail in five years' time. Hypothesis 3, concerning the extent to which the announcement of a policy path enhances the central bank's leverage over longer-term interest rates, is tested by examining whether or not the medium- and long-term yield effect of path surprises is stronger on the days when the central bank publishes its interest rate path forecast. This part of the analysis benefits from the fact that all three central banks under investigation pursue the practice of releasing their forward guidance – i.e. their inflation or monetary policy reports with their forecasts – on days when monetary policy decisions are also taken.

The main findings of the study are the following. First, we find that all three central banks have been highly predictable in their monetary policy decisions and that long-term inflation expectations have been well anchored in the three economies, irrespective of whether forward guidance involved the central bank publishing its own interest rate path or not. The first comparative analysis reveals that monetary policy surprises are found to be of similar magnitude for both the RBNZ and the Riksbank, and that there is no evidence that long-term yields are better anchored in New Zealand than in Sweden. The sub-sample analysis for Norges Bank reveals that policy surprises have become smaller since November 2005, when Norges Bank started to publish an interest rate path. This latter period was also characterised by very low volatility in the global economy and financial markets in general, however, which might also have contributed to lower policy surprises. Regarding long-term inflation expectations in Norway, there is no evidence that they have been better anchored since November 2005 than beforehand. These findings suggest that, if the central bank already operates under a monetary policy framework characterised by a clearly defined price stability objective and a high degree of transparency, the publication of an interest rate path does not appear to enhance the short-term predictability of monetary policy or the anchoring of long-term inflation expectations.

The second main finding, obtained from the comparison between the RBNZ and the Riksbank, is that the publication of an interest rate path appears to increase the sensitivity of medium-term bond yields to forward-looking monetary policy news and to reduce the sensitivity of bond yields to news about the current policy stance. In New Zealand, five-year bond yields are found to respond more weakly to the target surprise and substantially more strongly to the forward-looking path surprise on the days when the RBNZ publishes its interest rate path. In contrast to this, bond yields in Sweden are not found to have responded differently to monetary policy surprises on the days when the Riksbank published its report with the inflation forecast. This empirical finding suggests that explicit quantitative guidance, in the form of the publication of an interest rate path, may potentially enhance a central bank's leverage on the medium-term structure of interest rates.

The remainder of the chapter is structured as follows. Section 15.2 briefly discusses a few conceptual issues of central banks' own interest rate forecasts, namely how they are constructed and presented, what they mean and how they are related to market expectations of future policy rates. Section 15.3 describes the data and the construction of monetary policy and macro-surprises. Section 15.4 presents the empirical results and section 15.5 concludes.

15.2   Central banks' policy rate forecasts: conceptual issues

This section briefly discusses a few conceptual issues that it is useful to clarify before embarking on the empirical analysis. We start by briefly describing how central banks construct their own interest rate path forecasts.

Since June 1997 the RBNZ has published a forecast for the ninety-day bill rate, as well as for the inflation rate and other key macroeconomic variables, together with its *Monetary Policy Statement* (MPS), four times a year. The primary tool for the construction of the RBNZ's macroeconomic projections is the Forecasting and Policy System (FPS), a large macroeconomic model comprising more than 200 equations. Although the published projections are model-based, they also incorporate judgemental adjustments reflecting the views of the staff, the advisory Monetary Policy Committee and, ultimately, the governor. After convergence to a baseline projection has been achieved in an iterative process, the MPS with the central projections is eventually released under the authority of the governor. The interest rate path and the other macroeconomic projections are published without confidence or uncertainty bands.

Since November 2005 Norges Bank has published a forecast of its sight deposit rate, with confidence bands, together with its *Monetary Policy Report*, three times a year. Prior to that, Norges Bank published an inflation forecast that had been constructed on the basis of the assumption of, first, constant interest rates (CIRs) (from March 2001 until mid-2003) and, then, market interest rates (MIRs). Before publishing an explicit forecast of the policy rate path up to three years ahead, Norges Bank published from summer 2004 a 'strategy interval' for the policy rate four months ahead. The construction of the interest rate path and the forecasts of key economic variables are based on several macroeconomic models, a core model and a number of smaller models. In addition, Norges Bank also takes into account current statistics as well as information provided by its regional network and judgemental adjustments. The confidence bands of the interest rate forecast are calculated on the basis of the core model.

The Swedish Riksbank has published a forecast of its repo rate, with confidence bands, together with its *Monetary Policy Report*, three times a year since February 2007. Before that, the Riksbank initially used to condition forecasts on the assumption of a CIR. From October 2005 the Riksbank gave more prominence to projections based on MIR assumptions relative to those based on CIR assumptions, which were included only as an alternative scenario in the *Inflation Report* (now the *Monetary Policy Report*).

The Riksbank's forecasts are constructed on the basis of formal models and expert assessment. On the model side, models based on economic theory, notably a general equilibrium model of the Swedish economy called RAMSES, and more statistically oriented models are all used. The model forecasts are then examined by the sector experts on the basis of common sense and aspects of reality that the models are unable to capture. The experts' assessment and the results of the models then serve as the basis for the main scenario. The Riksbank publishes the main scenario together with uncertainty bands, which are calculated from historical forecast errors for implied forward rates with an adjustment for the systematic forecast error in order to capture the existence of risk premiums.

Figure 15.1 shows how the RBNZ, Norges Bank and the Riksbank present their respective interest rate forecasts in their regular reports. The figures reveal that the policy rate is forecast approximately two years ahead, reflecting the time horizon over which the inflation target is attempted or required to be met. While the RBNZ publishes only the point forecast, Norges Bank and the Riksbank publish the point forecast together with fan charts in order to visualise the uncertainty surrounding the forecast.

As is always stressed in the public communications of path-publishing central banks,[10] a published interest rate path is not a promise by the central bank. Rather, it is the central bank's best guess, or forecast, at the time of the publication of the forecast, of the future path of policy rates, conditional on the information available up to that date. Obviously, unforeseeable future developments will yield *ex post* a policy rate path that may look quite different from the expected paths that have previously been published. This becomes evident when we compare the RBNZ's track record of published interest rate paths with the one that was actually delivered, displayed in Figure 15.2. To put the volatility of the RBNZ's policy path forecast into perspective, we show in Figure 15.3 the vintage of market expectations of the Riksbank's policy rate (measured by implied forward rates) together with the realised policy rate path. As seen in the figure, market forecasts are also volatile and not very precise in predicting future policy rates. Nonetheless, this does not imply that markets and central banks are poor forecasters of the future policy rate; it shows merely that they change their mind as the facts change (see Goodhart

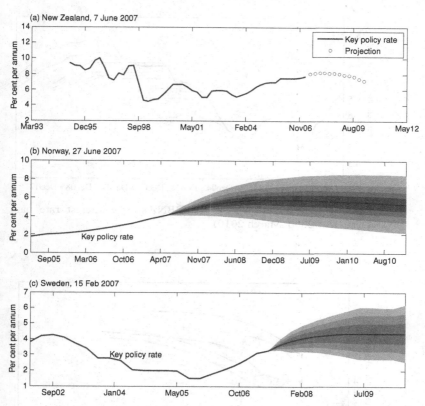

Figure 15.1 Key policy rate and interest rate paths for New Zealand, Norway and Sweden

and Lim 2008 for a recent empirical assessment of the (in)ability of central banks and markets to forecast the future path of policy rates).

In this context, it is also important to point out that the central bank's forecast of the policy rate path and implied market expectations do not need to (and usually do not) accord with each other, since markets and the central bank may have different assessments of the macroeconomic outlook. Indeed, path-publishing central banks commonly acknowledge that the alignment of market expectations with their forecasts is neither to be expected nor desirable.

However, discrepancies between the central bank's forecast and market forecasts can at times be picked up as an issue in the financial press. Such a discrepancy was particularly significant when the Riksbank began to publish an interest rate path on 15 February 2007. In its *Monetary*

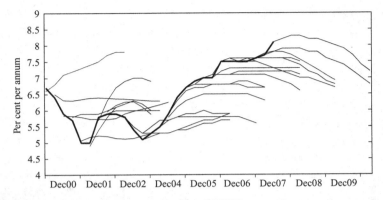

Figure 15.2 Track record for the RBNZ's own interest rate path (December 2000–March 2010)

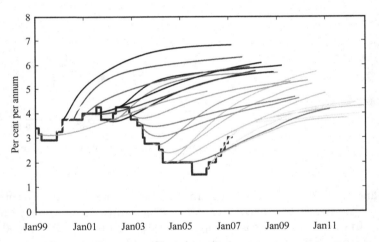

Figure 15.3 Track record for market-based forecasts of the Sveriges Riksbank's repo rate (January 1999–August 2012)

Policy Report, the Riksbank stated: 'The Riksbank's current assessment is that the repo rate needs to be raised by a further 0.25 percentage points in February and by another 0.25 percentage points during the coming six months. There could then be a pause before it is time for a further increase.' The release of the interest rate path attracted much attention

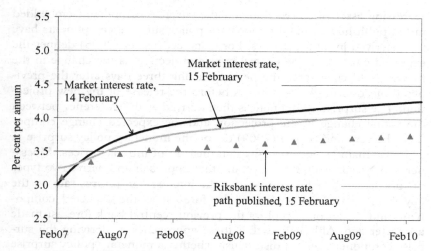

Figure 15.4 Riksbank repo rate forecast and market expectations, February 2007

in the media, as the path implied a much more accommodative monetary policy than that anticipated by the markets. As a result, market rates shifted down after the report's publication. However, market participants did not revise down the expected repo rate path fully, leaving a noticeable gap between the implied forward rates and the Riksbank's path over the one- to three-year horizon (see Figure 15.4). The Riksbank's deputy governor, Rosenberg, in a speech on the reactions to the publication of the Riksbank's own interest rate path in February 2007, played down the apparent differences between the markets' and the Riksbank's view about the future interest rate path (Rosenberg 2007): 'The fact that other agents make their own assessments of how the interest rate will develop is essentially very positive. One of the arguments put forward against a central bank presenting its own forecast for the interest rate path was that the agents in the financial market would then stop making their own analyses of interest rate developments. However, these misgivings have proved unjustified.'

15.3   Data and surprises

Deriving monetary policy surprises

The earlier literature gauging market reactions to the publication of central banks' interest rate paths has, in general, approached this issue by regressing asset price reactions on the surprise component embedded in the published path. The monetary policy surprise components have been derived in different ways. For instance, Archer (2005) defines the expected changes in the central bank's projection as the change in the market yield curve over the period starting three days after the previous projection until five minutes before the release of the new projection. The surprise component is then derived as the difference between the actual change in the projection and the expected change component. Ferrero and Secchi (2009) define the monetary policy surprise in a similar manner but use daily data instead of intraday prices. Moessner and Nelson (2008) take yet another approach and derive two types of surprises. Their first proxy uses the interest rate futures rate on the day prior to the publication of the forecast as the expected component, and the second employs the previous central bank forecast made a quarter ago. Although useful, these approaches to deriving the surprise component cannot distinguish whether a monetary policy surprise results from the actual monetary policy decision deviating from analysts' expectations or from the published path not being in line with market expectations.

To try to capture and elucidate what is driving the overall surprise, this study defines both so-called 'target surprises' and 'path surprises' for Sweden, Norway and New Zealand. There are, in general, two approaches to extracting target surprises: survey-based and financial-market-based measures. There are pros and cons for each. Survey-based expectations are usually collected a few days before the monetary policy announcements and, as a result, any news or events taking place between the collection day and the decision day are not reflected in the surveys. Another argument against surveys is that investors do not 'put their money where the mouth is'. On the other hand, analysts' expectations are publicly available, and an analyst would run a reputation risk if his estimate systematically missed the actual outcome. An argument in favour of surveys is that survey estimates should, in theory, reflect investors' 'true' expectations. This is contrary to expectations derived from financial markets, for which risk premiums can drive a wedge between the observed and true expectations. On the other hand, expectations from financial asset prices, apart from being derived from real bets by investors, are timely and can be extracted only minutes before the release of the monetary policy decision.

Most studies on asset price reactions to monetary policy news have been conducted on economies in which monetary policy expectations are easily available for long time periods (the United States, the euro area and the United Kingdom). However, as concerns the countries examined in this study – Sweden, Norway and New Zealand – data availability is more problematic. In particular, survey-based expectations are available only for the past few years (Bloomberg survey data are available for New Zealand from 2001 and for Sweden and Norway from 2003).

In order to use consistent data for the entire time series, we derive target surprises from financial markets for all countries. Daily changes (surrounding the actual decisions) in domestic one-month interbank rates are used to proxy for the surprise. In more detail, we employ the one-month STIBOR (Stockholm Interbank Offered Rate) rate, listed at 11:05 a.m., for Sweden; the one-month OIBOR (Oslo Interbank Offered Rate), set at noon each day, for Norway; and the thirty-day bank bill yield, also set at noon, for New Zealand. Interbank rates normally tend to be good approximations of short-term risk-free rates. The information content can, however, be distorted during periods of extreme financial stress. For instance, the turmoil that got under way in July 2007 sparked a sharp upturn in interbank volatility. Our results should not be distorted, though, as this period of financial turbulence lies outside our sample. For the sample under consideration, monetary policy decisions in Sweden and New Zealand have on all occasions been released earlier than the listing of interbank rates. Thus the standardised Riksbank and RBNZ surprise for a monetary policy decision taking place at day t is calculated as

$$S_t^{MP,j} = \frac{i_t^{1M} - i_{t-1}^{1M}}{\sigma} \tag{15.1}$$

where $S_t^{MP,j}$ represents the standardised monetary policy surprise at day t for country j ($j =$ Sweden, New Zealand), i_t^{1M} is the one-month interbank rate at day t and σ is the sample standard deviation of the surprise components. Norges Bank has throughout the sample announced its decisions no earlier than 14.00 (local time). As a result, the surprise component for Norway is calculated as $i_{t+1}^{1M} - i_t^{1M}$ in equation (15.1).

One caveat regarding the use of bank rates is that they contain credit and liquidity risk components, which can distort the information content. However, it is reasonable to assume that these components do not change substantially over very short periods of time, and, in general, target surprises derived from market-based measures tend to be very similar to survey-based indicators. For the euro area and the United States, the estimated correlation coefficient between the two is 0.75 for the ECB target surprises, and 0.8 for the Fed target surprises (see Andersson 2007). To check the accuracy of the market-based data used in this study, Figures 15.5 to 15.7 show scatter plots of target surprises using standard

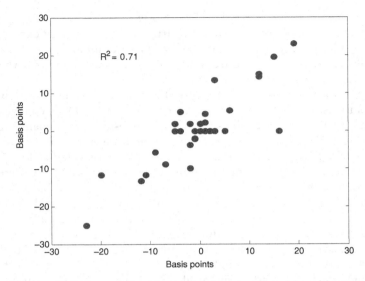

Figure 15.5 Survey-based (y-axis) and market-based (x-axis) measures of monetary policy target surprises for New Zealand, April 2001–June 2007

survey-based data (when available) and the market-based data (as described above).

As can be seen, the data points are scattered around the 45° line and the coefficient of the regression line is very close to one. The strong similarities between the two measures suggest that the market-based measure should accurately capture the investors' perceived surprise in the announced decision.

The second type of monetary policy surprises – path surprises – is intended to capture news about revisions in the future path of policy. Methods of how to derive path surprises were first developed by Gürkaynak, Sack and Swanson (2002). Later on, Brand, Buncic and Turunen (2006) and Andersson (2007) have applied slight variations of this method. This study defines the path surprise as the component of the change in around one-year-ahead three-month implied future swap rates surrounding the monetary policy decision that is uncorrelated with the target surprise. In other words, the component of the change in forward swap rates that cannot be explained by the target surprise is defined as the path surprise:

$$\Delta IFR_t^k = \alpha + \beta TS_t^k + PS_t^k \tag{15.2}$$

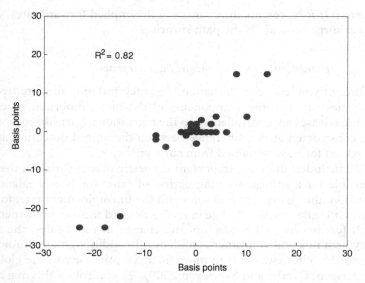

Figure 15.6 Survey-based (y-axis) and market-based (x-axis) measures of monetary policy target surprises for Norway, June 2003–June 2007

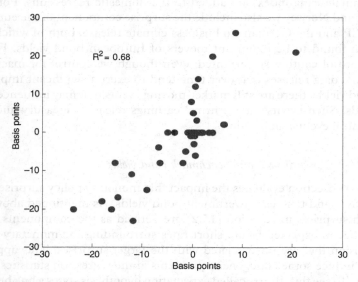

Figure 15.7 Survey-based (y-axis) and market-based (x-axis) measures of monetary policy target surprises for Sweden, October 1999–June 2007

where ΔIFR represents the changes in the implied forward rates, TS the target surprises and PS the path surprises.

Extraction of macroeconomic data surprises

In order to increase the estimation efficiency and minimise omitted variable bias, the surprise components of the most important macroeconomic releases are controlled for in the regressions. Surprise components are constructed as the difference between the official outcomes and the (median) forecasts obtained from surveys.[11]

We included the most important domestic macro-variables that were available for a sufficiently long period of time: for New Zealand, CPI inflation, the change in retail sales and the unemployment rate; for Norway, CPI inflation, the change in retail sales and the unemployment rate; and, for Sweden, CPI inflation, the change in retail sales, the unemployment rate and consumer confidence. In addition, many studies have found that US news tends to move financial prices across the globe (see Andersson, Overby and Sebestyén 2009). To control for this market feature, four US macro-surprises, namely those in CPI inflation, retail sales, non-farm payrolls and the Institute for Supply Management's (ISM's) manufacturing index, are added to the domestic regressions. For Sweden and Norway we also include the surprise component of the euro area HICP and the German Ifo business climate release, both of which have been found to be important movers of European bond yields. Finally, a word of caution is warranted: even though we control for macroeconomic data releases that over time tend to exert a significant impact on bond yields, there are still market-moving events that may influence bond yields. Such events can be firms' earnings releases, Treasury auctions, political events, and so on.

Forward rates and benchmark bond yields

This subsection evaluates the impact that monetary policy surprises have on five- and ten-year government bond yields. As mentioned above, the path surprises in equation (15.2) are derived as the components of the change in expected future short rates surrounding the monetary policy decision that are uncorrelated with the target surprises. This approach can induce some endogeneity problems in the regression statistics, however. To see this, the so-called expectation hypothesis states a link between short-term interest rates and long-term interest rates. This hypothesis is based on the general proposition that expectations about future short-term interest rates affect the current level of long rates. Thus the

n-period long-term nominal interest rate i at time t, i_t^n, can be expressed as

$$i_t^n = 1/n \left[E(i_{1,t}) + E(i_{1,t+1}) \ldots E(i_{1,t+n-1}) \right] + \theta_{n,t} \qquad (15.3)$$

where $E(i_{1,t+i})$ is the one-period yield that markets, at time t, expect to prevail at time $t + i$; θ is the term premium paid on an instrument with maturity n. Thus, as short-term interest rates are controlled by the central bank, monetary policy (in particular a policy surprise) also has an impact on long-term interest rates. With respect to ten-year bond yields, however, the endogeneity issue should be deemed relatively small, as it is derived from one small component in equation (15.3), namely the $E(i_{1,t})$ component. To account for this feature we add the five-year forward interest rate expected to prevail in five years' time to the explanatory variables. These forward rates have the additional advantage that, at least in theory, they should be unaffected by short-term business cycle news. As a consequence, central banks usually monitor these forward rates to gauge changes in market participants' long-term growth and inflation expectations.

The five- and ten-year (and the forward) benchmark bond yields are derived from Datastream, using the codes BMXX10Y and BMXX05Y (XX representing the two-digit country codes for New Zealand, Norway and Sweden).

15.4   Empirical analysis

To reiterate, the main aim of this chapter is to evaluate the effects of quantitative forward guidance provided by the RBNZ, the Riksbank and Norges Bank. Three avenues are pursued: the first concerns the predictability of monetary policy decisions, the second whether quantitative forward guidance has helped to anchor long-term inflation expectations and the third whether a move towards interest rate path publication increases a central bank's leverage on the term structure of interest rates. We use descriptive statistics to evaluate the predictability issue while regression analysis is employed to tackle the two latter points. Throughout this section we employ identical samples for RBNZ and the Riksbank (covering the period from January 1999 to January 2007). This enables us to compare two central banks that share similar policy frameworks, but differ in the sense that the RBNZ's is more explicit in its forward communication (via the publication of its own interest rate path). For Norway, the sample is split before and after the central bank's decision to publish its own interest rate path (in November 2005). Such a sample split helps to gauge the extent to which markets' reactions to Norges

Bank's communications changed after it decided to publish its best guess about future policy rates.

> *Hypothesis 1: does the publication of an interest rate path enhance the short-term predictability of monetary policy and help to avoid policy surprises?*

Predictability is of the essence for a central bank, because it enhances the effectiveness of monetary policy. In this respect it is common to distinguish between short-term predictability and long-term predictability. Short-term predictability is usually defined as the degree to which the public is able to anticipate upcoming monetary policy decisions. The longer-term dimension of central bank predictability has more to do with the fact that the public should be able to understand the central bank's monetary policy framework (see ECB 2006 and Blattner *et al.* 2008 for a more thorough discussion).

In this subsection we focus on short-term predictability and make use of the above-derived target and path surprises. Figure 15.8 shows the unconditional mean of both target and path surprises for the three economies. As is evident from the rather low level of target and path surprises, all three central banks have been successful in communicating their monetary policy intentions in a transparent manner. Furthermore, the target surprises are of similar magnitude for both the RBNZ and the Riksbank, while the RBNZ's path surprises, on average, have been slightly higher than those of the Riksbank. This latter feature suggests that the RBNZ's decision to publish its own interest rate path has not had any significant short-term predictability benefits, at least in comparison to the Riksbank.

For Norges Bank, it seems that its short-term predictability improved after the introduction of the interest rate path. In fact, both target and path surprises declined significantly after November 2005. It should be noted, however, that the period from 2005 to mid-2007 was characterised by a tranquil financial market environment. Such a favourable environment probably made it easier for market participants to anticipate upcoming monetary policy decisions.

> *Hypothesis 2: does the introduction of an interest rate path help to anchor long-term inflation expectations?*

To examine the extent to which the three central banks have been able to anchor long-term inflation expectations we use a standard regression framework. The Fisher hypothesis states that the yields offered on

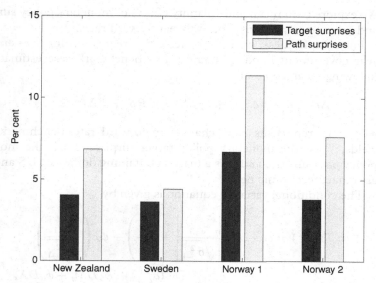

Figure 15.8 Average absolute target and path surprises of the Reserve Bank of New Zealand, the Riksbank and Norges Bank

Notes: Sample period for New Zealand and Sweden: January 1999–January 2007; Norway 1: March 2001–October 2005; Norway 2: November 2005–June 2007.

government bonds consist of three components: a real rate component, an inflation expectation component and a premium demanded for investing in longer-term securities. The real rate component is, in turn, closely related to an economy's growth prospects. By assuming that market participants' economic growth five to ten years into the future as well as the term premiums they demand over this horizon are broadly constant, changes in far-ahead forward rates should be related primarily to revisions in long-term inflation expectations, as seen through the eyes of investors (see Gürkaynak, Sack and Swanson 2005). Thus, if monetary policy (and other macroeconomic) surprises are unable to move the yields significantly on this long-term horizon, this would provide evidence that market participants' long-term inflation expectations are well anchored.[12]

To test this hypothesis we employ a standard exponential generalised autoregressive conditional heteroscedasticity (EGARCH) model proposed by Nelson (1991). This set-up is similar to previous studies investigating the effect of monetary policy surprises and communication on market interest rates (see, for example, Ehrmann and Fratzscher 2007).

We explore both mean and volatility effects of monetary policy surprises and macro-news surprises on five-year forward rates.[13]

For completeness, we also replicate this regression for five- and ten-year government bond spot rates. The benchmark case estimates the following mean equation:

$$\Delta r_t = \alpha + \beta \Delta r_{t-1} + \gamma_1 TS_t + \gamma_2 PS_t + \Phi X_t + \varepsilon_t \qquad (15.4)$$

where Δr_t represents daily changes in forward rates/benchmark bond yields, TS is the monetary policy target surprise, PS is the monetary policy path surprise and X is a matrix containing domestic, US and euro area macroeconomic news.

The conditional variance equation is given by

$$\ln(\sigma_t^2) = \omega + \phi_1 \left(\left| \frac{\varepsilon_{t-1}}{\sqrt{\sigma_{t-1}^2}} \right| - \sqrt{\frac{2}{\pi}} \right) + \phi_2 \left(\frac{\varepsilon_{t-1}}{\sqrt{\sigma_{t-1}^2}} \right)$$

$$+ \phi_3 \ln \left(\sigma_{t-1}^2 \right) + \phi_4 \left(\sigma_{t-1}^2 \right) + \phi_5 DM_t + \phi_6 DX_t \qquad (15.5)$$

where DM is a dummy variable equal to one on days of monetary policy decisions and zero otherwise and DX is a vector of dummies for the domestic, US and euro area macro-news (taking, respectively, the value one on days the news is revealed and zero otherwise). Two main results can be seen in Table 15.1. First, target and path surprises, across economies (and across samples in the case of Norway), have lower coefficient values and lower significance for the implied five-year-forward interest rates compared to the five- and ten-year spot yields. This suggests that long-term inflation expectations have been relatively well anchored in the three economies over the sample periods.

Second, this pattern also holds for the vast majority of domestic and foreign macroeconomic news. An important market mover appears to be the surprise in US non-farm payroll releases, which is found to move bond yields significantly for all three economies, across maturities, except for Norway over the more recent sample period. The fact that relatively few monetary policy surprises and macro-news exert significant influence on long-term forward rates contrasts with findings for the United States found by Gürkaynak, Sack and Swanson (2005). The authors state that 'our empirical results are all consistent with a model that we present in which private agents' views of [US] long-run inflation are not strongly anchored' (2005: 425). One plausible explanation for the contrasting results may be that all three economies included in this study have a clear inflation mandate that differs from the Federal Reserve's informal

Table 15.1 *Baseline results for New Zealand, Sweden and Norway*

	Five-year spot		Ten-year spot		Five-year-forward rate	
	Mean	Volatility	Mean	Volatility	Mean	Volatility
(a) New Zealand						
Lag	−0.01		−0.02		−0.03*	
Target surprise	3.43***		2.22***		0.94	
Path surprise	4.42***	−0.43***	3.56***	−0.31***	2.57***	−0.29***
NZ CPI inflation	2.43**	−0.02	1.78***	−0.01	1.49	0.02
NZ retail sales	1.17**	0.11*	0.79	0.10**	0.50	0.05
NZ unemployment	−9.68***	−0.12	−7.68***	−0.17*	−3.45	−0.02
US CPI inflation	0.33	−0.14	0.40	−0.09	0.51	−0.14*
US retail sales	0.85	0.12*	0.68	0.16**	0.39	0.11*
US NFP	2.01***	0.01	2.42***	0.09	2.63***	0.01
US ISM	1.55***	0.08	1.86***	0.14*	1.79***	0.08
(b) Sweden						
Lag	0.04**		0.03**		0.03	
Target surprise	1.73***		1.08*		0.53	
Path surprise	2.16***	0.07	1.84***	0.12**	1.41**	0.12**
SW CPI inflation	2.31***	0.06	1.20***	0.17*	0.25	0.12**
SW retail sales	0.59	0.04	0.29	0.05	0.02	0.22***
SW unemployment	−0.82**	0.03	−0.64*	−0.10	−0.58	−0.25***
US CPI inflation	0.37**	−0.05	0.29	0.01	0.25	0.14**
US retail sales	2.12***	0.01	1.79***	0.01	1.50***	0.09*
US NFP	2.67***	0.01	2.41***	−0.04	2.02***	−0.40***
US ISM	2.97***	0.47***	1.71***	0.49***	0.38	0.95***
EA CPI inflation	0.83**	−0.07	0.63	−0.18	0.72**	−0.55***
EA Ifo	0.81**	−0.14**	0.70***	−0.16**	0.54	−0.16***
(c) Norway 2001–5						
Lag	0.06**		0.09***		−0.08***	
Target surprise	3.73***		2.00***		0.36	
Path surprise	5.74***	0.28***	2.47***	−0.16	−1.35	−0.38***
NO CPI inflation	3.78***	0.04	1.84***	−0.06	−0.10	−0.14***
NO retail sales	0.46	0.31***	0.32	0.41***	0.39	0.17***
NO unemployment	−1.42	0.22***	−0.03	−0.02	1.40*	−0.16***
US CPI inflation	0.52	−0.05	−0.62	−0.12	−0.84	−0.19***
US retail sales	1.56*	0.08*	1.55**	0.27*	1.93***	0.03***
US NFP	1.90***	−0.47***	3.26***	0.02	4.42***	−0.24***
US ISM	1.82***	0.62***	1.47***	0.41**	0.51	0.51***
EA CPI inflation	−0.14	0.52***	−0.69	0.07	−0.69	0.15***
EA Ifo	1.43***	−0.35***	0.92**	−0.35***	0.76**	−0.20***

(cont.)

Table 15.1 (*cont.*)

	Five-year spot		Ten-year spot		Five-year-forward rate	
	Mean	Volatility	Mean	Volatility	Mean	Volatility
(d) Norway 2005–7						
Lag	0.04*		0.02		−0.20***	
Target surprise	4.19***		1.62		−0.36	
Path surprise	2.24*	0.12***	1.54*	0.20***	1.89	0.60***
NO CPI inflation	2.26***	0.52***	1.75***	0.23***	1.19	0.32***
NO retail sales	1.03	0.02***	−0.99*	−0.01	−2.30**	−0.07***
NO unemployment	−1.29***	−0.11***	−1.94***	−0.19***	−2.68***	0.03
US CPI inflation	−0.15	0.16***	0.06	−0.09***	0.53	−0.09***
US retail sales	1.30	0.16***	0.95	0.15***	0.63	0.43***
US NFP	1.62***	0.00	0.77**	0.14***	−0.41	−0.23***
US ISM	−0.14	0.06***	−0.83	0.06***	−1.45	0.46***
EA CPI inflation	−0.67	−0.02	0.77	−0.33***	1.14	−0.28***
EA Ifo	0.41	−0.46***	0.54	−0.04***	0.45	0.24***

Notes: NFP = non-farm payrolls. EA = euro area. * = significant at the 10 per cent level; ** = significant at the 5 per cent level; *** = significant at the 1 per cent level.

approach to a long-run inflation objective. This explanation is also supported by Gürkaynak, Levin and Swanson (2006), who find evidence that Swedish and UK long-term inflation compensation embedded in bond yields has been insensitive to economic news during the period when the economies have operated under a clear inflation-targeting mandate.

> *Hypothesis 3: does quantitative guidance in the form of interest rate path publication improve central banks' leverage over the term structure of interest rates?*

When an interest rate path is released, financial markets are provided with detailed quantitative information about the prospective future course of policy. One might therefore conjecture that, on these days, markets may be more reactive to the forward-looking communication, which would imply that bond yields respond more strongly to the path surprise. From a tactical central bank communication perspective, this would open a way to exert a larger influence (i.e. greater leverage) on longer-term bond yields. For instance, assume that a central bank wishes to steer bond yields in a certain direction and that history has shown that it is able to 'move the markets' more when it publishes a path. If that were the case, then the central bank would be more successful in steering the markets by direct forward guidance rather than by means of a speech or some other form of verbal guidance.

Owing to the limited number of interest rate paths published by Norges Bank between November 2005 and June 2007, the assessment of this conjecture is based solely on a comparative analysis of New Zealand and Sweden. To this end, we extend the EGARCH model estimated in the previous subsection by interacting the monetary policy surprises with a dummy variable D_t^{fguid}, which is equal to one on days when an interest rate path (in the case of New Zealand) and the inflation forecast (in the case of the Riksbank) was released and zero on the occasions when the two central banks only published the interest rate decision:

$$\Delta r_t = \alpha + \beta \Delta r_{t-1} + \gamma_1 TS_t + \gamma_2 TS_t D_t^{fguid}$$
$$+ \gamma_3 PS_t + \gamma_4 PS_t D_t^{fguid} + \Phi X_t + \varepsilon_t \qquad (15.6)$$

If quantitative forward-looking guidance induces increased central bank leverage on the term structure of interest rates, we would expect the coefficient on the dummy-interacted path surprise to be positive and significant. The expected size and sign of the coefficient of the dummy-interacted target surprise is not clear a priori. Obviously, the sample is relatively limited, and the results should be interpreted accordingly. There are thirty-four occasions for New Zealand when an interest rate forecast was released, and thirty-one occasions for Sweden when an inflation forecast was released.

Table 15.2 reports the estimated coefficients for the monetary policy surprises. For New Zealand, we find that the effect of the path surprise is consistently larger when an interest rate path was published (see panel (a)). However, it is significant only for the five-year segment. The effect of the target surprise, on the other hand, is found to be smaller, which could be interpreted as reflecting a shift in the bond markets' focus from the very near-term monetary policy stance (as captured by the target surprise) to the more distant monetary policy outlook (as captured by the path surprise).[14] The coefficient estimates suggest that the RBNZ can potentially obtain an enhanced leverage over medium-term bond yields on the days when it publishes a policy rate path, since the elasticity of the five-year bond yield to the path surprise is almost twice as large on these days as normally. For Sweden, interest rates do not show any extra sensitivity on the days the Riksbank publishes its monetary policy report (see panel (b)). Overall, these findings provide some mild support for the notion that the publication of an interest rate path forecast may enhance the central bank's leverage over medium-term interest rates.

Table 15.2 *Extended regression results for New Zealand and Sweden*

	Five-year spot Mean	Ten-year spot Mean	Five-year forward Mean
(a) New Zealand			
Target surprise	3.74***	2.99***	2.15***
Path surprise	2.96***	2.45***	1.77***
Target surprise DP	−0.65***	−1.85***	−2.98***
Path surprise DP	2.27**	1.63	1.17
Exclusion test	7.51***	5.14	2.65
(b) Sweden			
Target surprise	1.71***	0.88***	0.08
Path surprise	2.35***	1.79***	1.29*
Target surprise DR	0.12	0.33	0.56
Path surprise DR	−0.47	0.01	0.10
Exclusion test	0.33	0.06	0.43

Notes: DP = dummy path. DR = dummy rate. * = significant at the 10 per cent level; ** = significant at the 5 per cent level; *** = significant at the 1 per cent level. 'Exclusion test' reports the significance level of a likelihood ratio test of the null hypothesis that all dummy-interacted monetary policy variables can be excluded from the model.

15.5   Conclusions

The perceived primary advantage for a central bank of publishing its own interest rate path is that it would enhance the bank's ability to steer expectations, thereby enhancing the predictability of monetary policy, the anchoring of inflation expectations and the leverage of monetary policy over longer-term interest rates. This chapter has assessed these hypotheses in the following ways. First, we have tested if the publication of a central bank's own interest rate path can enhance the predictability of monetary policy – help avoid policy surprises and thereby reduce financial market volatility. This has been evaluated by examining the size of the three central banks' target and path surprises. Second, by examining the price sensitivity of long-term domestic government bond yields (both spot and forward) on derived path and target surprises, we have been able to evaluate if the publication of an interest rate path has altered investors' long-term inflation expectations. Third, one of the main arguments in favour of publishing an interest rate path is that it may improve the banks' leverage over the term structure of interest rates. We have tested this issue empirically by examining whether or not the medium- and long-term yield effect of path surprises is stronger on the days when the central bank publishes its interest rate path forecast. This part of the analysis has benefited from the fact that all three central banks under investigation always pursue the practice of releasing their forward guidance – i.e. their inflation or monetary policy reports with their forecasts – on days when monetary policy decisions are also taken.

The analysis has been based on two comparisons: first, a comparative analysis for the RBNZ and the Riksbank over a sample period in which the RBNZ, but not the Riksbank, published its own interest rate forecast; and, second, a comparative analysis for Norges Bank over two different sub-samples, when an interest rate forecast was published in the second sub-sample, but not in the first.

The main findings of the study are the following. First, we find that all three central banks have been highly predictable in their monetary policy decisions and that long-term inflation expectations have been well anchored in the three economies, irrespective of whether forward guidance involved the publication of the central bank's own interest rate path or not. The first comparative analysis reveals that monetary policy surprises are found to be of similar magnitude for both the RBNZ and the Riksbank, and that there is no evidence that long-term yields are better anchored in New Zealand than in Sweden. The sub-sample analysis for Norges Bank reveals that policy surprises have become smaller since November 2005, when Norges Bank started to publish an interest rate path. This latter period was characterised by very low volatility in the global economy and financial markets in general, however, which might also have contributed to lower policy surprises. Regarding long-term inflation expectations in Norway, there is no evidence that they have been better anchored since November 2005 than they were beforehand. These findings suggest that, if the central bank already operates under a monetary policy framework characterised by a clearly defined price stability objective and a high degree of transparency, the publication of an interest rate path does not appear to enhance the short-term predictability of monetary policy and the anchoring of long-term inflation expectations.

The second main finding, obtained from the comparison between the RBNZ and the Riksbank, is that the publication of an interest rate path appears to increase the sensitivity of medium-term bond yields to forward-looking monetary policy news and to reduce sensitivity to news about the current policy stance. In New Zealand, five-year bond yields are found to respond more weakly to the target surprise and substantially more strongly to the forward-looking path surprise on the days when the

RBNZ publishes its interest rate path. In contrast to this, bond yields in Sweden are not found to have responded differently to monetary policy surprises on the days when the Riksbank published its report with the inflation forecast. This empirical finding suggests that explicit quantitative guidance, in the form of the publication of an interest rate path, may potentially enhance a central bank's leverage on the medium-term structure of interest rates.

For completeness, it is important to note that there are other aspects in connection with a central bank publishing its own interest rate path on top of the predictability, inflation-expectations anchoring and leverage issues that have been the focus in this chapter. There are, for instance, further potential advantages, such as avoiding a number of technical problems associated with the adoption of the constant interest rate or the market interest rate approach in the construction of central banks' macroeconomic forecasts (see Goodhart 2009 for a thorough discussion of the alternative interest-rate-conditioning assumptions of central bank forecasts) and the establishment of a more forward-looking framework for internal policy deliberations. At the same time, there are also potential disadvantages. In particular, it might in practice be difficult for a monetary policy committee to agree on an entire future path of policy rates rather than merely on the level of the policy rate today (Goodhart 2001) – an argument whose relevance obviously grows with the size of the decision-making body.[15] In addition, for a central bank to publish its own interest rate forecast might be interpreted by the public as an unconditional promise (Mishkin 2004; Goodhart 2009); alternatively, central banks might be unwilling to revise their path for reasons of prestige (Gersbach and Hahn 2008), which might impede the required adjustments of the path to changes in economic conditions. These latter issues are difficult to test empirically. However, the fact, which we have documented in this study, that the RBNZ has over time made quite sizeable revisions in its published interest rate path without causing major disruptions in the markets or suffering a loss in credibility points to a potentially limited relevance of these issues. Finally, there is the issue of whether constructing a publishable interest rate path should be considered a pre-eminent issue for central banks with scarce resources.[16] This potential caveat might be qualified, however, if fewer resources needed to be devoted to other ways of policy signalling when a path was published.[17]

Overall, the relevance of the various potential advantages and disadvantages for a central bank of publishing its own interest rate path will depend to a large extent on the specific situation at the individual central bank, such as the importance of the inflation forecast in the monetary policy strategy and the size of the decision-making body.

NOTES

1. This chapter has benefited from comments and suggestions by the editors of this volume, Spencer Dale, Øyvind Eitrheim, Petra Geraats, Petra Gerlach, Charles Goodhart, Lars Heikensten, Jesper Johansson, Niels Lynggård Hansen, Christie Smith, Lars E. O. Svensson, Jean-Pierre Vidal and an anonymous referee. The authors would also like to thank seminar participants from presentations at the European Central Bank, the conference 'Central bank communication, decision-making and governance' at Wilfrid Laurier University, Waterloo, Ontario, the Sixth Norges Bank Monetary Policy Conference and the European Economic Association 2009 annual conference in Barcelona. The views expressed in this study are solely the responsibility of the authors and should not be interpreted as reflecting the views of the ECB or the Eurosystem.

2. Norges Bank started to publish an explicit policy rate path in November 2005, although a 'strategy interval' for the policy rate four months ahead had been published since the summer of 2004.

3. In 2007 the deputy governor of the Bank of England, Rachel Lomax (2007), stated that the Bank of England was considering publishing its own interest rate path, but more recent statements from the Bank of England's Monetary Policy Committee sound more dismissive. For instance, the Bank of England's chief economist, Spencer Dale (2009), recently stated that '[t]he Committee's preferred approach is to describe its assessment of the outlook for output and inflation, and allow the public and markets to make their own assessment of the likely future path of interest rates'.

4. For both the Swedish Riksbank and the Czech National Bank, the period over which an interest rate path has been published is still too short to allow an empirical assessment of its effects. For the Riksbank there is, however, an interesting study by Andersson, Dillén and Sellin (2006) investigating the effect of the various communication tools of the Riksbank (e.g. speeches, release of the *Inflation Report*) on market interest rates for the period before quantitative forward guidance was adopted.

5. Overall, there is strong evidence that the ability of financial markets to predict monetary policy has, in general, increased over the last decade, which provides evidence of the beneficial effects of the transparent approach to monetary policy adopted by central banks around the world in the recent past on the predictability of monetary policy. For a survey of the literature, see Blattner *et al.* (2008).

6. An interesting finding of the literature on this subject is that macroeconomic news appears to have a stronger and more significant effect on long-term interest rates or far-ahead forward interest rates in the United States (Gürkaynak, Sack and Swanson 2005) than in the euro area (Brand, Buncic and Turunen 2006; Beechey, Johanssen and Levin 2007) or the United Kingdom and Sweden (Gürkaynak, Sack and Swanson 2002), which is interpreted as suggesting that inflation expectations are less anchored in the United States than in these three other economies.

7. The Reserve Bank of New Zealand's inflation target is currently specified as a range for annual CPI inflation of 1 to 3 per cent over the medium

term. Before September 2002 the range was 0 to 3 per cent. The Riksbank's inflation target is an annual change in the CPI of around 2 per cent per year, with a tolerance range of plus/minus 1 percentage point.

8. Quantitative indicators of central bank transparency (see, for example, Eijffinger and Geraats 2006 and Dincer and Eichengreen 2007) commonly characterise the RBNZ and the Riksbank as being among the most transparent central banks in the world.

9. Norges Bank's operational inflation target is an annual consumer price inflation of 2.5 per cent over time.

10. A typical example is the statement by the deputy governor of the Riksbank, Irma Rosenberg (2007): 'I would therefore like to emphasise once again that the repo rate path we present in the *Monetary Policy Report* is a forecast and not a promise. The Riksbank cannot undertake, regardless of what happens in the economy, to follow the path published. The interest rate path is quite simply the best assessment we can make at a given point in time, given the information that is then available. New information may change the picture of the economy and then the Executive Board will have to rethink how we set the repo rate.'

11. The data were obtained from Bloomberg and Haver DLX.

12. A more direct approach would be to assess the anchoring of implied long-term inflation compensation backed out from the forward rates of nominal and index-linked bonds, as has been done by Beechey and Wright (2008) for the United States. We did not pursue this avenue here because of an insufficient number of on-the-run index-linked bonds for the three economies.

13. An alternative approach would be to gauge the impact on shorter forward rates, such as one-year implied forward rates in nine years' time. As benchmark yields (with high liquidity) are available in five-year and ten-year segments, we believe the information content in longer-term implied forward rates (e.g. a five-year-forward rate five years ahead) to be less distorted than shorter-term implied forward rates (e.g. a one-year-forward rate nine years ahead).

14. This pattern is similar to that obtained by Swiston (2007) in an assessment of the implications of the issuance of FOMC statements on the effect of monetary policy surprises on US bond yields. He finds that the introduction of the statements led to a reduction in the effect of the short-term monetary policy surprise and an increase in the surprise about the more distant prospective level of policy rates.

15. This point was challenged by Svensson (2003), however, who argues that agreeing on an interest rate path would not be more complicated than agreeing on an inflation or output growth forecast path. As a practical matter, he suggested letting each MPC member draw his preferred future interest rate path on paper and then taking the median of the individual paths.

16. This point was made by Lars Heikensten in a comment when our paper was presented at the Sixth Norges Bank Monetary Policy Conference.

17. Indeed, according to a comment made by Svensson at the Sixth Norges Bank Monetary Policy Conference, and also a speech by Rosenberg (2007), the Riksbank makes less use of signalling via, for example, speeches and statements since it has been publishing its own policy path.

REFERENCES

Andersson, M. (2007). 'Using intraday data to gauge financial market responses to Fed and ECB monetary policy decisions'. Working Paper no. 726. Frankfurt: ECB.

Andersson, M., H. Dillén and P. Sellin (2006). 'Monetary policy signalling and movements in the term structure of interest rates', *Journal of Monetary Economics*, 53(8): 1815–55.

Andersson, M., L. Overby and S. Sebestyén (2009). 'Which news moves the euro area bond market?', *German Economic Review*, 10(1): 1–31.

Archer, D. (2005). 'Central bank communication and the publication of interest rate projection,' Paper prepared for Sveriges Riksbank conference on inflation targeting. Stockholm, 11 June.

Beechey, M., B. Johanssen and A. Levin (2007). 'Are long-run inflation expectations anchored more firmly in the Euro Area than in the United States?'. Finance and Economics Discussion Paper no. 2008–23. Washington, DC: Federal Reserve.

Beechey, M., and J. Wright (2008). 'The high-frequency impact of news on long-term yields and forward rates: is it real?'. Finance and Economics Discussion Paper no. 2008–39. Washington, DC: Federal Reserve.

Blattner, T., M. Catenaro, M. Ehrmann, R. Strauch and J. Turunen (2008). 'The predictability of monetary policy'. Occasional Paper no. 83. Frankfurt: ECB.

Blinder, A., M. Ehrmann, J. de Haan, M. Fratzscher and D. Jansen (2008). 'Central bank communication and monetary policy: a survey of theory and evidence', *Journal of Economic Literature*, 46(4): 910–45.

Brand, C., D. Buncic and J. Turunen (2006). 'The impact of ECB monetary policy decisions and communication on the yield curve'. Working Paper no. 657. Frankfurt: ECB.

Dale, S. (2009). 'Inflation targeting: learning the lessons from the financial crisis'. Speech given at the Society of Business Economists' annual conference. London, 23 June.

Dincer, N., and B. Eichengreen (2007). 'Central bank transparency: where, why, and with what effects?'. Working Paper no. 13003. Cambridge, MA: NBER.

Drew, A., and Ö. Karagedikli (2008). 'Some benefits of monetary policy transparency in New Zealand'. Discussion Paper no. 2008/01. Wellington: RBNZ.

ECB (2006). 'The predictability of the ECB's monetary policy', *Monthly Bulletin*, January: 51–61.

Ehrmann, M., and M. Fratzscher (2007). 'Transparency, disclosure and the Federal Reserve', *International Journal of Central Banking*, 3(1): 179–225.

Eijffinger, S., and P. Geraats (2006). 'How transparent are central banks?', *European Journal of Political Economy*, 22(1): 1–21.

Ferrero, G., and A. Secchi (2009). 'The announcement of monetary policy intentions'. Economic Working Paper no. 720. Rome: Banca d'Italia.

Geraats, P. (2009). 'Trends in monetary policy transparency'. Working Paper no. 2584. Munich: CESifo.

396 *Andersson and Hofmann*

Gersbach, H., and V. Hahn (2008). 'Forward guidance for monetary policy: is it desirable?'. Economics Working Paper no. 08/84. Zurich: Center of Economic Research, Swiss Federal Institute of Technology.

Gjedrem, S. (2006). 'Monetary policy in Norway'. Speech given at Norges Bank's conference 'Evaluating monetary policy'. Oslo, 30 March.

Goodhart, C. (2001). 'Monetary transmission lags and the formulation of the policy decisions on interest rates', *Federal Reserve Bank of St. Louis Review*, 83(4): 165–81.

(2009). 'The interest rate conditioning assumption', *International Journal of Central Banking*, 5(2): 85–108.

Goodhart, C., and W. Lim (2008). 'Interest rate forecasts: a pathology'. Discussion Paper no. 612. London: Financial Markets Group, LSE.

Gürkaynak, R., A. Levin and E. Swanson (2006). 'Does inflation targeting anchor long-run inflation expectations? Evidence from long-term bond yields in the US, UK, and Sweden'. Working Paper no. 2006–09. San Francisco: Federal Reserve Bank of San Francisco.

Gürkaynak, R., B. Sack and E. Swanson (2002). 'Market-based measures of monetary policy expectations'. Finance and Economics Discussion Paper no. 2002–4. Washington, DC: Federal Reserve.

(2005). 'The sensitivity of long-term interest rates to economic news: evidence and implications for macroeconomic models', *American Economic Review*, 95(1): 425–36.

Holmsen, A., J. Qvigstad, Ø. Røisland and S. Solberg-Johansen (2008). 'Communicating monetary policy intentions: the case of Norges Bank'. Working Paper no. 2008/20. Olso: Norges Bank.

Lomax, R. (2007). 'The MPC comes of age'. Lecture at De Montfort University. Leicester, 28 February.

Mishkin, F. (2004). 'Can central bank transparency go too far?'. Working Paper no. 10829. Cambridge, MA: NBER.

Moessner, R., and W. Nelson (2008). 'Central bank policy rate guidance and financial market functioning', *International Journal of Central Banking*, 4(4): 193–226.

Nelson, D. (1991). 'Conditional heteroskedasticity in asset returns: a new approach', *Econometrica*, 59(2): 347–70.

Rosenberg, I. (2007). 'Monetary policy with our own interest rate forecast'. Speech at Riksbank. Stockholm, 6 June.

Rudebusch, G., and J. Williams (2008). 'Revealing the secrets of the temple: the value of publishing central bank interest rate projections', in J. Campbell (ed.). *Asset Prices and Monetary Policy*: 247–89. Chicago: University of Chicago Press.

Svensson, L. (2003). 'The inflation forecast and the loss function', in P. Mizen (ed.). *Central Banking, Monetary Theory and Practice: Essays in Honour of Charles Goodhart*, vol. I: 135–52. Cheltenham: Edward Elgar.

(2006). 'The instrument-rate projection under inflation targeting: the Norwegian example', in Banco de México. *Stability and Economic Growth: The Role of Central Banks*: 175–98. Mexico City: Banco de México.

(2009). 'Transparency under flexible inflation targeting: experiences and challenges', *Sveriges Riksbank Economic Review*, 1: 5–44.

Swiston, A. (2007). 'Where have the monetary surprises gone? The effects of FOMC statements'. Working Paper no. 07/185. Wahington, DC: IMF.

Woodford, M. (2005). 'Central bank communication and policy effectiveness', in Federal Reserve Bank of Kansas City. *The Greenspan Era: Lessons for the Future*: 399–474. Kansas City: Federal Reserve Bank of Kansas City.

16   Macro-modelling with many models

Ida Wolden Bache, James Mitchell, Francesco Ravazzolo and Shaun P. Vahey[1]

16.1   Introduction

We argue that macro-models in inflation-targeting central banks are too narrowly focused to provide accurate probabilistic forecasts. Despite the explicit consideration of model uncertainty afforded by Bayesian estimation techniques, the models prominent in central banks devote insufficient attention to 'uncertain instabilities'. Too much consideration is paid to refining a single preferred but inevitably misspecified model. A product of this oversight is that the 2007-vintage workhorse monetary policy models had little (or nothing) to say about the probability of 'tail' events, which now dominate the debate over the causes of, and remedies for, the recent global financial crisis.

In our view, the next generation of macro-modellers should address this deficiency while preserving the architecture of dynamic non-linear modelling. We propose a methodology adapted from the weather-forecasting literature known as 'ensemble modelling'. In this approach, uncertainty about model specifications – e.g. initial conditions, parameters and boundary conditions – are explicitly accounted for by constructing ensemble predictive densities from a large number of component models. The components allow the modeller to explore a wide range of uncertainties; and the resulting ensemble 'integrates out' these uncertainties using time-varying post-data weights on the components.

We provide two economic examples of the ensemble methodology. In the first, we consider a policymaker (recursively) selecting a linear combination of disaggregate predictives to produce an ensemble forecast density for inflation. Each component of the ensemble comprises a univariate autoregressive model using a single disaggregate series. In our second application, we utilise an ensemble of dynamic stochastic general equilibrium models, with the components differentiated by candidate break dates. In both examples, the ensembles outperform autoregressive benchmarks in terms of density forecast performance for Norwegian inflation.

The remainder of this chapter is structured as follows. In the next section, we set out the case for ensemble modelling to deal with uncertain instabilities. In section 16.3, we describe our examples. In the final section, we conclude with some suggestions for subsequent research.

16.2   Current macro- and ensemble modelling

We begin this section by motivating our approach to macro-modelling. Then we outline the relationship between ensemble modelling and the 'uncertain instabilities' literature in macroeconometrics. We complete the section with a discussion of the characteristics of the ensemble approach.

What just happened?

The recent global financial crisis has provoked considerable debate about the nature of existing macro-models. In particular, it has been argued that the models at the heart of policymaking in inflation-targeting central banks abstract from key aspects of financial plumbing that were the source of the crisis; and that, without these features, modellers and policymakers stood little chance of spotting the slump in activity. For example, Willem Buiter ('Maverecon', *Financial Times* blog, 3 March 2009) has argued that modern macro 'excludes everything I am interested in', echoing the thoughts of Goodhart on the dominance of macro-models without money and finance (see Goodhart 2007).

In response, central bankers are, no doubt, busy bolting bits of financial apparatus onto workhorse DSGE models, which abstract currently from many key features of the economy, not just the financial plumbing implicated in the current crisis. A narrow focus on inflation above other considerations represents, after all, the defining feature of an inflation-targeting regime. Leaving aside the issue of whether macro-models should be developed by bolting on new sectors after each unique crisis, whatever bits are added to today's model, the next generation of central bank workhorse models will remain highly abstract.

Of course, the early real business cycle literature – which kick-started the computational developments prevalent in modern workhorse macro-models – gave explicit consideration to the extreme degree of abstraction (see Karagedikli *et al.* 2010 for a recent review). Given this starting point, it seems surprising to us that inflation-targeting central banks typically focus on a single specification, estimated directly by the Bayesian equivalent of maximum likelihood. Why should simply allowing for informative priors on parameters yield a specification capable of producing accurate forecasts for the events of interest to policymakers?

Uncertain instabilities and ensemble modelling

A recent strand of the macroeconometrics literature considers 'model uncertainty' more widely, taking as its foundation the premise that the models are profoundly false. Durlauf and Vahey (2010) provide a summary in a special issue of the *Journal of Applied Econometrics* that focuses on the approach. On the forecasting side, this framework is sometimes referred to as one of 'uncertain instabilities'. The name implies that the estimated parameters of a single model will exhibit instabilities and that these can be difficult to identify in the real-time forecasting exercises confronting central banks. The dominant strategy in the forecasting applications combines the evidence from many models. For example, Clark and McCracken (2010) examine the scope for taking linear combinations of point forecasts in real time, motivated by the desire to circumvent the uncertain instabilities in any particular specification. (Jore, Mitchell and Vahey 2008 examine linear combinations of densities using the same US data.) In a series of studies, Stock and Watson (2001, 2004) have documented the robust performance of point forecast combinations using various types of models for numerous economic and financial variables.

Insofar as the 'uncertain instabilities' literature combines the evidence from many specifications, the prevailing approach has a Bayesian interpretation. The difficulty with applying conventional frequentist econometrics here is obvious: selecting a single model has little appeal if the usual model selection approach yields a specification that suffers from instability. This might happen either if the 'true' model is not within the model space considered by the modeller, or if the model selection process performs poorly on short runs of macroeconomic data.

Geweke (2010: 95) argues that standard Bayesian methods are ill-suited to the tasks of inference and prediction when the 'true' model is absent from the model space – what is sometimes referred to as an 'incomplete model space'. A number of econometricians, including Del Negro *et al.* (2007) and Sims (2007), have noted that ratios of marginal likelihoods overstate the difference between candidate models in the absence of the 'true' model from the model space. Using several examples, Geweke (2010: chap. 5) demonstrates the scope for pooling forecast densities to produce superior predictions, even if the set of components to be combined excludes the 'true' model. Hall and Mitchell (2007) draw attention to this property in their analysis of forecast density performance and combination at two institutions, namely the Bank of England and the National Institute of Economic and Social Research (NIESR).

Outside the econometrics literature, the benefits of density combination have been recognised for some time, as Garratt, Mitchell and Vahey (2009) observe. Over the last fifteen years meteorologists and statisticians have focused a great deal of attention on analysing statistical ensembles. The roots of the approach can be traced back to Josiah Willard Gibbs' contribution to thermodynamics. Loosely, the idea behind the ensemble approach is to consider a large number of component models, each of which is a replicant of the 'preferred' specification (the term 'replicant' is taken from the 1982 film *Blade Runner*; the equivalent term in micro-modelling is 'differentiated but otherwise identical'). Since each component could be viewed as an approximation of the current state of the 'true' but unknown specification, the components are considered together. The ensemble of components approximates the truth.

In the meteorological forecasting literature, the ensemble methodology is a response to the 'uncertain instabilities' problem. Density forecasts are generated from a common theoretical framework with slightly different initial conditions (measurements, auxiliary assumptions). The framework from which the component specifications are derived might allow for data, parameter and model uncertainty. In weather forecasting applications, the sensitivity to initial conditions stems from the chaotic processes considered. With practical forecasting issues in mind, two central questions are: (i) what components should be included in the model space?; and (ii) how should the ensembles be simulated? The researcher designs the ensemble component model space in order to explore the likely source of 'uncertain instabilities'. In meteorology and climate prediction, the analysis typically uses Monte Carlo simulation techniques.

Ensemble predictive methods are commonly deployed by the majority of weather prediction institutions worldwide. One example is the 'Ensemble Prediction System' developed by the European Centre for Medium-range Weather Forecasts. (For an early description of weather ensemble forecasting, see Molteni *et al.* 1996. Leutbecher and Palmer 1997 provide a primer on ensemble forecasting in meteorology. MacKenzie 2003 considers the impetus to ensemble modelling in meteorology provided by failing to assess the probability of severe storms (tail events).)

The experience of the global financial crisis indicates the limitations of designing monetary policy in the absence of precise information about probabilities. Even with explicit consideration of financial plumbing, it is hard to envisage that a single next-generation DSGE model will offer accurate (and robust) probabilistic forecasts. The ensemble methodology offers the scope to generate accurate density forecasts from large numbers of theoretically coherent models.

Characteristics of ensemble modelling

We conclude this section by highlighting some common characteristics of an ensemble modelling strategy for macro-modelling.

(1) The generation of forecasting densities, rather than point forecasts.
(2) Predictive density construction from a large number of component macroeconometric models.
(3) Forecast density evaluation and combination based on out-of-sample performance, rather than in-sample analysis.
(4) The component model weights vary through evaluation; ensemble densities have time-varying weights.

Studies in the economics literature that satisfy these criteria include (among others) those by Jore, Mitchell and Vahey (2008), Garratt, Mitchell and Vahey (2009) and Kascha and Ravazzolo (2010). Bjørnland *et al.* (2009) consider the performance of the Norges Bank's 'nowcasting' system, which also adopts the ensemble methodology. In these cases, the out-of-sample densities from many macroeconometric component models are directly combined into the ensemble using an 'opinion pool' (related work in econometrics by Wallis 2005 uses opinion pools to average model-free survey forecasts, rather than those from macroeconometric models, and Mitchell and Hall 2005 use opinion pools to combine forecasts from two institutions). These studies differ in the design of the model space and the number of components considered, as well as in the applied problem of interest. We discuss this opinion pool approach in considerable detail below when we analyse two specific examples. As we shall see, variants can produce symmetric or non-symmetric predictive densities.

Another strand of the ensemble economics literature uses informative priors and Markov chain Monte Carlo methods to produce ensembles. Maheu and Gordon (2008) and Geweke (2010) use mixture models to give non-Gaussian predictives while Andersson and Karlsson (2007) take an informative prior Bayesian approach to produce predictives from many vector autoregressions (see also the analysis of three macro-models by Gerard and Nimark 2008). Geweke (2010) discusses the relationships between density pooling and mixture modelling, and argues that the former presents a more coherent approach for incomplete model spaces. Clearly, both variants can be effective methods for combining densities in forecasting applications (in a related literature, Patton 2004, Geweke and Amisano 2008 and Maheu and McCurdy 2009 consider ensembles in various financial applications).

The mixture innovations approach to state-space models developed by (for example) Giordani, Kohn and van Dijk (2007) and Giordani and Kohn (2008) has a number of common features with ensemble macro-modelling. Both strategies aim to combine relatively simple components. In ensemble applications, the components are often conditionally – i.e. locally – linear Gaussian, but this is not required. The mixture innovation literature deploys the Kalman filter to conditionally linear Gaussian processes. (The ensemble Kalman filter can be used to approximate non-Gaussian processes with an ensemble based on simulated Gaussian measurement errors; see, for example, Mandel 2007.) Given the flexibility afforded by combination, the Gaussian components may not impair forecasting performance significantly. Ensemble macro-modelling applications also focus explicitly on out-of-sample density forecasting and, given the relatively light computational burden, a broader (and sometimes more eclectic) model space made up of candidate macroeconometric specifications.

16.3   Examples

In this section, we consider two specific examples of ensemble macro-forecasting for inflation: using an ensemble of disaggregates, and a DSGE ensemble. Both applications use Norwegian data and the opinion pool approach to ensemble density construction. We begin by describing the density combination approach used throughout.

Density combination

To summarise the approach, for each observation in the policymaker's out-of-sample 'evaluation period', we use forecast density combination to compute the weight on each component model. In each example that follows, the component models use a common time series structure. In the first example, each component considers a particular disaggregate inflation measure. In the second example, the DSGE components are distinguished by assumptions about break date timing. In both cases, the weights are based on the 'fit' of the component predictive densities for measured inflation. Given these weights, we construct ensemble forecast densities for measured inflation.

More formally, consider a policymaker aggregating forecasts supplied by 'experts' each using a unique component forecasting model. Given $i = 1, \ldots, N$ components (where N could be a large number), we define the ensemble by the convex combination also known as a linear opinion pool:

$$p(\pi_{\tau,h}) = \sum_{i=1}^{N} w_{i,\tau,h} g(\pi_{\tau,h} \mid I_{i,\tau}), \qquad \tau = \underline{\tau}, \ldots, \overline{\tau}. \qquad (16.1)$$

where $g(\pi_{\tau,h} \mid I_{i,\tau})$ are the h-step-ahead forecast densities for inflation from component model i, $i = 1, \ldots, N$, conditional on the information set I_{τ}.

We stress that each component model produces h-step-ahead forecasts for inflation; we are weighting the components only by the performance of their inflation forecasts in these examples, although multivariate weights are feasible. In the examples that follow, we also set $h = 1$ for simplicity.

Each component model uses data, dated $\tau - 1$ or earlier, to produce a one-step-ahead forecast density for τ. The non-negative weights, $w_{i,\tau,h}$, in this finite mixture sum to unity, are positive and vary by recursion in the evaluation period $\tau = \underline{\tau}, \ldots, \overline{\tau}$.

We emphasise that the ensemble forecast density could be non-Gaussian even if the component models produce Gaussian predictives. The linear opinion pool ensemble (16.1) accommodates skewness and kurtosis. The flexible structure resulting from linear pooling allows the data to reveal whether, for example, the ensemble should have fat tails or asymmetries. Kascha and Ravazzolo (2010) compare and contrast logarithmic and linear pooling. Logarithmic opinion pools force the ensemble predictives to be symmetric, but they accommodate fat tails (see also Bjørnland *et al.* 2009).

We construct the ensemble forecast density for measured inflation using equation (16.1). Implementation of the density combination requires a measure of component density fit to provide the weights. A number of recent applications in the economics literature have used density scoring rules. In the applications that follow, we utilise the continuous ranked probability score (CRPS), which, as (among others) Gneiting and Raftery (2007), Panagiotelis and Smith (2008) and Ravazzolo and Vahey (2009) note, rewards predictive densities from component models with high probabilities near (and at) the outturn. See Panagiotelis and Smith (2008) for an explanation of how the CRPS is calculated for each component density.

A disaggregate ensemble

Monetary policymakers regularly examine disaggregate inflation series for leading evidence of the inflationary process. The introduction of inflation targeting led central banks to focus much greater attention on the behaviour of inflation. One problem in doing so is that headline inflation can be volatile. A tradition common among inflation targeters considers the disaggregate inflation (or price) cross-sectional distribution but truncates and averages the distribution to provide a 'core' measure. A second approach excludes (zero-weight) particular disaggregates; the resulting measure is commonly referred to as an 'ex' core measure. Practitioners often propose that a key test of core inflation measures should be forecast performance (see, for example, Smith 2004).

In this example, we construct ensemble predictives based on the out-of-sample forecast performance of many component models, with each component model using a particular disaggregate series. The example follows closely the approach of Ravazzolo and Vahey (2009). Using US data, they label the combined forecast density the 'disaggregate ensemble core' inflation. We demonstrate below that the ensemble predictives provide accurate forecast densities for measured inflation. Moreover, the weights on the disaggregate components are non-zero throughout the evaluation. We conclude that the common practice of discarding disaggregate information by zero-weighting either groups or individual disaggregates – analogous to truncation and the 'ex' approach, respectively – is unwarranted from the perspective of assessing the probability of inflation events of interest. The example also illustrates the mechanics and flexible nature of ensemble modelling.

In our application, we decompose inflation in Norway into twelve disaggregates. These are: food and non-alcoholic beverages; alcoholic beverages and tobacco; clothing and footwear; housing, water, electricity and fuel; furnishings and house equipment; health care; transport; communications; recreation; education; restaurants and hotels; and miscellaneous goods and services. We emphasise that, in principle, our methodology could be applied to an extremely large number of disaggregates. For all inflation series, we work with quarterly growth rates. Restricting our attention to Great Moderation data, we start our sample with 1984Q1 and end with 2008Q4. The evaluation period for the predictives is 1996Q3 to 2008Q4; the period 1993Q1 to 1996Q2 we use as a 'training period' to initialise the ensemble weights. This application focuses entirely on one-step-ahead forecasts.

Within the core inflation literature, the horizon of interest varies, typically between one and eight quarters ahead. Although longer-horizon ensemble forecasts are possible (see, for example, Jore, Mitchell and Vahey 2008), we prefer to focus on horizons much shorter than the focal range of many inflation-targeting regimes. The results presented in this chapter cannot be interpreted as a test of the 'credibility' of the inflation-targeting regime (for further discussion of this issue, see Brischetto and Richards 2006).

Recall that we construct the ensemble by combining the predictive densities from all the disaggregate component models. Each component model uses a univariate autoregressive specification with four lags for a single disaggregate series. We construct the ensemble predictives for measured inflation by evaluating the disaggregate forecasts for measured inflation. In each recursion, we (recursively) centre the component forecasts on measured inflation, as described by Ravazzolo and Vahey (2009).

In effect, this step restricts the ensemble forecast densities to be unimodal but not symmetric.

To assess the calibration properties of the core ensemble density we follow Diebold, Gunther and Tay (1998) and compute probability integral transforms (PITs) and apply the Berkowitz (2001) likelihood ratio test for the independence, zero mean and unit variance of the PITs. The test statistic is distributed $\chi^2(3)$ under the null hypothesis of no calibration failure, under a maintained hypothesis of normality. We also report the average (over the evaluation period $T = \overline{\tau} - \underline{\tau}$) logarithmic score. The logarithmic score of the i-th density forecast, $\ln g(\pi_{\tau,h} \mid I_{i,\tau})$, is the logarithm of the probability density function $g(\cdot \mid I_{i,\tau})$, evaluated at the outturn $\pi_{\tau,h}$. As a result, the log score evaluates the predictives at the outturn only. We investigate relative predictive accuracy by considering a test based on the Kullback–Leibler information criterion (KLIC), which uses the expected difference in two models' log scores (see Mitchell and Hall 2005, Bao *et al.* 2007 and Amisano and Giacomini 2007). Suppose there are two density forecasts, $g(\pi_{\tau,h} \mid I_{1,\tau})$ and $g(\pi_{\tau,h} \mid I_{2,\tau})$, so that the KLIC differential between them is the expected difference in their log scores: $d_{\tau,h} = \ln g(\pi_{\tau,h} \mid I_{1,\tau}) - \ln g(\pi_{\tau,h} \mid I_{2,\tau})$. The null hypothesis of equal density forecast accuracy is $\mathcal{H}_0 : E(d_{\tau,h}) = 0$. A test can then be constructed, since the mean of $d_{\tau,h}$ over the evaluation period, $\overline{d}_{\tau,h}$, under appropriate assumptions, has the limiting distribution $\sqrt{T}\overline{d}_{\tau,h} \to N(0, \Omega)$, where Ω is a consistent estimator of the asymptotic variance of $d_{\tau,h}$. When evaluating the density forecasts we treat them as primitives, and abstract from the method used to produce them. Amisano and Giacomini (2007) and Giacomini and White (2006) discuss more generally the limiting distribution of related test statistics. Mitchell and Wallis (2009) explain the importance of information-based methods in discriminating between competing density forecasts.

We construct an ensemble one-step-ahead predictive density for measured inflation, which we refer to as DE12 (disaggregate ensemble with twelve components). As a benchmark we use a linear autoregressive model for aggregate measured inflation, with four lags, AR(4). We use uninformative priors for the AR(4) parameters with an expanding window. The predictive densities follow the t-distribution, with mean and variance equal to OLS estimates (see, for example, Koop 2003 for details). We use this AR(4) model as our benchmark in tests of relative forecast performance.

Before turning to the density evaluation for our ensemble, we summarise the point forecast performance. The root mean squared prediction errors (RMSPEs) of DE12 and AR(4) are 0.313 and 0.430, respectively. The Clark–West (2006) test for superior predictive accuracy (against the null of equal accuracy) indicates the superior performance of DE12, with

Table 16.1 *Forecast performance*

	LR	LS	LS-test
AR(4)	0.175	−1.057	
DE12	0.215	−0.615	0.001

Notes: 'LR' is the likelihood ratio *p*-value of the test of zero mean, unit variance and independence of the inverse normal cumulative distribution function of transformed PITs, with a maintained assumption of normality for transformed PITs. 'LS' is the average logarithmic score, averaged over the evaluation period. 'LS-test' is the *p*-value of the KLIC-based test for equal density forecasting performance of AR(4) and DE12 over the sample period from 1996Q3 to 2008Q4.

a test statistic of 2.61; the critical value for rejection of the null at 95 per cent is 1.65. Smith (2004) and Kiley (2008) discuss the point forecasting properties of various core inflation measures. Most fail to outperform simple AR benchmarks.

We turn now to the *ex post* assessment (i.e. at the end of the evaluation period) of the forecast densities from DE12 and the AR(4) benchmark. Table 16.1 has two rows – one for each. The columns report (reading from left to right) the Berkowitz likelihood ratio test (based on the PITs), the log scores (averaged over the evaluation period) and the *p*-values for the equal predictive density accuracy test (based on the log scores), respectively. Whereas both models appear well calibrated on the basis of the Berkowitz likelihood ratio, the final column shows that the AR is rejected in favour of DE12 using the KLIC-based test. DE12 delivers a statistically significant improvement in the log score at the 99 per cent level (reported in the second column).

The weights in DE12 display some variation through time. Table 16.2 reports the weights on the twelve disaggregates at three specific observations. It can be seen from the table that, generally, all disaggregate components have a non-zero weight, although the weight on 'Clothing and footwear' does drop to just below 2 per cent. (Geweke 2010 argues that even a zero weight is not sufficient to conclude that a component model has zero value for the linear opinion pool.) There does not seem to be a case for excluding the information on individual disaggregates, or groups of particular disaggregates, on the basis of these weights.

In Figure 16.1, we plot the median from our DE12 density forecast, together with the twenty-fifth and seventy-fifth percentiles from this ensemble density. The plot shows that the median of the DE12 core ignores several extreme values in the actual measured inflation series. Typically, the probability of inflation being less than zero is well below 25 per cent.

Table 16.2 *Disaggregate weights*

	1996Q3	2002Q3	2008Q4
Food and non-alcoholic beverages	0.138	0.128	0.117
Alcoholic beverages and tobacco	0.032	0.041	0.050
Clothing and footwear	0.031	0.017	0.016
Housing, water, electricity and fuel	0.105	0.091	0.070
Furnishings and house equipment	0.155	0.123	0.110
Health care	0.043	0.054	0.059
Transport	0.048	0.072	0.082
Communications	0.021	0.026	0.032
Recreation	0.136	0.161	0.159
Education	0.079	0.057	0.062
Restaurants and hotels	0.139	0.139	0.135
Miscellaneous goods and services	0.071	0.090	0.107

Notes: The columns report disaggregate weights for three observations, 1996Q3, 2002Q3 and 2008Q4.

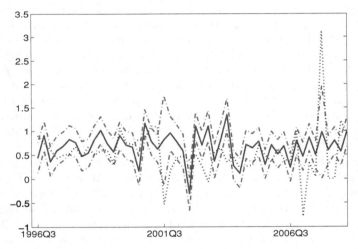

Figure 16.1 Inflation interval forecasts

Notes: The posterior meridian of the predictive density given by the aggregate ensemble DE12 is shown by the solid line, and actual inflation by the dashed line. The dash-dot lines are the twenty-fifth and seventy-fifth percentiles of the predictive density.

To provide further insight into the probability of tail events for inflation, Figure 16.2 provides the ensemble predictive densities at particular observations, namely 1996Q3 and 2008Q4, the first and the last values in our evaluation period. We see that the AR(4) benchmark produces

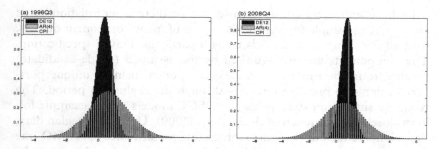

Figure 16.2 AR(4) and DE12 density forecasts

Notes: The histogram of the density forecasts is given by the AR(4) benchmark and by the disaggregate ensemble DE12 for the first and last forecasts. The realised values for CPI inflation are also provided.

density forecasts that are too wide, with a high probability mass attributed to (quarterly) inflation of greater than 2 per cent in absolute value for both observations. The DE12 predictives contain more mass in the regions around the outturn than the AR(4) benchmark, with minor departures from symmetry.

We conclude from this analysis that the ensemble approach provides a means of generating accurate forecast densities for measured inflation from disaggregate information. Moreover, the common practice of discarding disaggregate information by zero-weighting either groups or individual disaggregates is unwarranted in this density-forecasting context, as they do contain useful information about the future values of inflation.

A DSGE ensemble

Monetary policymakers typically use DSGE models as core workhorse models for forecasting and policy analysis. The introduction of inflation targeting led central banks to focus their macro-models on inflation issues. One issue in doing so is that the current generation of models is considerably more abstract than the large-scale Keynesian macro-models of the 1970s. Furthermore, the DSGE tradition adopted by ITers takes optimising behaviour by micro-agents as the cornerstone of model building. Despite the profusion of nominal and real rigidities adopted in the workhorse models, many critics argue that the models are fundamentally misspecified. We interpret this view as consistent with the incomplete model space concept developed by Geweke (2010).

In this example, we construct ensemble predictives for inflation based on the out-of-sample forecast performance of many component models, with all the component models using a particular DSGE specification. The components are distinguished by the assumed (single-candidate) break date in the sample, with each component using a unique post-break sample to produce forecasts through the evaluation period. The recursive simulation strategy for the DSGE models in this example follows closely the approach of Bache *et al.* (2009). Using Norwegian data, they compare the out-of-sample forecasting performance of NEMO (the Norges Bank core macro-model) with benchmark models. In our study, every component model is a replicant of NEMO, but with different start dates for in-sample estimation. We refer to the ensemble of DSGEs as the EDSGE, which we construct by using CRPS weights for measured inflation – that is, we treat the component models in exactly the same way as in the previous example, and eschew multivariate density scoring (multivariate extensions and a loss-based weighting of components pose no particular conceptual issues).

We emphasise that our EDSGE framework uses many very similar DSGE models. In each replicant DSGE, the agents and the government are assumed to have rational expectations. There is no learning taking place in any of our component models. In contrast, Svensson and Williams (2007) consider Markov jump-linear-quadratic systems that nest several prevalent, but relatively simple, macro-models.

It remains to be seen whether the Svensson–Williams approach will yield accurate forecast densities. We demonstrate below that the EDSGE provides accurate forecast densities for measured inflation using the same metrics for performance as in the previous (disaggregate) example. Since we have already described how the EDSGE is constructed, we simply summarise the DSGE model, before turning to the structure of the components and then the results.

NEMO is a medium-scale New Keynesian small open economy model with a similar structure to the DSGE models recently developed in many other central banks. In this example, we use a simplified version, motivated by the need to reduce the computational burden of producing the recursive forecasts for forecast density combination. The simplification involves modifications to the Bayesian simulation methodology and the steady-state behaviour of the model, as described below.

Bache *et al.* (2009: appendix) describe the NEMO economy in detail. Here we summarise the main features. There are two production sectors. Firms in the intermediate goods sector produce differentiated goods for sale in monopolistically competitive markets at home and abroad, using labour and capital as inputs. Firms in the perfectly competitive final goods sector combine domestically produced and imported intermediate goods into an aggregate good that can be used for private consumption, private investment and government spending. The household sector consists of a continuum of infinitely lived households that consume the final good, work and save in domestic and foreign bonds. The model incorporates real rigidities in the form of habit persistence in consumption, variable capacity utilisation of capital and investment adjustment costs, and nominal rigidities in the form of local currency price stickiness and nominal wage stickiness. The model is closed by assuming that domestic households pay a debt-elastic premium on the foreign interest rate when investing in foreign bonds. A permanent technology shock determines the balanced growth path. The fiscal authority runs a balanced budget each period and the central bank sets the short-term nominal interest rate according to a simple monetary policy rule. The exogenous foreign variables are assumed to follow autoregressive processes. To solve the model, we first transform the model into a stationary representation, detrending by the stochastic technology process. We then take a first-order approximation (in logs) of the equilibrium conditions around the steady state.

Estimation uses data on the following ten variables: GDP, private consumption, business investment, exports, the real wage, the real exchange rate, overall inflation, imported inflation, the three-month nominal money market rate and hours worked. We measure inflation with the (headline) consumer price index adjusted for tax and energy prices – known as the 'CPIATE' measure. The interest rate is the three-month money market rate, and the (seasonally adjusted) GDP variable excludes the oil and gas sectors. The national accounts data relate to the mainland economy – i.e. the total economy excluding the petroleum sector. See Table 16.3 for details about the data and the sources. Since the model predicts that domestic GDP, consumption, investment, exports and the real wage are non-stationary, these variables are included in first differences. We take the log of the real exchange rate and hours worked. All variables are de-meaned prior to estimation.

We estimate the structural parameters using Bayesian techniques in DYNARE (see Juillard 1996). The structural parameters are re-estimated in each recursion for the evaluation period. We construct the forecast densities by drawing 10,000 times from a multivariate normal distribution for the shocks. The standard deviations of the shocks are set equal to their estimated posterior mode. It should be noted that the (implicit) steady states vary by recursion through the evaluation period; we de-mean the data prior to estimation in each recursion. We emphasise that, as a result of this simulation approach, our components do not account for

Table 16.3 *Variable definitions and sources*

Observables	Description	Source
Y_t	GDP mainland Norway, per capita, s.a.	Statistics Norway
C_t	Private consumption, per capita, s.a.	Statistics Norway
I_t	Business investment, per capita, s.a.	Statistics Norway
M_t^*	Exports mainland Norway, per capita, s.a.	Statistics Norway
W_t/P_t	Hourly wage income divided by private consumption deflator, s.a.	Statistics Norway
RER_t	Import-weighted real exchange rate	Norges Bank
P_t	Overall price level adjusted for taxes and excluding energy prices (CPIATE), s.a.	Statistics Norway
P_t^m	Imported consumer prices adjusted for taxes and excluding energy prices, s.a.	Statistics Norway
R_t	Three-month money market rate (NIBOR)	Norges Bank
l_t	Total hours worked, per capita, s.a.	Statistics Norway

Notes: Observable variables in the estimation of the DSGE model; 's.a.' = seasonally adjusted.

parameter uncertainty and that the resulting predictives from each component are Gaussian.

We work with fourteen component DSGE models, distinguished by the assumed start date for in-sample estimations. The longest sample used starts in 1985Q2; the last sample starts in 1988Q3. The other variants explore every feasible start date between. Estimation is based on expanding window samples. The evaluation period for the predictives is 2001Q1 to 2008Q4; the period 1999Q1 to 2000Q4 we use as a 'training period' to initialise the ensemble weights. This application focuses entirely on one-step-ahead forecasts.

Before turning to the density evaluations for our EDSGE, we consider the performance of the point forecasts. The RMSPEs of the EDSGE and the benchmark AR(4) are 0.074 and 0.027, respectively. In other words, unlike the disaggregate ensemble in the previous example, our DSGE ensemble does not beat an autoregressive benchmark. This property stems from some mean bias in the components; none of the component models outperform the benchmark either. There may be scope to remove the forecast bias prior to combination (see, for example, Bao *et al.* 2009).

We turn now to *ex post* assessment (i.e. at the end of the evaluation period) of forecast densities from the EDSGE and the AR(4) benchmark. Table 16.4 has two rows, which refer to the EDSGE and the AR benchmark. The columns report the Berkowitz likelihood ratio test (based on the PITs), the log scores (averaged over the evaluation period) and the

Table 16.4 *Forecast performance*

	LR	LS	LS-test
AR(4)	0.101	−0.657	
EDSGE	0.226	−0.125	0.020

Notes: 'LR' is the likelihood ratio *p*-value of the test of zero mean, unit variance and independence of the inverse normal cumulative distribution function of transformed PITs, with a maintained assumption of normality for transformed PITs. 'LS' is the average logarithmic score, averaged over the evaluation period. 'LS-test' is the *p*-value of the KLIC-based test for equal density forecasting performance of the AR model and the EDSGE over the sample period from 2001Q1 to 20008Q4.

p-values for the equal predictive density accuracy test (based on the log scores), respectively. Whereas both models appear well calibrated on the basis of the Berkowitz likelihood ratio, the final column shows that the AR(4) is rejected in favour of the EDSGE using the KLIC-based test. The EDSGE delivers a statistically significant improvement in the log score at the 98 per cent level (reported in the second column).

We see in Table 16.5 that the weights on the different components in the EDSGE display little volatility over time. For the most part, all the DSGE components receive similar weight, which gives an indication of the individual plausibility of the components. The data suggest that a single DSGE model (a single break date) should not be used for density forecasting. We note, however, that an equal weight ensemble would perform nearly as well as our EDSGE with time-varying weights.

In Figure 16.3, we plot the median from our EDSGE density forecast, together with the twenty-fifth and seventy-fifth percentiles from the ensemble density. The plot shows that the median of the EDSGE is typically less volatile than the actual inflation series. Also apparent from this plot is the tendency for the runs of observations to occur outside the displayed percentiles. Clearly, there is scope to improve calibration by considering other candidate uncertainties – which could then be integrated out using the methods described in this chapter. We leave this avenue to be explored in a more complete analysis of DSGE ensembles.

Figure 16.4 provides the ensemble predictive densities at particular observations, namely 2001Q1 and 2008Q4. We see that the EDSGE density is much sharper than the AR(4) benchmark, and there are also some minor departures from symmetry.

Table 16.5 *DSGE weights*

	2001Q1	2004Q4	2008Q4
DSGE-1985Q2	0.076	0.072	0.072
DSGE-1985Q3	0.077	0.071	0.072
DSGE-1985Q4	0.072	0.074	0.072
DSGE-1986Q1	0.073	0.077	0.072
DSGE-1986Q2	0.070	0.073	0.070
DSGE-1986Q3	0.061	0.069	0.067
DSGE-1986Q4	0.070	0.073	0.070
DSGE-1987Q1	0.083	0.073	0.073
DSGE-1987Q2	0.083	0.071	0.074
DSGE-1987Q3	0.070	0.067	0.070
DSGE-1987Q4	0.061	0.071	0.073
DSGE-1988Q1	0.067	0.070	0.072
DSGE-1988Q2	0.067	0.070	0.072
DSGE-1988Q3	0.069	0.068	0.071

Notes: The weights, for three specific time periods, on the fourteen components, differentiated by the proposed break date, in the EDSGE. Each DSGE component is labelled by its break date.

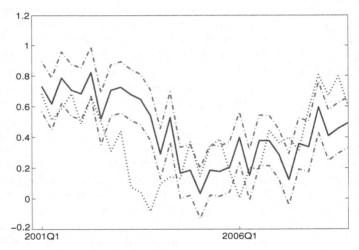

Figure 16.3 Inflation interval forecasts

Notes: The posterior median (solid line) of the predictive density is given by the disaggregate ensemble EDSGE and actual inflation (dashed line). The dash-dot lines are the twenty-fifth and seventy-fifth percentiles of the predictive density.

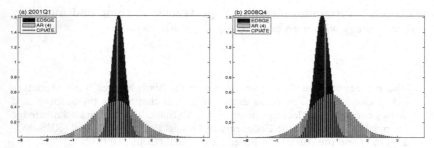

Figure 16.4 AR(4) and EDSGE density forecasts

Notes: The histogram of the density forecasts is given by the AR(4) benchmark and by the ensemble EDSGE for the first and last forecasts. The realised values for CPIATE are also provided.

We conclude from this analysis that the ensemble approach provides accurate forecast densities for measured inflation based on the DSGE components. The weights on the components indicate that none of the DSGE replicants are implausible and also that one component alone is not strongly preferred over the others.

16.4   Conclusions and ideas for further research

We have argued that the next generation of macro-modellers at inflation-targeting central banks should adapt a methodology from the weather forecasting literature known as 'ensemble modelling'. In this approach, uncertainty about model specifications (e.g. initial conditions, parameters and boundary conditions) is explicitly accounted for by constructing ensemble predictive densities from a large number of component models. The components allow the modeller to explore a wide range of uncertainties, and the resulting ensemble 'integrates out' these uncertainties using time-varying weights on the components. We have provided two specific examples of this modelling strategy.

The next generation of macro-models at inflation-targeting central banks could set aside the 'uncertain instabilities' problem and focus on these issues from the perspective of a single model; but a more promising route, we feel, is to explore model uncertainty explicitly. The computational simplicity of ensemble systems makes them very convenient for combining the evidence in many highly complex DSGE models, such as NEMO. Moreover, as our second example has demonstrated, the ensemble approach has the potential to produce accurate forecast densities from models used by policymakers in practice. Future work should explicitly allow for uncertainties regarding expectations, learning and monetary policy strategy within an ensemble framework.

NOTES

1. The authors are grateful to participants at the Sixth Norges Bank Monetary Policy Conference. The views expressed in this chapter are the authors' and do not necessarily reflect the views of Norges Bank. The authors acknowledge financial support from the Economic and Social Research Council (RES-062-23-1753) and the Australian Research Council (LP0991098).

REFERENCES

Amisano, G., and R. Giacomini (2007). 'Comparing density forecasts via likelihood ratio tests', *Journal of Business and Economic Statistics*, 25(2): 177–90.

Andersson, M., and S. Karlsson (2007). 'Bayesian forecast combination for VAR models'. Working Paper no. 216. Stockholm: Sveriges Riksbank.

Bache, I., A. Jore, J. Mitchell and S. Vahey (2009). 'Combining VAR and DSGE forecast densities'. Working Paper no. 2009/23. Oslo: Norges Bank.

Bao, L., T. Gneiting, E. Grimit, P. Guttop and A. Raftery (2009). 'Bias correction and Bayesian model averaging for ensemble forecasts of surface wind direction'. Technical Report no. 557. Seattle: Department of Statistics, University of Washington.

Bao, Y., T-H. Lee and B. Saltoglu (2007). 'Comparing Density Forecast Models', *Journal of Forecasting*, 26, 203–225. First circulated as 'A test for density forecast comparison with applications to risk management', University of California, Riverside, 2004.

Berkowitz, J. (2001). 'Testing density forecasts, with applications to risk management', *Journal of Business and Economic Statistics*, 19(4): 465–74.

Bjørnland, H., K. Gerdrup, A. Jore, C. Smith and L. Thorsrud (2009). 'There is more than one weight to skin a cat: combining densities at the Norges Bank'. Paper presented at the conference 'Forecasting and monetary policy'. Berlin, 24 March.

Brischetto, A., and A. Richards (2006). 'The performance of trimmed mean measures of underlying inflation'. Research Discussion Paper no. 2006–10. Sydney: RBA.

Clark, T., and M. McCracken (2010) 'Averaging forecasts from VARs with uncertain instabilities', *Journal of Applied Econometrics*, 25(1): 5–29.

Clark, T., and K. West (2006). 'Approximately normal tests for equal predictive accuracy in nested models', *Journal of Econometrics*, 138(1): 291–311.

Del Negro, M., F. Schorfheide, F. Smets and R. Wouters (2007). 'On the fit of New Keynesian models', *Journal of Business and Economic Statistics*, 25(2) 143–62.

Diebold, F., T. Gunther and A. Tay (1998). 'Evaluating density forecasts; with applications to financial risk management', *International Economic Review*, 39(4): 863–83.

Durlauf, S., and S. Vahey (2010). 'Introduction: model uncertainty and macro-economics', *Journal of Applied Econometrics*, 25(1): 1–3.

Garratt, A., J. Mitchell and S. Vahey (2009). 'Measuring output gap uncertainty', Unpublished manuscript. London: Birkbeck College.

Gerard, H., and K. Nimark (2008). 'Combining multivariate density forecasts using predictive criteria'. Research Discussion Paper no. 2008–02. Sydney: RBA.

Geweke, J. (2010). *Complete and Incomplete Econometric Models*. Princeton, NJ: Princeton University Press.

Geweke, J., and G. Amisano (2008). 'Comparing and evaluating Bayesian predictive distributions of asset returns'. Working Paper no. 969. Frankfurt: ECB.

Giacomini, R., and H. White (2006). 'Tests of conditional predictive ability', *Econometrica*, 74(6): 1545–78.

Giordani, P., and R. Kohn (2008). 'Efficient Bayesian inference for multiple change-point and mixture innovation models', *Journal of Business and Economic Statistics*, 26(1): 66–77.

Giordani, P., R. Kohn and D. van Dijk (2007). 'A unified approach to non-linearity, structural change, and outliers', *Journal of Econometrics*, 137(1): 112–33.

Gneiting, T., and A. Raftery (2007). 'Strictly proper scoring rules, prediction, and estimation', *Journal of the American Statistical Association*, 102: 359–78.

Goodhart, C. (2007). 'Whatever became of the monetary aggregates?', *National Institute Economic Review*, 200(1): 56–61.

Hall, S., and J. Mitchell (2007). 'Combining density forecasts', *International Journal of Forecasting*, 23(1): 1–13.

Jore, A., J. Mitchell and S. Vahey (2008). 'Combining forecast densities from VARs with uncertain instabilities'. Discussion Paper no. 303. London: NIESR.

Juillard, M. (1996). 'DYNARE: a program for the resolution and simulation of dynamic models with forward variables through the use of a relaxation algorithm'. Working Paper no. 9602. Paris: Centre pour la Recherche Economique et ses Applications.

Karagedikli, O., T. Matheson, C. Smith and S. Vahey (2010). 'RBCs and DSGEs: the computational approach to business cycle theory and evidence', *Journal of Economic Surveys*, 24(1): 113–36.

Kascha, C., and F. Ravazzolo (2010), 'Combining inflation density forecasts', *Journal of Forecasting*, 29(1–2): 231–50.

Kiley, M. (2008). 'Estimating the common trend rate of inflation for consumer prices and consumer prices excluding food and energy prices'. Finance and Economics Discussion Paper no. 2008–38. Washington, DC: Federal Reserve.

Koop, G. (2003). *Bayesian Econometrics*. Chichester: John Wiley.

Leutbecher, M., and T. Palmer (1997). 'Ensemble forecasting', *Journal of Computational Physics*, 227(7): 3515–39.

MacKenzie, D. (2003). 'Ensemble Kalman filters bring weather models up to date', *SIAM News*, 36(8): 1–4.

Maheu, J., and S. Gordon (2008). 'Learning, forecasting and structural breaks', *Journal of Applied Econometrics*, 23(5): 553–83.

Maheu, J., and T. McCurdy (2009). 'How useful are historical data for forecasting the long-run equity return distribution?', *Journal of Business and Economic Statistics*, 27(1): 95–112.

Mandel, J. (2007). 'A brief tutorial on the ensemble Kalman filter'. Report no. 242. Denver: Center for Computational Mathematics, University of Colorado.

Mitchell, J., and S. Hall (2005). 'Evaluating, comparing and combining density forecasts using the KLIC with an application to the Bank of England and NIESR "fan" charts of inflation', *Oxford Bulletin of Economics and Statistics*, 67(3): 995–1033.

Mitchell, J., and K. Wallis (2009). 'Evaluating density forecasts: forecast combinations, model mixtures, calibration and sharpness'. Discussion Paper no. 320. London: NIESR.

Molteni, F., R. Buizza, T. Palmer and T. Petroliagis (1996). 'The new ECMWF ensemble prediction system: methodology and validation', *Quarterly Journal of the Royal Meteorological Society*, 122: 73–119.

Panagiotelis, A., and M. Smith (2008). 'Bayesian density forecasting of intraday electricity prices using multivariate skew *t* distributions', *International Journal of Forecasting*, 24(4): 710–27.

Patton, A. (2004). 'On the out-of-sample importance of skewness and asymmetric dependence for asset allocation', *Journal of Financial Econometrics*, 2(1) 130–68.

Ravazzolo, F., and S. Vahey (2009). 'Ditch the ex! Measure core inflation with a disaggregate ensemble'. Unpublished manuscript. Oslo: Norges Bank.

Sims, C. (2007). 'Comment on Del Negro, Schorfheide, Smets and Wouters', *Journal of Business and Economic Statistics*, 25(2): 152–4.

Smith, J. (2004). 'Weighted median inflation: is this core inflation?', *Journal of Money, Credit and Banking*, 36(2): 253–63.

Stock, J., and M. Watson (2001). 'A comparison of linear and nonlinear univariate models for forecasting macroeconomic time series', in R. Engle and H. White (eds.). *Festschrift in Honour of Clive Granger*.1–44. Cambridge: Cambridge University Press.

    (2004). 'Combination forecasts of output growth in a seven-country data set', *Journal of Forecasting*, 23(6): 405–30.

Svensson, L., and N. Williams (2007). 'Monetary policy with model uncertainty: distribution forecast targeting'. Unpublished manuscript. Princeton, NJ: Princeton University.

Wallis, K. (2005) 'Combining density and interval forecasts: a modest proposal', *Oxford Bulletin of Economics and Statistics*, 67(3): 983–94.

17 Have crisis monetary policy initiatives jeopardised central bank independence?

Charles Goodhart[1]

These are extraordinary times for central banks. The wish that central bankers might become seen as useful, but boring, technocrats, rather like dentists, seems all too far from realisation. Let me start by reminding you that all the really serious financial crises have occurred in the aftermaths of periods of great economic success, and at times when inflation was *not* a serious issue, as, for example, in the United States in 1929, Japan in 1990/1 and almost everywhere in 2007/8. Before then, in the nineteenth century, crises often followed overexpansion on the basis of great technological breakthroughs, such as canals and railways, which had the effect of lowering prices. There are, indeed, good reasons, as Minsky has pointed out, why crises should follow overconfidence, as nemesis follows hubris.

The point of this, however, is to emphasise that successful control of goods and services inflation does not carry with it any assuredness of limiting, or even much mitigating, asset price bubbles and busts; and this would, I fear, remain so even if housing prices were to be correctly included in the inflation index, as should be done.

Achieving low and stable inflation does remain the priority, but it cannot be the be-all and end-all of a central bank's remit. This realisation has led to two different proposals. The first is to adjust central bank reaction functions so as to have them 'lean against the wind' of asset price bubbles and busts. The second is to find and employ *additional macro-prudential* instruments in order to dampen asset price fluctuations, and to maintain financial stability. In my view, the latter, *if it can be done*, would be far preferable.

The present constitutional position whereby the central bank uses its operational independence to hit a medium-term inflation target, mandated by government, is simple and straightforward and allows for clarity and accountability. It would muddy the waters, involving discretionary trade-offs, to have the central bank try to hit two, largely orthogonal, targets with a single instrument. In the current context in particular, with half the people fearing deflation and half fearing inflation, there is more need than ever for central banks to commit themselves to a fixed inflation target.

Central banks already have one instrument for achieving financial stability, in the form of liquidity provision. They were taken largely unawares by the scale and extent of the continuing need for liquidity from August 2007 onwards, and have been forced into unprecedented innovation since then. There must now be a rethink about how to charge banks, and other financial intermediaries, in advance for the liquidity insurance function that central banks fulfil; such a charge, whether it take the form of a direct payment premium, an additional capital requirement or whatever, should also serve as a counterweight to the incentive to run a large maturity mismatch.

Some additional regulatory controls over liquidity, though desirable, will not be sufficient, however. Generalised problems with liquidity almost always go hand in hand with concerns about solvency, as in 2007. If you could assume that I can and will certainly repay you, you would always lend to me unsecured at a risk-free rate – an invalid assumption that, alas, is incorporated into most macroeconomic DSGE models. Instead, liquidity and solvency issues are, almost invariably, intertwined. Indeed, liquidity only really has a rationale and meaning when solvency is a potential problem. Whereas central banks can provide liquidity, though, they cannot recapitalise banks or other systemic financial intermediaries by themselves. That can be done only by means of the minister of finance picking the fairly deep pockets of the taxpayer. This means that financial stability issues *have* to be decided and carried out jointly by the central bank, the Treasury and whichever institution is responsible for day-to-day supervision of the systemic financial institutions.

I see no sensible alternative to the adoption, or continuation, of some kind of tripartite committee, though I would rather have it normally headed by the central bank governor than by a politician or a Treasury civil servant. Quite where this need for fiscal/monetary cooperation on financial stability issues leaves the eurozone, except in rather obvious difficulties, remains to be seen. The problem with the operation of the Tripartite Committee in the United Kingdom, and its counterparts elsewhere, was not its structure and procedures (though, no doubt, these could be improved) but the lack of counter-cyclical instruments, in the form, for example, of time- and state-varying controls over capital requirements and mortgage lending. Even more important, when such requirements might have been applied in principle under the rubric of pillar 2 of Basel II, there was no keenness in practice to do so. Regulators and supervisors will always have to operate *against* the desires of the market, of the politicians and of the institutions, since 'taking away the punchbowl when the party is just getting going' wins no popularity prizes, and therefore central bank regulators *must* have their backbones stiffened by rules and *ex ante* commitments; but I have banged this particular drum often enough before now.

However, if there must be cooperation between the fiscal and the monetary authorities on financial stability issues, where does this leave the independence of the central bank? In principle, this does not worry me. An institution can carry out separate tasks, in which one set of such tasks is done independently, via a monetary policy committee with its attendant staff, and another set of tasks *jointly* via a financial stability committee (FSC), with its own staff. The MPC consists of specialised internal and external central bank appointees. The FSC would be wider, with a tripartite membership. Thus we normally separate pure monetary policy, in which the central bank has had independence delegated to it, from financial stability, for which decisions need to be taken jointly between the monetary and fiscal authorities.

Something of a spanner has recently been thrown into the workings of this separability theorem, however, in the guise of the recent adoption of quantitative easing (QE). This latter involves enormous fluctuations in the size of the central bank's own balance sheet, and puts the central bank in a position in which it can make either huge profits or massive losses. In short, the central bank's balance sheet has become risky, and central banks do not themselves have sufficient capital to absorb such risks.

At a time when the private sector is being asked to mark to market all such assets that are not being held to maturity, there are some interesting questions to be asked about the accounting principles being employed in central banks and in Ministries of Finance. After all, if one of the virtues of quantitative easing is its relatively flexible reversibility, we can hardly assume that all the assets being bought by central banks are to be held to maturity, can we?

One can hardly deny that QE drives a horse and cart through the thesis of the separation of fiscal and monetary policies. In a sense, this has already been recognised in a pragmatic way in the United Kingdom; we British tend to pride ourselves on being pragmatic rather than theoretical or ideological. Anyhow, the governor of the Bank of England has got the agreement of the Chancellor on the main modalities of QE – that is, the overall amount and the strategy of how and on what classes of assets the total funds may be spent – though the initiative has, I believe, come from the governor and the MPC, and the Chancellor has effectively indemnified the Bank against the risk of loss, and he, and the Treasury, then leave the MPC to get on with the application. The government has to be involved in setting the strategy but, equally, has to leave the operational tactics to an independent central bank. How far does that diminish the effective operational independence of the Bank of England? In my own view, hardly at all.

Can such a division of duties work so smoothly elsewhere, however, for example in the United States, where the separation of powers leaves Congress with control over fiscal policy, or in Europe, where Jean-Claude Trichet has no euro-fiscal counterpart? Does QE by the Federal Reserve represent, in part, a form of fiscal operation that has, for the time being at any rate, bypassed Congress? There are some in the United States who consider that QE raises some ticklish questions about the constitutional relationships between the Fed, the Treasury and Congress. For the moment this may be swept under the crisis carpet, but can it be so for long? The same is true in the eurozone. Could the ECB's Governing Council just decide off its own bat to – shall we say – treble the size of the ECB's balance sheet? What would happen if the member state governments were unhappy with this decision, as Angela Merkel would undoubtedly be?

There are some who will seize on the adoption of QE to argue that the separation of monetary policy, carried out by an independent central bank, from fiscal policy was from the start a dubious idea, and that the two policies should always have remained coordinated and under the control of the Treasury. I have heard a senior retired British Treasury civil servant muse along such lines.

Moreover, the kind of additional instruments that I and others have been proposing, in order to allow the financial stability committees of central banks to do their job effectively, such as time- and state-varying capital requirements, constraints on mortgage lending, etc., will, I believe, require supporting legislation, since they should be backed by appropriate sanctions, and sanctions need legal underpinning. It is quite likely, therefore, that there will need to be further legislation, virtually everywhere, both to reinforce central bank powers to implement financial stability and, perhaps, to sort out the constitutional difficulties that QE has exposed.

To conclude, the years 1993 to 2006 were in many ways a golden age. One aspect in which this was so for central banks was that it seemed that their constitutional and functional role had been largely and successfully clarified. One feature of the current crisis in general, and the adoption of QE in particular, has been to put this role back under review. We will see.

NOTE

1. This is the text of a speech given by Charles Goodhart at the dinner of the Sixth Norges Bank Monetary Policy Conference on 11 June 2009.

18   Inflation targeting: learning the lessons from the financial crisis

Spencer Dale[1]

Over the past year the United Kingdom's Monetary Policy Committee has responded to the dramatic deterioration in the economic outlook with an equally dramatic easing in monetary policy. Bank rate was cut by 4.5 percentage points in just six months and by 1.5 p.p. in November 2008 alone. That was the largest cut for twenty-five years and is twice the size of the reduction made by any other G7 central bank in the past eighteen months. The MPC also voted to purchase £125 billion of assets financed by the issuance of central bank money – an amount equivalent to around 9 per cent of UK GDP.

The scale of that easing took many by surprise, and some of the decisions may, at first blush, look rather courageous. Devotees of the British television show *Yes Minister* may recall that Jim Hacker, the hapless minister, became very nervous whenever Sir Humphrey suggested that a decision of his was 'courageous'. Central bankers can have similar instincts. When faced with big decisions, there is a temptation for caution to prevail: do interest rates really need to be moved by that much? Why not wait and see before resorting to the use of unconventional instruments?

Indeed, in the past the MPC has tended to move rates in relatively small, sequential steps. I would argue, though, that this is because, for much of the period since the establishment of the MPC, the outlook for inflation evolved relatively gradually. That all changed following the collapse of Lehman Brothers. Since the autumn of 2008 we have experienced an unprecedented sequence of events that has caused a substantial reassessment of the economic outlook and of the policy stance necessary to keep inflation on track to meet the target. As the economy slowed sharply and inflation threatened to fall substantially below the target rate, the MPC responded with unprecedented actions that had previously been confined largely to the realms of theory.

I believe that the operation of monetary policy during this period demonstrates the strength of inflation targeting in action. The clear numerical target, combined with a framework of transparency and accountability, imposes discipline on the Monetary Policy Committee.

424

Together, they ensure that we take the decisions necessary to bring infla-tion back to target, however 'courageous' these decisions might seem.

I do not think it is coincidence that arguably the two most significant monetary policy decisions taken by the MPC in the preceding twelve months – the decision to reduce bank rate by 1.5 p.p. in November 2008 and the announcement in February 2009 that the committee had sought approval to use the Asset Purchase Facility to conduct large-scale asset purchases – occurred in months in which the *Inflation Report* was published. The quarterly forecast round provides an opportunity for the MPC to reassess thoroughly its view of the economic outlook. This view is then explained and communicated via the *Inflation Report*, and in particular through the projections for GDP growth and inflation contained in the report. In both November and February the judgement of the committee was that, without further substantial easing in monetary policy, there was a significant risk of a large and persistent undershoot of the inflation target. Given the transparency of those judgements and the clarity of the target, it would have been courageous not to have taken the decisions we did.

Recent events must serve as a wake-up call for policymakers, however. The spectacle of banking runs, asset price falls and economic imbal-ances testifies that inflation targeting as currently operated is not suffi-cient. How should the macroeconomic policy framework in the United Kingdom be strengthened to reduce the likelihood of such events recur-ring?

One common suggestion is that the conduct of policy under inflation targeting should be modified to take greater account of movements in asset prices or economic imbalances that threaten the attainment of the inflation target, even if these risks may not materialise for several years. In principle, the remit given to the Monetary Policy Committee in the United Kingdom provides the latitude for policy to respond to such medium-term risks. In particular, the committee's objective is timeless: it is tasked with keeping inflation close to target 'at all times' in the future. Therefore, if the committee judged that intentionally undershooting the inflation target in the near term would help to reduce the risk of a much larger deviation from target in the future, it has the scope to follow such a policy.

However, a policy of 'leaning against the wind' is difficult to implement in practice. In part this reflects the difficulty of identifying changes in asset prices and economic flows that are unsustainable. At which point, for example, did the run-up in UK house prices over the past ten years cease to be warranted by a change in economic fundamentals, such as the rise in the number of households and the move to a low and stable inflation environment? Likewise, at which point did it become clear that sub-prime lending had ceased to be a beneficial financial innovation with the scope to allow people who had not previously had access to credit the chance to own their own home, and had instead become a source of international financial instability?

These are difficult judgements. They involve second-guessing outcomes generated by financial and economic markets. Policymakers will inevitably sometimes get the assessment wrong, with costly repercussions. These judgements cannot be ducked, though. Monetary policymakers have to form views about a range of uncertain and ill-defined issues, such as the level of potential supply and the credibility of policy. The sustainability of asset prices and economic imbalances are no different. Ultimately, a policy has to be set, even if explicit judgements are not formed.

Policymakers also need better tools to back up these judgements with actions. Short-term interest rates are a blunt instrument best deployed to maintain a broad balance between nominal demand and supply. They are not well suited to the task of managing asset price bubbles and economic imbalances. They may be wholly ineffective in addressing some types of imbalances, particularly those with an international dimension. Even for domestic imbalances, short-term interest rates would probably need to be held substantially higher for a persistent period in order to suppress rapid rises in asset prices or growing imbalances. Such policy actions could generate significant economic costs.

The practical difficulty of implementing a policy of 'leaning against the wind' in which the main policy instrument is short-term interest rates should not be underestimated. If, as policymakers, we were successful in preventing a bubble from inflating, it might appear as if we were responding to phantom concerns. The bubble or imbalance would be nowhere to be seen, but interest rates would be higher, inflation would undershoot the inflation target and we would appear to have inflicted unnecessary economic hardship. That could undermine public faith and support in both the inflation target and the MPC.

For me, the single most important lesson from the financial crisis is the need to expand the range of instruments available to policymakers. The inflation-targeting framework provides the scope to respond to asset price bubbles and to imbalances that threaten future economic stability. But short-term interest rates are not well suited to managing such risks.

The precise design of such instruments is now the focus of much work and analysis. It is likely that a range of instruments and initiatives will be required. These may extend beyond new regulatory instruments and should embrace the need for greater international policy coordination.

The ideal would be policy instruments and processes that are effective in preventing the build-up of asset price bubbles and economic imbalances and efficient in minimising the associated costs to the real economy. This would allow short-term interest rates to continue to be the primary tool for hitting the inflation target in the short to medium term, supported by the use of additional instruments to manage emerging imbalances that may pose substantial risks to economic stability further out.

Strengthening the policy framework in this way should lead to greater economic and financial stability; but we should not be lulled into a false sense that it will solve all our problems. Operating such a framework will continue to require finely balanced judgements and difficult decisions. Moreover, no policy toolkit can anticipate all future changes to the structure of markets and the economy, or to the shocks hitting them. The process of increasing the robustness of the macroeconomic policy framework should be seen as continuous, not a one-off response to the current crisis.

The inflation target remains a vital pillar of the macroeconomic policy framework and should continue to provide the focus for monetary policy. There are lessons that need to be learned from this financial crisis, though. Good policy frameworks should provide policymakers with the right incentives to take difficult decisions and the right tools to implement those decisions. Inflation targeting goes a long way: the clarity of the objective and the transparency of the regime acts as an important discipline on the Monetary Policy Committee, and short-term interest rates are, for the most part, effective in maintaining a broad balance between nominal demand and supply and so generating low and stable inflation. They are not well suited, however, to nipping incipient bubbles in the bud and restricting burgeoning imbalances. Policymakers need to make difficult judgements about asset prices and imbalances, but they also need effective and efficient instruments to enact those judgements.

NOTE

1. This is a revised version of Spencer Dale's contribution to the panel discussion at the Sixth Norges Bank Monetary Policy Conference. The remarks have not been updated to reflect subsequent events and policy actions. The author would like to thank Rohan Churm, Jens Larsen and Rob Wood for their considerable help in preparing these remarks. An extended version was delivered to the Society of Business Economists' annual conference on 23 June 2009; it is available at www.bankofengland.co.uk/publications/speeches/2009/speech395.pdf. The views expressed are the author's and do not necessarily reflect those of other members of the Bank of England's Monetary Policy Committee.

19 The financial crisis as an opportunity to strengthen inflation-targeting frameworks

Hans Genberg[1]

The topic we have been asked to address is 'Inflation targeting: where do we go from here?'. Based on the observation that inflation-targeting countries were not spared from the fall-out of the current financial crisis, a frequent reaction to questions of this type has recently been to argue that the inflation-targeting framework is fundamentally flawed and needs to be replaced (see, for example, Wolf 2009).

Although he does not subscribe to this view, are Jonung pointed out at the conference that, in a historical perspective, regime changes tend to happen as the result of crises, suggesting that inflation-targeting frameworks may come under pressure as a result of the financial crisis we are currently experiencing. For those of us who believe that targeting inflation is still the central role of monetary policy, the challenge is therefore to ensure that this pressure does not lead to abandoning the framework altogether but, rather, to improvements in its implementation.

Crises may lead to questions about the validity of the status quo, but they do not necessarily bring about regime change. To illustrate how they may in fact be taken as an opportunity to implement constructive reforms, I find it instructive to review how the monetary authorities in Hong Kong have dealt with crises affecting its currency board system. This system has endured for twenty-five years, even though it has been tested a number of times. I argue that the reaction of the authorities to crises was to render it more credible, both by reaffirming the fundamental objectives of the currency board system and by introducing modifications in its operation to make it more robust. Inflation-targeting central banks need to provide a similarly forceful confirmation of their commitment to the goal of price stability, while at the same time taking actions to improve the operational framework.

Even though it follows a fixed exchange rate policy rather than pursuing inflation targeting, I believe that the experience of the Hong Kong Monetary Authority provides useful lessons, because the performance and resilience of any monetary policy framework depends fundamentally on the credibility of the framework in the eyes of the private sector.

428

Although the HKMA has now achieved a high level of credibility, this has not always been the case. The system has come under speculative pressure a number of times, but each time the HKMA was able to withstand the pressure, and each time it took the occasion of the crisis as an opportunity to implement credibility-enhancing changes in the framework. I would like to illustrate this briefly by recalling two specific events: the speculation against the Hong Kong dollar during the 1997/8 Asian financial crisis, on the one hand, and the appreciation pressure in the 2004/5 period associated with speculation on a strengthening of the Chinese renminbi, on the other. In both instances the HKMA intervened forcefully in the foreign exchange market in order to stem the pressures, and it was ultimately successful.[2]

For my purpose here, however, the interesting point is the reaction of the HKMA *after* the crises. In both cases it combined a reaffirmation of the commitment to the pegged exchange rate with reforms of the operational mechanisms designed to make the currency board system more robust. In the first episode these reforms were introduced as 'seven technical measures', and they were intended to make the system less crisis-prone. In particular, they included the creation of an overnight borrowing facility at the HKMA that would reduce the likelihood of liquidity squeezes in the Hong Kong interbank market. The reforms introduced in the aftermath of the second episode included the creation of an explicit two-sided target zone band for the exchange rate with respect to the US dollar. This established a clear numerical value for the strong-side intervention point at which the HKMA would enter the market – something that had not existed theretofore. In both episodes, therefore, the actions of the HKMA appear to have increased the credibility of the currency board system (see Genberg and Hui 2009).

The relevance of the experience of the Hong Kong Monetary Authority for how inflation-targeting central banks might react to current critics is, I believe, twofold. First, they need to reaffirm their commitment to price stability as the cornerstone of their policy framework, and explain why the attainment of financial stability is perfectly consistent with this commitment. Second, they need to acknowledge that the *implementation* of the commitment to price stability will be reviewed and modified in order to ensure that subsidiary goals such as economic growth and, especially, financial stability will be appropriately taken into account.

What modifications in current practice seem most urgent? Some insights from Orphanides' contribution (Chapter 3) can be used to address this question. Orphanides emphasises three important aspects of inflation targeting: (i) an explicit quantitative definition of price stability; (ii) a transparent communication strategy; and (iii) the requirement that the central bank be 'sensitive' to objectives other than the primary one of price stability. I believe that it is in the third of these areas that improvements can be made in inflation-targeting frameworks. I wish to touch on one aspect on which I have written previously together with Sushil Wadhwani and Steve Cecchetti, namely the reaction of central bank policy to developments in financial markets.

The basic point of our earlier work was that central banks should take into account unusual developments in financial markets when they determine their policy stance. These developments may be related to movements in housing or equity prices, in exchange rates or in the growth rates of money and/or credit aggregates.

We may not yet fully understand the reasons for the unusual developments because they cannot be incorporated neatly into our models, but I believe that this should be a reason for re-examining the models rather than ignoring the unusual developments in the data.

In our original study on this topic, the formal example was related to equity price misalignments, but that was mainly an illustration of a more general point. It did have the unfortunate side effect, however, of presenting opponents with an easy straw man to pick at. The immediate response to our suggestions was to argue that central banks cannot identify bubbles in equity prices and, even if they could, it would be very costly to prick the bubble, because the policy interest rate would have to be increased too much.

We have come a long way since then. I hope it is now well understood that paying attention to developments in financial markets does not mean targeting asset prices, pricking bubbles or setting firm targets for growth rates of money or credit. Instead, it is completely compatible with a sensible definition of inflation targeting in which the inflation performance in the economy over the medium term can be improved if central banks are sensitive to the build-up in financial imbalances.

I am perfectly happy with the general point that our suggestion can be incorporated in a general targeting approach to determining optimal monetary policy trade-offs. I do not think that labelling is crucial, but I do think that it is important that we recognise that our models may not be perfect, and that we sometimes have to contemplate trade-offs between inflation at different time horizons rather than just the usual trade-off between inflation and output variability.

All this is not to say that it is easy to implement a strategy in which developments in financial markets are taken into account. I am encouraged, though, when I see more research efforts devoted to incorporating financial markets into monetary policy analysis, both at the empirical front and at the theoretical front.

The near-collapse of the financial system during the height of the current crisis has triggered a more fundamental questioning of the role of central banks, namely whether the objective of their policy formulation should be extended to ensure financial stability in addition to monetary stability. While many central banks already undertake assessments of the stability of their financial systems and publish financial stability reports in addition to inflation reports or monetary stability reports, these assessments do not typically lead to specific policy recommendations the way the inflation reports do.

Adding financial stability to the objectives raises a number of thorny issues. Is the central bank able to deliver financial stability using the policy tools at its disposal? Could there be trade-offs between measures to deliver financial stability and monetary stability, and, if so, how are they to be resolved? What implications does adding financial stability as an objective have for the governance structure of the central bank? The list goes on. In the remainder of this contribution I would like to touch very briefly on each of these issues.

In pursuing monetary stability – or, more precisely, price stability – the central bank can rely on (i) a relatively clear and precise definition of its objective, (ii) a body of theory and empirical evidence relating to (a) the determinants of price stability as well as (b) the relationship between the policy instrument(s) and the ultimate objective, and, finally, (iii) relatively comprehensive data on the variables relevant for carrying out the mandate.

With respect to financial stability, the situation is almost completely the reverse. There is no generally agreed definition of what constitutes a state of financial stability, let alone a single numerical indicator that could serve as a measure of the success or failure of the policymaker. In fact, financial stability is typically defined by its negative: the absence of financial instability. Even here, though, it has not so far been possible to define a set of numerical indicators that could form the basis for a clear policy strategy. The problem is that financial instability can take many forms. It can be reflected in the banking sector or in non-bank financial intermediaries, in short-term interbank money markets or in equity markets, in international financial flows or in exchange rate movements, etc.

Since financial instability can take many forms, there is no general model that can be relied on to account for all its manifestations, and to link these to appropriate policy instruments. Partial equilibrium models of individual markets do exist, and, although they can provide valuable insights about certain sources of financial instability, they are as yet not always well suited to providing recommendations with respect to specific policy actions.

As a matter of general principle, the Tinbergen rule states that a policymaker charged with achieving a certain number of policy objectives must be able to control an equal number of independent policy instruments. A central bank that is trying to achieve an inflation target while at the same time minimising the variability of output should, ideally, have two instruments, and adding a third objective related to financial stability would require yet an additional instrument. We may need to look beyond the traditional tools of the central bank for this.

The strictures implied by the Tinbergen rule and the related assignment problem should not be overstated, however. Even if additional policy instruments are available to deal with additional objectives, this does not imply that interest rate policy should be conducted completely independently of those other policy instruments. Coordinated actions involving all instruments are surely more efficient, as some occurrences of financial instability may be related to general financial conditions rather than circumstances particular to a specific sector. In addition, there may be situations in which there are conflicts between the achievement of price stability and the achievement of financial stability. For example, concerns about illiquidity in the banking system may call for some form of easing of regulatory standards, even if this may compromise the inflation objective at some time in the future. If the policy interest rate is raised as a pre-emptive measure, the original illiquidity problem may become more acute, potentially eliciting a further regulatory response that leads to an unstable interaction between the two policy instruments. In this case a coordinated policy response, in which the regulatory response and the interest rate policy are set cooperatively, is likely to produce a superior outcome.

Another situation in which the interest rate instrument may have to be used in part to deal with a latent financial instability problem could arise if the agency charged with financial stability policy does not act for some reason. In this case it may be that the central bank has a comparative advantage (in the short run) in using the policy interest rate, in a second-best solution in which it would trade off inflation and financial stability concerns.

The possible need for coordination between policies to deal with inflation, on the one hand, and financial stability, on the other, raises the question of whether both policy instruments should be vested with the central bank. The benefits from coordination speak for combining both instruments in the same agency. Against such an arrangement, it has been argued that assigning too many possibly conflicting goals to the central bank may negatively affect its credibility in carrying out its original objective of price stability. To guard against this, it may be desirable to separate clearly the different duties by creating a financial stability committee, which would be responsible for the analysis and policy recommendations with respect to financial stability policy. This committee would operate separately from the monetary policy committee, the primary responsibility of which would be to pursue price stability by setting the policy interest rate. Some organised form of coordination between the two committees would have to be designed, and the ultimate responsibility would have to be taken by the central bank governor. However the institutional arrangement is solved, the fact that there are clear links, and sometimes conflicts, between traditional interest rate policy and a newly created financial stability policy points to considerable communication challenges for the policy authorities.

These issues are just in the process of being considered by central banks and international bodies such as the Bank for International Settlements, the Basel Committee on Banking Supervision and the newly formed Financial Stability Board. Much theoretical and statistical work remains to be carried out in order for the pursuit of financial stability to be put on sound analytical and empirical foundations. Likewise, designing robust institutional arrangements, at both the national and the international levels, needs further analysis. The work has, in many ways, only just begun.

NOTES

1. This is a revised version of Hans Genberg's contribution to the panel discussion at the Sixth Norges Bank Monetary Policy Conference.
2. In the 1998 episode it also intervened in the local stock market to counteract the so-called 'double play', in which speculators simultaneously shorted the currency and the stock market.

REFERENCES

Genberg, H., and C. Hui, (2009). 'The credibility of the link from the perspective of modern financial theory'. Working Paper no. 02/2009. Hong Kong: HKMA.
Wolf, M. (2009). 'Central banks must target more than just inflation', *Financial Times*, 5 May.

20 'Leaning against the wind' is fine, but will often not be enough

Lars Heikensten[1]

Thank you for inviting me here to discuss inflation targeting twenty years on. It is now some years since I left active duty in a central bank. Participating in this panel has given me an opportunity, which I very much welcome, to summarise my thoughts on some of the monetary policy issues discussed today.

First, it is important to be clear what we mean when we talk about inflation targeting. Obviously, inflation targeting has to involve a target for inflation. In my world, that target also has to be explicit. I would therefore not think that a country could qualify as inflation targeting *ex post* – being perceived in retrospect as having tried to reach a target. This is sometimes claimed to have been the case for the Bundesbank, or, more recently, for the Federal Reserve. Acting in this way should be classified as *behaving like* an inflation targeter, not being one.

I also think that to be an ITer the target should be part of a wider framework, set up to make the bank clear and transparent. One should not only say in advance what one is aiming for, but it should also be possible to follow up in retrospect what has been delivered.

I do not believe that one can underestimate the importance of central banks trying to be open and clear during the recent decade and a half. This was a process clearly pioneered by the inflation-targeting central banks. In many cases it was decisive in their securing acceptance for their independence, and for the legitimacy and credibility obtained. It might be worthwhile to note that the independence of central banks has not – as far as I am aware – been questioned despite the present problems. This, surely, is an indication of how far we have come. This would not have happened without inflation targeting!

Did inflation targets play a role in setting the stage for the current crisis?

On a literal interpretation of this question, I would say that the answer is 'No', or 'Very little'. The crisis was caused by a *combination* of

434

macroeconomic imbalances, regulatory failures and monetary policy. Regardless of the relative importance of these factors, however, the problems emerged primarily in countries that did not have inflation targets (the United States in particular) according to my definition above; in fact, they often tried to distance themselves from inflation targeting.

Having said this, we can broaden the issue and ask if monetary policy played a role. The answer now is clearly 'Yes'! Does this mean, though, that the crisis could realistically have been avoided with another kind of monetary policy?

For small countries, the answer is in practical terms 'No'. It would not have helped Sweden very much to have run a more restrictive monetary policy from 2002 to 2006. The problems Sweden is confronted with now are on the whole related to a fall in exports and the management of two of our banks in the Baltics.

Is it true for larger countries or regions? Perhaps the answer here is 'Yes'. However, the present public discussion often overlooks the costs. It is as if there had been some magic, middle-of-the-road policy stance that would have delivered high GDP growth and at the same time could have curbed asset price increases. The crucial issue is empirical; how high would rates have needed to be to avoid or limit the crisis? Would that have been preferable to the policies followed? The jury, in my opinion, is still out. The answer will, among other things, depend on how deep this crisis becomes.

I recall a discussion I had with Joseph Stiglitz in the early 2000s, when he was in Stockholm to get the Economics Prize in memory of Alfred Nobel. I challenged him on US monetary policy during the preceding years. Had it not been too lax, encouraging a debt build-up, driving up equity prices, etc.? Would this not lead to a deeper downturn next time? On the whole he defended Alan Greenspan. His argument was that millions of Americans had been entering the labour force who otherwise would have remained outside. This had done wonders to income distribution, more than any other policy.

Having said this, I think that central banks should have 'leaned against the wind'. I will come back to this point, but I do not find it likely that a policy of this kind could have avoided the crisis altogether.

In my opinion, it is clear that most of the problems we are now confronted with are related to regulatory failures. These failures existed in individual countries, not least the United States, and had to do with the housing market, with the markets for derivatives of different kinds and also with a lack of supervision of systemically important 'non-banks'. Behind the problems was, among other things, a fragmented regulatory structure – again, not least in the United States.

Some of these problems are a reflection of a lack of understanding of what *could* happen. However, we should not be naïve. Let me give one or two examples. I read an article not long ago in *Newsweek*, in which Larry Summers (at the time the US secretary of the Treasury) was clear on having 'silenced' one of the regulators in the late 1990s from raising the issue of regulation in the derivatives markets. This was good business, and the United States wanted to keep it.

In addition, a lack of understanding is not the reason for inaction in Europe when it comes to supervision and crisis management. To a substantial degree it was known before the crisis what needed to be done. Nevertheless, it did not happen. If you look at the website of the Riksbank you will find several speeches from the early 2000s arguing for action. We advocated crisis exercises, more common supervisory principles, even one European supervisor. Why did we do that? Clearly, not because we were wiser. We had gone through a crisis in the early 1990s and we still remembered.

These discussions have now acquired some momentum. What I fear, though, is that if the European economy recovers, as now seems likely, the momentum will be lost and national interests will again take over. This would be a pity, because the crisis has clearly demonstrated that the very desirable financial integration has already gone further than the political systems regulating and guiding it.

In short, therefore, I would say that inflation targeting is not to blame for our problems. However, monetary policy is, to some extent. 'Leaning against the wind' would have made sense. To have really had an influence over the developments, though, and to have avoided the crisis, it would not have been enough. Other actions would have been needed, among them more of an international and systemic focus in regulation (for some early suggestions on what could have been done, see Contact Group on Asset Prices 2002).

Does inflation targeting need to be modified as a consequence of the crisis?

First, it needs to be noted that this is not a new question. During the ten years I spent in central banking the issue of how to deal with asset price movements was almost always on the agenda. The problems we are now confronted with are not a consequence of lack of awareness, but of the character of the issues, which are fundamentally difficult.

Inflation targeting was never, at least in my interpretation, only about inflation. In the Riksbank – at least since 1995 – we always looked at the real effects of what we were doing. Along with Mervyn King we underlined that we were not 'inflation nutters'.

The Riksbank law also makes the responsibility for financial stability clear: the bank 'should safeguard an efficient and stable payment system'. Even before we had the new law, the bank chose to follow closely financial developments that were perceived to be systemically important, particularly in the banks. Reports on financial stability with this focus have been published on a regular basis since 1997. If we saw major problems building up we were, from the late 1990s, clear in our communication that we would be prepared to act; interest rates might need to be raised to limit the risks for a future financial meltdown, with severe real consequences.

As can be seen, the majority of the Riksbank board members took a different view from that communicated by many central bankers, in particular Alan Greenspan. Morever, we advocated this view within the central banking community (for an account of this position, see, for example, Heikensten 2000; see also Ingves 2007).

I could perhaps say that there is another Alan Greenspan, whom we could have relied on when describing our approach. That is the one connected with the so-called risk management approach, characterised by Greenspan himself as 'understanding as much as possible the many sources of risk and uncertainty that policymakers face, quantifying those risks when possible, and assessing the costs associated with each of the risks'. This is precisely what I think we tried to do when we took asset prices into account!

Let me take two examples. In the late 1990s we followed the potential risks from the rapid increases in equity prices for the banking system, in particular. As it happened, most of the more audacious financial ventures were financed directly by rich individuals and not via the banking system. Thus the risks for financial stability were perceived to be manageable. For this reason, but also because we did not think that actions on our part would have much effect on the equity markets, the majority of the Riksbank board never referred explicitly to equity prices as a reason for an interest rate decision. We did not all agree, though, I might add. Some of my colleagues thought we should raise rates more quickly at the time, partly to slow down the equity price increases.

House price developments were also followed by the Riksbank. The risks here were judged to be higher, but perhaps not so much via the financial system as via the effects that falling house prices might have on household consumption. However, the fact that household savings were relatively high, at least compared to the United States and the United Kingdom, was regarded as limiting the risks. In the end, risks related to house price developments led the Riksbank to refrain explicitly from taking rates down on a few occasions during 2005, despite the fact that strict adherence to the target could have led to looser monetary policy.

Today I think we could have gone further; rates should perhaps not have been brought down as much during 2005 and should have been raised more quickly afterwards.

As we saw it, we could well decide not to do exactly what *strict* inflation targeting would imply but, instead, to factor in other aspects, whether or not they reflected financial or real concerns. The difficulty with this is not the intellectual framework, which is, in my view, still valid, but having a solid base for decisions and knowing when to act.

When a decision is taken to act – and not to follow the simple policy rule – it should be explicit and the arguments put forward should be clear. Thus merely referring to the development of credit or money aggregates in general would, in my opinion, not suffice, as long as the links between these measures and the issues at hand are not made clear.

The issues we are talking about are, in my view, too complicated to be summarised in some simple measure. Each situation has to be looked at separately. An asset price increase of a certain size might have very different impacts in one country from what it might have in another, and the impact might also change over time. The analysis needed is of the kind we tried to do – with varying degrees of success – in our *Financial Stability Reports*.

The short answer to this question is in general, therefore, 'No'. Inflation targeting is flexible enough for policy to 'lean against the wind'. Some central banks have done this, others not (and it does not seem as if inflation targeters have been doing it less than other central banks). The issues involved are difficult, however. Before acting, and 'leaning against the wind', central banks have to know what they are doing and to be able to motivate it. It goes without saying that this is not always an easy task. At the same time, there are good reasons to be cautious unless the motives are good and can be explained.

NOTE

1. This is a revised version of Lars Heikensten's contribution to the panel discussion at the Sixth Norges Bank Monetary Policy Conference. Lars Heikensten was deputy governor and then governor of the Sveriges Riksbank from 1995 to 2006.

REFERENCES

Contact Group on Asset Prices (2002). *Turbulence in Asset Markets: The Role of Micro Policies*. Basel: Contact Group on Asset Prices. Available at www.bis.org.

Heikensten, L. (2000). 'Six monetary policy issues'. Speech at Umeå School of Business and Economics, Umeå University. Umeå, Sweden, 7 November.

Ingves, S. (2007). 'Housing and monetary policy: a view from an inflation-targeting central bank', in Federal Reserve Bank of Kansas City. *Housing, Housing Finance, Monetary Policy*: 433–43. Kansas City: Federal Reserve Bank of Kansas City.

21   Inflation targeting, capital requirements
     and 'leaning against the wind': some
     comments

Sushil B. Wadhwani[1]

It is a great privilege to have been invited to this timely conference to discuss an issue of considerable importance.

Did the inflation-targeting regime play any role in setting the stage for the current crisis?

The current financial crisis has several causes, and it would be a mistake to focus on a single factor. At first sight, however, monetary policy was too loose in several countries, and, as a result, housing and credit market bubbles were allowed to develop. Had interest rates been higher during the boom, it is plausible that the bubbles would have been more muted, and, therefore, the damage caused to the real economy when the bubbles eventually burst would probably have been more limited. Moreover, interest rates would have been higher when the bubble burst, so there would have been more scope to cut them in an attempt to stimulate the economy before having to resort to the largely untested policy of quantitative easing.

Note that the inappropriate monetary policy does not represent a failure of inflation-targeting regimes per se (at least when targets have been set to be achieved over the medium term rather than at a fixed horizon). Instead, the problem appears to be that several central banks failed to operate an inflation-targeting regime in an appropriate manner. After all, several years ago some of us (see, for example, Cecchetti *et al.* 2000 and Cecchetti, Genberg and Wadhwani 2002) argued that inflation-targeting central bankers should 'lean against the wind' in response to asset price bubbles.

Why, then, did so many central banks not operate a policy of 'leaning against the wind'? I have discussed this elsewhere in greater detail (see Wadhwani 2008), but a representative response has been provided by Ben Bernanke (2002), who argues that

it is rarely the case in economics that the optimal amount of insurance in any situation is zero. On that principle, proponents of leaning against the bubble have argued that completely ignoring incipient potential bubbles, if in fact they can be identified, can't possibly be the best policy. . . . I believe that, nevertheless, 'leaning against the bubble' is unlikely to be productive in practice.

While I would not pretend that bubble identification is easy, it is important to recall that it is not historically unusual for private market participants to spot a bubble, but yet be unable or unwilling to bet against it. By contrast, central bankers are less subject to short-termist performance pressure, and should therefore find it easier to respond to such bubbles.

Another commonly advanced objection to an LATW policy is what Bernanke calls the difficulty of 'safe popping' – i.e. we might need a very large increase in interest rates to prick a bubble. However, LATW is *not* about pricking bubbles but merely adjusting interest rates to improve macroeconomic stability. Furthermore, if this crisis results in a multi-year period of disappointing output growth (as in Japan during its 'lost decade') then a mild recession in the pre-2007 period induced by LATW might come to seem to have been a price well worth paying. In his contribution, Spencer Dale (Chapter 18) has argued that it was risky for the central banks to have engaged in LATW, as, if they had got it wrong, it would have undermined support for the inflation-targeting regime. I would contend, however, that the failure to follow an LATW policy and the depth of this recession associated with the financial crisis have already dented the credibility of several central banks.

The fundamental problem is that both Federal Reserve and Bank of England policymakers supported the Greenspan doctrine that it was better to mitigate the fallout when it occurs rather than try an LATW policy. This 'mopping-up' doctrine failed because monetary policy becomes much less effective when balance sheets are impaired after the bursting of an asset price bubble. In addition, in 2008 the developed countries simultaneously faced an external inflation shock in the form of higher commodity prices, which reduced their ability to follow a more aggressive monetary policy. It would have been much better to have been pre-emptive and operated an LATW policy. Moreover, the 'mopping-up' strategy introduced an asymmetry in monetary policy setting, which further reinforced the procyclicality of the financial system. It is also the case that, after the internet bubble burst, 'mopping up' only sowed the seeds of the next bubble.

Does inflation targeting need to be modified as a consequence of the crisis and, if so, how?

Several central bankers have argued that the existing framework needs to be supplemented with an extra policy instrument – what now sometimes goes by the term 'macro-prudential' framework. If one could identify an instrument that works, this makes sense, as, on the Tinbergen principle, one needs as many instruments as targets. A candidate for a possible instrument that attracts much favour is time-varying capital requirements.

However, I worry that some of the discussion about the use of capital requirements might be promising too much. For example, Bean (2008) argues against LATW with respect to monetary policy by asserting that the required increase in interest rates would have depressed activity significantly, and 'I doubt that people would be prepared to accept the clear short-term costs of such a strategy in return for the uncertain long-term benefits'. He then points to the need for an additional instrument, such as time-varying capital requirements, as a substitute for using monetary policy that would not impose these short-term costs on the economy, and refers approvingly to the Spanish approach of dynamic provisioning.

I am sceptical that time-varying capital requirements would be less costly or are a credible substitute for LATW with respect to monetary policy. First, it is worth noting that increasing capital requirements will operate primarily through changing the spread between the lending rate and the central bank's policy rate. They could easily, therefore, have a significant macroeconomic impact on output and inflation. If time-varying capital requirements are to make bubbles less likely they must impose some short-term macroeconomic costs that are similar to those imposed by higher interest rates (albeit somewhat more targeted). It would be a mistake to deny that. Second, one must recall that the Spanish approach of dynamic provisioning did not prevent a significant housing market bubble emerging, in part because monetary policy was set inappropriately for Spain's needs.

More generally, standard theoretical considerations suggest that it is more efficient to set both policy instruments (interest rates and capital requirements) jointly to achieve one's twin objectives of price and financial stability, rather than rely on an independent assignment. It must also be noted with respect to capital requirements that it is highly likely that the financial industry will, over time, find ways to evade these requirements. It will therefore be critically important that monetary policy is also an LATW policy. One should not underestimate the harmful impact on productivity growth of some of the regulation that is likely to go hand in hand with the introduction of capital requirements.

In a UK context it may be that, in order to encourage the use of monetary policy to lean against the wind, the Chancellor needs to amend the annual letter that sets out the remit. At present it includes an example that discusses appropriate monetary policy in the face of a 'supply shock'. Perhaps it should now also discuss how monetary policy should behave as a bubble is emerging.

Finally, as we attempt to rebuild our monetary and regulatory frameworks, it may also repay us to look more carefully at the Australian and Swedish experiences, in which central banks did, to some extent, operate an LATW policy. One is particularly impressed by how Australia has fared during this crisis, even if one must accept that, for LATW to work effectively, the large economic regions need to do it too.

NOTE

1. This is a revised version of Sushil B. Wadhwani's contribution to the panel discussion at the Sixth Norges Bank Monetary Policy Conference. The author is extremely grateful to Roy Cromb, Steve Cecchetti and Hans Genberg for many helpful discussions. All remaining errors are, of course, the author's.

REFERENCES

Bean, C. (2008). 'Some lessons for monetary policy from the recent financial turmoil'. Remarks at conference on 'Globalisation, inflation and monetary policy'. Istanbul, 22 November.

Bernanke, B. (2002). 'Asset-price "bubbles" and monetary policy'. Remarks before the New York Chapter of the National Association for Business Economics. New York, 15 October.

Cecchetti, S., H. Genberg, J. Lipsky and S. Wadhwani (2000). *Asset Prices and Central Bank Policy*. Geneva: CIMB.

Cecchetti, S., H. Genberg and S. Wadhwani (2002). 'Asset prices in a flexible inflation targeting framework', in W. Hunter, G. Kaufman and M. Pomerleano (eds.). *Asset Price Bubbles: The Implications for Monetary, Regulatory, and International Policies*: 427–44. Cambridge, MA: MIT Press.

Wadhwani, S. (2008). 'Should monetary policy respond to asset price bubbles?', *National Institute Economic Review*, 206(1): 25–34.

Index

Printed in the United States
By Bookmasters